CW00924353

EMPIRES OF
THE IMAGINATION

EMPIRES OF THE IMAGINATION

POLITICS, WAR, AND THE ARTS
IN THE BRITISH WORLD, 1750–1850

HOLGER HOOCK

PROFILE BOOKS

First published in Great Britain in 2010 by
PROFILE BOOKS LTD
3A Exmouth House
Pine Street
Exmouth Market
London EC1R 0JH
www.profilebooks.com

Copyright © Holger Hoock, 2010

1 3 5 7 9 10 8 6 4 2

Typeset in Fournier

Printed and bound in Great Britain by
T. J. International

The moral right of the author has been asserted.

All rights reserved. Without limiting the rights under copyright reserved above, no part of this publication may be reproduced, stored or introduced into a retrieval system, or transmitted, in any form or by any means (electronic, mechanical, photocopying, recording or otherwise), without the prior written permission of both the copyright owner and the publisher of this book.

A CIP catalogue record for this book is available from the British Library.

ISBN 978 1 86197 859 2
eISBN 978 1 84765 223 2

Mixed Sources
Product group from well-managed
forests and other controlled sources
www.fsc.org Cert no. SGS-COC-2482
© 1996 Forest Stewardship Council
FSC

CONTENTS

PART II
EMPIRE, ARCHAEOLOGY, AND COLLECTING (*c*.1760–*c*.1850)

PART III
CAPITAL OF CULTURE (1815–c.1850)

For DE –
inspiration, always.

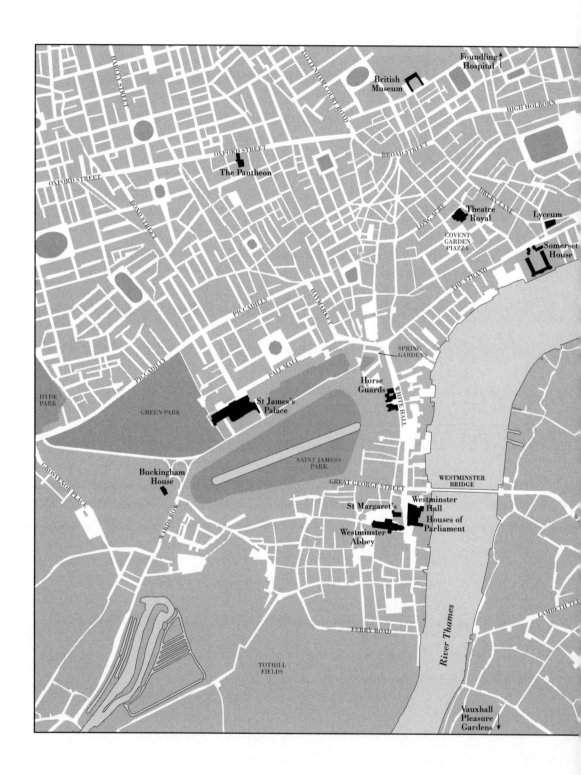

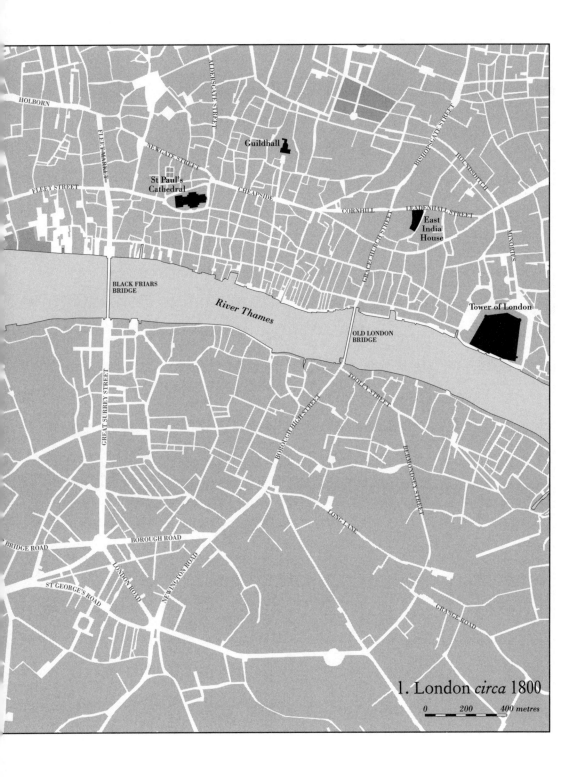

HOLBORN

FLEET MARKET

FLEET STREET

NEWGATE STREET

ALDERSGATE STREET

Guildhall

St Paul's
Cathedral

CHEAPSIDE

CORNHILL

GRACECHURCH STREET

BISHOPSGATE STREET

HOUNDSDITCH

LEADENHALL STREET

East
India
House

MINORIES

BLACK FRIARS
BRIDGE

River Thames

OLD LONDON
BRIDGE

Tower of London

GREAT SURREY STREET

BOROUGH HIGH STREET

TOOLEY STREET

BERMONDSEY STREET

LONG LANE

BRIDGE ROAD

BOROUGH ROAD

LONDON ROAD

NEWINGTON ROAD

ST GEORGE'S ROAD

GRANGE ROAD

1. London *circa* 1800

0   200   400 metres

GREAT
BRITAIN

Woolwich
London
Portsmouth
Le Havre
Paris

FRANCE

Venice Trieste

ITALY
Rome

Marseilles

Minorca

Naples Herculaneum
Pompeii

Corfu Bassae

Sicily

Zacynthos.
Ionian Islands

Navarino

Carthage

M e d i t e r r a n e a n   S e a

Malta

Cythera

Athens

Attica
Aegina

Crete
Rhodes

Black Sea

Constantinople

OTTOMAN
EMPIRE

Smyrna
Cnidus
Halicarnassus
Bodrum
Geronta

Alepp

LYCIA

Patara
Xanthus   Cyprus

SYR

Balbec

LEBANO

Acr

HOLY
LAN

Nile
Delta

Suez
Canal

Alexandria

Giza Cairo Bulaq
Memphis

SINAI

EGYPT

Valley of Biban Luxor
Karnak Thebes

Philae

Abu Simbel

Nile

NUBIA

SUDAN

ABYSSINIA

2. British Archaeological Sites in the Mediterranean and Near East

0   200   400   600   800 *kilometres*

Lake Balkhash

Aral Sea

Caspian Sea

Khorsabad

Kuyunjik (Nineveh)

Mosul • •
Nimrud

Euphrates

• Tehran

Tigris

myra

• Baghdad   PERSIA

Babylon•

Basra •   • Persepolis

Persian Gulf

Red Sea

Arabian Sea   INDIA

Bombay•

Cape of Good Hope

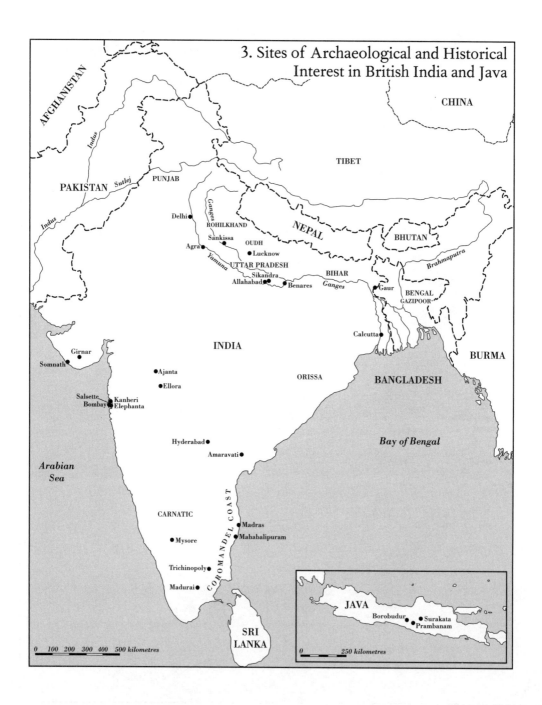

3. Sites of Archaeological and Historical
Interest in British India and Java

AFGHANISTAN

CHINA

Indus

PAKISTAN   *Sutlej*   PUNJAB

TIBET

Indus

Ganges

Delhi

ROHILKHAND

NEPAL

BHUTAN

Sankissa

Agra   OUDH

Lucknow

Yamuna   UTTAR PRADESH

Brahmaputra

Sikandra   BIHAR

Allahabad   Benares   *Ganges*   Gaur

BENGAL

GAZIPOOR

Girnar

INDIA

Calcutta

Somnath

BURMA

Ajanta

ORISSA

Ellora

BANGLADESH

Salsette   Kanheri
Bombay   Elephanta

*Arabian
Sea*

Hyderabad

Bay of Bengal

Amaravati

CARNATIC

C
O
R
O
M
A
N
D
E
L
   C
O
A
S
T

Madras

Mysore

Mahabalipuram

Trichinopoly

Madurai

SRI
LANKA

JAVA

Borobudur   Surakata
Prambanam

0   100   200   300   400   500 kilometres

0   250 kilometres

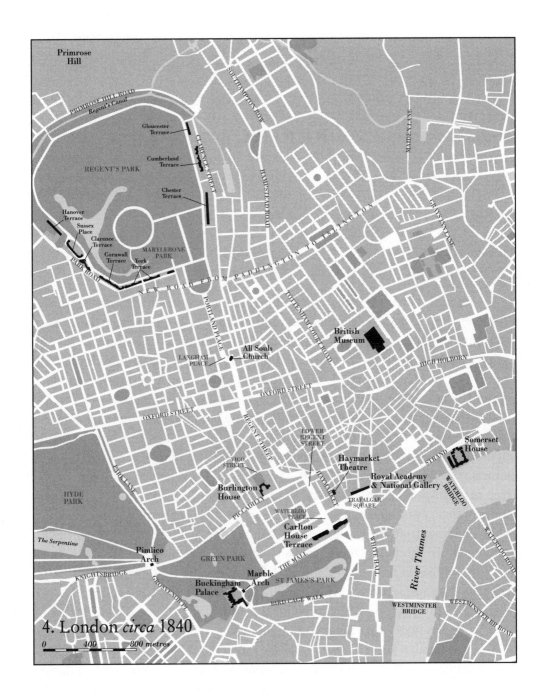

Primrose
Hill

PRIMROSE HILL ROAD
Regent's Canal

Gloucester
Terrace

REGENT'S PARK

CLARENCE STREET

Cumberland
Terrace

SOUTHAMPTON ROW

Chester
Terrace

HAMPSTEAD ROAD

Hanover
Terrace
Sussex
Place
Clarence
Terrace
Cornwall
Terrace
York
Terrace

MARYLEBONE
PARK

PARK ROAD

NEW ROAD FROM PADDINGTON TO ISLINGTON

GRAY'S INN LANE

MAIDEN LANE

PORTLAND PLACE

TOTTENHAM COURT ROAD

British
Museum

LANGHAM
PLACE

All Souls
Church

HIGH HOLBORN

OXFORD STREET

OXFORD STREET

REGENT STREET

LOWER
REGENT
STREET

Somerset
House

STRAND

VIGO
STREET

Haymarket
Theatre

WATERLOO BRIDGE

PARK LANE

Burlington
House

HAYMARKET

Royal Academy
& National Gallery

HYDE
PARK

PICCADILLY

WATERLOO
PLACE

TRAFALGAR
SQUARE

WATERLOO ROAD

The Serpentine

Pimlico
Arch

GREEN PARK

Carlton
House
Terrace

WHITEHALL

River Thames

KNIGHTSBRIDGE

GROSVENOR PLACE

Marble
Arch

THE MALL

ST JAMES'S PARK

Buckingham
Palace

BIRD CAGE WALK

WESTMINSTER
BRIDGE

WESTMINSTER BR ROAD

4. London *circa* 1840

0   400   800 metres

PREFACE

BETWEEN THE MID-EIGHTEENTH and the mid-nineteenth centuries, Britain evolved from a substantial international power but relative artistic backwater into a global superpower and a leading cultural force in Europe. This book explores some of the cultural, artistic, and imaginative work that Britons undertook to help the country to come to terms with the loss of the American colonies, to sustain the generation-long fight against Revolutionary and Napoleonic France, and to assert a growing empire in India. As Britain built a global empire, the British also built empires in their cultural imagination. Only a great power could wield the imperial reach and support the military capabilities to accomplish certain types of cultural endeavour. Officially sponsored cultural projects helped demonstrate the reach of the imperial state, legitimate its expansion, and mask its setbacks. The narratives of state, war, and empire were developed by erecting heroic monuments and public buildings from the Caribbean to Canada and Calcutta and by appropriating ancient cultures from the Mediterranean, Near East, and India.

With *Empires of the Imagination* I wish to suggest a framework for thinking about the relations between worlds of politics and worlds of art and culture. I do so, first, by exploring the role of art in political culture, for instance at state occasions and in the practices of national commemoration. Heightened sensitivity to the political potential of art in the public sphere was evinced by attacks on monuments in Revolutionary America and by the reception of American art in London during America's War of Independence. Notions of masculine heroism and its sculptural representation were subject to both political and aesthetic controversy.

Second, the prevailing view among historians has been that the structure and scope of the British state limited its cultural concerns. This book offers an alternative perspective. I analyse the cultural state's distinctly British nature. More than has been previously recognised, its boundaries were fluid and porous, it encouraged the dovetailing of public and private effort, and it was more responsive to demands for the provision of infrastructure for cultural endeavours.

Third, I examine war as a catalyst of cultural developments. Both the expansion and setbacks of the imperial fiscal-military state had cultural and artistic repercussions. Archaeological campaigns and the collecting of classical and Near Eastern antiquities for the British Museum were at once the means and the result of diplomacy; prize antiquities were both weapons and trophies in the Anglo-French struggle for international influence. The surveying and preservation of antiquities in British India were inextricably linked with the imperial project in the east.

Finally, I seek to put British experience in European context. In this period, concern for the social and political significance of the arts was growing across Europe. International competition was a key driver of cultural politics. Functional similarities among cultural states were often greater than rigidly formal comparisons and notions of British 'uniqueness' have suggested. Nonetheless, comparisons between British and, especially, French and Prussian approaches to commemoration and collecting serve to highlight the country's distinctive constitutional arrangements and political culture.

In this book I thus argue that the British state, politics, war, and empire were more significant sites and agents of cultural change than has generally been acknowledged. In addition to exploring these big themes, I seek to shed new light on issues such as national heroic aesthetics in relation to political culture, and the artistic careers and political lives of American painters during and after the American Revolution. Discussion of the relations between imperial officials and indigenous intellectuals and assistants in the archaeological field highlights the ambivalent and contested nature of Orientalism. Colonial encounters were informed by selective respect for the Orient, by cultural hybridity and intellectual dialogue, by British insecurities as much as by assumptions of Western superiority and imperialist exploitation. The narratives of war and empire, and narratives of the cultural politics of the imperial state, were inextricably connected. *Empires of the Imagination* seeks to suggest ways in which previously not well connected cultural, administrative, military, and imperial histories might be better correlated.

Throughout, I have sought to integrate material culture (the treatment, display, dissemination, and reception of objects) with archival studies and readings of printed sources. To the observant visitor of the British Museum, markings on objects tell potent stories, viz. the words 'captured by the British army in Egypt 1801', painted on the side of the Rosetta Stone, or the saw-marks engraved on other antiquities. Imperial officers, scholars, and artists who documented Indian antiquities in descriptions and drawings engaged in a mode of preservation. In studying the commemoration of military heroes, we need to pay as much attention to aesthetic conventions governing the representation of idealised bodies, allegories, and warriors' portraits as to battle histories, political culture, and codes of masculinity. Since contemporaries' experience of heroic monuments such as Nelson's or of battle paintings was often mediated by imagery, texts, and performance, I have made ample if necessarily selective use of a wide range of textual and visual genres. The captions accompanying the illustrations, intended to be read in conjunction with the main body of text, help contextualise sites, objects, and modes of display.

To illuminate the manifold ways in which the culture of power and the power of culture were interlinked in shaping the character of British public life, this book revisits key sites of British politics and culture in the company of royalty, military heroes, and famous painters, as well as of now little known characters: Westminster Abbey at the coronation of George III; an emerging, unique British military pantheon at St Paul's Cathedral; and the origins of world-famous collections of antiquities at the British Museum. In the now mostly forgotten memorials of American loyalists and of British war veterans in minsters and country churches across the British Isles, stories of private mourning merge with, or provide counterpoints to, the national experience of triumph and defeat. Beyond the British Isles, we trace the controversial transatlantic careers of America's leading painters during her War of Independence. In a period when the British state fought international culture wars over prize antiquities, we follow diplomats and explorers Lord Elgin, Henry Salt, Charles Fellows, Henry Layard, and Stratford Canning on archaeological campaigns from Greece, Egypt, and Asia Minor to Assyria. We accompany less well-known imperial officers and their Indian assistants studying antiquities while they were surveying Mysore and Java. Like their colleagues in the Mediterranean, and their common sponsors in London, they struggled with issues of plunder, heritage, and preservation that are as vital and controversial today. Finally, we return to Britain at the time of the Battle of Waterloo, when the flamboyant Prince Regent, later George IV, had London redesigned as a truly imperial capital city. British power was glorified in monumental arches, as well as in Sir Thomas Lawrence's paintings for what became the Waterloo Chamber at Windsor Castle. Subsequent generations of reform-minded politicians considered art galleries and historical monuments as a means of education for the many, dramatically expanding the notion of the cultural nation and advocating free access to national museums.

A book of such comparatively wide thematic and geographical range (whilst it does not aim to be a comprehensive cultural history of the period) is greatly indebted to the sophisticated historiographies of the British state, empire, and war, the literature on memory and commemoration, as well as new histories of art, collecting, and museums. When taking a stance on scholarly arguments, I have tried to stay clear of the sometimes vituperative debate between scholars; the endnotes do some of the scholastic duty. Reasons of space precluded a bibliography, but a full bibliography of the archival and printed sources I consulted in researching the book, and of the scholarly literature cited in the endnotes, is available on the book's dedicated website: http://www.holgerhoock.com/books/empires. The original spelling has been retained throughout; (sic) has not been used. I am grateful to Cambridge University Press for permission to use material in chapters 5 and 6 and in chapter 9 that has previously appeared in different shape in two essays: 'The British State and the Anglo-French Wars over Antiquities, 1798–1858', *Historical Journal*, 50:1 (2007), 1–24, and 'Reforming Culture: National Art Institutions in the Age of Reform', in Arthur Burns and Joanna Innes (eds), *Rethinking the Age of Reform: Britain 1780-1850* (2003), 254–70.

It remains for me to acknowledge with profound gratitude the help I have received since starting this project. At various stages my research has been generously supported by a British Academy Postdoctoral Fellowship, a Visiting Fellowship at The Huntington Library and Art Collections, California, and a Visiting Scholarship at Corpus Christi College and the History Faculty, Oxford. I thank the Master and Fellows of Selwyn College, Cambridge, and the President and Fellows of Corpus Christi, Oxford, who provided intellectual homes and polite sociability near the beginning and end of this project respectively, and intermittently along the way. The extraordinary privilege of a Philip Leverhulme Prize in History (2006) afforded me crucial space and time to complete the research and to write the book; I am hugely indebted to the Leverhulme Trust for enabling me to pursue multiple ambitious projects with an intensity that would simply not have been possible without such uniquely generous and flexible support. I am very grateful for a Publication Grant from The Paul Mellon Centre for Studies in British Art to help fund the illustrations. While this book was in the making, I had the good fortune to found the interdisciplinary research centre *Eighteenth-Century Worlds* and to learn from colleagues at the National Maritime Museum, Greenwich, and National Museums Liverpool. For their support at the University of Liverpool, I am especially grateful to Will Ashworth, John Belchem, Dmitri v. d. Bersselaar, Harald Braun, Andrew Davies, Charles Forsdick, Tom Harrison, Matt Houlbrook (now at Oxford), Robert Lee, Anne McLaren, Kate Marsh, Graham Oliver, Brigitte Resl,

Eve Rosenhaft, and Marcus Walsh. I salute the vision and appreciate the support of my former Heads of School Pauline Stafford and Michael Hughes, Dean Slater, and Deputy Vice-Chancellor Dockray.

Before returning to editing, my former agent Jonathan Jackson found this book an excellent home at *Profile*, where my erudite editor Peter Carson has been wonderfully demanding and supportive in equal measure. At *Profile*, I also thank Penny Daniel, Peter Dyer, Niamh Murray, Rukhsana Yasmin, and their colleagues for helping shape the manuscript into a handsome book, as well as copy editor Mark Handsley, cartographer Martin Lubikowski, and my publicist Valentina Zanca. For their assistance I am grateful to the staff of the archives, libraries, museums, and galleries on whose terrific collections this book is based. Frances Macmillan and Clara Paillard as project assistants helped me keep the managerial ship afloat. Valerie Didier and especially Ashlee Honeybourne carried out valued research assistance. Erica M. Charters offered particularly able research assistance and later took wonderful care of my teaching and of *Eighteenth-Century Worlds* when I was on leave to complete this book. She also nudged me to extend my scope, challenged my approach, informed my style – I owe so much more to her thoughtfulness and our conversation than any endnote could express. My non-historian friends (they all know who they are) and my parents (through difficult times for them) must have wondered why this book took so long to complete, yet offered a peripatetic scholar support and hospitality in Europe and North America. Special thanks also to Joshua Civin and Katherine Tang Newberger in Baltimore, Shelley and Mark Bookspan in Santa Barbara, Ulrich Gotter and Anke Hagedorn in Konstanz, and Jürgen Luh and Franziska Windt in Berlin for beautiful spaces, companionship, and shared dinners in various phases of research, writing, and editing. I have also treasured precious times away from the book with Maddie, David and Simon, Shel, Daniel, and Felix.

Audiences and commentators at conferences at the British Society for Eighteenth-Century Studies, Consortium on the Revolutionary Era, Institute of Historical Research, and National Maritime Museum, and at the universities of Cambridge, Manchester, Nottingham, Oxford, Yale, and York helped me hone the project. I owe much to the kindness and insight of readers of earlier draft chapters, including Malcolm Baker, Stephen Conway, Jas Elsner, Alan Forrest, Rachel Hewitt, Ludmilla Jordanova, Michael Ledger-Lomas, John MacKenzie, Peter J. Marshall, Jonathan P. Parry, Mark S. Phillips, Sujit Sivasundaram, Hannah Smith particularly, and Lucy Worsley. Much more than a picture researcher, Julia E. Hickey, a painter and writer, helped me think about images and shaped not just the captions. Joanna Innes and Heather P. Ewing read an early draft of the manuscript and made me think harder about conceptual and narrative frameworks; Heather's editorial help was truly invaluable. I have also benefited from conversations with many friends and colleagues who have given generously of their time and advice, most especially Bill Foster and Hannah Smith, and also Brian Allen, Luisa Calè, David Cannadine, Linda Colley, Jessica Feather, Sian Flynn, Julian Hoppit, Maya Jasanoff, Alex Kidson, Larry Klein, Andrew McClellan, Peter Mandler, John S. Morrill, Frédéric Ogée, Martin Postle, John Ray, Frank Salmon, David L. Smith, Gill Sutherland, Roey Sweet, Astrid Swenson, and Stella Tillyard. For a decade, I've been fortunate to enjoy the perceptive criticism and wise counsel of Joshua Civin and, longer still, of Ulrich Gotter, two outstanding thinkers and wonderful friends. My debt of gratitude to three scholars is growing by the year: John Brewer, Martin Daunton, and Ludmilla Jordanova, true mentors all.

London/Berlin/Washington, DC, Summer 2009

ABBREVIATIONS

AI/II	Mildred Archer, *British Drawings in the India Office Library*, 2 vols (London, 1969), vol. I, II
AR	*Asiatic Researches*
BL	British Library, London
BL, Add. MSS	British Library, Additional Manuscripts
BL, IOR	British Library, India Office Records
BL, OIOC	British Library, Oriental and India Office Collections
BM	British Museum, Archives
BMC	Frederic George Stephens and Mary Dorothy George (eds), *Catalogue of Political and Personal Satires in the British Museum*, 11 vols (London, 1870–1954)
FD	Kenneth Garlick, Angus Macintyre, Kathryn Cave (eds), *The Diary of Joseph Farington*, 16 vols (London/New Haven, 1978–84)
HC Journals	*Journals of the House of Commons*
HUN MSS	The Huntington Library, San Marino, California, Manuscripts
JRAS	*Journal of the Royal Asiatic Society*
NMM	National Maritime Museum, Greenwich
OHBE	*Oxford History of the British Empire*, various editors, 5 vols (Oxford, 1998–9)
P.P.	Parliamentary Papers

Proceedings	*Proceedings of the Asiatic Society,* ed. Sibadas Chauduri, P. Thankappan Nair (Calcutta, 1980–95), I: 1784–1800; II: 1801–1816; III:1, 2: 1817–1832.
R.A.	Royal Academician
TNA	The National Archives, Public Record Office, London

ADM	Admiralty
AO	Audit Office, series 12, 13: American Loyalists' Claims
CO	Colonial Office
FO	Foreign Office
HO	Home Office
LC	Lord Chamberlain
MPD	Maps and Plans
PC	Privy Council
T	Treasury
WO	War Office
WORK	Office of Works

UKNIWM	UK National Inventory of War Memorials

LIST OF PLATES AND ILLUSTRATIONS

Plates

I. Allan Ramsay, *George III* (1761–2). Oil on canvas, 248.9 × 162.6 cm. The Royal Collection 2009, Her Majesty Queen Elizabeth II. RCIN 405307.

II. François X. Habermann, *Die Zerstörung der Königlichen Bild Säule zu Neu Yorck / La Destruction de la Statue Royale à Nouvelle York* (Augsburg and Paris, *c.*1777). Hand-coloured engraving, 28.6 × 40.6 cm. Eno Collection, Miriam and Ira D. Wallach Division of Art, Prints and Photographs, The New York Public Library, Astor, Lenox and Tilden Foundations.

III. Joseph Wilton, *Equestrian Statue of George III*, tail and other fragments (1770). Marble pedestal (16.5 × 195.6 × 94 cm) and lead fragments. Collection of The New-York Historical Society, accession numbers 1878.5, 1878.7.

IV. Jonathan Trumbull, *Washington and the Departure of the British Garrison from New York City* (1790). Oil on canvas, 274 × 183 cm. City Hall, New York City. Photograph by Glenn Castellano. Courtesy of the Art Commission of the City of New York.

V. Benjamin West, *Fidelia and Speranza* (1776). Oil on canvas, 139 × 108 cm. The Putnam Foundation, Timken Museum of Art, San Diego.

VI. Benjamin West, *John Eardley-Wilmot* (1812), with West's framed painting *Reception of the American Loyalists by Great Britain in the Year 1783*. Oil on canvas, 105.4 × 148 cm. Yale Center for British Art, Paul Mellon Collection.

VII.   John Singleton Copley, *The Collapse of the Earl of Chatham in the House of Lords, 7 July 1778* (1779–80). Oil on canvas, 228.6 × 307.3 cm (support). Copyright © Tate, London, 2008.

VIII. John Singleton Copley, *The Death of Major Peirson, 6 January 1781* (1782–4). Oil on canvas, 251.5 × 365.8 cm (support). Copyright © Tate, London, 2008.

IX.   John Trumbull, *The Death of General Warren at the Battle of Bunker's Hill, June 17, 1775* (1786). Oil on canvas, 65.1 × 95.6 cm. Copyright © Yale University Art Gallery, New Haven, Connecticut. Trumbull Collection.

X.   John Singleton Copley, *Hugh Montgomerie, 12th Earl of Eglinton* (c.1780). Oil on canvas, 226.3 × 148.9 cm. Scottish National Portrait Gallery.

XI.   John Singleton Copley, *Elkanah Watson* (1782). Oil on canvas, 149 × 121 cm. Princeton University Art Museum. Gift of the estate of Josephine Thomson Swann. Photo credit: Bruce M. White. y1964–181.

XII.   Benjamin West, *The Apotheosis of Nelson* (1807). Oil on canvas, 100.3 × 73.7 cm. Yale Center for British Art, Paul Mellon Collection.

XIII. James Gillray, *Siège de la Colonne de Pompée: Science in the Pillory* (published 1799). Hand-coloured etching and engraving, 55.3 × 41.8 cm. Courtesy of The Lewis Walpole Library, Yale University.

XIV.   George Scharf, *A Lycian Tomb at Xanthus of the Style Resembling a Wooden Construction* (1844). Graphite drawing with white paint on toned paper, 75.5 × 55.5 cm. British Museum book of drawings: *1844 Expedition to Lycia and Xanthus,* number x.31. Copyright © The Trustees of the British Museum.

XV.   Robert Havell after James Baillie Fraser, *A View of Government House from the Eastward,* from Part I of Fraser's *Views of Calcutta and its Environs* (London, 1824–6), hand-coloured aquatint, 27.7 × 42.6 cm. Yale Center for British Art, Paul Mellon Collection.

XVI.   Thomas Hickey, *Col. Colin Mackenzie and His Assistants* (1816). Oil on canvas, 58.5 × 38 cm. British Library, India Office Library and Records. Copyright © The British Library Board, 2009.

XVII. J. Mustie, *Plan of the stupa excavation in June 1817. Inscribed: Plan descriptive of the present state of the Mound of Depaldenna at Amrawutty, showing what has been cleared out and what still remains to be removed, laid down from actual measurements, June 1817* (1819). Ink and watercolour on paper, 52 × 44.7 cm. Scale 20 feet: 1 inch. British Library, India Office, Prints and Drawings. Copyright © The British Library Board, 2009. WD 1061, fos 7–8.

XVIII. Joseph Nash, *Windsor Castle: The Waterloo Chamber, 5 June 1844* (1844). Watercolour and bodycolour over pencil, 28.2 × 36.8 cm. The Royal Collection 2009, Her Majesty Queen Elizabeth II. RL 19875.

Black and White Illustrations

22. James Heath, after Benjamin West, *The Death of Lord Viscount Nelson. K.B.* (1811). Line engraving, 51 cm × 64.5 cm. National Maritime Museum, Greenwich. PAH 8033.
23. Thomas Banks, *Monument to Captain Rundell Burgess*, St Paul's Cathedral, London (1798–1802). Courtauld Institute of Art, London.
24. John Bacon, *Monument to Sir John Moore*, St Paul's Cathedral, London (1810–15). Courtauld Institute of Art, London.
25. John Bacon, *Design for the Monument to Major-General Dundas in St. Paul's Cathedral, London* (c.1798). Design drawing. The National Archives, Kew [MPD 1/78].
26. William Holland (publisher), *The Sailor's Monument to the Memory of Lord Nelson* (1806). Hand-coloured etching, 24 × 34.4 cm. National Maritime Museum, Greenwich. PAG 8562 (MacPherson collection).
27. Richard Westmacott, *General Sir Isaac Brock* (1813-?). Marble monument, St Paul's Cathedral, London. Courtauld Institute of Art, London.
28. William Wollett, after Benjamin West, *Death of General Wolfe* (1776). Line engraving, 42.7 × 59 cm. Courtesy of the Library of Congress, Washington, DC.
29. E. W. Cooke, *Raising head to proper level opposite its pedestal in New Gallery (Gunners Installing Egyptian Sculptures at the North End of Robert Smirke's New Gallery)* (1834). Drawing, 26.1 × 32 cm. Copyright © Trustees of the British Museum, 2009.
30. *Perspective de l'Égypte, d'Alexandrie a Píale*, frontispiece to *Déscription de l'Égypte, ou, Recueil des observations et des recherches qui ont été faites en Égypte pendant l'expédition de l'armée française; publié par les ordres de Sa Majesté l'empereur Napoléon le Grand*, vol. 1 (Paris, 1809). Engraving. Asian and Middle Eastern Division, The New York Public Library, Astor, Lenox and Tilden Foundations.
31. *Rosetta Stone* (Ptolemaic Period, 196 BC). Excavated by Pierre François Xavier Bouchard from Fort St Julien, el-Rashid (Rosetta), Egypt. Width 72.3 × height 114 × depth 27.9 cm. View of left edge. Copyright © The Trustees of the British Museum, Gift of George III, 2009.
32. Marble block from the frieze of the Temple of Apollo Epikourios: *Greeks Fight Centaurs* (Phigalian, or Bassae, marbles, between 420 and 400 BC). Marble, length 161.25 cm. Copyright © The Trustees of the British Museum, 2009.
33. Charles R. Cockerell, *View of the Temple Jupiter Panhellenius in Aegina during the Excavations*, plate III in C. R. Cockerell *The Temples of Jupiter and Panhellenius at Aegina and of Apollo Epicurius at Bassae near Phigalia in Arcadia*

(London, 1860). Engraving by unknown artist, after drawing by J. M. W. Turner. Copyright © The British Library Board, 2009. 650.c.24.

34. H. Linton, after ? Gilbert, *Layard's Discoveries at Nimroud* (1852), published in *The Illustrated Exhibitor and Magazine of Art*, I (London, 1852), 145. Engraving, 14.5 x 17.3 cm. The Bodleian Library, University of Oxford: Per. 170 d.17, 1.

35. *The Xanthian Room Just Opened at the British Museum* (1848). *Illustrated London News*, XII, No. 298 (15 Jan. 1848), p. 15. Engraving. The Bodleian Library, University of Oxford: N. 2288 b. 6.

36. A. H. Layard, *Captives and Spoil brought to Assyria* (1845–7). Pencil and white paint on brown paper, 68 × 42cm. *Layard Original Drawings*, vol. 1 #69. Drawing after British Museum relief 'Campaigning in Southern Iraq' (640–620 BC) from Nineveh, south-west palace, room XXVIII, panels 9–11. Copyright © The Trustees of the British Museum, 2009.

37. *Shipping the Great Bull from Nimroud, at Morghill, on the Euphrates* (1850). *Illustrated London News*, XVII, no. 438 (27 July 1850), p. 72. Engraving, 24 × 15 cm. The Bodleian Library, University of Oxford: N. 2288 b. 6.

38. Percy William Justyne, *The Nineveh Gallery, British Museum* (c.1854). Wood engraving (clipped from a newspaper), 10.8 × 14.3 cm. Copyright © The Trustees of the British Museum, 2009.

39. J. C. Stadler, after Thomas Rowlandson and C. A. Pugin, *East India House, The General Court Room* [Old Sale Room] (1808). Coloured aquatint, 23 × 28 cm. Guildhall Library/LMA, City of London.

40. John Bacon, *Statue of Sir William Jones*, St Paul's Cathedral, London (completed 1799). Detail. Courtauld Institute of Art, London.

41. Thomas Daniell (1749–1840), *Gate of the Tomb of the Emperor Akbar at Secundra, near Agra* (c.1795). Hand-coloured aquatint, by and after Thomas Daniell, 45.7 × 59 cm. Part 1, Plate 9 of *Oriental Scenery* (London, 1795–7). Copyright © Victoria and Albert Museum, London, 2009.

42. Anon., *Architectural Model of Tirumala Nayak's Pudu Mandapa*, Madurai, India (1780–89). Commissioned by Adam Blackader. Copper alloy, 32.5 × 41 × 16 cm. Copyright © Victoria and Albert Museum, London, 2009.

43. Henry Salt, *Kenhery, Jagheyseer and Montpezir Caves* (London, 1818), reprinted in *Transactions of the Literary Society of Bombay*, I (1819), 41–52, plate [no. 4], facing p. 47. Engraving. The Bodleian Library, University of Oxford: Or. Per. 54.

44. James Phillips, after James Wales, *Interior View of the Principal Excavated Temple on the Island of Elephanta*, (1790); engraving after Wales's painting of 1785, after an initial drawing by James Forbes. Inside print line: 44.5 × 167 (image only: 37

× 65 cm). Copyright © The British Library Board, 2009. India Office, Prints and Drawings, P182.

45a and 45b. *One of the Smaller Temples at Brambanan in its Present State* and the same site '*restored to its original state*'. Plates juxtaposed in Sir Thomas Stamford Raffles, *The History of Java*, 2 vols (London, 1817; 1830), plate 22. Engraving after watercolour by the Dutch engineer H. C. Cornelius. Copyright © The British Library Board, 2009. 09055.b.38.

46. *Architectural Model of Marble Arch*, after a design by John Nash (*c*.1826). Plaster cast, 72.5 × 59 × 30.5 cm. Copyright © Victoria and Albert Museum, London, 2009.

47. Anon., *Plan of the Proposed Improvements at Charing Cross, St. Martin's Lane and Entrance to the Strand* (engr. Ingrey and Madeley, *c*.1824). Lithograph, 46 × 60 cm. Guildhall Library/LMA, City of London.

INTRODUCTION

SINEWS OF POWER AND EMPIRES OF THE IMAGINATION

Abu Taleb in London, 1800

In February 1799, Abu Taleb ibn Muhammed Isfahani set off from Calcutta to London.[1] For three decades, Taleb, a Shi'ite Indo-Persian scholar and a member of the north Indian Muslim service elite, had been working for Indian and British administrations at Oudh and in Bengal. He also made Indo-Islamic culture accessible to British imperial rulers through literary, historical, and political publications. After repeatedly fleeing from Oudh court intrigues into British protection at Calcutta, Taleb accepted the invitation of the Scots military officer and Persian translator for the East India Company, Captain David Thomas Richardson, to join him on his trip back to Europe. Taleb dreamed that he might found in London or Oxford a government-sponsored institute to teach Britons the Persian language and cultural skills they required to operate effectively in India.

Like other elite male Asians in the counterflow of empire, Taleb found that in Europe he rose in social standing. Passing through British-held Cape Town and through Dublin, he had learned that a bantering relationship with white, upper-class women gained him social prestige and access to powerful men. Portrayed by James Northcote, R.A. as a well-built, handsome man of noble countenance, Taleb had large almond-shaped eyes and a neatly trimmed moustache above sensually thick lips (fig. 1). In the Northcote portrait he is wearing a turban, a sash around the waist, and a scabbard. Taleb was soon fêted by the London crowds and newspapers as the celebrity 'Persian Prince' and was very favourably received at the court of King George III and Queen Charlotte. An accomplished gallant and flirt, Taleb gave

1. Anon., after James North-cote, R.A., *Portrait of Mirza Abu Talib Khan* (1801?).

himself up to 'love and gaity' and versified upon London's 'heart-alluring Damsels'. He cited the Persian poet Hafez to justify his enjoyment of the sensual pleasures of wine, music, and the occasional dance. Taleb revelled in the attention of aristocratic and polite society, and they in his, as he socialised for three seasons largely at their expense. He indulged in the varied entertainments the imperial metropolis had to offer: the opera, private masquerades, and balls, as well as the ubiquitous coffee houses and numerous clubs and societies. He met government ministers and attended debates in the House of Commons, where he likened the combative MPs to 'flocks of Indian paroquets, sitting upon opposite mango trees'.[2] As he mingled with freemasons, composers, artists, and Orientalists, Taleb loved how his 'wit and repartees, with some *impromptu* applications of Oriental poetry, were the subject of conversation in the politest circles'. British magazines acknowledged him as a 'man of considerable experience and knowledge of the world'.[3]

Yet Taleb was never much assimilated to British culture. The exotic yet unthreatening persona of the gallant, poetic Persian Prince served him well.[4] He took an active interest in collections of oriental manuscripts at Oxford, 'the most celebrated *Seat of Learning* of the Empire', whose stone-hewn buildings he compared with Hindu temples. Taleb was fascinated by Orientalist representations of South Asian culture in British paintings, botanical hothouses, and masquerades. He also saw the only major Indian country house in England, Sezincote in the Gloucestershire Cotswolds with its onion domes, multifoiled arches, and *chhatris* (corner pavillions).[5] Taleb met the upper-class Indo-Muslim women and bibis of retired Company officials as well as leading scholars such as Charles Wilkins and Sir William Ouseley.

Abu Taleb's visit fell at the halfway point of the period explored in this book, which saw Britain evolve from a substantial international power yet relative artistic backwater into a global naval, commercial, and imperial superpower as well as a leading cultural power in Europe. These developments, from the middle of the eighteenth century to the middle of the nineteenth, were not unrelated. In two seminal contributions to the history of eighteenth-century Britain, John Brewer first demonstrated the size and strength of the 'fiscal-military state' and then explained the transformation of the eighteenth-century cultural landscape in terms of the commercialisation of art, music, theatre, and literature in the polite public sphere.[6] But, as I will argue, the 'sinews of power' of the British imperial state at war also enabled and promoted projects which enhanced 'the pleasures of the imagination'.[7] To think and act big on the global stage required not only economic strength and military prowess, but manifestly also intellectual, cultural, and imaginative effort. As Britain expanded its global empire, Britons also built empires in their cultural imagination. And only a superpower wielded the military capabilities and imperial reach to accomplish certain cultural endeavours. Precisely the period around which Brewer's books end, the changing political, international, and imperial contexts at the turn of the nineteenth century, marked a transformative phase for British cultural politics and the cultural state.

Over the century between 1750 and 1850, the number and range of cultural sites and projects which the state (co)sponsored expanded significantly. These reflected, and in turn fostered, Britain's military and imperial experiences. War was a crucial catalyst of state engagement with certain forms of culture. Comparison, competition, and conflict with other nations provided important contexts in which Britons thought about national culture and cultural patriotism. Some of the imperial imagery Taleb encountered in London in 1800 had been commissioned or built to generate consensus and loyalty, to project a sense of purposefulness and patriotism as part of forging the imperial nation. In many instances this had required officials to be lobbied, and often it had necessitated legislation, parliamentary appropriations, or royal approval. But party politics and the desire for

3

individual aggrandisement often influenced discussions too. Monarchs, ministers, parliamentarians, and cultural players jockeyed for influence and contested notions of fame and heroic conduct. The politics of culture was shaped, too, by critiques of imperial hubris or exploitation, by debates over the plunder of antiquities, and by philistine or reforming attitudes to state sponsorship of culture.

The London that Abu Taleb came to visit had grown from a city of some 600,000 inhabitants in the early eighteenth century, roughly the same size as Paris, into Europe's largest city with a population of nearly one million in 1801. The British capital was the hub of the social season, scheduled around the parliamentary session and supported by a plethora of purpose-built entertainment venues. Europe's greatest centre of industrial production also formed Britain's single largest market for basic consumer and luxury goods, the guarantor of the country's trade credit, a pivotal *entrepôt*, and centre of the transport network on land. It was the workplace for more than half the country's doctors and lawyers; and the national stage for writers, artists, and musicians aspiring to prominence or glorying in fleeting stardom. London was also the seat of the royal court, government, and Parliament, and the head of the world's most expansive overseas empire. From this centre of international shipping, finance, and commerce, London's banks, insurance companies, docks, and merchant fleet connected the imperial metropolis with people, goods, and information all around the globe.[8]

It had taken several wars, fought on an ever-larger scale, mostly against France and Spain, for Britain to expand from a major European power with sizeable colonial possessions into the world's only imperial, naval, and commercial superpower. Since 1700, Britain had conquered Gibraltar and Minorca in the Mediterranean; Hudson Bay, Nova Scotia, Newfoundland, and Quebec in Canada; Florida and the trans-Appalachian lands, several Caribbean islands, St Kitts, as well as Senegal. After the Seven Years War (1756–63), the first truly global war, in which France had been defeated at sea, on land, and in the colonies, Britain also took control of Bengal and its 20 million inhabitants. Although after America's War of Independence (1775–83), Britain had lost its thirteen Atlantic seaboard colonies, the Floridas, the Western lands, Tobago, and Senegal, Anglo-American trade soon exceeded pre-war volumes. Britain then gained Trinidad and retained coastal Ceylon in the Peace of Amiens in 1802, the brief interlude in the French Revolutionary and Napoleonic Wars that were fought between 1793 and 1815. Over that period, the number of British colonies had risen from twenty-six to forty-three. Britain's sea routes to India were secured with bases from the Cape to Ceylon. In 1750, Spain and Portugal had still been major powers in the Atlantic world. The Mediterranean presence of France, Spain, and the Italian states had outweighed that of Britain, which was also just one of at least five powers with trading outposts in India. France was threatening to link its North American settlements to explore the unclaimed West. By 1850, of the other old colonial powers, only Spain still held Cuba and the Philippines, and the Dutch Indonesia, and France had invaded Algeria in 1830. The USA and Russia were only gradually mounting a challenge to the British Empire. By the time that this book ends, Queen Victoria's empire encompassed one quarter of the globe's land surface and one fifth of the world's population; it was unsurpassed in global reach and power.

Colonial policy was driven by Britain's need to finance defence and by an ambition to increase international trade, influence, and prestige – mostly in competition with France. Imperial expansion also followed the quest for plunder, land, professional advancement, and knowledge. As the volume of British trade tripled over the eighteenth century, trade with the wider world grew faster than that with Europe; by 1770, 60 per cent of British exports went to America, Africa, and India. Having a bigger merchant marine, and therefore a larger pool of trained seamen, gave Britain a distinct advantage over its arch-enemy France, as did the British state's capacity to extract three times as much revenue per capita through taxation as the French; it also funded ever more expensive wars through a uniquely trusted system of national debt, guaranteed by specific taxes levied by a representative Parliament. On the other hand, the limits in terms of Britain's sheer size, population, and therefore armed forces made sustaining a vast empire more chancy than its expanse and growth in this period might suggest. Smallness, however, also fostered cohesion and a shared determination by aristocratic, mercantile, and financial elites to jointly develop imperial investment and aggression. Beyond the expanse of Britain's formal empire, there were regions in which it exerted various degrees of informal influence by economic, political, and cultural means.[9]

National efforts of war and empire were underpinned not only by measurable sinews of power like taxation, debt, and soldiers, but also by more intangible factors. These included widely shared beliefs and values such as Protestantism, liberty, property, and a growing appreciation of the virtues of the monarchy. The very experience of empire was in turn a crucial political and cultural catalyst in the forging of the British nation. Historians have of late brought the imperial dimensions of British politics, social relations, and nationhood into increasingly sharp focus.[10] Just as state-building was a cultural as well as a political exercise, empire was not just a political project but to an extent a cultural artefact too: empire belonged to a geography of the mind as much as a geography of power. Culture and power, or mastering and understanding the empire, were linked in imagining and forging the nation. This pertained to mentality and material reality, to everyday life as well as notions of governance, race, religion, and manliness.[11] And, as part of the wider tendency of the metropolis to define the empire as a whole, visual culture developed a global imperial landscape. Topographical art – much of it created by military officers trained in military academies – valued the authority of first-hand experience, from the Scottish Highlands after the '45 to North America, the West Indies, and India, as well as on Admiralty-sponsored expeditions to the Pacific. Visualisation helped audiences at home imagine and conceptualise a globally connected empire; it could also help legitimise contentious imperial projects from the protection of slave societies in the West Indies to the regulation of empire in the East Indies.[12]

Although the London Abu Taleb came to know was truly a capital city, until the early nineteenth century it hardly looked like one (see map 1). Not for London the grand architectural visions of Vienna, Berlin, or St Petersburg. But imperial expansion and global warfare clearly marked the face of the metropolis. African and Asian people walked London's streets and were on display in its popular entertainment venues. Sugar, coffee, tea, and spices were consumed in coffee houses and in private homes.[13] Britons read in the burgeoning press about imperial conquests and setbacks, about the natural resources and peoples of the empire. At the Vauxhall Pleasure Gardens (which once advertised Abu Taleb's attendance to promote a charitable event), cultural consumption often revolved around patriotic and imperialistic displays. Promenades were decorated with triumphal arches and a temple of Neptune; Francis Hayman's paintings for the Grand Salon highlighted the magnanimity and charity of the conquering Generals Clive and Amherst during the Seven Years War; and the air rang with patriotic songs, celebrating the most recent battles won and calling forth a deeper patriotic and imperial aspect in the British national psyche.[14]

During Taleb's London visit, the young painter Robert Ker Porter's spectacular, forty-metre-long, semi-circular panorama of *The Storming of Seringapatam* attracted record-breaking crowds. It was among numerous paintings, plays, prints, pamphlets, and decorative art of all sorts inspired by the capture of Seringapatam in 1799.[15] The theatres offered their customary imperial fare: during Taleb's first season, Covent Garden showed *The West Indian* and – following Britain's triumph over Napoleon in Egypt – Drury Lane contributed to the newest wave of Egyptomania with a successful run of *The Egyptian Festival*. Imperial expansion was making its mark not only on commercial culture, but on official sites too. Indeed, Taleb experienced London at the cusp of a substantial growth in official imperial sites. Westminster Abbey, for instance, Britain's coronation church, was also the mausoleum of its distinguished statesmen, soldiers, and cultural icons. Imperial warfare in India and America had first entered the Abbey in the form of heroic monuments to men such as Admiral Watson and General Wolfe in the 1760s. America's War of Independence left but a few controversial traces in marble. Yet renewed imperial warfare and heroic death continued to register in the Abbey in the 1790s. When setting out from Bengal, Taleb's ship had been detained until the East India Company's Captain Cooke had captured the French frigate *La Forte*, which had been cruising predatorily in the Bay of Bengal; Cooke fell in the battle and soon joined the imperial heroes in Westminster Abbey.

Abu Taleb also visited the British Museum in Bloomsbury, 'a National Institution,' he explained, as 'the whole expense is paid by Government'.[16] The Hanoverians did not follow the lead of Continental princes in displaying royal collections to select publics, as happened between 1750 and the 1790s in Paris, Dresden, and Vienna.[17] Instead, the British Museum performed a national service as a public museum.[18] International competition over cultural property was played out in national museums. As Taleb was to discover in Paris in 1802, the Louvre was a rich 'repository of all the pictures, select statues, and other curiosities, plundered by Bonaparte and other French generals, from all the countries they have overrun'.[19] The British imperial state also enabled the British Museum to collect many of the world's most prized antiquities. In 1802, the armed forces sent the Rosetta Stone, a token of British victory over Napoleon, inscribed to this day: 'CAPTURED IN EGYPT BY THE BRITISH ARMY 1801' (see fig. 31). That year, Ambassador Elgin requested a large warship to demonstrate British naval prowess off Athens and to remove the caryatid porch of the Erectheum, as 'Buonaparte has not got such a thing, from all his thefts in Italy'.[20] In 1750, it was a select number of aristocrats who decorated their mansions with Roman and Greek antiquities. By 1850, Britain had not only acquired the Parthenon or Elgin Marbles, but, more widely, it had deployed its diplomatic, military, and naval capabilities in culture wars of informal empire with France and sometimes with German states. The new British Museum building, Robert Smirke's grand neo-Greek temple, was soon filled, as a result, with ornamental pillar-tombs from Lycia and giant winged, human-headed lions and bulls from Mesopotamia.

Britain had no doubt boasted cultural richness well before Abu Taleb's visit: English intellectual influence was felt in Europe through the philosophy and science of Bacon, Newton, and Locke and through Scottish philosophers' contributions to the European enlightenment. English literature and theatre were much admired and English garden design was beginning to be exported. But while most of the artists who had created the spectacle of Versailles in the previous century had been French, many of the leading artists in England even in the first half of the eighteenth century were foreign-born. The dominance of non-native sculptors, combined with connoisseurs' preference for Old Masters over contemporary British paintings, prompted much comment and considerable anguish. The trend, from around mid-century, to build institutions in the arts was partly driven by the desire of British artists and patrons to foster indigenous traditions in design and national schools of painting and sculpture.[21]

Promotion of native art was hailed as a patriotic act. Against the triumphant background of the Seven Years War, comparisons between the military and cultural might of Britain and that of contemporary France or ancient Rome helped justify demands for sponsorship of British culture. The 'rise of the imperial dream', in Matthew Craske's words, was accompanied and fostered by a culture that was increasingly 'consumed by the fantasies and realities of heroic war in foreign parts'.[22] Throughout much of George III's reign, official culture developed the narratives of state, war, and empire not only in heroic monuments in the metropolis and in public buildings and cemeteries across British India (chs. 1, 3, 4, 7), but also through the appropriation of ancient cultures from the Mediterranean, Near East, and India (chs. 5–8), and in the redesign of Regency London as an imperial, urban work of art (ch. 9).

One London site that unmistakably embodied the conjunction of military and cultural might and manifested the imagined links between the Roman and British empires was Somerset House, which first opened at the height of the American Revolutionary War in 1780. Located on the south side of the Strand halfway between the West End and the City of London, it was the most imposing public building erected in the imperial metropolis in the second half of the century, and one of Europe's grandest civic structures. It was also an important site of cultural and scientific endeavours. Offices servicing the world's mightiest navy cohabited with the Royal Academy of Arts, the Royal Society, and the Society of Antiquaries. The Royal Society, whose meetings Taleb frequently attended, was at the heart of Sir Joseph Banks's scientific empire, which stretched from the botanical gardens at Kew to India and the Caribbean.[23] The Antiquaries briefly hosted the Rosetta Stone on its arrival in London and also concerned themselves with the remains of civilisations which were now under imperial purview. In 1801, two portraits of Taleb (of the six that are known) were exhibited in the Royal Academy's annual show, alongside the usual panoply of paintings depicting British imperial warfare and models of heroic statues intended for metropolitan and imperial sites. Such statues rarely acknowledged one of the darkest sides of empire. In the Guildhall in the City of London stood the statue of the former Lord Mayor, William Beckford MP, the prominent absentee owner of Jamaican plantations and 3,000 slaves. Beckford, flanked by allegorical figures representing the City of London and Commerce & Navigation, is praised for upholding the 'City's traditional liberties'. His links with the slave trade and plantations lie unacknowledged, just as in the public memorials of other men involved in such activity.[24] It was only in commemorating those instrumental to the abolition of the slave trade in the British Empire in 1807, such as Granville Sharpe or Charles James Fox, that emblematic figures of kneeling, male, freed slaves were included in metropolitan statues. Imperial exploitation was rarely acknowledged in the physical landscape of the imperial capital; slavery and other forms of violence were mostly denied by metropolitan cultural representations.[25]

Also in the City of London stood East India House, the 'very extensive and superb' headquarters of the Company in Leadenhall Street in the City of London. Taleb ranked the seat of this imperial agency in 'political importance' next to the House of Commons.[26] As he approached, he would have been greeted by an allegory on the façade of benign Western rule and the promise of liberty in exchange for Eastern commerce. The building had recently been expanded, reflecting the dramatic change in Britain's Indian presence. It had evolved from largely seaborne trading relations to intermittent wars of conquest and, by this point, a very significant territorial dominion. This had prompted concern about the constitutional and moral implications of an Eastern empire of conquest. Yet, administrative reforms from the 1770s had been followed by the further militarisation of the aggressively expanding Company state. During Abu Taleb's stay in London, the Company opened the Oriental Repository, where fee-paying visitors could experience India as an exotic colony, with a miscellany of natural and man-made objects, including antiquities and trophies of war.[27]

The global scope of Britain's military and imperial concerns at the turn of the century was powerfully represented nearby, by another evocative set of trophies: the tattered enemy flags deposited in St Paul's Cathedral. Before Abu Taleb left London, the Cathedral also boasted its first national heroic monument. By 1820, some three dozen memorials – flanked by British lions as well as Indian elephants, Caribbean palms, and sphinxes – would commemorate the heroes of Britain's naval victories against the French, Dutch, and Spanish, the campaigns in Egypt, the Peninsula, North America, Nepal, and Ceylon, as well as the final defeat of Napoleon at Waterloo.

Taleb took the opportunity of the Peace of Amiens in 1802 to begin his journey home. He was disappointed that his initial plans for an Orientalist academy had not come off. At a stop-over in Paris he was much impressed with the cityscape, which 'in its exterior appearance, far surpasses London'.[28] Although he preferred the comfort of English domestic interiors and even English cooking, Taleb considered the French opera and especially the museum collections superior. His journey, aided by letters of recommendation from George III, took him through southern France, Italy, the Ottoman Empire, Persia, and Bombay. He arrived in Calcutta in August 1803, four and a half years after he had set out.

On his return, Abu Taleb found a city dramatically changed by the British. During Taleb's absence, Governor-General Wellesley had built a palatial Government House in Calcutta, at the same astonishing speed with which he was driving the aggressive expansion of British Indian territory. Imagery of the grand civic architecture of Calcutta, as well as of Bombay and Madras, circulated in Britain in the form of prints, paintings, and panoramas (see plate XV). Wellesley's defeat of Tipu in 1799 had also triggered Colonel Colin Mackenzie's pioneering physical and cultural survey of Mysore. His joint British–indigenous teams copied inscriptions, made hundreds of sketches, and collected texts, coins, and other antiquities (see plate XVI). Such imperial surveys, geared both to scholarly discoveries and to imperial governance, epitomised the inextricable connections between the culture of power and the power of culture.[29] Much to Abu Taleb's chagrin, the colonial government did not appoint him to any office after his return. He died in poverty before the Company's offer of a position as a Persian tutor at their college at Haileybury reached him.

Abu Taleb was an astute observer of both Indian and European societies. Like previous learned Indian travellers, Taleb recognised British political, technical, and military achievements, but he contested British and Christian cultural and moral superiority. He was outspokenly critical of the social and religious mores of the elite, gender relations, as well as the poverty, irreligion, and disorderliness of the working classes. Yet, whereas while he was in Europe he temporarily gained some prominence in the public discourse, he made no lasting impact and, ultimately, remained the turbaned, exotic curiosity whose analysis of European society was not taken very seriously there. Taleb was a transitional figure visiting the metropolis at a transitional moment in the history of the British Empire – after the loss of America and in the midst of a global war with Napoleonic France and aggressive British expansion in the East.[30] His encounters with the evolving face of imperial London showed the metropolis at the cusp of a significant growth in the number and visibility of official imperial sites. The places, objects, and representations, which Taleb, Londoners, and other Britons and visitors saw, rendered war and empire concrete and intelligible. They also reflected the increasingly prominent role played by the state in British cultural politics. At the same time, such representations had a creative potential of their own and helped shape political culture, and the very idea and practices of the cultural state. Having followed Taleb around the imperial capital, and before we explore these themes in detail, it is time to offer some definitions.

Concepts and Arguments

This book suggests a framework for thinking about the relations between two analytical categories: politics and culture, and more specifically about the notion of the politics of culture. By politics I refer to the pursuit and use of power through formal, institutional, and extra-institutional or informal means. Culture is a much more complex term, sometimes considered one of the two or three most difficult words in the English language, especially because it has multiple definitions of different orders of reference. For the purposes of this book I focus on three.[31] Most narrowly, culture refers to the arts – painting, sculpture, music, theatre, and literature – or what is sometimes called 'high culture'. The notion of 'the fine arts' as a system as we know it evolved in eighteenth-century Europe through the critical ordering of fields such as literature, painting, and music. This development was linked on the one hand to the processes of professionalisation and institutionalisation, and on the other to the evolution of national canons and the notion of a national heritage. To contrast culture with the state, the economy, or religion risks not appreciating the relations between culture on the one hand, and economic, social, and political structures on the other.

Secondly, and more broadly, 'culture' is used in line with the notion that culture forms a whole: culture here means the 'genius', 'humour', or 'spirit' of an age. This usage is in line with enlightenment histories of culture by writers like Voltaire, Montesquieu, Winckelmann, or Hume, who explained artistic production in terms of climatic determinism or historically contingent factors such as systems of government or the nature of societies. One problem with this notion of culture is that it is too organic, total, and homogeneous, and doesn't allow sufficiently for disagreement and contestation.

It is therefore helpful to consider culture, thirdly, as referring to the values and attitudes of a society, and the expression of such attitudes and values in collective representations. Culture here denotes the archive of stories a society tells about itself, including in works of art as much as in literature. It embraces the remembering of historical events and persons. Culture is a repertoire of practices through which humans provide meanings to their lives. Such cultural resources can be used in contestation as well as consensually.

We need some further preliminary definitions. By the British 'state' I mean first of all the formal institutions of state: the monarchy, national government, and Parliament, the diplomatic and armed services, as well as the formal institutions of imperial governance. Beyond these, I conceptualise the British state to encompass a wider, loosely connected network of institutions and influence, such as military academies, corporate bodies like the East India Company, and national cultural institutions such as the British Museum. Moreover, in order to appreciate the porous boundaries of the state it is necessary to look to scholarly and scientific networks and associations, and to organisations like the Royal Academy of Arts, which had more or less formal ties with the monarchy or government, variously lobbied or were consulted by government and Parliament, and helped the state to project influence in international and imperial spheres. Overlapping networks of officialdom and cultural players, of naval and military officers and metropolitan scholarly circles, shaped archaeology, collecting, and museum development; they drove imperial taxonomic projects from ethnography to natural history; and they forged ideas of national culture and identity.[32]

Nations, like all political communities, are imagined communities.[33] A key site of political and cultural imagination, and a space where new political culture is created, is the public sphere, that ground between the state and the private household that is public in as far as it is relatively accessible and relevant, but that is distinct from the state. The notion of political culture integrates ideas and values, communication and media, rituals, symbols, and habits, and the whole penumbra of informal political activities that relate to formal politics.[34] Art is premised on a range of social and political ideas and institutions. Much art is quite overtly political, making points about the nature of authority and legitimacy, about particular political actors and groups, or the ethics of public life.

The relation between worlds of culture and worlds of politics or power is therefore complex. Many cultural historians stress the interplay of ideas, language, and action, and the relations between meaning and symbols. Culture is not merely a reflection or expression of social experience or political reality; nor is it an autonomous entity. Instead, people's attempts to understand and to master the world around them are inextricably intertwined. The historian needs to consider both changing socio-political realities and the creative potential of cultural forms. Understanding the relationship of culture, ideas, symbols, and discourses to power requires that we investigate both how texts and artefacts work as systems of signification and how they were produced, used, interpreted, and circulated.[35] One recurrent example in this book concerns notions and practices of 'cultural patriotism'. By this I mean the expression of patriotic sentiment – a preference for, and an emotional identification with, one's own country – through the production, promotion, and consumption of specific cultural processes, events, and goods. The study of cultural patriotism needs to take seriously both the discourses of patriotism and its political sites, social scope, and cultural practices.

This book is also about the role of war in cultural history. War was not just, first, a catalyst of the emergence of the fiscal-military state after the Glorious Revolution and, second, a catalyst of notions of national identity and consciousness throughout the Second Hundred Years War with France (1689–1815). War played an important role, too, in the shaping of notions of national culture, the cultural nation, and the cultural state. Thus, the British state sponsored national military monuments as a way of promoting national culture and loyalist patriotic morale. Monument-building was the pursuit of war at a symbolic level. So was the collecting for the British Museum of certain types of classical and Near Eastern antiquities. International scientific and artistic exchange often continued even during periods of war. However, the supply of saltpetre for the manufacturing of gunpowder, botanical developments, and industrial espionage could become bones of contention; artists were liable to accusations of espionage when caught sketching fortifications. War cannot explain nearly all cultural development; nor was war relevant only for such cultural activity as related to the state. Yet, if one connects the narrative of the fiscal-military state to that of the cultural politics of its organisers, one finds that those running the fiscal-military state also often shaped the cultural repercussions of its success. 'Arms and Arts!' could be an effective rallying cry for artists and statesmen alike.[36]

As we explore the role of politics, the state, war, and empire as agents and sites of cultural change, and the role of the arts in political culture, this book is not directly concerned with the military and economic processes of empire-building and the fiscal and logistical aspects of warfare. Instead it analyses some of the cultural and imaginative effort that was invested to come to terms with the loss of the American colonies and to sustain the generation-long fight against Revolutionary and Napoleonic France; to appropriate classical civilisations in the national intellectual and cultural patrimony; and to assert a growing Indian empire over the insecurity of the thin red line, the questionable survivability of colonial rule itself. This book focuses less on campaign narrative than on representations of battles and heroes in monuments – and less on specific aesthetic developments than on the construction of cultural practices as patriotic or national.

However, it is crucial, I will argue, to appreciate the links too. For to understand who was considered eligible for heroic memorialisation requires an examination of the precise circumstances of their battles and deaths, at least as far as they were reported at the time to decision-makers and the public. Heroic representation needs to be explained in terms of political discourses as well as aesthetic conventions and codes of masculinity. To appreciate the achievements of archaeological expeditions means understanding the relative diplomatic leverage and military capabilities of Britain and its opponents in the Mediterranean and Near East. It requires studying the archives of the Admiralty and Foreign Office as well as the collections of the British Museum and Royal Literary Society. To explain the motivations and limitations of archaeological practice in British India, we need to understand the military, political, and imperial contexts which enabled and constrained them. Officially sponsored cultural projects depended on the reach of the imperial fiscal-military state and, in turn, they could legitimate its expansion.

It is important to put British experience back into European contexts. Across eighteenth-century Europe, there was growing concern for the significance of the 'fine arts', both socially in terms of the development of 'refinement' in complex, mobile societies, and economically, as developing the appetite for, and improving the quality of, manufactures. Moreover, the arts were a key expression of a distinctive 'national character' to help bind peoples to the emerging nation-states.[37] There were also broad similarities of trends in European cultural politics, such as professionalisation and institutionalisation, and, in the nineteenth century, the sacralisation and democratisation of the arts. Clearly, cultural politics in Europe was conducted in awareness of what was happening in other states and nations. Because international comparison, emulation, and, often, direct competition mattered to contemporaries, looking across the Channel can yield particular insights into British practices of collecting and commemoration.[38]

The British state and cultural politics by the late eighteenth century displayed features which put them in the Western European mainstream, and features by which they were distinguished. Yet the notion of British exceptionalism in cultural history has proven stubbornly persistent. While developments in the British state, social order, and industrial growth are increasingly seen as distinctive variants of wider European patterns, ideas about uniquely British ways of organising the nation's cultural life have not been tested as vigorously.[39] This is in part the result of the recently prominent notion that in Britain the visual and performing arts moved, comparatively early, from representational functions at court and in church to a commercialised culture in the public sphere. In France, Prussia, or Habsburg Austria, courts, monarchs, governments, and – especially in Catholic nations – the church promoted cultural endeavour. In Britain, 'high culture' became first and foremost a profitable leisure industry; investment in certain forms of culture was a private individual's marker of social status.[40]

This particular approach in recent cultural history has immensely enriched our understanding of the proliferation of cultural artefacts, institutions, and audiences.

Emphasis on the commercial, however, provides only limited insight into widespread contemporary preoccupation with what art could offer the nation.[41] Such emphasis can also constrain our understanding of what I call the politics of culture. By this I mean, firstly, the internal structures and workings of the distinct sphere of high culture – the ways in which those who made, disseminated, and appreciated and consumed art interacted within informal networks and formal organisations; and the languages such figures used to legitimise their actions. Secondly, and more broadly, studying the politics of culture involves considering how the cultural field related to the machinery and power struggles of British and imperial politics and the nature and personnel of the cultural state. Eighteenth-century British politics extended well beyond the formal institutions and official discourses of politics, to the languages of costumes, gestures, and performing arts. Satirical prints, exhibition spaces, and cultural rituals such as public dinners were all part of the wider political realm. The arts did not just stimulate the pleasures of the imagination in the cultural market place. They also served the aesthetic performance of politics and helped shape political culture.

The focus on a commercialised culture has encouraged thinking in somewhat simplistic dichotomies: market *versus* state; voluntary initiative and self-regulating professions *versus* public funding and state regulation; culture as commodity *versus* culture as official resource and national patrimony.[42] Indeed, historians commonly emphasise that there was a marked reticence about state promotion of the arts in Britain before the 1830s, especially when compared with Continental Europe. Parliamentary control over royal finances, Protestant reservations about the public role of the arts, the lack of state personnel, and a narrow notion of the state's responsibilities allegedly prevented it from playing a significant cultural role.[43]

This book makes the case that the formal institutions of state were more important players in British cultural life than has been recognised. We now understand the British fiscal-military and imperial state to have been more efficient and expansive, yet also more porous and open towards supporting private initiatives than previously assumed, and more so than was the case across most of Europe. Yet, as this revisionism has not yet fully extended to the cultural state, the prevailing view that the very structure and scope of the state limited its concern with culture remains largely intact. I argue that the 'cultural state' had a distinctly British nature: its boundaries were more fluid and porous, it allowed and often encouraged the dovetailing of public and private effort, and it was more responsive than has been recognised to demands for the provision of infrastructure and assistance for cultural endeavours.

The relationship between the state and civil society is worth reconsidering too.

The great variety of professional organisations founded mostly between the second third of the eighteenth and the first third of the nineteenth centuries – academies of art and music, learned societies, museums, and galleries – were all part of a vibrant, commercialised world of art and music. Yet, in manifold ways they were also linked to the world of politics and to the state. It is true that the French cultural state worked with a much heavier hand. The cultural institutions founded under Louis XIV's auspices – the royal academies for painting and sculpture, dance, inscriptions and letters, sciences, and architecture – had a near-monopoly of national talent.[44] But the equivalent academies and societies in Britain had a relationship with the state too, which those like the Royal Society, Royal Academy, or Society of Antiquaries at times activated to lobby or advise the crown, government, or Parliament. Moreover, private initiative could be justified or perceived within a framework of patriotic public policy and the context of international rivalry. Servants of the state, such as the diplomats Lord Elgin in Greece or Stratford Canning in the Ottoman Empire, strove to be recognised as cultural benefactors of the state and the nation.

There are instructive parallels between themes in this book and the much better researched relationship between the imperial state and science. Sir Joseph Banks as President of the Royal Society, Sir Roderick Murchison as Director-General of the Geological Survey, and Sir John Barrow, second Secretary to the Admiralty, institutionalised science as part of foreign policy and imperial administration. Exploration, mapping, resource reconnaissance, and commercial development on the one hand, and intelligence-gathering for imperial governance, foreign policy, and security on the other, were mutually enhancing. The most immediately useful sciences – botany, geology, and geography – led the way. The Geological Survey of Great Britain, the Royal Botanic Gardens at Kew with its imperial flora, and the Royal Geographical Society offered meeting grounds for officials and scientists. The state obtained intelligence relevant to imperial development; scientists stood to gain status, authority, and career opportunities.[45] Mapping and surveying were closely related to the archaeological techniques of mapping, inventory, and classification developed by military officers and imperial officials in India.

In this reassessment of British cultural politics, I will further argue that the similarities with Continental Europe were greater than rigidly structural or formal comparisons have previously suggested: similar functions were performed by different means. What is more, my analysis suggests a different choreography and chronology for the *pas de deux* of British-European cultural politics. In the best brief analysis of similarities and differences in Anglo-European cultural politics, Peter Mandler has argued that divergence increased in the Napoleonic period and in the aftermath of the great European wars of 1793–1815, followed by temporary convergence in the

1830s and 1840s, before divergence became again the main theme. This book proposes instead that the period c.1790–1815 was a transitional phase in British cultural politics, when the cultural state was first forged at metropolitan and imperial level. In my trajectory of change, the grand schemes of metropolitan building and collecting between c.1815 and the 1840s suggest greater continuity in state commitment to the arts throughout the first half of the nineteenth century.[46]

Just as the British parliamentary monarchy knew no single source of dominant power, there was by the middle of the eighteenth century no single, dominant source of cultural patronage either. The crown, government, Parliament, corporate bodies such as the East India Company, the Established Church, and municipal authorities all influenced the nation's cultural life in innovative ways.[47] To start with, the state defined frameworks for cultural practices. In the 1730s–90s, Parliament legislated on copyright for literature, engraving, music, and sculpture. From 1737, theatrical performances were subject to the approval of the Examiner of Plays. Customs duties regulated the importation of antiquities and of modern works of art. The Office of Works built government offices and improved royal residences. Politicians engaged impresarios to oversee the displays of transparencies, fireworks, and music, which transformed London's royal parks and streetscapes on the occasion of military victories, peace celebrations, and royal spectacles.

The British crown has traditionally been seen to lack the capacity and/or willingness, compared with Continental monarchies, to project a sense of kingship through cultural patronage. Parliamentary constraints and the existence of a commercial cultural sphere combined to limit royal cultural display.[48] When the French and Prussian monarchs built entire ensembles of palaces, the English and British monarchy did not have equivalent stages. It was not until George III and George IV first turned Windsor into the largest royal residence and George IV set himself on stage at Carlton House, the Brighton Pavilion, and the much aggrandised Buckingham Palace that the head of the global superpower lived on imperial scale. When eighteenth-century monarchs did dispense patronage, it was often as private patrons, and the main impact was to give social cachet. Nevertheless, the monarch did act as a *national* patron as well: George III founded the Royal Academy of Arts, promoted the cult of Handel, patronised moralistic history painting, chose designs for the first military monuments in St Paul's Cathedral, and transferred the Rosetta Stone – captured by his army in Egypt – to the British Museum. In his son, the Prince of Wales (from 1811 the Prince Regent, from 1820 George IV), the nation found one of its most aesthetically appreciative as well as extravagant royal cultural leaders since Charles I. George IV's penchant for grandiloquent ceremonial finally made London look more like the capital cities of Continental Europe.

The Established Church was an increasingly important patron of art and music in its own right. Although this subject requires a book of its own, we will touch on the ambiguous relationship between religion and the arts.[49] Protestant scepticism of cosmopolitan, aristocratic culture resulted in a call for *English* art, and sometimes in condemnation of the arts altogether as impious rivals to religion. There were strong evangelical reservations against promoting a secular cult of Handel and the same later of war heroes in the capital's cathedral. Religious thinking nevertheless influenced victory medals in the 1760s; Handelmania in the 1780s had a religious tinge; the cult of British Christian warriors in the 1790s was both enhanced and contested on religious grounds; and archaeological endeavours in Egypt and Assyria were advocated with reference to their potential to affirm biblical narrative. What the case of religion shows is that other axes along which contemporaries organised their identities could align or conflict with cultural patriotism, just as notions of patriotism were contested between political and cultural groups.

Many government ministers, members of both Houses of Parliament, and military and naval officers had wide experience of the arts. This was evident in their education and travelling and their patronage. Parliament, rather than just limiting court patronage of culture, offered a distinctly British forum for cultural politics. It founded the British Museum and sanctioned subsequent appropriations.[50] The parliaments of this period boasted dozens of important art-collectors, some accomplished amateur artists, as well as playwrights, musicians, and composers. Both Houses debated and formally decided on national monuments; the Treasury appointed the Committee of Taste, which consisted of collecting peers and connoisseurial parliamentarians, to supervise their design and execution.

Among the wider governing class, many of Britain's diplomatic representatives, imperial administrators, and military officers were steeped in the classics; they pursued their archaeological and antiquarian interests and collected antiquities on postings. Diplomats and imperial officials helped pioneer archaeological expeditions around the Mediterranean and Near East. East India Company officials – a colonial community which included more talented amateur artists than any other – commissioned thousands of drawings and paintings from both visiting British and resident Indian artists. They introduced metropolitan styles in architecture, sculpture, and painting to Calcutta, Madras, and Bombay, and they promoted the development of archaeology on the Subcontinent. Finally, the British state also employed artists: as engravers at the Mint, the Tower, the Stamp Office, and the Horse Guards; as architects and master masons; as drawing masters at naval and military academies, the training college of the East India Company at Haileybury, and the Board of Ordnance at the Tower; and as draughtsmen on military surveys, archaeological campaigns, and botanical, hydrographic, and geographical expeditions.

In brief, many among Britain's political elite took an active interest in cultural affairs. Politicians' cultural commitments blurred the lines between society and state. Scores of politicians, officials, and officers were involved with Britain's leading artistic, musical, and learned institutions: those which educated artists or musicians and such as offered patronage. At meetings of London's learned societies and at the Orientalist societies in Calcutta and Madras, clubbable and cultured politicians rubbed shoulders with antiquarians and archaeologists. Many embodied the overlap of interests and activities in the same person. Politicians helped run the British Museum and the Concert of Ancient Music, assisted in the development of the earliest provincial galleries, and set up London's Royal Academy of Music (1823) and National Gallery of Art (1824).

As the cultural and political players who populate this book interacted in informal networks and formal organisations, they developed a culture of association. Abu Taleb's attendance at the Royal Society and the Musical Society, and his reference to numerous clubs, testified to the sheer scope and vibrancy of associationism as a distinctive feature of British public life. Voluntary associations enhanced the pleasures of sociability, shared economic interests, and charity. Associations also acted as lobbies to shape legislative and executive policy on economic, political, and moral issues. In doing so, they developed the political skills and education of many who were excluded from formal politics. Politicians offered cultural societies the expertise of administrators and officers and access to the power elites. Overlapping circles of cultural figures and policy-makers created official and semi-official spaces to formulate and execute cultural policy. Associations assumed social and economic responsibilities that elsewhere (or in Britain somewhat later) were taken care of by governments or corporate bodies.[51] Some cultural organisations worked in that way too, but again it is mostly the porous boundaries between state institutions and the cultural sphere, and the sharing of authority between officials and artistic and scholarly figures, that interest me in this book.

Whereas this history focuses mostly on practices of Britain's political and cultural elites and on what is often referred to as 'high culture', in rituals such as coronations, national thanksgivings, state funerals, and in naval and military commemoration, the nation participated as more or less actively engaged and critical spectators. This book uses sources such as newspapers, engravings, and cheap guidebooks to examine the mediation of cultural politics. By the early nineteenth century, changing notions of 'national culture' and the prevailing ideas on state provision of culture fed into a national debate over access to cultural sites. The opening of national historic sites and contests over the accessibility of national monuments at St Paul's or the British Museum reflected demands for a broadening of the cultural nation. Strife over a more inclusive politics in the later eighteenth and the nineteenth centuries thus has parallels in the discourses and movements regarding the audiences and publics of culture. The representational culture of the court and church of the seventeenth century gradually gave way to the more accessible culture in the eighteenth-century public sphere. By the early nineteenth century, this fostered demands for increasingly inclusive cultural institutions and eventually widened access to national heritage.[52]

Themes: Politicisation, Commemoration, Collecting

The chapters that follow explore different ways of thinking about cultural politics and political culture. Alongside these big themes, I also aim to contribute to debates on more specific topics such as the politics and aesthetics of heroism and commemoration; the history of public collections and museums; notions of plunder and heritage preservation; and the relations between imperial officials and indigenous assistants in archaeological research.

Part I explores the politicisation of art and the themes of commemoration and memorialisation during George III's reign (1760–1820). In the American Revolutionary War and the French Revolutionary and Napoleonic Wars, history paintings and monuments visually defined a British hero. Studying the representation of war and of heroes illuminates both political culture and cultural politics. The controversial careers of American artists who painted in London during the American Revolution highlight the various ways in which art and politics related to each other. The study of national monuments shows how Britons' memories of war evolved over time and in space, as an increasingly complex commemorative geography emerged across London, the British Isles, and the Empire. In the 1760s, the narratives of war, state, and empire affected official monuments in Westminster Abbey. The following generation struggled with representing imperial disaster in public culture (chs. 1, 2). During the French Revolutionary and Napoleonic Wars, the building of a British pantheon at St Paul's Cathedral signified the pursuit of war at a symbolic level and pitted native talent against foreign achievement. After the fraught efforts of the American Revolutionary period, heroic representation was resurgent, though the politics and the aesthetics of commemoration continued to be contested. Comparisons with French and Prussian models will highlight the peculiar politics and styles of British memorialisation (chs. 3, 4). In British India, meanwhile, monuments to officers and intellectual leaders served to assert military-cultural prowess in the face of the thin imperial red line (Part II, ch. 7). After Waterloo, parts of central London were reimagined and rebuilt as a new social framework of royalist, national-imperial memory (Part III, ch. 9).

Part II analyses how the imperial state, politics, and art were intertwined in the conquest and representation of empire, and in the intellectual, imaginative, and material acquisition of foreign cultures. In studying the metropolitan and imperial cultural politics of archaeology and collecting, here too we start in George III's reign, but we move up to the middle of the nineteenth century, and occasionally beyond. Private individuals often collect to assert social claims, signify economic achievement, and demonstrate cultural acuity.[53] A *Leitmotif* of Part II is that nations and states collected for national prestige, and to display in their public spaces trophies of war and of imperial conquest. Diplomatic battles and international culture wars were fought over antiquities. In the Mediterranean and Near East, Britain's political, diplomatic, and military capabilities were pivotal to collecting in areas of both formal and informal empire (chs. 5, 6). In British India, where challenges from European powers were decreasing, archaeology involved the collecting of knowledge and objects for their own sake and for the purposes of imperial governance (chs. 7, 8). Orientalism – the knowledge gained by Europeans of non-European peoples, and the 'structures and ideologies of dominance that enabled and were themselves enabled by that knowledge'[54] – allowed for a broad spectrum of British-indigenous cultural and intellectual relations from genuine dialogue to domineering exploitation. The treatment of antiquities, from plunder to preservation, reveals a similarly mixed story.

Part III resumes the metropolitan story at Waterloo and takes it up to mid-century. A remarkable outburst of state sponsorship of artistic activity coincided with sustained rethinking of the relations between politics, society, and culture. As the cultural nation was defined in increasingly inclusive ways, cultural politics developed new languages and mechanisms. The state used art to display and glorify power in monumental architecture and in public spaces, and considered art and galleries as a means of education and social change (ch. 9).

The main thematic strands of this book – politicisation, commemoration, and collecting – are linked in multifarious ways, but especially by war, international comparison and competition, and by the role of the state in the nation's cultural life. Exploring the intersections of the art world with politics, war, and empire illuminates the character of British public life. It also sheds light on less conventional senses of political culture and on the nature of the cultural state and official culture. Another thread that runs through many chapters is the notion of cultural patriotism. At the accession of George III, British artists anticipated a bright new age of patronage for the national arts. Building monuments as an international contest on a symbolic level was fostered by, and enhanced, pride in the national arts. British artists and patrons who more or less consciously considered their cultural endeavours as 'British' balanced the desire to be seen to adhere and live up to common European standards on the one hand with the aim of promoting indigenous models and domestic producers on the other. Appropriating the physical remains of ancient civilisations in the face of international competition was also a matter of patriotic and imperial pride. In the early nineteenth century, the Prince Regent strove to outbuild Napoleon when he had parts of central London converted into a patriotic, neoclassical work of art and a truly imperial capital city.[55]

But it is in the London of autumn 1761, in the confident mood sustained by military and imperial triumph, that we start – just as courtiers and peers, artists and musicians, ordinary Londoners and noble visitors from abroad were preparing for the coronation of a young monarch.

LONDON, AUTUMN 1761: THE KING SHALL REJOICE

EMPIRE-BUILDING REQUIRED not only economic and military prowess, but also an intellectual and imaginative effort – for Britons to imagine and justify their national and imperial enterprise and to explain their national values to themselves and others. Ceremonial occasions were particularly potent moments to build this imaginative effort, and none more so than the rituals of a coronation. The coronation ceremony affirms a monarch's right to the throne in terms of tradition and customs as well as legality; the rituals and accompanying festivities provide charismatic legitimacy. In all these respects, eighteenth-century politics had performative and aesthetic dimensions. The study of coronation rituals and celebrations thus affords insights into political culture and cultural politics.[1] The coronation of George III in 1761 was framed by temporary artistic productions and elevated by sublime music. It gave rise to both official and commercial musical, literary, artistic, and theatrical productions. At the height of the first truly global war, there were rich opportunities to convey a confident, patriotic message of British imperial triumph under a reinvigorated monarchy.

~

Coronation day started early for the privileged few hundred individuals whose connections had obtained tickets for Westminster Abbey (fig. 2; map 1). The roads were hopelessly congested, as thousands of ordinary people streamed into London from across the country to witness the first coronation in over three decades. The

2. *Ticket for George III's Coronation at Westminster Abbey* (1761). Tickets with the holder's seat number added by hand depicted the enthroned royal couple underneath an arch prominently inscribed: 'S[enatus]P[opulus]Q[ue]B[ritannicus]'. Their Majesties are flanked to either side by high-rising and closely stacked nobility in coronation robes and coronets, and attended by allegories of Liberty, Britannia, and Fame.

German Count Kielmannsegge, in England specially for the coronation, took ninety minutes just to get from Pall Mall to Charing Cross. William Hickey, a boy at Westminster School, whose family set out in their coach at midnight, recalled that the noise of horses and coaches crashing into each other, breaking panels and windows, 'accompanied by the screeches of terrified ladies, was at times truly terrific'. Arriving at the Abbey around 7 a.m., the Hickeys and their party of twelve showed special tickets which had them ushered past the crowds, up a private staircase to their fifty-guinea box. They sat down to a 'hot and comfortable breakfast', after which some took a nap while young Hickey explored the Abbey.[2]

Meanwhile, the young royal couple began their day of twelve long hours in the public gaze. George had succeeded his grandfather George II in October 1760. One early Saturday morning, the old king had collapsed in the royal water-closet in the private apartments at Kensington Palace and died of heart failure. That November, he had been laid to rest in the royal vault in Henry VII's chapel at Westminster Abbey. Now, on 22 September 1761, the 23-year-old King George III and his teenage queen, Charlotte, had arrived in comparatively modest sedan chairs from St James's Palace at Westminster Hall, both the starting point of the procession to the Abbey and the site of the coronation banquet later that day. The newly commissioned State Coach (last used by Queen Elizabeth II at her 2002 Golden Jubilee) was a spectacular affair with its patriotic iconography of Britannia, Neptune, and Apollo. Alas, it was not to be ready until the state opening of Parliament the following year.[3] George III, in his first speech from the throne in November 1760, had proclaimed that, '[b]orn and educated in this country, I glory in the name of Britain'.[4]

Since 1066, every English and British monarch had been crowned at the Abbey. In 1761, a coronation service of great pomp, lavish trappings, and fine music was once more required. This was, not least, to reflect the unprecedented global triumphs Britain had been scoring since the imperial *annus mirabilis* of 1759, even though the new king could claim no credit. He was doing his bit, reported the *Bath Chronicle* on Christmas Day 1760, as George III, 'in consideration of the war with France, has forbid all French wines of any sort to be drank in the Palace', a saving estimated at £40,000 p.a.

Over recent weeks the land's grandest peers, and the scions of ancient families that had seen better times, had keenly attempted to ascertain who was entitled to attend the king at his coronation, confirmed their place in the several processions, or ensured they would serve as the bearers of bejewelled regalia. Others sought clarification regarding a place in the Abbey or a seat at the coronation banquet, a livery or a commemorative medal. In an impressively large petition with a massive seal, the Dean and Chapter of Westminster Abbey expressed their delight that the king preferred their church over others for his coronation – and they hoped that they and their families would not be entirely excluded from their own choir in favour of strangers.

Prices for good views of the procession were horrendously inflated: over 100 guineas to rent a room along the route, and between £300 and £1,000 for a house. A platform outside St Margaret's, Westminster, had apparently been rented for £2,400: 'the annual rent of palaces is offered for a single room for a single day'.[5] For most people it was a long day of waiting interspersed with all too brief moments of excitement. Captain William Owen was

> with a little party of friends in the scaffolding erected against the Exchequer wall in new palace yard where I paid three guineas for a place, of which I was most heartily tired before the whole was over, altho' we had taken care to provide a plentiful stock of wine, punch, beer, fowls, ham and neats tongue for the day.[6]

The connoisseur Horace Walpole's cunning plan of avoiding travelling by night or traversing congested London very early in the morning, by 'going to lie in Palace Yard', meant that he did 'not get a wink of sleep all night', what with the 'hammering of scaffolds, shouting of people, relieving guards, and jangling of bells'.[7] Coronation week brought excited confusion and threatened sensual excess: 'Oh! The buzz, the prattle, the crowds, the noise, the hurry!' Newspapers for September 1761 record anxiety that the sheer noise might kill the frail and sick, and noted hospital contingency plans for accidents and injuries.[8] There were also mishaps on the part of officials. The Bishop of Rochester would have dropped the crown, 'if it had not been pin'd to the Cushion'.[9] Amazingly, the masters of ceremonies forgot the Sword of State and the chairs for king and queen. A ceremonial sword was duly borrowed from the Lord Mayor, and craftsmen undertook last-minute constructions at the Hall. Around midday the procession finally set out for Westminster Abbey.

The anonymous satirical poem *The Coronation: A Poem, Humbly Addressed to Nobody who was There, by a Spectator*, vividly describes the 'tides of people' and 'acres of faces', from beggars and shopkeepers to scarlet- and gold-clad peers, the crowd jostling for the best places while constables pushed them back, and 'Caps, Hats, and Perukes, tumbled in the Mud'. 'All rush to Westminster; some Instinct-driv'n, | Others to steal, *and some to snatch what's giv'n*', that is, the left-over wine and perhaps some abandoned coronation medals. In a custom dating from plague-ridden centuries, the royal path was strewn with herbs, petals, and buds by the king's scarlet-clad Herb Woman, Miss Honor Battiscombe, and her six maids. Next came fifes and drums in scarlet livery, a drum major, eight crimson-velveted trumpeters, kettle drums, and another eight trumpeters. Drummers and trumpeters combined martial and court functions: they performed on battlefields from Dettingen to the Peninsula, but also on royal birthdays and weddings. Now came guards, followed – in an ascending scale of titles and magnificence of costumes and accessories – by the civic and state hierarchy, regalia-bearing bishops and peers, and then, under a canopy born by fifteen Barons of the Cinque Ports and with silver bells at its corners, her majesty the queen.

The skinny, tongue-tied, inexperienced queen, who was said to be 'far from well, with a nervous pain in her face and teeth' that day, was dressed in her coronation robes covered by a great diamond stomacher valued at £18,000, and a jewelled and embroidered silver tissue petticoat with 'Pearls as big as Cherrys'.[10] She wore a cap and crown, and a purple velvet surcoat with matching sleeves and a mantle trimmed with ermine and lace. The total bill for her coronation robes amounted to near £1,600, including payments to a pearl-stringer, to jewellers, and for a 'Sett of Coronation Locks'.[11] Until her wedding two weeks earlier a mere Princess of Mecklenburg-Strelitz, the bride had been chosen among eligible Protestant, mostly German, princesses according to character, health, and child-bearing ability. Walpole described the 17-year-old queen:

> She is not tall, nor a beauty; pale and very thin, but looks sensible and is genteel. Her hair is darkish and fine, her forehead low, her nose very well, except the nostrils spreading too wide; her mouth has the same fault, but her teeth are good.[12]

Finally, the king himself came into view, in his crimson silk parliamentary robes embellished with ermine, 'While joyful Britons trace | Sweet Mercy's Image stampt upon his Face.'[13] Walking under a canopy of cloth of gold, 'with a slow and exact pace, thro' increasing acclamations', George was accompanied by the master of the robes, gentlemen of the king's bedchamber, standard-bearers, captains, and 100 Yeomen of the Guard in crimson cloth breeches, gold-laced black velvet bonnets with crimson, white, and blue ribbands, and a basket-hilted sword with brass hilts and a silver handle. Their coats were 'of fine Crimson in grain Cloth lined with blue Serge, & guarded with blue Velvet Edged and laced with Gold Lace, with Rose, Thistle & Crown, Mottos & Scrolls', and the letters 'G.R.'.

Other men in uniform, namely the military, seem to have played a more prominent role in this than in previous coronations, and not just to fire volleys in salute. The short and narrow processional route, splendidly laid with near two kilometres of blue cloth, was guarded by 2,800 foot soldiers supported by numerous cavalry. Foot guards and units of light-horse and dragoons were also patrolling parts of London's West End.[14] At the height of the by now spectacularly successful war, the soldiers themselves were objects of national pride as the various regiments' banners and standards flew high along the coronation route. But the celebrated writer Dr Samuel Johnson sounded a warning note: the military was a potentially dangerous presence, 'since it cannot but offend every Englishman to see troops of soldiers placed between him and his sovereign, as if they were the most honourable of his people, or the King required guards to secure his person from his subjects'. Moreover, they were prone to insolent conduct which 'always produces quarrels, tumults, and mischief' among the people.[15]

Around 1.30 p.m., the king finally arrived at the Abbey, to be greeted by the fifes and kettledrums playing a march, soon joined by the organ and the assembled choirs of the Abbey and Chapel Royal and organ performing the Introit. The choir sang an unpretentiously homophonic *a capella* setting of 'I was glad when they said unto me' (Ps. 122.1–7), while the king and queen processed from the west door to their chairs beneath their thrones, covered in over sixty metres of gold tabby. The congregation got its first glimpse of the hired diamonds, valued at a staggering £375,000, which had been fitted into crowns, diadems, swords, and sceptres. Seats and galleries were covered with crimson serge and say, and green-and-red baize. A royal box had been built in St Edward's Chapel. There were galleries for ambassadors, seats for peers and peeresses in the transepts, and galleries raised over the altar for MPs, and over the choir screen for the musicians.

With Thomas Secker, the elderly Archbishop of Canterbury, presiding, the service got under way. Bishops and peers chanted 'God Save King George' and trumpeters sounded many a fanfare. Bishop Drummond of Salisbury's fifteen-minute sermon proclaimed the monarch's conception of his rights and his obligations towards his people. In contrast to previous eighteenth-century coronations, the ancient texts on allegiance under the penalty of damnation, or the Hanoverians' hereditary right to the throne, were no longer emphasised. Fifteen years after the last serious Jacobite challenge, the Hanoverians felt secure. Drummond expanded on two themes: first, that 'great and good Kings ... are the means, by which God blesses a people'; secondly, that 'the duty and end of Royalty is, to do judgment and justice'. For kingly government to serve the public good, a king required 'solid principles of wisdom and virtue ... a discerning spirit, strength and presence of mind', also a heart 'very resolute and steadfast in its integrity'. The king was to 'strengthen the bands, by which every society is knit together' and give a 'personal example of love to true religion and to the constitution', 'the best formed to convey peace and happiness to mankind'. The people's duty was to show a 'constant sense of due subordination, and a right conduct in our respective stations'.

As the bishop spoke, across the globe British and colonial forces were fighting Native Americans, Colonel Eyre Coote was taking Pondicherry in India, and the Spanish were entering the war against Britain. The bishop described the state of the kingdom as 'full of power and riches and honour; whose name stands foremost among the nations, and whose fame is raised to a pitch above the praise of former ages'.[16] In view of the continuing war, the archbishop had had to alter the line 'Thou shalt present him with the blessings of peace' to 'blessings of goodness' in the anthem 'The King Shall Rejoice in Thy Strength' (Ps. 21.1–2, 5–6).

Although the sermon was as short as protocol demanded, 'many thousands were out of the possibility of hearing a single syllable' and therefore 'took that opportunity to eat their meal, when the general clattering of knives, forks, plates, and glasses that ensued, produced a most ridiculous effect, and a universal burst of laughter followed.' Hickey's family enjoyed a splendid collation of 'cold fowls, ham, tongues, different meat pies, wines, and liqors of various sorts' which had been sent to their box the previous day and was now dished up by two servants. Grandees and royal household officials had made their own careful preparations: for the officers of the Board of Greencloth the Surveyor-General had installed 'a proper Staircase, Retiring Room and a Room for Entertainment'.[17] For those without such private arrangements, facilities had been set up in the Abbey where refreshments could be purchased, including chocolate, cold meats, and wine.[18] There were other diverting incidents to observe. When the queen wanted to visit her retiring-chamber behind the altar, a lady-in-waiting found the Duke of Newcastle 'perk'd up & in the very act upon the anointed velvet closestool.'[19]

At the political heart of the ceremony the king swore and signed the coronation oath, promising to govern according to the statutes, laws, and customs of his kingdoms, to exert justice and mercy, and to maintain the 'Protestant Reformed Religion Established by Law'. The king's anointing was prefaced by the ancient anthem 'Come, Holy Ghost' in the setting of the Master of the King's Band of Musicians, Dr William Boyce, for voices and organ, which looked forward to the gallant style of J. C. Bach and the young Mozart. Boyce, an organist, music editor, and the composer of 'Heart of Oaks', had succeeded Handel in 1759 and composed eight new coronation anthems. However, the backdrop for the most sacred act of the entire ceremony was Handel's now famous setting, composed for George II's coronation in 1727, of the ancient coronation text from the First Book of Kings, 'Zadok the Priest'. This text had been sung at English coronations since Edgar's in 973. The Archbishop of Canterbury had conveyed to Boyce the king's desire to have 'Zadok' 'performed as it was set for the last coronation'. Thus was founded the tradition of performing Handel's masterpiece of musical drama at every British coronation since.[20]

Set for double chorus, strings and basso continuo, two oboes, two bassoons, three trumpets, and percussion, this is the first anthem composed for an English service to include timpani. In contemporary ears, the combination of drums and trumpets must have rung military echoes. The anthem comes in three continuous sections. While the king moved slowly towards the altar and seated himself on a chair, with four Knights of the Garter holding a 'rich Pall of Silk, or Cloth of Gold' over him, the sound of broken arpeggios played by violins divided into three sections, and supported by woodwind, spread from the central crossing throughout the large, resonant Abbey and up the high Gothic vault. As the Archbishop of Canterbury anointed with holy oil the king's head, breast, and hands in the form of a cross, and the orchestra maintained its arpeggios, capped by high trumpets, and the timpani beat as if for a march, the massed choral forces entered with a blast of such shattering fortissimo and satisfying richness that it must have raised the hairs on every neck in the Abbey: 'Zadok the Priest, | and Nathan the Prophet, | anointed Solomon King'. The anthem's second part began at a faster tempo, in a lighter, dancing rhythm: 'all the People rejoiced'. The trumpets played increasingly exposed, brilliant fanfares and trills around the monophonic choir's phrases; the word 'rejoiced' was oft repeated, and the next caesura topped a further crescendo: 'and all the people rejoiced, and said': 'God Save the King! | Long Live the King! | God Save the King!' These chordal acclamations, delivered like hammer strokes, were supported by trumpets and timpani. The final theme, 'May the king live for ever, Hallelujah, Amen', alternated with joyful semiquavers and staccato chords of intertwining 'Hallelujahs' and 'Amens' until a triumphantly definitive 'Hallelujah' was reached. Final fanfares and powerful timpani brought the sacred scene to its monumentally jubilant conclusion.

One climactic moment now chased another. Around 3.30 p.m., the Archbishop of Canterbury placed the crown on the king's head. A man stationed at the top of the dome signalled to the guns in Green Park and – all the way down the river Thames – at the Tower to fire a salute, and the trumpeters in the Abbey sounded a fanfare. Answering their king's coronation, the peers and peeresses put on their own coronets and caps and the entire congregation, 'with loud and repeated shouts', acclaimed their new monarch: 'God Save the King'. While he had ceded the anoint-ment to Handel, for the act of coronation Boyce had one more rousing hymn in store. In a brief, electrifying opening, strings, trumpets, and timpani excitedly raced towards the first entry of the full choir, singing in highly rhythmic phrasing: 'Praise the Lord, O Jerusalem | Praise thy God, o Sion'. Passages sung in unison by the whole choir then alternated with contrapuntal settings before the anthem concluded in a majestic 'Hallelujah'. As the royal couple had only been married a fortnight before the coronation, Archbishop Secker had had the anthem's second verse changed from 'For Kings shall be thy nursing fathers, and Queens thy nursing mothers', to something more neutral, 'Behold, a King shall reign in righteousness, & Princes shall rule in judgement'.

The presentation of the Bible was followed by the 'Te Deum'. After the king was enthroned, the peers of the realm individually paid homage to their monarch, and silver coins engraved with his portrait were distributed. The choir with 'Instrumen-tal Musick of all sorts' performed the final anthem of the king's coronation proper, a nine-minute setting of 'The Lord is a Sun and a Shield', followed by drum beats, more trumpet fanfares, and acclamations. Then the queen was anointed, crowned, and enthroned to the sounds of Boyce's invigorating double-choir setting of 'My Heart is Inditing'. After all this, a full communion service was celebrated, before the king was again vested in his royal robes of purple velvet and ermine, handed his sceptre and orb, and to the accompaniment of a festive march processed with the queen through the Abbey's great west door. There the expectant populace greeted the crowned monarch and his consort to the sounds of some final rousing fanfares, a procession of drums, and the bells of Westminster Abbey and of all the churches of London.

After the service, young Hickey rushed to watch the coronation banquet at Westminster Hall with one of the tickets that his father had received from Lord Egmont in the nick of time. The Hall was illuminated by 3,000 candles, signifi-cantly more than in 1727, which had been regarded as the most splendid English

3. A. Walker, *The King's Champion enters West-minster Hall through a Triumphal Arch* (c.1761).

coronation to date.[21] It was dark by now, on this warm and close early autumn night. Walpole noted how, 'by a childish compliment to the King', the organisers had 'reserved the illumination of the hall till his entry, by which means they arrived like a funeral, nothing being discernible but the plumes of the Knights of the Bath, which seemed the hearse'.[22]

More faux pas had been committed. Although the organisers had thought of many logistical details, including a sluice 'of an admirable contrivance' built into the lower gallery 'for the reception of urinary discharges',[23] no provision had been made to accommodate the Barons of the Cinque Ports or the Lord Mayor of London and City dignitaries at dinner; the latter were given the table of the Knights of the Bath, who were moved to the table of some officers of state, who simply had to cede their dining rights. The wives of peers had to be content with the gallery and either clubbed their handkerchiefs to be tied together or lowered baskets to procure food and wine from those with privileged seats.

The coronation provided rich opportunities for image-making (fig. 3). The Hall's decoration combined references to imperial Rome, medieval England, and the Hanoverian dynasty's recent past. Just inside the main entrance stood William Oram's triumphal arch, modelled on the Arch of Titus, with trumpeters stationed on top. When the king and queen had taken their seats on raised Chairs of State, the

Lord Steward, the Lord High Constable, and the Deputy Earl Marshal, all on horse-back, ushered in the first of countless dishes which were to climax in a desert on which the 'confectioner had lavished all his ingenuity in rock work and emblemati-cal figure' representing 'Parnassus with abundance of figures of Muses, Arts, &c'.[24] Following medieval tradition, the king's champion – always the head of the ancient Dymoke family of Scrivelsby in Lincolnshire, clad in full armour – threw down a gauntlet, challenging anyone to dispute George III's right to the throne. In an anecdote which slightly stretches belief in equine longevity, his was the very horse on which George II in 1743 had led his troops into the successful Battle of Dettin-gen against the French, the last time a British monarch charged into combat at the head of his men.[25] At the height of the Seven Years War, either the masterminds of the coronation or sympathetic commentators seemed keen to see the young ruler linked with his family's (rather modest) martial achievements. By evening's close, numerous ladies had fainted from heat, and those who had not despaired at wax dripping on their fine dresses. But even Walpole had to concede admiringly that Westminster Hall was 'most glorious. The blaze of lights, the richness and variety of habits, the ceremonial, the benches of peers and peeresses, frequent and full, was as awful as a pageant can be'.[26]

The coronation deviated from those of the earlier Georges in certain respects. Accounts of the Office of Works suggest that attempts had been made to improve on 1727, with regard to better provisions for seating, conveniences, and lighting at Westminster Hall. But there was also a degree of muddling through: the king complained that few precedents were kept for the royal household to work to, 'the earl marshall's office had been strangely neglected'.[27] The heralds had even needed to advertise 'in the newspaper for the Christian names and places of abode of the peeresses'.[28] Yet, despite various organisational failures, mishaps, and confusions, the coronation was even for poet Thomas Gray a 'spectacle, w.ch in magnificence surpass'd every thing I have seen'.[29]

The loyal press stressed the good organisation, propriety, and dignity with which celebrations were carried off not only across the capital but throughout the country. This marked a significant change from the 'rough events' of 1714 and 1727, when all classes had mingled at bonfires and other revels at the coronations of the first two Georges. In 1761, the Privy Council forbade bonfires in Westmin-ster and restricted the use of torches. The *London Chronicle* denounced bonfires as 'a shameful nuisance and a scandal to government', and considered fireworks offensive to ladies, threatening miscarriages, burns, and disfigurements. But some leading politicians like the Duke of Newcastle lit bonfires outside their houses and served strong beer to the local populace in good-humoured defiance. The nobility's practice of hanging lamps was praised as 'compliments to our Monarchs, and signs of fidelity and affection'. [30]

Reports of celebrations across the country created an imagined community of a nation at war, united (remarkably so perhaps in comparison with ceremonies in subsequent decades) in loyal celebration of their young king's coronation. In Liverpool, Manchester, Bath, and other towns and cities around Britain, local elites used the opportunity to affirm their own exclusivity by dining and dancing in the splendour of their Town Halls, Exchanges, and the principal residents' houses. These elites also dished out charity, food, and drink to the poor. In Liverpool and Yarmouth, barrels of ale were even given to locally held French prisoners of war. Traditional bell ringing and illuminations were widespread, as they had been at previous coronations. In Gloucester, lady subscribers to the county infirmary raised donations at churches for poor 'young women of virtuous character' who were to marry before the king or queen's next birthday. This was part of a local celebratory programme which allowed the population to partake in the national event and demonstrate its loyalty, without incurring the hazards and cost of a metropolitan visit. [31] The national press reported on local celebrations, for instance in Winchester, where the event was greeted

> with great military pomp, and all other demonstrations of joy. At noon the regiments in the Camp ... went through various sorts of firing under a discharge of twenty-one pieces of cannon. In the mean time, the regiments in the city continued to fire.

This was followed by the obligatory fireworks, a dinner organised by the civic authorities for the army one evening, and the army's return invitation to an 'elegant ball' the following night. In Salisbury, coronation day was celebrated 'with great affection by all degrees of people'. After a cathedral service, the city's civic and military leaders, clergy, and gentry gathered to toast to a long and prosperous reign; they distributed moneys to the local militia and wine to the city companies to do the same. [32] And whereas George III had at one stage condemned the 'bloody and expensive war', his coronation was marked at least by those parts of the armed forces not engaged in active fighting that day. The army at camp in Wilhelmsdahl marched and fired a *Feu de Joye* and officers held celebratory dinners. [33] In the American colonies, newspapers carried detailed reports on London's festivities several weeks after the event, some complete with processional orders; the British government also briefed its colonial representatives, though in many places wartime conditions must have limited celebrations. [34]

~

A major occasion of state was also an artistic event. The coronation prompted not just new ceremonial music and ephemeral decorations and displays, but also paintings and plays. The best paintings that were created to mark the coronation are Allan Ramsay's portraits of the king and queen, easily the most impressive state portraits since Van Dyck had portrayed Charles I.[35] George III's portrait combines the grace of majesty with the reticent nature of the young monarch (see plate I). He looks out of the picture, composed and steady, standing in an elegant pose amid a magnificent setting of columns and drapery. The thickness and texture of George's ermine-lined and fringed coronation cloak are brilliantly rendered by the Scottish painter, who limits the regalia to an only half-visible crown and ceremonial sword, with the orb and sceptre absent.

The Society of Artists, Britain's first exhibition society, decorated their building in Spring Gardens with back-lit transparencies which associated the new king with his nation's naval prowess and the promise for a new era of artistic patronage. For its catalogue that season, William Hogarth produced a frontispiece in which a bust of the young king overlooks a lion-shaped fountainhead from which water pours into a watering-can held by Britannia. The allegorical lady waters three intertwined saplings, presumably of native oak: 'PAINTING', 'SCULPTURE', and 'ARCHITECTURE'. The inscription, quoting Juvenal in Latin, focuses on the centrality of the prince to artistic patronage: 'The hope and purpose of learning depend on Caesar only.'[36]

The accession of a new king who gloried in the name of Britain seemed indeed to signal to British artists the dawn of a bright new age of royal patronage. Imagery of martial prowess and religious piety, combined in the spectacular golden State Coach and later in Benjamin West's paintings at Windsor Castle, was considered appropriate to a great imperial nation. As the son of Prince Frederick – connoisseur, discerning collector, good amateur musician, generous patron of the national arts – George III had been tutored in drawing and architecture by several leading artists, including William Chambers.[37] He perhaps lacked the enthusiasm of his father and the connoisseurship of his eldest son, but he practised art patronage as part of his conscientiously exercised royal duties.

The coronation also gave rise to non-official and commercial musical, literary, artistic, and theatrical productions. Their aesthetic quality varies hugely, but they convey an overwhelming impression of great excitement and sensual richness. They also made some serious points rather effectively. The anonymous poem 'The Coronation' stressed the difference between foreign despotic countries and free

Britain: 'Where breathes a Nation, like Britannia free? | Where reigns a Monarch, so ador'd as Thee?' The song 'Great Britain's Glory and Happiness' had 'trumpets sound, and cheerful voice, proclaim this grand Coronation', 'every subject in his station'. And so Britain would beat the French and its commerce would flourish, as the songs, processions, and cannon resounded through the verses. Among the better poets who marked the occasion, Christopher Smart emphasised in Hymn 26, 'The Accession of King George III', that under George 'Our gallant fleets have won success, | Christ Jesus at the helm | And let us therefore kneel and bless | The sovereign of the realm' (ll.9–12).

The greatest coronation spectacle was staged by London's theatres. David Garrick's Drury Lane show re-created the event with a procession of 136 actors in thirty-four units, which followed as an after-piece on a production of *Henry VIII*. But it was upstaged by the extravaganza put on by John Rich, the 'God of Pantomimes, Jubilees and Installations', manager of the Theatre Royal, Covent Garden. His sumptuous show, staged at a cost of £3,000, went to tremendous lengths to re-create the costumes, sounds, and even the features of the Abbey:

> The whole of the Westminster choir sang all the time that the procession was passing across the stage, in exact imitation of the real procession. The same number of cymbals and trumpets were there; the bells were rung; and the guns and regimental bands in lines, through which the procession continually passed, were painted on the scenery … During the dinner when the scene representing the galleries in the Hall was filled with people, the coronation anthem, which had been performed in the Abbey, was sung to the accompaniment of a full band.

The *Court Magazine* found 'the number of persons, variety of the grandest dresses, and the amazing splendour of the whole appearance' beyond comparison. Count Kielmansegge was sure that 'there can hardly be any one in London, of high or low degree … who will not have seen the play at least once'. The piece saw sixty-seven performances in its first season; five seasons after the fact it was still enacted twenty-five times.[38] In Samuel Foote's *The Orators*, performed in 1762 at the Haymarket, the characters Tirehack and Scamber visit London from Oxford. Though pressed for money, they consider revisiting 'the Coronation; for you know we have seen it but nine times'. Cross-referencing in other plays was perhaps the ultimate sign of success (or notoriety) for a theatrical production.[39]

The crowning of George III allowed the nation at war to imagine itself. The all-enveloping sounds of drums, trumpets, chants, and cannon, and the sights of

35

splendid robes and impressive processions, formed the backdrop to a confident, nationalistic message of British imperial triumph under a young new monarch. A coronation was an exceptional moment in the life of the nation. But it was just one of the most dramatic among an infinite array of examples of how aesthetically performed politics and politically inflected art interacted in richly nuanced ways. Around the time of George III's coronation, Westminster Abbey also became *the* site for the commemoration of the nation's war heroes.

PART I

WAR, ART, AND COMMEMORATION
(*c.* 1750–1815)

AMERICA

Nationalising a Site of Memory

You here converse with Kings; with Heroes of all Kinds; with Philosophers &
Divines.

Peter Oliver, former Chief-Justice of Massachusetts Bay, visiting Westminster Abbey in 1777[1]

THROUGHOUT THE EIGHTEENTH CENTURY, Westminster Abbey enjoyed a unique status, not only as the site of coronations and mausoleum of kings but also as the pantheon of national heroes, enshrined in British literary memory in a famous essay by Joseph Addison in the *Spectator*. London guidebooks advertised the benefits of visiting the

> sumptuous and costly monuments erected in this venerable pile … It is certain that there is not a nobler amusement than a walk in this Abbey, among the tombs of heroes, patriots, poets, and philosophers; you are surrounded with the shades of your great forefathers … and grow fond of fame and virtue in the contemplation. It is the finest school of morality, and the most beautiful flatterer of imagination in nature. I appeal to any man's mind, who has a taste for what is sublime and noble, for a witness to the pleasure he experiences on this occasion; and I dare believe he will acknowledge, that there is no entertainment so various or so instructive.[2]

Foreigners were impressed to see common English people looking attentively at monuments and conversing about them with their companions. In the 1760s, a Frenchman, Pierre-Jean Grosley, marvelled at the range of visitors to the Abbey, which was 'incessantly filled with crowds … I have seen herb-women holding a little book, which gives an account of [the monuments, and] milk-women getting them explained, and testifying, not a stupid admiration, but a lively and most significant surprize.'[3]

Memory is social: people remember collectively, they remember publicly, and they remember interactively. Memorialisation enshrines certain events or persons in a group's notion of the past. It focuses on educating audiences, and it often involves contests and conflicts between those who, and over that which, they seek to remember. But memory and memorialisation are also always selective, and by virtue of being selective involve distortion and forgetting. Within the same polity, different social groups, political factions, and individuals construct potentially conflicting memories. The choice of events, 'heroes', and sites involved in memorialisation is a narrative process. As narratives often have arbitrary beginnings, simplify, and highlight individuals and events over structures and trends, memory can again become distorted.[4]

Monuments serve memory in a variety of ways, chiefly by forming records, by stimulating remembering, and by helping individuals to imagine and define themselves as members of a larger group, such as the nation. Like other objects, monuments have the capacity of allowing the content of communicative memory – the memories of the recent past shared by contemporaries and handed on between adjacent generations – to be detached from the conversation of specific social groups and to be transmitted and reworked over time into a part of (changing) cultural memory. Monuments 'enter' the person who visits, views, or contemplates them through the senses. Through their look, lustre, or feel, monuments evoke responses and recollections. This process of evocation is a dynamic dialogue between monuments, their founders, makers, and viewers in the construction of meaning. It is part of the wider dynamic process between the medium on the one hand, and experience and memory on the other.[5]

Disciplinary specialisation has meant that political historians sometimes do not pay enough attention to the aesthetic conventions and constraints imposed by artistic media such as monuments, while art historians have sometimes not appreciated the social and political contexts of commemoration. Studying the construction and contestation of memory requires exploring the agencies of remembering, the media, the politics of aesthetics, and the reception of memorialisation. It might be true that the British national elites were, on the whole, less concerned than their Continental counterparts about using the arts to engender national integration – such as Prussia using art, religion, and education to bind together the classes in a morally uplifting way in the early nineteenth century – as they considered Britain to be already comparatively well integrated. Yet, the building of monuments intended to inspire patriotic emulation qualifies this pattern. Representations of war and national identity in monuments were conditioned by, and in turn articulated, political cultures.

Between the 1720s and 1750s, Westminster Abbey ceased to be a space primarily for the commemoration of monarchs and of courtly loyalties. With the completion of the West Towers, the use of the West door as the principal entrance, and the shift of emphasis to the nave, instead it increasingly became a prominent site in London's public sphere. In addition to participating in the urban economy of display and leisure, in the second half of the century it became a site of national spectacle. Elite families, political factions, and various professions adopted the Abbey's nave and the north and south transepts as a forum where they competitively pursued their claims for public recognition through the erection of monuments. During the first two thirds of the century, the Dean and Chapter had used their right to permit burials and the erection of monuments, and the allocation of places for them, as an instrument of social patronage. The substantial fees levied for each of those permissions paid towards the upkeep of the Cathedral's fabric and to compensate the poorly endowed minor canons, who acted as paid tour guides. Under this system, many monuments commemorated men who had died without direct heirs. They expressed the gratitude to a benefactor rather than national acknowledgement of public service. As the French observer Jean A. Rouquet put it in 1755:

> the monuments which adorn the abbey church at Westminster, were not erected by the nation to honour the memory of illustrious persons ... To be buried in that church is a matter of mere private interest.[6]

Most of the hundreds of earlier statues and tablets in the Abbey were thus commissioned privately. This was true even of many military and naval monuments erected throughout the wars of the late seventeenth and the first half of the eighteenth centuries. Families and heirs to the estates of military and naval officers invested in memorials which ranged from modest statues to Roubiliac's theatrical monuments of various generals. Most of these military monuments suggest that the hero had been killed in battle; in fact, many had died away from the battlefield. Although some like Generals Wade and Warren had served with distinction, others do not seem to have seen any active service. The magnificence of most of these monuments thus belies their subjects' slight claims to martial fame.

From around 1750, some writers called for more public or officially sponsored monuments to commemorate military men. This was in part to help foster patriotic feeling after a period in which Britain had lacked consistent military and naval success. Admiral Vernon's monument (commissioned privately by a relative and beneficiary of the deceased) made reference to the increasingly vocal complaint that the times were not right for heroes.[7] If luxury and effeminacy were rendering the nation dangerously unprepared for war, the lure of immortal glory might enable a revival of patriotic heroism. This view gained urgency with the outbreak of the first skirmishes and then of full-scale war in 1754–6. By the *annus mirabilis* of 1759, the *London Chronicle* attacked the Dean and Chapter of Westminster Abbey for their indiscriminate sale of the right to erect monuments. This practice allegedly sponsored mediocrity, promoted self-interest, and deprived Britain's real future heroes of their due rewards. The policy encouraged

> family vanity, historical falsehood, jobbing articles, and ignorant statuaries; as well as the disgrace to national taste, the destruction of various kinds of marble, which ought to have remained in the bowels of the earth for the use of your

petitioners, who hope to employ the art of sculpture to more credit to their country … and it is with the greatest of regret they see the pavement and walls of your Abbey already possest by the names of generals never known but for their preferments; poets never mentioned but for their dullness; patriots never heard of but for their posts; and orators never known to pronounce a significant word, but the monosyllables, aye and no.[8]

The political and moral critique that the absence of self-sacrificial patriotism was a central problem of the effeminate age had found a new focus in the system of selling monumental positions in the Abbey.[9]

One obvious solution would have been a change in the power to commission and/or erect monuments in the Abbey. But the first formal national monument ever unveiled in the Abbey did little to change perceptions. In 1747, Parliament voted for the first monument to a supposedly national hero, Captain James Cornewall, who had fallen in an indecisive battle south of Toulon in February 1743. The British had carried a strategic victory in as far as France was never again in that war able to send a substantial military force to Italy by sea. However, the failure to win a decisive victory had led to bitter recriminations between the two jointly commanding British admirals. A partisan parliamentary inquiry and court-martials of both the admirals and several captains followed. The monument, concludes Doug Fordham, was 'less a celebration of Cornewall's heroism than a public denunciation of the "misconduct and misbehaviour" of those commanders who had returned to England alive'. However, when it was unveiled to the public in its very prominent position in the first bay of the nave, just inside the West door, in 1755, on the eve of openly declared war in Europe, the monument did set a precedent for national, parliamentary monuments, first in the Abbey, and from the 1790s in St Paul's Cathedral. It also was the first of several monuments honouring someone for their military service against the French with a memorial that has distinctively French elements, making it resemble contemporary *pompes funèbres*. But if it had been intended to inaugurate the transformation of the Abbey into a national shrine of national figures it was in many ways a false start. It reinforced impressions of the Abbey as a gallery of inconsequential or disputed figures commemorated by friends or factions.[10]

Private commissions, armchair generals, controversial naval figures, and ambiguously national monuments continued to enter the Abbey well beyond 1760. Yet, during the Seven Years War a new practice tentatively began of erecting monuments purporting to represent a broader public will. As part of the wider transformation of the Abbey's nave, which included the development of the poetical quarter as a national literary pantheon, three military monuments were commissioned by various public or quasi-public bodies. The general court of the province of Massachusetts Bay commissioned a monument to Brigadier-General George Augustus, 3rd Viscount Howe, who was killed on the march to Ticonderoga in 1758. The East India Company paid for a monument from Peter Scheemakers and James 'Athenian' Stuart of Admiral Sir Charles Watson (1714–57), who personified British naval dominance in Indian waters in the early Seven Years War. And Parliament honoured General James Wolfe, the conqueror of Quebec (d.1759), with a massive monument by Joseph Wilton.

The memorial to Watson featured the classically inspired, toga-clad admiral commanding the prostrate figure of a part European-style, bejewelled Calcutta, 'to be freed'. One breast exposed under her sari in a gesture of gratitude, Calcutta offers the riches of the East to Watson. She is juxtaposed with a magnificently muscular, chained Indian warrior with shaved head and topknot. He is described as a chained native of Chandernagore, the French enclave bombarded by Watson and captured by Clive in 1757.[11] Pierre-Jean Grosley, a Frenchman visiting London in 1765, spied British triumphalist arrogance, 'in all the pride of Asiatic pomp and magnificence. His statue … has on each side … a lofty palm-tree loaded with trophies and the spoils of the vanquished.'[12] British responses instead focused on Watson's compassionate, merciful treatment of the defeated enemy, embodied in the female marble figure of 'Calcutta freed'. Watson's palm branch symbolises victory, yet it may also stand for the peace and stability he brought to the region. The London press described the monument in sentimental terms, and felt it justified British imperial conquest as a 'means of extending the province of British liberty into exotic realms'.[13]

The monument to Wolfe further consolidated the Abbey's shift towards a truly national site of memory. The structure, the outcome of an extensive and well-publicised national competition, combined neoclassical and religious references with naturalistic reportage in a new patriotic language for British sculpture. Wolfe's monument, in which the Prime Minister William Pitt the Elder took a close interest, was the first memorial built as state propaganda.[14]

Those who commissioned public monuments did so ostensibly to promote virtuous and heroic conduct and loyalist patriotic sentiment among the nation. The narrative of the public monument in this period is to a large extent the narrative of war, state, and empire.[15] The Abbey's transformation into an official pantheon continued with the Earl of Chatham's funeral and national monument (1778–84), anticipating subsequent developments at St Paul's. However, the newly designated national site continued to be subject to partisan strife. In the monuments to

Howe, Wolfe, and Townshend (d. near Ticonderoga, 1759, private monument), the history of British officers was interwoven with that of America under the Abbey's roof. Commemorating the casualties of the next war was going to be much less straightforward.

A Civil and a Global War

At the conclusion of the Seven Years War, the nation's huge war debts amounted to some £132m. The British government sought an imperial solution and planned to raise revenue by enforcing existing commercial regulations and by raising external and internal taxation. The American colonies, which at that time were taking some 20 per cent of the value of British exports and supplying 30 per cent of imports, were to pay taxes and to contribute towards their own defence. The colonists mostly accepted that they needed to contribute to their own protection, although they perceived their threat level to have significantly lowered upon the fall of Montreal in 1760. Colonial assemblies insisted on their autonomy in internal policy, including taxation. What started as an economic dispute soon became a constitutional and ideological struggle over notions of representation and sovereignty. Parliament asserted its absolute sovereignty and formulated increasingly interventionist policies; most British politicians considered internal taxes entirely uncontroversial. But urban radicals and Protestant dissenters, many merchants, and parts of the intelligentsia and press were sympathetic to the patriots' concerns.

Americans opposing parliamentary taxation demanded the same rights of representation which they assumed belonged to all British people. After initial parliamentary requisitions, Americans began to reimagine the empire as a confederation of states bound together only by allegiance to the same crown. As all colonies had been established by order of the king, and had never been annexed or incorporated by Act of Parliament, they resisted imperial attempts at taxation. Parliament was increasingly considered corrupted by 'evil ministers', denying the colonists the rights of 'freeborn Englishmen'. Their approach failed to appreciate the changes which British constitutional practice had undergone in Great Britain whereby the monarch could no longer act without parliamentary consent. Suggestions for the reordering of the empire as a series of elements under the overarching arbitration of the crown were not thinkable for the majority of the British political class.[16]

George III saw himself as the father of his subjects, British and colonial. He took care of their welfare; they in turn owed him love and obedience. For George the notion of the nation as a family with the king as its father was more than an allegorical commonplace. It resonated on a deeply personal and emotional level. When his 'rebellious children' in America threatened to defect, and honour and duty failed to bring them back into the family fold, then force was unavoidable.[17] The war took its toll: on ordinary Britons through the sheer scale of mobilisation and rising unemployment and on George III too. In the spring of 1783 the king drafted a statement of abdication. With America lost, Ireland stirring, and his attempts to form a patriotic government above faction and party abortive, the king felt that he was 'no longer of utility to this Empire'. He offered to resign his crown and all dominions to the Prince of Wales and to 'retire to the care of my Electoral dominions, the original patrimony of my ancestors.' But George never gave his abdication speech and instead accepted the burden of kingship with which he had been born.[18]

America's War of Independence was the only major war lost by the British in the eighteenth century. This was despite unprecedented military efforts. Between 1775 and 1783, one in every seven or eight British adult males was under arms – a total of some 320,000 soldiers and sailors, 60,000 militia, and 110,000 Irish and British volunteers. Some 30,000 German mercenaries augmented the force still further. As Britain was fighting its former colonists on their own ground, it had to transport all men and supplies 4,800 kilometres across the Atlantic. In the previous war, the Royal Navy had successfully protected Britain's Atlantic supply lines at most times, but now Britain lost command of the sea at crucial moments. The entry of France and Spain into the war in 1778–9 multiplied its strategic problems.

This was indeed a global war. When the French intervened in 1778, followed by the Spanish and Dutch, British power was threatened in the Caribbean, at Gibraltar, and in north-eastern India. In 1779, there was an acute invasion threat to the homeland. Britain gradually reallocated army and naval resources away from America to home defence and the Caribbean, while meeting further commitments in the Mediterranean, West Africa, and India. A brief loss of British control of the seas isolated Yorktown during the hurricane season of 1781 – just long enough for it to fall. After the nadir of Yorktown, most of Britain's forces in North America were confined to three seaports, and the struggle had to all intents and purposes been lost. The French and Spanish conquered Minorca, St Kitts, and Nevis, though Britain managed to defend Jamaica as well as Gibraltar.[19]

The war was a crisis of British identity as much as of the British state, empire, and economy. In an imperial civil war, with both sides internally divided, and when supporters and opponents of American independence asserted both sameness and difference between Englishmen and Americans, identities were ambiguous and confused.[20] Against this background, British and American artists working in Britain sought to assimilate political and military events in and through art. They did so in part in artistic genres that traditionally celebrated triumph – public monuments as well as history and battle paintings. In the eighteenth century, ancient mythology and Christianity were fused with experience and individual-ism in these highest genres of art. History painting and monumental sculpture were ranked thus according to the mental effort required to produce them, and the intellectual pleasure derived from them. As both genres were used to define visu-ally a British hero, whose death evoked a moralising fervour, and although certain iconographical forms, postures, and gestures overlapped, they each had distinct modes of representation. Both genres sought to resolve the contradictions between classical theory and modern sensibility. As modern history paintings and monu-ments drew not from the ancient past, but from contemporary events, viewers brought with them knowledge from newspapers, pamphlets, sermons, and the talk of coffee houses and taverns. Their viewing of these works of art, and of the repro-ductive engravings which circulated much more widely, was further mediated by poetry and prints, plays and panoramas. A broader and more diverse public could therefore appreciate modern history, marine, and battle paintings, as well as public monuments.[21]

THE ART OF REMEMBERING
AND FORGETTING

O Memory! thou fond deceiver.

Oliver Goldsmith, 'Ode to Memory', from *Oratorio of the Captivity*

WHAT MADE A BRITISH HERO in this war? Did cultural representations
of war with America articulate, distort, or evade the difficult imperial realities?
Were the celebrations of exceptional military achievement in the East and West
Indies anything more than sophisticated exercises in forgetting much more important losses? An anonymous pamphlet considered enthusiasm over the retaining of
Gibraltar to deflect attention from the vastly greater loss of America, 'preferring
thus ... a few acres of barren rock, to the largest and most fertile extent of territory
that ever a nation was possessed of'.[1]

A war that was variously represented as a rebellion, revolution, civil war, and an
international and global conflict demanded complex choices for the commemoration of heroism. Led by the British king, government, and Parliament, the official
commemoration of figures and events in an imperial civil war was often fraught. It
also reveals the instability of the very notion of the heroic. Exploration of patterns of
commemoration needs to involve studying the gaps in the official visual and commemorative record. Looking briefly at private efforts of memorialisation undertaken
by Britons and by American loyalists offers a way to explore the selective emphases of
official commemoration.[2] Political and military conflict was intertwined with a struggle over cultural symbols of authority. The day in July 1776 when the Declaration of
Independence was read in New York City was marked by a dramatic act of king-killing.

Melted Majesty

In the mid-1770s, New York City had become the 'seat of war'. In such a contested space, public art attracted violent passions. To commemorate the repeal of the Stamp Act in 1766, the city commissioned a statue of William Pitt the Elder. Sitting now in the House of Lords as the Earl of Chatham, and advocating reconciliation with the colonies, this former British Prime Minister was an American patriot hero. Admirers regarded him 'in the sacred Light of having a second Time been the pre-server of this Country'. They then also voted for a statue of George III, mostly to forestall royal jealousy. The official rationale was 'to perpetuate … the deep Sense this Colony has, of the eminent and singular Blessings derived from Him, during His most auspicious Reign'.[3] But, as the New Yorker William Smith remembered, 'if they had not voted for a statue for Pitt, the King would have had none, for in truth they were disposed to give none'.[4]

In spring 1770, the New York press reported that the statues of George III and Chatham, both by Joseph Wilton, sculptor to the king and the empire, had arrived onboard the aptly named *Britannia*. Wilton's larger-than-life-size equestrian statue of the king stood on a five-metre-high marble pedestal. The statue was accorded an already symbolic site: it was placed on the Bowling Green at the foot of Broadway in Lower Manhattan, the spot of the 1765 Stamp Act Riot. Initially intended for Chatham's monument, the original fence (its crowns long since cut off) still marks the statue's site. The gilt statue was the first public monument ever to be erected in New York City. It was also quite possibly the first public monument in North America, and the first equestrian monument of George III anywhere in his domin-ions.[5] This stood in marked contrast to his counterparts in France, Denmark, and Portugal, or even to his own British predecessors. The monument was inaugurated in style, with a procession, patriotic music, and a 32-cannon salute.

Wilton's pedestrian statue of Chatham was erected a few weeks later at the inter-section of Wall and Williams Streets to the 'Acclamations of a great Number of Inhabitants'.[6] The marble figure, wearing the long robes of a Roman senator, held a partly opened scroll of the Magna Carta in his right hand; the left was outstretched in an oratorical posture, or a gesture of appeal. The inscription on the south side of the pediment declared that the statue expressed the colony's gratitude for the politician's services to America. There was no praise of the king in the inscription on his monument.

It was not long before the statue of the king attracted political controversy. An anti-graffiti, anti-desecration law was put into place in 1773 to discourage vandal-ism. And yet there were demonstrations of loyalty too. Even a year after the Boston Tea Party – and the fierce British reaction to colonists' agitation for representation

– the colonial governor, city authorities, and 'better sort of people' had 'uncovered' themselves in front of the statue of George III to acknowledge the blessings of his reign. They praised the repeal of the Stamp Act, army contracts, and the fact that 'the ministry did not mean to enslave the colonies, as the people of New England foolishly imagined'.[7] But all across the thirteen colonies, respect for the monarch, and for royal motifs and rites, was eroding gradually in the wake of the Boston Tea Party, the Quebec Act (seen as evidence of the establishment of popish government in 1774), and Britain's hiring of Hessian mercenaries in 1775.[8]

New York soon became a central battleground of the war, and the statue's fate reflected this. The city was of the highest strategic significance. It was an easily defensible naval base and served as the southern gateway to the Hudson Valley–Lake Champlain route north into Canada. By early summer the British, under the dual command of the brothers Admiral Richard Viscount Howe and General William Howe, amassed some 32,000 troops on Staten Island, in the harbour of New York City. Ten British ships of the line and twenty frigates with a total of 1,200 guns controlled the waterways surrounding the city, along with several hundred smaller craft and transport, making it appear to rifleman Daniel McCurtin 'like all London was afloat'.[9] Over 18,000 Continental soldiers were quartered in New York, then a city of less than one square mile, its wide, regular streets lined with trees and elegant houses, churches, and public buildings. Washington's headquarters was at No. 1 Broadway, the elegant house known as the Kennedy Mansion, which over-looked George III's monument.

When a copy of the Declaration of Independence reached New York, on 9 July 1776, General George Washington ordered that it be read to his Continental army. Washington hoped that the declaration would serve 'as a fresh incentive to every officer and soldier to act with fidelity and courage' as now the 'peace and safety of his country depends (under God) solely on the success of our arms', and also because there was a 'state possessed of sufficient power to reward his merit and advance him to the highest honors of a free country'.[10] In its brilliant preamble, the declaration set forth powerful Enlightenment ideals: 'That all men are created equal; that they are endowed by their Creator with certain inalienable rights; that among these are life, liberty, and the pursuit of happiness'. These were declared as self-evident truths, despite the social and racial inequalities that divided Revolutionary America. Much of the declaration consisted of an angry catalogue of royal abuses of power. The reign of George III, it said, had been 'a history of repeated injuries and usurpations, all having in direct object the establishment of an absolute Tyranny over these States.'[11]

By early evening, Continental soldiers and a crowd of New Yorkers had marched on the hated king's most prominent representation in the city. The large equestrian statue was made of lead and gilded in gold leaf. Showing the king in Roman garb, it was probably based on the statue of the Roman emperor Marcus Aurelius, a reference picked up by the New York papers.[12] The assailants vaulted the fence encircling the statue, looped ropes around the horse and rider, and tore it down. It landed with a tremendous thud, and one or several men began to saw at the king's head. Spectators, who had been cheering on the king's attackers, fell silent. It had been treasonous merely to insult the king with words: now his image was being toppled, the king's body killed. The mutilation of the royal head continued. Men chipped away the nose, clipped the laurel wreath, and otherwise disfigured it; they even, according to one source, 'drove a musket Bullet part of the way through his Head'.[13]

It is not clear who exactly was involved in the violent attack on the Bowling Green. The Sons of Liberty and various other patriotic citizens, soldiers, and officers claimed responsibility at the time, or have been credited or blamed since. We find a strong hint as to at least some of the perpetrators' identity in General Washington's reaction the next day. He made it clear he did not doubt that the perpetrators 'were actuated by zeal in the Publick Caus', but since it had 'so much the Appearance of Riot & want of order in the Army' he directed that 'in future Such things Shall be ... Left to be Executed by Proper Authority'.[14] Approving the motive, if not the method, of removing the king's representation, Washington confirmed that troops had been prominently involved in this gesture of defiance and patriotic triumph in a city threatened with British occupation. Other attributions made at the time are fanciful, but through their sheer existence they suggest just how momentous an act the attack on the king's statue was. An instantly produced, coarse American loyalist drama entitled *The Battle of Brooklyn; a farce in two acts, as it was performed on Long Island on Tuesday, the twenty-seventh day of August, 1776, by the representatives of the Tyrants of America assembled at Philadelphia* blamed Washington himself for the destruction of the statue.

Knowledge of the king-killing spread quickly. The *Pennsylvania Journal* of 17 July printed a letter from New York: 'the equestrian statue of George III, which Tory pride and folly raised in the year 1770, has, by the Sons of Freedom, been laid prostrate in the dirt – the just desert of an ungrateful tyrant!'[15] Newspapers elsewhere quoted an eyewitness of 'this ominous fall of leaden Majesty, looking back to the original's hopeful beginnings [who] pertinently exclaimed, in the language of the Angel to Lucifer, "If thou be'st he! But ah, how fallen! How chang'd!"'[16] Cynical and bitter comments appear in private journals too. Isaac Bangs, a 24-year-old lieutenant from Massachusetts, recorded the events with venomous energy in his journal:

Last night the Statue on the Bowling Green representing George Ghwelph alias George Rex ... was pulled down by the Populace. ... The Lead, we hear, is to be run up into Musquet Balls for the use of the Yankies, when it is hoped that the Emanations of the Leaden George will make as deep impressions in the Bodies of some of his red Coated & Torie Subjects, & that they will do the same execution in poisoning & destroying them, as the superabundant Emanations of the Folly & pretended Goodness of the real George have made upon their Minds.[17]

News of the event served as a loose framework into which both patriot and international artists inserted their own provocative and imaginative representations. In Augsburg, Franz X. Habermann in 1777 hastily produced a series of fantastical prints based on real events in the American War (see plate II). In the nineteenth century, national histories were illustrated with images of the scene. In the 1820s, crude woodcuts by John Barber's New Haven workshop depicted a standing king, apparently copied from Habermann, with crown and sceptre, being pulled down by a cheering crowd of men amid a plume of smoke.

All across America, in the days and weeks after the proclamation of the Declaration of Independence, crowds engaged in the safe and effective symbolic destruction of royal authority. Everywhere, streets named after the king and queen were being renamed. Most famously, Boston's King Street became State Street, and King's College in New York became Columbia. In cities from Massachusetts to New Jersey and Philadelphia, royal coats of arms of carved and painted wood were taken down from court houses, churches, and even from shops, taverns, and coffee houses, and destroyed in various rituals.[18]

Some iconoclastic actions were particularly violent. In Boston, the 'King's Arms [were] taken down and broken to pieces in the street, and carried off, by the people', just as Tom Paine's hugely popular *Common Sense* had envisaged the symbolic transfer of monarchical to popular sovereignty in a quasi-Eucharistic scene. In Huntington, Long Island, a pole with a flag dedicated to liberty and George III was used to make an effigy – complete with wooden crown and broadsword, blackened face, and feathers reminiscent of the king's black and Indian allies. Wrapped in the Union flag, it hung on a gallows, exploded, and burned. In Dover, Delaware, a portrait of George III was burned to 'destroy even the shadow of that King who refused to reign over a free people'. In Savannah, Georgia, a numerous crowd staged 'a very solemn funeral procession' and interred the mock king in front of the Court House, committing 'his political existence to the ground – corruption to corruption – tyranny to the grave – and oppression to eternal infamy'.[19]

Back in New York, the various parts of the royal and equine anatomy from

George III's dismantled statue became contested property.[20] The king's severed and mutilated head was carried off in a night-time procession to the tune of 'The Rogue's March', typically the musical accompaniment for a tarring and feathering. As the British were closing in on the city by late July, American patriot soldiers took the statue's head to Fort Washington, Upper Manhattan. The plan was to mount it on a pike in front of the Blue Bell Tavern in the same way that the British treated executed traitors or criminals. But British engineer Captain John Montressor arranged for the American spy Corbie and the loyalist John Cox to steal the head and bury it. By November 1776, Montressor sent it via Lady Gage to Lord Townshend in London, 'in order to convince them at home of the Infamous Disposition of the Ungrateful people of this distressed Country'.[21] Thomas Hutchinson, the former governor of Massachusetts and unofficial leader of the American loyalist exiles, in 1777 saw it at the Townshends' house:

> Lady Townshend asked me if I had a mind to see an instance of American loyalty? and going to the sopha, uncovered a large gilt head, which at once appeared to be that of the King. The nose is wounded and defaced, but the guilding remains fair; and as it is well executed, it retains a striking likeness.[22]

That is the head's last recorded sighting to date.

~

All but the statue's head was transported to Litchfield, Connecticut, a pivotal American military depot. On 29 June, the Provincial Congress had ordered the removal of lead from private New York homes – windows, sashes, drapery weights – to make bullets. Newspapers from New York to Pennsylvania reported that the lead from the statue too was to be recast into bullets, 'to assimilate with the brains of our infatuated adversaries, who, to gain a pepper-corn, have lost an empire'.[23] The statue was delivered to Oliver Wolcott, one of Connecticut's principal delegates to the Continental Congress and commander of fourteen regiments of the state militia. In a shed in Wolcott's orchard, ladies moulded the lead into 42,088 bullets. Ebenezer Hazard commented wryly to General Gates that George III's 'troops will probably have melted majesty fired at them.'[24]

Over the past two centuries, several pieces of statue have resurfaced at Wilton, Connecticut (see plate III). It seems loyalists stole and buried or otherwise hid as many parts as they could get their hands on while the convoy was stopping en route to Litchfield and the patriots were apparently getting drunk. Among the recovered parts are several portions of the saddle, saddle mountings, and saddle-cloth; a piece of rippled horsetail, still showing some faded spots of original gilding; a horse's flank with a small piece of the king's decorated saddle; a fragment of the horse's foreleg, and the king's left arm. Today, some 700 kilograms of king and horse still remain unaccounted for. The incident itself is little known outside specialist circles. But in the American Revolutionary period, the king's statue was only one of the more spectacular examples of how public art could become a site for political contest, popular passions, and violence, and of how contested images crystallised – or indeed shattered – loyalties, identities, and memory.

Representations of rulers – in the form of coins, heraldic signs, monuments, and paintings – have always been fundamental to asserting their presence in their realms and their authority among their subjects. And regime change often prompts the removal, defacing, or replacing of statues. The English Republic in 1649 ordered that symbols of the Stuart dynasty were not only to be removed from churches and public buildings but also to be defaced. A statue of Charles I at the Royal Exchange in London was decapitated and inscribed: 'Exit tyrannus Regum ultimus, anno primo restitutoe libertatis Angliae 1648'. The equestrian statue of George I erected by Sir Richard Grosvenor in Grosvenor Square in 1726 was vandalised by Jacobite opponents of the Hanoverian regime.[25]

Public humiliation of the king's mutilated image echoed the humiliating punishment meted out by American mobs to royal officials before the war, by patriots to (suspected) loyalists on the eve of the war, and by British mobs to some pro-American sympathisers. It was paralleled in text by Thomas Paine's incendiary rhetoric against the 'royal brute' in Common Sense, his attack on monarchy and hereditary succession.[26] The taking of the head reversed the coronation ceremony by 'crowning' transgressors with goose quills and marching them out of town.[27] Moreover, with the memory of Charles I's execution lodged firmly in the political thought and visual imagery of the period, the attack on the king's statue stood in the tradition of tyrannicide.[28] The humiliating parade of the king's leaden head according to well-rehearsed rituals usually reserved for traitors continued the demonstration of insult and disgrace.

The attack on the monument, the subsequent contest over the head between patriots and loyalists, and the recovery and hiding by loyalists of other pieces of statue are patterns that are also familiar from ancient Rome. In republican and imperial Rome, a variety of penalties was intended to limit or erase the memory and images of traitors or aspirants to tyranny, most prominently 'bad' emperors from Nero to Domitian. The penalties encompassed the destruction of public and private portraits, usually with their accompanying inscriptions; reworking a portrait into that of another person; recycling an entire statue or monument by melting down bronze statues, overwriting inscriptions on marble, or turning around and reusing marble slabs; the disfigurement or defacement of images, especially on monuments and coins; and the general erasure of the name from inscriptions and documents. The popular term for these sanctions – mostly officially decreed by the Roman Senate, the emperor, or the army, but sometimes carried out spontaneously – is *damnatio memoriae*. Such practices transformed what had been originally built as celebratory imperial monuments into dramatic reminders of a ruler's humiliating fall. Attacks on the sensory organs, eyes, nose, mouth, and ears, were particularly common: a mutilation of the emperor in effigy which paralleled the abuse of traitors' or tyrants' corpses.[29]

The example of Rome shows furthermore that attempts to erase memory also to some extent memorialise their victims. Post-mortem disgrace contains two linked and contradictory impulses, the 'urge to remember the villain so that his fate may be a warning to others and an equal or opposite tendency to forget him, to obliterate his name and career as if he had never existed'.[30] The perpetrators of violent acts wish to preserve traces as trophies of triumph and mementos of destruction. They indulge a desire for symbolic permanence that contradicts the impetus for total obliteration: hence the victor's flag waving over the enemy's ruins, or the destroyed monument's empty pedestal standing as a warning for the audience.[31] Remembering and forgetting, infamy and oblivion, are therefore often closely related tendencies.

The emphasis of the act of sacrilege lies on the deliberate and conscious attempt to desecrate the memory of the person. But even the erasure of a name from public monuments could serve a dual purpose if it was clear whose name was being erased. And if an inscription on an honorific monument was erased without the destruction of the statue itself, the act would not immediately abolish the victim's memory, though it might render them anonymous over time. Which will be read as evidence of the act of erasure, and which will be seen as a failed attempt at achieving historical oblivion: decapitating a statue, or removing it and leaving an empty pedestal behind?[32]

The British army occupied New York City. The restored governor and the army observed once again a full royalist calendar, just as the British forces and their German allies did wherever they happened to be in command in North America.[33] The British removed all liberty poles erected by the Sons of Liberty and the army seized the homes of avowed patriots and reclaimed them for the British monarch by painting 'GR' on their doors.[34] But New York nevertheless witnessed another monumental decapitation. In Royall Tyler's play *The Contrast*, the moderately literate Jonathan wanders around New York City: 'I went to see two marblestone men

4. Joseph Wilton, *Statue of the Earl of Chatham* in New York City (1770, mutilated *c.*1777). Via a corporation rubbish heap and the Fifth Ward Hotel in 1864, the marble torso made its way from its original residence on the intersection of Wall and William Streets to its current abode at West 77th Street, the New-York Historical Society.

and leaden horse that stands out ... doors in all weathers; ... one had got no head, and t'other weren't there'.[35] The latter was of course George III's equestrian monument. The decapitated statue was Chatham's, which had apparently been attacked during the night of 29/30 November 1777, St Andrew's Day. After the statue's head had been cut off, its right arm with the Magna Carta was severed just underneath the shoulder. The torso remained standing until 1788, when it was removed to allow for the paving of Wall Street (fig. 4).[36]

In the early nineteenth century, reports started to appear which had it that the statue had been attacked by British soldiers in retaliation for the destruction of George III's statue.[37] This version persists in the standard history of American sculpture and on the website of the New-York Historical Society.[38] Yet, decapitating and severing the right arm of the representation of a former (and still living) British premier – even in the case of a statue commissioned and revered by New York patriots – would seem to indicate at least confused loyalties. Chatham had never argued for independence, though he had advocated reconciliation.

Were British soldiers in New York City symbolically divesting the self-proclaimed American patriots of their British hero, his head, arm with Magna Carta, and with them their claim to traditional English libertarian or oppositional patriotism?[39] There is considerable doubt that the attackers were indeed British soldiers, though no concrete and plausible alternative has yet emerged. Whatever their identity, if by decapitating Chatham his assailants were seeking to render the statue anonymous, the fact that the inscription appears not to have been erased would have limited their success. The sacrilege therefore primarily drew attention to the act itself. New Yorkers – patriots and loyalists alike – and the occupying British forces would have seen evidence perhaps of an attempt to avenge the king, perhaps to desecrate, if not erase, Chatham's American patriot memory. When Chatham died just months after his New York image had been mutilated, the British state honoured his memory with a funeral and monument in Westminster Abbey. Even these supposedly national acts, however, did not unfold uncontested.

Compensatory Triumphalism

Lord Chatham fell in the Senate – not by daggers, nor by the thunder of Lord Suffolk's eloquence.

Thomas Hutchinson, c.1778[40]

On 7 April 1778, the Earl of Chatham, long ill in body and mind, collapsed dramatically in the House of Lords during a speech advocating reconciliation with the American colonies, short of accepting their Declaration of Independence. He was taken from the chamber to his country seat at Hayes, where he expired on 11 May, 'a glorious and voluntary sacrifice | In the cause of his Country'.[41] In death, Chatham continued to divide the political class as he had done during much of his lifetime. Chatham – formerly Pitt the 'Great Commoner', the independent 'patriot minister' – was in the 1770s still held up as a friend to the City of London and a patriot 'scourge of complacent courtly power'. Yet, George III denied the City of London's request to bury Chatham at St Paul's, because the House of Commons had already voted for a state funeral and monument in Westminster Abbey.[42] The wartime premier who had presided over unprecedented imperial expansion in Canada, America, and India during the Seven Years War was to be granted the highest official honours. After lying in state at the Palace of Westminster, on 9 June, the visionary elder statesman was buried in the Abbey's north transept.[43] The national authorities hoped to shape closely the interpretations and meanings of Chatham's funeral and commemoration.

Even as he was being admitted to Westminster Abbey, there was an attempt to privilege specific memories over others. To the king, Chatham had been an inconsistent politician who had been afflicted by hypochondria and depression in equal measure. George III had made it clear he would find it offensive if the parliamentary honours complimented Chatham's 'general conduct', rather than specifically 'his rousing the Nation at the beginning of the last War, and his conduct whilst at that period he held the Seals of Secretary of State'.[44] Indeed, the initial proposal for Chatham's memorialisation came from the opposition. Pro-City MP Isaac Barré proposed a state funeral, Richard Rigby suggested a monument as a lesser alternative, and Edmund Burke argued for both. Far from a dignified, bipartisan debate on the commemoration of a statesman and national hero, the discussion caricatured the long-standing contest between the City and the court and government.[45] Only two peers with court connections (among forty noblemen in total) and some twenty MPs attended the funeral. Among them were the opposition leaders Burke and the Marquis of Rockingham, carrying a 'picture of Britannia weeping over the arms of Chatham', as well as General Burgoyne, the defeated military leader turned bitter opposition politician. For them, Chatham had become a man of peace who to his last gasp had condemned the folly of imperial civil war.[46]

Chatham's national monument took six years to complete, and was unveiled in March 1784, when Britain's total defeat in America was still a gaping national wound. The dramatic portrait of the orating Chatham evoked memories of his aggressive direction of the triumphant Seven Years War, as much as his opposition to the current imperial conflict.[47] In its allegorical bombast, imagery of the fortitude of the determined war leader merged with that of the prudence of the statesman who had a vision of a maritime and commercial empire. London magazines published the inscription alongside engravings and descriptions of the monument, explaining that the statue bore historical testimony to both the nation's gratitude and its artists' improvements: 'Roman virtue is here eternised by Grecian elegance'. Foreign visitors reported, however, that it appeared to downplay Chatham's achievements by occupying a dark recess.

Having been prevented from burying Chatham at St Paul's Cathedral, the City of London commissioned a monument; it was completed well before the national memorial was ready. John Bacon's ambitiously baroque, tomb-like affair was publicly unveiled in the Guildhall in October 1782.[48] It too celebrates Chatham's seminal contributions to British imperial expansion and his support of political liberty – as war leader, protector of commerce, and wise governor. The inscription ends on the theme of commemoration itself:

TO WITHHOLD FROM THOSE VIRTUES; EITHER OF THE LIVING OR THE DEAD,
THE TRIBUTE OF | ESTEEM AND VENERATION, IS TO DENY TO THEMSELVES THE
MEANS OF HAPPINESS AND HONOUR ... | THE BRITISH NATION HONOURED HIS
MEMORY WITH A PUBLIC FUNERAL, AND A PUBLIC MONUMENT | AMONGST HER
ILLUSTRIOUS MEN IN WESTMINSTER ABBEY.

Although the City's monument was erected in competition with the government's, it nevertheless cross-referenced the national acts of commemoration. Both the national and the metropolitan monuments emphasised former imperial triumph over the current crisis.

Such a strategy, of harking back to the earlier days of imperial success, was one that the East India Company also readily indulged in. In the mid-1770s, the Company set up a monument in Westminster Abbey to Major-General Stringer Lawrence (1697–1775), its second commission after the Watson memorial. Lawrence had largely been responsible for the Company's successful resistance to the French on the Coromandel coast in the 1750s. As commander-in-chief of all Company forces in India, Lawrence distinguished himself in the relief of Tritchinopoly and the Battle of Sugarloaf Rock, and in the defence of Madras.[49] William Tyler's £700 monument required two earlier, private monuments to be moved to make space, thus physically reinforcing the trend from private to semi-public commissions. The major's portrait bust stands on a plinth with his coat of arms. The pedestal is carved with the fortified Rock of Tritchinopoly, which Lawrence and Clive had secured from the French and their allies in 1751, and with the city and the encampment. There are allegorical figures of Fame (or History) and, pointing to the major's bust, of Britannia (or the Company), at whose feet lie various conquered French and Indian flags. History holds a tablet which succinctly summarises Lawrence's achievements:

DISCIPLINE ESTABLISHED
FORTRESSES PROTECTED
SETTLEMENTS EXTENDED.
FRENCH
AND INDIAN ARMIES
DEFEATED
AND
PEACE CONCLUDED
IN THE CARNATIC.

Just as Chatham's monument was being unveiled, the East India Company commissioned its third Abbey monument, this time to commemorate the (Protestant) Irish general Sir Eyre Coote (Thomas Banks, 1784–9).[50] Coote's Abbey monument was perhaps the least controversial of the (quasi-)official military memorials of the American Revolutionary War period. It is a reminder that Britain's commitment was global: in India, the British were fighting both Hyder Ali and the French. The inscription links Coote's achievements in the Seven Years War on the Coromandel coast with his last and most glorious campaign, the defence of the Madras Presidency against Hyder Ali and Tipu Sultan in the first Mysore War (1781–2), before death 'interrupted his career of glory'. A brilliant tactician, Coote defeated Hyder Ali at Porto Novo, Pollilore, and Sholinghur.

Coote's massive pyramidical white marble monument shows a seated, life-size nude Mahratta or Hindu captive weeping beside a trophy. The captive provides the key to reading the monument: starting with his feet at the viewer's eye level, the composition unfolds along his body, around a winged figure of Victory, up and along her arms to rest on Coote's medallion portrait, which Victory hangs on the palm tree behind the armour. Banks's memorial received much praise, especially for the anatomy of the captive and the 'sedate dignified character of its grief'. The commission for the Abbey monument was fortuitously well timed to divert some attention away from the allegations of misconduct against Warren Hastings and wider charges of Company ineptitude and iniquity.[51]

With the monument to Coote, and the earlier ones to Watson and Stringer Lawrence, the Company had thus honoured conquests spanning the Seven Years and American Revolutionary Wars. They balanced the fraught official commemorative efforts relating to the American colonies, and located British India within the global Anglo-French struggle. Over the coming half-century, more expansive conquests would be remembered on the Subcontinent itself, in London, and in provincial sites across the British Isles, as the Company state turned into an aggressively militaristic ruler over vast parts of India (chapter 7).

Undaunted Briton or Sentimental Spy?

The only monument in Westminster Abbey which commemorates an action in the North American theatre of war does not honour a soldier's heroic death in battle. Instead the memorial, commissioned by George III, remembers the death by hanging of a gallant, sentimental young officer named Major John André. To the Americans he had been a spy, conspiring with the American General Benedict Arnold to hand over the strategically important West Point, the 'Gibraltar of America', to the British. For the British he was a martyr – a highly accomplished gentleman-officer who had served his country with distinction and faced his death with courage and sentimental grace. But such a controversial fate raised doubts in Britain too. When Mary Shackleton, a young Irishwoman visiting London in the summer of 1784, found André's monument temporarily boarded up, she speculated 'in what light his death could be placed for tho' we love his character, which was brave & amiable, yet sure the cause in which he fell, a spy, was inglorious.'[52] André's story posed fundamental questions about the very notion of masculine heroism and about commemoration at a time of imperial crisis.

Born in Paris or London to Huguenot parents and educated in Geneva and Göttingen, André joined the British army in 1771 and served in Canada and the American colonies from 1774, before becoming aide-de-camp to Sir Henry Clinton, commander-in-chief of the British forces in America. From 1779, André handled Clinton's intelligence correspondence and secretly communicated with the gifted, driven, yet temperamental American General Benedict Arnold. Arnold had made significant contributions in the early Canadian campaigns of the war and at Saratoga, but became frustrated over promotion and pay.[53] At a secret meeting on the shore of the Hudson river in the early hours of 21 September 1780, Arnold handed André papers with full details of the defences of West Point. As André's sloop, the *Vulture*, had been forced downriver by American outpost fire, he accompanied Arnold to a farmhouse at Haverstraw behind American lines, to await nightfall on the 22nd. Urged by Arnold, André exchanged his uniform for civilian clothing. By accepting papers and changing out of his uniform he had fatally violated two essential instructions of his commanding officer.

On the night of the 22nd, André rode back towards British lines through Westchester County. He had passed the American outposts and was in the notionally neutral no-man's-land, when near Tarrytown he ran into a patrol of three American militiamen. André mistook them for British soldiers and identified himself as a British officer on important business for General Clinton. Only when the militiamen revealed their identity did André show them his false pass. Yet the compromising papers tucked into André's stockings were discovered and André was arrested as a spy. Lieutenant-Colonel Jameson, who commanded the outposts, sent André's papers to Washington but had the officer himself taken to Arnold at West Point. Major Tallmadge, head of American intelligence, soon comprehended the full extent of the plot, a fast courier was dispatched, and André was put in custody in a windowless room at the dragoon headquarters at South Salem. Lieutenant Joshua King, the duty officer, noticed the powder in André's hair and was certain he had no ordinary person in charge.

Arnold fled just in time on the morning of 25 September, ironically using the

Vulture to make the escape behind British lines that had eluded André. That same day Washington personally took command of shoring up the defences of West Point and alerted American forces within 150 kilometres. The plot – a 'scene of the blackest treason' – made the American high command still fear an attack by 25 September.[54] Under a very substantial armed guard to fend off any British raiding parties, André was moved to the main army camp at Tappan. There, a formal court was assembled to consider the question he himself had raised: was he a soldier or a spy?[55]

On 29 September, the high-profile military court of inquiry set up by George Washington and chaired by Major-General Nathaniel Greene assembled at an old Dutch church at Tappan. Charges were levelled that André had disguised himself behind enemy lines, with a feigned name, false passport, and civilian clothing, and moved with a treasonous purpose and papers. In short, he had 'assumed the character of a spy'. André defended his honour and his life by arguing that he had found himself an involuntary prisoner behind American lines and had only donned civilian clothes to escape. He appealed for Washington to exchange him for an American officer in British custody, whose fate might otherwise reflect his. Yet the Board concluded that André ought to be considered a 'Spy from the enemy; and … agreeable to the law and usage of nations … he ought to suffer death' by hanging.[56] Clinton's efforts to save André failed, as did Washington's attempts to have Arnold abducted from New York. André demanded an officer's privilege of death by firing squad, instead of being hanged as a spy.[57] But that request was declined, and its failure recounted in the British press, and reprinted in annotations to poetic and dramatic renditions of André's story on both sides of the Atlantic.[58] After a stay of just twenty hours to allow for a final, inconclusive, Anglo-American parley, André was executed by Washington's orders at noon on 2 October. In his last letter to General Clinton, André had sought to take any feeling of guilt or responsibility from him and expressed himself 'perfectly tranquil in mind, and prepared for any fate, to which an honest zeal for my King's service may have devoted me'.[59] On the morning of 2 October, he had shaved, had his hair powdered by his servant Peter Laune, and dressed in a freshly laundered ruffled shirt, vest, neck cloth, and gold-trimmed jacket, with polished boots over the breeches. Eyewitnesses noted how he said farewell to his guards and American officers, bowed politely to his executioners, mounted a baggage wagon which had been driven underneath the cross-tree, blindfolded himself, and pulled the rope around his neck. Making use of his privilege of speaking some final words, he simply asked the surrounding gentlemen to bear witness that he met his death 'like a brave man'. His body was buried in a nearby grave. Initially marked only by a small pile of stones, a few days later someone planted cedar trees at either end and a peach tree on the grave.

The American officers observing André during the ten days between his arrest and execution had experienced mixed emotions. They were impressed equally with André's 'elevated sentiments' and his manly bravery on the scaffold. Major Benjamin Tallmadge had witnessed the 'affecting spectacle' of André marching

> to the destined ground with as much ease and cheerfulness of countenance as if he had been going to an Assembly room. Tho' his fate was just, yet to see so promising a youth brought to the gallows drew a tear from almost every spectator.

Tallmadge, who left the site 'in a flood of tears', was convinced that, had André 'been tried by a Court of Ladies, he is so genteel, handsome, polite a young gentleman that I am confident they would have acquitted him'.[60] Alexander Hamilton, then an aide to Washington, wrote a letter later reproduced in loyalist, patriot, and British newsprint. André had acted on the scaffold, Hamilton hymned, 'with a composure that … melted the hearts of the beholders' so that, 'in the midst of his enemies, he died universally esteemed and universally regretted.'[61]

Back home in Britain reactions were strong and bitter. André was celebrated as a gallant officer and martyr who had met his untimely death with fortitude and resolution. Samuel Johnson pronounced that Washington's order showed 'his heart of Nero's colour dy'd'.[62] The British press reported that General Clinton had difficulty restraining his troops' desire to revenge André's martyrdom.[63] The newspapers (in articles soon reprinted in the New York loyalist papers) were outraged that the Americans had not honoured the military code of civility. Men of the higher ranks could spy without losing their honour. Generals and commissioned officers were gentlemen and as such were not to be hanged like paid peasant spies.[64] This argument mirrored André's own defence: acting as a spy would have been incompatible with his condition in life and his honour. Washington was torn between the European officer code with which he had grown up when fighting with British imperial forces, and the tactical need of the American commander-in-chief to placate an American public and the rank and file of a Revolutionary army incensed by Arnold's horrible treachery and hostile towards the generous treatment of captured enemy officers.[65] However, André's movement between the lines, and the military board's findings that he had violated the very military code to which he and his superiors appealed, constituted a solid enough basis to proceed with the execution.

André's death fell at the height of the Anglo-American cult of sensibility, and

André had performed his final days as a veritable triumph of sentiment. He reso-nated with a late colonial American culture of sensibility, grounded in earlier theo-logical debates, moral philosophy, and scientific and medical discourses. In the period of the American Revolution, the ideals of sensibility pervaded novels and captivity narratives. In America, sensibility was not in conflict with militarism. The opposite was true. Officers used sensibility as a means of proving social distinc-tion. Commemoration of André – in prints, songs, and poems, in Britain, North America, and Continental Europe – perpetuated notions of the sentimental British soldier-hero which had first come to prominence in the Seven Years War. During that conflict, military manliness and sensibility had been conflated by artists and writers in Britain.[66]

André was also remembered in a more conventional heroic mode.[67] The French Major-General the Marquis de Lafayette judged André 'a charming man who con-ducted himself throughout, and died, like a hero'.[68] Americans too praised André's 'appearance of Philosophy & Heroism' who 'received his fate with greater forti-tude than others saw it'. Washington himself, 'pronounced that he had met his fate like a brave man'.[69] The emphasis on manly heroic bravery was stronger still among British responses. According to newspapers, the major had evinced 'the undaunted spirit of a Briton and [the] patriotic resolution of a Citizen of Rome or Athens'; he was to be compared with the Roman hero Mucius Scaevola in terms of their 'congenial bravery ... the same confidence, the same strength of mind, and inflexibility of Soul'.[70] After the execution, General Clinton had let his army know that André's reputation as a gentleman officer of the highest integrity and honour remained unblemished.[71] Even Anna Seward's famous *Monody* did not mourn her friend André exclusively for his literary and artistic gifts and romantic tragedy. She also hoped that his fate would inspire 'the fiercest lions', that is the British army. Dedicated to Clinton and denouncing the 'Remorseless Washington' as a 'cool determin'd Murderer of the Brave', the *Monody* ends by expressing the hope that the 'injur'd André's memory shall inspire | A kindling Army with resistless fire'.[72]

It was possible then in Britain, as it was in America, for a man to be imagined as both a sentimental *and* a brave, courageous officer in the conventional heroic mould. André's heroism was not demilitarised. His own last words, and those of many British commentators, highlighted the major's courage and bravery. George III, the British head of state, honoured André first and foremost as a brave officer and servant of the state who, as the inscription on his monument puts it, while 'employed in an important but hazardous Enterprise, fell a Sacrifice to his Zeal for his King and Country'.

George III's monument to André at Westminster Abbey was designed by the

5. Robert Adam and P. M. van Gelder, *Monument to Major-General John André*, Westminster Abbey (*c*.1780–82). All figures on the sarcophagus bas-relief are animated for sorrowful and subtly dramatic effect. André and Washington are depicted in slightly fuller relief. At the foot of the tree on which André is to be hanged sit a child and a woman wringing her hands, either Mercy and Innocence, or – more likely in this realistic narrative – American civilians.

celebrated Scottish neoclassical architect Robert Adam, one of the two joint architects of the King's Works, and it was sculpted by P. M. van Gelder (fig. 5). There were, in theory, numerous options for the designers. Adam briefly considered a generic image of a fallen hero; he could also have evoked the parallel with Mucius Scaevola. Instead, a reclining mourning figure of Britannia is joined by a lugubrious British lion on top of a sarcophagus on whose front is a small-scale narrative relief in modern costume. The relief, for which there were no obvious models, shows Washington's campaign tent, where a soldier sits crumpled with guilt. Washington receives what is most likely Clinton's demand for André's release. At right, two soldiers gingerly lead André away to the outline of a Continental firing squad. Despite this suggestion of a gentleman's death, André's left arm is gesturing towards the fuller relief of a hanging tree at far right. His right hand clutches the blindfold. Some responses described the structure as a 'strange memorial', even 'the most unfortunate monument in the whole Abbey'. But the reviewer for the *Gentleman's Magazine* not only praised André's gallantry and fortitude but also appreciated the jointly mourning figures of Britannia and the lion.[73]

Yet reviews disapproved of the apparent inversion of heroic representation on the bas-relief of André's monument: Washington was

> the capital figure … employed in the legal exercise of an acknowledged authority; whilst the poor Major is dragged from his presence like a criminal, and scarce seems to attract the notice of any other part of the assembly, but those who have laid violent hands upon him.

If viewed without guidance, the *British Magazine* continued, 'we should have represented it as a trophy to perpetuate the fame of General Washington, in the act of consigning to due punishment some atrocious offender against the sovereign states of America. Surely the brave, ill-fated Andre, should have been the hero of the tale!'[74] At least the Americans' refusal to show 'magnanimity and sympathy' was revenged by someone 'knocking Washington's head off the bas-relief'.[75]

It is instructive to view André's monument in its spatial and temporal contexts. Its placing in the Abbey could be read to suggest comforting symbolic coherence, yet also painful historical discontinuity. André's monument was situated near several others commemorating different types of violent death in imperial conflict across roughly a century. These include Adams's memorial to the 'equally unfortunate and brave' Colonel Roger Townshend, who had fallen near Ticonderoga in 1759. Memorials to other victims of war in North America, such as Wolfe, were nearby.[76] The juxtaposition could also work to André's disadvantage. A German visitor, Sophie von la Roche, pointed out the obvious difference between Townshend and André: 'The latter condemned to hang for a thoughtless action', while Townshend fell 'at his post on the battlefield'.[77]

An American visitor, John Quincy Adams, needed neither the comparison across British history nor between Washington and André to find the British choice of 'hero' dubious if not outright pitiful: 'how much degenerated that Nation must be, which can find no fitter Object for so great an honour, than a Spy'. The artistic representation of a spy-hero was going to be difficult in the best of circumstances. André's association with sentimental manly grace, and the comparison with Washington, rendered his position as a British hero during the imperial crisis even more complex.[78]

The same year that André's monument was completed at the Abbey, Benedict Arnold – now a financially secure brigadier-general in the British army – arrived in

England with Marquis Cornwallis. Arnold had been vilified in America as Lucifer and Judas and had had his effigy paraded and burned, hanged, and exploded in the streets. A crowd destroyed his father's tombstone in Norwich, Connecticut. Americans used to say that if possible they would cut off Arnold's leg, which had been wounded during his valiant leadership of patriot forces in what became known as the Battle of Freeman's Farm, and bury it with full military honours while hanging the rest of the body on a gibbet. London magazines described Arnold as a detested traitor due to whom André had fallen a martyr. Yet Arnold was consulted by George III and the cabinet. An American loyalist, who observed Arnold and his wife read the inscription on André's monument, overheard him remark: 'If I had succeeded, as I hoped, in re-uniting the Empire, I too might have found a place and a monument here'. Instead, 'His life was shame, his epitaph was guilt.'[79]

The only monument to Arnold is in the grounds of the Saratoga National Historic Park. It commemorates the general's single honourable limb of the Battle of Freeman's Farm fame. Sculptured in bas-relief upon the slab are a cannon, an epaulet, a wreath, and a military boot for a man's left leg. There is no name on either side of the slab, but on its reverse is an inscription explaining that the monument was erected by 'John Watts de Peyster |Brev: Maj: Gen: S.N.Y. | 2nd V. Pres't Saratoga Mon't Ass't'n:' in memory of the 'most brilliant soldier' of the Continental army, who had been wounded on this spot during a decisive Revolutionary battle in October 1777. The official Saratoga Monument, a monumental stone obelisk built on the occasion of the battle's centenary, features large bronze plaques with politico-military narratives of the Anglo-American struggle, including of 'The Wounding of General Arnold in the Brunswick Redoubt'. On the obelisk's façade, niches accommodate heroic statues to Generals Horatio Gates and Philip Schuyler and Colonel Daniel Morgan. The fourth niche, facing the battlefield due south, is empty …

Damage Control

André's story was never likely to result in very straightforward acts of national commemoration. But even the memorialisation of an exceptional, triumphant victory in this period, when inspected closely, shows how conflicted and ambiguous 'national' commemoration had become. By 1781, a shift to a direct French confrontation was Britain's 'only means left for a renovation of our glory'.[80] On 12 April 1782, a British fleet of thirty-seven ships commanded by Admiral Rodney, made battle with a French fleet of thirty-three ships under Admiral Grasse near a group of little islands between Dominica and Guadeloupe. In the confusion of the Battle of the Saints (Les Saintes), British ships unintentionally 'broke the line' of the French fleet in three places, cutting off Grasse's flagship and a few ships around her, but allowing the bulk of the French fleet to escape. Rodney took five ships, including the flagship, with the siege artillery in this substantial if not overwhelming victory. But as the war was going so badly overall, there was a sense of relief and euphoria that Britain had scored a victory against multiple enemies. Histories written in the immediate aftermath of the war stressed that the victory

> so elevated the spirits of Britain, and so depressed the hopes of France, that had it taken place prior to the surrender of lord Cornwallis, that event would have been less influential in disposing the nation to peace.[81]

Rodney's battle was as significant in ending the war in the Caribbean as York-town had been in North America. Britain's West Indian colonies stayed loyal during the revolution, partly because their white minority populations relied on military protection against slave revolts, and their sugar economy depended on the protected metropolitan market. As the centre of Atlantic trade and the cockpit in the Anglo-French struggle for naval and maritime supremacy, the West Indies accounted for a fifth of British trade and one eighth of British merchant tonnage and seamen. Each year, some 300 merchant ships sailed from the British West Indies to London, mostly bringing sugar and rum. The substantial plantation owners and big merchants, and many other British men and women of middling rank, had a direct investment in this trade. The islands embodied Chatham's vision of a mercantile 'Empire of liberty' of trading outposts and maritime colonies – although it was of course dependent on an economic universe built on slavery. After St Eustatius had been recaptured and St Kitts and Nevis (as well as Minorca) had been lost between November 1781 and February 1782, Rodney's victory protected Jamaica from capture and restored British mastery of the oceans. It preserved a vital strategic asset and boosted national morale. Together with Howe's relief of Gibraltar and Hughes's resistance to Suffren in the Bay of Bengal, it also helped secure more favourable terms under the Treaty of Versailles in 1783. As the Secretary of State, the Earl of Shelburne, stated confidently at the Paris peace negotiations: 'It is enough to lose one world; it is not necessary to lose a second.'[82]

Throughout the British Isles, townspeople illuminated their windows. In the poetic hyperbole of instantly composed songs and ballads, Rodney's glory outshone that of Roman emperors and even the glow of the stars. The admiral and his most famous battle also became the subject of popular memorabilia – from gold rings to brass, silver, and pewter shoe buckles, from Chelsea porcelain jugs and earthenware mugs to Liverpool cream ware plates, and from long-case clocks to a

6. *Earthenware Sifter* (*c.*1782). Staffordshire mask mugs shaped as the head of Lord Rodney are only surpassed in humorous ingenuity by this double-headed pottery vessel inscribed 'Lord Rodney', which is pierced at the top to function as a flour sifter. This is an unusually poor likeness of Rodney compared to most ephemeral commemorative objects, which permeated everyday life with instantly recognisable images of the admiral.

coconut flask depicting Rodney's *Formidable* breaking through the French line (fig. 6). Citizens in Shropshire erected an obelisk as a more permanent monument to the memory of Rodney's 'glorious victory', while William Roscoe and others would soon lay out Liverpool's grandest Georgian residential street in the admiral's name. John Mells, a Lincolnshire customs officer, summed up the general sentiment when he wrote over-optimistically:

> [t]he Spirit of the British Lion is at last roused and notwithstanding Great Britain has had to contend with the House of Bourbon America and Holland not one of these powers dare fairly meet her either on the Ocean or in the Field.[83]

The victory of the Saints enabled the British people to ignore the disastrous failure of the war overall. Government and Parliament planned to match popular enthusiasm with official recognition. Rodney received a barony and a generous pension. The Commons now also voted its *only* American Revolutionary War monument in Westminster Abbey – a massive white marble structure in honour of the highest-ranking casualties, Captains William Bayne, William Blair, and the Rt. Hon. Robert Manners.[84]

Rodney's new accolades and the captains' memorial were officialdom's attempt to capitalise on a story of exceptional success in a disastrous war. They wished to use Rodney's victory to balance pessimism over previous defeats and the all but certain loss of the American colonies. The government was driven also by a desire for damage control; they had embarrassingly sent a replacement for Rodney just before his great triumph. Damage control in *defeat* was familiar to London audiences. Battle accounts and images such as Serres's 1780 exhibit, *The Engagement between the Foe and the June off Brest, 10 Sept 1778* (RA 1780, cat. no. 20, commissioned by Captain Hon. T. Windsor), emphasised the protracted resistance that British forces maintained against superior forces. The Saints, however, prompted the unusual spectacle of damage control not in defeat but in victory.

Rodney himself enjoyed a mixed reputation.[85] On the one hand he was an outstanding commander-in-chief and a popular hero who had led the naval force in the capture of Martinique during the Seven Years War, crushed a Spanish squadron in January 1780, and delivered desperately needed troops and provisions to the besieged Gibraltar that same spring. On the other hand, Rodney had only returned from debtor's exile in France in 1778, embarrassingly bailed out by the French Marshal de Biron. Rodney's haughty approach to fellow officers had been controversial. His tactical judgement was not perfect, and, most damagingly, Rodney was accused of being diverted from his main strategic and operational tasks by the lure of the wealth of the neutral Dutch island St Eustatius. Rodney captured its huge warehouse stores and some 180 merchant ships, including British-owned goods. James Gillray celebrated this multi-million-pound scoop in his print *The Dutchman in the Dumps*, in which the Dutchman proclaims himself 'undone', while 'America now | To Old England might bow'.[86] Rodney justified the confiscations of British merchants' goods on the grounds that they had traded with the enemy, but the House of Commons set up an inquiry, and the Rockingham government dispatched a replacement for Rodney, Admiral Hugh Pigot. The admiral's victory over the French fleet at the Saints came as a major embarrassment. Rodney had supported the previous North administration and criticised the then Rockinghamite opposition. It seems that victory celebrations in parts of the country were orchestrated by North supporters aiming to discomfort the new administration.[87]

To avoid drawing more fire from the opposition, Admiral Lord Keppel and Charles James Fox, the First Lord of the Admiralty and Foreign Secretary responsible for substituting Rodney, praised him effusively and proposed votes of thanks in both houses. The Commons committee appointed to investigate the St Eustatius affair was discharged. Even the award of a British barony to Rodney was an exercise in damage control: the Irish peerage apparently preferred by the king would not have removed Rodney from the British House of Commons.[88]

Parliament's only vote for a national monument in Westminster Abbey in the American Revolutionary period thus takes on much more complex connotations. All parties could agree on the merits of the captains' heroic sacrifice and wished to celebrate with gusto the successful defence of Caribbean assets. But the address

7. Joseph Nollekens, *Monument to Captains Bayne, Blair, and Lord Robert Manners*, Westminster Abbey (*c.*1782–93). Britannia gazes mournfully at the captains' portraits, an empathetic lion cowers behind a Union Jack shield, and Neptune reclines on a seahorse. Out of a detailed relief of swirling sea rises a rostral column upon which a cherub fixes the captains' portrait medallions. Behind, three ships stack upward against the triangular back-stone, which implies a plane receding dramatically into the sky, upon which a winged Victory crowns the scene with a wreath.

for a monument was moved by Bamber Gascoygne, the opposition MP for Truro who had supported North's government. Once a monument had been agreed on, the Treasury directly oversaw the commission from the Royal Academician Joseph Nollekens (figs 7, 8). The Prime Minister himself attended most meetings. The captains' sacrifice appears to have been emphasised at least in part to help deflect attention from the government's embarrassing timing over Rodney's replacement. Perhaps adopting the fairly traditional format with a rostral column, which echoed earlier naval monuments in the nave, was also intended to help gloss over the contentious context of the commission.[89] On close inspection, Parliament's only commission for a military monument in the American Revolutionary War was not a straightforward, consensual, national affair.

Private Grief and Pride

If national, official, public commemoration was so conflicted in this period, how did private individuals memorialise death in the American War? Families commissioned monuments to casualties or veterans of the American Revolutionary War in

8. J. K. Sherwin, after Thomas Stothard, *The Death of Lord Robert Manners* (1786). Representations of heroic figures and events circulated in plays, prints, and ephemera. Manners, the second son of the Marquis of Granby, a hero of the Seven Years War, was visually the most widely recognised of the three captains commemorated at Westminster Abbey (fig. 7). By 1783, Stothard's painting was exhibited at Mr Haynes's, at Cockspur Street and Pall Mall. Manners is here dying heroically – if historically incorrectly – cradled in the arms of his crew amidst raging action.

Westminster Abbey, and in cathedrals and minsters, parish churches, and country graveyards across the British Isles.[90] Such memorials exist for earlier wars too, but the practice seems to have become more widespread from mid-century. In *The Theory of Moral Sentiments* (1759), Adam Smith had designated sympathy for the dead as a foundation of social sympathy. Mourning and honouring the dead was a tribute for the moral value with which the dead endowed the living. Mourning is a personal experience and one that can constitute communities. In this period, obituaries and the epitaph-obituary often linked the private and public virtues of the deceased. Many of these monuments served both private and public functions – as affective performances by and for families and friends, as well as patriotic rallying points for communities which imagined themselves as part of the wider nation at war.[91]

In some cases, the explicit purpose of private commemoration was to inspire emulation. In Westminster Abbey, in 1784, a white and coloured mural tablet by Robert Adam, with a shield of arms at the bottom and surmounted by a crest and a large gilded coronet, was erected in the niche next to the east doors of the cloisters, to commemorate William Dalrymple, eldest son of Sir John Dalrymple, Bart, a baron of the Exchequer in Scotland. William had been a midshipman who, as the inscription put it, 'preferred to a life of indolence and pleasure the toilsome and perilous profession of a seaman, when his country was in danger'. He was killed, aged eighteen, in an engagement with a French ship off Virginia in 1782. William's commander testified that he was a 'worthy and deserving youth, who, had he lived, would have been an ornament to his profession'. His 'once happy parents, in whose fond eyes he appeared to promise whatever could be expected from genius, spirit, and the best gift of God', he left 'a kind and melting heart, the endearing remembrance of his virtues'. They inscribed their prayer 'that there may never be wanting to the British youth the spirit to pursue that line of public honor which he marked out for himself and for them!' By erecting a monument at the heart of the imperial metropolis, this member of the North British establishment and his family framed their private grief in the language of patriotic service; public recognition of their son's and their own sacrifice may have made it more meaningful and bearable to them.

A wife's and mother's sacrifice for the empire is powerfully evoked by an elaborate white marble tablet in Chichester Cathedral. It commemorates her 16-year-old son, Lieutenant George Pigot Alms, who fell in action against the French fleet in the East Indies (as indicated on the central panel) while his father, James, commanded another ship in the same action:

HE LIVED THE PRIDE AND HOPE OF HIS PARENTS; | THE DELIGHT AND ADMIRATION OF HIS FRIENDS; THE RISING ORNAMENT OF HIS | COUNTRY; AND FELL GLORIOUSLY IN THE DISCHARGE OF [THE] DUTIES OF HIS | PROFESSION HONOURED AND LAMENTED BY ALL WHO KNEW HIM. | IMPRESSED WITH THE BITTEREST AFFLICTION AT THE TIME | THAT HER HUSBAND WAS STILL FIGHTING HIS COUNTRY'S BATTLES IN | INDIA, | HIS FOND, AND DISCONSOLATE MOTHER | CAUSED THIS MONUMENT | TO BE ERECTED.

While it was not uncommon for a monument to be addressed to both private and public audiences, such emotive power was rarely achieved by national monuments.[92]

Several privately commissioned monuments across London and various counties in England, Scotland, and Ireland commemorate specific actions by now mostly obscure officers. Among them is a memorial in St Nicolas Church in Great Bookham, Surrey, to Cornet Geary (b.1752) who was killed in an American ambush of British Light Dragoons in New Jersey in December 1776. In the anonymous monument, sharpshooters are seen crouching in the woods beside the road down which the British soldiers march, with Britannia mourning above. Other casualties in American theatres include William Home, Lord Dunglass, Lieutenant and Captain in the Coldstream Guards, who was commemorated for dying of wounds received in the Battle of Guilford Courthouse in 1781. Major A. Campbell's memorial in St Marylebone, London, lists his service in the Duke of Cumberland's American Rangers in 1775–8; wounded at Bunker Hill and Brandywine, he died in Spain aged forty-one. In Salhouse parish church, Norfolk, the Dalrymple family erected a black marble monument to their son, an infantry officer who returned 'with impaired health' from North American service and died in 1784, still only twenty. Families like Dalrymple's did not necessarily require specifically heroic service to commemorate their own.

This was true of naval families too. Francis Astley is commemorated by an ornamented white stone tablet in St Peter's, Melton Constable, Norfolk, for dying aged twenty-one in an engagement between the frigate *Arethusa* and a French frigate off the French coast in 1778. In St Peter and St Paul's, Fareham, Hampshire, is a memorial to Captain Michael J. Everett, who was killed by a cannonball on HMS *Ruby* off Hispaniola in 1779, aged twenty-six:

SMIT IN THE HOUR OF YOUTH'S JUST OPENING BLOOM | TH'ASPIRING HERO FOUND AN EARLY TOMB. | BLUSH NOT TO WEEP, BUT O'ER THE HONOURED BIER, | WITH VIRTUE AND HIS COUNTRY DROP A TEAR.

In the parish church of Grouville, in the Channel Islands, a granite stone remembers several grenadiers who died repelling the French invasion at La Roque Plate in January 1781. A grave in Ulverston, Cumbria, commemorates an unknown sailor of HMS *Princess Amelia* who fell in the Battle of the Dogger Bank in August 1781, an event that would have been familiar to contemporary Royal Academy audiences.

It was straightforward to celebrate service against the traditional French and Spanish enemies, or against unruly imperial subjects, where victory, or death, could be commemorated in a less inhibited way. Service against Americans was less easily and commonly celebrated. But by focusing on individual acts of heroism and sacrifice, on exceptional battles won, on successful single-ship actions, or simply on young, dear lives lost, private memorials integrated the American War more seamlessly in the commemoration of previous and later conflicts than national memorials could. On some monuments, an officer's American service appears as part of a longer career. Lieutenant-Colonel J. Stapleton's monument in St Mary's, Thorpe, Surrey, lists his staff appointments in America in 1776–83 and his subsequent service as inspector general and secretary of the barrack department in 1794–1817. On Cornwallis's red marble tablet in the Guards' Chapel in Westminster (lost through enemy action in 1944), his American stint had featured simply as 'Lieut.-general on service in America 1776–81', followed by his Irish and Indian appointments; no mention is made of Yorktown. An officer who served with Cornwallis, Lieutenant-General Sir J. Stuart KB, had his severe wound inscribed on his nearby monument, together with his subsequent service in European and Egyptian campaigns in 1793–1805.

For over half a century, private memorials continued to be erected in numerous churches and cathedrals to veterans of the American War. The Battle of the Saints was the only event that attracted instant and sustained commemorative investment well into the nineteenth century. It was also the only battle which was both a British triumph and produced 'heroes' to be commemorated locally and nationally. At least four monuments erected in England and Scotland between c.1789 and 1847 commemorate veterans of the Battle of the Saints – from a granite wall tablet in Edinburgh's Greyfriars Church in memory of Rear Admiral Sir Charles Douglas, Bart (d.1789), to a wall tablet in St Mary's, North Mymms, Hertfordshire. The latter, surmounted by a crest which includes a sailor with a flag, commemorates Admiral Sir Davidge Gould (d.1847) as 'the last surviving captain' of Nelson's Battle of the Nile (1798). Even the memory of the exceptional triumph of the Saints was superseded, if not erased, by the greater and less ambiguous victories of the 1790s.

'There will scarcely be a village in England without some American dust in it'[93]

The visual record of major British military defeats in the American War is unsurprisingly very limited. It is perhaps more remarkable that no official commemorative effort appears to have been invested to honour the many thousands of American loyalists who passively or actively supported the crown throughout the war – the 20,000 or so men who fought in loyalist regiments, or the 80,000–100,000 who went into exile in Canada, the Caribbean, Britain, or elsewhere. Substantial numbers had suffered verbal and physical abuse or arrest during the Revolutionary period, and most of the exiles and refugees lost all or much of their property for taking a stance for the British king and government. A significant number died for their loyalism.

Throughout the 1780s, over 3,000 loyalists pursued claims with the parliamentary commission established to consider loss of property, office, or income. Eventually some 2,300 petitioners were awarded a total of £3 million, a third of the amounts claimed; some ministers received parishes; 203 loyalists drew pensions for the loss of office.[94] Yet the initial honeymoon between the British government and exiled loyalists, such as it was, was short-lived. And the British state methodically considered the losses suffered by loyalists, but it never memorialised their loyalism, not even if it included military service and bodily sacrifice.

The absence of official commemoration might be due to the fact that there were relatively few really prominent loyalists, but mostly rather 'ordinary' colonists of the sort who never were commemorated anyway. Similarly, the British state would not commemorate ordinary British soldiers or sailors until the middle of the nineteenth century (chapter 3). Official commemoration was perhaps also avoided because loyalism was simply an expected duty not considered worthy of special honours. Moreover, official acknowledgement might have bolstered exiles' case for compensation. Ultimately, loyalists created great awkwardness as far as various shades of British opinion were concerned. Supporters of the war might feel embarrassed at the lack of support given to the loyalists, even by governments that they supported. Opponents of the war regarded the loyalists as politically suspect – authoritarian in sentiment, and supportive of North's detested government. In any case, loyalists were now often seen as unwelcome reminders of national defeat. There was, in other words, almost a consensus that the loyalists were best forgotten, not remembered.[95]

Yet loyalist families and friends made public statements in the form of monuments in churches and cathedrals in their country of exile. Some read like a proud and defiant continuation of their subject's campaign for recognition. In Westminster Abbey, today probably the least well known of the American Revolutionary monuments is that of the only American loyalist who was privately memorialised in what was then the primary British pantheon. This is the memorial to William Wragg, a fierce loyalist who had been prominent in South Carolina. Wragg, whose memorial tablet of white and coloured marble is in the south choir aisle, was born in 1714 in South Carolina as the son of a plantation owner.[96] Taken to England to be educated at Westminster School, St John's, Oxford, and at the Middle Temple, William practised the law and operated the British side of the family business from London before he inherited his father's rice plantations. He returned to South Carolina around 1750, entered public life, and as a member of first the upper and then the lower house was often involved in controversy. He opposed non-importation and other patriot policies; in 1775, Wragg refused to sign the Continental Association.

The General Committee placed him under house arrest, not at Charleston like other loyalists, but instead treating him 'with greater inhumanity; by banishing him in this sickly season to his Plantation [near Dorchester on the Ashley river], cutting him off from all society with his family & friends, & to add to his distress he left Mrs Wragge big with Child'.[97] His town house and offices were converted into barracks.

In South Carolina, especially in the Back Country, there was a strong loyalist minority, possibly even a majority, made up of large landed proprietors like Wragg and their tenants. What made Wragg's fierce independence seem particularly dangerous to the patriots was that he voiced his views in the capital, Charleston. In 1777, Wragg refused to swear the oath of allegiance to the state and to forswear allegiance to the British king. These commitments were required from all voters, office holders, and suspected opponents of the Revolution by a Provincial Act. Some southern loyalists evaded the requirement, others submitted, but many, like Wragg, were banished from the colony, either to England or to the West Indies.[98]

Wragg sailed for England via Amsterdam on the *Commerce* but was shipwrecked in a violent storm just twelve hours off the Dutch coast. Wragg was with the other passengers in the roundhouse when the ship struck. He sought to help the crew but was thrown down by a wave and hung on to a rope until he was too battered and exhausted. After he had died, the vessel broke up; most passengers floated ashore on part of the deck attached to the roundhouse. Wragg's infant son, from his second wife, Henrietta, was saved by their slave Tom Skene who supported him on a piece of wreckage. As a reward, Tom was set free by the boy's mother and settled on a piece of land near their plantation with a servant, a horse, and a cow.

In England, Wragg's sister obtained the Dean and Chapter of Westminster Abbey's permission to erect a memorial tablet to Wragg not in the country church where their mother lay buried, but instead at the heart of the national-imperial pantheon (fig. 9). The inscription on Wragg's monument struck what had by then become a typical balance of the public and private, but gave prominence to his politics and fate:

SACRED TO THE MEMORY OF WILLIAM WRAGG, ESQ:^R OF SOUTH-CAROLINA WHO, WHEN THE AMERICAN COLONIES REVOLTED FROM GREAT BRITAIN INFLEXIBLY MAINTAINED HIS LOYALTY TO THE PERSON AND GOVERNMENT OF HIS SOVEREIGN AND WAS THEREFORE COMPELL'D TO LEAVE HIS DISTREST FAMILY AND AMPLE FORTUNE. IN HIS PASSAGE FOR ENGLAND BY THE WAY OF AMSTERDAM HE WAS UNFORTUNATELY SHIPWRECK'D AND DROWNED ON THE COAST OF HOLLAND, THE 3:^D DAY OF SEPTEMBER, 1777.[99]

9. Richard Hayward, *Monument to William Wragg*, Westminster Abbey (*c.*1780). Detail. With a more grim and emphasised narrative than the monuments that surround it, this small sarcophagus presents Wragg as a tiny figure desperately clinging to the railing of a half-submerged vessel. The central action is devoted to Tom, Wragg's slave, helping his young master on to a coffin-like plank amidst curling waves. At right, the lowest level of relief atmospherically delineates the nearby Dutch coastline.

Through his sister's efforts, the American loyalist who had given up country, wealth, and family for his convictions had found final recognition in the English House of Kings, accompanied in this unlikely iconography by his slave, whose selfless loyalty to his 'kind master' was rewarded by freedom and (anecdotal) bucolic happiness in South Carolina.

Beverley Minster in east Yorkshire features the marble wall monument to Brig. General Oliver DeLancey.[100] DeLancey, the son of a Huguenot émigré from Normandy, and one of the wealthiest and most powerful citizens of the colony of New York, had fought alongside British troops during the French and Indian War. In the American War, DeLancey raised a loyalist brigade and was the senior loyalist brigadier-general in the British forces. His English-educated son rose fast in the ranks of the British army while his nephew James led the 450 men in DeLancey's Refugee Corps in raids on rebel properties. In 1777, DeLancey's son-in-law, William Draper, petitioned the British government to appoint the Brigadier-General as Lieutenant-Governor by way of partial compensation for the losses which he had suffered through 'his very Loyal, Steady & manly Behaviour in Support of Government'.[101] When Oliver DeLancey sought asylum in Britain in 1783, witnesses testified that he had consistently been 'an active, Zealous Loyalist attached to Great Britain from principle.[102] His pivotal role was acknowledged in British publications after the war. DeLancey claimed losses totalling £108,957 (twenty-three of his houses had been burned by the rebels); he received some £23,000. After his death in Beverley in 1785, his grave in the minster was marked by a black marble slab with a simple inscription giving his name, his native place of 'New York in North America', and his date of death and age. His nearby monument is a plain white marble wall structure composed of a large rectangular panel carrying the inscription, topped by an unadorned pyramidical form. The inscription establishes DeLancey's impeccably loyalist credentials and tremendous personal sacrifice.

In Chester Cathedral there is a large wall monument to Frederick Philipse of Tarrytown on Hudson (1720–86), who had been a loyalist member of the assembly of New York in 1750–75. In 1776, 'Fred III' had mobilised a local association in the picturesque Westchester County against the Revolutionary movement, but was 'seized on by a party of American Volunteers from New York and carried from his Family a Prisoner into Connecticut'. Released on parole by Governor Trumbull after six months, Philipse and his large family took refuge in New York until the British evacuation in 1783. Five of his sons fought on the British side, two fell; Philipse stressed that purchasing their commissions had left him in debt. He claimed over £40,000 in compensation for confiscated lands at Philipsburg Manor (his son later found that the entire estate had been confiscated and claimed over £150,000), as well as considerable sums for lost rental income, livestock, three slaves, and personal effects. The inscription on Philipse's Chester monument echoes his testimony to the commissioners, where he had described himself as acting 'from the firmest Principles of Loyalty and Attachment to the British Government' and protested against the 'usurped Legislature of New York' which had had his estates confiscated.[103] Indeed, the defiant inscription on the large wall tablet, which is framed by pilasters and surmounted by a crest, lays out the loyalist case in language reminiscent of the petitions submitted in their thousands:

> Firmly attached to his Sovereign and the British Constitution, he opposed, at the Hazard of his Life, the late Rebellion in North America; and for this faithful Discharge of his Duty to his King and Country, he was Proscribed, and his Estate, one of the largest in New York, was Confiscated, by the Usurped Legislature of that Province.

And so he bore his losses, exile, and complete reversal of fortune.

Families continued to perpetuate the memories of loyalist sacrifice into the following decades. On the south wall of St Margaret's Church, Westminster, directly adjacent to the Abbey, is a monument to Barnardus Lagrange (d.1797) and his son, James Brazier.[104] Barnardus was a lawyer with a lucrative practice worth £400 p.a. and 350 acres of real estate in Middlesex County, New Jersey. At the outbreak of the revolution he was such a strong and vocal supporter of Great Britain that he and his family became the focus of ferocious verbal and physical persecution. Exiled to England in the late 1770s, by the late 1780s he resided in Westminster. In his petition to the parliamentary claims commission, Lagrange detailed that already in 1775

> he was carted at New Brunswick in Effigy, his house attacked for the purpose of exposing him personally to the Rage of an inflamed Populace. That he has been publickly advertised as an Enemy and Traitor to his country, and his personal Safety rendered so precarious

that he went into hiding and later joined the British army under Howe on Staten Island. Now aged sixty-two, with four children and ten grandchildren, he suffered from want of resources 'in consequence of his Loyalty Zeal and unshaken Fidelity to his Sovereign'. Lagrange claimed over £8,300 in compensation for his losses. He received £2,638 and a pension of £120, plus £240 p.a. for a lost wartime income as an attorney of some £400 p.a.

The wall monument at St Margaret's by Henry Poole consists of a triangular upper part with arms, and the main section which is virtually filled with two eulogies by Lagrange's grandson. It stands in memory of Lagrange:

> (AN AMERICAN LOYALIST) WHO DIED ON THE 10TH OF DECEMBER 1797 | AGED 77 YEARS |AND OF HIS SON | JAMES BRAZIER LAGRANGE ESQUIRE, | WHO DIED THE 25TH OF FEBRUARY 1823 | AGED 62 YEARS … AND OF | THE DAUGHTER AND SISTER OF THE ABOVE | MRS FRANCES DONGAN, THE WIDOW OF | LIEUT.COL. EDWARD VAUGHAN DONGAN; | (ALSO AN AMERICAN LOYALIST) | WHO DIED ON THE 17TH OF APRIL 1831 | AGED 75 YEARS.

Forgoing explicit funereal euology, the repeated parentheses – '(an American loyalist)' – served to explain why the family were taking such a prominent space in the imperial metropolis.

Loyalists' monuments were not commissioned by official bodies or English host communities but by the loyalists themselves. Access to public spaces – even if it need not signify more than the economically self-interested tolerance of local clergy – at least afforded loyalists prominent posthumous displays. Largely, and conveniently, forgotten in the founding myth of the American republic, some of them used these spaces to remind their country of exile of their loyal sacrifice. They have left modest but moving markers in the topography of British national and imperial memory.

Conclusions

Between the extreme cases of attempts to erase memory and nationally consensual commemoration there are subtle processes of selective remembering, displacement, and distortion of memory. Representing the heroic amid imperial crisis and defeat was a challenging and in many ways fraught exercise. The conflicted and contested nature of most instances of commemoration in the American War notwithstanding, the institutions and personnel of state and church clearly considered official memorialisation a worthwhile investment. Begun in the Seven Years War, and sporadically attempted during the American War, national monument-building was one way in which officialdom could try to shape the national imagination. Topical interest in recently fallen military heroes was often high, and the public's foreknowledge of the subject matter substantial. While monuments usually took several years to complete, design drawings, exhibition models, discussions in the press, and other imagery of the hero in circulation could keep the subject in the public mind. The impact of specific instances of official memorialisation depended on an individual officer's prior reputation, the manner of his death, and his wider public imagery. Also important were the temporal and spatial contexts in which he was remembered. So was his capacity to foster political divisions or consensus – to serve certain political agendas, or indeed none. Individual reputations and political contests could jeopardise official efforts at consensus-building and patriotic celebration. Parliament's commissions of monuments to Chatham and Rodney's captains were driven by factions intent on promoting their partisan heroes and, in different ways, on projecting compensatory triumphalism. Chatham's statue ended up being an ironic reminder of the dramatic reversal of national fortunes. The memorialisation of Rodney's captains was threatened to be overshadowed by factional wrangling over their commander. The king's memorial to Major André not only demonstrated the instability of British notions of heroic masculinity, but also appeared, unintentionally, to ennoble Washington.

The British state did nothing to preserve the memory of defeat, for understandable reasons. There is only one tiny, inconspicuously grey slab remembering General Burgoyne in the cloisters of Westminster Abbey, set there by private hands.[105] While the state let the memory of loyalist sacrifice fade, families like Wragg's challenged

81

the state even at the heart of the national site of commemoration. Loyalists learned from the dozens of private monuments in parishes and cathedrals across Britain, which could integrate the American Revolutionary War more easily than official monuments in the commemoration of British conflicts. It was during the French Revolutionary and Napoleonic Wars that the invention of a new military pantheon at St Paul's Cathedral crystallised a vigorous revival of notions of British masculine heroism and their sculptural representations. Despite an unprecedented surge of popular patriotism, promoted by officialdom, there remained, however, considerable scope for political, cultural, and aesthetic contestation (chs. 3, 4).

Experiences and perceptions of the American Revolutionary War and the wider imperial conflict were represented in other public artistic media too. National monuments were intended to remain in the public eye in perpetuity. The equally high-minded and public genre of history paintings also often enjoyed prolonged exposure to the public gaze. Their initial appearance – to many tens of thousands of viewers at the Royal Academy or in solo-exhibitions – was well publicised and critiqued. Engravings produced after such paintings ensured wider audiences; and even if bought by private collectors, paintings might remain accessible to a select public, or eventually end up in the public collections of the early nineteenth century. In the peculiar circumstances of the American Revolutionary War, a painting could attract attention on account of the politics of the artist – especially if he was an American in London or a British supporter of the American Revolution. In the next chapter, I want to continue the analysis of the cultural politics of the American Revolutionary War by shifting the perspective from those commissioning and being remembered in monuments to the politics of a set of mostly American painters. They include some of the most famous artists of the eighteenth century. Others are not now widely known, but they are no less fascinating for the insights their careers and works afford into the cultural politics of the period.

2

TRANSATLANTIC JOURNEYS

Rival of Greece, in arms, in arts
Tho' demm'd in her declining days,
Britain yet boasts uncumber'd hearts,
Who keenly paint for public praise;
Her battles yet are firmly fought
By chiefs with Spartan courage fraught:
Her painters with Athenian zeal unite
To trade glories of the prosp'rous fight,
And gild th' embattl'd scene with Art's immortal light.

William Haley, 1785[1]

Political contests being neither pleasing to an artist or advantageous to the Art itself

John Singleton Copley, 1770[2]

THROUGHOUT THE AMERICAN REVOLUTIONARY WAR, British audiences saw certain kinds of patriotic imagery flourish. Scores of paintings of the Royal Navy's encounters with the French, Spanish, and Dutch fleets were exhibited at the annual Royal Academy shows. The military establishment, under attack for its failures and perceived corruption, used art to portray a favourable image of itself. The defenders of Gibraltar and Jamaica, General Elliot and Admiral Rodney, were painted by the nation's leading artists. Their sieges and battles were re-enacted in dramatic spectacle and musical comedies on London's stages. Theatre, fiction, and exhibition paintings spread awareness of George III's visits to the naval dockyards at Chatham and to Portsmouth, as well as to the military encampments at Windsor, near Salisbury, and on Warley Common in Essex. Engravings brought imagery to wider audiences, as did transfer-printed pottery and mass-produced mementos, such as Josiah Wedgwood's ceramic heads of popular admirals and earthenware mugs and jugs depicting their battles. Along with the Battle of the Saints, perhaps the most widely depicted episode of the entire war was the siege of Gibraltar; by 1783, reviewers complained that the audience's patience was worn out by looking at floating batteries and the rock.[3]

So there had been plenty of opportunities for British painters to work in various genres throughout the war and its immediate aftermath. Yet, in 1789, it seemed to one frustrated British artist that American painters unfairly dominated London's artistic scene:

> Mr. West paints for the Court and Mr. Copley for the City. Thus the artists of America are fostered in England, and to complete the wonder, a third American, Mr. Brown of the humblest pretenses, is chosen portrait painter to the Duke of York. So much for the Thirteen Stripes – so much for the Duke of York's taste.[4]

During the imperial civil war itself, the position of American artists had seemed much less secure. There were a good many of them. Benjamin West and John Singleton Copley were 'a magnet for aspiring American painters, deprived in the turmoil and relative isolation of the new Republic of proper training, experience of good paintings and public support.'[5] West, originally from Pennsylvania, thrived as the king's history painter; his fellow Academician Copley, a Bostonian, specialised in commercial one-man shows of patriotic British history. The permanently resident West and Copley were counted among the British School, but their presence attracted younger American artists. These included Copley's fellow Bostonian, the talented (if now little known) Mather Brown, and the visionary John Trumbull, the son of the last royal governor of Connecticut who went on to paint a series for the rotunda of the United States Capitol. This colony of American-born artists made up an informal American academy at West's studio; some of them also studied at the Royal Academy.

The work and apparent success of these American painters had a political as much as an artistic import in the Revolutionary period. This chapter is a case study in the politics of painting, a notion which encompasses the subject matter of a work of art, the circumstances of its creation, display, viewing, and impact, as well as the political beliefs and actions of the painter. Some works of art made thinly veiled references to the Anglo-American crisis. Henry Walton's painting *Plucking the Turkey*, exhibited at the Society of Artists in 1776, can be read as a pro-British statement of popular sentiment against the ungrateful colonies, represented by the bird which was so closely associated with America that Benjamin Franklin advocated it be adopted as the national symbol instead of the bald eagle.[6] But the politics of painting that I wish to explore is more encompassing and multi-layered. As British politics was increasingly polarised in the later eighteenth century, the personal politics of artists became relevant to their public reception. American artists who were working in London's divisive atmosphere during the Revolutionary War years were judged in part by their political views and actions, and by the political views their works expressed or implied. American patriots and loyalists, those with ambiguous or conflicting loyalties, and pro-American British artists all had to learn to negotiate the relationship between their artistic and political lives. Few managed, or could afford, to separate them. Some of these artists are today better known than others, but together they manifest the range and depth of transatlantic artistic links. Exploring the political beliefs and actions of individual artists in relation to their artistic careers and the specific works they created sheds light on the multifaceted relationships that existed between 'politics' and 'art'. It illuminates the role of the visual arts in political culture, the ways in which visual transactions occurred between the two sides of the Atlantic, and the negotiations over the recent past in which artists were involved.

Janus-Faced Patriots: Benjamin West and John Singleton Copley

The most prominent American-born painter in London was Benjamin West (1738–1820). After the conclusion of the Seven Years War in 1763, West had partially made his reputation with a series of paintings depicting instances from the North American theatre of that global war for empire. These scenes, mostly classically derived compositions in North American settings, showcased ideals of British imperial expansion and heroism. They range from the full-length portrait of *General Robert Monckton* (c.1764) and *General Johnson Saving a Wounded French Officer from the Tomahawk of a North American Indian* (c.1764–8) to, most famously, *Death of General Wolfe* (1770–71).[7] Now, as Britain and its American colonies were heading for conflict in the 1770s, West did not hide his sympathies for the patriots. But George III's confidence in the royal history painter remained unshaken. The king valued West's views on the personalities of American leaders and confided in him when he was depressed over political events. George III was said to appreciate

West's attachment to the land of his birth, and did not doubt his essential loyalty to his adoptive country and royal master. West nevertheless judged it prudent not to follow up on his earlier scenes of previous colonial exploits. This does not mean, however, that his sympathies during the American Revolutionary War had no impact on his painting practice. While his single largest group of works in this period was royal portraiture, including, at its most splendid, a full-length portrait of George III as commander-in-chief,[8] West also painted several images which can be read as commentaries on the American Revolution by analogy.

West's conflicting allegiances found visual expression in an ambiguous allegory centred upon the two cardinal virtues of Faith and Hope (see plate V). *Fidelia and Speranza* was the last in a series of three major subjects which West painted from Spenser's *Faerie Queene* for exhibition at the Royal Academy in 1772–7. Spenser's original text was a thinly veiled critique of Elizabeth's rule. West's appropriation of *The Faerie Queene* expressed at once criticism of, and concern for, the monarchy and his pious patron. Dressed in modest classical robes with arms gracefully intertwined, Speranza is holding an anchor and Fidelia a large copy of the New Testament and a grail-like chalice. As depicted from the vantage point of the House of Holiness, this painting juxtaposes a serene and sheltered space, occupied by maidens of Christian virtue, with the stormy landscape at lower left from which Una leads the dispirited Redcross Knight. An emblematical reading assumes that Redcross stands for a 'mentally worn and physically injured monarchy'. Una is leading the spiritually broken Knight (St George and/or George III) to rehabilitation at the House of Holiness. Resident there are Fidelia and Speranza, the main characters in the painting. They are the 'prescriptive balms' who alone can restore the Knight from 'the increasingly miserable plight' in the closing cantos of book 1 of *Faerie Queene*, and, by analogy, restore the king and monarchy from the current crisis.[9]

Between *c.*1775 and 1782, West also painted an intriguing series of images representing the restoration and military consolidation of constitutional monarchy in late seventeenth-century England. They were probably all commissioned by Richard, Lord Grosvenor, later Earl Grosvenor, who bought West's *Death of Wolfe* in 1771. West started with the most recent events, two key battles with which William III had confirmed his hold on the English crown after the Glorious Revolution of 1688–9. In the Battle of La Hogue the English and Dutch fleets had defeated the French fleet carrying a French–Irish army to England in 1692, thus ending Louis XIV's design to restore James II to the throne. In West's scene, the exiled James II is shown as a tiny figure watching from a distant cliff the destruction of the French fleet and with it his hopes of returning to the English throne. The *London Courant* praised the painting's 'beautiful effect' and patriotic credentials.

There was something so 'strikingly characteristic in the contest between the British and French officer in the boat, that Hogarth himself could not have refused it his admiration. This is true English history.'[10]

Others, however, criticised what they saw as the introduction of 'indecorous anecdotal scenes' and objected to the 'disgraceful attitude of the French officer in the boat, and the sailor aiming a blow with his fist at a drowning man ... a circumstance too ludicrous for the sublimity of such a composition'.[11] The incident in the right foreground – of a frenzied sailor aiming a final knock at an already half-submerged, wide-eyed adversary – is a rare concession to the messy, deadly nature of battle, made particularly poignant by the fact that here it occurs alongside the more familiar topos of the victorious British saving defeated enemies from drowning.

Yet West's painting offered an uplifting historical tale of bravery and patriotic victory at a moment of national crisis, especially when French invasion threats loomed large in public consciousness in 1778–9. That it occupied an important place in British national memory became clear when in 1785 a historian of the American War sought a comparison for the 1782 Battle of the Saints: 'Never did France, since the famous Battle at La Hogue ... sustain so complete and ruinous a defeat as on this memorable day.'[12] A generation later, William Paulet Carey, the (Irish) propagandist-in-chief for modern British art, would claim that the engraving of West's *La Hogue* along with those of *Death of Wolfe* and *Death of Nelson* functioned as virtual battle sites, on which 'England fought her battles over again, and will continue to fight and conquer her enemies to the end of time.'[13]

In 1778, West painted *The Battle of the Boyne*.[14] On 1 July 1690, on the banks of the river Boyne, William had defeated the forces of James II and crushed the Stuarts' hold on Ireland. West represents William on a white horse as the central figure, in a composition reminiscent of the Marcus Aurelius monument on the Roman Capitol (which West would have known) with Prince George of Denmark and the Duke of Ormond behind in the far left. James II is absent, as he was during the battle. West's choice of subject had clear contemporary resonances. In the late 1770s, Ireland was in turmoil and British–Irish relations were being redefined. In 1778, the Irish Parliament, supported by Lord North's British government, eased the penal laws so that Roman Catholics could again own and inherit land on the same terms as Protestants. At the same time, there was concern that the 8,000-strong Irish Volunteers force, established to defend Ireland against a possible French invasion, might also be turned against British authority. By 1782, Ireland obtained a greater degree of legislative independence. In contrast to the highly volatile and fluent contemporary situation, West had depicted a problem essentially resolved – the Catholic cause controlled, the country subdued.

After showing the two post-Glorious Revolution paintings at the 1780 Academy exhibition, in 1783 West exhibited a picture addressing the restoration of monarchy in 1660, *General Monk Receiving Charles II on the Beach at Dover*. The most intriguing painting in the series, however, is *Oliver Cromwell Dissolving the Long Parliament*.[15] On 20 April 1653, Cromwell had dissolved and expelled the Long Parliament which had been sitting since 1640. According to Hume's *History of England*, a widely used source for history paintings at the time, Cromwell accused various MPs of being a whoremaster, adulterer, drunkard, and extortioner, then had soldiers empty the chamber, and locked it.[16] In the painting, Cromwell orders a soldier to remove the mace. Other identified figures include Sir Henry Vane, Speaker Lenthall being pulled from his chair by Colonel Thomas Harrison, as well as Generals Fairfax, Lambert, and Fleetwood, and Cromwell's bare-headed son-in-law Henry Ireton (who, in fact, had been dead since 1651).

West's first three paintings had showcased the themes of the crown secured, France defeated, Ireland subdued, and the constitutional monarchy consolidated, both domestically and internationally. Cromwell was, to say the least, an ambiguous figure for the politically ambiguous West on which to conclude his series.[17] In colonial America, Cromwell had represented the notion of a standing army, the usurpation of the powers of the legislature, enthusiasm for colonial empire, and the navigation acts. During the Revolution, there was modest praise for Cromwellian foreign affairs and electoral reform, but overwhelmingly he was used as a foil to the seventeenth-century English heroes of liberty, Sydney and Hampden. If the Revolutionaries were largely anti-statist, a revolution of the Rump and the Commonwealth was one thing, but the Protectorate was quite another. Loyalist critics of the Revolutionaries, however, branded them as devotees of 'Old Oliver's Cause'.[18] There were contrasting images of Cromwell in England too. On the one hand, he represented violent opposition and tyranny. For others, however, he was a strong, patriotic 'leader associated with national vigour, pride and prosperity', even a reformer. The latter image was evoked specifically in the context of a critique of George III's handling of North American and Irish affairs in the late 1770s.[19] Perhaps Cromwell's highly ambiguous image made him the perfect choice for George III's history painter, as ultimately no single reading could be fixed on the painting and its author's intentions.

By 1783, Benjamin West was able to rejoice at America's victory. In his initial enthusiasm he planned a series of Revolutionary subjects. Charles Willson Peale sent visual evidence of American uniforms and suggested various topics. West's paintings, to be engraved as 'The American Revolution', would, as far as we can tell, have covered the cause and development of the conflict, as well as its chief battles and alliances. The project would have allowed West to establish himself as the new nation's leading painter. It also seemed economically attractive, as there was likely to be both American and European interest in the engravings.[20]

West started with a message of conciliation: *Signing of the Preliminary Treaty of Peace in 1782* (1783–4). The painting shows on the left-hand side John Adams, Benjamin Franklin, John Jay, Henry Laurens, and William Temple Franklin, secretary to the American commissioners. Of the Americans all but Benjamin Franklin sat for West during visits to London. West copied Franklin's portrait either from a copy of a Joseph Wright portrait or from a miniature, both by Joseph-Siffred Duplessis. The blank right-hand side of the unfinished painting – which was to have shown the British commissioner Richard Oswald and his secretary Caleb Whitefoord – is intriguing. Did Oswald, of whom no other portrait existed, refuse to sit because he was considered decidedly ugly, or because he did not want to be commemorated on the occasion of Britain's historic defeat, or both?[21] In 1817, John Quincy Adams understood that West still wanted to complete the painting for the US Congress. Yet the picture remained unfinished. It was also the only painting of West's projected series that was undertaken. Realising that the topic was after all too sensitive for the king's history painter to touch, West encouraged his disciple Trumbull to assume the mantle of the American republic's first history painter (see below, p.000).

Probably also in 1783, Benjamin West had first painted *Reception of the American Loyalists by Great Britain in the Year 1783* (see plate VI). The original painting is lost (if it ever existed), but we can see a representation of it in the background of the portrait of John Eardley-Wilmot (signed and dated 1812), exhibited at the Royal Academy in 1812 as 'Portrait of J. E. Wilmot, Esq., who adjusted the losses, claims and compensations of the American loyalists'. An engraving was also published as the frontispiece to Wilmot's *Historical View of the Commission for Enquiring into the Losses, Services, and Claims of the American Loyalists* (London, 1815). As an English MP, Wilmot (1750–1815) had opposed the war. In 1782–3, he reviewed the loyalist pension list and in 1783–90 sat on the parliamentary compensation commission for loyalists. Wilmot – who had disagreed with the loyalists' demand for the forceful submission of America, but respected their principled stance – seems to have been particularly generous in awarding pensions.[22]

West's use of the colour white calls attention to three key elements of the scene: Wilmot's dignified profile, the papers through which he acts – REPORT OF LOSSES AND COMPENSATION TO THE AMERICAN LOYALISTS, and a letter to *The Right Hnble William Pitt* – and, in the framed picture, the floating allegorical figures of Religion and Justice as they extend the mantle of Britannia to the expectant loyalists. At far right are West and his wife. In a cloud in the background two cherubs bind together the fasces of Britain and America, symbolising the restoration of peace and amity between the nations. The loyalists are led by William Franklin, the exiled last royal governor of New Jersey and Benjamin's son. He had been arrested in 1776 and in 1780–82 had served in New York before being sent to petition George III on behalf of the loyalists to perpetuate the war. He only arrived after the peace treaty had been signed. Franklin is joined by Sir William Pepperell, the only American-born baronet, who left Boston for England in 1775, became chairman of the Loyalist Association in 1779, and liaised with the claims commission from 1783 as a member of the Board of Loyalist Agents.

Among the group of loyalists are lawyers, clergy, and officials at the front and dark-hatted Quakers towards the rear; a well-dressed gentleman and woman with child perhaps represent merchant families. Prominently positioned along the central viewing axis from bottom left to top right, leading the eye to Britannia, is a large, statuesque Native American chief who extends one hand to Britannia and points with the other to a war widow and orphans. A freed black man and children look up to Britannia. Poor white exiles including widows and orphans were indeed awarded small charitable subsistence allowances, often well into the nineteenth century, though the terms of the commission envisaged only compensation for property.

West imagined an enlightened post-Revolution empire receiving an all-inclusive American loyalist community – from the pillars of white colonial society to the equally suffering beneficiaries of British benevolence: the poor whites, blacks, and Native Americans. For Simon Schama, this was, 'even by the romantic standards of the late eighteenth century ... an outrageously self-serving fiction'. West's freed, sturdy, and noble black reaches out with hope to touch Britannia's mantle. In fact, only blacks proving that they were free-born had been likely to be seriously considered for property compensation, as slaves joining the British army were assumed not to have had any property.[23] Shadrack Furman was granted £18 p.a. for having 'reportedly been blinded and crippled by a band of Revolutionaries who had tortured him in 1781 to make him reveal his knowledge of Cornwallis' troops'. Only very few other former slaves received £5–10 each, and even fewer an annual allowance.[24] And while 8,000–10,000 black loyalists were to be free in the post-revolutionary British world (in Canada, Britain, Sierra Leone), as Maya Jasanoff has shown, Britain continued to enable loyalist slave ownership in Canada, Florida, the Caribbean, and the Bahamas, so that '[e]ven by conservative estimates, 50 percent more blacks left the colonies as slaves of loyalists than as loyalist freemen.'[25] Equally, only the Mohawks under the skilled leadership of Joseph Brant achieved relocation to Canada, whereas Britain's southern Indian allies faced the cession of Florida to

Spain. With British policy towards loyalists of various ethnicities ranging from liberally inclusive to harshly exclusive elements, West's image was neither wholly fact nor entirely fiction. Once again he had excelled in painted ambiguity.

~

Benjamin West was joined at the Royal Academy by another American, John Singleton Copley (1737–1815), who painted British patriotic imagery throughout the war. Copley had spent his early career as a portrait painter in pre-Revolutionary Boston, where he had tried to appear politically neutral and accepted roughly equal numbers of commissions from both sides of the developing political divide. Around 1772, Copley had portrayed Samuel Adams for Adams's Revolutionary friend John Hancock. Adams points with one finger at the Massachusetts charter and in his right hand firmly grasps a document recording the protest of Boston citizens over the Boston Massacre. This is the only Copley portrait of a political figure in conflict, but by itself it does not allow us to infer whether Copley's sympathies lay with Adams and the common citizenry, or with the 'Tories' who opposed Adams as a populist tribune. In 1773, Copley had unsuccessfully tried to mediate between the tea consignees (which included his in-laws) and rebels in Boston to prevent civil war. Once the war with Britain had started, Copley wanted the patriots to win. Works of art were already provoking intense emotions. A pre-Revolution-mob entered Harvard Hall to cut the 'heart' from Copley's portrait of Governor Sir Francis Bernard – a visceral, violent kind of attack more familiar from figurative sculpture like George III's in New York. Copley's portrait of the radical Thomas Hollis, hanging next to Bernard's, seems to have been left intact.[26] Copley departed Boston for London just before the outbreak of war in 1775. Like in his American period, as a portraitist in the imperial metropolis Copley carefully maintained a business-enhancing political neutrality, or at least the appearance thereof.[27]

In 1779, Copley was elected a full Royal Academician, and the following year he exhibited a single painting at the RA's opening show at Somerset House, the spectacular *Major Hugh Montgomerie* (see plate X). The picture skilfully avoided any reference to the current imperial crisis. Instead it commemorated Montgomery's involvement in the Seven Years War, which had resulted in British mastery of North America. It seems likely that artist and sitter jointly worked out the portrait's complex approach. The painting was related to specific events in the 1760 razing of Cherokee villages on the South Carolina frontier during the Seven Years (or French and Indian) War, as indicated by the burning of a town in the background. Montgomery had served as a subaltern in his cousin Archibald's regiment with other British and colonial and Native American forces. The initial encounter left over a hundred Cherokees killed or captured. But when the imperial forces moved further into Indian territory they had to break off the campaign in the face of determined resistance. In 1779, Montgomery's current regiment had experienced a mutiny. Ironically, the Highlanders fighting in the 1760s had only recently committed themselves to the British crown, while the Cherokees in the American War fought loyally on the British side. In negotiating recent Anglo-American military history, Copley's portrait implied a warning of the potential cost of rebellion, and perhaps, too, a critique of the decline of British manliness.[28]

Copley moved further beyond portraiture to history and profitably rode the wave of British patriotism. He spent two years from spring 1779 to 1781 painting *Death of Chatham* (see plate VII). When the City of London rejected Copley's painting as their official memorial to Chatham in favour of Bacon's monumental sculpture, as discussed in chapter 1, Copley's painting became a speculative venture. Copley could bank on the profits from its exhibition and subsequent sale as well as from the subscription fees for an engraving to be made after the painting. In spring 1781, Copley displayed the painting in a one-man one-picture show at a private venue at Spring Gardens. His printed brochure was also used as a press release.[29] When nearly 20,000 visitors paid a shilling each in the first six weeks, the Royal Academy worried about the effect such competition had on its audience figures. Many more would have read descriptions in the newspapers or heard the painting discussed, and many eventually bought the much delayed engraving executed by Francesco Bartolozzi.

Radical writer William Godwin explained in his *History of the Life of William Pitt* that the scene of Chatham's collapse owed its grandeur to the magnitude of the issues at stake: war, peace, and independence for the colonies, but it was undoubtedly enhanced by 'the age, the infirmities, the unabated vigour, and immortal patriotism of the hero.'[30] Transcending the limitations of his human frame through his determination and convictions, Chatham had achieved heroic status. He also had preserved his mastery of histrionics. With a superb sense of drama, Chatham had fallen underneath the Armada Tapestry in the House of Lords. Just moments before collapsing, Chatham had recited England's proud history of self-defence in the face of foreign invasion – from the Danes and Normans to the threats of the Spanish Armada and later French and Spanish attempts.

The painting cast Chatham as a great orator, statesman, empire-builder, and patriotic martyr; a military hero dying in the act of defending the empire he had proudly helped to build.[31] At centre right is the collapsed Earl of Chatham, surrounded by his three sons and his son-in-law and supported by the Dukes of

Cumberland and Portland. The nearby Duke of Richmond has just finished speaking. To the left and rear are grouped some of the great officers of state, the bishops and other peers are in the left foreground, and the Lord Chancellor and judges are seated on the woolsack. Copley's painting was ingenious and sensational in more ways than one. Benjamin West had revolutionised history painting with his *Death of Wolfe* by depicting a contemporary rather than an allegorical, mythological, scriptural, or classical event.[32] Copley took this a step further and depicted a contemporary *political* rather than military event. What is more, this was an event that was not removed in place, as Wolfe's death at Quebec had been, but a moment of greater imaginary proximity. Copley elevated portraiture – the genre for which he had been famous in Massachusetts – by introducing it into a patriotic historical painting. He was thus adapting the genre of history painting to combine historical reportage with political journalism to such an effect that monuments, for instance, could not achieve. Copley himself considered

> uniting the value of living characters to the dignity of an Historical Fact an advantage that will be rising in every succeeding age, and which no other Picture extant has to boast of in any degree equal to this.[33]

Among the lively press coverage of Copley's painting were highly specific political readings, such as reviews which studied the political implications of the grouping and individual expressions of the figures. The *St James's Chronicle* pointed out that those around Chatham and the minority leaders were planted 'to the utmost Advantage', while the group around Lord Mansfield, the only to be depicted seated, seemed to have the appearance of 'sharpers'.[34] Only Chatham's relatives and supporters to the left show any overt emotions of distress, contrasting with the largely controlled emotions of most other peers. The reviewer for the *London Courant* on 11 June 1781 emphasised that the first impression was of 'drapery in motion', a veritable 'war of dress', before going on to criticise the picture's emotional flatness:

> Whether it be *literal* or *allegorical* death we see before us, almost every face, the sons perhaps excepted, tells us that the object of their looks is neither dead nor dying; their features, their motions have not more energy than what any assembly would have had on any sudden occurrence, however trifling; as much emotion, the same curiosity or surprise must have been expressed, had the hero's crutch failed, or his seat broke under him, as he rose.[35]

This critique was particularly damning as it was then a theoretical and artistic commonplace that the 'expression' of figures was crucial to a viewer's ability to understand the story of a painting.[36] After ten weeks at Spring Gardens, Copley removed the painting to the Gresham lecture room above the Royal Exchange, where it remained a favourite display with American refugees in London.[37] It seems that, in the safety of London at least, Chatham could be the hero of loyalist Americans as much as he was the patriots' in New York. In hindsight, Chatham's proposals for reconciliation may have appeared more appealing from the vantage of London exile at the end of the war, than New York recaptured at the beginning. Well composed and brilliantly executed instances of patriotic history, and a sense of realism and reportage combined with the theatrical and emotional, were to become Copley's hallmark.

In 1784, Copley scored another triumph with *The Death of Major Peirson*, today in the collection of Tate Britain in London (see plate VIII). Here he took a minor victory and turned it into a major heroic event.[38] On the night of 5 January 1781, some 900 French troops had landed on the British Channel Island of Jersey, seized the capital St Helier, and forced the imprisoned British commandant to agree a surrender. The British forces, however, ignored the order to lay down arms and under the ranking British officer, 24-year-old Major Francis Peirson, recaptured the capital and defeated the invasion. Peirson was mortally wounded by enemy fire. The picture became a much-needed patriotic morale booster after a war lost in North America. Copley exhibited *The Death of Major Peirson* along with *Death of Chatham* in the Great Room at 28 Haymarket from May 1784. For the admission fee of one shilling, visitors received a brochure with the proposal for an engraving, and a description of the picture complete with a key to the portraits of some of the officers.

The painting is an example of the constant visual transactions that occurred across the Atlantic. It is in some ways a reworking of the print by Paul Revere and Copley's half-brother Henry Pelham of the Boston Massacre, when British soldiers had killed five colonists in 1770. There are clear similarities of composition, such as the confinement of the battle to the urban square in the foreground, the row of soldiers calmly firing in unison (already in the print a rewrite of history), and the mirroring of Peirson's grouping with wounded colonist and supporters to the left. In the Copley, the setting of St Helier's market place, with George II's statue at the centre, as well as the portraits and uniforms make for a high degree of realism. British reinforcements march over Town Hill in upper left. In the lower left a British sergeant covers his wound and gestures towards the dying major in a pose directing the viewer's gaze to the central group with Peirson and the Anglo-French battle in the foreground. That central group is composed of officers of the 95th regiment and one officer of the Jersey militia, who carry Peirson off the battlefield, strewn with the dead and dying.

While giving much realistic detail, Copley also massaged his facts for propagandistic and dramatic effect: for instance, he shifted the place of Peirson's death to centre-stage and beefed up the role of the 95th regiment at the expense of the 78th regiment of Highlanders, who had resisted embarkation from Scotland to Jersey for three days for fear of being sold to the East India Company. The diagonals of officers and bayonets, the steep hill hovering in the background, the smoke and contrasting light and shadows convey the drama and confusion of battle. Copley had painted, in Emily Neff's words, a truly 'epic nationalist picture that conveys the heat of battle, a surprise victory, and model heroes through dazzling displays of paint.'[39]

Copley mirrored Peirson's insubordination by breaking the artistic conventions of order and unity and painting two if not three narratives: Peirson's death, his putative black servant's retaliatory action, and the women and children fleeing the scene.[40] The function of the black servant, exacting vengeance (possibly wholly fictitious, for no contemporaneous account appears to mention such a man), was to draw in the viewer and to gesture towards the popular topos of the loyal servant. Copley ignored the alleged cowardice of Peirson's superior (who in fact had been placed by the French as a hostage in the front line and had his hat shot through before being court-martialled by the British). By also focusing not on Peirson's insubordination but on the heroic death-and-revenge sequence, Copley emphasises notions of duty, patriotism, control, and the possible justification of insubordination. The rightward thrust of the painting's composition leads our eyes to rest, ultimately, upon the women and children, who are the only group that, instead of exuding stoic calm, looks bewildered. The mother, protectively clasping her baby, looks back in horror; her friend appeals for divine intervention; the young boy clings to the mother's shawl and barely avoids stepping on a fallen soldier's lower arm. He is the outsider in the picture who looks straight at the viewer, anything but the youth ready to be instructed in the lessons of heroism. Copley thus combined an exemplary (though contemporary) heroic narrative with the sentimental narrative of women and children in distress, part of an emerging trend towards affective immediacy in history painting. This paralleled a historiographical shift from masculine historical composition to sentimental narratives in the works of Hume and others, which engaged readers in a sympathetic response to history.[41] But Copley's juxtaposition is an uneasy one: by conveying a sense of terror and loss of control, Copley's group of women and children introduces a sceptical note, even, perhaps, a critique of war, into the heroic masterpiece.

As Copley was putting the finishing touches to the painting, the press was already publishing his description to whip up interest; positive reviews of the portraits and costumes, and of the painting's composition, colouring, and chiaroscuro, followed.[42] The *General Evening Post* judged the 'performance ... truly dramatic; it excites pity and horror in the mind of the spectator like the tragedies of Shakespeare'. Copley's work was not only appreciated in aesthetic terms, but he was also on safe British patriotic ground. To depict victory over the traditional French enemy was much more straightforward than trying to make sense of the killing of fellow (if rebelling) Englishmen. Indeed, various papers described the Jersey event as one of the most honourable actions of the war. Thanks to Peirson's 'gallant exertions', 'great effort and military skill', the British had defeated a superior force.[43]

Only once, when the Anglo-American conflict was virtually concluded, did Copley deviate from his otherwise strictly neutral stance as a portraitist (see plate XI). In 1782, he painted the American merchant and ardent supporter of the Revolution Elkanah Watson. A native of Plymouth, Massachusetts, Watson had previously conveyed dispatches to Franklin in France and from Franklin to Priestley and Burke in London. In 1782, he invested 100 guineas apparently from an insurance claim for goods lost in the siege of Gibraltar (or from a bet at Lloyd's that Howe would relieve Gibraltar) in a grand portrait by his fellow countryman. Watson recounted how the painting turned into a political statement:

> The painting was finished in a most admirable style, except the back-ground, which Copley and myself designed to represent a ship, bearing to America the intelligence of the acknowledgement of Independence, with a sun just rising upon the stripes of the union, streaming from her gaff. All was complete save the flag, which Copley did not deem prudent to hoist under present circumstances, as his gallery is a constant resort of the royal family and the nobility.
>
> I dined with the artist, on the glorious 5th of December, 1782, after listening with him to the speech of the King, formally receiving and recognizing the United States of America into the rank of nations. Previous to dining, and immediately after our return from the House of Lords, he invited me into his studio, and there with a bold hand, a master's touch, and I believe an American heart, attached to the ship the *stars and stripes*. This was, I imagine, *the first American flag hoisted in old England*.[44]

More than just a depiction of a successful, gentlemanly merchant and his transatlantic trading emporium, Watson's portrait had become a comment on America's new place in the world. The bright sun announcing the rise of the new republic mirrors the notion of the westward migration of the arts – from Greece and Italy via France, Flanders, and Holland to England, and now America – their path paralleling the passage of liberty depicted in the Revolutionary allegories of Peale and Barry (see below). With *Watson*, Copley had allowed himself just once to indulge his American patriotism. The picture remained largely a safe, private gesture, however, as it appears not to have been exhibited during his lifetime. Even if some people might have seen the portrait in the artist's studio, it did not contribute to the wider politico-cultural debate.

Copley manoeuvred the faultlines of British artistic politics with great adeptness. A Royal Academician, but otherwise not closely tied to the monarchy, Copley explored the possibilities of public art to imply subtle critiques even in overtly patriotic subjects, as in *Montgomerie* or *Major Peirson*. In the process he created some profitable and well-received, innovative masterpieces in the genre of patriotic modern history painting. Copley's fellow Academician West sought to balance his political sympathies with his royal appointment. By playing with deliberate politico-artistic ambiguity on the registers of allegory and historical analogy, the king's history painter, too, struck a delicate balance. Meanwhile, some of the younger American painters whom West was teaching were eager to establish themselves as artists on the London scene. They are today less well known but their stories suggest the scope of politico-artistic transactions across the Atlantic at that time: they too negotiated the politics of paintings each in his own way.

Pragmatic Loyalists? Ralph Earl and Mather Brown

Among the younger Americans who were propelled into voluntary or forced exile in Britain by their political attitudes and actions was Ralph Earl (1751–1801). Earl was at heart a loyalist who sought to act pragmatically. Avoiding military service to pursue his artistic career, he was, however, forced to take a political stance and go into exile in Britain. Mather Brown (1761–1831), another pragmatic loyalist, came to London of his own choice in 1781. While Earl seems not to have expressed his politics very clearly in his art, Brown established himself as a portraitist of American republican leaders, exiled loyalists, and British royalty. Though these artists clearly strived to reconcile politics with the need to attract clients, not all of those may have cared about politics but instead simply sought the best artist they could afford.

Earl, born as the eldest of four sons of a prominent landholder in Worcester County, Massachusetts, was set to inherit the family estate. He was, however, intent on pursuing an artistic career.[45] When in 1774 Earl declined to serve in his father's militia company, he was disinherited and publicly accused of disloyalty to the colonial cause. Settling in New Haven, he nevertheless obtained commissions to portray prominent patriots. His life-size portrait of Roger Sherman commemorated the sitter's service at the First Continental Congress in Philadelphia in 1774. Earl also painted a pendant portrait of fellow delegate Eliphalet Dyer. Conflicting sources report that in 1775 Earl marched with the Connecticut governor's guard to Concord, or – more likely, given his previous stance – travelled there as a tourist after the battle. In any case he sketched the battle sites of Concord and Lexington and collaborated in the production of four historical prints. Nevertheless, when he was called before the New Haven Committee of Safety in October 1776 and refused to take up arms, he chose exile over prison, but went into hiding with the 'Friends of Government'. In April 1777, the press declared Earl one of several men publicly impeached on the charge that they refused to take up arms against George III's army. That same spring Earl appears to have been instrumental in warning British troops against being cut off from the east end of Long Island. When arrested, he was again offered the options of service, prison, or exile, apparently in deference to his father's position. Earl again chose exile. Disguised as a servant of Burgoyne's Quartermaster-General, Captain John Money, Earl was taken via Providence and Newport to London, where he arrived in April 1778.

In January 1779, Earl petitioned the British government for support: his loyalism to the British crown and his refusal to take up arms had caused him to be disinherited and driven into exile. Earl also cited his role in tipping off the British on Long Island which had prevented 'Blood shed and plunder'. Earl believed that, had it not been for his father's standing, he would have been sentenced to death, as the 'rebels were suspicious of his corresponding with the British Officers'. Captain Money certified the veracity of Earl's account and believed him to be 'now in great Distress'.[46] There is no record of any government response. Nor do we know much of Earl's first four years in England, probably spent mostly in Norwich.

Then, in 1783–5, we find Earl exhibiting four male portraits at the Royal Academy, including one of Admiral Richard Kempenfelt, whose portrait he had apparently painted from life by 1782; the painting was completed after Kempenfelt's death later that year, with the man of war in the background taken from an engraving after Tilly Kettle's Royal Academy portrait of that year. In 1784, Earl exhibited *A Master in Chancery Entering the House of Lords*, one of his best English works. Masters in Chancery acted as legal functionaries in the Court of Chancery and the House of Lords. In the sitter's hand are portions of bills passed and repealed in 1775 to restrict trade with the northern and southern colonies, perhaps a suitably ambiguous attribute for the pragmatic loyalist Earl to paint.

In 1785, Earl returned to the United States of America. There he put to good use the experience he had gained of London's international portraiture style as he portrayed men from both sides of the recent political divide. In 1785–6, his subjects included a range of recent American 'heroes', such as Captain Silas Talbot of Rhode Island, and loyalist or Englishman Thomas Barrow in New York. When Earl was incarcerated in that city's debtors' prison in 1786–8, the Society of the Cincinnati (an association of officers who fought in Washington's Continental army) some-what surprisingly provided a market for official portraits. Similarly, after his release Earl continued to portray Revolutionary heroes from Prussian Baron von Steuben to Lt-Gov. Oliver Wolcot. These commissions testify to Earl's range of contacts, his relatively low-key status as a mostly passive loyalist, and perhaps also to the sheer shortage of competent artists. Yet Earl had been sufficiently suspicious to the patri-ots to be driven into exile. There is little doubt of his self-identification: he refused to take up arms and claimed compensation as a loyalist. In post-war America, Earl swiftly reintegrated himself, not least by tapping into the market for commemora-tive Revolutionary portraiture, his former stance either forgiven, or conveniently forgotten, by the war's patriot heroes.[47]

Mather Brown was another pragmatist, from a family split between loyalists and patriots. He came to London of his own volition in spring 1781, armed with an introductory letter from Benjamin Franklin in Paris.[48] Brown enrolled in the Academy schools and became another of West's American students. He enjoyed a busy metropolitan social life as 'handsome young Brown' and initially used his loyalist networks to get commissions. Brown exhibited *Harrison Gray* at the 1783 Royal Academy, portrayed Frederick W. Geyer and his own loyalist uncle the Rev. William Walter in 1784, and made book illustrations inspired by the London-based loyalist Mrs Fleming. In 1784, Brown supported his uncle the Rev. Mather Byles's claims before the compensation commission. But then, in 1785–6, Brown painted some of America's founding fathers – first the US ambassador to London, John Adams, then Jefferson, the new US ambassador to Paris who was on a London visit (unlocated); Adams paid for a replica.[49] In 1786, Jefferson in return commissioned from Brown a portrait of Adams (Boston Athenaeum), and in 1787 of Thomas Paine too (probably not executed); at least one further portrait of Adams followed (1788). Perhaps for Adams and Jefferson, the more prominent Copley was uncom-fortably closely associated with British patriotic history.

By 1786, Brown's London town house was said to contain almost 100 portraits of Americans 'lined up against the walls according to their Patriot or Loyalist sympa-thies'. There were also portraits of various public figures and beautiful women; most of these had probably been painted, without commission, as an advertising strategy. In a significant expansion of his patronage base, in 1788 Brown painted not only the hero of Gibraltar, General Heathfield, but also the king's two eldest sons, the Prince of Wales and the Duke of York. The Prince he depicted in one of his beloved fancy military uniforms, with guns firing in the background and warships out at sea. Both portraits were exhibited to critical acclaim at the 1789 Royal Academy.[50] Brown was appointed official portrait painter to the Duke of York; in 1790 Brown assumed the same position in the household of Prince William, the future Duke of Clarence and William IV. Pragmatically entrepreneurial, young Brown had established himself as portraitist of the American republican leadership *and* of British royalty.

British Radicals: James Barry and Robert Edge Pine

A few British artists are known to have supported the American cause. The brilliant, irascible Irish Catholic painter James Barry (1741–1806) criticised Britain's social and political order and the government's Irish and American policies.[51] Several others, such as Thomas Stothard and Richard Westall, kept radical company and gave visual expression to a radical domestic agenda, supporting for instance the Society for Constitutional Information and parliamentary reform.[52] Among those British artists who supported the American Revolution, at least one of some prominence, Robert Edge Pine (fl.1730–88), appears to have felt so strongly about his politics that he emigrated to America after war's end.

In spring 1776, Barry had exhibited at the Royal Academy *Death of General Wolfe* and *Portraits of Barry and Burke in the Characters of Ulysses and His Companion Fleeing from the Cave of Polyphemus*. Both paintings can be read as indirect comments on the disintegrating situation in North America. In December that year, Barry published his first politically motivated print. The etching and aquatint *The Phoenix or the Resurrection of Freedom* (1776) was a fierce republican attack on the king and court and celebrated the passage of liberty from Britain, where it had died, to America (fig. 10). Barry was using the medium of print, which reached wider audiences, to propagate the notion of opposition to the war as a patriotic duty. Liberty's flight is described in the margin:

> O Liberty thou Parent of whatever is truly Amiable & Illustrious, Associated with Virtue, thou hatest the Luxurious & Intemperate & hast successively Abandon'd thy lov'd residence of Greece, Italy & thy more favor'd England when they grew Corrupt & Worthless, thou hast given them over to chains & despondency & taken thy flight to a new people of manners simple & untainted.

Fragmented writing on a tombstone attacked the king's repressive policies, which prohibited his subjects from communicating with 'those Audacious Assertors of

10. James Barry, *The Phoenix or the Resurrection of Freedom* (1776–1808). In one of Barry's most radical prints, Britannia has died. Once-English liberties, now suppressed in Britain, have fled to America's shores, where the Temple of Liberty is open to all. At left, Father Time honours the memory of classical civilisations where civil liberties flourished. The sun has followed freedoms and the arts westward to illuminate the background of the print. Barry indicates his sympathy for the Americans by including a self-portrait at far right among Britannia's mourners: the republican thinkers Milton, Locke, Sydney, and Marvell.

human Rights on the other side of this Atlantic'. Britannia's bier is inscribed: 'This … Monument to the Memory of … [Brit]ish Freedom[.] a Corrupt degene … [ra] te Nobility & Gentry, dissipated … poor … rapacious & dependent upon the … Court'. In a reference to the government's assault on the Habeas Corpus Act, a paper marked 'Habs Corps' peeps out from the back of the coat of the chained figure in front of the bier. Over the next couple of years, Barry produced further allegories which more or less overtly criticised the war with America and its consequences, or commented on the politics of domestic reform. But *Phoenix* remained his boldest public political statement, which Barry had judged prudent to leave unsigned. The reference 'U & C fecit' may refer to *Ulysses and Companion*, and the figure with the long straight nose may be Edmund Burke, who was critical of government policy on America. In 1782, Barry turned down an opportunity to travel to America to paint the heroic exploits of General Washington; he probably expected his ongoing

11. Joseph Strutt after Robert Edge Pine, *America. To those, who wish to Sheathe the Desolating Sword of War. And, to Restore the Blessings of Peace and Amity, to a divided People* (1781). According to Pine's own description, kneeling in the storm at left is 'America, after having suffered the several evils of war, bewailed its unhappy cause, and lamented over the victims of its fury – her ruined towns – destroy'd commerce … On the appearance of Peace, is represented in an extacy of gratitude to the Almighty – Heroic Virtue presents Liberty attended by Concord – Industry followed by Plenty and her train for a group expressive of Population; and ships denote Commerce.' As does Barry in *Phoenix*, Pine uses light to denote blessings or favour.

project of painting a grand cycle of murals at the Society of Arts at the Adelphi to bring him recognition and commissions at home.

∼

The only prominent British painter to emigrate to the United States after the war was Robert Edge Pine. There he sought to establish himself as a painter of American Revolutionary history. Pine, the son of a London engraver, was described as 'a very small man – morbidly irritable'.[53] He held republican views which were encouraged by contacts with Thomas Hollis. He also repeatedly portrayed John Wilkes, the popular radical London politician whose pro-American views Pine shared, as well as the historian Catherine Macaulay as a Roman matron. In the decade or so before the American Revolution, Pine had painted history that could be read to have anti-monarchical overtones, for example *The Surrender of Calais to Edward III* (exhibited 1760) and, in a critique of the notion of monarchical infallibility, *Canute Reproving His Courtiers for Their Impious Flattery* (exhibited 1763 and 1768). In 1771, Pine displayed at the Society of Artists *Earl Warren, making reply to the writ commonly called 'Quo warranto' in the reign of Edward I*, quoting the historian Rapin on the subject of the ancient liberties of the English people against the king. Pine painted a huge allegory 'expressive of the Oppressions and Calamities of America, also the great Revolution with which it pleased Heaven to terminate the infernal War' (1778). Only Joseph Strutt's engraving of *America* (London, 1781) survives today, dedicated to 'Those, who wish to Sheathe the Desolating Sword of War [and] to Restore the Blessings of Peace and Amity, to a divided People' (fig. 11).

Having made the acquaintance of George William Fairfax, a Virginia landowner and friend of Washington's, and of Benjamin Franklin's friend Samuel Vaughan, in 1784 Pine emigrated to Philadelphia: 'I think I could pass the latter part of my life happier in a Country where the noblest Principles have been defended and establish'd than with the People who have endeavoured to subdue them'. A local printer produced a handsome catalogue of Pine's paintings which he exhibited from October 1784 in an apartment in the Philadelphia State House; 25 cents bought admission and a copy of the catalogue. Fairfax provided Pine with an introduction to George Washington by sending him a print of *America*. Pine, the introduction enthused, was 'as true a Son of Liberty as any Man can ever be', who had lost his business and made enemies in Britain by publishing *America* and declaring his political leanings. Now compelled to make a new start, there was 'not a person in England, that merits a better reception in America than the unfortunate Gentleman [whose] only fault was his good wishes to our Country'. The figure of Heroic Virtue in the painting, Fairfax claimed, represented Washington. Pine also used his political credentials, as manifest in his actions and his art, to fend off the Philadelphia Assembly's criticism of the City Council's decision to allow him rent-free space for his exhibition. Pine was confirmed as a 'constitutional citizen' and in 1786 was elected to the American Philosophical Society and enrolled in the Philadelphia militia.

By then Pine had for a year or so been travelling to paint the portraits of a range of generals and legislators, including Washington's, for a projected series of at least eight paintings with subjects from the Revolution. It is not clear what was to blame for Pine's slow progress. Perhaps the lack of cooperation of some sitters played a part. John Dickinson, who had opposed the Declaration of Independence when it was voted on because he (rightly) anticipated it would lead to full-out war, declined: 'I cannot be guilty of so false an ambition as to seek for any share in the fame of that council'. By the time of his death in 1788, Pine had started at least four Revolutionary paintings, all now untraced: *The Capture of Lord Cornwallis and the Colors Laid before Congress*, a subject no British artist in Britain dared to paint; *General Washington Resigning His Commission to Congress*; and *General Washington under the Character of Fortitude*. An oil copy of *Declaration of Independence* by Edward Savage as well as his engraving after that copy survive as the only physical evidence of Pine's American Revolutionary project – showing contemplative men engaged in the earnest act of voting for the new republic's independence.

~

The most bizarre contribution any artist made to the American Revolution was that of the Scot John Aitken, alias John the Painter (1752–77).[54] After an apprenticeship to an Edinburgh artist, followed by a life of crime in London, a brief jaunt to Virginia, and more thievery in England, in 1776 Aitken tried to aid the American cause by seeking to destroy all six British royal dockyards. Aitken procured modest financial and lukewarm moral support from the American commissioner in Paris, Silas Deane. With an ingenious incendiary device which he claimed would allow him to set fires undetected, Aitken damaged a rope house at Portsmouth and wreaked considerable destruction at Bristol before being apprehended in a nationwide manhunt. Imprisoned at Clerkenwell, Aitken foolishly confessed to another painter, John Baldwin, who promptly reported everything to the Admiralty. Aitken's trial was the most celebrated of the decade. Convicted within a few hours, he was hanged on 10 March 1777 from the mizzen mast of the *Arethusa*, specially erected on Portsmouth Common. The case produced rival biographies, trial accounts, spoofs, 'histories', and the confession Aitken had dictated while awaiting execution. None of his paintings survive. All that is left of John the Painter are his (supposed) relics – a pistol, a vial of turpentine, and a mummified finger turned tobacco stopper.

'The peaceful muse outweighs political warfare': Charles Willson Peale

At least two prominent American patriots saw active military service and served as politicians, diplomats, and possibly spies, while also leaving their mark as the most distinguished painters of the Revolutionary era: Charles Willson Peale (1741–1827) and Jonathan Trumbull (1756–1843).[55] Peale supported the so-called anti-proprietary party in Maryland in the early 1760s and joined the Sons of Freedom before fleeing in 1765 to New England to escape his creditors, and then to London to train with West. While in London, Peale painted for the Virginia legislature a large allegorical portrait of Chatham as a Roman orator. It depicts Chatham 'in a Consular Habit, speaking in Defence of the Claims of the AMERICAN Colonies, on the Principles of the BRITISH Constitution'.[56] The representation of Pitt in classical dress rather than the robes of a peer of the realm had a political as well as an aesthetic function: it associated Pitt with Roman republican heroes of liberty and avoided offending the sensibilities of those in America who had questioned Chatham's stance when he moved from the Commons to the Lords. In a broadside accompanying the engraving which was produced from the painting, Peale described his intentions by quoting Montesquieu: 'the *States which enjoy the highest Degree of Liberty are apt to be oppressive of those who are subordinate … to them*.'[57] References to Anglo-American traditions of (now fragile) political liberty were combined with hints at violence. In the left background, Inigo Jones's Banqueting House in London, from which Charles I had been led to his execution in 1649, indicates what might happen to monarchs when English laws and liberties were violated. As an American artist in London who sympathised with the colonial patriots, Peale was an obvious choice to portray the former British Prime Minister turned American hero.[58]

Peale's artistic practice was politically engaged in many ways. Both before his London sojourn and after his return to America in 1769, he painted emblematical designs, banners, placards, and battle flags to help the Revolutionary cause in Maryland and Massachusetts. His portrait of John Beale Bordley (1770), a Maryland planter and republican official, was also an allegorical warning of the consequences of arbitrary power and the suppression of liberty (fig. 12).

Peale employs layers of space to depict Bordley's position as challenger. Bordley, an advocate of American autarky, is shown clothed in brown homespun and standing in a peach orchard. The background, where a sheep meadow receives sun, refers to America's agricultural self-sufficiency. To the left, under dark skies, British soldiers guide away a horse with sheepskin, products of American industry. The theme of tyranny pervades the foreground, where the visual narrative moves to the colonists' case against British usurpation of American products and rights, and the rejection of the new customs impositions signified by the torn paper at Bordley's feet. The suggested solution is the restoration of English historical precedent, law, and justice. Bordley leans on the carefully balanced book of law – 'Nolumus

12. Charles Willson Peale, *John Beale Bordley* (1770).

Leges Angliae mutari' ('We are unwilling that the laws of England be changed') –
and points to the figure with the scales of justice and cornucopia of the blessings
springing from the just application of law. If the carefully balanced book of law falls,
through Britain losing the goodwill of sensible men like Bordley, and if political
liberty cannot be preserved from the apparent corruption of the constitution, Peale
seems to suggest, then Americans will seek redress in a radical sense of 'natural'
law: the book rests on a natural rock, and the law is represented amid American
landscape and fauna. Native American jimson weed – a poisonous plant at the
statue's base – warns of the dangerous consequences of any encroachment upon
American civil liberties.[59]

Peale has been described as 'a living advertisement for the values of republicanism, most especially the conviction that individuals should subordinate their personal well-being to the greater good of the community'. While Peale in 1769–73 did establish himself as a leading American portraitist, he also put much of his energy into politics. His association with the patriot cause probably cost him loyalist patronage and possibly hindered his career in the 1770s. Yet Peale was critical of artists who appeared to put profit before principle. Everyone's role in the Revolution would be scrutinised and artists' conduct in the present crisis would help shape the future of the arts. In August 1775, Peale wrote to Edmund Jenings of the day 'when my brush should fail, that I must take the Musket'. In the event he managed to combine painting with politics, although the balance of his activities varied. In 1776, he was to paint more portraits than in any other year, albeit primarily miniatures – easier to carry and keep safe in a period of war, amid frequent displacement and occasional plunder. That year, Peale also joined both the militia and a political grouping called the Furious Whigs. As a lieutenant in the Philadelphia militia he saw active service around the city, and in the Continental army under Washington in New Jersey. Peale thrived on campaigning and combat, however much he retrospectively minimised this aspect in his autobiography to emphasise his pacifism. Between 1777 and 1780, he served as the chairman or member of over thirty committees, as agent for confiscated loyalist estates in Philadelphia, and as a representative in the Pennsylvania state legislature. Clearly aligned with the republican cause, Peale nevertheless advocated moderation when civilian affairs threatened to turn violent.[60]

In 1779, the Supreme Executive Council of Pennsylvania commissioned Peale to paint the portrait of *George Washington at Princeton* (1779) for their Council Chamber. The commission resembled the practice of hanging royal portraits in British colonial capitals to focus and symbolise imperial loyalty. In Peale's portrait, Washington is wearing a blue and buff uniform and the commander-in-chief's blue sash and leans on the barrel of a captured cannon. Two Hessian flags (captured at Trenton the previous week) are beside him and, at his feet, a British ensign lies on the ground to the left, and a blue battle flag with thirteen stars flies above. In the left middle distance a mounted soldier gestures towards red-coated prisoners being led away under guard. Peale had himself seen action at Trenton and Princeton, two of Washington's greatest victories which boosted the morale of American patriots. The portrait was so popular that Peale made at least eighteen copies for clients as diverse as the French ambassador and the American diplomat Henry Laurens; the latter's picture was captured by a British cruiser and brought to Britain as spoils of war.

In 1780, Peale contributed a two-faced effigy of the traitor Benedict Arnold to a political parade by the Furious Whigs. But then he and other radicals lost re-election to the Pennsylvania legislature as their party fell out of favour in the turbulent world of Pennsylvanian Revolutionary politics. Disappointed that the war might have affected his reputation, Peale concluded that 'the peaceful muse outweighs political warfare' and withdrew from active politics. Nevertheless, throughout the 1780s he continued to present himself *as an artist* in the role of the public servant who had sacrificed career advances and profit during the war and painted Revolutionary leaders for posterity at little or no remuneration. Indeed, from the mid-1770s onwards, Peale had been capturing the faces and events of the Revolution. By 1783, Peale had painted some three dozen portraits of military and other Revolutionary leaders for a 'Gallery of Great Men'. This Revolutionary portrait pantheon – today partially yet impressively preserved in the Second Bank of America in Philadelphia – was to help the nation-building process. Americans could recognise key characters of the Revolution and the gallery could help them 'think nationally instead of locally or individually'. The bust portraits were all painted in the same size and presented in oval frames. They were a visual civics lesson, as an emphasis on character instead of specific action democratised notions of heroism. The political class of moderate republican men and miscellaneous European officers who had fought with the patriots was capable, through reason, virtue, and the right public action, to achieve admission to the pantheon. On the other hand, women, ethnic minorities, 'ordinary' Americans, and loyalists were omitted from this gallery. Peale also excluded most of his radical compatriots, his fellow Furious Whigs of the 1770s, and prominent anti-Federalists of the 1780s, though he did paint his friend Thomas Paine. Peale's selective Revolutionary pantheon, and his portrayal of some former political adversaries from 1782–3, seemed poised to attract maximum support for his museum. By 1784, the portrait gallery had forty-three paintings (rising to seventy in 1804, 180 in 1818), with Revolutionary figures being joined by men of science and religion, as well as a group in whom Peale had a special interest, nonagenarians and centenarians.[61]

In 1783, the General Assembly of Pennsylvania gave Peale the equivalent of £600 to build a Roman Triumphal Arch as the centrepiece of the celebrations for the signing of the peace treaty. The tripartite arch, some twenty metres wide and twelve metres high, spanned Market Street, one of downtown Philadelphia's main thoroughfares. Dressed with Ionic pillars and balustrades, it was decorated with backlit transparencies of war heroes thrashing redcoats, Indians building wilderness churches, and a laurel-crowned Washington as Cincinnatus returning to the plough. Atop the central arch, with the Latin motto, 'By divine favor, a great and new order of the ages commences', stood the Temple of Janus, shut. Transparent panels, illuminated by 1,100 lamps, honoured the war dead. The enormous structure was topped by the figure of 'Peace', which was to descend with goddesses and to light with a torch hundreds of rockets. Tragically, the whole structure of varnished paper and cloth over scaffolding burned down when some early rockets set it alight. The artilleryman was killed and others badly burned, including Peale, who also broke several ribs. After spending three weeks in bed to recover from the disaster, Peale valiantly started a local fund-raising effort and reconstructed the arch. To him, the episode was a lesson in hubris punished.[62]

Peale was a rare blend of a patriotic man of action – in the field and the committee room – who also used his creative mind in the service of the political cause he supported. Among his wide-ranging interests, which also encompassed natural history, was a broad spectrum of visual culture from political ephemera to his lasting Revolutionary portrait gallery. Only one of his contemporaries matched Peale in the combined impact of his political and painting practice.

'To his country he gave his sword and his pencil': John Trumbull

John Trumbull, the aristocrat among early American artists, was the son of the last royal governor of Connecticut, who remained in office as patriotic governor during and after the Revolution. Educated at Harvard, young Trumbull was intended for a legal or clerical career.[63] He nevertheless tutored himself in art by studying Harvard's modest art collection, and by reading European art history and theory in the library, including Hogarth's *Analysis of Beauty* (1753). In 1775, faced with a choice, he engaged as a patriot. Unlike Ralph Earl, who perhaps avoided military service at least in part in order to pursue an artistic career, and much like Peale, Trumbull initially involved himself actively in politics and war. As Adjutant of the First Regiment of Connecticut in 1775, he saw and heard the Battle of Bunker Hill from a distance. In 1776, he became Deputy Adjutant-General with the rank of Colonel, and made his most important military contribution to the war in the form of a plan for defending Fort Ticonderoga. The following year, Trumbull failed to have the terms of his commission as Deputy Adjutant-General of the army for the Northern Department amended by the Continental Congress so as to state the correct date at which he had started his responsibilities; he resigned in a sulk.[64]

In 1780, Trumbull went on a family business venture to Paris. It is possible he also discharged a secret political–diplomatic mission concerning the French–Dutch–British conflict in the West Indies.[65] In the event that the business project failed, Trumbull had secured permission to go on to London to pursue artistic training, provided he engaged in no political activity. While studying at Benjamin West's studio in 1780, Trumbull, like his master, did not entirely hide his political sympathies. He wrote at one stage: "'Tis the sword only that can give us such a peace, as our past glorious struggles have merited. The sword must finish what it has so well begun."[66] On 20 November 1780, Trumbull was arrested on treason charges. The evidence is inconclusive. Trumbull himself suspected that he had become the victim of American loyalists bent on revenging André (the news had reached London five days before). Trumbull was of equal rank and thus seemed 'a perfect *pendant*': 'the resentment of government marked me as an expiatory sacrifice.'[67] Trumbull told magistrates that he was 'an American – my name is Trumbull; I am a son of him whom you call the rebel governor of Connecticut'. He detailed his military service and asserted that he had 'had the honor of being an aide-de-camp to him whom you call the rebel General Washington.' Trumbull calmly added the thinly veiled threat that his treatment at British hands would be mirrored by that of British POWs in America.[68]

On West's pleas, the king guaranteed Trumbull's life, but George III declared he could not secure his release. Just as Ralph Earl would be painting Revolutionary leaders in his New York prison cell in 1786–8, Trumbull painted while incarcerated in London's Bridewell. He even sent exhibits to the Royal Academy. Ironically, his portrait of Washington had been published as an engraving by Valentine Green in early 1780 (by 1783 it would also be adapted for a frontispiece for the London magazines). In 1782, Edmund Burke secured Trumbull's release on condition that he leave the kingdom within thirty days. At £100 each, Copley and West jointly posted half the bond. Trumbull subsequently helped his brother provision the American army, but by January 1784 he had returned to London with the intention to work with West, followed by studies in Italy. His correspondence conveys a sense of homesick loneliness, guilt at defying his family's wish for a more conventional career in America, and competitiveness with other over-achieving male members of the family. Within months of arriving back in London, Trumbull exhibited *The Deputation from the Senate Presenting to Cincinnatus the Command of the Roman Armies*. His rendering of Cincinnatus was an unmistakable likeness of Washington. The message was clear: no British or other European leader would have had the grace or confidence to make the disinterested gesture of a Cincinnatus or a Washington, namely of resigning supreme military command and returning to their plough. Soon Trumbull embarked on his lifetime project: painting the history of the American Revolutionary War.[69]

In the mid-1780s, Trumbull told a correspondent: 'I am now ... employ'd writing in my language, the History of our Country.'[70] In a letter to Thomas Jefferson, Trumbull explained that his chief motivation to resume painting had been the wish of commemorating the great events of our country's revolution. I am fully sensible that the profession, as it is generally practiced, is frivolous, little useful to society, and unworthy of a man who has talents for more serious pursuits. But, to preserve and diffuse the memory of the noblest series of actions which have ever presented themselves in the history of man; to give to the present and future sons of oppression and misfortune, such glorious lessons of their rights, and of the spirit with which they should assert and support them, and even to transmit to their descendants, the personal resemblance of those who have been the great actors in those illustrious scenes, were objects which gave a dignity to the profession, peculiar to my situation.[71]

Much later, when he wrote his autobiography in 1841, Trumbull's self-image was that of the artist as patriotic visual historiographer who was well equipped to record the events of his time. Trumbull's 'History of our Country', which he started in London and Paris in the mid-1780s and completed half a century later in the rotunda of the Capitol in Washington, DC, became his famous Revolutionary War series.[72] Undertaken with the encouragement of Benjamin West, the project promised to solve the dilemma of painting serious art for America, where there was not much demand for any genre other than portraiture. Trumbull, like West previously, also reckoned with substantial American and French markets for engravings; the prints for *The Battle of La Hogue* had just earned West 1,500 guineas. The project allowed Trumbull to combine his patriotism with his artistic interests. Like Copley, whose influence on Trumbull was very strong, he used his skills as a portraitist in painting history. Recent Anglo-American and American history, especially military history, was an obvious niche for Trumbull to move into. Copley and West, dependent on the king's and the British public's support, were wise to largely avoid the subject area; Pine's series was making little progress; and Peale was focusing on his 'Gallery of Great Men'. Like Peale, Trumbull could draw on his familiarity with the look of British and American officers and soldiers, and with the events and actors he was to paint. These were important assets in a period when authenticity and realism in history painting mattered.[73]

Trumbull started his series with paintings of battles in which both sides had scored victories. They focus on heroic sacrifice, military martyrdom, and the universal values of magnanimity and chivalric bonds between officers of all nations.[74] *The Death of General Warren at the Battle of Bunker's Hill, June 17, 1775* (1786) shows *American* military martyrdom in the context of a *British* victory (see plate IX). But it juxtaposes the death of the American General Joseph Warren, at the moment when the British troops press beyond the American fortifications, with that of the

British Major Pitcairn. Both scenes are highlighted in the image as if by spotlights. The painting's moral is of gentlemen-officers' virtue and universal humanitarian values. The British officer Major Small is shown preventing a grenadier from bayoneting the dying Warren. American soldiers, Lieutenant Grosvenor, and his black servant express their concern for Warren and respect for Small's generosity. Trumbull quoted the pictorial strategies of his influential contemporaries West and Copley in the service of differently toned politico-moral representations. Like Copley in *Peirson*, Trumbull employs strong diagonals and alternating bands of light and shadow to intensify the chaotic nature of his scene. Although *Warren* is more vividly coloured than any of West's paintings, Trumbull's use of orange tints to warm his whites was perhaps inspired by his teacher. Like Copley's *Chatham* and *Peirson* and West's *Wolfe*, this was no eyewitness account, but Trumbull's painting was unusual in its strong effect of authenticity: not only was he familiar with the main characters and the lie of the land, but he had seen the fire and smoke of Charleston burning.[75]

Abigail Adams, the ambassador's wife, praised Trumbull's work for preserving national history: 'Looking at it my whole frame contracted, my blood shivered, and I felt a faintness at my heart.' He had taught 'mankind that it is not rank nor titles, but character alone, which interests posterity'.[76] William Dunlap, another student of West's during the 1780s, later criticised Trumbull for his representation in terms that were very similar to earlier British criticism of Major André's monument in Westminster Abbey. While West in *Death of Wolfe* had represented the martyrdom of a national British hero, Trumbull depicted

> the moment of the overthrow of his countrymen, and the triumph of their enemies. The death of Doctor Warren … is an incident of minor consequence compared with the repeated defeats of the veterans of Great Britain, by Prescott, Putnam, and the brave undisciplined Yankee yeomen … Surely one of these moments of triumph might have been chosen by an American painter for his picture.[77]

Quite apart from exaggerating the prominence of British officers, Dunlap entirely missed the point: generosity towards a defeated enemy was standard behaviour for classical heroes, whose spirit Trumbull was seeking to evoke. Nevertheless, the painting could serve a partisan point, too. When Trumbull came under suspicion from the French Revolutionary authorities in 1797, *Bunker's Hill* helped him prove his anti-British and Revolutionary spirit.[78]

A second British victory was the subject of *The Death of General Montgomery in the Attack on Quebec, December 31, 1775* (1786). It shows the moment when the Continental general Richard Montgomery died during a daring night-time attack from a blast of grapeshot fired by British-Canadian forces defending the batteries outside Quebec. Montgomery, an Anglo-Irishman had been a Captain in the British army before resigning his commission, emigrating to New York in 1773 and accepting a commission in the Continental army in 1775. Second in command to General Philip Schuyler on the Canadian expedition, he had been killed by cannon and honourably buried by the British. Benedict Arnold and others appreciated that Montgomery's body was shown 'Every possible mark of distinction'.[79] Yet some patriot poems, sermons, plays, and pictures soon reinvented the story: Montgomery had been slain by Native Americans, and his mangled body displayed by the British commander, who called for American prisoners to be tortured and cannibalised. The invasion of French Canada was thus a preventative move to forestall the imminent unleashing by the British of Indian warfare. Trumbull's version is true to the sudden shock of the explosion which killed Montgomery. The figure of the native warrior, like the poses, central slumping figure, and overall composition are reminiscent of West's *Wolfe*, though the brushwork and palette are more dramatic than in the staid West.[80] Trumbull's initial choices were perhaps meant to generate maximum transatlantic appeal by emphasising the transnational value of magnanimity. Like British statesmen such as Burke, he also considered the Canadian campaign a brilliant achievement despite its outcome. But the appearance of ambiguous loyalties was not appreciated by the US Congress, which did not adopt these subjects for the Capitol.

Washington's magnanimity and kindness were a model of sublime heroism. Two of the paintings Trumbull started in 1786–7 took American victories for their subjects. *The Death of General Mercer at the Battle of Princeton, January 3, 1777* (unfinished version 1786–8) shows British grenadiers mortally wounding the general. The victory resulted in Washington gaining control of most of New Jersey. Mercer was clubbed and bayoneted by the British when he refused to beg for mercy; removed from the battlefield, he died nine days later. Trumbull also undertook *The Capture of the Hessians at Trenton, December 26, 1776* (1786–1828), a scene from an overwhelming American victory which focuses on the victors' magnanimity towards the fallen Hessian Colonel Rall. The rationale was, again, to give 'a lesson to all living and future soldiers in the service of [their] country, to show mercy and kindness to a fallen enemy, – their enemy no longer when wounded and in their power'.[81]

In 1786–7, Trumbull also began *The Sortie Made by the Garrison of Gibraltar, November 27, 1781*, in a clear bid to court the British public. Trumbull knew that with his American paintings he 'had given offense to some extra-patriotic people in England'. The Gibraltar scene was taken from the night-time British sortie to destroy Spanish breastworks. It shows the Spanish officer Don José de Barboza who had refused the offer of British help when he lay dying. Trumbull later explained that, once again, he had wanted to celebrate 'noble and generous actions, by whomsoever performed'. The Gibraltar scene, like Bunker Hill, focuses on universal values. If the lesson had been lost on the British public in the former painting, it was perhaps more obvious with a Spanish protagonist being treated with British magnanimity in the context of a major British success. Still, this was a depiction of the heroic death of an *enemy* officer. When he exhibited a version of the painting in 1789 in a large hall he rented for over £150 in an auction house in the fashionable Spring Gardens, Trumbull was apprehensive that his critics would use his politics against him: 'every tingling tongue of Envy will be busy in recalling all my past sins of Rebellion in America, of Spyship & Imprisonment [and] of connexions in France'. In his later recollection, however, despite his lack of

> family connections or friends to support me, but with the remembrance of my adventure in 1780 still rankling in some minds, it attracted the public attention in a satisfactory degree. The military were partial to it, and I seldom looked into the room without being cheered by the sight of groups of officers of the Guards, in their splendid uniforms.[82]

The printer's bill for admission tickets suggests that the exhibition was only a modest success, possibly because it was competing with the Royal Academy exhibition and Boydell's Shakespeare Gallery. Despite private appreciation from Thomas Jefferson to Horace Walpole, there were also fewer than 240 subscriptions to the print.[83]

In 1786, Trumbull had started composing *The Declaration of Independence, July 4, 1776* (1786–93, 1817–20), which shows Jefferson's drafting committee presenting their report to John Hancock, President of Congress. Jefferson provided an eyewitness account and a (slightly faulty) sketch of the room. Both Jefferson (who considered Trumbull's project a 'national work') and Adams advised Trumbull that in the interest of authenticity the painting ought to include both the declaration's signatories and its opponents, such as John Dickinson, the Quaker from Delaware who had refused to sit for Pine's version of the subject. Trumbull eventually included forty-seven portraits, of which he painted thirty-six from life, nine from existing portraits, one from a description helped by memory, and one purely from memory. Most prominently, Jefferson in a red vest at the centre of the reporting group is laying the document before the president in the *ad locutio* pose of military leaders and statesmen; Adams is dead-centre in Charles I's pose in a famous Van

Dyck portrait; Franklin faces the viewer.[84] There are links to the battle paintings in Trumbull's series, in the form of trophies taken from the British. But *Declaration* essentially depicts the triumph of an idea, and a moment of silence – the founding fathers holding their breath as participants in a momentous event.

Finally, in 1786–7, Trumbull also commenced studies for *The Surrender of Cornwallis at Yorktown, October 19, 1781* (1787–c.1828). By late 1787, he painted fifteen French officers into *Cornwallis*, Major-General Charles Ross into a small version of the *Sortie*, and Jefferson into the *Declaration*. He was thus shifting the balance of the series from commemorating dead heroes and martyrs to painting surviving officers and statesmen. The series would later also include *The Surrender of General Burgoyne at Saratoga, N.Y., October 16, 1777* (1791–c.1816). Key British defeats were subjects that no British artists in Britain attempted, though Pine in America tried. By ending on such a theme, Trumbull had gone full circle from the earliest scenes of British triumph. These last two subjects, along with the *Signing of the Declaration of Independence* and *Washington Resigning His Commission*, adorn the US Capitol's rotunda today.[85]

Conclusions

American painters during the Revolution were public figures, invested both in image-making and in political agendas, and highly alert to the impact of painting their loyalties. They negotiated the relationships between their artistic and political lives as they tried to maintain or expand a critical and commercial support base on at least one side of the Atlantic. Their work speaks to the constant visual transactions across the Atlantic and the negotiations over the recent Anglo-American past in which they were involved as artists. Art contributed to political ephemera and symbolism and negotiated contemporary Anglo-American politics and recent history by way of analogy or more or less oblique or explicit references. Permanent London residents like West and Copley kept their political sympathies largely to themselves and put their professional careers first, although not without painting the occasional political ambiguity, or risking being read ambiguously as they followed various strategies of painting by historical analogy and allegory. Several younger American painters were either genuine loyalists, or disguised their pro-American stance, or kept quiet on political affairs to pursue training and practice. While some artists were struggling to reconcile politics with the need to cultivate clients, the latter may not all have cared about artists' politics and simply preferred the best artist they could afford. Mather Brown, and others such as Thomas Spence Duché, stayed on in Britain after the war and painted variously the portraits of loyalists for their American relatives, British society figures and royalty, or Revolutionary subjects. Loyalists such as Ralph Earl quickly rebuilt their support base across Revolutionary political divides. Earl, either a pragmatist or a largely passive loyalist, exploited the market for commemorative Revolutionary portraiture. Charles Willson Peale likewise composed his Revolutionary, national pantheon for maximum post-Independence appeal. Peale and John Trumbull claimed artistic leadership as national historians in the genres of portraiture and history. Theirs was a vision (shared by the British exile Pine) of a new republican nation capable of honouring artists with bountiful commissions of national heroes and Revolutionary military victories.

The last visual statement in this chapter shall belong to Trumbull, who was both politically the most prominent of the artists discussed here, and the most important visual historiographer of the American Revolutionary War. Trumbull negotiated the balance between adherence to neoclassical conventions in history painting and his desire for artistic leadership in America and transatlantic commercial success. But he never left his true loyalties in doubt. In 1790, President Washington gave Trumbull fourteen sittings to paint his portrait into the *Capture of the Hessians at Trenton*, *Death of General Mercer*, and *Surrender of Lord Cornwallis at Yorktown*. At the end of these sittings, Trumbull did a small portrait of the president as a gift for Martha Washington. When the Corporation of the City of New York commissioned an over-life-size copy of that portrait for the City Hall, Trumbull repeated the figure and horse as in Mrs Washington's portrait, but appropriately presented the victorious American commander on the occasion of the evacuation of New York by the British in 1783 (see plate IV). In the background, therefore, ships and boats with the last of the British army are leaving the shore, and Broadway lies in ruins. Washington's informal pose, his right arm draped over the saddle, the other on his waist, is reminiscent of Thomas Gainsborough's portraits of *Col. St Leger* and *George, Prince of Wales*, both exhibited at the Royal Academy in 1782. In an exquisite visual pun, Trumbull contrasts the large and modest general George standing in front of his horse with the tiny, empty pedestal of the former equestrian statue of King George, tucked to the side of the equine's right foreleg.[86]

LONDON, SPRING AND SUMMER 1784

IN THE MONTHS THAT FOLLOWED the end of war in 1783, churches across Britain rang to the sounds of preachers who decried the imperial disaster in stark terms.[1] William Keate at Bath reflected a sense of post-war crisis when he pointed out the danger that the astronomically high national debt, domestic party strife, and foreign enemies watching for their next chance, might 'all conspire to the over-throw of this once flourishing state'.[2] Dissenting preachers like William Bennet in Moorfields saw Britain's imperial humiliation as divine chastisement. A costly civil war had been waged at a huge expense of treasure and blood, leaving thousands of British 'hardy Veterans and valiant Youths' dead. The national trauma was

> that his Majesty's own empire has been the seat of such dreadful devastation – that fellow-Protestants, friends, and relatives by birth and blood – whose religion was the same – whose interest was one – whose comfort and glory so much depended on mutual confidence and affection – who, in a state of union, might have been a terror to the world – have been left in Providence to take the field against each other, and to embrue their hands in each other's blood!

The sheer scale of national humiliation was astounding, and painful: 'have we not, in one stroke, suffered a dismemberment of empire, such as was never heard of or known before?'[3] Other preachers encouraged their congregations and readers to heal through selective remembering.[4]

Performances of art and music also engaged London audiences and the wider

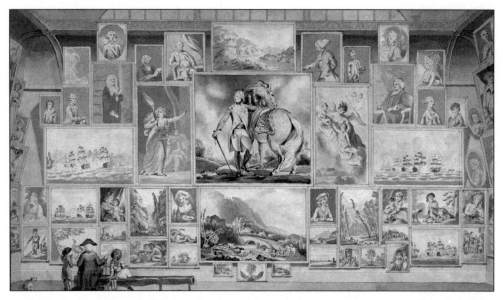

13. Edward Francis Burney, *The Royal Academy Exhibition of 1784: The Great Room, North Wall* (*c*.1784).

cultural nation in that first post-war season. The annual show at the Royal Academy at Somerset House, London's grandest public building shared by the world's mightiest navy, was a site where the imperial nation imagined itself visually. On the courtyard façade, four statues by Joseph Wilton represent the four continents. Europe, Asia, and Africa bear cornucopias 'loaded with tributary fruits and treasures'. America, however, is shown 'armed and breathing defiance'. This curious piece of sculptural propaganda on the building opened at the height of the American Revolutionary War was by 1784 a reminder of Britain's recently painful imperial past.[5] In that spring, however, the Academy's visitors saw imperial themes pervade the exhibition walls in what amounted, in Mark Hallett's words, to a 'powerful reassertion of the nation's military prowess and a remarkably coherent iconography of Britishness at a time of crisis' (fig. 13).[6]

Dominating the north wall of the Great Exhibition Room was President Sir Joshua Reynolds's arresting portrait of the Prince of Wales in a red military coat and the blue Garter ribbon, resting his left arm on a charger's saddle and his right hand on a sword. It was flanked by another royal portrait by Benjamin West and a Shakespearean subject by Henry Fuseli, and, further to the margins, by two large paintings by Dominic Serres of recent British naval victories in the Caribbean.[7] Among a total of twenty-six works by marine painters in this show was Robert Edge Pine's *Lord Rodney in Action aboard the Formidable*. Along with *Lieutenant*

General William Amherst d. 1781, this was Pine's politically safe valedictory exhibit before he sought exile in America.

More military-naval subjects greeted the spectators: sequential images of naval actions, a genre harking back to seventeenth-century Dutch art; views of the successful recent defence of Gibraltar; a frigate chasing a cutter by honorary exhibitor Lieutenant W. Elliot; portraits of naval and military officers; and Francis Wheatley's *Alderman Barnard Turner* as a colonel of the city militia. With the third marine picture of the Battle of Quiberon Bay of 1759 to be exhibited since 1777, the 1784 show also constructed a narrative of repeated national naval success. Memory and commemoration was a theme too: in *Britannia, Hibernia & Scotia Exhibiting the Names of Their Great Commanders in the Late War*; designs for statues of naval commanders; and a mezzotint by Valentine Green of Chatham's monument, unveiled in Westminster Abbey that same year. The most prominent image by an American artist was probably Trumbull's *Cincinnatus*.

The Academy audience was offered a highly selective, morale-boosting visual diet from the lost war. But they were also confronted with the violence inherent to continued imperial expansion. John Webber's *A Party from the Resolution, on Captain Cook's Last Voyage, Shooting Sea Horses* (i.e. walruses) was faced on the west wall by Johann Heinrich Ramberg's *Death of Captain Cook* at the hands of Hawaiians – in the words of Martin Myrone a 'crude confrontation between the bestial racial other and the enlightened white hero' who had lived and died a gentleman to the last.[8] Finally, an alternative path to heroism was sketched out by James Northcote's large canvas, *Captain Inglefield Escaping from his Ship the Centaur*, hung centrally on that west wall. After commanding the 74-gun *Centaur* in the Battle of the Saints, in September 1782 Captain John Nicholson Inglefield was returning with the booty convoy to England when his ship sank in a hurricane. Inglefield was later court-martialled for abandoning the vessel with just ten of the crew of 600. Acquitted, he published a popular account in which he explained how his love of life had prevailed. Instead of classical or biblical heroic self-sacrifice, Inglefield offered a new exemplary narrative which, according to the *British Magazine and Review*, gave 'hints to those brave adventurers who are so valuable in a maritime country'. The figures of Inglefield and his crew saving themselves in the pinnacle, with a young, long-haired boy being rescued from the water at the eleventh hour, are rendered in heroic terms. By making the contest of man *versus* nature the subject of his epic canvas, Northcote gave prominence to physical heroism and fortitude in a non-military context.[9]

These marine, naval, and military displays constructed national narratives. Imagery of the struggles and landscapes of empire made visible the imperial nation on the site, which was at once the official HQ of the patriotic British School and a central node in Britain's naval administration. Marine and naval painting was a means by which Britons told themselves about heroic action, national values, and national and imperial identity. The intellectual and imaginative effort of national recovery and healing after imperial disaster was just as important as imaginary empire–building was at times of promise and triumph. At this very same moment, music too helped the cultural nation sense optimism and pride.

~

The most spectacular cultural event of the 1784 season was a series of concerts to mark the twenty-fifth anniversary of the death of George Frederick Handel (and the centenary of his birth which had been misdated to 1784 rather than 1785). These five concerts, the greatest musical event of the century, drew thousands of listeners and received unprecedented news coverage. By embracing the naturalised British composer in a quasi-sacred performance in the confessional state, George III started reinventing himself as a popular monarch. The first concert, at Westminster Abbey, featured sacred and royal music such as the *Dettingen Te Deum*, the funeral anthem for Queen Caroline (George II's queen), the funeral march from *Saul*, and the coronation anthem 'Zadok the Priest', by then a regular piece on the cathedral and concert repertoire, as well as choruses from oratorios such as *Joshua* and *Israel in Egypt*. The second concert was staged at James Wyatt's Pantheon (1769–72), which Fanny Burney's Evelina thought had 'more the appearance of a chapel, than of a place of diversion', and whose spectacular domed, cathedral-like hall looked indeed like a mixture of Rome's Pantheon and Constantinople's S. Sophia.[10] The secular and more cosmopolitan programme featured extracts from Handel's operas alongside concerti by Corelli, ending on Handel's coronation anthem 'My Heart is Inditing'. The third concert, back at the Abbey, saw 251 instrumentalists and 275 singers perform the *Messiah* for some 4,500 people. The success of the Abbey concerts led to slightly modified repeats in early June, which constituted the fourth and fifth concerts.

Defining national styles in music is a tricky issue; but by the middle of the eighteenth century, the English style was quite different from much Italian music, and maintained allegiance to high-baroque idioms. It was through composing oratorios that Handel had transformed his image from that of a somewhat rough, 'Gothic' German composer to an English cultural icon who articulated national identity in his music.

Oratorio was a form of musical drama for soloists, chorus, and orchestra. It was set for the theatre, not the church, but oratorio was not staged. As a form of entertainment, it combined piety and national pride. Oratorios were performed by native singers and players and their texts were in English, taken from the Bible, other religious texts (*Messiah*), or classic English authors such as Milton (*Samson*), Dryden (*Semele*), or Spenser (*Occasional Oratorio*). They were given further respectability by frequent use at benefit concerts, such as the annual charity performances for the Foundling Hospital from 1750. In 1784, £6,000 from the proceeds of the ticket sales at the commemorative concerts and receipts from the publication of Charles Burney's history of the Commemoration went to the Society of Decay'd Musicians, of which Handel had been a generous founding member.

Crucially, Handel's libretti allowed political and moral readings. The history of biblical Israel was presented as an English or British national epic: the call for unity in the face of war in *Israel in Egypt*; the fear of a French invasion, as well as a rebellion, in *Judas Maccabaeus*, after the defeated Jacobite rebellion of 1745–6; or the Ark of the Covenant standing for the British constitution in *Joshua*. Oratorios also defended religious orthodoxy in the struggle against alternative spiritual offerings such as rationalist deism, and the *Messiah* and other oratorios duly celebrated the mysteries and prophecies.[11]

The performance of Handel as a national ritual climaxed in the 1784 Commemoration.[12] It brought together various strands of metropolitan and provincial music-making. These included London's Concerts of Antient Music (1776–1848), whose aristocratic directors were the organisers of the Commemoration. The exclusive concerts established a diverse, cosmopolitan, sophisticated musical repertoire. Handel's slow and reflective opera arias and the grand choruses from the oratorios sat alongside sixteenth- and seventeenth-century madrigals, Corelli, as well as concerti, operas, and sacred works from the first half of the eighteenth century. This emerging canon of recognised great works allowed for a moralising reading of the music. 'Ancient music' formed a bulwark against 'degraded' modern music, considered to be dominated by profit-making, vulgar fashion worship, and sheer virtuosity. In political terms, a Tory, High Church tradition of learned music was transformed by the 1780s into a less partisan form, in which state and church remained, however, the foundations.

Another influence on the Commemoration were the metropolitan and provincial music meetings and choir festivals. Over the century, cathedral festivals grew in length and in the number and quality of performers; they also moved from new music to old, gradually enshrining Handel at their core. These gatherings established a musical public beyond regular concert goers. Choral concerts were grafted on to provincial civic calendars. At the Three Choirs festivals, held from around

1718 in Gloucester, Hereford, and Worcester, the *Messiah* (performed annually throughout 1757–84) could integrate communities across the divides of party, class, or religious belief, though Handel as a local ritual also assumed locally specific socio-political colouring. By 1784, Handel was clearly part of the national musical tradition in ways which had the potential to merge the learned and cosmopolitan approach of the aristocratic Concerts of Antient Music with the more popular and national strands of the music meetings.

In London in late spring 1784, the composer and music critic John Marsh was preparing for the forthcoming concerts. He repeatedly checked up on preparations at the Abbey and the pantheon and received a personal briefing from the chief impresario, Joah Bates.[13] This Cambridge-educated organist and conductor of comparatively modest northern English background was a mid-level mediator between the worlds of politics and culture. Bates was a civil servant protégé of the Earl of Sandwich as well as the manager of his musical affairs and director of the Concert of Antient Music (1776–93). In May, Marsh went to the Festival of the Sons of the Clergy to have a comparison 'of the effect intended' by over 500 performers at the forthcoming Commemoration. Sixty performers sounded indeed 'weak and languid'; the planned masses would better 'fill the lofty & extensive *nave* of the Abbey'. The sheer quantity of performers planned for the Commemoration was greater even than at the grandest historical occasions anywhere in Europe that Burney or his foreign witnesses could remember.[14]

Such large forces – the printed list of performers runs to five pages of three columns each – relied on the vibrant musical scene of the capital. Over the previous century, there had been a gradual shift of musical patronage from the court, church, and aristocratic households, to the capital's theatres and assembly rooms. A veritable explosion of concerts just before George III's accession made them pre-eminent among London's entertainments in the first few decades of his reign. Entrepreneurial musicians combined various sources of patronage and income – from the Chapel Royal and King's and Queen's Band, the venues of collective aristocratic patronage such as at the Italian Opera and the Concerts of Antient Music, as well as churches, municipal and military bands, and commercial concerts at Drury Lane and Vauxhall Gardens. Only London could then supply such forces, and the Commemoration would become a model for monumental performances across the British Isles and further afield.[15]

On the big day, Wednesday, 26 May 1784, John Marsh saw his hairdresser at 7 a.m., had coffee, chocolate, and muffins at a coffee house in New Palace Yard, and approached the Abbey just as a long train of coaches was arriving. Marsh was 'obliged to push & squeeze as much as I could to get near the door'. At 9 a.m., 'we

14. [E. F. Burney], *View of the ORCHESTRA and Performers in Westminster Abbey during the Commemoration of HANDEL* (1785). Contemporaries admired James Wyatt's theatrically raked platform for orchestra and choir, and the terraced audience galleries in both aisles. The kettle and tower drums are being vigorously beaten on either side of the organ. Facing the orchestra, and backing on to the choir screen, was the Gothic royal box, with stalls for the hierarchies of state and church on either side.

123

all thronged into the Abbey, in w'ch there was pretty near as great a squeeze as in mobbing it into the pit at the theatre on a crowded night'. Remarkably no mishaps occurred 'except disshevell'd hair, and torn garments', as another commentator wrote later (fig. 14).[16]

Listeners and viewers were transported by the sublime spectacle of celestial music staged in the Abbey's sacred space. Above the orchestra was placed the organ 'in a Gothic frame, mounting to, and mingling with, the saints and martyrs in the painted glass on the west window'. The choir seemed to be 'ascending into the clouds ... as their termination was invisible to the audience'.[17] The seating plan made hierarchy visible, with special boxes for royalty and peers. The concerts' social inclusivity became a subject for satire, and one writer ridiculed how 5,000

> pleasure hunting people of all descriptions and from all parts of the kingdom were assembled, some dressed, some undressed, some noble, some ignoble, some vulgar, some fashionable, a small number that understood music, and a great number ... to whose ears the sacred songs of the blind fiddling chaunter in St Paul's church yard would have been equally delightful, as the full band and chorus in the Abbey.[18]

The *European Magazine* also detected a sense of the anarchic public in carnival mood: 'here we had all the youth, beauty, grandeur, and taste of the nation ... grouped in all the natural and easy appearance of the *pêle-mêle*'.[19]

At noon the court arrived and then, finally, appeared the king and queen with Prince Edward and three of the princesses, though they entered silently and not, to one pro-government paper's regret, to a ceremonial march.[20] Yet, this dramatised the impact of the first piece of music, which evoked the king's coronation in the same space twenty-three years earlier. As Lord Sandwich gave the sign, John Marsh was quite awestruck when

> the whole force of the orchestra with all the voices, full organ, trumpets, trombones, double drums, etc., burst upon us all at once, in the words 'Zadok the priest' etc. the force & effect of w'ch almost took me off my legs & caused the blood to forsake my cheeks.

Sylas Neville too found the 'effect of the first crash of such a band ... astonishing. Wonder mixed with pleasure appeared in every countenance'.[21] For Marsh the following movement 'was all ecstasy'. After the overture from Esther came the Dettingen Te Deum, which had been 'composed for a military triumph'. The numerous trumpets and various types of drums specially made for the occasion were 'introduced with great propriety'; the double-base drums 'except the destruction, had all the effect of the most powerful artillery'. The 'Tower-drums', a hemispherical type of kettle drum, had been specially brought over from the Ordnance stores, where they had been deposited as the Duke of Marlborough's trophies from Malplaquet (1709). The Te Deum served as a bombastic musical and symbolic performance of military triumphalism in the wake of imperial disaster.

After the secular concert at the Pantheon the following day, the third concert, on 29 May, saw over 500 musicians perform the *Messiah* at the Abbey. Burney considered the climaxing Hallelujah Chorus 'the triumph of HANDEL, the COMMEMORATION, and of the musical art.' As the orchestra

> seemed to ascend into the clouds and unite with the saints and martyrs represented on the painted glass in the west window, which had all the appearance of a continuation of the Orchestra, I could hardly refrain, during the performance of the Allelujah, from imagining that this Orchestra, so admirably constructed, skilled, and employed, was a point or segment of one of these celestial circles. And perhaps, no band of mortal musicians ever exhibited a more respectable appearance to the eye, or afforded a more extatic and affecting sound to the ear, than this.[22]

The choice of site was crucial to the patriotic purposes of the events. The Gothic coronation church of English and British kings communicated the nation's continuing grandeur through strong sensual impressions. The Venetian count Benincasa considered the jubilee an honour to mankind, but one of such 'grandeur and sublimity' that only the great English nation was 'capable of planning and executing'. Benincasa was enraptured by the sight of the Gothic temple being filled with 'the most beautiful and wealthy inhabitants of the first city in the universe', and that 'prodigious Orchestra, which never before had existence on the earth; and which by its admirable arrangement seemed like Music itself, to descend from the skies.'[23]

The Handel Commemoration was predominantly a patriotic British, and an Anglican and 'conservative', ritual. It had the potential to unite yet also to exclude. The patriotic spectacle promoted the king as the leader of the aristocracy and the nation. The organisers of the concerts came from relatively broad regional and political backgrounds and enjoyed varying relations with the monarch in 1783–4.[24] This is significant against the background of recent national politics. In spring 1783, the coalition of convenience between Charles James Fox and Lord North had forced itself upon the king. George especially detested Fox as the notoriously womanising and gaming Prince of Wales's tutor in debauchery. In December, the king rid himself of the government by killing Fox's contentious East India Bill through the constitutionally unacceptable bullying of members of the House of Lords. George sustained his new, 24-year-old Prime Minister, William Pitt, in a minority government until the following March, when the king dissolved Parliament just halfway into its seven-year term. The Foxites were being routed as Pitt was returned with a majority of 100. George III had finally come of age politically during the crises of the early 1780s, and Pitt's national triumph rewarded him with relative political stability until 1801.

At the Handel concerts, the king's supporters in the Lords and moderate opposition politicians dominated. Charles James Fox and some of the other more fervent opponents of the government were conspicuously absent. Foxites and radicals attacked the concerts as luxurious displays of the corrupt, closed aristocratic system of patronage, a critique that grew stronger over subsequent years. If the court and administration's intention was to stage a reunion of the political elite after the severe constitutional and political crises of the previous two years, then their success was limited.[25]

Both newspapers favouring and those opposed to the administration appreciated the Commemoration as a nationally and historically significant event and a potential force for civic harmony. Yet both sides also scored partisan points. The fervently oppositional *Morning Herald* sniped at sloppy ticket distribution and snarled at the Lord Chancellor's ecclesiastical partisanship.[26] The pro-government *Morning Post* gloried in Fox's defeat in the recent Westminster election:

> From the effect of the music in the Jubilee, softening and humanizing the hearts of men of both parties, a correspondent thinks it were proper to have a good band of music in St. Stephen's Chapel [of the House of Commons]. Mr Fox's petition might be accompanied with "Fallen is the Foe," etc., and the committee sit to the Dead March in *Saul*.[27]

For the *Public Advertiser*, the Commemoration was a triumph not just of the Prime Minister but of the British constitution: 'his Majesty's assent was with it … the Aristocracy also supported it … and last not least in all matters of entertainment and expense by the *Majesty of the People*'.[28]

One particular ideological criticism related to the use of churches as the state's cultural branch. The Evangelical poet William Cowper lamented:

> A religious service instituted in honor of a Musician, and performed in the house

of God, is a subject that calls loudly for the animadversion of an enlighten'd minister, and would be no mean one for a Satyrist, could a poet of that description
be found spiritual enough to feel and to resent the profanation ... it would surely
puzzle the Pope himself to add anything to [Handel's] Canonization.[29]

The 1784 concerts confirmed Handel as a national hero. John Brewer writes
that his oratorios became an 'essential ingredient in Britain's patriotic repertory of
"ancient" and pious music, a repertory that stood against foreign innovation and
invasion'. This reading grew, if anything, more compelling from the American to the
French Revolution.[30] The memory of the London festivals helped music meetings
throughout the British Isles to prosper; Handel was soon performed in secular halls
too. Handel as a local ritual had an integrating function in Birmingham, Leeds, and
Norwich, where genteel Whigs and dissenters led charity oratorio performances.
But they were more partisan in the narrower social bases in the north, where they
were organised by industrial and artisanal dissenters independently of the gentry.

Not everyone agreed with the massed forces and the sonic effects of Handel's
thickly textured music in the Abbey: 'The force of music does not depend entirely
on an increased harmony'. But the site and the combined sensual impact of sights
and sounds left strong impressions on many spectators, who tried to express their
reactions to such sublime sensual near-overload. Neville was amazed at 'so many
voices, such prodigious kettle drums, that most powerful instrument the trombone
& the loftiness of the place so well adapted to give the highest effect to musical
sound', though he wondered what an effect the same performances would have
had in 'a magnificent Italian church'. The Irish playwright John O'Keefe, a friend of
chorus master Samuel Arnold, let himself be happily overwhelmed by the 'immense
burst of sound' at the first concert, only to have to retreat because of claustrophobia.
One newspaper commented on the *Messiah*: 'The immense volume and torrent of
sound was almost too much for the head or the senses to bear – we were elevated
into a species of delirium.'[31]

The sublime emotions, tears, and ecstasy experienced by those present notwithstanding, the Commemoration also marked a change in the conduct of musical
audiences of Handel and later Haydn. Previously, at the opera, oratorio, and instrumental concerts, the public had 'chatted, moved from box to box and seat to seat,
and paid only intermittent attention to the performance'. But at the 1784 Commemoration the audience had listened with silent, awed attention.[32] During the Coronation Anthem, from the 'first sound ... to the final close, every hearer seemed afraid
of breathing, lest it should obstruct the stream of harmony in its passage to the ear'.
The Te Deum was performed to 'the most mute and eager attention in the audience'.

Indeed, 'such a stillness reigned, as, perhaps, never happened before in so large an assembly. The midnight hour was never sounded in more perfect tranquillity'.[33]

Handel's oratorios were also hits in the English cultural export market; the London Commemoration was reviewed from Berlin to Boston. Although there had been some earlier performances in Florence, Vienna, and Hamburg, as well as in North America, the success of London's 1784 concerts triggered a wave of monumental performances around Europe.[34]

~

The Handel jubilee reaffirmed the king's authority and asserted the value of a national unity that was orchestrated around the crown. Until 1784, George had taken little interest in Handel, yet by attending a whole series of concerts and by encouraging Handelmania after the festival, George presented himself as the nation's moral and cultural leader. The monarch posed as protector of the civic verities of honour, liberty, and loyalty, which were key to the oratorio libretti, and as the upholder of excellent musical taste. George III promoted a series of further commemorations in five of the following seven years; these only ended in 1791 amid royal–aristocratic strife.[35] When, in 1784, the king had spontaneously demanded an encore of the 'Hallelujah' chorus in the *Messiah*, he began to perform his own apotheosis. The royalist Burney hymned that this was 'to the great satisfaction of all his happy subjects present'.[36]

With the international conflict settled and William Pitt's government consolidated after his electoral triumph in 1784, the king still remained involved in the business of government. But now that the suspicions of double-dealing and accusations of bad government, which had haunted his early reign, had been lifted, George's biographer Stella Tillyard explains how he began 'to step back from his intense emotional involvement in the nation's politics.' The king's personal virtues and habits, his economy, fidelity, and piety, gradually came to match the public mood. Embracing the quasi-sacred performance of Handel as a national ritual was a part of that synchronisation. An assassination attempt in 1786, and soon dramatic illness and the nation's recognition of the frailty of the king's physical body, endeared George to his subjects and furthered his apotheosis.[37]

The king now also invested in rehabilitating chivalry and the Gothic in a royal and national cultural programme. From c.1786 to 1789, Benjamin West painted seven large scenes from the life of Edward III, Queen Philippa, and the Black Prince for the Audience Chamber at Windsor Castle. They represent the king and prince fighting the French and showing magnanimity in victory. Edward III was one of Windsor Castle's greatest builders as well as the founder of the Most Noble Order of the Knights of the Garter in 1348. The paintings were exhibited at the Royal Academy (1787–94) and then hung in the Audience Chamber, which George III envisaged as a Garter Throne Room.[38] West had by then already started work on one of the most extensive projects in British art history, namely three dozen Old and New Testament scenes for a new Chapel of Revealed Religion at Windsor. However, in autumn 1788 this work was thrown into uncertainty, like the rest of court life, when George III suffered what has been thought to have been a serious porphyria attack. For half a year, as the king appeared to have gone mad, the Whig opposition tried to install the Prince of Wales as Regent. Yet Pitt's government held out just long enough for the king to recover by spring 1789.

The king's history painter marked the occasion with the emblematic picture *George III Resuming Power in 1789*. The monarch – illuminated by a burst of divine light – strides confidently towards the throne with the crown and sceptre, the royal standard flying on Windsor Castle's Round Tower behind. To the left of the throne, members of the House of Lords stand in front of a Corinthian column inscribed 'Honour' and listing the number of peers who had voted for the king. Members of the Commons gather in front of a Doric column, 'Virtue', also with their number of votes. To the right, the doctors who had cured the king stand in front of a Doric column of 'Science'.[39]

The king's recovery prompted repeated illuminations of the streets of Windsor and of London's public buildings. A celebratory dinner was held at St George's Hall at Windsor Castle. Over 750 localities and groups from around Britain presented loyal addresses to the king, twice as many as the total of all petitions prompted by the seven most controversial issues since mid-century.[40] George III wanted the nation to celebrate the monarchy with patriotic and pious pomp. When the next grand scene of royal apotheosis was enacted at St Paul's Cathedral, the Prime Minister and top clergy acted as choreographers-national. They also inaugurated an unprecedented and more formally codified programme of state investment in patriotic culture. As Britain fought a world war against Revolutionary and Napoleonic France, a unique military pantheon evolved at St Paul's. Like governments in war-torn Europe, Britons built memorials as a way of pursuing the conflict at a symbolic level. In doing so, they developed their own ways and styles of heroic commemoration.

BRITAIN, EUROPE, EMPIRE

'PRETENSIONS TO PERMANENCY'

A Temple of British Fame

On St George's Day, 1789, King George III and his still young Prime Minister, William Pitt, reinvented St Paul's Cathedral in the City of London as a site of national ceremony. For the first time in nearly a century, since Queen Anne had celebrated the Duke of Marlborough's victories in the War of the Spanish Succession, the Cathedral was thrust into the national limelight.[1] On 23 April, the king and queen triumphantly processed in a glass coach drawn by eight cream-coloured horses, past cheering crowds and buildings decked in crowns and flags, from Westminster to the City of London. As the procession arrived at St Paul's, the band played 'God Save the King' and the guns at the Tower fired a salute. The king had personally chosen the Psalm (100), 'Make a joyful noise unto the LORD, all ye lands … Enter into his gates with thanksgiving', and the Old Testament lesson, 'And in that day thou shalt say, O LORD, I will praise thee: though thou wast angry with me, thine anger is turned away, and thou comfortedst me' (Isaiah 12). In his sermon, the Bishop of London asserted that the king 'in his person, [represents] every thing that is dear and valuable to us, as Men, as Britons, and as Christians'. After the bitter divisions of the Regency crisis, the congregation and the nation at large were asked to 'let this day be the æra of general harmony and concord'.[2]

St Paul's Cathedral, rebuilt by Sir Christopher Wren after the Fire of London in the late seventeenth century, was a point of geographical and psychological orientation for Londoners, Britons, and foreign visitors alike. As a landmark in London

15. Thomas Malton, *Interior View of the Transept of St Paul's Cathedral* (1797).

topography it featured prominently on the scenic itineraries of public buildings and historic tours outlined in London guidebooks. Hundreds of engravings and paintings circulated; there were majestic depictions of St Paul's from across the river in Greenwich, close-up views from along Fleet Street and up Ludgate Hill, and panoramas of the London cityscape as seen from the Cathedral's dome, the first such structure in the British Isles (fig. 15).

While British and polite foreign tourists marvelled at the sublime spectacle of the vast edifice, many were annoyed with the rushed twopence-tours of the Great Model, Geometrical Staircase, Library, Whispering Gallery, and Bells. Foreigners also expressed their disgust with the 'void, barren' space and the 'disagreeable effect of the nudity' in the Cathedral.[3] For until the 1790s, the only decoration was scenes from the life of St Paul barely visible high up in the cupola. These were by Sir James Thornhill, who had been chosen (so the Archbishop of Canterbury said) as the only Englishman and Protestant among five competitors for the task. There were also standards taken 'at different times from the enemies of England, *at the price of blood'* – the Duke of Marlborough's Blenheim colours and Wolfe's Canadian trophies framing the nation's recent martial history.[4]

For much of the century, anti-Catholic sentiment and a puritan fear of idolatry had severely circumscribed church patronage of the arts. As late as 1773, a plan under the auspices of the Royal Academy to introduce historical paintings and monuments to St Paul's had been vetoed by the ecclesiastical authorities, ostensibly on grounds of fear of idolatry. By the century's end, however, the Anglican hierarchy accepted that (the right kind of) art and church music had the capacity to teach Christian virtues and inspire piety. Changing political circumstances had helped; the French Revolution revived a desire for the church as a defender of Christian culture in the face of French cultural and atheistic anarchy.[5]

In 1791, the Cathedral authorities finally responded to the hopeless cluttering of Westminster Abbey with monuments. As Sainte-Geneviève, the patron church of Paris, was being converted into the French Revolutionary Panthéon, St Paul's was styled the 'Temple of British Fame' or the 'National Temple of Fame'.[6] Some thirty national military monuments had been erected in the Cathedral by the time Napoleon was defeated at Waterloo in 1815. The Cathedral was most famous as the place of military heroes – Nelson's tomb lay at the very heart of the crypt under the dome. But with the funerals of cultural leaders such as the composer William Boyce (1779) and Sir Joshua Reynolds (1792) and the monuments to Reynolds, the lexicographer Dr Johnson, and the Orientalist Sir William Jones, London's emblem was fast becoming a British cultural shrine. The monarchy, and the civic and military branches of the state, used the Cathedral as a primary site for national celebration, mourning, and commemoration.[7]

Today, this national pantheon is hardly noticed by the millions of Cathedral visitors. Some may linger for a moment or two in front of individual statues, but since many monuments have been moved from their original positions, and as most of the heroes other than Nelson are hardly household names, not many will have a sense of the scheme as a coherent project. To fully understand the pantheon, we need to re-create it in our imagination as both an ambitious political and a cultural and artistic experiment. And because such politico-cultural projects were conceived in competition with other nations, a comparison with French and Prussian commemorative practices will help highlight the British pantheon's particular qualities.

As Britain embarked on a very long conflict with France, it became the senior partner or leader in changing coalitions of Europe's old monarchies. The British monarchy and the person of the king increasingly focused the nation's loyal devotion. Many in France initially saw the Panthéon in Paris as the answer to

Westminster Abbey, which Voltaire had misrepresented as the site where *the state* selected the British nation's great men for burial and commemoration (while, as we have seen, in fact almost all monuments had been privately commissioned). In the 1790s, the Constituent Assembly converted the church of Sainte-Geneviève into a temple of the fatherland to receive the bodies of great men, 'beginning with the era of our liberty'.[8] This Panthéon was to be the central sanctuary of the new regime, an educational centre where tombs, monuments, and ceremonies would help form the new citizen by emulating the example of the great man.[9]

Voltaire's description better fitted St Paul's, which the British compared with French commemorative efforts. Les Invalides, inaugurated by Napoleon as the French temple of military glory, also served comparable purposes to St Paul's in their respective national contexts. They both were spaces for military state funerals. Victory celebrations at Les Invalides corresponded to national thanksgiving services at St Paul's. Under the dome of St Paul's, French colours were dedicated as British trophies, while medals of the Order of the Legion of Honour were awarded under the dome of Les Invalides. But Napoleon, who derived a large part of his legitimacy from his success as a war leader, also turned Les Invalides into the necropolis of France's military heroes and used its impressive spaces for military ceremonial. He ordered the ritual translation of the remains of the seventeenth-century general Henri Turenne and the burial of his military commanders at Les Invalides.[10] In 1800, the veterans of France were also given supreme guardianship over recently captured enemy flags from the (lost!) Egyptian campaign and Italian triumphs. But British visitors during the Peace of Amiens noted gleefully (though probably with patriotically selective eyesight) that only a handful among the hundreds of foreign flags were English, while St Paul's displayed many more French trophies. After the stupendous victories of Jena and Auerstedt in 1806, Napoleon supervised the transferral of Frederick the Great's sword and decorations from Potsdam: Napoleon's dynasty and nation were to guard the memory of a great soldier whose own decadent successors were considered incapable of doing so.[11]

Against the backdrop of these French developments, the British state invested in an innovative, coherent, and expensive programme of commemoration. While the statues of statesmen continued to be erected in Westminster Abbey, Parliament invented a British military pantheon at St Paul's.[12] This was a project wholly unprecedented in British history, built by and for an embattled nation in need of reassurance. French Revolutionaries had killed King Louis XVI, were executing some 16,000 supposed internal enemies in the Terror, and were seeking to export their ideals by war and conquest; in Britain it was feared that radical sympathisers would provide a fifth column in the event of a successful invasion. Pitt's government limited political liberties. It also sponsored a propaganda campaign to encourage loyalty to the crown and draw attention away from those calling for political reform. Over the next decade, men were urged to join one of the mobilised land forces – the army, militia, or volunteers – and many hundreds of thousands did. Subscriptions for the war effort raised millions of pounds from all parts of the country and virtually all sections of society. In this context, in Britain, as elsewhere in war-torn Europe, to build monuments was to pursue the war by other means. In the pantheon, British politicians and artists sought to embody notions of patriotism, national stereotypes, and perceptions of the French enemy. At St Paul's, with an investment of which only the state was capable, the British were thus trying to beat the French at their own propagandistic game. In the process, they developed their own ways and style of commemoration.

Monuments to war heroes were intended to appeal to Britons' reason and to their emotions. In 1811, William Attfield, a 21-year-old student at Oriel College, Oxford, won the Chancellor's English prize competition for his essay on 'Funeral and Sepulchral Honours'.[13] Monuments to illustrious men, Attfield explained, prompted emulation by the few men who were born for heroic action and with a love of glory. The less heroic majority were still inspired by 'monumental edifices whereby the gratitude of the nation would perpetuate the glory of its benefactors'. For, if even the historical narration of great deeds aroused virtuous feelings, how much stronger would the impression be if memory was prompted by sculptured memorials with inscriptions and 'the very image and countenance' of the persons commemorated. Monuments spoke

> to the feelings of the spectactor with a language and an eloquence which he only could resist who is more or less than man. These scenes of august and sacred imagery are indeed a school for the public mind: they are the national galleries furnished and adorned, not with pieces of rare art, but with monuments of exalted virtue; to give a model of noble taste and design in the true business of man, and rear artists of enterprise, patriotism, and magnanimity ... sepulchral honours [also] strengthen the attachment ... for our native land.[14]

Attfield's piece encapsulates standard contemporary views on the potential of commemorative monuments: he stressed the didactic and moralistic potential of monumental sculptures and sites, and their capacity to promote emulation. He appreciated the immediate sensual, emotional, and intellectual impact of the commemoration. By referring to the 'sacred imagery' and the 'national galleries' of virtue, Attfield related the concept of the monument to sites of pilgrimage, the mausoleum, and the museum. He engaged with the belief, rooted in Greek thought, that the 'great man' lives on in his monument and in the memory of those who are meant to view it. Finally, monuments promoted the national arts and fostered patriotism among both artists and the wider nation.

The medium of sculpture was considered the most pedagogically effective form of public art: the solid marble promised eternity; the medium forced the artist to focus on a single expressive gesture; the three-dimensional medium was more life-like than painting; and, theoretically at least, monuments were easy to set in scene in ceremonies staged around them. The code of the monument bears an analogy with the code of the nation: both need to be 'realised' and completed by the person who thinks of the nation and who contemplates the monument. A monument as a symbolic representation of the nation enables viewers to identify themselves with that larger entity. As a collection of 'great men' of a society or nation, and the physical site of their representation, a 'pantheon' is a particularly potent manifestation of the national monument, which seeks to perpetuate a moment in a nation's history, an event, person, or group of persons, and thus to encapsulate national identity in a permanent symbol.[15] The hope was that by highlighting patriotic and heroic values, public sculpture commemorating military achievements would foster emulation.

As with war literature, it is difficult to ascertain whether monuments actually inspired others to sacrifice their lives, rather than offering comfort that the sacrifice of others was duly acknowledged. Perhaps inspiration was mostly gained in personal contact with fighting friends and relatives, in competition with peers, and in the direct emulation of officers? But studies of the relations between soldier and citizen show that the 'raising of willing armies is best accomplished when military ideals are maintained at a simmer and their representations and values are kept fresh by commemoration [and] national myths'.[16] Contemporaries clearly believed that monuments were there 'to delight, astonish, elevate, or sway the *minds* of others, through the medium of their *senses*'.[17] And the political elites certainly invested in the pedagogical power of national monuments and considered pantheon-building an integral, if secondary part of the war effort.

Those who could not visit London or pay their way into the Cathedral might see prints of the national monuments. Contemporaries' participation in commemorative culture, and their experience of monuments, was indeed mediated by all sorts of imagery – heroes' portraits in oil and on pottery, representations of battles in panoramas, paintings, and prints, and of gallant sailors on textiles, patch boxes, fans, and other emotionally charged and useful memorabilia (see fig. 6). Britons made sense of the national monuments in relation to written and spoken texts, including military gazettes, sermons, heroes' biographies, and poems; and their appreciation of the pantheon was framed by public spectacles, from military plays, aquatic and equestrian drama, ship launches, and Nelson's quasi-regal processes through the country to victory and peace celebrations, including at St Paul's itself.

There has been a perception that the British state was either unable or unwilling to produce spectacles to impart a special sense of grandeur in the fashion of Europe's absolutist rulers and revolutionary regimes. Revolutionary France undoubtedly placed great significance on the arts as a means of political education and propaganda. Even at the height of political crises, the Committee of Public Safety set up art competitions. The Directory considered republican museums, civic temples, triumphal arches, and victory columns. Architectural projects were increasingly militaristic (though the amount of propaganda art actually built was meagre) and the painter Jacques-Louis David organised grand civic and military spectacles for the Revolutionaries and Napoleon.[18]

But Britons too used processions, art, and music to dramatic effect – not only at coronations, but at national thanksgivings, troop and fleet reviews, and occasionally at the funerals of national heroes. This is particularly true of the period of the French Wars. Against the backdrop of spectacular French Revolutionary festivals, St Paul's became the centre of the nation's ceremonial life. To distinguish British ceremonies from French pageantry, the British focused on the monarchy, aristocracy, and the church, and stressed the antiquity of British customs in the face of new-fangled ideals across the Channel.[19]

By holding a national thanksgiving service in December 1797, the king and government sought to boost public morale after the invasion crisis of the summer and the naval mutiny at the Nore, which had in part been inspired by political radicalism. The Foreign Secretary, Lord Grenville, advocated the need for the 'raising of people's spirits': 'if we had done in this war half that our enemies have done to raise the courage and zeal of their people, we should not now be where we are'.[20] The service marked the start of an unusually concerted government campaign to mobilise the population behind the war effort. This involved the expansion of volunteering, the launch of the 'voluntary contribution', and the official demonisation of the enemy and of internal opposition. It also featured a government-sponsored project for a national naval pillar, the first attempt to raise a heroic monument by public subscription.

The service was full of pageantry and drew on traditions both recent and historic. It was modelled partly on the 1789 service, and partly on the Elizabethan spectacle at the old St Paul's after the defeat of the Armada just over two centuries before. Enemy flags were paraded through London's streets past well-behaved crowds estimated to be an astonishing 200,000 strong – roughly the size of the amassed militias of England and Wales at the height of mobilisation. French, Dutch, and Spanish flags captured in battles from the Mediterranean to the Cape were carried by 250 marines and ordinary seamen, a controversial decision which was backed by the king and set a precedent for Nelson's funeral in 1806. After the first lesson the flags were ceremonially deposited on the altar. Pitt had chosen 2 Samuel 22 – David's song to the Lord after He had rescued him from his enemies – as the text for the sermon. He advised that sentences on the naval mutiny be omitted from the draft. Bishop Pretyman praised commanders for their zeal and skill, and seamen for their intrepid spirit, and emphasised 'that God, who governs the world by His providence, never interposes for the preservation of men or nations without their own exertions'. While '[t]he King appeared devout', although he put 'occasionally his glass to His eye', Pretyman lauded the navy and explained the war with France as a struggle for English liberties, for Christianity, and for national independence against an enemy who had insulted the majesty of heaven.[21]

The service symbolised the links between the state, the church, the navy, and the City of London, the commercial heart of the Empire that the navy was fighting to protect. The king, government, and Anglican hierarchy sought to create an image of British national unity against the background of the recent mutiny, divisive tax policies, and economic hardship.[22] The 250 seamen and marines played a key role in this patriotic performance. Britons of all classes could participate – whether as part of the procession, among the thronging crowds, or as newspaper readers or spectators of the engravings published around the occasion. But taking on the French in the business of 'raising the people's spirits' was not only an ambitious but also an ambiguous undertaking. Conservatives did not like the obvious connections with Revolutionary ceremonial, and denounced the parading of other ranks as a 'Frenchified farce'. Moreover, whereas some criticised the projection of state power in a church, for others the occasion was a successful Christian counter-cultural riposte to France's Revolutionary festivals.[23]

Throughout the British Isles, Anglican and dissenting preachers painted a terrifying picture of the French atheistic monster from whom only divine providence, a pious monarch, and the Royal Navy had thus far protected Britain.[24] The public feast day allowed ordinary Britons all around the country to participate imaginatively in national affairs. Thomas Butler, whose Yorkshire family firm manufactured spades and shovels, pudding dishes and pokers, recorded in his diary:

> Today is appointed by Royal Proclamation to be a day set apart to return thanks to Almighty God for his Wonderful deliverances wrought for us in Giving us three Such Signal Victories over our Enemies at Sea ...| The King in all his Royal

16. Isaac Cruikshank, *The Victorious Procession to St. Pauls or Billy's Grand Triumphal Entry* (11 Dec. 1797).

Attire: With all the Peers in their Robes &c &c &c are to March in procession to St Paul's – and there to dedicate to the Lord the Colours taken in the forementioned Engagements: at the same time to render thanks to the Almighty for such remarkable Instances of his favor: and humbly to Implore Divine assistance in future: so that our Enemies may never have power over us.

Mr. Miles gave us an excellent Sermon this morning on the Occasion.[25]

Back in London, ordinary people found difficulty celebrating naval victory in the face of heightened taxation; indeed, radicals used the occasion to demonstrate against Pitt's tax rises. Isaac Cruikshank made a print (fig. 16): the Prime Minister is riding a muzzled bull (John Bull) on a heavy saddle made of taxes. On the day, Covent Garden produced a 'new Musical Farce', *Britain's Brave Tars; or, All for St Paul's*, which focused on the fiscal prudence of Londoners hiring out their apartments to spectators.[26] The Prime Minister was hissed, heckled, and pelted on his way to the Cathedral; in various parts of London, he was burned in effigy. Cavalry had to escort Pitt back to Downing Street.

If the 1789 service had set the scene for the martial pantheon at St Paul's, the ceremony in 1797 helped trigger its initiation. By August 1798, George III at St James's Palace put crosses against his favourite design for each monument: Charles Rossi's Captain Faulknor; John Flaxman's Captain Montague and John Bacon's Captains Harvey and Hutt, all casualties of the 'Glorious First of June' 1794; the same sculptor's Major-General Dundas, the first army officer admitted to the pantheon, for amphibious operations in the West Indies; and Thomas Banks's design for a statue of Captain Rundell Burgess (Battle of Camperdown). It was the Treasury, initially under Long's direction, which chose positions for the monuments, negotiated clerical permissions and fees, and supervised the execution of statues. Over the next quarter-century, a total of £117,075 (over three times the sum Parliament spent on the Elgin Marbles in 1816 prices), and many hours of parliamentary debate and connoisseurial consideration, would be committed to building the pantheon. The first three monuments were erected in 1801–5 on the inside of three of the four great piers at the entrances to the north and south transepts, demonstrating the aim to develop a spatially coherent ensemble.[27]

Between 1798 and 1801, the House of Commons voted another four monuments: to Captain Westcott (Nile); to Admiral Howe, with 'an Inscription expressive of the public Sense of his great and meritorious Services in the Course of a long and distinguished Life', with particular recognition of his 'brilliant Victory ... over the French Fleet on the 1st Day of June 1794'; to Captains Mosse and Riou (Copenhagen); and to General Abercromby (amphibious operations in Egypt).[28] In 1802, the Treasury set up regular administrative procedures: a committee for national monuments, popularly known as 'The Committee of Taste', of initially seven leading connoisseurs and collectors chaired by Charles Long, was appointed to supervise competitions, select designs, award commissions, and supervise the progress and erection of monuments. They included men who also distinguished themselves as collectors of British paintings and classical antiquities, such as Sir George Beaumont, Charles Towneley, Richard Payne Knight, Henry Bankes – a published historian of Rome and unofficial parliamentary spokesman for the British Museum – the Marquises of Buckingham and Stafford as well as Thomas Hope. The government wanted national monuments to 'be the best Testimonies of the Taste of the age in which such works are executed.' By drawing on the expertise of both private and public figures, the state gradually developed coherent administrative procedures out of ad hoc arrangements. External expert advice was to ensure coherence of designs and use of space. Standard prices were fixed for commissions, relating military rank to the price and hence, to a degree, to the format and size of monuments: admirals and generals (and prime ministers) in marble were worth 6,000 guineas, captains 4,000. A Royal Academy committee of architects, sculptors, and painters advised on appropriate sites. When the Committee of Taste demanded alterations to designs, and occasionally even amalgamated several into one, artists were understandably frustrated with a method which would lead to the 'alternative of insipidity or deformity'. In 1802, for instance, Charles Rossi was asked to execute the monument to Captains Mosse and Riou at 4,000 guineas, 'partly from his design for Lord Howes monument and partly of an Idea proposed by the Committee'.[29] Even for the prime commission, the monument of Nelson, the Committee of Taste charged John Flaxman with largely executing Richard Westmacott's design.

The death of Admiral Nelson at Trafalgar in October 1805 had initiated a third phase of pantheon-building. The Treasury now set the sums for individual commissions, drafted contracts, and paid instalments. The Committee of Taste ran national competitions, exhibited designs at the British Gallery (the display space of the British Institution recently founded by the same connoisseurial circles), and inspected sculptures on site.[30] For Prince Hoare it was a self-evident patriotic duty that national commissions went to British artists. He objected to the famous Italian sculptor Canova making a monument to Nelson:

> Are we to be taught to make statues, who have made men worthy of being immortalized by the statues? Are the heroes of our navy and army to die for their country, that some half-starved foreigner may live by making monuments for them? ... We might as well run to French captains to command our men of war, as import foreign artists to be employed upon our national works.[31]

All monuments were erected in the north and south transepts and the entrance to the choir. As far as possible in a scheme spanning eleven distinct phases over a quarter-century, monuments were placed so as to maintain symmetries both of military rank and of type of monument, both within and across the transepts. Thus, the highest-ranking officers, Nelson (see fig. 21) and the Marquis Cornwallis, were allocated the most prominent spaces against the two great piers on the north and south sides of the great eastern arch between the dome and the choir; in a juxtaposition of Trafalgar casualties, they were overlooked by Nelson's captains Cook and Duff. The positioning of monuments also prompted correspondences of form. The Moore and Collingwood monuments, which occupy matching positions in the south transept, are both long and low-lying, Admiral Collingwood's body resting on an antique prow, General Moore's being lowered into his grave. The pantheon clearly seemed to engage the public consciousness. Perceived violations of principles of arrangement were criticised in the papers, for instance when the joint monument to Captains Mosse and Riou (with its two sad lions on one sad sarcophagus) was allocated a position corresponding to those of the much more senior Admiral Howe and General Abercromby.[32]

From around 1810, hierarchical principles of arrangement were not strictly adhered to and the monetary value of individual monuments decreased. From 1812, we find smaller monuments, wall tablets, and reliefs, and two heroes commemorated in one monument. In part this reflected a decrease in available space, a return to the mural monument typical of churches, and a concomitant concern with the preservation of the architecture of walls, columns, and arches. But, then,

17. Valentine Green, *The British Naval Victors* (published 1799). Popular portraits of Nelson, St Vincent, Howe, and Duncan are set among oak trees symbolic of steadfast English strength, and framed in drapery with details commemorating Britain's naval victories from 1794 to 1797. Dedicated to the king and watched over by God's eye, this commercial miniature pantheon celebrates naval supremacy under divine protection.

half the monuments in the pantheon were in fact voted between 1810 and 1815 for roughly a third of the scheme's overall expenses. The single largest group was nine monuments to eleven casualties of the Peninsular campaign. The others reflect the truly global dimensions of Britain's war and include honours to casualties of campaigns in Canada, the United States, Nepal, and Flanders, ending with monuments to Generals Picton and Ponsonby, who fell at Waterloo in 1815.

For those fighting a global war, the connections between battles and sites, regiments and ships, and heroes represented in the pantheon were real (fig. 17). In November 1798, the surgeon Gillespie at the Naval Hospital on Martinique noted in his journal the local illuminations for the Battle of the Nile (fought on 1 August) and the death of Captain Westcott, under whom he had previously served. Captain Hardinge had been onboard Miller's *Theseus* when it exploded at the siege of Acre; their monuments went up in St Paul's within roughly a decade from one another. Major-General Craufurd (pantheon 1812) led the charge at the Battle of Busaco in 1810 with the battle cry: 'Now, Fifty-second! Avenge the death of Sir John Moore!'

(pantheon 1809). *London Scenes* (1824) crowded twenty-three heroes into four stanzas; here are the first two:

> In monumental marble stand
> Nelson and Collingwood;
> Those brave defenders of our land, -
> The noble and the good.
>
> Fam'd Howe, and Abercrombie too,
> With gallant Moore, are here;
> Cornwallis and Dundas we view,
> and Crauford claims a tear.[33]

The Napoleonic-era pantheon was completed in 1823 when monuments were voted to the Earl St Vincent (who had then just died) and to Admiral Viscount Duncan to commemorate their lives dedicated to naval service in general, and particularly their 1797 victories over the Spanish and Dutch fleets respectively. Since the security now enjoyed by Britain was in large measure due to the Royal Navy, it was considered appropriate to honour these two admirals in peacetime, in the hope that they might inspire future generations. The imaginative effort maintained military ideals well into the post-war period.[34]

The Politics of Glory

The St Paul's pantheon needs to be understood as both a phenomenon in political culture and in cultural politics. It speaks to the constitution of the cultural state and to British political culture, reveals partisanship in heroic memorialisation, and highlights contests over the degree of inclusiveness of commemoration. The pantheon was jointly built by the crown, Parliament, and government. The crown traditionally recognised martial valour and achievement by creating Knights of the Order of the Bath (KB). Between 1793 and 1814, sixty-seven KBs were awarded. Membership of the Order, originally limited to thirty-five, expanded to seventy-two after 1812. In 1801, Nelson represented the king at a makeshift ceremony of investiture on board the *St George* in Kioge Bay, near the scene of the Battle of Copenhagen. Making Sir Thomas Graves a KB, Nelson expressed the hope

> that these honours conferred upon you will prove to the Officers in the service,
> that a strict perseverance in the pursuit of glorious actions, and the imitation of

144

your brave and laudable conduct, will ever insure them the favours and rewards of our most gracious Sovereign, and the thanks and gratitude of our country.[35]

The monarch had other ways to single out commanders for special attention. After Howe's victory against the Brest fleet, George III held a 'naval levee' onboard Howe's ship at Spithead and presented him with a diamond-hilted sword and a naval medal on a gold chain.[36] In 1797, the king also publicly thanked Duncan, though not Jervis, finely grading the degrees of royal attention bestowed on various admirals.

The highest, and most permanent, honour in the gift of the crown was of course a peerage. Thirty-three generals and admirals were ennobled between 1780 and 1830 (compared to three in 1750–79, although there were then also fewer peerages in general). Twenty-five of these remained in active service after they had been elevated. The award of peerages to military leaders was part of a broader shift towards rewards for distinguished public service, also encompassing civilian administration and diplomacy.[37] Armed service saw the greatest increase of all categories in 1750–1830, with inter-service rivalries intensifying competition over peerages. As with other honours, the rank of peerage to be awarded had to match primarily the rank of the officer, although specific achievements were also considered.[38] An important change in the crown system of honours for meritorious military and naval service was the extension of the award of medals to ships' commanders and battalion officers. After the Glorious First of June gold medals were awarded to flag officers and captains who had fought in successful fleet actions. Similarly, field officers in the army received medals from 1806.[39]

While the crown and government awarded titles and medals, Parliament had its own ways of recognising military service. This is hardly surprising, given that some 400 or just over 20 per cent of the MPs sitting in the British Parliament between 1790 and 1820 had served in the regular army at some stage, plus some 100 in the Royal Navy. During the wars of 1793–1815, 135 army officers were elected as MPs. The average number of army officer MPs returned to each Parliament between 1790 and 1818 was 136 (seventy-seven active), and of naval officers twenty-five. Some forty army officers each had served in the West Indies and India; twenty-five in Egypt; nearly 100 in the Peninsular War; twenty-five fought at Waterloo; several naval officer MPs had fought major battles. At least fifteen officer MPs died in or as a result of military action, forty more bore conspicuous wounds and mutilations. Seven of the army officers in the St Paul's pantheon, as well as Cornwallis, had been MPs, including two who were killed while serving in the House (Picton and Ponsonby at Waterloo), and three naval officers before they were elevated to the British peerage (Rodney, Howe, Jervis). In addition to officers in the regular forces, about half of the roughly 2,000 MPs served as militia or volunteer officers. Officers thus brought a considerable amount of military and naval expertise to the House, even if their parliamentary impact was limited. With most officer MPs sporting their uniform, the British Parliament had, in Linda Colley's trenchant formulation, 'not just become a military headquarters conducting a world war for territorial integrity, empire and property. It looked like a military headquarters as well.'[40]

Appreciative, then, of martial service, Parliament awarded pensions to officers: £3,000 to Jervis (St Vincent, 1797); £2,000 to Nelson (Nile, 1798). Parliament's most common mode of acknowledging military valour and victory was the formal vote of thanks, widely publicised in the press and pamphlets. After the first major battle of the war on the Glorious First of June, the Commons thanked Admiral Earl Howe 'for his able and gallant Conduct in the most brilliant and decisive Victory obtained over the *French* Fleet'. Certain named rear-admirals and all captains and officers also received the thanks of the House. In November 1797, peers were specially summoned to attend the Lords when the Lord Chancellor conveyed the thanks of the House to Admiral Lord Duncan for his service, especially the recent victory over the Dutch fleet and his stamina during the mutinies.[41]

Monuments as a relatively new form of honouring officers also spoke to Britain's constitutional system and political culture. Formally, the king and Parliament were the pantheon's joint founders: the monarch granted the Commons' formal request to give directions for monuments to be erected. With the king and later the Prince Regent taking a close interest in military spectacle, the pantheon's potential as a permanent focus for loyal commemoration and celebration was enhanced by its association with the monarchy as an important symbol of national unity. In this respect, the commemorative cultures of Britain, Napoleonic France, and Prussia were similar.

However, equally important was the role of Parliament in British political culture, and its enhanced role in honouring military service and organising national commemoration. Indeed, in Britain, monuments belonged more in the parliamentary than in the royal sphere: heroic monuments were decreed by 'the gratitude of the Nation and the wisdom of Parliament'.[42] Resolutions for the monuments were usually part of a wider range of parliamentary acknowledgements of naval and military service. Previous votes of thanks to officers were cited to justify a monumental award to heroes. Parliament had itself inscribed on monuments as the new (joint) fountain of honour, 'erected at the public expence', or at 'the national expence'.[43] Faulknor's monument was 'erected | By the British Parliament'. Burgess's inscription referred to the 'unanimous act' of the national legislature by which the country had enrolled his name among its heroes. Occasionally, a Commons vote was even incorporated verbatim in an inscription:

MAJOR-GENERAL THOMAS DUNDAS
DIED JUNE 3ᴰ 1794. AGED 44 YEARS:
THE BEST TRIBUTE TO WHOSE MERIT AND PUBLIC SERVICES
WILL BE FOUND IN THE FOLLOWING VOTE OF THE HOUSE OF COMMONS
FOR THE ERECTION OF THIS MEMORIAL
5TH JUNE, 1795. RESOLVED NEMINE CONTRADICENTE
THAT AN HUMBLE ADDRESS BE PRESENTED TO HIS MAJESTY, THAT
HE WILL BE GRACIOUSLY PLEASED TO GIVE DIRECTIONS, THAT A MONUMENT
BE ERECTED IN THE CATHEDRAL-CHURCH OF SAINT PAUL, LONDON,
TO THE MEMORY OF MAJOR-GENERAL THOMAS DUNDAS, AS A
TESTIMONY OF THE GRATEFUL SENSE ENTERTAINED BY THIS HOUSE, OF
THE EMINENT SERVICES WHICH HE RENDERED TO HIS COUNTRY,
PARTICULARLY IN THE REDUCTION OF
THE FRENCH WEST INDIA ISLANDS.

The foundation of the pantheon thus shifted the focus of national honours and commemoration from the government and crown towards the state in its distinctly British configuration, with Parliament at the centre.

Partisan Immortality

On the face of it the British were building a largely non-partisan pantheon, which contrasted with the highly partisan French Revolutionary Panthéon. At the Panthéon, mortality became transient. Successive regimes believed that they could decree immortality to signal their belief in the stability of the Revolutionary order. In fact, the Panthéon was largely an unsuccessful attempt to give permanent expression to Revolutionary ideals in a temple of great men. Its pedagogical value was seriously depreciated by frequent regime change. And as critics of the very notion of the Revolutionary pantheonisation of individuals pointed out, what was worth commemorating was less the individual action but rather the safeguarding of the Revolution itself.[44] After Mirabeau's funeral in the Panthéon in April 1791 his dealings with Louis XVI were revealed: his remains were removed on the occasion of the pantheonisation of Marat in 1794. One British visitor complained that although the Panthéon initially had been dedicated to men of genius and to civil or military servants to their country, it had now become a 'receptacle of departed maniacs'.

He ridiculed the inconsistency of throwing the remains of Mirabeau, the 'libertine advocate for public freedom', into the Seine as a royalist, while those of the royalist Voltaire stayed in the Panthéon. After Mirabeau's removal, the site received the 'corrupt carcases of that wretched little demoniac, Marat, and a multitude of *other sages*, who had rendered themselves worthy of immortality, by their villainies, their buffoonery, and their insanity'. Alas, before long 'Marat was tossed into the common sewer'.[45] Mirabeau's remains would have been restored to the Panthéon under the Directory in 1797, if only they could have been found.[46] British travellers during the Peace of Amiens ridiculed how the traffic of heroes in and out of the Panthéon reflected the frequent changes in the political regime.[47] Under Napoleon, the Panthéon's role changed from a national shrine of charismatic Revolutionary figures to the site where the emperor's loyal servants were commemorated. The Panthéon, now returned to the church, in 1806–15 received forty-two imperial dignitaries – eighteen generals and admirals, plus ministers and senators, cardinals, and a sprinkling of artists and scientists. Less politically volatile than during the Revolutionary era, the Napoleonic pantheon was biased in favour of imperial favourites.

While in Britain the progress of the war naturally determined the chronology of votes for individual monuments, and while Parliament influenced the selection of heroes, it was the government of the day that organised competitions. This handed successive administrations the power to use their control over timing to maximise the benefit they might reap from naval and military victories. Government propaganda regularly marketed the war – in the domestic press and London-based Francophone journals – by boasting of victories, excusing defeats, and justifying general strategy. The monuments, and the debates surrounding them, also provided such marketing opportunities.

The timing of the first competition manifestly followed a political logic. Over four years after the first monuments had been voted by Parliament, a competition was finally prepared in parallel with the great Naval Thanksgiving in December 1797. The design competition was run concurrently with the passing of the Defence of the Realm Act, which popularised civil defence, and with the collection of Pitt's 'voluntary contribution' of £2.8m in 1798. Viscount Castlereagh, the Secretary for War who built up local militias to the strength of 200,000, also became the government's chief spokesman on national monuments. As Foreign Secretary he would later reiterate that there was

> no better mode of providing for the defence of the country – of laying by a stock of public spirit and personal valour, upon which national security could more safely repose, than in the proper distribution of national honours.

Monuments preserved the memory of the dead and provided an incentive to the living, 'conducing at once to maintain the glory and the safety of the empire'.[48] The pantheon was grounded in, and in turn fostered, the notion of *fama*, a secular form of ensuring immortal glory, and *pietà* – the duty of surviving relatives and wider collectives to keep the honourable memory of the dead. Admiral Nelson exemplified how the modern British hero shaped his own cult and *fama* during his lifetime; with his state funeral, monument, and pilgrimages to his tomb and monument in St Paul's, *fama* and *pietà* merged.[49]

A political logic governed not only the pantheon's foundation but also successive phases of its expansion. The second competition, for instance, was set up immediately after the vote for the monument to General Abercromby of Egyptian fame (see fig. 18) Following Nelson's destruction of the French Fleet in 1798, Abercromby's victory over the French army in 1801 vindicated the British army's reputation after its European defeats throughout the 1790s. The government sought to capitalise on his triumph by refocusing public attention on the pantheon project. The proposal by Henry Addington, the Prime Minister, also underlined the continuity of government commitment to the pantheon after Pitt's resignation and the truce with France. Finally, the injection of new momentum into the project just after the foundation of the United Kingdom can be linked to the fact that Abercromby was the first prominent *Scottish* officer thus honoured. His monument celebrated Scotland's enhanced military role in the United Kingdom and the empire.

A major turn in the fortunes of war in a particular theatre could equally determine governmental timing over monuments. When the British captured Ciudad Rodrigo the French lost the strategic initiative in the Peninsula. By early 1812, the British parliamentary opposition had also made a *volte-face* and stopped publicly criticising Wellington's campaign and the government's conduct of the war. The government commissioned monuments to sustain this new political momentum. The offensive operations of 1812 climaxed in the Battle of Salamanca, and the victory at Vittoria in June 1813 effectively liberated all northern Spain except Catalonia. Within weeks, monuments were voted to the fallen heroes of both these battles, together with a monument to the first commanding officer killed in the new war with the United States, Major-General Brock (see fig. 27). Like the authorities in allied Prussia and arch enemy France, the British government was more adamant than ever that national martial honours such as monuments to the heroes of Baltimore, New Orleans, Kalunga, Bayonne, Bergen, and Waterloo were a vital means of boosting national morale by extending national and imperial defence into the realm of the imaginary.[50]

Partisanship over national heroism went further than governments attempting to time competitions strategically. Indeed, there was something of a tradition of political controversy in the commemoration of British officers, especially at Westminster Abbey.[51] The monument of one of the most prominent naval officers of the middle of the eighteenth century, the oppositional hero Admiral Vernon, was privately erected by a relative and beneficiary. It praised the distinguished officer as one who had 'retired, without Place or Title' and was isolated from public affairs, having only the 'testimony of a good conscience' as his 'reward'.[52] It is not surprising then that in the French Wars, government and opposition MPs alike again used (the now much more frequent) parliamentary debates on monuments for factional point scoring.[53] Press reports enhanced the impression of partisanship – the column inches and emphasis given to opposing views expressed the editor's political conviction.

Some monuments were proposed by the government of the day in an effort to contain opposition criticism of the conduct of the war. In January 1809, General Sir John Moore fell while successfully repulsing a French attack on the British army waiting to embark after its famous retreat to Coruña. With hindsight we know that Moore had done the allied cause a great service by diverting the French from the immediate advance to Lisbon and Seville. But when his army returned to England battered and in rags it provoked a political furore. Despite distrusting Moore, partly because he was associated more with the Whigs, ministers had appointed him commander of the 26,000-strong British army in Spain in 1808. At Coruña the dying general had anticipated posthumous controversy over his reputation: '*I hope the people of England will be satisfied! I hope my country will do me justice!*'[54]

As soon as news of Moore's death reached London, the struggle over his memory began. The Foreign Secretary, George Canning, had wanted to lay all blame on Moore, but the general's heroic death altered the terms of the political debate. The government felt compelled to change tack. It now led the tributes to Moore, moved parliamentary thanks to the British army, and called for a monument in St Paul's to the commander. Opposition speakers lauded Moore but were scathing about the government's 'ignorance and incapacity' – which, said Lord Moira, had sacrificed 'British blood and treasure' in a futile operation. But Castlereagh played the statesman. He reminded the House of Moore's last wish that his country should honour his memory and admonished the opposition that it ought not to mix the 'venom of party-feeling with sentiments more suited to the present solemn occasion'. The government would answer for its conduct were an inquiry to be conducted. The highly partisan contest over Moore's reputation intensified over subsequent decades, but the government's tactical move had, for the time being at least, blunted the attacks of the parliamentary opposition.[55]

Who's Allowed to be a Hero?

The politics of glory was contested not only with regard to those commissioning monuments, but also with respect to the criteria for eligibility for the pantheon. Occasionally, the very frequency of awards was queried. In 1795, Sir William Pulteney, by then a government supporter, criticised the House for being 'niggardly' in bestowing honours. He charged that British military advancement was governed by money rather than distinction, in contrast to other countries where 'any extraordinary act of skill or bravery was constantly rewarded'. Charles James Fox, a prominent opposition leader, agreed with the government on the need to keep honours limited and hence more coveted.[56] Similarly, the poet Robert Southey complained that Parliament seemed finally

> to have discovered the nakedness of this huge edifice, and to vote parliamentary monuments to every sea captain who falls in battle, for the sake of filling it as fast as possible. This is making the honour too common … It is only to those who are remembered that statues should be voted; only to those who live in the hearts and in the mouths of the people. 'Who is this?' is a question which will be asked at every statue; but if after the verger has named the person represented it is still necessary to ask 'Who is he?' the statue is misplaced in a national mausoleum.[57]

To an extent, the St Paul's pantheon was a parliamentary extension of the traditional system of honours granted by the crown and government. As with peerages and medals, monuments commemorating military and naval commanders were awarded as a function primarily of military rank. Commanding officers dying in the moment of victory were honoured with monuments to commemorate their leadership, strategic skills, or cautious foresight. Abercromby, Nelson, Cornwallis, Moore, and Ross were promoted as role models for subordinate officers, crews, and troops.[58] Commanders who survived important battles and died either peacefully, whether in active service or in retirement, or in later, less important action, were honoured with monuments as lifetime achievement awards. Particular acknowledgement was then made of their most important battles: Rodney and the Saints; Howe and the Glorious First of June; Duncan and Camperdown.

The highest-ranking junior officers killed in a significant battle often received a monument if all superior commanders survived. In rare instances they were sometimes included alongside their fallen chiefs. When Admirals Bowyer and Pasley each lost a limb but survived 1 June 1794, Captain James Montague as the highest-ranking casualty was memorialised.[59] Major-General Hoghton and Colonel

Cadogan, who died in the command of brigades in Sir Rowland Hill's 2nd Division at Albuera (1811) and Vittoria (1813) respectively, entered the pantheon as their superiors all lived.[60] Captain George B. Westcott was the highest-ranking British casualty in the Battle of the Nile in 1798. He received a monument, although his ship, the *Majestic*, overshot its likely intended position and mishandled the attack on the *Heureux*. It was essential to commemorate the highest-ranking officer killed in a victory on a new scale: a battle in which the Royal Navy destroyed or captured eleven French ships of the line plus two frigates.[61]

Tensions over the eligibility of particular men for the pantheon are manifest throughout the war. Captain Robert Faulknor (1763–95) first distinguished himself in the West Indies at the capture of Fort Royal on Martinique and the conquest of Guadeloupe in 1794. Surgeon Gillespie characterised Faulknor as a fiery hero:

> he seemed to be possessed of an insatiable thirst for glory, the whole turn of his conversation was on the acquisition of military fame and the signalizing himself in battle, he seems to have been ardent and impetuous in his disposition, though to have possessed a singular presence of mind in the greatest danger.[62]

Faulknor was killed in January 1795 in a brilliant frigate action, later recorded in vivid detail in the monument's inscription:

THIS MONUMENT WAS ERECTED
BY THE BRITISH PARLIAMENT
TO COMMEMORATE THE GALLANT CONDUCT
OF CAPTAIN ROBERT FAULKNOR,
WHO ON THE 5TH OF JANUARY 1795,
IN THE THIRTY-SECOND YEAR OF HIS AGE
AND IN THE MOMENT OF VICTORY
WAS KILLED ON BOARD THE BLANCHE FRIGATE
WHILE ENGAGING LA PIQUE, A FRENCH FRIGATE
OF VERY SUPERIOR FORCE
THE CIRCUMSTANCES OF DETERMINED BRAVERY, THAT DISTINGUISHED THIS ACTION,
WHICH LASTED FIVE HOURS, DESERVE TO BE RECORDED.
CAPTAIN FAULKNOR HAVING OBSERVED THE GREAT SUPERIORITY OF THE ENEMY,
AND HAVING LOST MOST OF HIS MASTS AND RIGGING,
WATCHED AN OPPORTUNITY OF BOWSPRIT COMING ATHWART THE BLANCHE,

AND WITH HIS OWN HANDS LASHED IT TO THE CAPSTERN,
AND THUS CONVERTED THE WHOLE STERN OF THE BLANCHE INTO ONE
BATTERY;
BUT UNFORTUNATELY SOON AFTER THIS BOLD AND DARING MANOEUVRE,
HE WAS SHOT THROUGH THE HEART.

In the Commons, Whig opposition leaders had demanded a monument to Faulknor's daring and heroic actions: would any of the 'great Heroes of England' honoured with monuments 'think themselves disgraced by an association with the gallant Faulknor'? The government opposed the motion, not because they did not consider Faulknor a valiant officer but because it was wrong to discuss individual merit and to reward any one-off and small-scale as opposed to 'general actions'. Such a precedent might invite unacceptable claims for honours for distinguished lieutenants and even midshipmen. The motion for a monument was nevertheless carried. What the case had shown was that – while modern, highly organised warfare valued simple obedience more than individual heroism – the pantheon possessed the potential to bridge obedient state service and the heroic: the heroic was admitted to the pantheon, though never below the rank of captain.[63]

On his design drawing, Charles Rossi indicated that Captain Faulknor's monument was to be 'an Allegory representing a Warrior falling in a Naval Action at the Moment of Victory'. The poorly conceived statue depicts Faulknor naked and dying in the embrace of Neptune, who is seated with a trident and a monstrous fish while a pretty Victory offers a laurel wreath. Faulknor's case nevertheless set a precedent for monumental honours to other young captains such as George Nicholas Hardinge, 'a stripling in years, yet … a veteran in achievements',[64] as well as for middling-ranking army officers of the Peninsular War.[65]

As Faulknor's inscription specifies, and as even Hardinge's not especially high-profile case shows, the selection of officers for the pantheon – both supreme commanders and more junior officers – was often justified with reference to the notions of precise heroic timing and of defeating a superior enemy. The topos of commanding officers dying 'at the moment of victory' relates the St Paul's pantheon to an important trope in the code of the warrior hero. Though mortally wounded, he would continue fighting in super-human fashion to present an example and leadership to his men. If eventually he had to die this was only after witnessing the victory he had delivered. The ideal was rehearsed in poetic eulogies and parliamentary rhetoric.[66] By contrast, Captain Hardinge's heroic timing in the Indian Ocean was less than perfect as he died, slightly prematurely, 'in the path to victory'. In his monument, a winged, mourning Victory holds a wreath in her hand that she was not quite able to give to him, but, as if by way of compensation, 'VICTORY' is set in larger letters than the rest of his monument's inscription.[67]

Alongside heroic timing, the topos of a victory achieved over enemies of superior strength was frequently evoked. In 1809, Castlereagh justified Hardinge's monument: it commemorated 'death connected with victory, and met by the opposition of an inferior to a superior force.' The inscription on Captain Hardinge's St Paul's monument expressed the motive in the manner of a bookkeeper: 'TO GEO. N. HARDINGE, | CAPTAIN OF THE ST. FIORENZO, 36 GUNS, 186 MEN. | WHO ATTACKED, ON THREE SUCCESSIVE DAYS | LA PIEDMONTAISE, 50 GUNS, 566 MEN.'[68]

~

If the scope of honours even for officers was contested, extending monuments to the ranks seemed out of the question, despite, or perhaps because of, the fact that the level of mobilisation of British working men after 1798 was not again reached until the First World War. Battle accounts highlighted the heroic mind-set and actions of ordinary fighting men. The 14-year-old William Henry Dillon was a gunner on the lower deck of the 74-gun HMS *Defence* on 1 June 1794. He was disgusted by the unceremonious throwing overboard of dead sailors, but then he met a young man who had lost part of an arm, yet

> was quite cheerful, not seeming to mind his misfortune … It was a very gratifying circumstance to witness so many acts of heroic bravery that were displayed on board our ship. Patriotic sentences were uttered that would have done honour to the noblest minds: yet these were expressed by the humblest class of men.[69]

Expressing similar demotic heroism, a seaman on the *Victory* allegedly remarked while his arm was being amputated: 'Well, this by some would be considered a misfortune, but I shall be proud of it, as I shall resemble the more our brave Commander in Chief.' Association by amputation was only surpassed by simultaneous death, occasionally written up in heroic code even by ordinary seamen seeking to console relatives: 'Pray, inform their poor friends of their death, and remind them that they died at the same time as Nelson, and in the moment of glorious victory!'[70]

Pleasure garden songs and entr'actes presented victory as a triumph of British valour and sacrifice shared by all ranks. The brave tar was a ubiquitous fictional presence in plays, novels, and popular music. Dibdin's *The Soldier's Grave* calls for a tribute and commemoration of an anonymous soldier's last sacrifice. A popular mezzotint commemorating the battle, *Jack's Return after Lord Howe's Glorious*

Victory, stressed the participation of the ordinary sailor, though the caption also alluded to the potential for mutiny in the navy: 'Our fleet has engag'd and the French as expected, | And wish'd by all ranks, save a few disaffected, | Have not only been *tuck'd up* but also *dissected*.' While maritime portraiture was confined to officers and rarely showed 'the men' in the way portraiture of country gentlemen might include servants, numerous well-circulated prints represented the tar as the loyal, chivalric, heroic supporter of Britannia.[71]

Yet, official acknowledgement of these heroic services of the ordinary fighting man was limited. To be sure, Parliament frequently voted thanks to crews and troops, usually praising their valour in disciplinarian language. Clerics in thanksgiving sermons also increasingly extended their praise to the lower ranks among Britain's intrepid seamen.[72] But the state did not honour ordinary seamen with medals or monuments. Medals for *all* British seamen in a battle were instead designed and struck on the initiative of, and financed by, private individuals flaunting their patriotism. Alexander Davison, Nelson's prize agent, issued unnamed medals to the officers and men present at the Battle of the Nile, and medals to the seamen on HMS *Victory* after Trafalgar. A Birmingham manufacturer, Matthew Boulton, also gave medals to 14,001 Trafalgar veterans.[73]

In Prussia, by comparison, King Frederick William III founded the Iron Cross to reward distinguished military service. Small cast-iron Maltese crosses decorated with a sprig of oak, the king's initials, crown, and the year of the campaign were awarded not only to officers but also to common soldiers, militia members, and volunteers. This reflected the demotic nature of Prussia's mobilisation. By March 1814, over 6,600 2nd Class, 331 1st Class, and three Grand Crosses had been awarded.[74]

By contrast to the innovative Prussian policy, it was only after Waterloo that the British government issued the first official campaign medal for all veterans. In 1855, Queen Victoria presented Crimean medals to all ranks, an occasion which she felt 'united high and low and brought *all* equally together as heroes ... the first time that a simple Private has touched the hand of the Sovereign'.[75] As with medals, so with monuments. The pantheon of select officers marginalised the ordinary serviceman. This was notwithstanding the fact that the armed services, and the navy in particular, offered opportunities for professional and social advancement to men of comparatively low social origins. Captain Westcott is said to have been the son of a baker in Honiton but his skill and bravery secured him promotion from cabin boy to captain in the Battle of the Nile. Yet the pantheon did not do much to emphasise the relative inclusiveness of the armed services. Only half a dozen monuments in St Paul's include representations of ordinary soldiers or sailors. General Abercromby's is the earliest of these monuments (fig. 18). Abercromby is the central hero in this composition

18. Richard Westmacott, *Monument to Sir Ralph Abercromby*, St Paul's Cathedral (1802–5). The depiction of a battle scene, the spiral composition, and the representation of an ordinary soldier were relatively rare among Westmacott's work and among Committee of Taste commissions. Below the frightened horse, a battered and faceless French soldier reaches in vain for what will be Britain's battle trophy. The cold, expressionless sphinxes situate the scene geographically and contrast with the energy of the central composition.

– but the Highlander loyally catching the falling general is also given a prominent place, although the face of the foot soldier who stands in a (literally) supportive and hierarchical relationship to his genteel equestrian officer remains unseen.[76]

Several other monuments in St Paul's to officers include mourning tars and Tommies who appeal to an inclusive community of addressees and acknowledge the ordinary serviceman's presence, though without elevating him to the status of the hero. For example, in the monument of Captain Duff a bare-chested, kneeling tar is sobbing over the captain's tomb. In Hopper's monument of Major-General Hay falling into the arms of a very muscular, scantily draped figure representing Valour, the hero is lamented by a sentinel. Smaller than the officer and allegorical figure, the sentinel occupies a different time and space, contemplating death, or representing life as a foil to death. His inclusion acknowledges the general's duty to his loyal men. George L. Smyth speculated that the bare-chested soldier leaning halfway over the double tomb of Generals Craufurd and Mackinnon by Bacon was meant to represent a Highlander. Maria Hackett in her *Popular Account of St Paul's* identified the male figure helping to lay General Moore to rest in Bacon's monument as a Spanish soldier, though others like Smyth thought it represented Valour; the confusion or conflation of ordinary servicemen with allegorical figures perhaps reflects the insecure status of the former.[77]

Even the occasional inclusion of soldiers and sailors in monuments marks a departure from earlier commemorative practice. This may reflect the notion – increasingly prominent since the Seven Years War – that a leader's relationship with his men counted towards his status as a public hero. Abercromby for instance was generally praised for having been loved by his troops, for his kind attention to their welfare. The affection Captain Duff enjoyed from his crew apparently kept them from joining the mutiny in 1797. The relief on the pedestal (now lost) of the Duncan monument showed 'a seaman with his wife and child, illustrative of the regard in which Lord Duncan's memory is held by the poor but gallant companions of his achievements.'[78]

Francis Chantrey's innovative relief memorials to Hoghton, Bowes, and Cadogan added a new dimension to the representation of heroes in St Paul's. While retaining the focus on the gloriously dying officer hero, these memorials show the men doing the actual fighting. Although they remain anonymous and in the background, they manifestly are the focus of the dying heroes' attention. They include overlapping figures of uniformed men charging or storming enemy positions in an orderly manner. Seen half in profile behind each other, in a manner probably inspired by the Parthenon frieze, these monuments combine the archaic composition of overlapping figures with modern historical reportage. Hoghton led a brigade of fusiliers in one of the most costly battles in the Peninsular War, at Albuera in 1811, when more than half the men in his brigade were lost. Captain Thomas Henry Browne recorded how Hoghton 'at its head, its brave Commander, whilst cheering

19. Sir Francis Chantrey, *Monument to Colonel Cadogan*, St Paul's Cathedral (c.1815). On the design drawing for the monument, Chantrey had narrated that when Cadogan received 'the wound which occasioned his Death he requested to be carried to the Top of a Hill [to] contemplate the Brilliant Victory which his gallantry had contributed to achieve.' A soldier bends to counter Cadogan's weight as others rush ahead of the fallen. Cleverly positioned, Cadogan looks towards both the light of battle and a window in the cathedral's south transept.

it on to the charge, fell, pierced with wounds.'[79] Chantrey shows the general, already wounded on the ground, a horse's grotesque head remembering the fall, and in a last effort propping himself up on his right arm. With his left arm he points his men, who are charging with levelled bayonets, in the direction of victory. The flag horizontally divides officer from soldiers, and acts as a curtain which will fall when Victory lets go to crown the dead hero.

Bowes, who had had no business as a general officer leading the storming of the fort of San Gaetano at Salamanca, is shown falling on the breach, his right foot standing imperiously on a disabled enemy gun. The inscription records his death 'WHILE LEADING THE TROOPS TO THE ASSAULT'. An obituary reported how the wounded Bowes had returned to the field to cheer on his temporarily repulsed troops, when he was fatally shot. Smyth appreciated Chantrey's historical reportage, 'a representation of the dying officer, borne along by his men, with his face still turned towards the enemy'.[80]

Finally, in the monument to Cadogan, two of the men supporting him are waving their hats, either cheering the men on to victory, or marking the moment of victory (fig. 19). Seen from several metres below it is not evident that they are on a hill, and the background profiles of common soldiers appear subtle.

Britain was slow to erect a general war monument to all the fallen and veterans. Although general battle monuments were being built in France and Prussia from the 1790s, it was 1815 before Parliament moved to approve one. In Continental countries, the broadening of commemoration corresponded with the demotic nature of war mobilisation under general conscription (France 1792–3, 1798; Prussia from 1813 to 1814). It also reflected the concept of the citizen-soldier and the promise of political participation for all (or all educated) fighting men. The nature of a country's military constitution, the specific socio-political order for which a hero was supposed to be dying, the prospect or actuality of political rights, and the mode of their posthumous commemoration were all linked.[81]

One model which many Britons were aware of was Revolutionary France, which erected tablets or monuments listing the names (or at least the numbers) of the fallen. When he visited Paris during the Peace of Amiens in 1802, the British painter Joseph Farington was startled by such democratic commemoration. Viewing a 'very large tablet' in Les Invalides he saw 'inscribed the Names of Soldiers who during *the Wars of the Revolution* distinguished themselves in battle. Some of them were Corporals &c. Rank made no difference in the claim to distinction.'[82] There were projects for war memorials for each Parisian *département*. The Vendôme Column, the Colonne de la Grande Armeé commemorating Napoleon's campaign of 1805, was originally planned as a war memorial for the soldiers of the *département* of the Seine who had died for country and liberty, with the names of outstanding officers and brave soldiers inscribed (1799). The statue as eventually built consists of a gigantic column with a spiral relief of military scenes commemorating the Grand Army and topped by a colossal statue of the emperor. As a French variation on the Roman serial campaign relief carving, to an extent it could be 'read' by the illiterate. The definition of both the objects and addressees of commemoration was inclusive.[83]

In addition to the Panthéon and Les Invalides, beginning in 1806 Napoleon converted the incomplete Church of la Madeleine in Paris into a 'Temple de la Gloire' for the Grande Armée. The Madeleine also became a depositum for conquered monuments, weapons, and standards. The inscription on the façade announced: 'de l'Empereur Napoléon aux Soldats de la grande Armée'. Marble tablets listed all who served in the battles of Ulm, Jena, and Austerlitz by army units; gold tablets named all the fallen; and silver tablets remembered the soldiers fielded by each *département*. Bas-reliefs of regimental colonels and marble statues of the marshals of the Grande Armée set apart the officer class. Hierarchical order under imperial leadership was combined with the inclusive commemoration of all casualties and veterans.[84]

Prussia, too, built general war monuments. Frederick William III in 1793 had erected a war memorial in Frankfurt, dedicated to the eighty Hessian troops who had fallen under the Duke of Brunswick in the reconquest of that city from the French Revolutionary army in 1792. It listed all the fallen in order of their military rank, top-down from colonel to private. This first collective monument in a German territory carried the patriotic dedication: 'To the noble Hessians, who fell here, victorious, in the fight for the Fatherland'. The king thus acknowledged the French Revolutionary principle of equality, but integrated it in a conservative, monarchical, patriotic vision.[85]

Beginning in 1807, discussions on how to commemorate all fallen soldiers took place within the context of Prussian army reforms. In 1813, the king decreed 'a lasting memorial' to those who had fallen and could not be awarded the Iron Cross. All warriors who would have earned the Iron Cross according to the unanimous testimony of their superiors and comrades were to be commemorated with simple memorial tablets, paid for by the state, in their regimental church. Memorial tablets were also to be erected at the community's cost in parish churches, inscribed: 'in this parish died for king and fatherland', followed by all names, with those who would have earned the Iron Cross listed first. Finally, requiems were to be celebrated in honour of all heroic warriors. To demarcate the boundaries of official commemoration, the king refused to sponsor privately initiated projects. This royally decreed cult of the warrior hero sought to promote patriotic readiness for individual and collective sacrifice, and preserve the memory of the nation's heroic armed citizens. The tablets were part of the symbolic cannon, which also included commemorative coins, victory celebrations, and illuminations for leaving and returning troops. Now often lost, damaged, or forgotten, these memorial tablets were then omnipresent throughout the Prussian provinces. Towards the end of the war, several German princes and governments and Austria (in the peripheral territory of Mähren) also sponsored more inclusive commemorative practices.[86]

Against this international background, the British authorities were aware that they risked provoking demands for wider political rights if and when they sponsored unprecedented mass mobilisation, especially after the mutinies of 1797. Some voices, including in Parliament, were already calling for national monuments to acknowledge the importance of ordinary servicemen (see fig. 22). There were even well-advanced ministerial plans for a more inclusive honours system in Britain, in the form of a Naval Order of Merit (1797) and a Naval and Military Order of Merit (1805–6). Three classes would each have combined the criteria of rank and individual achievement. The abortive proposal probably echoed too closely Napoleon's Legion of Honour (1802). It might also have been thought that a slightly more exclusive honours system, such as the gold medals, ensured that the rewards were more highly prized by the officer class. The British ruling orders remained uneasy about the political ambiguities that general battle honours and a more inclusive commemorative culture might have been seen to carry, and which could have been exploited by those who demanded political participation for all fighting men. An expanded concept of the state's acknowledgement of the heroic still extended only to officers above a certain rank.[87]

As they built a national pantheon with 'pretensions to permanency', the British state and artists developed their own ways and style of commemoration. These reflected the specific constitutional structures and political culture of Britain. The occasional inclusion of ordinary soldiers in these monuments and the state's refusal to widen the scope of commemoration any further suggests the potential of culture to be a determining force rather than representations just reflecting pre-existing political agendas. To fix in marble the contributions which ordinary fighting men made to the defence of the realm might risk inviting claims for broader citizenship rights. Yet, within these limits, the founders of the St Paul's pantheon – George III, the Westminster Parliament, successive governments, and their advisers – had mounted a more or less explicit, robust response to the Revolutionaries' Panthéon and Napoleon's Les Invalides. Parliament's key role differentiated this British pantheon from monarchical, Revolutionary, and Napoleonic modes of commemoration. Parliament also provided the space for political contests over the general principles guiding the award of honours, the merit of specific heroes, and their due rewards. Although Britons were wont to ridicule the ever-changing composition of French pantheons, there was considerable scope for partisan politics at the ostensibly national pantheon at St Paul's, too. Successive governments sought to harness the propaganda potential of naval and military victories to defend and market their conduct of the war, inspire an ethic of service in the armed forces, and inculcate patriotism in a nationalistic public.

To pursue the complex and ambitious agendas implied in national memorialisation, close attention had to be paid, too, to the strategies of artistic representation. In this process, the relationship between European neoclassical aesthetics and the desire for a specific, modern, British heroic aesthetics had to be negotiated.

4

MODERN HEROES

BY TELLING PERSONAL AND NATIONAL STORIES, the St Paul's monuments were intended to inspire awe, boost national morale, and kindle the desire for emulation. This required careful design and strategic modes of representation. Each monument is one particular artist's response to a particular dead officer's reputation, the manner of his death, his battle legends, and the political circumstances at the time of the commission. Yet, in seeking to present a national heroic iconography, the sculptor works also within aesthetic conventions of representing idealised bodies, allegories, and realistic portraits and costume. Moreover, he represents both the story of an individual man and a moment in the nation's history and ideals of heroism, manliness, and sacrifice. While the heroic discourse made much of bodily sacrifice, of the piety of the British warrior hero, and of his patriotic death for the nation, in their monuments for St Paul's sculptors appeared largely to avoid violent and religious references. This is partly explained by sculptural conventions and by the particular site. But the performance and perception of military heroes were also shaped by complex notions of military masculinity. These incorporated ideals of bravery and courage, magnanimity and humanity, and sensibility and self-control. The study of the politics of monumental aesthetics needs to consider the full spectrum of possible representations as well as the silences implied in the monuments as built. It is the (often conflicted) interplay between the practices and notions of cultural patriotism, masculinity, and sculptural aesthetics in the creation of modern British heroes that this chapter seeks to illuminate.

Naked Captains

One of the main challenges faced by British sculptors charged with representing contemporary military heroes was to negotiate the requirements of academic tradition and of a modern audience. It is helpful to make an excursion back to the height of the Seven Years War and Parliament's national monument of the quintessential imperial hero of his age, General James Wolfe, as it set an important precedent for the marriage of allegory and realism in the representation of modern British heroism (fig. 20).[1]

A large number of design drawings and models was submitted for Wolfe's monument. The winner was the young, internationally educated, British sculptor Joseph Wilton. As we have seen, he would soon go on to make the monuments of Chatham and George III for New York City as well as any number of monuments across the British Empire. In the quest for an appropriate sculptural language, Wilton could assume that the nation at large was familiar with Wolfe's story from numerous official and commercial renditions. To inspire continued loyalty and emulation in viewers of national monuments, the sculptor had to construct a permanent and timeless memorial while at the same time retaining Wolfe's popular resonances and accessibility. To a large extent this boiled down to the question: how could the heroic ideal be combined with narrative, reportage, and naturalism?

Wilton's monument is in three sections: a bronze relief, by Wilton's former Italian travel companion Capitsoldi, of boats disgorging the troops at the foot of the cliffs near Quebec, with the British lines drawn up on the heights above; on top of the base two alert and aggressive British lions, and a neoclassical sarcophagus with the inscription quoting the House of Commons resolution. This in turn is topped by the death scene. The near-nude, muscular Wolfe, right hand to his breast, is reclining on a sofa, supported by a grenadier; to the rear, in low relief, a Highland soldier is leaning against his pike, directing Wolfe's gaze to Victory. Wolfe's tunic, hat, and rifle lie on the ground, and a French flag is under the general's feet. The scene is set against a tent, with foliage framing its peak, to create a triangular upper section possibly reminiscent of a field hospital.[2]

Academic aesthetic theory required classical forms and allegory for art to transcend the specifics of time and place, to inspire by conveying timeless notions of beauty, virtue, and truth. Sir Joshua Reynolds, President of the Royal Academy, demanded idealised form and the avoidance of familiar objects and modern costume in public sculpture. But if Westminster Abbey, like Vauxhall Gardens, was going to function as part of an increasingly inclusive public sphere – for a public much wider than those able to read allegory – then naturalism and narrative reportage became more important.

The usual focus of the discussion about the heroic ideal *versus* historical veri-similitude and naturalism is Benjamin West's adaptation of the *pietà* formula to a supposedly historically correct representation of the death of General Wolfe of 1770–71 (see fig. 28). West's history painting of a hero's death on an epic scale combines a wide range of classical references with much particularised detail in the figures, costumes, and the background narrative of the main actions of the day. It successfully plays the academic tradition and the consumer-orientated modern formula towards the middle. But the problems had already been worked through at the height of the Seven Years War – by Francis Hayman in a series of historical paintings at Vauxhall Gardens, and by competitors for Westminster Abbey monuments, especially Wilton's *Wolfe*.[3]

In Wolfe's drapery, in the laurel wreath with which Fame flies towards him, and in the shroud, tent, and flag, Wilton's monument anticipates neoclassical designs. The winged Fame visiting from heaven to crown the naked, dying martyr-hero in a scene of quasi-deification reflects the transfer of the rituals and iconography of martyrdom and sainthood to the culture of national heroism. Yet, although Wolfe died at the moment of victory, he is perhaps represented as much as a vulnerable man of feeling as a man of action. This is a monument both of nationalistic triumph and of sentiment. Finally, alongside allegory and neoclassical detail there is much naturalism and reportage. Apart from the bas-relief, Wolfe's head in the monument resembles Wilton's earlier busts of Wolfe. There was also speculation as to whether the Highlander was based on a particular soldier. In any case, the iconographic particularity of the Highlander – symbolic of the incorporation of former enemies of England into the Anglo-British state and its imperial project – helps locate Wolfe, the general of Irish descent who had been among the victors of Culloden and died near Quebec, as a truly British imperial hero.[4]

The monument was not unveiled until 1773, in circumstances very different from those of 1759–60. Commissioned perhaps in part to celebrate the first minister, Pitt, as much as the general, the statue was erected when Pitt was critical of the government of the day, when empire in America increasingly appeared to be a liability, and when notions of heroic masculinity themselves were coming under scrutiny. As we saw, the American Revolutionary War had offered limited scope for the further development of a national heroic iconography. The naturalistic reportage and narrative in the Wolfe monument appear, however, to have been increasingly appreciated.[5] Later military monuments would benefit from Wolfe's aura as a national and patriotic commission which successfully married allegory and reportage, Christian and pagan iconography, and understated triumph with sentimentalism. Flaxman for one justified his choice of faithfully portraying

20. Joseph Wilton, *Monument to General James Wolfe*, Westminster Abbey (1760–73). Detail.

Nelson (fig. 21) as lifelike and, in the interest of general accessibility, of discarding allegory:

> Divine attributes, moral virtues or national characteristics, represented by allegory, are addressed to the speculation of the philosopher, or the imagination of the poet – but ... general feelings are more gratified by the likeness of the man.[6]

Wilton, then, had set an important precedent and model for the representation of modern heroism. But while many sculptors negotiated the complicated relationship between allegory and realism, not all did so successfully. A major row erupted over one of the earliest monuments in St Paul's, that of Thomas Banks's Captain Rundell Burgess. Burgess was a casualty of the battle against the Dutch fleet at Camperdown in 1797. The memorial depicted a larger than life-size figure, scantily draped, with a portrait head on top of a nude body (fig. 23). The strange naked man is greeted by a winged Victory handing him a sword over a hefty, phallic cannon

21. John Flaxman, *Monument to Horatio, Viscount Nelson*, St Paul's Cathedral (1807–18). Largely after Westmacott's design, Flaxman created a noble portrait of Nelson that does not fully present either realism or neoclassical idealisation. This is a broadly pleasing Nelson to whom the public could relate. The slight proportions of the admiral are heightened and broadened, a fur-lined cloak both conceals and acknowledges the amputated arm, and incisions add a spark of life to the eyes. A motherly Britannia directs two young seamen's attention to Nelson's inspirational and dignified form.

between them, balls on the ground. One London guidebook of 1807 condemned the indecency:

> an *English* Captain of a man of war, suffering with fortitude, dying at the moment of victory? Obliterate the inscription; and who is he? Not a Briton. We have no *naked naval Captains*. If a man would redden with shame and indignation at barely being asked to enter a friend's house stripped, how is it that we dare prophane the house of God with such indecent representations? … These *Roman* fancies are absurd to the last extreme … in the name of propriety, let future statues for St. Paul's be Britons in their features, their actions, and their habits.[7]

Allan Cunningham, a contemporary biographer and critic of artists, demanded a national aesthetics which would set contemporary monuments apart from classical and neoclassical templates: 'every-day noses and chins must not be supported on bodies moulded according to the godlike proportions of the Greek statues'. After all, no British warriors went naked into battle, and 'no antique mould is necessary when a British hero is to be celebrated by a British artist'. Charles Robert Cockerell

22. James Heath, after Benjamin West, *The Death of Lord Viscount Nelson* (1811). Some artists who played a key role in the creation of the St Paul's pantheon elsewhere included ordinary servicemen in commemorative art. West's painting, seen by tens of thousands at his house in 1806 and again at the 1811 Academy, includes portraits of ordinary seamen. A key which accompanied the publication of Heath's engraving identifies, for example, no. 25, 'Saunders, a seaman', kneeling before Nelson and laying a Spanish flag at his feet, or no. 58, 'Sanders, a Powder Boy'. Their energetic countenances emphasise both the joy of victory and – by contrast with his wilted body – the tragedy of Nelson's fall.

similarly criticised the Italian sculptor Antonio Canova's design for the Nelson monument: 'What is the English tar to say when he sees his beloved Nelson in a Roman petticoat?'[8] When he deliberately confused allegory and realism in Captain Burgess and his goddess, Cunningham's concern was with the intelligibility of monuments:

> That Victory, a modest and well-draped dame, should approach an undrest dying man, and crown him with laurel, might be endured – but how a well-dressed young lady could think of presenting a sword to a naked gentleman [goes] far beyond all … notions of propriety.[9]

23. Thomas Banks, *Monument to Captain Rundell Burgess*, St Paul's Cathedral (1798–1802). Realistic sculpture helped the wider public recognise their heroes by specific physical traits. Yet realism was at odds with the aesthetic demand for works embodying the qualities of classical Greek sculpture. The mixture of realistic and idealising elements could be aesthetically unsatisfactory and didactically ineffective. And even without a phallic cannon, balls on the ground, and a sword delivered, many considered near-naked representations of modern men in churches indecent.

This line of critique resonated with contemporary psychological thinking, which held that the lesser the distractions from the connections between ideas, the greater the power of association.[10]

For military Scots, costume carried the connotation of bravery and model heroic leadership.[11] Scottish regiments were transformed into icons of national valour. Scottish regiments were overwhelmingly Lowland in personnel, yet they were distinctly Highland in spirit. The image of the military hero in tartan kilt was itself a tradition only invented in the middle of the eighteenth century. Highland units were the most showy-looking in British service. Cathedral guides emphasised Scotland's distinct claim to fame as exemplified by Sir Ralph Abercromby and Sir John Moore.[12] Their monuments were regionalised by juxtaposing the dying hero with anonymous Highland soldiers, another cross-reference to Wilton's *Wolfe* in the Abbey (see fig. 18). Artists depicting battles and heroes' deaths in a vein similar to Westmacott's Abercromby recognised the patriotic value of regional dress and helped create an imagery of Scottish national militarism, and a mythology of loyalty proven by military service (see plate X). From the middle of the eighteenth century, military and imperial service had become the most important means of social, material, and cultural advancement for Scotsmen. Scots were the arsenal of Britain's empire, which, in terms of conquerors, administrators, and settlers (as well as missionaries, merchants, and botanists) was distinctly Anglo-Scottish.[13] When the army built national regiments, by the 1800s, 80 per cent of Scottish recruits entered Scottish regiments. The representation of Scots officers in St Paul's, and, more generally, the frequent representation of Scottish military men in the art of the Napoleonic period, reflects the hugely disproportionate number of Scots serving in the British army in both the officer corps and rank and file, and the important and growing role Scotland was playing in the defence of the British Isles and the empire.

Bodily Sacrifice

A pantheonised officer was expected to have endured multiple injuries over his career and to have died in battle with stoic calm and determination. It was the Scots General Sir John Moore who would demonstrate better than most the heroic virtue of accumulated bodily sacrifice (fig. 24). In a preview of his heroic potential, early on in the same battle in which Abercromby had long concealed his mortal wound, Moore was injured in the leg but kept going. He displayed 'a force of exertion almost incredible to many when the severity of the wound was ascertained'. Moore made the ultimate sacrifice in the Battle of Coruña when a cannon shot struck him on the left breast and threw him from his horse. He mounted again and showed no sign of pain. It was soon realised, however, that his

> shoulder was shattered to pieces, the arm was hanging by a piece of skin, the ribs over the heart broken, and bared of flesh, and the muscles of the breast torn into long strips, which were interlaced by their recoil from the dragging of the

24. John Bacon, *Monument to Sir John Moore*, St Paul's Cathedral (1810–15). Moore is tenderly lowered in a composition reminiscent of Ulysses laid down on the coast by the Phaeacian sailors. As sculpted, Moore's body appears pristine and whole – a contradiction of truth and of the monument's own description of his death, 'slain by a cannonball'.

shot. As the soldiers placed him in a blanket his sword got entangled, and the hilt entered the wound.

Moore declined having it removed: "*It is as well as it is. I had rather it should go out of the field with me.*" And in that manner, so becoming a soldier, Moore was borne from the fight.' Having recommended meritorious officers for promotion and inquired after the safety of friends and staff, Moore finally died. When the Secretary for War, Viscount Castlereagh, proposed a monument he too rehearsed the topoi. For the mortally wounded general, 'life was but a secondary, a trifling object of consideration.' When he observed the British advance, Moore 'seemed to derive new and increased vigour from the scene, as if the approach of death was forgotten in the approach of victory'. William Hersee's rapidly composed stanzas envisaged Moore's commemoration:

Long shall the weeping Briton mourn thy Fate –
Long shall he tell of thee the pensive tale
That, when the Vict'ry claim'd the day elate,
Thy Corse lay bleeding in Corunna's vale.[14]

In eighteenth-century medical and psychological thinking, military bravery and the warrior's capacity to suspend his *sensibilité* in peril of death was an 'illustration of the more-than-human in man'. The successive mutilations in one or more battles, like Nelson's over his long-suffering heroic career, were often described in great detail.[15] But it was not just the bodily sacrifice of commanders but that of subordinate officers too which was widely and graphically reported at the time. In the Peninsular War, an obituary of Major-General Bowes recorded that he had been 'wounded in two places, shot through the thigh and bayoneted' in the storming of Badajoz. Heading his brigade, he was injured early in the subsequent Battle of Salamanca. With his wound barely dressed, he returned to the field to cheer on his men, when he was shot. In that same battle, Major-General Le Marchant died 'with 36 balls in his body, while advancing and cheering at the head of his men', and Major-General Sir William Ponsonby fell 'pierced with seven lance wounds'. Wellington's Ciudad Rodrigo dispatch stated severe losses among top brass. Major-General Mackinnon's body, along with well over 100 men, was never found after the retreating French had exploded a magazine in the ditch of their retrenchment before they abandoned the garrison rampart.[16] And in anticipation of a major battle, Ponsonby's fellow Waterloo casualty Sir Thomas Picton kept injuries sustained in the Battle of Quatre Bras secret. At Waterloo he fought with two broken ribs and internal wounds, his body swollen and blackened, as was later recounted in Parliament. This sacrifice ensured that his last battle and death would be written up in heroic code:

> when the moment came which called for his great example, the hand of death, which it is supposed was even then upon him from the wound alluded to, could not, while sufficient life yet remained, check for a moment his lofty courage.

His monument has perhaps the strongest male allegory in St Paul's: in the taller Celtic warrior who guides the British lion, Britannia, who faces him with laurel wreath, had finally found her male counterpart after Waterloo.[17]

The St Paul's monuments barely reflected the corporeal heroism which served contemporaries as a framework within which to conceptualise heroes and their deaths. The sculptors of the national monuments mostly effaced wounds, mutilations, and the ugly realities of heroic death. The pathos of the heroic discourse of field dispatches, parliamentary debate, magazines, and memoirs contrasts with iconographic reticence. Sculptors' hesitation in depicting bodily mutilation in St Paul's monuments must be partly due to the notion that sculpture ought to be idealising not idolising. Although wounds were to be found in antique sculpture, for instance in the group of the Gaul committing suicide with his wife (Arria and Paetus), this aspect of classical sculpture was not adapted here. Sculptural conventions also demanded that the narrative, not just (or even primarily) visually descriptive appearance and surface treatment, depict heroism. The artist seeks to do only what is necessary to convey his ideas. Moreover, depictions of bleeding men might not be considered heroic, and would render an image time-specific (pre-death) or trap the hero in a state of continual suffering.[18]

At St Paul's, representations of army officers dying in battle are quite rare. Westmacott's Abercromby (see fig. 18) shows him falling wounded from his horse, though the wound itself is covered. A few other monuments depict the modern warrior as critically injured, like General Bowes falling wounded on the breach of San Gaetano, Salamanca, his right foot placed imperiously on a disabled enemy gun. A classicised General Sir William Ponsonby is shown reaching in death for glory and fame, indeed perhaps the only 'glorious fall' in St Paul's, with a hovering Victory crowning him as the sword glides out of his dying grip and the wreath barely touches him. Hoghton is suspended between life and death. Collingwood's corpse, his profile still and peaceful and his breast bared, lies on an antique prow, as a kneeling Britannia cradles his head and leads him to float to the other life. By only showing sarcophagi and mourning soldiers, monuments such as that of Craufurd and Mackinnon perhaps acknowledge implicitly that the bodies were badly hurt. But the multiple lance or shot wounds, the hideously disfigured bodies, which the wider heroic discourse made so much of, are never explicitly shown. Flaxman presents Nelson as if in command on deck, avoiding any classical nudity or allegory in the main figure, recognisable enough, yet idealised by making his mutilated body look 'whole' again and perfect. Monuments such as Moore's (maimed by a cannonball, but sculpted smooth and whole), Brock's, or Pakenham and Gibbs's totally deny bodily harm. By and large, the darker sides of battle and of heroic death are avoided at St Paul's.

Christian Warriors

One possible further explanation of this reticence may have to do with religious sentiment. Religion was both a unifying and a potentially divisive factor in British public life, in the forging of a national identity, and in the politics of national com-memoration. British governments tapped into the tremendous propagandistic potential of loyalist preachers. Most Anglican clergy accepted the inevitability of war and taught that divine providence protected God's elect nation. Adherence to reli-gious principles, loyalty to king, and national unity were the nation's duty towards the soldiers and sailors who sacrificed their lives.[19] The actions and achievements of national heroes were frequently represented in patterns of Christian virtue. Indeed, the concept of individual sacrifice for the higher good, informed by antique and Christian precedent, was central to patriotic discourse and iconography through-out Europe. Ideas about Christian soldiers had been around throughout the eight-eenth century. With Wolfe's Westminster Abbey monument, British sculptors had a model for transferring imagery of Christian martyrdom to statues of military heroes.[20] Yet in the 1790s, the glorification of militaristic ideals in a cathedral of the Established Church created tensions.

There had always been influential counter-traditions to 'the heroic' in eighteenth-century Anglo-Scottish philosophy, historiography, and fiction. These drew on general pacifist impulses fed by Roman stoicism, Christian beliefs, and humanism. Joseph Addison and Richard Steele mocked the chivalric in polite satire. Alexander Pope explored the ambiguity of heroism which combined courageous achievement with cruelty and corruption: 'All that rais'd the Hero, sunk the Man.' John Locke held the classical syllabus and its focus on battles and conquests responsible for vandalism and cruelty to animals. A later debate about corporal punishment as the appropriate method to instil knowledge, virtue, and self-discipline in pupils reveals similar scepticism. Enlightened historiography explained the rise of civil-ity and civilisation through commerce, not the traditional concept of honour: the latter and martial prowess were now attributed to a less civilised stage in societal development. This line of thought supported the anti-duelling case of Evangelicals and others, while proponents of duelling, and those in favour of corporal punish-ment in schools, held that fostering an ambition for honour and manly hardiness produced excellent gallant soldiers of the kind required by an imperial nation.[21]

Some of the strongest resistance to the celebration of earthly heroism in mon-uments sited in churches came from Evangelicals and Methodists. Their reaffir-mation of revelation had important implications for attitudes to death. Edward Young's influential *Night Thoughts*, first published in 1742–6 and going through half a dozen editions between 1790–1820, presented life as transient, and immortality as the essence of Christianity. James Hervey, in his widely read 'Meditations among the Tombs', showed distaste for 'bribing the vote of fame, and purchasing a little posthumous renown' for the expeditious death of a mortal in the necessary service of his country, since this was dwarfed by Christ's voluntary death for his enemies.[22] By the 1790s, for many dissenters war signified divine chastisement, moral wrong, or a threat to liberty. Edmund Butcher, preaching in Sidmouth, Devon, warned of those who set nations on a course of war for their personal gain and those 'as are fond of that sanguinary phantom military glory: the laurels they acquire must cost humanity dear, they are steeped in tears and blood.'[23]

Contemporary Europe offered various examples of the conflation of religion and heroism. In Revolutionary France the profane cult of Revolutionary martyrs, and the quasi-religion of *la patrie* and of the ideals of liberty and equality, supplanted Christian notions of martyrdom. The new, non-transcendental immortality resided in the memory of posterity. The mystique of the sovereign Revolutionary nation and its mutilated martyrs was expected to supply the spiritual conviction to give soldiers courage to die for the *patrie* (as much as religion had inspired their predecessors to die for the king). The corpses of those who had died violent deaths, whether on the battlefield or by assassination, were exhibited in state funerals. In macabre displays, the half-naked corpses with their mortal gaping wounds or blood-stained clothes were dramatic reminders of the martyrs' sacrifice. By appealing to the sentiments of horror, pity, and desire for revenge, the displayed victim served as a metonym of the Revolution.[24]

In Prussia, a cult of death for the fatherland and blood sacrifice on its altar was celebrated in poems, songs, and sermons, and at swearing-in ceremonies and the consecration of colours.[25] The sculptor Johan H. Gast designed a monument to his only son, Carl H. A. Gast (1796–1813), who fell in the 'holy war for king and fatherland', and for 'all the sons of the fatherland, who sacrificed their lives for the just cause'. Underneath the altar of white Carrara marble is a sacrificial plate of red porphyry, its redness indicating the blood tribute of those fateful times and white spots standing for the many who had fought.[26]

In Britain, there was also significant overlap between Christian theology and the notion of patriotic example. The formation of a naval and military pantheon within a church was tolerated during wartime. From the admission of the first monuments in 1791, the British Temple of Fame had the 'additional sanction of religion'. When George III brought the French military banners to St Paul's for a Thanksgiving in 1797 to testify to God's protection of Britain, he was seen as imitating David laying the spoils of victory before the Temple at Jerusalem. In the crusading rhetoric of the *Sun* newspaper this turned into the invocation of 'a war of Virtue, Order and Religion, against Crime, Anarchy and Atheism'.[27]

Although public worship in the armed services had been neglected for much of the eighteenth century,[28] the British hero was often represented as particularly pious, for instance in James Stanier Clarke's widely read *Naval Sermons* (1798), reprinted as *Sermons on the Character and Professional Duties of Seamen* (1801). Religious symbolism framed ship launches and the dedication of regimental colours. On national days of fasting and thanksgiving, God's blessing was evoked for the armed forces. Nelson's family background and his piety were seen to reflect on the values of the British polity and nation. Admiral Duncan after the Battle of Camperdown and Nelson after the Nile demonstrated conspicuous religiosity by holding thanksgiving services on their flagships.[29]

The 1797 naval mutinies brought the need for religious education in the navy to the fore, although, still, not even every large ship had a clergyman. The Society for Promoting Christian Knowledge and the Naval and Military Bible Society distributed tens of thousands of bibles among the army, as well as tracts, prayer books, Psalters, and testaments, and (as previously in the century) religious literature like Josiah Woodward's *The Soldier's Monitor*. The government eventually became so concerned about absenteeism among regimental chaplains that it empowered commanding officers to hire local clergy as full-time chaplains for each brigade. This hints at the recognition that religious apathy deprived the army, first, of an important tool in the fight against immoral behaviour in the army; second, of a potential source of group identity, especially if chaplains had been appointed to minister to the needs of Presbyterian Scots and Catholic Irish recruits; and, third, of an ideological-emotional weapon in the fight against Britain's enemies.

However, few of the secular heroes at St Paul's display martyrological imagery. In the British context, this was also a departure from resurrection monuments at Westminster Abbey, such as General Hargrave's, where the defeated figure of Death seems to be falling down on the spectator, and the 'figure of the general is supposed to be just re-animated, and rising in an ecstasy of joy from the tomb in which he had reposed'.[30] In many other depictions of the death of British heroes, too, like Benjamin West's *Sketch for a Monument to Lord Nelson*, the rituals and paraphernalia of Christian martyrdom were transferred to heroic iconography (see plate XII). In the Royal Academy catalogue of 1807, West described his design as integrating painting, 'best calculated ... to give allegorical figures their full effect, and to form a composition expressive of Lord Nelson's nautical achievements, and the immortality of his greatness', with sculpture, 'to give the sepulchre its appropriate character', and architecture, to 'inscribe on [the] frieze the honours which Parliament decreed to the family of Nelson.'

The St Paul's pantheon – as a concept and in its iconography – negotiated the tensions between the religious and secular notions of a pantheon in distinctive ways. There are no *pietàs*, no scenes of apotheosis, no resurrection-type monuments.

The sculptural language even of a monument such as that of Nelson does not correspond readily with the wider discourse of heroic suffering. Nelson is shown as if still in command on deck, in naval uniform and boat cloak – not at the moment of death or in a scene of deification. Captain Westcott's monument is an exception: the falling, dying or dead captain is propped up by a winged Victory who is holding aloft a laurel wreath. The captain's eyes are closed, directed towards the ground, while Victory looks away from him and slightly upwards; both seem removed, not present. But almost all other monuments at St Paul's employ retrospective imagery, celebrating the achievements and virtues of the officers, rather than depicting death as a moment of birth, and deploying prospective imagery looking forward to an afterlife. A sense of the horror or promise of death is largely missing.[31]

The distinctly British nature of the pantheon could be made more intelligible, and the glorification of military action in a church more palatable, by presenting the act of dying for God's elect nation as a mission in defence of civilisation against the barbaric enemy. The key story in the St Paul's pantheon is that of the death of Major-General Thomas Dundas (1750–94), and of his French and British memorialisation. Dundas had commanded a brigade of light infantry at the capture of Martinique, St Lucia, and Guadeloupe. Shortly after becoming governor of Guadeloupe, Dundas succumbed to yellow fever at Basse Terre and was buried on 4 June in the main bastion of Fort Matilda. The French then recaptured the island, the British evacuated the fort, and the French commissioner Hugue ordered Dundas's body to be disinterred and 'fed to the birds'. His burial place would be marked by a monument with the following inscription:

> This ground, restored to liberty by the valour of the Republicans, was polluted
> by the body of Thomas Dundas, major-general and governor of Gouadaloupe
> for the bloody [King] George the Third.

That same year, the National Convention banned French soldiers from taking British POWs, now considered agents of tyranny, and as such undeserving of mercy. In 1795, the House of Commons voted a monument in St Paul's Cathedral to Dundas's services in the West Indies, which 'occasioned a gross Insult to his Remains'. Dundas was the only officer entering St Paul's who had neither died in battle nor been a supreme commander: French desecration was his claim to fame.[32]

The Dundas story was rehearsed not only on the floor of the House but in newspapers, magazines, and cathedral guides. According to one popular contemporary history of the West Indies, the first measure of the French commissioner Hugue

25. John Bacon, *Design for the Monument to Major-General Dundas in St Paul's Cathedral* (c.1798).

(previously a hairdresser and publican on Guadeloupe) had displayed 'the baseness and ferocity of his character.' Dundas's tomb,

> which a generous enemy, in every civilized part of the earth, would have held sacred, was immediately destroyed by orders of this savage despot, and the remains of the deceased hero dug up and thrown into the river Gallion ... This mean and cowardly display of ineffectual vengeance, was made the subject of boasting and triumph in a public proclamation.

Hugue was then alleged to have continued his vengeance against the sick and wounded British prisoners. He also freely used the guillotine to repress political opposition on the island, proving himself fully worthy of his bloody patron, Robespierre.[33]

Bacon's winning design (fig. 25) was described as a colossal Britannia paying 'a tribute of honour to the memory of her valiant Defender' in the form of the general's bust, 'whose remains were treated with so much indignity by the Enemy'. Britannia, with an acquiescent lion at her side, is accompanied by a smaller figure representing Sensibility, on whose left 'is a boy presenting an olive branch, indicating that the only just object of war, is the attainment of lasting and honourable peace.' On the plinth/tomb are

> small bas-reliefs figures representing (true) LIBERTY flying to BRITANNIA, and protected by her against ANARCHY, who is deciphered by a human head in one hand, and in the other a flaming torch. Anarchy is also aided by another figure, HYPOCRISY, who follows with a smiling mask, by which she partly conceals a ferocious countenance.

When the monument was unveiled, *The Times* pointed to Hypocrisy's features, 'expressive of the most ferocious and horrid barbarity'.[34]

The story fed into Revolutionary reportage in Britain which had begun to dehumanise the French from the mid-1790s. French soldiers in particular were depicted as plundering, raping, murdering *banditti*. Francophobe clergymen across Britain condemned the 'modern VANDALS the FRENCH', mirroring French Anglophobe propaganda against the English 'barbarians'. This type of French anti-English vitriol, first prominent during the Seven Years War, returned from around 1793, when the Convention claimed that, once again, their English opponents had 'wilfully set themselves outside the universal (and French-centred) human community', and then revoked the customary privileges of POWs.[35] At the same time, British clergymen, fearful of domestic insurrection, preached political and spiritual opposition to the French Revolution and its attack on Christian religion. Should those wicked French 'monsters', those 'vipers', the 'slaves of despotism', who combined the 'grimace of the Monkey with the savageness of the Tyger, as he who knew them well has described them (Voltaire)', invade Britain, then disastrous consequences would ensue: political and social anarchy, the eradication of Christianity, unimaginable bloodshed, and the destruction of Britain's very way of life. Hence the purpose of the war was not so much glory and gain, but rather the protection of English or British religion, liberties, honour, and national independence. Any victories Britons won were owed to divine protection of the elect nation and the combination of national valour with British discipline.[36]

The stories of Dundas's French and British memorials extended this mutual Anglo-French vilification into the realm of monumental propaganda. However, even in Dundas's monument, there is no direct Christian imagery. Moreover, in Bacon's design drawing, the general's feet protrude from the sarcophagus in a dramatic representation of the sacrilege; this violent, macabre element of the design was edited out before the monument's realisation for St Paul's.

Codes of Masculinity

The absence of the physical horrors of war from St Paul's can further be explained in terms of different codes of military masculinity which coexisted with some tension throughout the eighteenth and early nineteenth centuries. Masculine identities are social and cultural constructs, which are always understood and experienced in relation to each other, to notions of femininity, and to other categories of social and cultural difference, such as class or religion. Masculine identities are asserted and imagined in a variety of ways, including in cultural and artistic representations.[37]

The St Paul's pantheon was a site where the evolution from eighteenth-century notions of male politeness to imperial Victorian 'Muscular Christian' heroics was negotiated. Eighteenth-century representations of British soldiery and imperialism in various media often emphasised both decorous manly sentiment and sensibility as well as compassionate battlefield clemency and magnanimity in victory, rather than aggressive and bombastic virility.[38] At Westminster Abbey, military monuments balancing the representation of active military triumph with softer, contemplative, and Christian virtues gradually gave way to more overtly triumphalist imagery after c.1758–9.

At St Paul's, alongside those monuments which were built as a function of the military rank of the officer remembered, others commemorated the spectacularly (and often recklessly) brave actions of individuals, especially young captains and middle-ranking army officers, who had managed to fall 'in the moment of victory'. They reflect and contributed to a more general revival of militaristic ideals among the British elite. Starting a trend that would peak in the mid- and late Victorian era, public school education increasingly emphasised competitive physical hardiness, aggressive manliness, and a classical curriculum (instilled with the birch rod), which glorified the heroic and patriotic achievements of men of rank.[39] Thus, with this type of monument the male elite in Parliament (with a significant naval and military element amongst them) adopted a muscular pose and admitted individual military bravura into the pantheon.

But the ideal of the humane, compassionate, and magnanimous British warrior survived the return of more aggressive, militaristic, conquering notions of patriotism.[40] The trope of British magnanimity in victory drew on traditions stretching back to Cicero, Seneca, and the Bible. Steele's *Christian Hero*, seeing some twenty editions between 1701 and 1820, had posited religious faith as the basis for the heroic man who combined physical strength and courage with magnanimity and forgiveness. The notion pervades the songs, plays, and sermons of the Seven Years War. And it is visible in its art, most famously, perhaps, in Francis Hayman's paintings of General Amherst and Lord Clive for Vauxhall Gardens and Edward Penny's *The Marquis of Granby Relieving a Sick Soldier* (1764), portrayals of military leaders embodying the highest virtues in David Hume's ethics – mercy, generosity, benevolence.[41] Hume's *History of England* and Benjamin West's cycle of paintings at Windsor emphasised not Edward the Black Prince's and Edward III's conduct in battle but the courteous consideration of the vanquished by their conquerors. And during the French Wars, didactic publications for soldiers, such as *The Military Mentor* (1804), defined the British warrior not only in terms of courage, valour, and love of country, but also of 'humanity': the horrors of war needed to be softened by 'this amiable virtue'.

The notion of British 'national humanity' demonstrated by its victorious navies and armies was also repetitively propagated in sermons preached onboard battle ships and during thanksgiving services on shore, in private battle accounts, parliamentary rhetoric, and in battle paintings. On the stage and on canvas, British sailors were constantly saving defeated, drowning enemies – Spaniards at Gibraltar in 1782, Frenchmen on 1 June 1794 and again at Trafalgar, where British tars demonstrated 'those exalted principles, which it had been the glory of ancient France to cultivate, and which it has been the endeavour of modern France to extinguish.'[42] British sailors' chivalrous conduct was matched on land. The Glorious First of June was celebrated at a moonlight review of 6,000 troops near Portslade, complete with *feu de joie*, cannon shots, and chants of 'Rule Britannia'. Lord Minto noticed a 'fine trait of English humanity … shown by the populace' when the wounded French prisoners of war disembarked: the crowd turned quiet when told that their huzzas were bad for the captured invalids, and only continued when the latter had safely arrived at a hospital.[43]

From the 1730s, there had been military concerns about the softer forms of masculinity. Politeness, the main technique of self-fashioning for eighteenth-century Englishmen, was modelled on the French and was best achieved in the company of women. It therefore bore the danger of compromising the identities of English men, both as men and as English. Philosophers like Hume sought to reconcile the ideals of politeness and courage to validate new styles of male conduct. A superior form of courage now encompassed both warriorship and refinement attained through polite sociability.[44] At mid-century, General Wolfe embodied the blend of courage and martial vigour with a polite, refined character. Similar notions persisted throughout the Napoleonic Wars. Army surgeon Gillespie described the affable Captain Westcott as 'a Man of the most even temper, pleasing Manners and mildness of Character which the Bustle of a life spent in the Navy and much at Sea could not shake'. General Sir John Moore was remembered as not only a 'very clever man and a good general', and a gallant 'fine, noble, brave fellow', but also as 'most courteous in his manners, whenever he gave any orders to the officers or men'. And the novelist Jane Porter found in Sir Sidney Smith her 'idea of a Hero – which always contained a vast deal more, than physical strength, or mere martial skill', for he was not only an accomplished linguist and classical scholar, but also a gentle and a candid man.[45]

Since the middle of the eighteenth century, artists and writers in Britain had also conflated military manliness and sensibility. Unlike the active quality of magnanimity exercised by those in control and power, sensibility responded to external conditions. Captain Riou, on his way to the battle of Copenhagen in Nelson's task force, was petitioned by some Danish sailors in the British fleet to be transferred on to a ship bound elsewhere: they did not want to leave the British navy, but they did not want to fight their compatriots either. Riou was reported to have complied tearfully.[46]

It was a revival of chivalry which helped the gentleman to be refashioned as masculine in the late eighteenth and early nineteenth centuries. The chivalric revival was manifest in Gothic architecture, including George III's neo-Gothic building programmes at Windsor and Kew; in antiquarian research in medieval ballads and weaponry; in translations and editions of medieval romances and chronicles; and in Scott's novels and his compilation, *Minstrelsy of the Scottish Border*. It also prompted historical works on the Middle Ages and the Crusades, and books which described a code of conduct for modern man, such as Kenelm Digby's *The Broad Stone of Honour* (1822).[47]

As a code of universal values, chivalry refers to ideas of justice, generosity, courage, faith, loyalty, and courtesy. These were virtues which many in the early nineteenth century held to be inherent to the British character. While achievable not only by elite or military men, chivalric ideals were especially important to the imagination and conduct of the British warrior. Notions of superior courage, chivalry, and self-control came together in the demand for compassionate restraint towards civilians. Among the heroes pantheonised at St Paul's, this was exemplified, *inter alia*, by General Picton.

British soldiers, much like their Prussian counterparts, were trained in self-discipline and were expected to combine valour with restraint towards civilians.[48] Armies had a rational interest in limiting the degree to which soldiers were emotionalised and brutalised. Just as reckless courage and senseless sacrifice were too costly given the expenses of recruiting, equipping, and training soldiers, excessive plunder and violence against civilian enemy populations complicated warfare in enemy territory. The notion that self-control needed to circumscribe courage was key to the conflation of sensibility and militarism in the second half of the eighteenth century.[49]

One British 'hero' who is commemorated at St Paul's challenged the rhetorical skills of his supporters more than most when they sought to portray him as humane, restrained, and moderate. Major-General Robert Ross, an Irish-born, highly decorated infantry commander, had led the audacious expedition against Washington DC in 1814. This was a controversial assault on the symbolic heart of a new nation. The British under Ross burned the Capitol, Treasury, War Office, military barracks, stores of weapons and gunpowder, the office of the *National Intelligencer*, the national archives and library, and the White House. Ross was killed by American sniper fire in the subsequent advance on Baltimore – which, as a port and fort, many saw as a less controversial target.[50] In the Commons debate on Ross's national monument, the radical Samuel Whitbread lamented that

> the gallant Ross was obliged to concur in a transaction so discordant to every example of the civilized world, so abhorrent to every [principle] of legitimate warfare … We had done what the Goths refused to do at Rome, when Belisarius represented to them, that to preserve works of elevated art was an act of wisdom but that to destroy them was to erect a monument to the folly of the destroyers.[51]

In the controversy over the commander's humanity, Whitbread clarified that it had been 'happy for humanity, and the credit of the empire' that the revenge instructions had been carried out by a moderate and just officer. Others like Ponsonby and Captain Harry Smith, Junior Adjutant to Ross, stressed that Ross had prevented more indiscriminate destruction as allegedly advocated by Admiral Cockburn. Several MPs even characterised Ross as tender and gentle, both on and off the field.[52] In Ross's rather strange, triangular monument, a winged, bare-breasted Fame descends to crown his bust, a disconsolate Britannia recumbent is weeping, while a large, muscular, and almost naked figure of Valour, with a lion-mask loin-cloth, beholds the bust with pleading intensity and lowers an American flag on the hero's tomb.[53]

The imagery of Britannia at St Paul's, and the female code she represents, is designed to complement the male code of military, humane, compassionate manliness. As with the ideal and practices of politeness, albeit in very different ways, military manliness was supposed to be shaped by the company, expectations, and influence of women. Domesticity and sensibility were not only the virtues of loving fathers and husbands but necessary prerequisites for patriotic valour, so that these men were prepared to risk their life in defence of their womenfolk.[54] Women's status as patriotic subjects thus depended on their capacity to bring forth their lovers' and sons' bravery and masculine patriotism.[55]

However, in Britain, women's war effort was not recognised in any official way, as it was, for instance, in Prussia. There, the Luisenorden complemented the Iron Cross from 1813 in recognition of women's empathy and sacrifice. Some British women acted as nurses, messengers, or spies, and even served as soldiers or sailors, but generally women were absent from the field of combat. They did, however, experience war in manifold ways, and war placed many demands on their physical, material, and emotional resources. Female interest in the war was promoted by a range of factors, from fear of the consequences of a French invasion to sexual fantasies of heroic lovers. Women sponsored subscriptions, knitted clothes, and funded, made, and presented regimental colours. They thus contributed to the war effort in ways which rendered compassionate domesticity relevant in public contexts. But war also underlined women's secondary role in the national imagination.

Yet the feminine was incorporated in British sites of collective memory. Throughout the eighteenth century, the figure of Britannia was represented in two guises: as the ideal of Georgian femininity, virtuous mother, and lover; and as the armoured protectress of her children and of the righteous in battle. Typically she would be seen to be inspiring patriotism, in charge of the fierce British lion, rather than fighting herself. Women admired, inspired, yet also required male valour and protection: Britannia as symbol both of womanhood and of the country was in need of defence. Female domestic virtues complemented and kindled masculine heroism. In Gore and Skerrett's monument, two classically dressed women touch closely, like mourning lovers left behind. Cook's monument features a rather motherly Britannia. In Collingwood's, the rigidness of the admiral's body and boat contrast with Britannia's soft arms, her hand gently cradling his head. Flaxman's Nelson features a figure of a motherly Britannia showing the heroic model to two young seamen. The connection between motherly femininity and education resonated with the contemporary notion that women read much history and were particularly affected by the power of example. In these monuments, which looked to female and male audiences, Britannia thus allegorically accompanied the compassionate warrior to St Paul's.

'The conquering hero comes – Dead! Dead!'

The ceremony which probably had a more powerful impact than any other on the national imagination during the French Wars was Nelson's official funeral at St Paul's in January 1806. Any joy Britons felt at the destruction of parts of the French fleet at Trafalgar was tempered by the devastating loss of Nelson. A state funeral was to symbolise the transformation of Britain's greatest hero into a national deity and attempt to rally the nation behind a show of national mourning and gratitude.

Nelson's body was returned to Britain in a barrel of brandy on board *Victory*.[56] It was laid in a coffin made of timber from the mainmast of the French flagship at the Battle of the Nile, *l'Orient*, and lay in state in the Painted Hall in Greenwich from 5 to 7 January 1806. Tens of thousands came to pay their respects. On 8 January, it was again Handel's powerful music – muffled drums and pipes playing the dead march from Handel's *Saul* – which framed this pivotal moment in the nation's public life, as a two-mile procession of black-draped boats escorted the coffin underneath a canopy topped with ostrich feathers in a royal barge up the Thames. The following morning, a solemn crowd of several tens of thousands lined the streets from Whitehall to Ludgate Hill. Minute-guns boomed as a formidable army of some 10,000 troops, together with Greenwich Pensioners, seamen and marines of the *Victory*, thirty-one admirals, cabinet ministers, the Lord Mayor of London, and seven royal princes accompanied Nelson's funeral car, modelled on the *Victory* from the Admiralty to St Paul's. Sir Peter Parker, Admiral of the Fleet, instead of a member of Nelson's family, had been chosen as chief mourner, to signify the navy's importance to the state. Tears

> did not flow from the soft sex only, but every man, who had a heart capable of feeling, yielded to emotions of sorrow, which the illustrious character so well deserved. The scene was particularly affecting, when the spectators exclaimed, with reverential enthusiasm, 'the conquering hero comes. *Dead! Dead!*'

The inclusion of ordinary sailors in state ritual in 1797 had set a precedent and by 1806 was viewed less apprehensively. Many were touched by the 'exhibition' of perforated enemy colours by *Victory*'s sixty seamen; only those insusceptible to merit and patriotism did not look with

> particular reverence to such ... gallant fellows ... These men, whom no dangers could daunt, whose nerves would stand unshaken before the most menacing terrors of death, seemed deeply depressed by the fate of their commander.

Shortly before one o'clock, infantry bands and cavalry trumpets heralded the arrival of the funeral procession at St Paul's:

The great western gate was opened, and the winds that were thereby admitted gently waved the French and Spanish ensigns captured at Trafalgar, compelling them to a reluctant tribute to the memory of their immortal captor.[57]

Since 11 a.m., the seats under the dome, the choir, and in the nave had been filled by some 7,000 ticket holders, mostly selected from the higher ranks of society. At the end of the four-hour-long burial service, as night was falling over wintry London, and the artillery fired a salute and the infantry three volleys, the Garter King at Arms proclaimed the style, titles, and dignities of the deceased peer, ending, unusually and dramatically, with the exclamation: 'the Hero, who, in the moment of victory, fell covered with immortal glory.' The choirs of St Paul's, Westminster Abbey, the Chapel Royal, and St George's Chapel, Windsor, sang an adapted version of Handel's 'His Body is Buried in Peace'. When at 5.33 p.m. a concealed lift started lowering the coffin into the crypt, the protocol asked for the sailors to fold up the colours and place them on a table. Instead, the sailors unexpectedly, but with intuitive coordination, rent one of the flags, perhaps *Victory*'s ensign, into pieces, to preserve them as relics. The future Dean, Henry Milman, then a young boy, recollected: 'I heard, or fancied that I heard, the low wail of the sailors who bore and encircled the remains of their admiral.'[58] In one-off ceremonies more than in commemorative effort intended for permanency, the valour of ordinary servicemen was acknowledged by the prominent inclusion of the sailors. It probably helped that they were there to mediate the worship of the officer hero. But during a ceremony choreographed by the College of Arms in a quasi-royal fashion, the sailors' final act of defiance mirrored Nelson's frequent flouting of the authorities: Nelson remained the popular, maverick hero as much as the state's outstanding serviceman.

On many the event made a lasting impression. Lady Bessborough did not consider 'grand ceremonies and processions ... the Genius of the English Nation, and therefore they usually fail; but in this instance I must say I never saw any thing so magnificent or so affecting, and well managed'. Even those who could not attend in person felt part of a virtual national community of mourning and commemoration:

Thy memory shall be embalmed in our grateful affections: and history shall record, that a whole nation, sensible of their obligations to thee, by their presence or their sympathy attended thy funeral, and followed thy awful remains to their august and final abode.[59]

185

That week, St Paul's was truly the kingdom's heart, the focal point of the national imagination. Britons participated on many levels. In the provinces, bells tolled, parades and assemblies were held, and sermons read and prayers said. Hull restaged the entire lying-in-state. Lincoln Assembly Rooms exhibited a replica coffin. Provincial theatres re-enacted the metropolitan street procession and Manchester theatre the funeral itself. Special editions of journals and prints rendered the occasion in word and image. All aspects of Nelson's funeral, as well as his last battle, were depicted in prints, on commercially produced ceramics, glasses, and silver-rimmed horn beakers, on enamel boxes, pendants, brooches, and on funeral fans, and even on hurriedly produced furniture. Such commemorative objects later mediated visitors' experience of the pantheon, and served them as aides-memoire. There were also glass paintings of Nelson's death and funeral, and a plethora of prints, especially of the funeral car, which merged the popular genre of pasteboard ship models on the London stage with heraldic art. The funeral car itself was to be preserved at Greenwich Hospital 'as a Monument'. In spring 1806, Westminster Abbey installed Catherine Andras's life-sized wax figure of Nelson as a rival tourist attraction to the tomb in St Paul's.[60]

In the era when cemeteries were separated from churches, the interment of a national hero in a metropolitan cathedral created a place of pilgrimage. Vergers at St Paul's had shown off the burial place even before the funeral. Now the crypt with his tomb was immediately included in the Cathedral tour. Nelson's coffin was encased in a Renaissance sarcophagus of black marble, originally designed for Cardinal Wolsey and later intended for Henry VIII. Nelson's tomb quickly became a hallowed (and commercialised) site of pilgrimage of the British Christian Empire, shown by the ghostly light of lanterns handed down in procession from verger to verger. Across Europe, national pantheons inhabited temple-like structures, often removed from conurbations and placed on an elevated site. Many such quasi-sacred sites were planned, if not realised, in Britain and France. The designs for a Prussian national monument to the wars of liberation in 1814–15 belong in this category, as does Leo Klenze's Walhalla, first conceived in the 1800s. The concepts and structures of the mausoleum, the pagan pantheon, and the modern museum merged in those shrines to national worthies.

The notion of immortality implied in the stories of the St Paul's heroes is not the Christian notion of an afterlife, but the memory of future generations. As Sheridan's inscription on Nelson's monument in the Guildhall put it: 'THE PERIOD TO | NELSON'S FAME | CAN ONLY BE | THE END OF TIME'.[61] The British pantheon, as the burial place of the national hero, combined the Christian custom of burying a saint's body in a sacred monument with an 'Enlightenment sensibility underlying the need to preserve the individual's memory among the living.'[62] In the personal cult of Nelson, Christian terminology and ritual had been transferred to nationalism.

Despite the distinctly Anglican nature of Nelson's funeral, public participation was much broader. By the early nineteenth century, St Paul's was a truly national emblem, a temple of Britishness whose appeal appeared to reach well beyond Anglicanism.[63] The limits of appropriating St Paul's as a pantheon of mortal warriors seemed to have been reached when some proposed to erect Nelson's monument under the centre of the dome, preferably raised on a pyramid, making it the focal point of the church. Although artists like Flaxman and Bacon entertained notions of Christian sculpture, Flaxman, for one, objected – this was bordering too closely on unacceptable idolatry.[64]

As the Royal Academy's first Professor of Sculpture, Flaxman explained that his appointment had only become necessary when the art of sculpture was rising in popularity, and 'native achievements had called the powers of native sculpture to celebrate British heroes'.[65] National monuments, commissions from native artists, notions of patriotic art, and an evolving national heroic aesthetics were all closely intertwined. The reluctance to conflate secular heroism too closely with quasi-religious notions and the avoidance of martyrological imagery at St Paul's were only some of the ways in which the British state and British artists set their national commemorative culture and heroic iconography apart from contemporary European practices. In the shift from Westminster Abbey to St Paul's Cathedral as the new national site of mourning and memory, the shift from the American to the French Wars, and from mid-century sentimental heroism to a revival of chivalry around the turn of the next century, Britons had developed specific representational strategies to negotiate notions of religion, masculinity, and bodily harm. The relationship between military practices and experiences and their representation in national monuments was complex. Artists and their official patrons chose from a wide spectrum of representational possibilities; this involved numerous disjunctions as well as silences.

CODA

IMPERIAL SITES OF MEMORY

ST PAUL'S ATTRACTED SUSTAINED PUBLIC INTEREST and streams of visitors. But disputes over its accessibility went right to the heart of defining the cultural nation. Not everyone who wanted to make the pilgrimage to St Paul's and Nelson's tomb could do so. This provoked ironic and sarcastic responses, such as the print *The Sailor's Monument*, published right after Nelson's funeral (fig. 26). By the time Flaxman's statue was finally unveiled at St Paul's in 1818, Nelson had already been commemorated privately and publicly on numerous estates and in very many towns and cities across the United Kingdom, where civil society commissioned monuments by public subscription. Multiple sculptural reference points helped create a virtual national community of mourning and commemoration. They also demonstrate how local and trans-local politics intersect with investment in the commemoration of a national hero.[1] Nelson, who had briefly visited Barbados in 1777 and Quebec in 1782, was an imperial hero too; as early as 1809, a group of Montreal citizens erected their Nelson monument by public subscription in Place Jacques-Cartier.[2]

Physical and imaginary sites of memory, such as the imperial and national topography of sites associated with Nelson, order and embody collective memory.[3] By way of a coda to this section, let us visit a few British imperial sites of memory in North America and India. At some of these, British imperial and colonial contributions to memory-making coincided. And although our primary framework remains official commemoration, those practices overlap with personal memory.[4] We will end by returning to Nelsonian sites, and two brief examples of how the

26. William Holland (publisher), *The Sailor's Monument to the Memory of Lord Nelson* (1806). Jolly Jack Tar stands sulkily in his backyard looking at his own crude memorial to the admiral, with a legend reading: 'I'll be no Twopence Customer at S.ᵗ Paul's!' The admission fee limited physical access to the national pantheon for many ordinary Britons. Only during some twenty hours of services a week did access remain gratis: 'Service is over,' went the notorious cry, 'and tuppence for all that wants to stay.'

THE SAILOR'S MONUMENT.. to the Memory of Lord Nelson.

imperial hero became the focus for anti-imperialist attacks in the 'Irish Troubles' and in the post-colonial Caribbean of the twentieth and twenty-first centuries.

India: 'A rivalship of public gratitude'

Within days of Nelson's death in 1805, the man who would soon face him in marble at St Paul's died in India. He was the outstanding military leader of British India of his generation – the Marquis Cornwallis. His memorialisation allowed various imperial narratives – of conquest, civilian reform, and benign rule – to be highlighted. Both the British state at home and officialdom and British-Indian society on the Subcontinent invested in commemorative practices; in India these were seen as a friendly competition between the Presidencies.

Cornwallis had delivered a decisive British victory in the Third Mysore War in 1791–2, which was especially widely visualised. Satirical prints criticised initial failures and alleged corruption and greed. Maps, paintings, and illustrated histories claimed authenticity in their celebration of victory. Imagery transferred the accusation of despotism from the British to Tipu and celebrated perceived British benevolence in the so-called 'hostage pictures'. The handing over of Tipu's two young sons

189

to Cornwallis to guarantee that Tipu would abide by the terms of the treaty was depicted by Robert Home (who had been present on the spot), Arthur W. Devis, the American Mather Brown, and Henry Singleton, as well as in stage productions and transparencies from London to Dublin and the Caribbean. The iconography of British military conduct harks back to Hayman's paintings of Granby, Clive, and Coote, and, as we have seen, was widely picked up in Napoleonic-era British culture. In the British imperial imagination, the representation of Cornwallis as the paternalistic symbol of imperial conquest cushioned the shift towards more aggressive expansion and authoritarian rule. The British presence in India, previously much critiqued as avaricious, corrupt, and inhumane, was now often imagined as a triumph of British humanity over indigenous despotism and cruelty. Home exhibited *Reception of the Mysore Princes by Lord Cornwallis* at the 1797 Royal Academy alongside his *The Death of Colonel Moorhouse at Bangalore, 1791* (1793–4), a large canvas that resonated with West's *Wolfe* and Copley's *Peirson* (see fig. 28, plate VIII). Moorhouse is shown dying amid British and Indian troops in the storming of the Pettah Gate: British martyrdom balanced the plight of the young princes.[5]

In Britain, Cornwallis had been made a marquis for his 1792 victory and received the thanks of Parliament and the freedom of the City of London. After his death, he won parliamentary marble accolades at St Paul's. The pyramidical group shows the life-size statue of the marquis on a truncated column, a stately, slightly plump figure wearing the robes of the Garter, his outstretched right arm holding a scroll. Two figures below represent the British Empire in Europe – seated, in classical garb, at once imperious with spear and shield (as if posed for battle), yet contemplative with eyes cast down – and the British Empire in India. The latter stands bare-breasted (more attention is given to her anatomical detail than elsewhere in the monument), wearing a heart-necklace, her empty hands folded in front of her, and gazing up submissively to the governor.[6]

The inscription on his St Paul's monument asserts Cornwallis's military conquests but also his civilian leadership in a paternalistic empire. He had reorganised the Company's revenue, commercial, and judicial branches in the so-called Cornwallis Code or Bengal system. Both his roles were acknowledged by commemorative practices in British India, where monument-building had in fact preceded metropolitan activity. In 1792, the British residents in Madras had raised £2,000 towards a statue to commemorate Cornwallis's victory over Tipu Sultan and his retirement as Governor-General.[7] Thomas Banks's statue stands in a pose similar to the Apollo Belvedere, with his left hand on his hip and the right hand turned out in greeting or as if giving directions. Fierce debate on classical *versus* modern dress had resulted in a compromise: a military uniform is covered by the voluminous robes of the

Knight of the Garter. The pedestal relief narrates the familiar handing over of Tipu's sons – the scene of Indian humiliation and British benefaction. The monument was unveiled in 1800 on the Parade Grounds of Fort St George as the first public commemorative sculpture executed in Britain to be erected on the Indian Subcontinent. The metropolitan art public saw prints of the sculpture, and models and drawings at the Royal Academy (which had supervised the commission), displayed alongside scenes from the Battle of the Nile and views of the new East India House. The Cornwallis statue – paid for by the 'PRINCIPAL INHABITANTS OF MADRAS | AND ... THE CIVIL AND MILITARY SERVANTS OF THE EAST INDIA COMPANY' in the Fort St George Presidency – was later moved to an Ionic temple in front of the Secretariat in order to preserve it from adverse environmental conditions.[8]

~

Meanwhile, an elaborate Anglo-Indian commemorative programme was under way in Calcutta. In 1793, its British inhabitants had started a subscription towards an equestrian statue. By 1803, as British magazines were reviewing the monument by John Bacon the Elder and the Younger, it was making its passage on the *Earl Howe*. Bacon had it accompanied by his assistant Robert Fox as he was 'fearful that the workmen in India are incompetent to put together the Colossal Group'. The statue consisted of a duplicate of the elder Bacon's statue for East India House, here flanked by seated figures of Prudence and Fortitude, with the attributes of Hercules between them. The inscription highlighted Cornwallis's political consolidation of Bengal and its defence against Tipu's 'unprovoked' aggression. Cornwallis stood at Calcutta as a Roman proconsul whose ancient European power and modern nation brought India prosperity by law as well as arms. The monument was eventually erected in Calcutta's neoclassical Town Hall on the Esplanade, which became a hall of British fame. Cornwallis was joined by John Bacon the Younger's statue of Wellesley in court robes and by Richard Westmacott's of Warren Hastings as a scholar accompanied by a Hindu Brahmin with a manuscript and a cross-legged Muslim scholar reading a book. Brahmins and Muslim scholars in Anglo-Indian monuments (they also appear with Company servant Josiah Webbe and Major-General Close in St Mary's, Madras) articulated the imperial narrative of protecting indigenous cultural traditions in the face of tyrannical, anti-intellectual rulers.[9]

When Cornwallis died in 1805, shortly after starting his second spell in India as Governor-General and commander-in-chief, General Orders proclaimed that the Company, British India, 'the 'Native Powers of India', his Sovereign and his country, and Europe at large would honour the memory of a man to whose 'splendid and important Services ... in different quarters of the Globe' the 'records of the British Empire in Europe and Asia bear ample testimony'.[10] Within weeks of Cornwallis's death, a subscription opened at Calcutta's Bank of Hindustan for a mausoleum over Cornwallis's grave at Ghazipoor. Separate committees oversaw the fund-raising in India and in the United Kingdom.[11] Special invitations to subscribe were sent to the British residents of various Indian cities, Ceylon, and Penang, and to indigenous inhabitants of Calcutta. The British residents of Madras, however, prioritised their own subscription for a cenotaph on the Mount Road to Cornwallis, from whose victories, just administration, and patriotic virtue they felt they had benefited.

Monument-building on the Indian Subcontinent had become an explicit 'rivalship of public gratitude' between the presidencies and their British elites.[12] The heavy octagonal building of the Ghazipoor mausoleum consists of a raised Tuscan-Doric peristyle around a central cella with sarcophagus, covered by a coffered semi-spherical dome.[13] By order of the Company directors, Flaxman created a marble statue, topped by an urn with decorative mouldings; four panels show the hero's portrait medallion in military uniform and mourning figures of a Hindu and a Muslim in the attitude of mourning above an English epitaph, and a European soldier and a sepoy with an epitaph in Urdu. The lengthy English inscription praises Cornwallis's victories and gives an imperialist reading of the benefits of British rule for both colonists and colonised.[14] Perhaps not all Cornwallis hero worship was imperialist propaganda, though: the site seems to have become a venerated shrine where indigenous people placed offerings.[15] That indigenous people could be central to an imperial officer's military strategy and to his memory was shown just a few years after Cornwallis's death – in British North America.

Canada: Wampum and Memorials

After the end of America's War of Independence, over 30,000 American loyalist refugees settled in the Maritimes. They went mostly to Nova Scotia, with its rough North Atlantic seaboard and the farming land of the Annapolis Valley. It was, along with Quebec, the only part left of Britain's North American Empire by 1783. When, from 1806 onwards, Napoleon's Continental Blockade had stopped all European trade with Britain, imports from New Brunswick, Nova Scotia, and Lower Canada (the old French heartlands of Quebec) replaced Baltic timber. Commercial and territorial antagonisms with the United States erupted in the War of 1812.

Among the final generation of British heroes whose reputations were won on North American battlefields was Major-General Sir Isaac Brock. Today much better known in Canada than in Britain, his commemoration demonstrates that

192

the memory of a British hero could be evoked both in the name of British imperial unity and of an emerging sense of national unity among British and indigenous people in Canada.

Brock, born on Guernsey in 1769, entered the British army just after the American War at the age of fifteen, rising swiftly by purchase to the rank of lieutenant-colonel by 1797. After European service, Brock led his 49th Regiment of Foot to the Canadas. To his admirers, Brock was the 'beau-ideal of military manhood, six foot two … broad-shouldered and deep-chested, active, athletic, keenly intelligent, and thoroughly sympathetic'.[16] He was a demanding but humane and charismatic military leader who could motivate both white soldiers and Indian warriors. In October 1811, Brock took command of all troops in Upper Canada, combining that position with chief civil administrator, or President, of Upper Canada.

Tensions over neutral shipping and British impressment of American seamen had been intensifying since 1803. By 1812, Brock reinforced the province's defences and courted First Nations.[17] There were an estimated 10,000 warriors in the Great Lakes region, including some 1,600 in Upper Canada. Brock appreciated that, if he wanted to secure the cooperation of the First Nations and inspire the population of Upper Canada with confidence, he had to show British military strength and capture the American posts of Michillimackinac and Detroit in case of war. In autumn 1812, some 500–600 Grand river Iroquois, Mississauga, Delaware, and Ojibwas joined the British on the Niagara peninsula. After his coup in capturing Fort Mackinac, where Brock's native allies first induced psychological fear in the enemy, Brock concluded an alliance with the Shawnee chief Tecumseh, one of the most influential leaders among the First Nations. Brock bluffed the American General Hunt into surrendering the fort of Detroit, 3,500 troops, and some 60,000 square miles of American territory, a feat which could not have been achieved but for the presence of Tecumseh's warriors. Brock also committed the British to the Shawnee's vision of an independent native territory, urging the Prime Minister to consider his allies' position in future peace negotiations.

In the autumn of 1812, both the British and Americans secured their defensive positions along the Niagara river. Outnumbered three to one by the Americans, Brock had to divide his regulars and local militia between Fort Erie and Fort George, leaving Queenston, between the two forts, only lightly garrisoned. Early in the morning of 13 October, the Americans attacked across the Niagara. Despite heavy British fire and treacherous river currents, most of the first wave reached the Canadian shore across from Queenston. Half the force headed up the embankment towards Queenston Heights, eighty metres above. Brock, wearing his full gold and scarlet dress uniform and a sash from Tecumseh, had meanwhile galloped eleven kilometres from Fort George to Queenston. Americans now reached the top of the promontory and forced the British from the Heights after they had spiked their biggest cannon. Brock led a bold frontal assault up the escarpment with only two companies and some militia, between 100 and 200 men in all, and gained the gun on the Heights. Already slightly wounded by a bullet, Brock charged further to drive the Americans to the edge of the Heights when – an easy target at a towering, dressy 190 cm – he was shot at short range with a rifle, the ball entering under his left breast and passing out by the right shoulder. He urged that his fall was not to be noticed lest it 'impede my brave companions from advancing to victory'. Later in the day the reinforced British Canadians, together with some 500–600 native allies, counter-attacked and won indeed a decisive victory.[18]

Brock's death, however, was a substantial loss for British imperial defence and for the British Canadians. And it was a particularly tragic loss for their native allies, who had played an important part at Queenston and with whom no British leader enjoyed a standing similar to Brock's. There were both Anglo-American and native mourning rituals. Brock's body lay in state in Government House until 16 October, when a funeral procession led by detachments of the 41st and militia, the general's horse and servants, and army surgeons and a chaplain conducted Brock (and his dead ADC) to Fort George. The caskets were carried between rows of more than 5,000 men: the militia and First Nations warriors faced regular soldiers, all resting on their arms reversed. The Americans had agreed to extend the ceasefire and asked permission to pay their military respects. Cannon thundered at Lewiston and Fort Niagara as well as at Fort George as Brock and his aide were interred in the same grave in the York battery at the British fort.[19]

Having first joined the Euro-American ceremony, Brock's native allies then separately paid their respects in their traditional way. On 6 November, a 'General Council of Condolence', a ritual mostly associated with the conclusion of diplomatic negotiations and performed as a cultural renewal, was held at Fort George. The Six Nations' speaker presented eight strings of white wampum to Brock's British and Canadian comrades, to

> wipe away your Tears, that you may view clearly the surrounding objects, we clear the passage in your throat that you may have free utterance for your thoughts, and we wipe clean from Blood the place of your abode, that you may sit there in comfort without having renewed the remembrance of your loss by the remaining stains of blood.

Wampum were 'beads arranged in strings or belts that served a mnemonic purpose as well as one of mutual empowerment through gift exchange'.[20] The Indians further presented a large white belt of wampum, that

> the remains of your late beloved friend and commander General Brock shall receive no injury we cover it with this Belt of Wampum, which we do from the grateful sensations which his friendship towards us continually inspired, as also in conformity with the Customs of our Ancestors, and we now express with the Unanimous voice of the Chiefs, and Warriors of our respective Bands the great respect in which we hold his memory, and the sorrow and deep regret with which his loss has filled our hearts.

Five more strings of wampum confirmed their continued brotherhood in arms.[21]

In Brock's case, unlike with Cornwallis, metropolitan monument-building anticipated colonial practice. Viscount Castlereagh, the Foreign Secretary, emphasised how Brock had inspired the population of Upper Canada with confidence and a 'sense of the value of their connection with [the United Kingdom], highly favourable to the frustration of the enemy's designs', a reference to Brock's character, civil administration, and steadfast belief in the defensibility of the province. Castlereagh proposed a monument as 'an animating example to future officers who might be entrusted with similar duties in His Majesty's more remote dominions'.[22]

The monument appropriates the visual formula of the *pietà* scene used so successfully in Benjamin West's *Death of General Wolfe* (1771) – a virtual imperial altarpiece merging Christian devotion with civic and especially colonial duty (figs 27, 28). The *pietà* form harks back to religious depictions of lamentations, most notably for the death of Christ. West had employed it to combine grand history with the celebration of milder virtues at a time when British heroism itself was in doubt. Westmacott's Brock used the *pietà* to highlight both a British heroic revival and the crucial role played by Brock's native allies.

In West's painting of *Wolfe*, the concerned glances of those surrounding the dejected dying hero contrast with the Indian's 'expressionless gaze' which, writes David Solkin 'serves to define an otherness which is both un-British and uncivilised'. The Royal Academy's 'unheroic audience' was asked to mourn a leader, yet also to celebrate the death of heroism and 'its victorious replacement by their own ideals of a sympathetic humanity'.[23]

Westmacott's relief monument shows Brock expiring in the arms of a soldier. Behind Brock a helmet and sword rest on top of several stacked stones, a votive record supposedly erected by the commander's companions. The memorial shares the lamentation formula and the figure of the single Indian with West's painting.

195

27. Richard Westmacott, *General Sir Isaac Brock*, St Paul's Cathedral (1813–?).

28. William Wollett, after Benjamin West, *Death of General Wolfe* (1776).

But it appeals to an audience that was participating in a revived patriotic cult of heroism. It also includes the 'Indian' in a much more significant role as one out of only two figures attending the hero (the medium and format of the relief monument limit the number of figures that can be included). He faces the British soldier in whose arms the hero expires. Standing upright (unlike West's kneeling Indian), apart from Brock's upper torso, the Indian's is the only nude body for the sculptor to demonstrate his competence in that important aspect of the art. In contrast to the 'expressionless gaze' of Wolfe's Indian, Brock's looks down on the dead general in a meditative expression of composed sadness, not unlike the British soldier, who – though holding on firmly to the general – is actually looking away from him in the direction of the Indian. In Westmacott's own description, the Indian was paying 'the tribute of regret [Brock's] bravery and humanity elicited'. Westmacott had probably read accounts of the Indians' participation in the funeral and condolence ceremonies. The marble Indian stands in for the many First Nations warriors who had paid their last respects to their most important British ally. Westmacott's Indian, 'natural man' responsive to Brock's human qualities, pays equal tributes with the British soldier to a hero in the national pantheon, and to a humane British leader who had (though, ultimately, in vain) sponsored the Indians' quest for an independent territory.

Transatlantic commemoration of Brock led to his reinterment in a monument, an anti-imperial attack, and a second, culturally more inclusive national Anglo-Canadian memorial. By 1815, the Assembly of Upper Canada decreed a Brock monument near Queenston. It was financed partly from public funds, partly by subscription. Eventually built in the 1820s, it combines elements from two proposals, namely that of a high tower, on Queenston Heights, with a mausoleum for Brock's remains, and of a monumental column similar to Lord Nelson's Montreal monument. In 1822, on the tenth anniversary of his death, some 8,000 people witnessed Brock's re-entombment in the base of the still incomplete forty-metre-high Tuscan column. On Good Friday, 1840, the monument was severely damaged in an explosives attack carried out by the anti-British Irish-Canadian Benjamin Lett. Just three months later, over 5,000 Canadians met on Queenston Heights to dedicate themselves to building a new monument. The event manifested the first stirrings of Canadian nationalism encompassing both white and aboriginal communities; the latter were also prominent among the subscribers to Brock's new monument. The committee assured them that the monument would

> tell their great Mother the Queen, and all their White Brethren, that the brave and grateful Indians have not forgotten their glorious leader and friend, who

197

flew to their defence in the time of danger, and that they have helped to build the tomb over his grave.

On 13 October 1853, the fortieth anniversary of his fall, Brock's remains were ceremoniously reinterred at the base of the new monument, adorned by statues of other warriors and lions. A sealed bottle, with a sketch of Brock, his date of death, and the reasons for the reinterment, was placed under the foundation stone. Of the dedication ceremony in 1859, coincidentally the year when Lett died, the *New York Times* reported that some of the First Nations were present, but that they kept 'largely aloof', and that there was nothing offensive to Americans in the speeches. Atop the sixty-metre Corinthian column of Queenston stone, then second in height only to Wren's column to the Fire of London, Brock still stands proudly, five metres tall and sword in hand, surveying the battlefield with a spy glass. Brock is today largely forgotten in Britain; even the plaque erected to Brock's memory at St Peter Port Church, Guernsey, was dedicated by the Ontario Department of Public Records and Archives. Across Ontatio, by contrast, places, schools, and B&Bs are named after Brock. The Saviour of Canada's alleged last words, 'Surgite! Push on!', form the motto of Brock University on the Niagara Peninsula. And the pressure group Citizens for a Canadian Republic have considered Brock among the Canadian leaders (Tecumseh being another) to replace the Queen on Canada's currency.[24]

New York to London: André Returns Home

The history of transatlantic commemoration had already come full circle the year before Brock's first reburial, when in 1821 the remains of Major John André had been repatriated from Tappan, New York, to be entombed near his monument in the south aisle of Westminster Abbey. The cult of André, manifest on both sides of the Atlantic, combined and sometimes integrated commemoration by the hierarchies of state and church with highly personal memoralisation and mementos. Most histories of the American War published in Britain since its conclusion had perpetuated the earlier portrayal of André as the polite, accomplished British martyr. Prompted by the ceremonial removal of the English-born General Richard Montgomery's remains from Canada, where he had died serving with the American 'rebels', to New York in 1818, the British consul in that city, James Buchanan, and the Duke of York as commander-in-chief of the British army, arranged the exhumation of André's remains and their removal to England. The 'exchange' of two military martyrs had the potential to inspire both national pride and international reconciliation. André's official exhumation also made possible the creation of personal mementos.

On the morning of Friday, 10 August 1821, Consul Buchanan led a large party by carriage to Tappan, where they were awaited by an American contingent.[25] Around 11 a.m., the diggers set to work, cautiously removing earth with shovels till they hit the coffin. Despite rumours of grave robbing, the skeleton was found undisturbed, although the skull had come apart from the neck joints and the roots of the peach tree had wrapped themselves around it. Small tufts of hair and the leather cord that had bound the queue were later sent to André's sisters in Bath. At Tappan, under the gaze of an 'attentive crowd of both sexes', the bones were placed in a sarcophagus of polished mahogany, the exterior panels of crimson velvet edged with gold, and its interior lined with black velvet. Local ladies proffered garlands to decorate the bier and six young New York ladies had sent a myrtle tree and a poetical address to accompany the body to England, along with the cedar and peach trees.[26]

The disinterment of André's remains prompted tensions between genteel society and an Anglophobe populace still harbouring resentment from the War of 1812. Nostalgic pride in the Revolutionary generation and their achievements was resurgent. While most showed 'respectful tenderness ... a few idlers, educated by militia training, and Fourth of July declamation, began to murmur that the memory of General Washington was insulted by any respect shown the remains of André'. These provocateurs were soon too drunk in a tavern to defend Washington's memory. But, clearly, André's role in the Revolution was still seen as controversial. Respectable society could perceive André as a symbol of genteel bravery and sentimentality, as they had done in 1780. But critics continued to label him a spy unworthy of special treatment, and denounced his disinterment as a disgrace to the memory of his captors and President Washington.[27]

The interment ceremony at Westminster Abbey was a low-key affair. A second part was added to the inscription on the plinth of André's monument to record the repatriation of his remains from Tappan. Again bridging official and personal commemoration, the Duke of York presented a gold-mounted snuff box – made from one of the cedar trees which had grown near André's grave – to the Rev. Mr Demarat to thank him for protecting the site against vandalism and from relic hunters. The peach tree from André's New York grave was replanted in the king's garden behind Carlton House.[28]

The *Gazetteer of the State of New York* dismissed all this as great British government-sponsored pomp:

> the memory of the spy and the traitor, are, however, alike consigned to infamy, snuff boxes, royal dukes, poetry, and sickly morality, fable, fiction, American clergymen, Westminster Abbey, and the 'monument' to the contrary notwithstanding.[29]

But when Lydia Maria Child in the early 1840s found the spot of the former grave in the middle of what was now a potato field, marked by 'a rude heap of stones, with the remains of a dead fir tree in the midst', she recorded that both 'tree and stones are covered with names' – presumably of visitors carving their names to mark the occasion and join their memories to André's.[30]

Personal responses to public sites of memory were undoubtedly more idiosyncratic and varied than the sparsely surviving documentation allows us to ascertain. People viewed monuments not just for detached historical and aesthetic edification, but for emotional reasons, often with their personal stories in mind. For some, standing in front of a military monument triggered campaign memories and allowed them to relive the moment. In the early nineteenth century, a possibly apocryphal story has it, Londoners observed the last surviving veterans at Wolfe's monument in Westminster Abbey 'lingering for hours, following with the end of their staffs the march of their comrades up the shaggy precipice, and discussing the merits of the different leaders.'[31]

The controversy over André's national monument led to a peculiar desecration at the Abbey. The statue was reported to have been 'wantonly damaged within a short period after it was erected, and several of the heads were broken away'. As early as the 1800s, London guidebooks had referenced the monument as 'proof of the necessity for shutting the nave against passengers ... It is nearly broken to pieces; the head of several figures being broken off.' Some suspected the choir boys of playing hockey with the heads in the cloisters:

> Often has the head of Washington or André been carried off, perhaps by republican or royalist indignation, but more probably by the pranks of West-minster boys: 'the wanton mischief', says Charles Lamb, 'of some schoolboy, fired perhaps with some raw notions of Transatlantic freedom. The mischief was done', he adds, addressing [the poet Robert] Southey, 'about the time that you were a scholar there. Do you know anything about the unfortunate relic?' Southey, always susceptible at allusions to his early political principles, not till years after could forgive this passage at arms.

In the Victorian period, the 'chest' in which André's remains had been transferred was still being preserved in the Abbey's St Blaize's chapel. Americans continued to visit André's monument in Westminster Abbey: 'many a citizen of the great Western Republic has paused before the sight of the sad story.'[32]

In 1879, a few years after the United States had celebrated the centennial of independence, a memorial of reconciliation was erected where André had died near Tappan, New York. The monument explained that André's remains had been removed to the Abbey. It quoted Washington's tribute to André, celebrating 'those better feelings which have since united two nations one in race language and in religion with the hope that this friendly union will never be broken'.[33] The special relationship encouraged American relic hunters too. By 1884, *The Times* of London claimed that André's and Washington's heads in the Abbey had each been replaced thrice. It blamed American tourists for 'taking home samples of what they see in "the old country"'.[34]

Imperial Hero or Villain?

Irreverent choirboys and irresponsible tourists were one kind of menace to a national monument's physical integrity. In the post-colonial era of the twentieth and twenty-first centuries, some of the most prominent imperial Nelson statues attracted much more violent anti-imperialist sentiment. Ireland had commemorated Nelson in 1808 with a very tall fluted Doric column topped by the admiral's statue in Dublin's Sackville Street (now O'Connell Street). On the fiftieth anniversary of the Easter Rising, 8 March 1966, the upper half of the pillar was blown up by Liam Sutcliffe, a member of the IRA, in protest against British imperialism.[35] British army engineers demolished the remains of the pedestal and the area was paved over. Only in 2003 was a monument by the English architect Ian Ritchie, the 125-metre-high Spire, erected for £4m. Nicknamed by Dubliners 'The Spike', the stainless-steel needle rises from a seven-metre diameter bronze disc set in the ground and tapers gradually from over three metres wide at the base to a mere fifteen centimetres near the top. Of Nelson's statue, only the severely damaged stone head survives in the Dublin Civic Museum, a poignant relic of Ireland's imperial and post-imperial pasts.[36]

Likewise in the Caribbean, after Barbados gained independence from the United Kingdom in 1966, Nelson's statue became embroiled in the debate about the history of imperialism and slavery. The monument had been erected on Barbados in 1813, designed by Westmacott, to commemorate 'their ILLUSTRIOUS DELIVERER', 'The Preserver of the British West Indies | in a moment of unexampled peril'. Nelson was further memorialised in 1905, at the centenary of his death, with a halfpenny postage stamp showing the monument framed by palm trees. But independence prompted a controversy over the propriety and meanings of a British imperial statue at the symbolic heart of a newly sovereign nation. Was Nelson to be seen primarily as an upholder of slavery and British imperialism, or a protector of Barbados from the French and thus indirectly an enabler of eventual Barbadian independence? First, Nelson's bronze statue in Trafalgar Square was turned by

180 degrees so the British admiral no longer looked down on the square and the Broad Street shopping district; the traditional wreath-laying on Trafalgar Day also ceased. In 1999, the government renamed the square National Heroes' Square and proposed that Nelson's monument be replaced by a statue of independence leader Errol Walton Barrow. The legendary Calypso singer The Mighty Gabby sings: 'Take down Nelson and put up a Bajan Man'.

As I completed this book in 2008, the Barbados National Trust voted to leave the statue in place. A report of the meeting in the *Barbados Free Press* prompted several dozen bloggers to continue the long-running debate on the history, politics, and aesthetics of Nelson's monument. Ought Nelson to be retained for reasons of historical truthfulness, to demonstrate the maturity of an independent nation, or simply for touristic gain ('the true national hero to those that matter ... the british tourists and west coast property owners', in the words of one blogger)? Or should the statue, like other trappings of empire, be removed to a maritime museum, or even be disposed of in less respectful ways? More fanciful contributions credited Nelson for saving not just Barbados but Africa (the Nile!) from French dominance. Others used the discussion to push broader agendas, wishing to throw Nelson out of the island along with all foreigners, or comparing Nelson's 'taking a bullet for his nation' with current leaders retiring with offshore bank accounts. The possibilities of reimagining this site of imperial and post-colonial memory seem endless; the debate on Barbados looks set to go on ...[37]

∼

It is another set of debates, which also began at the turn of the nineteenth century, and still preoccupy politicians and cultural leaders today, that we turn to in the following section. The wars commemorated at Westminster Abbey and St Paul's, and Britain's military and diplomatic capabilities more broadly, were also the contexts for key archaeological campaigns in areas of formal and informal empire. As antiquities became trophies of war, eliding the different meanings of monuments, and as Western Europeans appropriated the physical remains of ancient civilisations from the coasts of the Mediterranean and the depths of the Near East, the overlapping worlds of politics and culture had to grapple with issues of plunder, heritage, and preservation.

PART II

EMPIRE, ARCHAEOLOGY, AND COLLECTING (*c*.1760–*c*.1850)

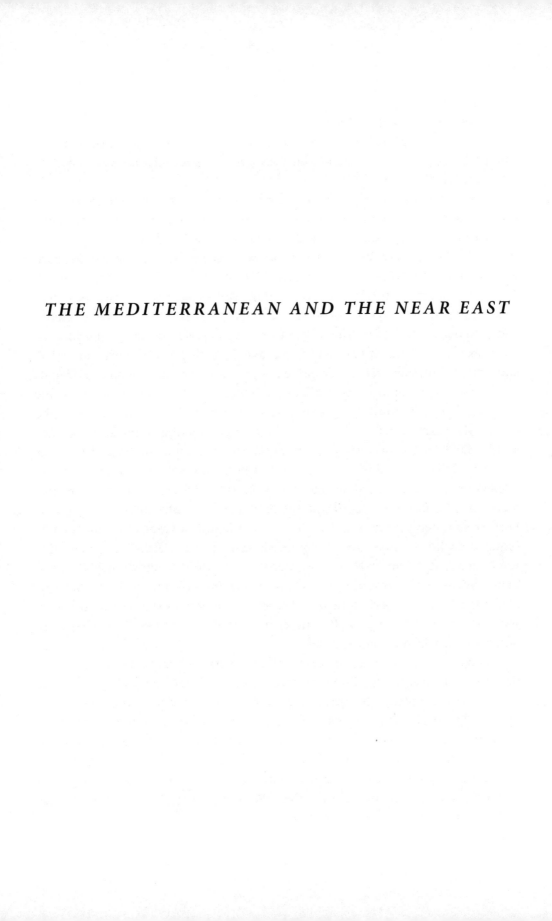

THE MEDITERRANEAN AND THE NEAR EAST

Bona rapta pone leno.
Lay down you thief the stolen goods.

Anagram of Napoleon Bonaparte, scribbled on to the final page of a notebook of

Captain Francis Beaufort, surveying the coast of Karamania, *c*.1811.[1]

IN THE LATE EIGHTEENTH and first half of the nineteenth centuries, Britain had vital spheres of interest between the western Mediterranean and the China Sea (see map 2). Egypt was of strategic and commercial significance, as it provided the overland route between Africa and Asia, and the maritime passage to the East. Between 1798 and 1801, the British expelled Napoleon from Egypt to protect India. The supposed French threat also prompted the British army to increase its regular Indian establishment to over 26,000 by 1801; these forces could now be effectively deployed outside India too. The Levant Company operated from Aleppo, Smyrna, the ambassadorial seat at Constantinople, as well as the small factories at Tripoli and Acre. To forestall French Levantine designs around 1800, Britain extended its involvement with Turkey. After the loss of Minorca in 1782 (it was recaptured only temporarily in 1798 until 1802), a new network of island bases was set up in the central Mediterranean, first focused on Malta, then extending to the Ionian Islands and Corfu; the latter was retained after 1815 and a protectorate was established over the Ionian Islands (until 1864). An Anglo-Turkish commercial convention in 1838 opened up the eastern Mediterranean and the entire Ottoman Empire to British merchants. Tariffs were reduced and Britain received 'most-favoured-nation' status. Further east, between 1798 and 1808, an India Board of Control Residency was set up at Baghdad, three government missions made it to Persia, and an embassy was established at Tehran. Basra – reached overland from Aleppo to Baghdad, and thence by river boat – was a key transit port in the East–West trade. From the 1820s to the late Victorian period, fears of French and Russian expansion into British spheres of interest, but especially with regard to the Ottoman and Persian empires, occupied officials in Britain and India.

As important as those regions were for their geostrategic and commercial potential, they were also of increasing significance to the British cultural state and the cultural nation. Indeed, the intellectual effort to explore and appropriate ancient lands and their physical remains was as crucial in some of these areas as the strife for territorial or commercial empire. The remains of ancient civilisations provided rich spoils for European imperial states engaged in wars of collecting and eager to claim ancient empires for their national cultures. Britain, it was argued, gained national prestige by capturing antiquities that were either of high aesthetic value like the Parthenon Marbles, or illustrative of the history of ancient art. They might be primarily of historical, philological, and literary importance, such as antiquities from Asia Minor, Egypt, or Assyria. Finally, interest in the Near East was also rooted in the project of uncovering the circumstances of biblical narratives.[2]

The political and the cultural coincided in this contest over symbolic resources. Classical and Near Eastern antiquity constituted an imperial frontier in an ideological sense. First, Western scholars, and increasingly governments and national museums too, sought to control the meanings of antiquity and claim inheritance, in terms of systems of governance, the accomplishments of a civilised society, or cultural excellence. Second, archaeological research was seen to be a means of informal imperialism. Cultural nationalism and the rivalry of nation-states were increasingly important in the building of national museums such as the Louvre, the British Museum, and the royal museums in Berlin. In this sphere, a cultural state was as strong as cultural and political actors' ability to draw on the state's fiscal-military and imperial capacities. For Britain, more than in other countries, it was public–private partnerships that determined success in the international competition over antiquities.

Public–Private Partnerships

Today the British Museum is famous for its extensive collections of ancient monuments. But for the first half-century of its life it possessed but few antiquities, reflecting their relative inaccessibility. Unusually for a European museum, the British Museum also lacked a royal collection at its core, although not all royal collections prominently contained antiquities at that time. There were a few objects: in the 1760s, George III, his Prime Minister, the 3rd Earl of Bute, and the Lethieullier family added a mummy with its decorated case, architectural slabs, a limestone relief, and a coffin to the small bronzes, amulets, and four mummies which had been among the 160 Egyptian objects in the founding collections of Sir Hans Sloane. In 1772, Parliament bought Sir William Hamilton's first collection of Greek vases for £8,410.[3] However, it was not until the early nineteenth century that outstanding collections arrived in rapid succession, starting with large objects which the British army captured from the French in Egypt in 1801–2. In 1805, Parliament acquired Charles Towneley's marbles for an astonishing £20,000, partly in order for Britain to be seen to compete (in morally irreproachable ways) with Napoleon's Italian art loot. In 1814, the Towneley vases, terracottas, and bronzes were added. In 1815, the first great body of original Greek sculpture arrived in the form of the sculptured frieze of the Temple of Apollo at Bassae in the Peleponnese, and in 1816 the Parthenon or Elgin Marbles. These were joined at Bloomsbury between the

1830s and 1850s by remains of other ancient civilisations from Asia Minor to Mesopotamia and central North Africa.

An extraordinary range of outstanding collections had thus been acquired as the result of direct or indirect state intervention. Nevertheless, there has been a perception that, in contrast especially to France but also Prussia, the British national collections were formed to a large extent by the generous donations of private individuals. The state supposedly looked on with indifference, or, at best, occasionally bought antiquities on the cheap from enterprising travellers or diplomats. In fact, however, the acquisition of the British Museum's main collections of antiquities, their quality, and their sheer scale can only be explained with reference to the power and reach of the British military and imperial state and its considerable investment of material and human resources in archaeological enterprise. International competition, the harnessing of diplomatic and military resources to archaeological work, and the dovetailing of private and public interest added up to a substantial programme of public patronage. This is easily missed or ignored by approaches that only consider Continental European ideal types of official or public patronage and designated public bodies like Napoleon's Egyptian Commission on the Sciences and Arts.[4]

Filling the British Museum with antiquities was an aspect of the wider relationship between the state and the arts. But rather than thinking in terms of a simplistic dichotomy of private versus public interest, it is important to recognise that various and overlapping modes of acquiring antiquities coexisted. State interest in archaeological enterprise and acquisitions for the British Museum reached a new level in the Napoleonic period and experienced its first heyday in the 1830s to early 1850s. This is in part explained by the increasingly urgent patriotic impulse for rival nations to wage war by cultural means. In the diplomatic and military struggles over the remains of ancient civilisations, British ministers, officials, and officers increasingly invested national pride in the British Museum, especially as Napoleon was expanding the French national collections. On a more modest scale, but with similar motivations, Prussia, smaller Continental European countries, and later the United States also joined the race. National museums enshrined cultural authority, which in turn symbolised diplomatic influence, political prestige, and military power. Acquiring and displaying prize antiquities was becoming key to the cultural politics of major Western European nation-states.[5]

Just how aggressively competitive international collecting had become by the 1790s is evident in the French ambassador Choiseul-Gouffier's instruction to his Athens agent, Consul Lucien Sebastian Fauvel: 'Take everything you can, lose no opportunity to loot everything which is lootable in Athens and its surroundings

... Spare neither the dead nor the living.'[6] Choiseul-Gouffier was one of the great art patrons of his age, and the grandest of French Grand Tourists. In the 1770s and 1780s, he had travelled through Greece to Constantinople with a suite of scholars, had dispatched his artists to paint views of Egypt and the Levant, and sent numerous antiquities to the Louvre.[7] Against the strictest prohibition, Fauvel bribed his way to obtaining a segment of the Parthenon frieze and a metope which were lying amongst the ruins. But before long, the French Revolutionaries declared Choiseul-Gouffier a traitor and ordered Fauvel to care for the collections as French national property.

The peculiarly British approach to collections development, namely by public–private partnership, was recognised in the late nineteenth century by Adolf Michaelis, a German professor of classical archaeology at Strasbourg. Michaelis recounted how the British Museum had been set up in 1753 by a parliamentary grant and public lottery to house a combination of purchased and bequeathed collections. Its antiquities department (he summarised correctly) was based on donations and purchases at first, but then on the Egyptian booty and the results of official expeditions:

> The State has ... liberally devoted regular and extraordinary subsidies to this grand national institution. With signal success it has recommended its diplomatic representatives in classic lands to keep the interests of the British Museum ever before their eyes, and it has liberally supported their researches. Not unfrequently officials have been chosen with special regard to their capacity for such work.[8]

Here in a nutshell is the explanation of the British approach and success in collecting antiquities by public–private partnership, by a combination of regular and spontaneous funding, and with diplomats and other officials acting as the archaeological arm of the state. The professional duties and status of diplomats, officers, or army doctors often facilitated archaeological activities. One of the themes of the following two chapters is how private and public interests dovetailed or conflicted in various ways.

For certain types of campaign, infrastructure of a particular nature and scope was required. The state was one of the main suppliers and often proved responsive to requests for diplomatic, logistical, and financial support. Scholarly societies and other semi-public bodies assisted also. Even though by the nineteenth century there was almost a routine expectation that state support would be forthcoming, this does not necessarily mean that the British government or Parliament were actively formulating a vision for the British Museum. The historian's task is to illuminate the conditions under which the state was most likely to commit resources, and to dissect the arguments which were advanced to justify such investment. Did private enterprise merely adopt the fig leaf of public interest and official support? To what extent were private motives – from genuine archaeological interests to diplomatic career tactics – translated into public policy? And if international rivalry was one key driver, was the attempted mobilisation of state resources by archaeologists more likely to succeed as and when the government sought to exert influence in a given region?

The characters featuring in these chapters pursued varied interests when travelling around the Mediterranean and the Near East. These ranged from educational travel, archaeological and architectural research, and scientific interests in geology, mineralogy, geography, and botany, to the quest for profit, power, or prestige. In the eighteenth century, British Grand Tourists marvelled at the remains of ancient Rome, the antiquities of Naples, the recent discoveries at Herculaneum and Pompeii, and the Greek and Roman remains of Sicily. Aristocrats and landed gentry collected primarily Roman and Greek sculptures, chiefly to decorate their country houses.[9] Encouraged by the presence of the Levant Company, the number of private travellers to the Levant increased in the eighteenth century, mostly young men with an interest in antiquities. That interest was often motivated by the desire to identify biblical or classical sites. Although Palmyra, Balbec, and Persepolis were investigated, relatively little certain knowledge of their history was acquired. Some learned men travelled in Upper Egypt, such as Richard Pococke, who also visited the Holy Land, Syria, and Cyprus between 1737 and 1740. In the following generation, James Bruce travelled on the Nile, through the Sudan desert, and to Abyssinia. Others traversed the Red Sea or crossed overland through Egypt to and from Suez. Journeys by camel from Aleppo to Baghdad, by river boat to Basra, and thence by ship to India became increasingly common.

Modern transport soon reduced travel times rather drastically. Marseilles to Alexandria in the 1820s could be a month-long sail, but in 1843 P&O steamers made Southampton to Alexandria in half the time. Henry Salt in 1802–3 took six months to travel from London via the Cape of Good Hope to Bombay; in 1843, Bombay could be reached in six weeks, including a five-day overland transit from Alexandria to Suez. In the 1850s, British-built railway lines from Alexandria to Cairo and from Cairo to Suez, and from 1869 the Suez Canal, transformed the transit of Egypt and further enhanced the country's significance in European–Asian trade.

Many journeys resulted in publications. In the 150 years up to Napoleon's expedition, the French had published some twenty-seven travel accounts of Egypt, the

English and British sixteen; in the period 1798–1850, fifty-four French accounts compare to 114 British; only in the 1860s did French again outnumber British publications. Beyond national accounting, however, rich cross-referencing and cross-fertilisation between authors of various nationalities suggests the continued vitality of the European republic of letters.[10] Over the half-century from 1775 to 1825, seventy different book titles appeared in English about the Levant, many of them reviewed at length in the literary magazines. Most focused more on antiquity than on the contemporary societies which their authors had encountered. There was also a revival of interest in Greek classical studies, manifest in growing travel, research, and publications on Greece and Asia Minor. This trend peaked with the more systematic and ambitious archaeological and topographical research undertaken in the early nineteenth century. More than the truly learned few continued to dabble in archaeological activity, and new types of illustrated press fostered an interest in archaeology among wider audiences.

While French and German scholars had been advancing the history of ancient art and classical studies from the middle of the eighteenth century, serious British interest in the history of classical art developed only towards the close of the century, with the studies of a triumvirate of Grand Tourists and outstanding collectors: Richard Payne Knight, an eccentric but perceptive critic, Charles Towneley, and, with regard to painted vases, Sir William Hamilton, the British ambassador to Naples otherwise remembered for his vulcanology and voluptuous Emma, his wife and Admiral Nelson's mistress.[11] Alongside Grand Tour collecting and private archaeological exploration, the British began to specialise in non-governmental, yet semi-public or semi-official patronage. This was exemplified by the Society of Dilettanti's expeditions to Athens and Asia Minor.[12] The resulting publications – *The Antiquities of Athens* (vol. I, 1762, dedicated to George III; vol. II, 1814) and *Ionian Antiquities* (1769) – inaugurated a new phase in the acquisition of antiquities. As national rivalry fired the ambition of British governments, archaeological enterprise around the Mediterranean and beyond was inextricably linked to military and diplomatic struggles for influence and power. Well into the nineteenth century, the initiative of private travellers and archaeologists and of individual diplomats continued to be important to British archaeological success. However, increasingly the British also used their military prowess and diplomatic influence to survey, excavate, and remove antiquities which otherwise might have made their way to Paris, Munich, or Berlin.

Yet British governments and Parliament still stopped short of formulating a coherent public policy that would have committed the state to the systematic, long-term expansion of the British Museum's collections. Indeed, this story of overall intensifying state commitment also features setbacks and counter-examples. Bavaria snatched up the Aegina marbles. Consul-General Henry Salt's second collection was purchased for the Louvre in 1826. In the view of some, the Treasury underfunded the Assyrian campaigns of the 1840s. Archaeological pioneers encountered other obstacles and limitations, as work was seasonally impossible in certain areas, and insecure in others. However, even if state support for archaeological endeavours was often still organised ad hoc, there were strong underlying assumptions and, after 1800, a fast expanding list of precedents which supported the regular commitment of resources. In some cases, precedent of official support came about because individual diplomats such as Lord Elgin were determined to acquire sculptures by any means possible. But on the whole, from the Napoleonic Wars onwards, logistical support, naval vessels and government transports, as well as diplomatic effort, often seemed relatively easy to mobilise.

If archaeological enterprise continued to be pursued partly in an ad hoc manner, private archaeologists as well as individual diplomats and officials nevertheless needed to have access to the relevant levels of government for opportunities to be seized effectively and efficiently. They also had to shape opinion and to ensure the allocation of adequate resources. Access was facilitated by the intimate connectedness of Britain's cultural and socio-political elites. Private explorers and individual diplomats used various channels from British Museum curators and scholarly networks to British Museum trustees and direct ministerial and parliamentary contacts. Networks of politicians, diplomats, and archaeologists shaped opinion on archaeological enterprise and the role of the state. Politicians and diplomats – most of them steeped in the classics, some very well travelled, and a few even published classical scholars in their own right – rubbed shoulders with archaeologists, architects, Egyptologists, and comparative linguists in London's polite clubs and learned societies. The latter, until the late nineteenth century, were more important than the universities in furthering emerging disciplines such as Egyptology.

In the Secretary of State's office and later the Foreign Office there was a tradition of literary-minded under secretaries, such as Robert Wood, the extensively travelled archaeologist, linguist, Hellenist, and author of *The Ruins of Palmyra* (1753) and *The Ruins of Balbec* (1757), of which French editions were printed almost immediately. Wood then took up a political career as an MP and undersecretary of state in the Foreign Office. At the same time he helped draw up the instructions for the Dilettanti's first expedition to Asia Minor in 1764. Similarly, diplomats in the eighteenth century pursued antiquarian and archaeological interests, and sponsored artists and architects. This is true not only of Sir William Hamilton at Naples, collector and dealer in painted vases. Around 1750, the British resident at Venice, Sir James

Gray, together with James Porter, British ambassador to Constantinople, arranged for James Stuart and Nicholas Revett's proposal for an architectural expedition to Athens to be published in both London and Venice. Gray also masterminded their election to the Dilettanti, of which he was a founding member and his brother Colonel George Gray the secretary and treasurer. The tradition was continued by men such as William Richard Hamilton, Stratford Canning, and Henry Creswicke Rawlinson, who feature in the chapters that follow.

Not only diplomats but military officers, too, had an antiquarian tradition, which they developed both within the British Isles and abroad. In Scotland, the officer William Roy, one of the inspirations behind the later Ordnance Survey, had moved on from the Military Survey of Scotland (1747–55) to map camps and stations constructed during Agricola's campaigns in the Scottish Lowlands; his contemporary, Captain Robert Melville, also discovered Roman camps.[13] At the turn of the nineteenth century, as the British army was briefly getting involved with Egyptian monuments, hydrographers with the Royal Navy also studied classical topography and antiquities from Asia Minor to central North Africa. Armies continued the antique practice of bringing monumental spoils of war from campaigns in Egypt to Afghanistan. And, as we shall discover in chapters 7 and 8, it was in British India that this military antiquarian tradition found one of its richest fields yet.

∼

Networks of politicians, diplomats, and officers, and of travellers and archaeologists, shared a classical outlook and brought the state's resources to bear on collection-building. Travelling Egyptologists like James Burton could draw on their scholarly contacts in the Dilettanti, Royal Society of Literature, Royal Geographical Society, and African Association to lobby the government. Scholarly travellers such as the historical topographers William Gell and Lieutenant-Colonel William Martin Leake became clearing houses of archaeological information for fellow scholars and government officials alike. Classical topography was the mapping of modern landscape in terms of classical geography. Gell travelled extensively on scholarly and diplomatic missions in the eastern Mediterranean, led the Dilettanti's second Ionian expedition (1811–13), and published widely on Troy, Attica, and Italian antiquities. In 1814, he was knighted for services in the eastern Mediterranean, presumably for both his diplomatic work in the Ionian Islands in 1803 and his scholarly efforts. From 1830, as the Society of Dilettanti's 'Resident minister-plenipotentiary' in Italy, he conducted an extensive international correspondence and was a member of academies from Paris to Berlin. The main reason for Leake's extensive travels was military: he spent much time between c.1799 and 1810 surveying parts of the Ottoman Empire from Greece to Egypt. His particular interests included topography, ancient remains, and ethnographic description. He represented British interests at Ali Pasha's court at Joanina, saw action in Egypt in 1801, and was on the brig *Mentor* when it sank with a consignment of Elgin's marbles. Leake published widely on the topography of ancient Greece, as well as on inscriptions, coins, and Egyptian monuments and hieroglyphics, held offices in the Dilettanti and the African Association, and helped found both the Royal Society of Literature and the Royal Geographical Society.[14]

Characteristic of the British hybrid approach, the British Museum Board of Trustees comprised private benefactors, the leaders of the learned and artistic professions, *and* the principal officers of church and state. In May 1818, the trustees of the British Museum, meeting in Bloomsbury, considered whether ministers and 'Public Functionaries' abroad should be used systematically to acquire collections for the Museum.[15] The adoption of such a recommendation by the Museum and government would have formalised a policy which was *de facto* already in operation, for instance with respect to multilingual inscriptions in Egypt. The importance of state endorsement was stressed by Giovanni d'Athanasi in *Researches and discoveries in Upper Egypt under the direction of Henry Salt*: since 1815, excavations in Egypt had 'always [been] done through the medium of the Consuls' who received exclusive permits.[16] One of Salt's successors as Consul-General, Sir Charles Augustus Murray, in 1849 offered to the Museum the collection of ancient gold coins assembled by the late Viceroy Ibrahim Pasha on his campaigns in Syria, Upper Egypt, and Achra. Uncertain whether he ought to communicate with the government or the trustees of the British Museum, Murray chose the Marquis of Lansdowne as an 'influential member of Both': 'I am quite aware that in my official capacity, I am not authorised to make any Purchases on account of the Govt. without previous Instructions', he wrote. But he wanted to secure what might prove to be 'an important national acquisition, before my Colleagues had got scent of it.' French and Russian competition, by the way, would double the price.[17] And Charles Thomas Newton told Henry Austen Layard in 1852 that permanent residence and official position in a territory gave an archaeologist a clear advantage over mere visiting agents, not least because he was thus better able to ascertain the true market value of antiquities.[18] In brief, overlapping circles of scholars and curators on the one hand, and of archaeologically keen politicians, officials, diplomats, and officers on the other, deployed resources of the British state to further collections development. The boundaries demarcating the semi-public and official spaces within which these actors moved were as permeable and fluid as the dual identities of officials and collectors.

One of the reasons why it was easier to persuade government and Parliament to commit resources to certain archaeological enterprises than it was to convince them, for instance, to patronise modern history painting was the importance of the classics to the world view of the elites. For there was a long-standing political as well as cultural tradition which lauded classical achievements, and a tradition of gentlemanly collecting, especially of Roman and Greek antiquities, among Britain's governing elites.[19] A classical education remained dominant for the ruling orders well into the nineteenth century, reformed to include ancient history at Oxford in 1830 and Cambridge in 1851, and philosophy in the Oxford Greats. The public schools mapped out literary and actual itineraries for the Grand Tour to Italy, on which Britain's classically educated future rulers collected editions of ancient authors, eighteenth-century deluxe folios on ancient architecture and sculpture with engraved plates, as well as ancient monuments and modern copies. While socially and culturally exclusive, the classics were disproportionately influential through the men setting the political, moral, and religious tone of the late Hanoverian and Victorian age. In the eighteenth century, it was an idealised image of republican Rome that English aristocrats referred to for their model. From the Seven Years War, the governors of the British Empire identified with the Roman imperial paradigm and adopted and adapted its material legacy. Napoleon's appropriation of Rome made the Greek republican model increasingly attractive to British imperialists.

The acquisition of classical relics by Grand Tourists was an expression of their knowledge of ancient cultures and sites; their appropriation and adaptation as models for British audiences was one aspect of colonialism. As the range of ancient civilisations that were recovered widened, so did the specific reasons advanced for supporting diverse archaeological enterprises. The valences of antique remains ranged from aesthetic to historical, linguistic, and religious rationales. Sometimes they were contested, as in the case of the aesthetic appreciation of Assyrian sculpture, but in all these aspects modern Western engagement with antiquity involved the competitive appropriation of symbolic resources. Abu Taleb reversed Westerners' critique of Indians who idolised aesthetically poor sculptures when he ridiculed Europeans for fetishising antique statues:

statues of stone and marble are held in high estimation approaching to idolatry. Once in my presence, in London, a figure which had lost its head, arms, and thighs, and of which, in short, nothing but the trunk remained, was sold for

40,000 rupees (£5000). It is really astonishing that people possessing so much knowledge and good sense, and who reproach the nobility of Hindoostan with wearing gold and silver ornaments like women, should be thus tempted by Satan to throw away their money upon useless blocks.[20]

Although the classics were in many ways socially exclusive, antiquities mattered not just to the educated few. The arrival of major archaeological collections in Bloomsbury made national news. Ancient civilisations increasingly captured the popular imagination. By the second third of the nineteenth century, magazines and best-selling books related the adventures of intrepid archaeologists who rediscovered ancient civilisations in dangerous lands.[21] Accounts of the hazardous journeys across deserts and oceans of the gigantic sculptures from Luxor, Xanthus, and Nineveh gripped popular audiences. The thousands who visited the Museum also read about how the English polymath Thomas Young raced the brilliant French linguist Jean-François Champollion to decipher the hieroglyphs. The latter eventually 'cracked the code', but Young's substantial contributions are honoured by his epitaph in Westminster Abbey: he 'first penetrated the obscurity which had veiled for ages the hieroglyphics of Egypt'.[22]

Antique marbles also sparked controversy. Satirical prints attacked the government for spending money on antiquities when the country could not even afford to feed its veteran seamen, a dig, in part, at the relative exclusivity of the concern with antiquities. Others lampooned the government's 'niggardly grants' that did not do justice to the discoverers' 'fine English spirit of research'.[23] In an argument still raging today, Lord Byron challenged Elgin's right to remove the precious heritage of Greece. The British and French accused each other of the barbaric use of chisels, saws, and gunpowder to cut antiquities into manageable pieces. And even among British political and archaeological circles there was fierce debate between those seeking to avoid national shame by damaging antiquities in removing them to Britain and those who preferred a mutilated monument in Britain to ceding any to France.

Around 1800, restrictions on access to the British Museum were gradually eased. In response to calls from in- and outside Parliament, the general public was more generously admitted to the national collections that it funded. Annual visitor figures soared accordingly, to exceed 50,000 by 1818. Crowds of all ages and social classes were particularly large on public holidays. In 1808, the first *Synopsis* had been published as a general guide to the collections; it went through some sixty editions until specialised catalogues replaced it by the end of the century. The *Synopsis* shows the Museum's ambiguous attitudes towards its dual mission. For

29. Edward William Cooke, *Raising Head to Proper Level Opposite its Pedestal in New Gallery* (1834). A detachment of gunners was needed to move the colossal, two-toned granite bust of the 'younger Memnon', in fact Rameses II, into the British Museum's new gallery. The floors in the temporary passage connecting the Towneley gallery to the new building were strengthened, and the men used tackle capable of lifting up to sixteen tons.

this substantial publication – while providing a concise history of the Museum and a room-by-room overview of the collections – asserted that the 'chief use of the Museum' was to assist scholars and artists in their studies and work. To satisfy the 'curiosity of the multitudes, who incessantly resort to it in quest of amusement', was 'a popular, though far less useful application of the Institution'.[24] The debate over the degree of accessibility and social and cultural inclusiveness would continue well into the 'age of reform' (chapter 9). There was thus an international and a domestic aspect to the 'national argument' that the British Museum collections ought to be built up proactively, and that the expanding galleries should be accessible to the nation, or at least to those who could make best use of the collections on behalf of the nation – its scholars, artists, naturalists, and everyone of 'decent appearance' and with a modicum of education. The combination of this bifocal national argument and of references to the aesthetic, scholarly, or religious valences of the physical remains of various ancient civilisations allowed archaeologically committed individuals and networks to manipulate the machinery of state for the benefit of the British Museum collections.

A wide range of state agencies aided collections development. The Foreign Office and its diplomats regularly organised the removal to ports of antiquities which private individuals had asked the Museum to accept as donations; the Admiralty and Royal Navy provided transport; the Treasury granted customs exemptions; the Admiralty offered free storage at arsenals from Chatham to Woolwich; and detachments of gunners helped install the often massive sculptures in Bloomsbury (fig. 29). Even private donations often required such state help to facilitate their arrival at the British Museum. From the French Revolutionary to the later Victorian period, a clear shift of emphasis occurred as far as acquisitions for the British Museum were concerned, from primarily individual, private, or semi-official to increasingly official and national operations. This shift was initially fostered by intensifying international competition during two decades of global warfare, which enabled the scaling up of Britain's archaeological operations. Indeed, many of the extensive collections of sizeable objects excavated and transported in the first half of the nineteenth century would have been almost impossible to acquire for the lone explorer, private merchant, or diplomat acting without considerable state support.

The following two chapters track the unfolding of state-supported archaeological activities around the Mediterranean and the Near East in times of war and peace. Moving in roughly chronological order of discovery from Egypt and Greece to Asia Minor and Assyria, they seek to illuminate the nuances of public–private partnerships, the precise nature and degree of state involvement in collecting antiquities, and the connections between archaeology, diplomacy, and culture wars. Although there are variations over time and across the geographical regions, taken together the cases amount to a pattern and narrative, if not to an entirely coherent and systematic official policy. International competition was a constant motivation for state investment in archaeological expeditions. National rivalry was a *Leitmotif* both in public rhetoric and in the language of individual archaeologists lobbying for support. However, although we will encounter numerous Anglo-French pitched battles in the field, this did not necessarily spell the end of the continuity of the cosmopolitan republic of letters in Europe.

THE SPOILS OF WAR

'Memorable Trophies of National Glory'

In 1798, Napoleon sailed from France with an expeditionary force of thirteen ships of the line and a 31,000-strong army to conquer Egypt and prepare the way for a possible advance to India.[1] Later that year, Admiral Nelson destroyed Napoleon's fleet in the Battle of the Nile, and in 1801 General Abercromby defeated the army which Napoleon had left behind in Egypt. In the first major state-sponsored *land* mission of scientific exploration and collecting, Napoleon's army was accompanied by a 167-strong Commission on the Sciences and Arts led by Dominique Vivant, Baron Denon, an artist, diplomat, Egyptologist, and later director of the Louvre. The military campaign largely determined the prospects for exploration and research. But the military and scientific missions shared the object of appropriating the territory, both materially and intellectually, and some of the army's missions turned also archaeological. According to Denon, the joint operation sponsored a muscular, military antiquarianism: 'If a fondness for antiquities has frequently made me a soldier, on the other hand, the kindness of the soldiers, in aiding me in my researches, has often made antiquaries out of them.'[2] On 27 January 1799, Desaux's division rounded a bend of the Nile and came in sight of the temples of Luxor and Karnak. The army paid spontaneous tribute to antiquity by coming to a halt and bursting into applause: 'Without an order being given, the men formed their ranks and presented arms, to the accompaniment of the drums and the bands.'[3]

Some missions of Napoleon's army became devotedly archaeological, if only

30. Frontispiece to *La Description de l'Égypte* (1809). A richly decorated frame is employed to both claim and reveal Pharaonic antiquity from Alexandria to Aswan. Alexander, Pompey, Caesar, Mark Anthony, and Augustus all came to Egypt, strategically located at the juncture of three continents, to seek power. Here, in the guise of a nude Apollo or Alexander, Bonaparte follows their conquest in a chariot. He is trailed by twelve muses returning the arts to their legendary origins in Egypt.

because engineers measured monuments and related them to their topographical and hydrological environment in order to determine the lie of the Nile and consider the possibilities for irrigation. By also seeking to link the history of Pharaonic civilisation to the history of the earth, and to make studying Egypt's past the prerequisite for plans to administer the conquered territory, they introduced Egyptology as a discipline at the intersection of geology, geometry, architecture, and archaeology. After the Egyptian expedition had failed militarily, and Napoleon could no longer deploy scholarship as a tool of imperial governance, in 1802 he endorsed the publication of *La Description de l'Égypte* as a state project: the lavishly illustrated volumes presented the expedition as a cultural triumph. Initially, scholarship had been seen in part as a tool of imperial governance; in the end, scholarly results had to substitute for territorial conquest (fig. 30).[4]

Although the British army travelled without a scientific corps, some were aware of the wider historical, political, and cultural contexts and implications of their expedition. In December 1801, Lieutenant George Meredith of the Royal Marines asked his commander-in-chief for permission to remove a tin Cap of Liberty which

French soldiers had fixed on a strong pole on top of Pompey's Pillar in Alexandria as 'a double memento of sovereignty and intrepidity'. Meredith asked to be allowed to substitute 'our insignia more worthy so exhalted a situation' and requested an order be given 'to destroy so conspicuous a trophy of the Triumph [of] France over the friends and allies of Great Britain'. British sailors did indeed then remove the Cap 'in token of victory'. Thomas Walsh, captain in the 93rd Regiment of Foot, asserted that nothing could 'exceed the beauty of this fine monument of ancient architecture'. Andrew Pearson, an outstanding NCO with a lively interest in the customs of the people that his regiment encountered on their tours of duty, later recollected how, during the Egyptian expedition of 1802, 'like other travellers', the army had explored antiquities such as the catacombs near Fort Triangular. Pearson also remembered how they collected mummies in pyramids by decoying Bedouins away with coins, ascended the Great Pyramid, and measured Pompey's Pillar, 'the most beautiful specimen of granite I ever saw ... polished so bright that it appeared as if it were newly finished'.[5] (See plate XIII.)

Under the Treaty of Alexandria which concluded Anglo-French hostilities in Egypt in 1801, the French savants were to 'hand over all antiquities found by them and to relinquish all rights to any seized at sea by the naval blockade'. The French argued that their antiquities were the officers' private property, and then removed several key objects to secret locations in town and on a hospital ship in the harbour of Alexandria. General Menou's official version deviated:

> The monuments that can be considered public remained in the hands of the English, but I shall forcefully demand the return of a stone covered with inscriptions that was found in Rosetta, when I was commander there. I had declared it to be my own property and I assure you Citoyen Ministre, that this property in truth belonged to the Republic. I dare to hope that you, as a friend of the arts, will use all your influence to see to it that this precious monument is not lost to France.[6]

The British were aware, however, that the French scholars 'were the servants of the Republic, and their works were contracted for as national property'.[7] General Hutchinson explained that his demand for the antiquities mirrored Napoleon's example in transferring Roman art treasures, such as the Apollo Belvedere, to Paris. An eyewitness overhearing the heated exchange between the French and British generals noted that Menou's exclamation 'Jamais on n'a pillé le monde' 'diverted us highly, coming from a leader of plunder and devastation'.[8]

Thus the British eventually retrieved fifteen antiquities, some under military

31. *Rosetta Stone.* Spoils of war.

escort. Among these were two small obelisks from Thebes and Upper Egypt, three large hieroglyph-covered stone sarcophagi, including those of Nectanebo II and Hapmen, a colossal ram's head and colossal fist of Rameses II, and statues of the lioness-goddess Sehkmet. Most famously, there was Menou's Rosetta Stone, part of a broken dark-grey granodiorite stela, inscribed with a priestly decree which affirms the royal cult of the 14-year-old Ptolemy V Epiphanes in the year 196 BC. This artefact was crucial because of its trilingual inscription in hieroglyphic script, demotic Egyptian, and Greek. It was seized by the energetic collector the Rev. Edward Daniel Clarke and Lord Elgin's private secretary, William Richard Hamilton, supported by a detachment of artillery. Having allowed the French to take a cast, Colonel Hilgrove Turner conveyed the stone, in a strong case and separate from the other antiquities, on the *Egyptienne* to Portsmouth, from where it was moved via Deptford, the London Customs House, and the Society of Antiquaries at Somerset House to the British Museum. The Secretary of State, Lord Hobart, oversaw the triumphant progress of this 'proud trophy of the arms of Britain (I could almost say *spolia optima*), not plundered from defenceless inhabitants, but honourably acquired by the fortune of war'. In Parliament, the foundation of the

British Museum's Egyptian collection was discussed as entailing the acquisition of 'memorable Trophies of National Glory' 'by His Majesty's victorious Arms'. In a series of engravings, to be published under royal patronage, the Museum objects were advertised in 1803 as 'a GLORIOUS TROPHY OF BRITISH PROWESS, which the VANQUISHED THEMSELVES have been compelled to supply'. Visitors at the British Museum mostly crowd in front of the iconic object. Yet walk around the glass case and you'll notice that to this day the Rosetta Stone has inscribed, in fading paint, on its left edge its status as a token of victory: 'CAPTURED IN EGYPT BY THE BRITISH ARMY | 1801' (fig. 31).[9]

'Collecting-furor'

Egypt continued to occupy both military strategists and the builders of national collections of antiquities. After the 1801 surrender of the savants' collections, and the departure of most armed forces, the Anglo-French scramble for more winnings continued. Egyptian antiquities had acquired high prestige value in London and Paris. Egyptomania – already in evidence in Freemasonry's symbolism and Mozart's *Magic Flute* – reached new heights in European fashion and architecture. During the Peace of Amiens in 1802–3, hundreds of British politicians, artists, and collectors flocked to Paris to see Napoleon's European art loot which was filling the Louvre, not least its new antique galleries, unveiled in 1800. The catalogue opened: 'The majority of statues exhibited … are the fruits of the conquests of the Army of Italy'.[10] Many among the British ruling elite envied Napoleon's thorough attempt at a *translatio imperii* from Rome to Paris. In 1803, the British Museum founded its own Department of Antiquities and by 1808 the Royal Navy helped install in the completed Towneley Gallery the spoils of 1801 – the first Egyptian monumental stone sculptures known in Western Europe and the first entire collection acquired by the British state in this unfolding war over antiquities.[11] Although the aesthetic preference for the perceived naturalism and humanistic scale of Greek art was unassailable, there did develop in early nineteenth-century Britain an Egyptian aesthetic too, with a safe if subordinate place in the historical ordering of objects. Theories of cultural relativism of the kind advocated by the German writer Johann Gottfried Herder defended the importance of Egyptian objects as manifestations of native religion and as links to the biblical and classical pasts of European civilisation.[12]

Egypt under the reforming and expansionist Viceroy Muhammad Ali was meanwhile opening up further to foreign advisers who helped build modern schools, factories, prisons, and armed forces, and to diplomatic missions. At the end of the Napoleonic Wars, the British Foreign Office instructed the Consul-General, Henry

Salt (1780–1827), to collect for the British Museum. He brought to the task the prestige of the victorious power. Salt, a Lichfield-born man of middle-class background,
had previously studied with Royal Academicians, then travelled with Viscount Valentia in India and Abyssinia, and undertaken an expedition to Abyssinia on behalf
of the African Association to organise Red Sea trade. That trip secured him membership in the African Association and Royal Society. With the patronage of Sir
Joseph Banks, the President of the Royal Society, Salt was appointed British Consul-
General to Egypt in 1815. Salt found a match 'in rank and in collecting-furor' in his
French rival, the Piedmont-born Vice-Consul, Bernardino Drovetti, who had initially been appointed by Napoleon and made France Egypt's closest European ally.[13]

Richard Burton claimed that Salt and Drovetti had divided the Nile valley into
spheres of influence in which they commanded firmans and native workforces: the

> Nile-land was then, as now, a field for plunder; fortunes were made by digging,
> not gold, but antiques; and the archaeological field became a battle-plain for two
> armies of Dragomans and Fellah-navvies.[14]

But rarely did the spheres of influence remain separate; as Salt, Drovetti, and their
associates engaged in a protracted and often fierce war over Egyptian antiquities,
much depended on the balance of Anglo-French political leverage on Muhammad
Ali.[15] Some of the main battles in this war were fought over obelisks from Philae
and Luxor. There was also Salt's successful attempt to remove the three-metre-high
granite bust which was then called the head of the Young Memnon (and was in
fact that of Rameses II, see fig. 29). Salt was helped by Belzoni, the Padua-born
circus strongman turned successful Egyptological entrepreneur, and donated the
sculpture to the British Museum jointly with Jean Louis Burckhardt, the Swiss-
born Sheikh Ibrahim, who published widely on his journeys to Nubia, Syria, and
Arabia in 1810–17.[16]

Another major area of competition was multilingual inscriptions, vital to help
decipher hieroglyphs. Here, government policy (formulated with the advice of
learned societies) and diplomacy in the field dovetailed with private enterprise.
In 1815, the Foreign Office instructed Salt to recover the missing fragments of the
Rosetta Stone, thought to contain twice as many hieroglyphic characters as the
stone at the British Museum, and 'other Stones & fragments with hieroglyphic
inscriptions', which British army officers and travellers had allegedly spotted in
Alexandria and Cairo. Prompted into action by a Society of Antiquaries memorandum, the Foreign Office assured Salt that in 'affording an assistance so valuable to
literature & Science' he was to charge all expenses to the government.[17]

In 1819, Salt had conceded failure, but luck struck in 1826 for the private traveller and Egyptologist James Burton, who discovered a trilingual stone set in the doorway of a mosque he referred to as Emir Yakir, adjacent to the erstwhile French Institute in Cairo. A traveller and copyist rather than a scholar, Burton was nevertheless one of the earliest Egyptologists. In 1822, he had participated in a geological survey of Egypt for Pasha Muhammad Ali, partly intended to find coal. He then joined Robert Hay and John Gardner Wilkinson in 1824, and the following year went up the Nile with Edward William Lane. Burton camped at the site of ancient Thebes, recorded the opened tombs in the Valley of the Kings, and was probably the first to enter KV5, the tomb of the sons of Rameses II. He continued to Abu Simbel and then returned to Karnak to excavate the Granite Sanctuary and discover a new kings' list. In Cairo, Burton prepared sixty-four plates and printed *Excerpta Hieroglyphica* (4 parts, 1825–8). It was while working on the *Excerpta* that Burton in 1826 discovered the trilingual stone. Burton sketched the stone, whose exposed part was some one and a half metres long and four metres wide, with twenty lines of hieroglyphs, twenty-seven of Euchorial, and fifty-nine lines of Greek. He planned to discreetly remove the tablet and repair the entrance to the mosque in order to soothe local feeling.[18]

Yet, the stela quickly became a diplomatic bargaining chip. Representations by British envoys to gain Muhammad Ali's permission to take the tablet to Britain were unsuccessful. Burton concluded he had been 'thwarted solely by a French party' and redoubled his efforts 'to prevent this stone from being clandestinely removed to Paris'. Yet the British position in Egypt had significantly weakened since the days of Nelson, Abercromby, and Salt. Muhammad Ali now received extensive French military advice and technical assistance. The British were outmanoeuvred by the young French polymath Jean-François Champollion, who had cracked the hieroglyphs in 1822. He became the founding curator of the division of Egyptian works of art established by Charles X in 1826 at the Louvre. Champollion had bought Salt's second collection – some 4,000 pieces of exceptional variety and quality – for the French crown for £10,000, making the Louvre at one stroke the world's pre-eminent collection of most types of Egyptian antiquities. For those supporting state-sponsored collecting in Britain, this was particularly vexing since Salt had previously offered it to the British government for an annual pension of £600. In 1828–9, Champollion led an official Franco-Tuscan expedition to Egypt, during which he found hundreds of examples of writing which proved that their alphabet was good. When shown the trilingual tablet by a careless British nobleman, Champollion lobbied Drovetti that its acquisition 'would be a notable and important victory over British arrogance, and an excellent opportunity to console France for the painful loss of the Rosetta monument'. Muhammad Ali added the trilingual stela to his presents to the French king on the occasion of Drovetti's imminent retirement.[19]

Burton was only allowed four days' exclusive access to the Stone to prepare a rough copy of the inscriptions. British diplomatic and scholarly networks sought to ensure for Burton 'all the credit for previous discovery and transcription as well as to inform the world of my right of property in the same'. John Barker, Salt's successor as Consul-General and a serious collector of antiquities in his own right, arranged for transcriptions to be sent securely to Britain, and thence across Europe. A 'necessary manifesto' against Champollion was prepared for publication in the British and French press. Barker accused Champollion and Drovetti of thinking 'that the arts of Courtiers consist of nothing but duplicity & falsehood', and denounced the conduct of the French in Egypt as 'much decried by the Turks as by the Europeans'. Scholarly contacts in London campaigned internationally to secure Burton's right of discovery and transcription, spreading the word, for instance, to the University of Leipzig, one of the earliest centres of Egyptological studies. In 1836, the British Museum bought many of the 420 lots of Burton's Egyptian collection at a Sotheby's sale. But the 'Caristie Stone' itself, as it has come to be known, had entered the Louvre as one of its proud possessions, more for having been snatched from under the eyes of the British than for its actual value: when it was removed it was discovered that it only represented half of the original stela; most characters were illegible and some appeared only when struck by the light from certain angles. Yet the Caristie Stone had confirmed how much the chances of acquiring or losing an antiquity depended on the relative diplomatic clout and cunning of the respective bidders.[20]

In 1835, the British government made three proposals for a state-aided British Museum acquisition policy: 'travelling naturalists and others' might be employed to collect for the Museum; naturalists and 'persons versed in antiquities' could accompany Admiralty expeditions; or consuls, British ministers, and other government officials abroad could be used to acquire collections. The trustees supported the final option, which resonated with their own 1818 proposal and with established practice.[21] After they had let Salt's second collection go to France, the Treasury enthusiastically acquired his third collection at the asking price, partly because it was unlikely that British representatives would acquire similar collections again. The trustees also noted Muhammad Ali's restrictions on excavations and export ban on antiquities as decreed in 1835, although these were not strictly enforced for several decades.[22]

I. Allan Ramsay, *George III* (1761–2). Ramsay, one of His Majesty's Principal Painters in Ordinary, mostly lived on the success of his brilliant state portraits of the king and queen, and the fees that his studio earned from producing some 150 copies of the pair for the royal family, colonial governors, British ambassadors, corporations and institutions, and as gifts for foreign sovereigns and privileged subjects. The portraits also circulated widely through engravings by William Wynne Ryland.

II. François X. Habermann, *Die Zerstörung der Königlichen Bild Säule zu New York* (*c*.1777). In this imagined scene of the destruction of George III's New York equestrian statue, a standing figure is pulled down by a few patriots and many of their slaves; copies in reverse of this German print appeared almost immediately in Paris.

III. Joseph Wilton, fragments and pedestal of the *Equestrian Statue of George III* in New York (1770, destroyed 1776). By 1783, the slab of the stone pedestal was being used as the tombstone for a British officer, Major John Smith. After 1804, it was a doorstep to the Van Voorst family mansion in Jersey City. They would also exhibit it as the 'corner-stone of liberty' in their garden before sending it to the New-York Historical Society, where over time it supported half a dozen other pieces. Some of the surviving lead fragments of the statue were temporarily arranged on a gallery wall and set with the pedestal against a painted outline.

IV. Jonathan Trumbull, *Washington and the Departure of the British Garrison from New York City* (1790). General George Washington and his horse dwarf the empty pedestal of the former statue of King George.

V. Benjamin West, *Fidelia and Speranza* (1776). The king's history painter cautiously used allegory to express his conflicting Anglo-American allegiances. Only Faith and Hope can restore the British monarchy and George III, here represented as the dispirited Redcross Knight, from the current crisis.

VI. Benjamin West, *John Eardley-Wilmot* (1812). The framed painting within the painting, West's *Reception of the American Loyalists by Great Britain in the Year 1783*, imagines a mostly fictitious, post-Revolution world in which an all-inclusive American loyalist community comes home into imperial Britannia's benevolent fold.

VII. John Singleton Copley, *Collapse of the Earl of Chatham in the House of Lords* (1779–80).

VIII. John Singleton Copley, *The Death of Major Peirson, 6 January 1781* (1782–4).

IX. John Trumbull, *Death of General Warren at the Battle of Bunker's Hill, June 17, 1775* (1786). Although not an eyewitness account, Trumbull's painting of American heroic sacrifice and of the universal value of magnanimity in the context of a British victory used his familiarity with locality and characters to strongly authentic effect.

X. John Singleton Copley, *Major Hugh Montgomerie* (1780). Striding dramatically into the foreground in a pose weighted like the Greek statue Apollo Belvedere, this larger than life-size portrait of Montgomerie depicts him amidst his military achievements in the French and Indian War. His right hand brandishes a sword, the left pointing to the 'successful enactment of his commands'. In the background, Highlanders overcome Cherokee in hand-to-hand combat and a burning settlement sends clouds billowing up and around the sky to frame Montgomerie, unruffled by combat. The glowing orange warmth of the war fire infuses the cool-toned painting with a foreboding heat, yet no colour competes with the vivid red of Montgomerie's 77th Highlanders uniform.

XI. John Singleton Copley, *Elkanah Watson* (1782). Oil on canvas, 149 × 121 cm. Princeton University Art Museum. Gift of the estate of Josephine Thomson Swann. Photo credit: Bruce M. White y1964–181. In what was possibly the first American flag hoisted in Britain, this portrait of an American merchant contains a rare visual reference to Copley's patriotism.

XII. Benjamin West, *The Apotheosis of Nelson* (1807). With mourning seamen and representatives of England, Scotland, and Ireland attending its base, West's tripartite allegorical memorial is virtually an altarpiece. The painted part was published in 1809 as the frontispiece to Clarke and M'Arthur's *Life of Nelson* and adapted for a portico at the Royal Naval College, Greenwich.

SIEGE DE LA COLONNE DE POMPÉE. —— *Etched by J.º Gillray, from the Original Intercepted Drawing.* SCIENCE IN THE PILLORY.

XIII. James Gillray, *Siège de la Colonne de Pompée: Science in the Pillory* (1799). When the Royal Navy captured personal letters from disillusioned French officers in Egypt, they were published in London. Gillray offered this depiction of desperate savants with the assurance that it was etched 'from the Original Intercepted Drawing'. The text describes a letter from General Kléber recounting the approach of an Ottoman army, which forced the French to retreat to Alexandria, where 'a party of the Scavans, who had ascended Pompey's Pillar for Scientific Purposes, was cut off by a band of Bedoin Arabs, who, having made a large pile of straw and dry Reeds at the foot of the Pillar, set Fire to it, and rendered unavailing the gallant Defence of the learned Garrison, of whose catastrophe the above Design is intended to convey an idea.'

XIV. George Scharf, *A Lycian Tomb at Xanthus* (1844). Scharf was a highly skilled draughtsman, as evidenced by the convincing perspective of the tomb and lush, varied rendering of vegetation. He has placed himself into the scene – confidently sketching away – both in party with, yet in contrast to, the admiring natives.

XV. Robert Havell after James Baillie Fraser, *A View of Government House, Calcutta* (1824–6). Government House forms the backdrop to the equally orderly British street life of guards, horsemen, and carriages with genteel Britons, while local inhabitants with oxcart and palanquin are spectators at the margins of the scene, and the empire.

XVI. Thomas Hickey, *Col. Colin Mackenzie and His Assistants* (1816). Mackenzie, a military engineer and pioneering surveyor in India, fostered unusually close working relationships with indigenous assistants in the quest for colonial knowledge.

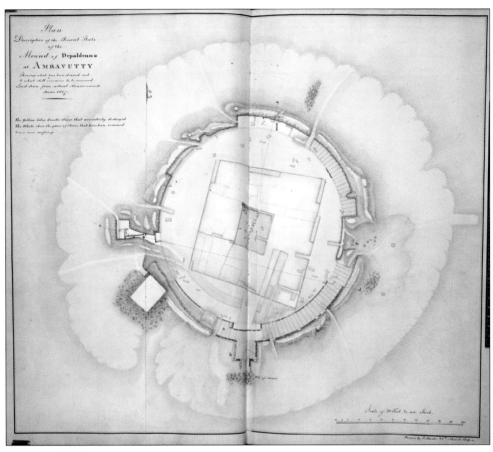

XVII. J. Mustie, *Plan of the Amaravati Stupa Excavations in 1817* (1819). Of the sculptures that once adorned the sides of the Amaravati stupa and the stone railing that surrounded it, less than a third have been identified. In this plan, yellow denotes stones that are entirely destroyed. The white shows the places of stones that were removed and are now missing.

XVIII. Joseph Nash, *Windsor Castle: The Waterloo Chamber* (1844). In the 1830s, Horn Court in the North Ward of Windsor Castle was roofed over to create the Waterloo Chamber. The pierced timber ceiling and panelled walls with Gibbons carvings from the former St George's Chapel provide the setting for Lawrence's magnificent series of portraits. Queen Victoria commissioned this depiction of her leading Tsar Nicholas I of Russia in to dinner during his State Visit.

XIX. Sir Thomas Lawrence, *George IV* (1821). This swagger portrait of a flamboyant and implausibly young king is among the grandest portraits ever painted of a British monarch. George wears the collar and ribbon of the Garter, and the collars and badges of the Golden Fleece and the Hanoverian, Guelphic, and Bath Orders. His right hand lays claim to the *Table des Grands Capitaines*, commissioned by Napoleon in 1806 and given to the Regent by Louis XVIII in 1817. This version is now thought to have been commissioned on the occasion of the king's visit to Ireland in 1821. One of numerous other (studio) versions hung in the Waterloo Chamber (plate XVIII).

XX. Sir Thomas Lawrence, *Arthur Wellesley, First Duke of Wellington* (1814–15). This triumphant portrait of the Duke of Wellington in his new field marshal's uniform and the ribbon and collar of the Garter underneath a Roman-style arch dominates the Waterloo Chamber (plate XVIII). He holds aloft the Sword of State, his own baton resting on the ledge beside. In the background we glimpse the procession to the thanksgiving service held at St Paul's Cathedral in July 1814.

'Friends of Greece'

The French Wars of the 1790s and 1800s deflected Grand Tourists largely to the fringes of the Mediterranean that remained open through British naval supremacy. This included Egypt (disturbances in Upper Egypt had kept most Europeans out for the previous half-century) and the Holy Land, but travel especially increased in the Balkans and particularly Greece after 1809, when Anglo-Ottoman relations were restored. James Dallaway's *Constantinople Ancient and Modern* (London, 1797) was the first book for the English 'tourist'. In 1810 in Athens, one could meet Lord Byron along with several other young aristocrats, Henry Gally Knight, the artist Giovanni Battista Lusieri, the architect Charles Robert Cockerell, and Fauvel, the antique-dealing French diplomat. The Ottoman Grand Tour first peaked in the 1810s; by the 1830s and 1840s, for some travellers it had even displaced the Grand Tour centred on Italy:

> No man is now accounted a traveler, who has not bathed in the Eurotas and tasted the olives of Attica; while, on the other hand, it is an introduction to the best company, and a passport to literary distinction, to be a member of the 'Athenian Club', and to have scratched one's name upon a fragment of the Parthenon.[23]

But while a neoclassical outlook was widely shared among European ruling and social elites, even cosmopolitan expeditions soon turned into national rivalries. In 1811, several architects and artists in Athens founded Xeneion, a cosmopolitan association of 'friends of Greece' in search of ancient monuments.[24] They included the British architects Charles Robert Cockerell and John Foster, Prince Ludwig of Bavaria's agent, Baron Haller von Hallerstein, as well as men from the south-western German Kingdom of Württemberg, Denmark, and the Baltics. The British and German members of Xeneion discovered a large number of sculptures at the Temple of Aphaia on the island of Aegina, dating from c.500–470 BC (see fig. 33). Cockerell – one of many British architects, like Wilkins, Robert Smirke, and Barry, who undertook study visits to the ruins of Greece and the Middle East – bought the marbles cheaply from the local elders. In great secrecy, he had them taken out of Ottoman reach to Athens, where the international archaeological–artistic community

> considered them as not inferior to the remains of the Parthenon … Fauvel, the French consul hardly recovers the shock, although an excellent man … the finding of such a treasure had tried everyone's character most powerfully.[25]

227

On Fauvel's advice the collection was shipped for greater safety to Zante, an Ionian island under British occupation, for public auction on 1 November 1812. Meanwhile, Cockerell's father Samuel Pepys, an architect and official surveyor, together with William Richard Hamilton (of Rosetta Stone and Elgin Marbles experience) had persuaded the Prince Regent to offer £6,000 for the collection. The British government was to send a transport and warship to Athens to transfer the marbles. But when HMS *Pauline* arrived in November 1811, Captain Perceval was only able to pick up some of Lord Elgin's marbles and to transport the Aegina marbles from Zante to the greater safety of Malta, as Foster and Cockerell had urged. The impending sale was now advertised in the European press, and connoisseurs lobbied their princes and governments to bid. The Society of Dilettanti persuaded Lord Liverpool's government through William Richard Hamilton that Britain must acquire the marbles. Taylor Combe FSA FRS, the Oxford-educated numismatist and archaeologist, and Keeper of the Department of Antiquities at the British Museum, was to attend the auction with full powers to buy. Combe found the marbles at Malta and assumed that the auction was going to take place there as well. In December, he thought he had made a bid for £8,000 when in fact in November the marbles had already been sold for a similar sum at the preappointed venue on Zante to Prince Ludwig of Bavaria's art agent, Johann Martin von Wagner. The French had miscalculated. The British had botched the operation. Allegations that Wagner – in order to keep Combe in the dark – had bribed Georg Gropius (the Berlin-born British Vice-Consul at Trichery who had the power of attorney to sell the marbles) were never proved; Gropius probably had forgotten to inform the Englishman out of sheer inefficiency. A British attempt to buy the marbles from the Crown Prince failed, as did a petition to the British government to deny export permission from Malta on the grounds of improper procedure. Instead, the marbles were restored by the famous Danish sculptor Thorvaldsen and in due course displayed in Munich.

For the British, the Aegina debacle was soon followed by national triumph. In 1812, members of Xeneion found a spectacular thirty-metre long frieze of the ruined temple of Apollo at Bassae in the then densely wooded mountains of southwestern Arcadia. The Doric temple was built of limestone around 430 BC, reportedly by Ictinus, one of the Parthenon's architects. The frieze is carved with two mythical battles of Lapiths fighting Centaurs and Greeks fighting Amazons (fig. 32). In 1814, General Sir James Campbell, Bart, commandant of the Ionian Islands and representing the Prince Regent and British government, bought the marbles at an auction on the island of Zante for the equivalent of £15,000. By October 1815, fifty-one cases of the so-called Phigalian Marbles arrived safely at the British Museum. Together with a piece of the same frieze, which John Spencer Stanhope

32. *Marble block from the frieze of the Temple of Apollo Epikourios* (between 420 and 400 BC). The Bassae marbles represent fighting, biting, charging figures in two battles (Greeks *versus* Amazons and Lapiths *versus* Centaurs) with no clear victory or continuous narrative. Because each slab was carved separately with little sculptural overlap, the sequence is uncertain. Originally, they were vividly painted with purple, red, and green vestments on a bright blue background, and wore polished metal weapons and helmets. When found, twenty-three slabs of frieze had fallen from their position seven metres above the floor and close to the ceiling of the Temple of Apollo.

had purchased from a local peasant and donated to the museum in 1816, and further parts presented by Peter O. Bronsted in 1824, the marbles were fixed into the walls of the small room adjoining the Elgin Room.

The case of the Parthenon (or Elgin) Marbles at face value appears to be the most difficult example to accommodate in a revisionist account of the role of the state in British collecting. As is well known, in the first decade of the nineteenth century, Lord Elgin shipped some 200 tons of sculpture, including large parts of the Parthenon frieze, to Britain. After initial hesitation, the British government and Parliament resolved to confer 'honour on the arts as well as on the arms of this country' by buying the marbles for the British Museum for £35,000. This was significantly less than the £62,440 Elgin claimed he had spent on their acquisition. It appeared that the heroic private individual had been exploited by an ungrateful state and country, even if one takes into account post-war economic depression. In fact, however, Elgin's project would have been inconceivable, from start to finish, without the input of considerable state resources. It was the surrender of Egypt by the French to the British in 1801, which led directly to Lord Elgin obtaining the Ottoman firman allowing him to work on the Parthenon site in Athens. This firman from the Caimacam (the second-highest official when the Grand Vizier was on campaign) to the Governor and Chief Justice of Athens was a specially prepared letter of much higher authority than the ordinary 'official permissions' used by numerous travellers as passports. Elgin's firman allowed him to take pieces found in digging, but not pieces of the building. In strictly formal terms, Elgin proceeded on his own private initiative, but he acted on the assumption that his archaeological and collecting activity was an obvious and accepted part of his public function as a diplomat in the region. He therefore expected both access to the logistical resources of the state and compensation for any financial outlays he might incur. As early as September 1801, Elgin asked for a large British warship to appear off Athens to persuade local 'publick opinion of our watchfulness & ability to protect them' and to remove what he considered a prize antiquity to England:

> I have been at a monstrous Expence, at Athens ... what I have secured, is more valuable than anything that ever went to England and I have more at my Command. But this cannot be got without a large ship and English sailors, and the appearance of the English Colours.

Referring probably to the removal of the entire caryatid porch of the Erectheum, this would 'do a very essential Service to the arts in England. Buonaparte has not got such a thing, from all his thefts in Italy.' As he was shipping the first two metopes to England, Elgin emphasised that they had been 'repeatedly refused to the gold and influence of France in the zenith of her power' and were now to 'prove of inestimable service in improving the National Taste' in Britain. Later he claimed that he could have bought himself free when he was Napoleon's prisoner of war in France had he ceded his marbles (which he had sent separately) to the emperor.[26]

Throughout the Napoleonic Wars, there were many British warships in the eastern Mediterranean, though not many called at the Piraeus, and captains were not keen to weigh and slow down their ships with heavy cases. Yet, when they *were* available, 'no one questioned Elgin's right to use Royal Navy ships and British government transport vessels to carry home his collection of marbles even although they were private property'.[27] Over the course of several years, Elgin's marbles made their way not only by private merchantmen and chartered ships but also by Royal Navy and government transport vessels, mostly via Alexandria or Smyrna, and usually via Malta. When Elgin's own small brig, the *Mentor*, sank with seventeen cases off Cythera, William Richard Hamilton had divers recover the cargo and Admiral Nelson ordered a transport to Cythera to pick up those marbles that were retrieved for safe convoy to Malta. There the *de facto* British governor ensured their safe transferral to England, where Elgin discovered them at the Customs House in 1806. Finally, by helping the grounded troopship HMS *Braakel* to refloat in the

Piraeus in December 1802, Elgin's agents obliged the captain to embark forty-four cases of sculptures, the largest shipment thus far; it arrived in England in 1804.

Anglo-French competition was as tangible in Athens as it was in Cairo. In 1803, the Royal Navy seized Choiseul-Gouffier's collection of marbles on *l'Arabe*; Admiral Nelson ordered that the marbles be sent to London. When Fauvel in turn seized cases of Elgin's marbles in 1804 and in 1806–7 (when Britain and Turkey were briefly at war), British dominance of the eastern Mediterranean prevented the French from carrying them off. In 1808, William Hamilton sought to remove Elgin's collections by a combination of financial incentives to the Voivode and a show of British naval strength. With Anglo-Turkish peace restored in 1809, British diplomacy and naval capabilities secured the retrieval of Elgin's remaining collections. When Elgin argued that the collection had been formed in his public function as ambassador on behalf of the British nation, he therefore did so in the knowledge that from initial access to the Parthenon, via protection of antiquities on site, to their safe and partially state-paid transport to Britain, official involvement had been crucial to his project throughout.[28]

Spoliation or Preservation?

The tensions between the eighteenth-century tradition of cosmopolitan cooperation and emulation on the one hand, and Anglo-French competition on the other, pervaded archaeological discovery and publications. Justifying his bilingual publications during the Seven Years War, Robert Wood had written in 1757 in *The Ruins of Balbec*, 'We consider ourselves as engaged in the service of the Republick of Letters, which knows, or ought to know, neither distinction of country, nor separate interest.'[29] But by the early nineteenth century, national rivalries had raised the stakes of archaeological discovery. Even a cosmopolitan group like Xeneion, which was seeking to maintain international cooperation in the field, encouraged the members' respective home countries to vie for possession of their finds. In 1814, the Society of Dilettanti committee reviewing Gell's expedition to Smyrna, Eleusis, Samos, Halicarnassus, Cnidus, and Lycia urged swift publication. The expedition had facilitated the travel of others and they might publish their own results first. After all, LeRoy had published

> with the view of claiming for his nation, the merit of having been the foremost in making known to the world the beauties of Grecian Architecture, before the preconceived and published intentions of Revett and Stuart could be carried into effect.[30]

The fissures within the republic of letters operating across rival nation-states had opened up even within London's learned societies. However, in 1828 – the very year when Champollion was fighting the British in Egypt over the trilingual tablet discovered by James Burton – the French Egyptologist was elected a Foreign Member of the Royal Society of Literature. In 1829, he was even shortlisted for a King's Medal as the 'author of many important discoveries, and works to illustrate them, in the Hieroglyphical Literature of Ancient Egypt'. In the end the medals were awarded to the Renaissance historian William Roscoe and philologist Baron Sylvestre de Sacy. At the same time, the Society helped defend Burton's right to the find of the tablet against Champollion's supposedly unfair competition. When in 1844 the two governments and their national museums agreed on the joint procurement of casts from Parthenon sculptures, it was a rare late example of Anglo-French cooperation, driven on the British side by sheer necessity. Whereas Prussians, French, and Italians collaborated in running the Instituto di Corrispondenza Archaeologica in Rome, the only notable Englishman among them appears to have been the collector and scholarly dealer James Millingen.[31] The British dominated the Egyptian Society, founded in Cairo in 1834: of some 110 members in 1843, two thirds were British, with the French the second largest group, followed by a few Italians, Germans, and Americans. Even a national expedition, such as Richard Lepsius's official Prussian campaign in the early 1840s, was a 'true Babel of languages', with English represented by Joseph Bonomi and others, while

> French and Italian serve as a medium of communication with the authorities, our chance guests, and the Levantine merchants; in Arabic we command, eat, and travel; and in very capital German we consult, chatter, sing, and live.[32]

There were no formal international agreements on the rights to archaeological discoveries. Arguments about the preservation of antiquities in situ *versus* their removal to Western museums, ostensibly for preservation, aesthetic appreciation, and edification, started to be rehearsed in this period. Edward Daniel Clarke was probably in a minority to suggest – when faced with French procrastination over handing over their Egyptian spoils in 1801 – that whoever possessed the greater ability to understand the past should have the right to inherit its physical remains.[33] From Egypt to Assyria, it was more commonly asserted that whoever found an antique site or object had a legitimate claim to it: 'they say it is God's property, and he gives it to whom he pleases'.[34]

If a country lost out on a particular set of antiquities, there were several typical rhetorical reactions. Often the losers accused the winners of spoliation. In 1821, for

33. Charles R. Cockerell, *View of the Temple Jupiter Panhellenius in Aegina during the Excavations* (1860). Amid fallen fragments of sculpture, men search, dig, carry, and measure antiquities; their leaders pore over plans and documents in the campaign tent. Related images show men feverishly swarming the temple with sticks and ropes to prop up and take away slabs.

instance, the French stonemason Lelorrain used chisels, saws, and gunpowder to remove the Zodiac of Dendera – carved on stones three feet thick – in the temple to Hathor, on the bank of the Nile opposite Qena, for the collector Sébastien Louis Saulnier. Saulnier argued that having the Zodiac in France would compensate for the British conquering the Rosetta Stone and acquiring the Head of Memnon and the Obelisk of Philae. French papers alleged that Salt tried to prevent its removal through agents, who were fooled by Lelorrain displaying a pocket handkerchief as the French flag, which he claimed would be insulted if the British intervened. Lelorrain embarked the Zodiac for Marseilles, rescuing it – according to Saulnier – from 'natives' as well as 'certain Europeans … that appear zealous for the preservation of antiquities'. In Britain, the *Quarterly Review* asserted that Salt had never considered committing 'so barbarous an act as that of destroying the most perfect monument that remained on the banks of the Nile'. The *Quarterly* also printed a letter by Henry Bankes, the Pittite parliamentarian, Roman historian, and Trustee of the British Museum, in which he denied consorting with Salt over the removal of the Zodiac: 'I have always deprecated, in the strongest manner, such spoliations of existing and

233

entire monuments, such as that temple is'.[35] The Prussian General-Lieutenant Frei-herr von Minutoli, who led an officially sponsored scientific expedition to Egypt in the early 1820s, and even some other French savants, disapproved too. However welcome the efforts of the new enlightened government of Egypt to allow monuments to be transferred to Europe, Minutoli hoped that no one would imitate such an example of ruthless greed ('rücksichtsloser Habsucht').[36] The Zodiac was bought by Louis XVIII for the Louvre for the equivalent of some £6,500. By the 1830s, it was the French Consul-General Mimaut who warned Muhammad Ali that locals were quarrying the temple of Dendera for a cotton cloth factory.

Examples of wanton Western destruction of monuments are legion. In 1813, the Swiss traveller Jean Louis Burckhardt saw the bust of the 'Young Memnon' at Thebes. The French savants had drilled a hole in the statue's right breast and turned it face up, intending to blow off the head to make the seven-ton statue transportable. Belzoni at Philae discovered that a set of reliefs of Osiris in judgement, which he had cut from the walls of the Temple of Isis and had left awaiting shipment to Alexandria, had been smashed by Drovetti's agents; the words 'operation monque' had been inscribed in charcoal.[37] In 1829, the British accused Champollion of planning to cut out the bas-reliefs from the side of the tomb of Osiris in the valley of Biban. As 'an Englishman and a lover of antiquity', Egyptologist Joseph Bonomi felt it was his duty to dissuade Champollion from 'so Gothic a purpose at least till you have permission from the present Consul General & Mohammed Ali.' Bonomi, who had studied at the Royal Academy before travelling as a salaried artist on Robert Hay's 1824 Egyptian expedition and producing the engravings for Burton's *Excerpta*, was one of several British expatriates who favoured preservation of antique remains in situ over removing them to Britain. They also included Hay, who fought against 'spoiling Egypt of her Ancient Monuments!', Wilkinson, and, albeit in a more complex manner, James Burton. Regarding Osiris's tomb, Champollion answered that, as a Frenchman, he recognised no authority in Egypt other than Muhammad Ali, and certainly not the British consul; Burton would one day have the pleasure of seeing the reliefs in the Musée de France. In undertaking this project, Champollion claimed he acted as 'a true friend of antiquity, as I am removing these monuments with the aim of preserving rather than selling them.' For the British in Egypt, Champollion's appropriation of the tomb was

> on a par with his conduct in the case of the Trilingual inscription and if it is not purely French is at all events quite of the Napoleon school in which Mons. has been educated.

When the British found no way of intervening with Muhammad Ali, Bonomi in collusion with an Italian called Rossalini, but against Burton's urging, cut out a bas-relief for the British Museum. Their dubious justification now was that the tomb would be destroyed within five years if rain got into it again.[38] Some writers already saw greater complexity and questioned the assumption of an automatic Western right to discoveries. With reference to the removal by French 'savage plunderers' of the sarcophagus of Nectanebo II, the *Edinburgh Review* had reflected whether conquest gave the British the right to appropriate such objects, and whether 'the feelings' of their previous owners had been 'sufficiently consulted'.[39]

As the Rosetta Stone was travelling to Britain in 1801, the occupying forces in Egypt had obtained permission from the Ottoman Empire to remove a fallen obelisk which they called Cleopatra's Needle. In the words of a veteran of the campaign, the obelisk, 'close to the theatre of those glorious achievements whereby Egypt was wrested from the dominion of Buonaparte', ought to be moved to 'the Metropolis of the British Empire … to commemorate the Victories of the British Arms in Egypt'. But after considerable efforts involving thousands of British troops, military commanders ordered a stop to the project, ostensibly because it unduly diverted resources.[40] By 1821, a writer in the *European Magazine* urged reticence in victory, and suggested the obelisk serve as a trans-national memorial to all the fallen of the Egyptian campaign:

> We have been charged with lukewarmness and apathy for not causing this stupendous and unrivalled trophy to be erected in London, as it would then be calculated to keep alive the recollection of that effectual blow, which was given by the English army to the ambition of Napoleon. In the metropolis we do not require such a memento … as we are the conquerors, I think we should act much more nobly were we to let the obelisk to be preserved where it now is, in memory of those of the contenting parties, who shed their blood upon the spot.

He continued his argument in terms of preservation in situ *versus* collecting:

> Much as I desire to see my country enriched with whatever is valuable or excellent, I cannot subscribe to the opinion which advocates the transportation of these interesting relics. As long as they remain on their own soil, they are classically important; but the moment they cross the seas … they are converted into toys and puppets – mere objects of curiosity … for few understand the hieroglyphics, and they are appreciated only by the connoisseur and the historian:

whereas in the East, they call forth the most delightful associations, and they are in character both with the climate and with the other antique monuments around them ... Whether we regard 'Cleopatra's Needle' as a specimen of the antique, as a testimonial of 'British glory', or as a monument to the deceased, all association must be spoiled when we behold it surrounded by the hum and bustle of a crowded city.[41]

The same author complained that the dispersal of objects with hieroglyphs without a systematic record of their locations severely limited their scholarly accessibility and use. He hoped that in future a record could be kept, facilitated by consuls and agents, so that a literary and linguistic history could be built up. Isolated monuments in European museums were of purely aesthetic interest; as historical record they had lost their significance. This chimed with what Antoine-Chrysostome Quatremère de Quincy, a French authority on aesthetics, had declared as early as 1796: only the full context of the creation of a work of art would fulfil the pedagogical functions that others attributed to museums.[42]

Today still the most hotly contested British Museum antiquities in terms of the question of cultural heritage and potential repatriation are the Parthenon or Elgin Marbles. Accused of plunder as early as 1803, Elgin argued that in the light of a quarter-century of recent military and naval tourism, his removal of their marbles was their rescue from casual pillaging and a market in broken-off pieces run by the Ottoman soldiers of the fortress. Yet he had quite clearly exceeded the authority granted in his 1801 firman. His secretary had threatened to have officials removed from their posts if they obstructed removal. Very large sums of money were also paid, in the case of the Military Governor some thirty-five times his annual salary. William St Clair, who has uncovered these details, concludes that this was 'imperialism in action, destroying not only monuments but the local administrative and legal infrastructure.'[43]

When negotiations between Elgin and the British Museum and the government for the purchase of his collections for the nation had reached a stalemate in 1815, Elgin petitioned the Commons to investigate the circumstances of the acquisition of the marbles and to establish whether and at what price they ought to be purchased for the nation. Nicholas Vansittart, Chancellor of the Exchequer, accepted Elgin's petition and affirmed the government's 'desire of conferring honour on the arts as well as on the arms of this country'.[44] The 1816 parliamentary inquiry vindicated Elgin against the charge of spoliation. The report was drafted when France's earlier boastful claims that the centre of the Western cultured world had shifted from Rome to Paris were put to shame by the forced return of its imperial spoils under British military and political superintendence. As France's loss met England's gain, Waterloo became England's Battle of Marathon and the Elgin Marbles her 'Triumph of Excellence'.[45] The artist Benedetto Pistrucci designed medals to commemorate Waterloo and the Elgin Marbles' acquisition, thus revealing expectations for a new age of greatness and articulating a connection between contemporary Britain and Periclean Athens as champions of liberty and artistic regeneration. Let Britain, her parliamentary class proclaimed, adopt the altogether different paradigm of freedom-loving, Periclean Athens, a sea-faring city and empire, and afford

> an honourable asylum to these monuments of the school of *Phidias*, and of the administration of *Pericles*; where secure from further injury and degradation, they may receive that admiration and homage to which they are entitl'd, and serve in turn as models and examples to those, who by knowing how to revere and appreciate them, may learn first to imitate, and ultimately to rival them.[46]

Those who claimed the political inheritance of Athenian good governance and political liberty had the right to its physical remains and a duty of care. While such a narrative of rescue and stewardship was not unique to the British Empire, the presence of the highest achievements in art history in London helped legitimate the British Empire as uniquely caring, intellectual, and artistic.[47]

Different travellers and antiquarians put forward a variety of justifications for the removal of ancient objects, depending in part on what they considered to be the main cause of their suffering in situ. Thus, Elgin's secretary, William Richard Hamilton, emphasised the 'zeal of the early Christians' as well as the Turkish artillery explosion on the Acropolis in the late seventeenth century, whereas Edward Daniel Clarke developed a mineralogical theory of the decomposition of stone (and invented a method to 'date' ancient monuments through chemical analysis).[48] In response, Byron had attacked the practice of removing antiquities and what he considered its spurious justifications in canto II of *Childe Harold's Pilgrimage*, his metaphoric account of his Greek travels, and in *The Curse of Minerva*:

> Then thousand schemes of petulance and pride
> Dispatch her scheming children far and wide,
> Some East, some West, some everywhere but North,
> In quest of lawless gain they issue forth.
> And thus, accursed be the day and year!
> She sent a Pict to play a felon here![49]

Neither war nor the corrosive passage of time, but sheer imperial greed of men who lacked aesthetic sensibility (however strongly they professed curatorial concerns), was the worst enemy of antiquities.

The perceived relationship between classical worlds and the modern inhabitants of antique lands had a direct bearing on the arguments over the appropriation of the symbolic resources and physical remains by Western nations.[50] Not that many of those professing Hellenism (an interest in ancient Greece) were also Philhellenes and loved modern Greece and its inhabitants. Indeed, many Western travellers and commentators could barely repress their contempt for what they saw as the barbarous ignorance and indifference of the modern inhabitants of Greece towards the physical remains of Greek antiquity. Those like Johann Joachim Winckelmann, Edward Gibbon, and Richard Chandler were quite explicit. A few travellers such as Stuart and Revett, W. Eton, and the Frenchmen Pierre-Augustin Guys in the 1770s and Lafayette in the 1820s stressed the continuities between ancient and modern Greeks, but the dominant view was that the connection had been lost. European Philhellenes returning from Greece in the mid-1820s wrote disappointed and often bitterly unbalanced accounts in which they described the modern Greeks as cruel and barbaric. Some saw them as the degenerate descendants of a historically sophisticated civilisation; others considered them as a people who suffered both from a barbaric past and social backwardness in the present. In the 1820s, the Cambridge don and Anglican clergyman Thomas Smart Hughes referred to the modern Greeks as 'that unfortunate race, occupants of the soil, if not the legitimate descendants of those heroes, whose names still shed a blaze of glory over the land which contains their ashes.' Theories about the racial discontinuities between the ancient and modern inhabitants of Greece and about northern Europeans as the racial or cultural heirs of the ancient Greeks helped justify the national appropriation of the Parthenon Marbles by Britain.[51]

Westerners mostly dismissed local practices concerned with ancient remains as evidence of irrational and naïve ignorance and superstition. However, Greek people engaged with ancient things in meaningful ways, if rarely before the early nineteenth century, in order to protect or preserve them as monuments and heritage in modern Western archaeological terms. Local populations often venerated antiquities for their supernatural and mystical properties, and resisted their removal or destruction lest epidemics or poor harvests follow. By incorporating ancient objects above the front doors of new buildings, people sought to bring their protective qualities into the present. Greek people also attributed to antiquities animate properties and agency; certain statues were seen as bodies that had been mutilated and petrified by magicians for the duration of the Turkish occupation.

If and when Greece was freed, the statues would be transformed into their former bodies. The spirits within the statues, often referred to as Arabim, were frequently heard moaning, either when a statue was being removed, or when others like the Erechtheion caryatids called out for their sister taken by Lusieri.[52]

Classical archaeology and the preservation of Greece's classical ancient heritage became important to the ideology of the independence movement and to nation-building in the young Greek state. Hellenised Greek intellectuals, who had adopted the Western ideal of Hellenism, reclaimed ownership of classical antiquity as their heritage. In 1826, the provisional government of Greece declared antiquities national property which belonged to the state, although this did not prevent government agencies from donating, exchanging, or selling antiquities, for instance when the first governor of Greece, Kapodistrias, allowed the French to export antiquities excavated at Olympus during the 1829 Morea expedition. In 1827, Muhammad Ali had been sent to crush Greek independence; during the last Ottoman siege of Athens in 1826–7, the Greeks defended the Acropolis as a talisman of their civilisation. As in 480 BC, when the Persians had sacked the city, oriental barbarians seemed again to be besieging Athens. The British obtained a firman from the Sublime Porte, the Ottoman Empire, that the monuments of Athens should not be damaged in the fighting (while Greek intellectuals appealed to the fighting Greeks to protect classical monuments). The monuments survived with only slight damage, although William St Clair judges that 'this happy result was due more to bad shooting than to respect for the firman'.[53] An Anglo-French-Russian coalition eventually defeated Muhammad Ali's forces in the Battle of Navarino; Greece's independence was finally consolidated in 1830. One key element in the European powers' rhetoric to justify intervention on behalf of the Greeks had been the status of their land as the cradle of civilisation, as well as the fact that they counted as a fellow Christian nation under Muslim rule.[54] After only partially effective attempts at antiquities preservation during the war, the new state – initially under the influence of the German archaeological officials of the (Bavarian) Greek King Otto – enacted legislation to control excavations and exports and founded the Archaeological Service and the first archaeological museum in Aegina. When the Aegina collections were relocated to Athens, the Hephaisteion functioned as the National Archaeological Museum and the Propylaia, Parthenon, Temple of Athena Nike, and other structures also served as repositories for architectural fragments, sculptures, and inscriptions until purpose-built museums were erected in the 1860s and 1870s. Sites such as the Athenian Acropolis were 'purified' from post-classical accretions, key monuments were restored, and sites were designated as archaeological monuments, with admission fees and guards enforcing the ban on removing antiquities.[55]

As for Egypt, Constantin-François Chassebœuf, Comte de Volney, had already asserted in the late eighteenth century that antiquarianism was an argument for colonising Egypt. The antique land was the heritage of Europe, not of its current inhabitants. In 1835, the year in which Muhammad Ali banned the export of antiquities, the French Captain E. de Verninac Saint-Maur had no imperialistic scruples:

> France, snatching an obelisk from the ever heightening mud of the Nile, or the savage ignorance of the Turks ... earns a right to the thanks of the learned of Europe, to whom belong all the monuments of antiquity, because they alone know how to appreciate them. Antiquity is a garden that belongs by natural right to those who cultivate and harvest its fruits.[56]

The stewardship narrative of legitimation was so powerful that not just winners, but even losers in archaeological competitions emphasised that it was paramount that *any* Western European nation 'rescued' antiquities from 'barbaric natives'. After Choiseul-Gouffier had comprehensively lost out to Elgin in the fight over the Parthenon Marbles, he admitted to feeling 'a twinge of envy'. Yet 'all art lovers' must rejoice that 'these masterpieces have been rescued from the barbarism of the Turks and preserved by an enlightened connoisseur who will allow the public to enjoy them'.[57]

In the 1840s, the British Museum was to justify its instructions to Layard in Assyria in similar terms. This line of thinking relates to the tradition of earlier travellers to Italy berating the locals for neglecting or destroying antique remains, for instance by partially dismantling the Colosseum to build the Farnese Palace. It also reinforced the British claim to cultural superiority and to being the worthy heir of the Greek and Roman civilisations. In this respect it carried a Western imperialist notion that the modern inhabitants of ancient lands were uneducated, incapable and unworthy of looking after precious ancient remains. Therefore it was permissible to 'protect' antiquities by removing them from sites where allegedly they were at risk (fig. 34). When critics condemned state-supported archaeological activity as cultural imperialism, apologists countered that the Parthenon or Elgin Marbles had merely been 'borrowed' from the Athens of Pericles, which was seen as a civilisation as liberty-loving as modern-day Britain. They were 'a proud trophy ... because they are not the price of blood shed in wanton or ambitious wars', a swipe at the imperialist tyrant Napoleon's ruthless confiscation of Greco-Roman statues from Italian, German, and Austrian collections. At the British Museum, the Parthenon Marbles were safe from barbaric local peoples and the greedy approaches of other, less discerning European nations.

34. H. Linton, after ? Gilbert, *Layard's Discoveries at Nimroud* (1852). As quoted in the adjoining article, 'France and England divide the glory of having rescued from the underground darkness and oblivion of twenty-five centuries, some of the most magnificent remains of the old world.' A shirtless, shoeless Arab hoists a basket of rubbish away from the site of excavation, where another has thrown up his hands in surprise or anxiety at the unearthed image. As a third man points aggressively at the romantically illuminated slab, the well-dressed Layard remains calm, with instructive pointer in hand. This engraving contrasts the ignorance of the locals with British heroism to legitimise the political and intellectual appropriation of Mesopotamia.

French writers would make exactly the same points. Denon thought he had proved the basic ignorance of modern Egyptians when he reported how a Sheik asked him whether the ruins of Luxor had been erected by the English or French (although he may have missed the irony). With local ignorance taken for granted, the imperial rivals had to be rhetorically taken care of. In addition to the 'violence of the Turks', the monuments had to fear 'the hands of certain Europeans. I shall mention no names, but merely observe that they are not French.'[58]

In 1829, the new British Foreign Secretary, Lord Aberdeen, had intervened in these debates with a dose of *Realpolitik*. Aberdeen had himself travelled extensively in Italy, Asia Minor, and Greece. At Athens, he excavated some tombs and shipped to Britain several minor gravegoods, one foot from a Parthenon metope, the relief of a lady's toilet seat from Amyclae, an altar from Delos, a female torso from Corinth, and some coins. He was a published classicist and avid collector, a Fellow of the Society of Dilettanti and the Royal Society, long-term Trustee of the British Museum, as well as President of the Society of Antiquaries. Aberdeen believed that it was permissible to remove antiquities to save them from destruction, for instance with regard to the Parthenon. Yet he also acknowledged that principled concern about Western spoliation could be neutralised by the pressures of *Realpolitik*. Writing to Lieutenant-Colonel Leake, who was worried about French spoliation of Greece, Aberdeen feared that as the British gave the Greeks 'no pecuniary assistance' they could hardly interfere: 'If the French, for their subsidy of four hundred thousand francs a month think proper to take payment in antiquities, it would not be very gracious in us to oppose the bargain.'

The reference was most likely to French excavations at Olympia during the concurrent military expedition to the Morea to enforce the evacuation of the Peleponnesus by Egyptian forces. Aberdeen hoped that Greek pride and self-interest would combine with French honour to prevent the worst:

> the French who exhibited so much virtuous indignation at what they called the spoliation of Athens by the English, may feel some shame at the thought of imitating the proceeding on a greater scale.[59]

The Greek authorities contravened their own recent decrees and allowed the French to take sculptures from the Temple of Zeus.

When the next opportunity arose for the British Museum to acquire a very substantial collection of the remains of a newly rediscovered ancient civilisation – from Lycia in Asia Minor – it was a private effort that was gradually turned into an official, reasonably well-funded, military-style operation. Indeed, the case of Lycia demonstrates just how much the well-oiled machine of the Foreign Office, Admiralty, and Royal Navy could achieve if thrown behind an archaeological enterprise. State commitment on this new scale might in part have been encouraged by the desire to project informal influence in the Ottoman Empire through a military-archaeological campaign during the Middle Eastern crisis of the late 1830s and early 1840s. And although field operations were a very long way yet from reaching modern archaeological standards, the government and British Museum now also sought to take a more conscientiously preservationist approach.

ANTIQUE DIPLOMACY

Triumph at Xanthus

ANCIENT LYCIA WAS A SEA-GIRT, mountainous area in what today is western Turkey. Richard Pococke (1704–65) had visited that region in 1739–40 as part of his tour of Greece and the Near East. In 1764, the classical scholar Dr Richard Chandler together with James Stuart and the painter William Edmund Pars explored parts of Greece and Asia Minor. On behalf of the Society of Dilettanti, and following Stuart and Revett in setting new standards of precision in documentation and representation, they drew ruins and transcribed inscriptions. The resulting publications include the first part of *Ionian Antiquities* (1769) and Chandler's *Travels in Asia Minor* (2 vols, 1775).[1] Then, in 1811, Captain Francis Beaufort (1774–1857), a scientifically talented Irish naval officer, was commissioned by the Admiralty to survey the southern coastline of Turkey on the frigate HMS *Frederiksteen*. Beaufort paid special attention to studying the ruins accessible from the sea. While the primary task of the expedition was to 'settle the hydrography and to ascertain the naval resources', Beaufort felt strongly that

> the venerable remains of former opulence and grandeur, which every where forced themselves into notice, were too numerous and too interesting not to have found some admission among the more strictly professional remarks; and indeed they were often necessarily combined with the operations of the survey.[2]

Beaufort hoped that his expedition would inspire further inquiries into ancient history and modern science: 'The professional duties and habits of a seaman, preclude that fullness of detail which the artist and the antiquary alone can supply.'[3] In October 1811, Beaufort wrote to his parents from the *Frederiksteen*, giving his mother a brief, atmospheric account of his discoveries: 'antiquities I meet at every Step, Temples Pillars Theatres Palaces, & Aqueducts, Magnificent towns and spacious Harbours – huge mountains and luxurious Valleis'. He was also finding 'some most singular natural curiosities' and curious geological features. Beaufort then addressed a learned discussion to his father, whom he wished he could introduce to the antiquities near Karamania. The 'quantum of classical knowledge amongst us all is too little to make much of them', though they often could decipher ancient names. But with a 'learned Doctor … much more might be effected', he continued, before transcribing and discussing inscriptions and sets of characters in Greek and other scripts.[4]

Among other sites, Beaufort identified Patara, the ancient harbour he found mentioned in Strabo and Livy, but which was now filled up with sand and cut off from the sea, at the mouth of the river Xanthus. Patara was thought to be the seat of the ancient Oracle of Apollo. Since a recent Society of Dilettanti expedition was going to be reported on shortly by William Gell, in his published work Beaufort gave but a brief account of the site, including the town walls, temples, altars, sculptures, Greek and Latin inscriptions, a theatre, and a pit which he thought might have been the Oracle's seat. Local peasants told Beaufort that

> at a short distance in shore, were ruins of far greater extent than those of Patara. They are probably the remains of Xanthus, described by Strabo as the largest city of Lycia, and celebrated for its singularly desperate resistance to the Persian and to the Roman arms.[5]

Beaufort had temporarily been joined by Cockerell after the latter had discovered the Aegina and Bassae Marbles. Beaufort's mission was ended prematurely by an attack of some Turks on his boat crew in which he was severely wounded. Beaufort had persuaded Cockerell to remove, for greater safety, from his Greek vessel to the larger *Fredericksteen*. After several scary encounters with locals, Cockerell took marines with him for protection when he studied the ruins of Pompeiopolis. Yet, one fine June day in 1812, when the shore party exploring the Ayas Castle went bathing and turtle hunting, they were attacked: one man was killed, Beaufort was wounded in the hip. His journal, after hundreds of pages of the most enthusiastically detailed coverage in word and image of his explorations, stops abruptly after a rather scientific account of a 'particularly rascally' fellow taking direct aim at him from behind a rock, as Beaufort had just made it to his boat:

fortunately the ball struck the stern which turned it a little out from my groin but entering the middle of the thigh struck the bone close to the trocanta[r] (hip joint) and most singularly turning inwards instead of being deflected off, it passed through the thick muscles and penetrating above 10 inches of flesh it made its exit about an inch from the rectum.[6]

It was a dramatic reminder that scientific operations required a credible Royal Navy presence for security.[7] Beaufort would go on to become Hydrographer to the Admiralty (1829–55) and oversee the production of over 1,000 charts, co-found the Royal Geographical Society, and promote surveyors who shared his antiquarian interests. In a similar vein, Captain (later Admiral) Thomas Spratt used his naval hydrographic surveys to collect materials for books on Crete and Lycia; he presented parts of his collections of marbles to the British Museum and Cambridge University.[8]

The art of the ancient Lycians was virtually unknown in Western Europe until 1838, when the Englishman Charles Fellows travelled up the river Xanthus from the mouth at Patara and discovered the Lycian capital, Xanthus, with its highly ornamented pillar-tombs. Fellows's *Journal Written During an Excursion in Asia Minor* (1839) inspired the numismatist Edward Hawkins, Keeper of Antiquities at the British Museum, and the trustees to secure government support to retrieve as a 'desirable requisition for the Museum' the antiquities Fellows had discovered. The drawings of temples, tombs, and other monuments in Fellows's journal were attractively lithographed by Charles Hullmandel. The Foreign Office and the ambassador at Constantinople were to procure a firman. The Admiralty ordered the local commander-in-chief to supervise the removal of the antiquities via storage on Malta to England. Before the first cache of marbles even arrived in England, Fellows was preparing a second private tour to Xanthus, now with the immensely talented George Scharf as his draughtsman. The British Museum provided introductions to consuls and sought a blanket order from the Admiralty to 'naval officers employed off those coasts' to assist Fellows in transporting any objects he might choose for the British Museum. But the firman was not secured and Fellows returned to England without any sculptures.[9]

After Fellows had undertaken one private and one semi-private expedition in the face of French and some Prussian competition, but had been unable to remove the large objects he had excavated, the Foreign Office and Admiralty organised two official, military-style operations on a much larger scale. It helped that Anglo-Ottoman relations were then improving with the resolution of the Middle Eastern Crisis in 1840–41. Muhammad Ali had sought to balance his position against the

Sultan's vis-à-vis Britain and France, playing them against each other, until Louis XVIII changed his pro-Egyptian stance for a British alliance. The British had seen the expansionist Muhammad Ali (in 1839 he had occupied Syria) as a threat to the stability of the Ottoman Empire and a risk to their own strategic priorities. Lord Palmerston forged the Convention of London with Russia, Austria, and Prussia, demanding that Muhammad Ali evacuate Syria. The Royal Navy supplied Lebanese insurgents with weapons, captured Beirut, bombarded Acre, and paraded a gunboat off Alexandria. Muhammad Ali withdrew his army to Egypt and forswore emancipation from the Porte. He lost his Syrian holdings but gained the title of Viceroy of Egypt in hereditary succession. If previously Britain had been the guarantor of Ottoman suzerainty, now it further consolidated its presence in the Middle East and developed closer relations with Egypt.[10] Indeed, it is perhaps not too far-fetched to consider that the government was responsive to requests for official collaboration on the archaeological enterprise with a view to using all means available for extending its influence in the Ottoman Empire.[11]

Fellows's accounts and drawings by now had persuaded the trustees of the British Museum that the architectural sculptures from Xanthus were 'worthy of a place in the National Gallery of Antiquities'. The Museum was further spurred into action by what appeared to be renewed French as well as Austrian and Prussian competition. When Fellows warned that the 'unaccountably long delay' on the British side was making the acquisition of the monuments 'very doubtful', the Admiralty delegated a ship to assist with the removal.[12] A firman was finally granted as an expression of Anglo-Ottoman friendship for the removal of antiquities to the British Museum.[13] Fellows's team – including a naval shore party of nearly twenty men – excavated, documented, and reconstructed architectural and sculptural finds during the winter of 1841–2. When the responsible naval captain apparently contravened his orders by refusing to ship the marbles to Malta, Fellows left eighty-two fully catalogued cases of sculptures under the protection of the Pasha of Rhodes's cavasses. Fellows feared for the success of the campaign:

> Before me lay a mine of treasure just opened, and all ... at our disposal; I had ... no difficulties or wants but to communicate with Malta for the simple boats and machinery required. This was refused ... A year might pass over before the treasures would be safe in English custody; ignorance of the peasantry, the curiosity or wantonness of travellers, might do them injury, or political changes might check the expedition.[14]

Yet, in 1842, the British Commander-in-Chief in the Mediterranean had the

35. *The Xanthian Room Just Opened at the British Museum* (1848). The *Illustrated London News*, one of the most popular weekly newspapers of the middle and lower classes, advertised itself as a guide for those who could not attend the Museum. It presents the Xanthian Room as a long corridor flanked by lion sculptures, with the Tomb of Payava on the left and Harpy's Tomb on the right. The perspective lines of the high ceiling and dramatic permeation of natural light on to the far wall showcase the Ionic (or Nereid) Monument as the leisurely wanderers' destination.

marbles retrieved by a very substantial naval party. From Fellows's measurements, Royal Engineers had calculated their weight to be some eighty tons. Commander Frederick Warden of the *Medea*, an 835-ton paddle-steamer survey vessel, and the much larger *Monarch* with some 160 men recovered the treasures. By Christmas Eve, seventy-eight cases, including hundreds of pieces of the Ionic Monument and nine cases with the Harpy Tomb frieze and animal slabs from the city walls of Xanthus, had arrived via Malta at the British Museum (fig. 35).[15]

Public and critical acclaim for the Ionic Monument and the Harpy Tomb seemed to support the trustees' request for government authority to resume operations at Xanthus on an even larger scale. The aim was to discover parts missing from monuments that were already in the Museum, as well as important new antiquities, as these sculptures illustrated the history of Greek art. Antiquaries such as the Comte de Caylus and Winckelmann had developed the notion of the 'great chain of art', namely that all cultures of antiquity were interconnected, and that in a finite evolutionary development Greek art of the classical period marked the aesthetic apex to which all other art ascended or from which it descended. Fellows asserted that few Continental museums could display ancient sculpture as an illustration of the history of art, as hardly any had collections with known dates and countries. The British Museum by contrast had the Parthenon and Phigalian Marbles, the Ionic Monument from Xanthus, as well as Lycian (and soon Nineveh) sculptures. As the Lycian antiquities raised important questions about liminal areas in Greek civilisation and helped reconstruct the history of Greek sculpture, much was expected, asserted Fellows, of the British by European archaeologists.

Aware of recent German historicist museum practice, and perhaps seeking to strike a compromise between Quatremère and dominant approaches, Fellows insisted that the arrangement take into account the original archaeological context of the sculptures. That meant placing marbles and casts in relation to each other and to the region as a whole and giving a feel of the landscape in which they had been discovered. Although there was thus a unique chance for a historical arrangement to make 'our National Institution of Instruction the envy of all others', the trustees, advised by the sculptor and Royal Academician Sir Richard Westmacott, overruled Fellows. Instead they chose a traditional picturesque arrangement and highlighted the most classicised features among the works. In Berlin, Lepsius would soon cause controversy by his historical display which privileged even the most heavily damaged Egyptian fragment that could be dated by royal names over the most beautifully preserved, but externally undated, pieces, which ended up in the dark so-called mythological room of the Prussian king's museum. Westmacott further alienated Fellows by giving greater prominence within the arrangement to the Nereid Monument (see fig. 35) over the Lycian ones, which Fellows considered to be relatively old and evidence of the artistic talent of a people living in Xanthus before the Greeks. This blatant disregard of Fellows's expertise, and rather curt communications, came from a museum which was also indebted to Fellows for donations of dozens of specimens of natural history.[16] Before long, however, a parliamentary inquiry criticised the trustees for relying on the advice of a private gentleman to the apparent exclusion of the views of the head of department (and, implicitly, Fellows).[17]

Arguments over the display did not prevent further expeditions. Ahead of his third journey, Fellows's political paymasters developed guidelines for the most ambitious British state-sponsored archaeological expedition yet. William Richard

Hamilton, now a Museum trustee (1838–58), intervened together with the Prime Minister, Robert Peel, himself an *ex officio* trustee, when Fellows wanted to saw up 'the Obelisk at Xanthus having an inscription in Lycian Characters on its four sides'. Fellows's excuse was that if he did not, then 'the French would soon remove it entire to Paris'. Hamilton pleaded that the government ought to 'prevent such a stigma from being cast on our national character, as that of wantonly destroying works of art which we could not remove, in order that others might not have the merit of possessing a monument'. He conceded that there were 'some, whose love of & zeal for Antiquity is undoubted, who would prefer the mutilated monument in this country, to the risk of leaving it to fall into the hands of the French'. Yet, prompted by the Prime Minister, the trustees ordered that no sculpture ought to be removed if there was a reasonable chance that it would remain intact and unharmed in its original position.[18]

Once the parameters for excavation, preservation, and transport were established, Fellows was officially put in charge of the archaeological aspects of a joint British Museum–Admiralty expedition. His section was to include 'a Draftsman, a young architect, and a foreman of masons and carpenters' from England plus two Maltese stone sawyers. If previously diplomats had advanced funds for archaeological enterprises in the hope for later reimbursement, the trustees appealed to Fellows's professional pride and patriotism to justify the lack of a salary or fee. Fellows even had to advance expenses for tools, gifts for peasants, and the hire of cattle. After consultation with Fellows, an expeditionary force was set up, establishing procedures that the Admiralty used in subsequent campaigns. Fellows was consulted on housing at Xanthus, weather conditions, and equipment. Naval commanders studied the difficulties that had attended the previous expedition, especially with respect to the removal of antiquities across challenging terrain, their embarkation at less than ideal anchorages and in difficult nautical conditions, and the severe toll which hard work in a difficult climate took on the men's health. From those researches were estimated the minimum manpower and communications and transport capacities required.[19]

The competent Frederick Warden – recommended for his previous experience and his 'judgement, his perseverance, and resources' – led the *Medea*'s complement of seven officers and sixty-one seamen, augmented by a number of officers and men from the admiral's flagship the *Queen*, a new screw-steamship of 3,099 tons, whose Lieutenant John Massie commanded the landforces at Xanthus. The *Medea* functioned as a supply ship and received cases of antiquities; the survey vessel *Devastation* was also to pick up crates in January 1844.[20]

The weekly medical and scientific reports of Dr Alexander Armstrong, the

Assistant Surgeon in charge of the medical side of the expedition, combine detailed descriptions of the excavations with observations on the local Greeks, Turks, and Gypsies, and medical updates on cases of fever and diarrhoea, occasional wounds, bad contusions, and a cataract. First, though, Armstrong sketched the local topography: a fairly flat lower valley connecting the sea and ruins in a 'richly wooded plane', with olive, fig, myrtle, and plane trees growing on mostly sandy soil, but fertile ground in the flood areas. The hilly upper valley to Mount Taurus was 'also highly wooded, & very picturesque':

> The Ruins of Xanthus occupy a high and commanding situation from which there is a most picturesque & romantic view of the Plane beneath the neighbouring mountains & the sea. The hill is covered with the remains of Temples buildings Sarcophagi &c.[21]

Lieutenant Henry Temple set up a Halfway Station as a signal station between the camp and the ship, which was to be manned by two midshipmen, a sergeant, and four to six marines. There were also a depot for stores and a collection point for crates of marbles. Within a week of their arrival, a road was built to the camp. A headquarters was established in the stone granary at Koonik. Soon there was a separate house for naval officers; the men lived in ten prefabricated huts. A hospital tent, a forge, carpenter's workshop, store, and munitions houses completed 'Queen's Town'.

Warden established clear chains of command and division of labour on site: 'the locality and objects of research and labour are to be pointed out by M:r Fellows, but … the taking down what may be required; the embarkation; and every process dependent upon manual labour; or the application of the purchases and machinery' were under the direction of a naval officer. The naval personnel were 'at all times to take the greatest care to guard against these relics suffering from accident, or the carelessness of any one'. Yet at the same time Maltese sawyers and British sailors were ordered to cut off tomb lids to reduce their weight, using gritty sand specially imported by the navy from North Africa. Any coins found on the expedition were to be considered government property and handed over to Fellows. In order not to 'excite the jealousy' of the local population, the men were issued only with limited firearms for self-defence against locals and wild beasts.[22]

Repeatedly, the camp received groups of keen visitors. Richard Hoskins, master of the *Beacon*, who was engaged on a survey of the Cragus Mountains to the west of Xanthus, came to report to his captain on the river and the best mode of transporting the marbles to the coast.[23] Lieutenant Thomas Abel Brimage Spratt, assistant surveyor of the *Beacon*, and the young naturalist Edward Forbes, who joined the naval expedition in 1841, were also studying the Cragus, along with the artist and amateur archaeologist the Rev. Edward Daniell, who had joined the *Beacon* after travelling in Greece and the Levant. Spratt and Forbes dedicated their book of travels to Daniell, who died of a fever during later, independent travel.[24] A group of five scholars led by Gymnasialprofessor Augustus Schönborn from Posen, who had discovered the frieze of the Heroon of Gölbasi-Trysa in 1841, also passed through during an extensive expedition to Asia Minor, apparently inspired by Fellows's first publication. Sponsored by Prussian officialdom, they studied the natural history, geography, and ancient inscriptions of Lycia, although Schönborn's attempts to secure funding for the removal of the reliefs to Berlin failed. Was the competition already checking on the progress of the British party?

George Scharf kept a pocket-size travel journal in which he recorded the progress of the excavations, life in camp, local topography and flora and fauna, various excursions undertaken by the party, the first wild boar of the season (shot by the Turks but eaten by the British), and his own sketching activities. These ranged from the most detailed close-up of an individual sculpture to panoramic views of the entire site (see plate XIV). Significant finds improved morale. 10 November 1843: 'in the afternoon an important piece of a Lion in archaic manner, the men are working with greater spirit & alacrity'. 4 December: the hind quarter of the bas-relief lion had been found the previous day, and now a remarkable 'angle stone belonging to the great Frieze now in the British Museum. Its preservation is far better & more complete than any single slab of the series previously discovered'. On 11 December, an interesting slab from the Ionic Monument was found with a riding Amazon dressed in a short chiton trampling upon a fallen soldier. From mid-December, sailors were hauling crates to the Halfway Station, from where they were taken on pontoons downriver and to the ship. In mid-January, the coloured mosaic pavement of the Roman baths was exposed.

But the captain's log and officers' correspondence suggest that excavations had not been going all that well thus far: 'A Frieze or two, one or two animals in fragments, fragments of several Statues, and smaller pieces which may be made available hereafter probably are the extent of our success from the excavation.' But then, near the so-called Horse Tomb, the team discovered a tomb with 'a well defined figure of the fabulous animal called the Chimaera'. The 'Chimaera Tomb' was estimated to weigh twelve tons and was to be cut into four pieces for removal. Despite several cases of illness, including the Italian caster who was sent home, and one death from fever, soon excavations picked up speed, and larger pieces were cut and packed, and cases and crates transported to the lower station.[25]

One January night, Scharf returned from a moonlit excursion to the camp and heard the welcome sound of the sailors singing. He thought it was 'In the days when we were gypsing, a long time ago',[26] but coming closer he realised they had adapted 'gypsing' to 'marvelling' (or 'marble hunting'). With local flute-players joining in the merriment, Scharf jotted down six stanzas. Here is the second:

All hearts are gay, all eyes beam bright,
If a <u>curio</u> they spy   [curiosity]
and when a corner stone they sight
Their clamours reach the sky.
With bas reliefs & statues too
We <they> quickly fill the crates
The Turks they view this sight so new
And wonder fills their pates.

After the digging comes the packing and the cheerful dragging of the marbles over tough terrain. These British sailors on special archaeological secondment concluded their song in the evocation of girls and friends, and of queen and country.

During this campaign, Fellows also led several expeditions to Pinara, Cadyanda, and other Lycian cities to make casts of inscriptions and of sculptures and architectural elements that were impossible to remove to England. After the last crate of the Chimaera Tomb was taken downriver on 6 March, Fellows embarked with Scharf for Malta. Between June and November, 114 cases of sculpture and casts arrived via Malta at Portsmouth Dockyard and Woolwich. Fellows, the trustees, and the Admiralty congratulated each other: the country and the lovers of ancient art, Fellows stressed, were indebted above all to the government's commitment. In the first recognition of its kind, in 1845 Queen Victoria knighted Fellows for 'Services rendered … in the removal of the Xanthian Marbles to this Country'.[27] By then, the next state-supported archaeological enterprise was already underway – this time on the banks of the river Tigris.

The Lion of Nineveh

The Assyrian sculptures in the British Museum and Louvre mostly date from c.900–600 BC, when the kingdom of Assyria dominated most of the Middle East from Iran to Egypt, before it collapsed under attacks from Babylonians and Medes.[28] In the early nineteenth century, the region (largely modern-day Iraq) lay at the far eastern fringe of the Ottoman Empire and was composed of semi-autonomous *pashaliks* each governed by a pasha. The rediscovery of the ancient Near East began in earnest from around 1810 by army and navy officers, engineers, and military and civilian officials of the East India Company. In 1825, the British Museum acquired the collection of Claudius James Rich (1787–1821) – the Company's first Baghdad resident and author of travelogues on Kurdistan, Babylon, and Persepolis – some fifty pieces of Assyrian pottery, bricks, and fragments of a stone sculpture or bas-relief. Rich's presence in the region had had defensive geostrategic objectives: in the wake of Napoleon's Egyptian adventure he was to secure British interests in Mesopotamia, as well as overland and river routes to India. As so often, the imperial effort was to produce cultural (side-)effects.

When Julius Mohl, the secretary of the French Asiatic Society, saw the Rich collection in London, he secured funds from the French government to appoint Paul Emile Botta as archaeologist-consul and sent him and an artist to work in Assyria.[29] It was Botta's (initially illegal) excavations of the Palace of Sargon II at Khorsabad in 1843 which inspired the British traveller Austen Henry Layard, who was to become the central figure in the Western rediscovery of Assyria. Layard had been born in Paris of Huguenot stock and spent much of his childhood in Italy. His interest in archaeology and the Middle East had been aroused by Fellows, who was a guest at Layard's family home. Layard qualified as an attorney in London and set out in 1839 to practise as a barrister in Ceylon. Commissioned by the Royal Geographical Society to research the terrain on the overland route, he instead, however, travelled to Constantinople, Jerusalem, Mosul, and Persia.

Layard had all the qualifications required by an archaeologist in Mesopotamia: education, courage, physical strength, and wide experience of dealing with Arabs and Turks. On one occasion he took decisive action when his raft was plundered: he seized a local sheik as a hostage and got his stolen ropes and felts back. British magazines and newspapers had reported Botta's activities as early as 1843–4.[30] Botta initially shared descriptions of his discoveries with Layard – fifteen chambers of a palace and walls covered with inscriptions and sculptures showing sieges and naval manoeuvres. While Layard, diplomats in Constantinople and Mosul, and London-based museum specialists urged that Britain had to prevent the French from 'monopoliz[ing] the field', the British Museum was initially reluctant to commit resources to excavate materials of as yet unproven significance.[31]

Stratford Canning, the British ambassador at Constantinople, took on Layard as an unpaid attaché and used him to gather information on various trouble spots in the Ottoman Empire. Canning also began to privately finance excavations at Nimrud, the Assyrian capital in the ninth and eight centuries BC. For Canning, archaeology in part provided a cover for operations in the region, and it was a means of staking claims in the Near East/ancient Assyria in the face of international rivalries. Association with the national project of acquiring outstanding antiquities was also a potential means of advancing Canning's diplomatic career. Similarly, Layard seems to have invested in Assyriology as a means towards achieving recognition and fame, and encouraged aspiring young diplomats to see archaeological enterprise as a career move:

> If you are determined to return Eastward and to seek for a consulate you may depend upon it that your name brought before the public connected with fresh discoveries at Nimrud would be of considerable service – and would almost, I think, ensure you something.[32]

Archaeology was both a means and a result of diplomacy. In Egypt in the 1820s, John Barker had already shared the same notion. After twenty-eight years of service, latterly as Vice-Consul in Alexandria, the 'most ineligible Consulate' in the gift of the government, he had desperately been hoping to succeed Salt in his £1,600 p.a. job. Since Barker had little 'interest' in the Foreign Office, he had feared, somewhat embittered, that 'some Young man, who has been in Egypt, and acquired a taste for Egyptian Antiquities, may, through Parliamentary influence, supplant me'.[33] But then voices such as the *Quarterly Review* of 1818 had accused diplomatic personnel of negligence if they did not use their positions for research:

> If some of our consuls have merited the reproach of having made their public station subservient to their private interests, and of wholly neglecting those researches into objects of literature or science which their situation might have brought fairly within their reach, the names of Bruce, Davison and Salt may [be] safely mentioned as honourable exceptions from it.[34]

In the 1830s and 1840s, several geographical and geological expeditions in the Near East were jointly funded by scientific societies and the government, and run under the auspices of the Royal Geographical Society, with the multiple aims of gathering political and scientific data, and projecting a low-key British presence in sensitive territories. Such expeditions investigated navigable rivers, mineral resources, and potential to stimulate trade, at the same time as they located sites of ancient cities and historical manuscripts.[35]

In late 1845, Stratford Canning sent the heads of a warrior and of a eunuch following a king with a fan, discovered by Botta near Khorsabad, to Sir Robert Peel. Stratford believed them to be the first examples of Assyrian sculpture to reach

England. Peel gave them to the British Museum for 'a limited time' and allowed casts to be taken.[36] At the mound of Nimrud meanwhile, Layard employed a very large work force of Nestorian Chaldaeans from the Kurdish hills as excavators, and less strong Arabs for earth-carrying tasks. With Botta suspicious of his intentions, Layard had had tools made secretly in Hormuzd Rassam's workshop and had left under pretence of going on a wild boar hunt. He was accompanied by Henry James Ross, a British merchant in Mosul, a servant, and a cavass. Early nineteenth-century techniques of excavation were based on the knowledge that the palaces had been built of sun-dried mudbricks which had collapsed when the buildings were abandoned. This left the stone panelling which had covered the walls up to the height of some two or three metres and remained in place with earth on either side. Excavators such as Botta and Layard followed that panelling around the corners and through the doors. Layard's team immediately discovered stone slabs with battle scenes, richly bedecked horses, and the siege of a walled city. He suspected the machinations of the French consul lay behind impediments thrown in his way by 'the wicked Pasha of Mosul'. In 1841, the French had pitched their consular-archaeological tent in that commercial and manufacturing hub some 300 kilometres north of Baghdad, which the British had previously 'taken'. Layard saw a chance that his finds might reach Europe before Botta's, which would be 'very important for our reputation' (the national 'we' here conveniently elided with the royal plural of the ambitious explorer). He had 'a scheme which I think will defeat them and secure us all we want for ourselves, and much more for the benefit of the world at large'.[37] The *Athenaeum*, a London-based arts and science journal, then just abandoning its accustomed political neutrality, in 1846 attacked the apathy of the British government, in contrast to the French, who had

> a king and government who are prompt to ... promote any enterprise which can reflect honour on the national reputation for taste and intelligence ... the money spent by the French is said to amount to nearly 30,000 £ ... in any undertaking of this nature private munificence can scarcely be expected to keep pace with national; and you can imagine how mortifying it must be to Mr. Layard to find, after a year's indefatigable exertions – crowned too with such brilliant results – that nothing has been done by the British Government to mark its interest in his labours ... Such neglect is discreditable to the English ministry.[38]

Similarly, the *Builder* reported a meeting of the Royal Institute of British Architects in 1846. Anxious to direct the attention of the government to Layard's discoveries, it was argued that 'We owed much in England to individual Enterprise, and that too,

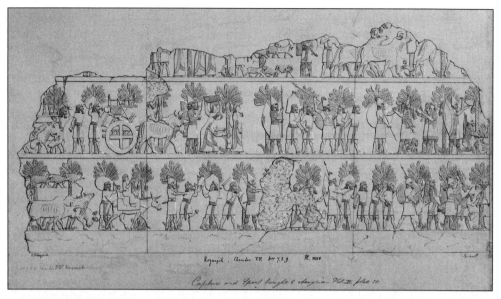

36. A. H. Layard, *Captives and Spoil brought to Assyria* (1845–7). Nineveh's most impressive building was the south-west palace, an administrative centre with elaborate decorations illustrating the king's achievements. This three-level narrative relief shows Assyrian soldiers – identified by their helmets – piling up booty such as weapons and furniture. Prisoners are led through groves of date palms, accompanied by their families and possessions, to the Assyrian headquarters at right, where one soldier presenting several enemy heads is awarded a bracelet.

on the part of non-professional Men' such as Belzoni and Fellows. 'M.:r Layard was of the same class; he was a solicitor travelling for his health, but by his enterprise & good judgement he had succeeded in making what must be considered some great discoveries'[39] (fig. 36).

By summer 1846, Layard had had his hitherto provisional authority formalised by the Grand Vizier, who ordered that 'no obstacle should be put in the way' of him taking

> ancient stones on which there are pictures and inscriptions …which are present in desert places, and are not being utilised; or of his undertaking excavations in uninhabited places where this can be done without inconvenience to anyone; or to his taking such stones as he may wish amongst those which he has been able to discover.

Layard would later romanticise the moment:

I read by the light of a small camel-dung fire, the document which secured to the British nation the records of Nineveh, and a collection of the earliest monuments of Assyrian art.[40]

Canning's covering note advised, now that Layard had permission to 'excavate and export to your heart's content', he nevertheless ought to exercise 'discretion and moderation' with locals.[41]

With the help of diplomats, the East India Company, and the Royal Navy, Layard shipped about a dozen cases of antiquities by rafts of inflated sheep skins (which imitated the mode of transport of the ancient Assyrians) from Baghdad to Basra, and thence via Bombay to England. By June, they were deposited in a new room west of the Front Hall of the British Museum as marbles 'purchased' under a recent agreement with the Treasury to buy 'certain antiquities discovered by persons acting under [Stratford Canning's] direction in Kurdistan'. Layard had narrowly lost the race for the first exhibit. Botta's first finds had travelled via Mosul and Basra to Le Havre and Paris. On 1 May 1847, King Louis-Philippe inaugurated the first display of Assyrian artefacts in Western Europe at the Louvre.[42]

Yet Canning was still optimistic that 'Montagu House will beat the Louvre hollow'. He had briefed Peel about his and Layard's early successes and had persuaded the government to refund his expenses (more easily than Elgin a quarter-century earlier, though the sums were much smaller) as well as to fund future Assyrian expeditions.[43] The trustees devised the most detailed set of instructions yet for an official expedition. First, proper procedures were established for the 'preservation of monuments of Antiquity' in terms of excavating and documenting finds. Second, should he encounter foreign competition, Layard was to conduct himself in a spirit of peaceful cosmopolitan coexistence and 'honourable liberality' and

confine himself to those localities where his priority of occupation or other circumstances admit of no rival pretensions. The saving the Monuments of the distant past in ancient Assyria from destruction and bringing them out of their present concealment to the illustration which European knowledge may be able to throw upon their meaning and history, is an object to be ... promoted by whatever agency ... Nor can any thing have a more direct tendency to teach the natives some respect for the remains of the great works of art ... than the leading them to believe that the Europeans desire to possess these remains ... because of their connections with ancient nations and languages, and of the hope which the study of these affords of contributing to the more extended cultivation of learning and taste, and the prevalence of those principles of justice

37. *Shipping the Great Bull from Nimroud, at Morghill, on the Euphrates* (*Illustrated London News*, 1850). Nautical, military, racial, and commercial imagery fuse in this depiction of the Great Bull, presented as both booty and commodity, as it is being swung on to the merchant brigantine *Apprentice*. On the shore, a small punt, a flagless pole, and the horizontal toiling of Arab workers contrast with the ship's firmly vertical stance and the massive Union Flag hanging on its guard ship – the British Indian steamer *Nictoris*. Arabs in the foreground gaze upon Britain's assertion of technological and cultural superiority, the representation conveying oriental admiration for Western wisdom.

and benevolence, by which only ... the general concord and prosperity of the human race is to be attained.

After this had been expressed in the characteristically paternalistic language of Western cultural superiority, Layard was nevertheless enjoined to exercise great caution and respect in his dealings with the local authorities and to leave the locals with 'an impression entirely favourable to the British character'.[44]

Dissatisfied with the allocation of a relatively modest £1,500, Layard personally supervised excavations, drew sculptures, copied inscriptions, and made casts until, his funds exhausted, he returned to London in the summer of 1847. Accounts in the Layard papers speak of the sheer logistical complexities of these operations: diggers, basket-fillers, and carriers needed to be paid; food bought for overseers; government officers required to be accommodated and paid; presents purchased for local sheiks and for local farmers to compensate for taking objects through their corn fields; paper purchased for copying inscriptions. And then there were the costs associated with removing the objects: wood, nails, and iron screws for cases; mats, felts, and cotton for packing; ropes and tackle; skin for rafts, or fees for hiring rafts, raftmen, pilots, as well as watchmen on the river banks, and other expenses of embarkation and transport by various means.[45]

Sculptures such as the black obelisk of Shalmaneser III and the headless seated statue from Kalah Sharkat arrived in Britain on government transports and private ships. On Layard's request via the British Museum trustees, the East India Company provided specialist tackle from Baghdad. Between autumn 1848 and late 1849, various government and chartered private vessels docked at Chatham with dozens of cases of sculptures. In the autumn of 1850, HMS *Apprentice*, a merchant brigantine, specially refitted and rigged to cope with the heavy colossal, winged, human-headed lion and bull from the palace of Ashurnasirpal II, delivered its cargo (fig. 37). Layard had urged that valuable sculptures ought not to be sent on 'vessels but little calculated for such cargoes thereby greatly increasing both the risk and expence'.[46] The *Illustrated London News*, which it is estimated reached over half a million readers, illustrated a panegyric on 'Shipping the Great Bull' with Orientalist imagery.

In 1849, an acrimonious dispute erupted between Layard and a group of British antiquaries at Bombay over the packaging of some Nineveh material. Hawkins had written in late 1848 that on unpacking the treasures in London he had been filled with

> wrath and indignation with the barbarians who unpacked the cases at Bombay without I suppose authority and then jumbled them together without any care, mixing in the same box, glass stone and metal, and separating portions of the same object into different boxes. The paper impressions from inscriptions have unfortunately suffered from wet. What to do in sorting and arranging all these things without your assistance I know not.[47]

With the publication of Layard's sensationally successful *Nineveh and Its Remains* in early 1849, a contretemps erupted. The antiquaries in Bombay contested Layard's version in the *Bombay Times*: Layard alleged 'Goths and Barbarians' to have damaged his objects in Indian transit. In fact, those were the same people who had enabled him to carry out early research, threw their own repository open, promoted publication, and provided instruments for anyone to use. Quoting the *Quarterly Review* on the 'negligence or unwarrantable curiosity' of Bombay antiquaries by which the Nineveh sculptures had been damaged, the *Bombay Times* continued the strong defence of the local antiquaries. Objects arriving damaged at the British Museum had been packed at the site of excavation and never unpacked, but must have come lose or damaged in transit. Those unpacked and displayed, and the obelisk of which a cast had been taken at Bombay, had arrived perfectly preserved. The Bombay scholars and government, who could not hope to see the objects in the British Museum, had taken the greatest care of the objects.[48]

The government's decision to order a refitted ship to Basra as well as a rumoured further funding commitment of £20,000 were in part prompted by the impression which the sculptures had made on Prince Albert and the cabinet who had been taken around the collections by Hawkins. But as much as VIP tours around the collections, the popular appeal of his sculptures and the success of the first English archaeological bestseller, *Nineveh and Its Remains*, had encouraged the trustees and government. Allies in the Foreign Office, the Oriental Secretary at Constantinople, Charles Alison ('Write a whopper with lots of plates'), and Layard's savvy publisher, Murray, had all understood that an illustrated excavation adventure mixed with exoticism and biblical allusion would benefit Layard's career and pockets. It was also expected to enhance the prospect of the extraordinary sculptures still lying in packing crates at the Basra docks being brought to England. Layard's book was rapturously received. The *Illustrated London News* added to public pressure on the government by contrasting the half-hearted British approach with that of the French government which, 'with its accustomed liberal sympathy in the cause of science, stepped in, and most nobly assisted M. Botta'.[49] At long last, French action, so the most popular weekly of the reading English middle and lower classes claimed, seemed to prompt some 'eleventh hour' funding by the British ministry.[50] The *Illustrated London News* fascinated a large readership with illustrated accounts of discovery, excavation, removal, and installation of objects in the British Museum, interspersed with coverage of the Louvre collections, and illustrated spreads of new Assyrian museum pieces, published just ahead of popular holidays. Layard reprinted excerpts from other publications in his *Popular Account of Discoveries at Nineveh* (1852). The *Athenaeum* of July 1849, which had lampooned the British government's 'niggardly grant' as 'one unworthy of a great nation in a matter of such remarkable literary interest', asserted that the

> fine English spirit of research displayed by Mr. Layard, and his known unwillingness to profit in pocket by his discoveries when the British nation is a purchaser, should have been met by a nobler return than they have yet received from the representatives of the British people.[51]

Elgin had been left out of pocket and Fellows asked to make do without a salary for his Lycian services; Layard's case showed that the public–private partnership was still not working to everyone's satisfaction.

In 1849, the Foreign Secretary, the 3rd Viscount Palmerston, finally appointed Layard to the salaried embassy staff at Constantinople, 'as a reward for past services in the cause of literature', formalising his status as a consular archaeologist parallel to Botta's. Nominally he was to work on the Turco-Persian boundary question, though in fact he conducted excavations at Kuyunjik (Nineveh). The geographer-diplomat in the field provided cover for, and had intellectual affinity with, the consular archaeologist's work, a pattern that was replicated in British India.[52] Layard's sponsors – Lord Ellesmere, Charles Arbuthnot, and the Duke of Wellington – had told Palmerston that he was 'one of those men of whom England seems to have a monopoly, who go anywhere, surmount anything and achieve everything without assistance, patronage or fuss of any kind.'[53] The Foreign Secretary furthered several scientific-political expeditions as a means of projecting a British presence in sensitive Near Eastern territories. It was on his request that another appointee to the Turco-Persian boundary commission was the geologist William Kennet Loftus, who combined the gathering of intelligence for the War Office with scientific investigations and collecting antiquities for the British Museum.[54]

Although he was still only granted £3,000 or £3,500 for excavations at Kuyunjik between October 1849 and April 1851, Layard nevertheless opposed a new private Nineveh Fund, because it threatened to confuse in the official and public mind his ambitions for state-funded expeditions. Layard was also desperate about the unsuitable artists he had been given to work with:

> a mere boy, very willing and industrious, but not the person any enlightened government would dream of sending … It is to me … a matter of deep regret that such an opportunity has been lost of carrying thro' an undertaking of so much interest in a manner worthy of the British Government. I feel heartily ashamed when I compare my published drawings with those of the French. With the subjects, we had enough to have produced a ten times' finer work than our neighbours.

And when the boy-artist drowned while bathing, to be replaced by a certain Hodder, Layard wrote in despair to Sir Henry Ellis that the French had sent four 'first-rate men', especially the experienced Flandin: 'How Mr. Hodder – ignorant of the country, its languages, and its customs – can compete with them I am at a loss to conceive, if the Trustees wish to continue the researches creditably to the country.'[55]

After payments for the artist, a doctor, and Hormuzd Rassam – a Protestant convert from Mosul who worked as Layard's secretary and paymaster – barely more than £900 was left for the actual excavation and transport of sculptures to Basra in the first season. According to Hawkins, the small size of the grants was due to the general state of the country's finances, but also to trustees' fears that Layard might not use larger funds responsibly – what a contrast to Prussian officialdom's confidence in Lepsius when it had doubled his Egyptian expedition budget a few years earlier: 'A capable man must be given sufficient means and be trusted implicitly if he is to achieve the best possible results.'[56] As the Porte was showing an 'incipient desire ... to collect materials for establishing a museum of its own', the renewal of Layard's permission to excavate was now also conditional upon him submitting one specimen of any multiple objects he might find to the Ottoman authorities.[57]

Like other antiquities, Assyrian remains were evaluated in historical-antiquarian, aesthetic, religious, and national terms. Deciphering the Assyrian script, cuneiform, was a dimension of Anglo-French archaeological and linguistic competition. Layard discovered the cuneiform library of Ashurbanipal (r. 668–627 BC); its 20,000 tablets of cuneiform texts were to provide the key for much of modern scholarship on Mesopotamian literature and science. For many, the value of Assyrian sculptures lay not primarily in their intrinsic aesthetic value, but in their interest to literature, philosophy, scriptural scholarship, and the history of oriental peoples. For the Orientalist Samuel Birch at the British Museum they were

> a new feature in the history of art. The remains of these people are most intimately connected with Biblical learning, and tend to prove the truth of many passages in scripture and elucidate the customs of the Hebrews and other Oriental People.[58]

Responses to Layard's excavations and reviews of his *Nineveh and Its Remains* praised the biblical historicity of his work and made spiritual claims to the region to justify Britain's imperial presence in the Middle East.[59]

National honour was again at stake in competing with France, in this case not least over deciphering cuneiform.[60] Sir Henry Creswicke Rawlinson, a cavalry officer, diplomat, and gifted linguist, asserted that the 'marbles of Nimrud will be ... an honour to England, not in the exclusive department of art, but in that more worthy field, a general knowledge of the early world'.[61] In 1853, the devout Layard was awarded the freedom of the City of London for demonstrating 'the accuracy of Sacred History'.[62] But Layard also appreciated the character of Assyrian *art*, and

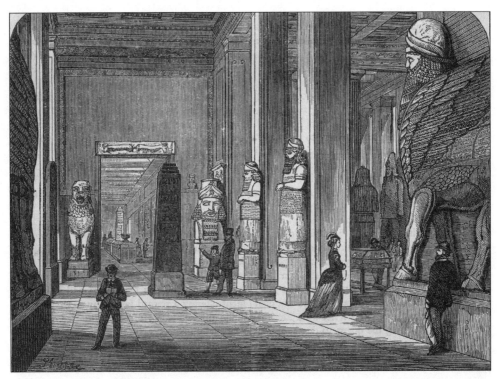

38. Percy William Justyne, *The Nineveh Gallery, British Museum* (*c.*1854). In 1852, the saloon completed a series of chambers – seen receding at left – which connected the Egyptian via the Assyrian to the Phigalian and Elgin galleries in a continuous narrative of ancient history and of Britain's imperial prowess.

the combination of sculpture and painting in bas-reliefs, in which the sculptured reliefs were subservient to the colour laid on them: 'I think the Nimroud basreliefs will furnish new ideas on the history of the Arts'.[63] He praised their anatomical knowledge, composition, sense of *mouvement*, and 'exquisite taste'. In a drawing of a relief at the north-west palace in Nimrud, which depicts a ritual scene of the king being purified with water by courtiers and protective spirits, Layard meticulously represented the delicate ornament of Assyrian royal dress with light pencil-work; he used black and red watercolour to call attention to the few areas of the frieze with traces of paint.[64] Indeed, breaking free from a merely antiquarian framework, Layard's aesthetic appreciation of the Assyrian artefacts – they were better than the Egyptian, if not at the level of classical Greco-Roman antiquity – allowed them to reach the wider audience of the middle-class *Art-Journal* as well as the *Penny Magazine* rather than just the rarefied readership of the *Athenaeum*.[65] In 1852, the Nimrud Central Saloon opened at the British Museum with finds from Layard's excavations at both Kuyunjik (Nineveh) and Nimrud. The saloon was popular with a 'daily throng' of visitors. In its display, Assyrian remains were ordered according to provenance, historical narrative, and instruction rather than by aesthetic or architectural considerations (fig. 38).

Rawlinson, who disagreed with Layard's aesthetic evaluation and instead grouped Assyrian with Egyptian and indeed Indian sculpture, nevertheless secured further (small) Treasury grants: £500 in 1851 for Loftus to explore Susa, and annual grants of £1,500 to continue researches in Assyria in 1852–4. Rawlinson also sent the British consul at Basra, J. E. Taylor, to excavate at the sites of Ur (Muqayyar) and Eridu (Abu Shahrain). French interest in the region revived too, when the French Minister of the Interior saw the British Museum collections in 1851. He used diplomatic channels to have casts made from numerous Lycian and Assyrian sculptures. He also secured 78,000 francs from the national exchequer to fund an expedition to 'Mesopotamia and Media' and to continue Botta's work in Assyria, where Victor Place was appointed the new consul at Mosul. When in 1853 Rassam found a slab of Ashurbanipal's large-scale lion hunt, he claimed the site for his country, 'because it was an established rule that whenever one discovered a new palace, no one else could meddle with it, and thus, in my position as agent of the British Museum, I had secured it for England.'[66] He had in fact discovered the finest sculptured Assyrian palace, built by Ashurbanipal around 645 BC on the northern side of Kuyunjik. Rassam excavated till May 1854, then Loftus (on behalf of the Assyrian Excavation Fund) and the British Museum's agents worked alongside each other before merging their operations. In 1853, the Crystal Palace Company acquired unclaimed sculptures and Layard advised on the Assyrian Court at the Sydenham Crystal Palace.

Meanwhile, international interest in Assyrian sculptures was spreading. In 1852–4, an application for specimens of duplicate sculptures was granted to an American missionary for the Smithsonian and other US venues; similar applications were made or expected from representatives of Austria and Sweden. Frederick William IV of Prussia, who had bankrolled Lepsius's expedition and publications over the previous decade, offered £500 to the Assyrian Excavation Fund for duplicate sculptures for the Royal Museum in Berlin. In spring 1854, the East India Company's steam-frigate *Achar* conveyed 118 cases of antiquities from the Gulf to Bombay. A second steam-frigate, the *Feroze*, brought sixteen cases of the consul Taylor's discoveries at Ur and some of Loftus's in southern Babylonia also to Bombay. Both cargoes arrived in England onboard the sailing ship *Merchantman* in early 1855. The following spring, the East India Company's *Christiana Carnell* brought a further 106 cases direct from Basra, including the famous slabs depicting the lion hunt of Ashurbanipal. When the Crimean War limited the transport capacities of the French and British fleets, both countries agreed to ship a final selection of their most recent discoveries on the private transport *Manuel* hired by the French navy. The last Assyrian sculptures thus arrived in Britain in June 1856 at the London Bridge Dock onboard HMSS *Soho*. They came from Le Havre, where they had been conveyed by the French from Basra via Bombay and the Cape, in exchange for some materials that the British could spare from their excavations at Nimrud and Kuyunjik. There was also a smaller amount of finds from Victor Place's excavations at Khorsabad. But the flotilla of boats and rafts bringing the French finds to Basra had been looted by armed Arab bands with the loss of the vast majority of French finds – including 120 cases of Place's excavated objects plus many of the pieces ceded by the British to the French, and eighty cases destined for Berlin; those for the British Museum mostly survived.[67]

The Wonders of the World

After his return to Britain in 1851, Layard used his celebrity to start a political career. He was now sometimes called the 'Lion of Nineveh' in respectful and playful reference to Ashurbanipal the supreme lion-slayer, who had adopted the myth of Gilgamesh in the decoration of his throne room at Nineveh. The archaeological reach of the British state, however, did not slacken with Layard's departure from the field.[68] In 1852, Charles Thomas Newton resigned as assistant in the Department of Antiquities at the British Museum and took up a string of consular offices in the Mediterranean.[69] After Layard had blazed the trail, Newton enjoyed government funding and substantial diplomatic, military, and naval support to excavate the mausoleum at Halicarnassus, one of the seven wonders of the ancient world, from *c*.1856 to 1859. Hundreds of cases of sculptures and architectural fragments reached the British Museum. Newton returned there in 1861 in a senior post and campaigned successfully for major government grants for further expeditions and acquisitions.

Charles Somers, Lord Eastnor, on behalf of Stratford Canning, visited the Crusader Castle of St Peter at Bodrum while on a mission to the embassy at Therapia. He reported on forty-two sculptures, to him equal in quality to the Elgin Marbles, which had been set into the walls of the castle by the Knights Hospitallers of Saint John in the late fifteenth and early sixteenth centuries. These were stones of the mausoleum at Halicarnassus which Queen Artemisia had constructed in 353–351 BC for King Mausolos and other members of the Hekatominid dynasty of ancient Caria. The external walls overlooking the harbour incorporated three pieces of an

Amazon frieze around a Crusader shield and one slab from a centaur frieze. Many more were set into the internal walls, but those were very difficult to access for Europeans. Richard Dalton on Lord Charlemont's expedition of 1749 had drawn the sculptured friezes and had them engraved. Luigi Mayer, the Piranesi pupil who created pictorial encyclopedias of vast parts of the Ottoman Empire on behalf of the ambassador Lord Ainslie and Lord Guilford, made an inexact composite view of the interior in 1797.[70] In the 1810s, first Bankes and then James Mangles and Charles Leonard Irby had tried in vain to remove the marbles. The improvement in Anglo-Turkish relations in the late 1830s created new opportunities for archaeological enterprise. In 1838, a commercial convention opened up the eastern Mediterranean and the entire Ottoman Empire to British merchants. The capture of Acre did for Stratford Canning what British success in Egypt had done for Elgin. The 1840 convention for the pacification of the Levant further consolidated the situation.

When in June 1844 the Oriental Secretary, Charles Alison, called on his way to Syria at Bodrum and reported on the remains of the mausoleum, Canning felt encouraged to redouble his efforts. In 1846, after several abortive attempts, he gained permission to extract the Parian marble slabs from the walls as a personal gift to him from the Sultan. Getting ready for the mission at Constantinople, he confessed to his wife his anxieties: 'Oh! if they should stick in the wall! Oh! if they should break in coming out of it! Oh! if they should founder on their way to England!' While he was fretting, Canning also had supreme confidence in the significance of his project:

> I shall be disappointed if the new Ministry and the Corn Laws be not thrown into the shade by these celebrated marbles, which it has cost me nearly three years of patient perseverance to obtain.[71]

By February, Canning reported to Sir R. H. Inglis from Constantinople that sixteen cases, weighing a total of some twenty tons, were on their way to Malta on HMS *Siren*. These contained twelve of the seventeen slabs and showed Amazons and Greeks in combat. He had himself only seen imperfect sketches at that stage, but suggested Inglis look up their merits in Clarke and Anacharsis, Pliny, or Vitruvius. By August, the *Acheron* was sailing from Malta to Portsmouth, whence the marbles were transported to Woolwich to arrive finally at the Museum in September. The trustees thanked Canning for his present in the same letter in which they sanctioned £2,000 for Layard. The twelve slabs were arranged temporarily in the Phigaleian Room. By 1851, twelve sets of casts were put at Canning's disposal.

Charles Thomas Newton, who had been a contemporary of John Ruskin at

Christ Church and was recruited in 1840 to be Hawkins's assistant in the British Museum's Department of Antiquities, resigned in 1852 to become the British Vice-Consul at Mytilene on the island of Lesbos. While a minor diplomatic position, this was a major departure for a British Museum archaeologist.[72] In this new role, Newton was able to contribute more to the Museum than from Bloomsbury. He was aware that the reputation of the Museum collections over the previous half-century had in good measure depended on a succession of diplomats and officers with archaeological interests. The Museum gave him some limited financial support and instructed him to seize opportunities to augment its collections.

Despite a chronic shortage of funds, in January 1855 the British Museum acknowledged an 'extensive collection of marbles, inscriptions, vases, and other antiquities from Greek islands', with a further four cases of inscriptions following in the summer. After two visits to Bodrum in 1855–6, where Newton enjoyed easy access to the castle, he returned to London in the summer of 1856 to lobby for a proper expedition. He claimed he had been inspired by Beaufort's survey of Karamania to search for the mausoleum, and also used Spratt's chart in lobbying the authorities. In the favourable climate at the end of the Crimean War, and with support of the Foreign Secretary, the Earl of Clarendon, Newton received a firman to retrieve and remove some lions from the mausoleum. The Foreign Office granted him £2,000, a warship for at least six months to supply food and water, and a lieutenant of the Royal Engineers and four sappers, including a photographer. The steam corvette *Gorgon*, commanded by Captain Towsey, Newton's 'mainstay and sheet anchor'[73] in the management of men and practical matters, set out with 150 men under Lieutenant Murdoch Smith RE as commanding officer and Corporal William Jenkins, who was highly respected by the Turkish workforce, the photographer Corporal B. Spackman, and Lance-Corporals Patrick and Francis Nelles, a smith and mason who both spoke Greek. Also with the party were the painters Roderick Stanhope and Val' Prinsep, who proved quite useless, and Newton's friend George Watts. The *Gorgon* sailed from Spithead in October 1856. Excavations commenced on 24 November but were hindered by the constant need to negotiate the purchase of houses and fields from Turkish locals.

False starts were made, including at the site first identified by Spratt.[74] After Christmas, efforts were transferred to a site north of Aga's Konak, the excavation's HQ, and by 7 January 1857 Newton's team thought they had found the correct site. In fact this had been identified (unacknowledged by Newton) by Robert Murdoch Smith, and was roughly the site located by Newton and Cockerell, who in turn had used an old Admiralty chart by Graves and Brock as well as ancient literary sources. The excavation opened up a very large area in the form of the quadrangular cutting in the rock for the basement of the mausoleum, as well as the north-east corner of the surrounding *temenos*, with a vast quantity of architectural and sculptural fragments, including on the west side of the site the Persian Rider, to the east a seated statue, and further east four pieces of the Amazon frieze, parts of a quadriga, and behind the *peribolos* wall a pile of large marble slabs and statues. Some slabs were identified as steps of the pyramid that had topped the mausoleum. Despite Newton's firman, the Turkish minister of war ordered the castle commandant to remove the best Bodrum lions from the walls of the mausoleum to bring them to Constantinople. In the nick of time, Canning managed for a renewed firman to arrive on the *Swallow* to prevent the caique leaving for Kos to transfer the lions to Constantinople. In June 1857, the *Gorgon* sailed from Bodrum, with 218 cases and packages and a full inventory for the Foreign Secretary, Clarendon; its arrival at Woolwich was announced on 22 July.

There was no space at the Museum after the recent Assyrian arrivals so that the new sculptural fragments were temporarily arranged in a timber and glass shed on the colonnade to the west of the main entrance. The lesser sculptures and mosaics went into basements under the North Library. In April 1858, the Canning marbles were moved from the Phigalian Room and incorporated into the arrangement. At Bodrum, meanwhile, the government store-ship *Supply* had replaced the *Gorgon*. The Rear-Admiral Superintendent at Malta had been instructed to provide further tools, iron, steel, Crimea huts, and tents. Excavations continued, restricted only by residents' refusal to move from the site. Instructed by the Foreign Office, by November Newton took part of his work force to Cnidus, leaving Smith and Jenkins in charge of work at Bodrum; the rationale was that by opening up a new site the deadlock with Bodrum residents might be resolved. Newton asked Lord Lyons for a small guard of marines to protect his party against robbers and pirates, especially since Cnidus lacked an anchorage and the ship had to anchor at Bodrum.

At Cnidus, Newton was joined by the draughtsman Richard Popplewell Pullan (1825–88), an architect and archaeologist sent by the Foreign Office to survey the mausoleum. He then moved to Newton's excavations at the theatre at Cnidus and the so-called Demeter sanctuary, where fragments of sculpture, inscriptions, terracotta figures, lamps, and other small objects were retrieved. Further discoveries were made at the Temple of the Muses and the Necropolis. The most important find occurred (on a local tip-off) five kilometres from Cape Crio. In a month-long operation, a colossal lion lying face down was raised, lowered into a reinforced packing case, and hauled on a sledge on a specially constructed six-metre-wide road, which zigzagged down to near sea level. From the cliff the lion was lowered with the help of ship's tackle on to a raft and from there on to the *Supply*.

Newton, Jenkins, and sixty Turkish workmen also excavated ten archaic Greek seated statues, which were half-buried near the Temple of Apollo at the Greek village of Geronta, the ancient Didyma. They had first been identified in the Society of Dilettanti's *Ionian Antiquities*. Newton reported to Clarendon that he thought he had found a 'connecting link' between the Egyptian and Greek antiquities in the British Museum and procured the requested firman for their removal. The *Supply* took the sculptures from Geronta, 111 cases of antiquities collected at Bodrum since the *Gorgon*'s departure, plus 106 blocks from the north *peribolos* wall of the mausoleum complex, as well as fifty-seven cases from the excavations at Carthage of the American-born Dr Nathan Davis, who was associated with the British consulate, plus one case with a sarcophagus from Sidon sent from Malta. It arrived at Woolwich in late November 1857 and the marbles were at the Museum by January 1858. Total funds were now confirmed to be £4,000 for expenses incurred on site, and £1,000 for payment of accounts in England. A little later an additional £2,000 was granted to complete work at Cnidus, but then in spring 1859 spending was capped at £2,000, including the expenses already incurred in England; taking into account the expenses of the previous six months, that in effect ended the campaign and the workmen were paid off. Newton packed up in June 1859 and sailed via Rhodes (to buy for the British Museum some vases and gold objects which had been excavated by Salzmann and Biliotti) and Malta to England, which he reached by late summer.

The same year, Newton became consul at Rome, but, following the retirement of Hawkins at the age of eighty in 1861, he assumed the newly created post of Keeper of Roman and Greek Antiquities at the British Museum, with Samuel Birch at Oriental Antiquities (including Egyptian and Assyrian). Newton exploited his new status to lobby successfully for substantial parliamentary grants for major acquisitions. He did so by approaching trustees, writing in the press, and using his personal acquaintance with Gladstone. Newton supported many excavations; some continued to receive help from the Admiralty. He was also involved with founding the Society for the Promotion of Hellenic Studies in 1879, the Egypt Exploration Society in 1882, and the British School in Athens in 1883. In 1880, he had been appointed to the inaugural Yates chair in classical archaeology in the University of London.[75]

Conclusions

The careers of Layard, the diplomat turned archaeologist turned politician, and of Newton, the curator turned diplomat turned politically well-connected curator, epitomise the tradition of British diplomats taking an active interest in archaeology and collecting. This stretched from Gray and Hamilton in Italy to Elgin, Hamilton, and Salt in Athens and Egypt, and Stratford Canning in Assyria and Halicarnassus. They embodied the overlapping private and public interests in archaeology and collecting. They were equally well connected in officialdom and in London's learned societies. Playing antiquities as diplomatic bargaining chips, these men also saw acquiring internationally sought-after antiquities as integral to their diplomatic careers – either as a self-defined duty, as in Elgin's case, an official commission as with Salt, or as a means of advancing their career prospects, as Stratford Canning and Layard did, and as the latter advised other aspiring diplomats to do. Few were entirely above the motives of profit or prestige. Archaeologists and their collaborators mobilised considerable administrative, financial, diplomatic, and military resources by arguing that Britain gained national prestige not just from the conquest of lands, but also by capturing antiquities of supreme aesthetic value (Parthenon Marbles), those illustrative of the history of ancient art (Lycia), or those which were primarily of historical, philological, and literary importance (Egypt, Assyria). A particularly powerful argument with regard to both Egyptian and Assyrian remains was that they could help illuminate or corroborate the Bible.[76]

The cross-Channel competition over antiquities had a direct impact on the development of British collections. Such development was contingent upon access by archaeologists to, and the commitment of, particular ministers, officials, diplomats, and officers. Crucial too were national technological, naval, and military capabilities, and the state of international relations. At the archaeological front line (however central or peripheral to Anglo-French imperial geographies), Anglo-French archaeological antagonism tended to be particularly fierce in wartime. Archaeological diplomacy in peacetime – Burton's in Egypt, Fellows's in Lycia, Layard's in Assyria – proceeded by covert means (machinations, rival petitions to Ottoman and local authorities, carefully engineered procrastination, and the accusatory rhetoric of spoliation) rather than by physical prevention of access to sites, or the conquest or forceful removal of a rival nation's collections. Yet while the weaponry varied, British success or otherwise in accessing archaeological sites from Lycia to Assyria, in acquiring objects such as the Caristie Stone in Egypt, and in protecting Greek sites from spoliation by others, was contingent upon the state of bilateral relations with the Porte, the respective regional balance of Western (predominantly Anglo-French) influence, and the Mediterranean naval balance of power. Collecting was often part and parcel of imperial expansion.

The capacities and agendas of the imperial fiscal-military state were crucial to the potential, scope, and success of archaeological endeavour: imperialism furthered archaeological projects. In turn, archaeology could be a means of imperial policy and a tool of imperial governance. However, archaeological diplomacy and collecting wars occurred not only in regions of acute imperial competition but also in those which were predominantly of interest for the symbolic resources and physical remains of their ancient civilisations. Archaeological campaigns could also serve informal imperialism, by ensuring that Britain had a low-level local presence and might exert influence in territories of the unstable Ottoman Empire. The timing of particularly vigorous British state interest and investment in archaeological campaigns across the Ottoman Empire, for instance in the years around 1840, at the very moment when British governments were concerned about the empire's stability and British influence, might not be entirely coincidental. The presence of a few warships, the diplomatic negotiations over firmans, and the information gathered around an archaeological campaign helped stake claims in such areas.

There was considerable continuity across periods of both war and peace in the assumptions among the British governing elites about the importance of building the Museum collections. These beliefs were sufficiently strongly held and widely shared to ensure that a degree of diplomatic and logistical support for archaeological endeavours was forthcoming when lobbied for, and especially whenever the British government had diplomatic leverage and military capabilities in the region concerned. While the precise combination of private and public efforts varied from case to case, after state-directed competition over antiquities had first come into prominence during the Napoleonic Wars, the post-Waterloo era saw a gradual shift from individual, private, or semi-official to fully-fledged official and national operations of growing scale, logistical complexity, and systematic commitment of resources.

British cultural politics and public cultural patronage relied on the dovetailing of private and public interest. As with the practices of commemoration, the collecting of antiquities reveals many nuances and a wide spectrum of state involvement; it also demonstrates the value of functional rather than formalistic international comparisons. Once ideal types of Continental European public patronage are abandoned, and different modes and degrees of semi-official and official patronage are appreciated, a substantial, if not entirely consistent and coherent programme of British public patronage is revealed. The classic dichotomy of a non-state-centred Britain contrasted with a statist France requires continued refining. Both countries used diplomats as the archaeological arm of the state: Choiseul-Gouffier and Fauvel in Constantinople and Athens around 1800, Drovetti in early nineteenth-century Egypt, and Botta and Place in Assyria in the 1840s faced British ambassadors and consuls who collected just as actively and aggressively as they did. Without a considerable involvement of 'bureau and barrack',[77] the British Museum would not have acquired some of its most important and extensive collections in the face of fierce cross-Channel competition. Britain's ambition, investment, and achievement in the monumental wars and archaeological diplomacy of the first half of the nineteenth century were considerable. To that the galleries of antiquities in Bloomsbury testify to this day.

As these case studies have indicated, relationships between imperialism and archaeology were complex.[78] The shores of the Mediterranean and the ancient lands of the Near East were an imperial frontier between Britain and France throughout much of this period. They were also a pivotal theatre in the struggle for control over the meanings of antiquity and the physical remains of ancient cultures. The cultural politics of archaeology shaped debates over spoliation, collecting, and preservation. These debates were influenced by the perceived relationships between ancient and modern inhabitants of antique lands (racial or cultural continuity or not), and the perceived conduct of both modern inhabitants of antique lands and of the imperial rivals towards antique remains (practices and rhetoric of spoliation, damage, sensitive trusteeship).

The Anglo-French consular collecting rivalry in Egypt continued into the 1840s and 1850s, with the representatives of other powers like Austria, Belgium, and Sweden–Norway playing minor roles. When the British expanded their empire in India, they found vast areas full of very different antiquities.

INDIA

The munificence and liberality of the Honorable East India Company, in promoting works of science, in the extension of useful knowledge, and in the encouragement of the arts, will remain a lasting monument of their fame, and may be read with pleasure and admiration when the records of conquests, victories, and splendid aggrandizement are consigned to utter oblivion.

William Petrie, 1807.[1]

Give us time ... for our investigators and we will transfer to Europe all the sciences, arts, and literatures of Asia.

William Roxburgh, 1790.[2]

The shores of Asia have been invaded by a race of students with no rapacity but for lettered relics; by naturalists, whose cruelty extends not to one human inhabitant; by philosophers, ambitious only for the extirpation of error, and the diffusion of truth. It remains for the artist to claim his part in these guiltless spoliations.

Thomas and William Daniell, 1810.[3]

It is equally our duty to dig and discover, to classify, reproduce and describe, to copy and decipher, and to cherish and conserve.

Lord Curzon, c.1900.[4]

Empire, Culture, Knowledge

BRITAIN'S PRESENCE IN INDIA changed dramatically between the middle of the eighteenth century and the early nineteenth (see map 3). From enjoying largely seaborne and stable trading relations, it moved to intermittent wars of conquest and a very significant territorial dominion. By 1850, the entire Indian Subcontinent was under the control of the East India Company state. As the Company was transformed from a trader to the sovereign of a vast Indian empire, British expansion was driven by rule of force and by negotiation; by the violent subordination of indigenous populations and by the empire's capacity to build alliances with colonised elites to a shared, if unequal, benefit.[5] Information-gathering and interventions in India's cultures were integral to colonial state formation. As a corollary of imperialism's military-economic dimensions, 'colonial knowledge' was compiled and produced at the instigation of the imperial authorities to assist them in controlling and administering the colonial territories. Indian learning was also promoted with a view to improving imperial governance. Indeed, the British state employed scientific expertise on the colonial frontier earlier and more fully than at home. In India, more than anywhere else in the British Empire, imperial administrators and soldiers carried forward the imperial project in cultural terms. The anti-intellectual traditions of much of military and administrative history, and the anti-military inclinations of much cultural and intellectual history, have until recently constrained the study of the cultural, intellectual, and imaginary legacies of empire-builders. But those who conquered, administered, studied, and collected the empire were hybrid types – the gentleman-amateur, the scholar-administrator, and the gentleman-officer-scholar.[6]

By 1830, India was Britain's most important imperial asset. British-Indian trade outpaced any other imperial commerce and the Company was vital to Britain's credit system. A huge army in India supported British interests in other parts of the world. The East India Company, first established in 1600, had developed within the commercial environment of a chartered monopoly company, but it owned the rights to protect itself, to wage war, and to govern small territories given to it by Indian authorities.[7] As the Mughal empire – the central Asian dynasty that had ruled over most of northern India since the sixteenth century – fragmented in the face of internal rebellion and external threats, the Emperor gave the Company in 1765 the *diwani* or land revenue rights to Bengal, Bihar, and Orissa. The East India Company thus earned £3m in additional revenue and became the effective ruler of Bengal's 20 million people. It had also made gains in the west around Bombay and in the south and was the dominant power along the Coromandel coast.

In the British-Indian state, political consolidation was accompanied by an emphasis on military considerations and values, albeit under civilian supremacy. This was legitimised with reference to constant threats from within and without India, including the risk of Napoleon uniting with Tipu's Mysore against the British in India. Militarism was fed by the need to fund the expanding armed forces, by the quest for financial gain and security of officers and men, and by a belief in the fragility of civil institutions and the lack of political stability in India.[8]

By 1800, the Company state was at core a version of the British fiscal-military state.[9] The growth of Indian territories under British influence was sustained by a largely Indian army that expanded from 2,500 men in 1744 to nearly 230,000 by 1820. War in India was funded by revenue extraction and subsidies from Indian rulers. The military establishment consisted of three separate armies each composed of sepoys (native formations drilled and equipped on the European model), royal regiments paid for by the Company in India, and Company regiments of Europeans. The Third Mysore War (1791–2) marked the first British national war on the Subcontinent: for the first time, crown forces were the dominant partner with the Company. In addition to Company and army officers, the Indian 'services' comprised administrative and commercial Company servants and some civilian specialists; all were reasonably well salaried and promoted by strict seniority, and many had followed their grandfathers, fathers, and uncles in the service. With the army's domineering presence, military culture 'moulded the structure and ethos' of much of Indian colonial society and the British-Indian 'garrison state'.[10]

The expanding military presence focused public attention at home. This was partly a response to the loss of America. It also related to anxieties over expansion in the East regarding war spoils, a potential conflict between conquest and commerce, and the constitutional and moral implications of the abuses of British governors. There was concern that imperial corruption might not only affect the indigenous populations but also corrode the values of metropolitan society and ultimately threaten despotism in Britain. From the 1770s, these anxieties triggered parliamentary inquiries into the Company's affairs. Subsequent legislation integrated the Company more firmly and coherently in the British state. William Pitt's 1784 India Act created a Board of Control (six members of the Privy Council, and a president sitting in the British cabinet) to effectively oversee foreign, defence, civil, and fiscal policy in India. In fact, the Company's Examiner of Indian Correspondence continued to influence policy-making, and the primary administrative functions of the Company and its commercial arrangements remained in place.[11] As elsewhere in the British Empire, considerations of power politics in the metropolis and the colony were inextricably linked with imperial encounters of the intellect and the imagination.

The Outward Appearance of Power

Empire-building was an intensely visual affair. The East India Company's headquarters in London featured elaborate allegorical programmes on the exterior and the interior (fig. 39). The pediment above the Ionic portico entrance shows Britannia offering her right hand to kneeling India, who is pouring out the Treasures of Asia. King George III is in the centre in Roman armour, holding a shield of protection over Britannia. He is the head of the empire, assisted by Religion and the virtues of Justice, Order and Wisdom, and Integrity.[12] Inside, the allegorical programme took on a more commercial focus. The overmantel on John Rysbrack's elaborate marble chimneypiece showed *Britannia Receiving the Riches of the East* (1728), and Spiridone Roma's ceiling painting in the Revenue Committee Room, *The East Offering Its Riches to Britannia* (1778), featured Persia's silks and rugs, China's tea and porcelain, and India's pearls and jewels. The directors' General Courtroom was adorned by a series of landscapes of Company settlements in India, St Helena, and the Cape.

39. J. C. Stadler, after Thomas Rowlandson and C. A. Pugin, *East India House, The General Court Room* (1808). Before the rebuilding of East India House around 1800, quarterly auction sales of the Asian goods imported by the Company had been held in the General Court Room. Across from the barrier sit the presiding director and officials. The commanding poses and gestures of the largely Romanised marble statesmen and military heroes contrast with animated, less stately bidders.

Such imagery of the maritime and commercial aspects of the Company's work was echoed by numerous other paintings and prints circulating outside Company HQ. It had celebratory and commemorative functions, and the Company may have promoted it to disguise controversial shipping policies and alleged corruption.[13]

At and beyond Company HQ, officials promoted notions of civilised politeness and heroic yet magnanimous conquest; they emphasized a paternalistic, improving, and civilising ideal of imperial rule, rather than one of Mandevillian luxury and rapacity. All manners of visual genre and media were used to justify the imperial project: sketches, maps, and paintings of coastal profiles; ephemera such as fireworks and transparencies; enduring imagery like prints, portraits, and history paintings; and the most permanent physical structures of empire: civic architecture, and funerary and commemorative monuments.

Indeed, the British asserted their imperial presence in India in commemorative and funerary monuments and in civic architecture on the colonial frontier. There were very few resident professional architects with the East India Company. Most public and many private buildings in British India were designed by military engineers and other junior officers, who were largely self-taught and found their examples in training manuals, pattern-books, and in British and foreign architectural treatises.[14] From 1794, some professional training was available at the surveying school in Madras, where talented draughtsmen like the mathematician and astronomer, John Goldingham and his fellow engineer Thomas Fraser were active, and later at Addiscombe College (1809) and the Royal Engineers Institution at Chatham (1812).[15] The officer-architects designing British colonial, civic buildings mostly reproduced the prevailing British (and European) styles of any given period: baroque classicism and Palladianism in the eighteenth century, and Greek Revival architecture in the early nineteenth. Colonial structures were often adapted to suit local needs: some features were exaggerated to enhance their magnificence, and others added to improve circulation of air.

The leaders of the Company state around 1800 were among the grandest architectural patrons of their time (see plate XV). Under Richard Wellesley, Lord Mornington (later Marquis Wellesley), Governor-General between 1798 and 1805, the British in India followed a more coherent, aggressively expansionist imperial policy, stressing 'the power and dignity of the state, the morality of conquest and British racial superiority.'[16] In 1805, Wellesley would be recalled owing to disagreements with the Company directors over economic policy (he had managed to treble the Company's debt) and to allegations that he had exceeded his authority over the foundation of Fort William College and patronage issues. Not least controversial were his pro-consular style and the sheer cost of his bombastic cultural statements. Wellesley presented himself as the direct representative of the king. His endless chain of titles serried Roman triumphal addresses, European chivalric honorifics, and Indian distinctions of rank. Wellesley also insisted on demonstrating British power through ceremonial and palatial architecture.

Most British public buildings in India in this period were neoclassical, reflecting the values of Greece and Rome. British visitors to Calcutta and Madras in the late eighteenth and early nineteenth centuries made comparisons with Mediterranean cities of classical antiquity. By 1800, Calcutta was one of the largest cities in Asia; its British and European community lived largely set apart in white mansions in the southern part of the city. Likewise, the European part of Madras, with its 'long collonades, with open porticoes and flat roofs', offered the eye of the painter William Hodges 'an appearance similar to that which we conceive of a Grecian city in the age of Alexander'.[17] Specific references to classical antiquity were part of wider efforts by empire-builders to relate the new, unusual, and often threatening territories and cultures of the East to their familiar models. This helped render the Indian empire 'safe'.

In Calcutta, one axis of public buildings led from the civil arm of authority around an expansive square dominated by the barrack-like Writers' Building to the military arm in the vast open space of the *maidan* by the gigantic Fort William, the premier symbol of British military might in all Asia. The secondary axis embraced the Council House, the Courts, and the Doric Town Hall. At their perpendicular intersection stood Government House.[18] With its triumphant lion-and-sphinx-topped neoclassical gateways and trophy-studded grounds, Government House best embodies the Governor-General's ambitions.[19] Designed by Charles Wyatt, an officer in the Bengal Engineers, it was modelled on Kedleston Hall, the Curzon family seat in Derbyshire (which Wyatt's uncles had helped build).[20] Raised on a high basement platform to enhance its visibility, it drew heavily on antique examples. The Marble Hall evoked a Roman atrium, with classical figures and deities looking down from the ceiling, and life-sized busts of the twelve Caesars lining two walls. Legend had it they had been captured from Napoleonic warships; more likely they had been reproduced from those at Kedleston, linking the British and ancient empires as in the dining rooms of countless eighteenth-century English country houses. The slightly later east gate, which also drew on an English country house precedent, that of Robert Adams's gateway to Syon Park just outside London, was decorated with two sphinxes and a huge lion striding the pediment, holding a globe of the world in its paws (see plate XV).

On 26 January 1803, 800 European guests followed Wellesley's invitation to a ball to inaugurate his marble palace and to celebrate the Peace of Amiens. Temporary Temples of Fame and Valour had been erected in the 26-acre grounds, where mock-classical wall reliefs and marble vases evoked the atmosphere of a Roman emperor's country estate. Among the spoils of war were two brass cannon, inscribed 'Seringapatam, 4th May 1799'. These were set on wooden gun-carriages with muzzles shaped in the form of a tiger's head; the wheel-spokes resembled tiger's paws. As the British Empire in the East expanded, brass cannon from Afghanistan and a huge gun mounted on a winged dragon from Nanking would join trophies at Government House.

In Madras, the Governor (1798–1803), Edward, Lord Clive, the son of Clive of India and a collector of Indian art and artefacts, rebuilt Government House as an imperial site of memory (1800–1802). He commissioned a vast new Banqueting Hall, modelled on the Parthenon. Designed by Goldingham, the head of the

Company's surveying school, the hall took the form of a Greek temple with Doric columns, its broad flight of steps guarded by stone sphinxes. The pediments were embellished with the names and trophies of Plassey and Seringapatam and the ceiling decoration inside showed banners, fasces, and eagles. Imperial generals and governors from Coote to Cornwallis and Wellesley looked down from the walls. Opened by Clive *fils* with a ball for the principal residents and officers to celebrate the peace with France in 1802, the hall functioned like a pantheon or Heroum.

The Company directors did not necessarily share the desire of some of their local representatives for monumentalised posturing. When the directors criticised Wellesley for spending £167,000 on Government House, Lord Valentia sprang to his defence. Passing through on his Grand Tour of the East, Valentia considered India 'a country of splendour, of extravagance, and of outward appearances'. He felt India ought to be 'governed from a palace, not from a counting-house; with the ideas of a Prince, not with those of a retail dealer in muslins and indigo': this would disprove French allegations of the 'sordid mercantile spirit' of the British.[21]

Before Wellesley was recalled in 1805, Lord Clive had also been criticised for excessive expenses, not least for building in the exaggerated style of ostentatious native princes. Such metropolitan criticism notwithstanding, monumental civic architecture continued to express the ambitions of empire-builders in British India. In Bombay, Colonel Thomas Cowper, Bombay Engineers, built a temple-fronted Town Hall inspired by the Parthenon opposite the cathedral (in 1820–33). A portico with six fluted Doric columns (made in England) leads to a tall, three-aisle Corinthian Hall. In an example of the adaptation of Greek Doric to Indian contexts, there are projecting *jhilmils* (window hoods). The structure accommodated the Bombay Asiatic Society, Assembly Rooms, and other polite and learned societies, and the bill of £60,000 was shared between the Company, a subscription, and a lottery win. Alongside the mints, clubs, and churches of British India, the hall is one of its finest neoclassical structures. Militarism manifested itself architecturally, too. Forts, citadels, and government houses asserted the imperial presence in the presidential cities, and town planning privileged open grounds, parade routes, and fortified perimeters. Military architecture also influenced civilian design such as bridges, gaols, and the opium godown in Patna.[22]

As British residents and advisers embedded themselves in native courts, native princes built representational architecture for them. In Hyderabad, the Resident, James A. Kirkpatrick, oversaw the building of an imposing complex with triumphal arches surmounted by goats' heads and the royal arms centred on a magnificent palace, broadly modelled on Calcutta's Government House (1803). Architecture was presented as an instrument of policy. The Resident of Hyderabad explained in

1811 that indigenous princes and people judged 'power and authority by no other standard than the external marks of it'. This defied the Company directors' parsimonious caution: 'the keeping up of an outward appearance of power will in many instances save the necessity of resort unto the actual exercise of it.'[23]

Alongside monumental architecture, funerary monuments on the colonial frontier also became important political systems.[24] Bombastic tombs in cemeteries in India in the early eighteenth century allowed Britons to insert themselves into the cultural politics of late Mughal India. But over subsequent decades, practices of death and commemoration increasingly became markers of British difference and exclusivity. British communities who felt threatened by Indian princes, French rivals, and potentially overpowering alliances of both, interpreted British deaths as martyrdom at the hands of inhuman Asians and heroic sacrifice in the service of imperial dominion. As the militaristic and the civilising strands of Anglo-Indian empire-building were consolidated from around 1790, representations of death helped to forge a new sense of imperial community in India and to project British power as necessary and virtuous back home. Memorials articulated power relations and competing visions of the purposes of empire; they could signify concern about the thinness of the imperial red line as much as confident bombast. As markers of personal bereavement in imperial settings, they connected personal memories with the national-imperial project, and served as rallying points for the small British communities in (latently) hostile environments.

The most famous Anglo-Indian burial site of this period was Calcutta's walled South Park Street cemetery (1767), where burials took place after dark by torchlight. The burial ground featured simple marble slabs, neoclassical cenotaphs, obelisks on square podia, pyramids, small brick houses, classical rotundas, stuccoed, painted temples, and monumental tombs with canopies on very high pillars. The 1,600 graves represent the hierarchies of colonial officialdom and a wide range of ordinary citizenry, male and female. From the 1790s, memorial compilations supported community-building and imperial self-justification. Biographical information on important figures and martyrological lists of those who had conquered British India were published to guide succeeding rulers. Private individuals – widows, friends, and fellow officers in semi-official mode – erected monuments to fallen officers and soldiers. At South Park Street, a monument to Colonel Deane Pearse (d.1789, aet. 47), Commandant of the Artillery, recites his imperial service from Guadeloupe and Havana to Bengal and honours equally his dutiful and able command and his benevolence and warm friendship.[25]

Funerary monuments were mostly built with a colonial British audience in mind. But in some cases they united European and indigenous contributions. J. P. Parker's monument to Sir David Ochterlony, the hero of the Gurkha Wars and of the 1816 Nepal expedition, boasts a 55-metre tall Greek Doric column, crowned with a bulb-iform cupola, which stands atop a stylobate placed on an 'Egyptian', almost cubic, pedestal. The inscription reads: 'The people of India, native and European, to com-memorate his services as a Statesman, and a Soldier, have, in grateful admiration, raised this *Column*'.[26] Other heroes or events prompted separate commemorative efforts. Maria Nugent visited a battlefield where Sir Robert Abercromby, a veteran of the Seven Years War, had fought Rohilla chiefs. The monument to British offic-ers, looked after by a female fakir, struck Nugent as an 'ugly pyramidical building, without any inscription'. The memorial to the Rohilla chiefs, 'in the oriental style, and rather pretty', was a place where the poor Muslims prayed and worshipped a sainted chief.[27]

Hybrid cultural forms provide further evidence of the impact of British archi-tecture on indigenous elites – whether as imperial domination or a constructive negotiation between imperial power and the colonised. In some cases, European style was simply superimposed on to an Indian structure. When, after the conquest of Delhi in 1803, the Mughal palace became the British Residency, grand Ionic columns were fixed to its façade: hybridity here marked conquest.[28] Certain Indian princes also incorporated European design elements in their building. The *zamind-ars* (large landowners) in Bengal erected neoclassical palaces in Calcutta and on their country estates. This did not necessarily imply a desire for an Anglicised life-style, however. Often all it showed was a superficial adoption of European elements, such as stucco decoration of Corinthian pilasters on the walls of an Indian skeleton structure.[29]

Yet some Indian rulers seemed to read British architecture as a manifestation of a great power that had shown itself capable of conquering large swathes of India. They consciously adopted and adapted elements in Muslim, Hindu, and Jain archi-tecture – in the Tomb of Mushirzadi, Tipu Sultan's Mosque, and the Sitambara Jain Temple. Around 1800, Raja Serfoji II of Tanjore (r.1798–1832) built a palace in hybrid style. Educated by Western missionaries, and reinstalled by the British in 1798, Serfoji soon filled it with English imagery and furniture, and a European-style cabinet of curiosities. He commissioned drawings of his palace and monuments in a mixed Anglo-Indian style, and gave pen-and-ink drawings on English paper by local artists to various company representatives, some of which ended up in the Company's museum.[30] The Nawab of Murshidabad's palace, an Italianate varia-tion on Calcutta's Government House, was designed by General Duncan Macleod (1780–1856, Bengal Engineers). Other Indian princes and some wealthy private individuals followed suit. Among the mansions in Calcutta was the 'Marble Palace'

(1835–40) of the wealthy Brahmin and patrician Rajendra Mullick. This freely conceived Palladian structure was also India's first museum of European and Europeanesque *objets d'art*, from Old Masters, Sèvres vases, and Venetian mirrors to figures from Dresden, swords from Spain, and a full-size bronze of an English cow. Designed to educate the public, it represented, in Maya Jasanoff's phrase, a form of 'collecting back'.[31]

The most important Indian neoclassical builders were the nawabs of Oudh at Lucknow, which in 1775 became the capital of Oudh under British suzerainty. Several buildings absorbed forms and motifs from European buildings, mixing Indian cusped with classical round arches, *chattris* with pediments, or Mughal balustered columns with classical columns and pilasters. But European influences were also more eclectic. Some buildings referred to English baroque, and mixed it with Indianised elements, as seen in the elongated Ionic columns on the façade of Dilkusha House. The neo-Palladian Residency and its banqueting hall and neoclassical structures such as the Sher Darwaza stood side by side with picturesque sham castles like Khurshed Manzil and the Greek revivalist Tarawali Kothi. Almost all these structures were again designed by military engineers, often following closely the patterns in *Vitruvius Britannicus* or specific British buildings. Hybrid Indo-European styles were Nawabi variations on English, mostly classical, themes, with very free adaptations of plans, elevations, and decoration. Some designs were inevitably more successful than others. Most were criticised by purists in either tradition. But they constitute a distinct architecture that influenced large parts of India: the Qaisarbagh (1848–50), more vast than the Louvre and Tuileries combined, epitomises the synthesis (or incoherent jumble) of opposed cultural traditions.[32]

Indomania and Orientalism

For most of the eighteenth century, India had been marginal to metropolitan cultural concerns. But there was a close connection between the rise and consolidation of the British-Indian empire and the forms of British cultural involvement with India. Up to the last third of the eighteenth century, many Britons in India were being 'Orientalised' and some Company officials engaged closely with native cultural traditions. Yet, growing distance from the indigenous population increasingly became the official policy. In the presidency towns, the British were physically set apart in 'white towns' with the infrastructure and amenities of British urban polite society. Calcutta, for example, 'struck visitors as a dislocated outpost of Europe, as if Regency Bath had been relocated to the Bay of Bengal'.[33] Even in large army cantonments, Britons lived as increasingly self-sufficient communities with their own libraries, racecourses, and assembly rooms. Formal Indian participation was limited, except in Bombay with its adaptable Parsis, and in token Mughal court settings such as the Anglo-Mughal Hyderabad with its social and racial mixing.

At home, during periods of war and heightened imperial anxiety, Indian affairs were briefly central to political debate and the wider public consciousness. Yet, alternating with moments of Indomania, and alongside much ignorance and indifference, outright Indophobia also existed in metropolitan society – fuelled by evangelicalism and notions of 'moral improvement', and by pressure to legitimise empire with reference to Indian backwardness.[34] In India itself, there had been little British design until 1800 to Anglicise the Subcontinent. The Company avoided challenges to Indian culture that could have threatened the stability of its rule; awareness of religious sensibilities continued to inform British policy well into the nineteenth century.[35] The relationship between Orientalisms, and civilisational categories such as language and religion on the one hand, and race on the other, was complex throughout the late eighteenth and the nineteenth centuries. After ideals of Westernising social 'uplift' and modern citizenship had shaped the British imperial mission in a more 'martial, nationalistic, paternalistic, moralistic, and racially pure' mould, after the 1857–8 Mutiny the *ancien régime* of Indian princes and maharajas became the bulwark of the raj.[36]

Scholars have interpreted British-Indian cultural relations in terms of Orientalism: the knowledge gained by Europeans of non-European peoples, and the 'structures and ideologies of dominance that enabled and were in themselves enabled by that knowledge'.[37] For those like the American anthropologist Bernard S. Cohn, the British deployed forms of linguistic, legal, aesthetic, and symbolic knowledge to further the imperial project.[38] Others such as the British historian Christopher Bayly, by contrast, have focused on the use of received indigenous knowledge in the making of empire. He explores the information gaps and panics, which developed when the British replaced older forms of information-gathering with new, more scientific modes. Sometimes this weakened the imperial state, for instance when it failed to detect the strength of anti-colonial sentiment in the 1850s. The former approach sees the imperial state imposing colonial discourses. The latter – while sharing the premise that knowledge underpins power – focuses more on indigenous agency, the local pragmatics of knowledge production in negotiation between Britons and Indians, and the inherent weaknesses of the imperial project. The Company relied on Indians and on indigenous forms of governance, trade, social interaction, and labour. In particular, the conquest of India depended not just on military superiority but on sophisticated intelligence systems too, of running-spies, news-writers, political secretaries, *munshis*, traditional Mughal networks of agents, and other indigenous informants.[39] Some imperial officials interested in Indian antiquity similarly relied closely on native assistants. Their dialogue and cooperation produced, as we shall see, new forms of imperial-colonial knowledge in the archaeological field.

Military success gave the British primacy over other Europeans in India and unique access to the sources of Indian culture. British intellectual interest in the precolonial history of India developed in the context of debates about conquering and ruling the Subcontinent. Company servants acquired expertise in sketching, cartography, geology, natural sciences, languages, and history for administrative and strategic considerations: for military planning, surveying, statistical exercises, and bureaucratic routines. But such skills were easily adapted to wider intellectual pursuits and made officials generally inclined 'to adopt empirical approaches to questions of colonial knowledge'.[40] Empire-builders compiled knowledge of India in the forms of maps, surveys, and assembled objects, as well as in histories, dictionaries, grammars, and translations of ancient texts, especially those of legal interest. The expansion of knowledge was not just a by-product but a precondition of empire. Information – collected, translated, and classified – was as important as guns and economic monopolies in establishing and consolidating imperial domination.[41] Many imperial administrators conceptualised the colonial encounter as the appropriation of territory by naturalists and Orientalists: 'Give us time,' the botanist William Roxburgh bragged in 1790, 'and we will transfer to Europe all the sciences, arts, and literatures of Asia.'[42] If surveying, mapping, botany, and anthropology were all colonial enterprises, history was a colonial enterprise too, both because it celebrated Europe's history by contrast with others, and because it was closely related to consolidating the governmental regimes of the British in India.

In their encounter with Indian cultures, the British envisaged themselves as a modern, civilised Western people facing an oriental, Eastern 'other'. There were enduring notions of Eastern 'oriental despotism', of India as a land with no laws and property. Explanations of the causes of despotism shifted over the eighteenth century from deterministic notions of the 'enervating climate' to assumptions of enduring cultural and racial characteristics. Muslim conquest was thought to have left India with little capacity for improvement, its people mere passive partners in the colonising project. The authoritarian paternalism of the British raj was a variant of European enlightened despotism; the conquest of Mysore was presented as its liberation.

From the late eighteenth century, India was reimagined as an empire of improvement and enlightenment, and this trend was reflected in new categories of heroic monuments to benign rulers and intellectual leaders. Augustus Clevland, Governor Jonathan Duncan of Bombay, and Governor-General Lord Bentinck were memorialised for their roles in pacifying western hill peoples, ending infanticide in Benares, and abolishing sati.[43] As the national mission in India was increasingly defined in terms of bringing 'improvement' to a backward indigenous population, the colonisers' need to exult their own race, religion, and civilisational achievements involved the denigration of indigenous culture. The reimagining was helped by refocusing 'official Orientalism' from the Persian literature of Indo-Muslim governance to Sanskrit and the mysteries of ancient Hinduism. The European enlightenment traced a historical narrative from classical civilisation via long middle ages of 'barbarism and religion' to recent enlightenment through reason and commerce. It found an analogy in the development from classical Hindu civilisation via a dark age of barbarism and religion to modern colonial enlightenment.[44]

Contrasting with the vision of oriental despotism and Western improvement was another view of India in which Hindu culture was appreciated for its past civilisation. This ancient land was now seen to be excluded from the progressive world led by 'modern Europe' through cultural backwardness and eternal decay, if not in everyone's estimation any longer by religious superstition. Serious study of ancient Indian cultures was driven by late eighteenth-century Orientalists such as the judge and scholar Sir William Jones, a precocious Oxford man and the most accomplished European scholar to go to India in the eighteenth century, founder of the Asiatic Society of Bengal and of modern linguistics. His work ranged from Indian chronology, music, and dramatic literature to ancient astronomy, botany, the history of chess, and the cure of elephantiasis. He looked to the study of ancient Hindu culture to answer questions on the origins of peoples, the history of the world, the relations of languages, the diversity of religions, and the evolution of legal systems and forms of governance. For administrative convenience and out of enlightened curiosity, Governor-General Hastings, William Jones, and their associates in the Asiatic Society urged the understanding of Sanskrit and of Hindu legal traditions. Oriental languages were taught to future civil servants and army officers at special Company colleges, primarily to enable the young men to serve the needs of empire. 'Original texts' were constructed to represent codices of Hindu and Muslim law, which could and should be enforced in Company courts. This undermined notions of oriental despotism, but also crudely simplified Indian historical experience. Early Orientalists, supported by artists like William Hodges in India and Sir Joshua Reynolds in England, further pursued aesthetic agendas in the expectation that European art and literature had something to gain from India.

Although the British end of this story is quite heavily London-centred, the wider intellectual contexts reached far beyond the capital. New disciplines such as economics, geography, and proto-anthropology, very much rooted in a wider world of empire and informal empire, were being forged in the vibrant intellectual climate of the universities and learned societies of late eighteenth-century Scotland, and especially Edinburgh. A range of philologists and historians of India in the early nineteenth century shared a Scottish enlightened background and applied a 'philosophical' framework to the history of Indian civilisations and the study of contemporary society. These men included administrator-scholars such as William Erskine, John Leyden, Mountstuart Elphinstone, and John Crawfurd, all of whom had some connection with the University of Edinburgh in 1788–1803 before they went to India.[45]

In British India, as in other spheres of formal and informal empire, war, conquest, and the requirements of imperial governance were key catalysts of cultural politics and agents of cultural change. The practices of early British-Indian archaeology allow us to study the relationship between imperial warfare and complex notions of Indian pasts, as well as the relationship between Orientalists, officials, and indigenous people. The following two chapters explore the institutional settings, the methods, and the results of early British-Indian archaeology. The antiquities of India added a novel and vital dimension to the cultural politics of the British Empire.

7

ANTIQUITIES OF INDIA

THE BRITISH EMPIRE TRANSFORMED Western appreciation of the antiquities of India between the late eighteenth and late nineteenth centuries. From the sixteenth century, some travellers from the Low Countries, France, and the British Isles,
missionaries and scholars among them, had studied aspects of India's past. Sailors
and other travellers visited monuments in west and south India, such as Kanheri,
Elephanta, Ellora, and Mahabalipuram. Some also described the Islamic architecture of Bijapur in the Deccan, and a few ventured as far as Agra and Delhi, one of the
most ancient cities in the world. By the middle of the eighteenth century, systematic
scholarly interest is first evident in descriptions of monuments of western caves and
temples in southern India by A.-H. Anquetil-Duperron and Carsten Niebuhr. In
the second half of the century, British curiosity about ancient India developed in the
contexts of the transformation of imperial rule, the rise of British antiquarianism,
and growing Western philosophical interest in India as a home of ancient cultures.

At first sight, British imperial engagement with Indian antiquities seems to
resemble what we found around the Mediterranean and Near East. The British
imperial state enabled officers and civilian officials, artists, and travellers to be in
India in the first place. It provided many of them with skills, access, protection,
and logistics to study sites, collect objects, or restore ancient architecture across the
Subcontinent. But the story of early British Indian archaeology differs in crucial
ways from the one told in the previous chapters on classical and Near Eastern
archaeology. Appreciating these differences helps us understand how and why
British officials and scholars engaged with the antiquities of India.

Western attitudes towards Indian antiquities differed from those towards the physical remains of classical and Near Eastern antiquity. Indian antiquities were deemed to be of lesser aesthetic value. India was also not easily assimilated to the Christian narratives which helped frame engagement with the Near East. The primary interest in the antiquities of India was therefore historical and scholarly. Their study would help understand the past of India's civilisations and ancient Indo-European cultures. Concern with antiquities was also political: some of that research was expected to provide insights relevant to imperial governance.

Virtually all commentators rated the perceived naturalism, humanistic scale, and sublime beauty of classical Greek art more highly than its colossal and curious Indian equivalents. By contrast to the great chain of Egyptian, Assyrian, and Greek art, oriental cultures were categorised as inferior.[1] The physical remains of Greece's past were appropriated in Western narratives as part of their own histories, and collected at the Louvre and British Museum. Indian objects were mostly displayed in special colonial museums. The early Indian Repository at East India House was more akin to early modern cabinets of curiosity, which sought to evoke the spectators' wonder, than to enlightened museum collections, validated by the objects' intrinsic and contextual meanings.[2]

Orientalists nevertheless tended to locate Indian civilisation with reference to European classical antiquity. They searched for shared origins and for resemblances between Hindu and classical gods; for matching chronologies of the origins of cultures; for analogies of the structure of religions and languages; and for Greek influences and comparisons in specific examples of Indian architecture and sculpture. The Mughal architecture of the Muslim rulers in the north, with its curvilinear vocabulary of bulbous domes, multi-lobed arches, and baluster-shaped supports, seemed most aesthetically familiar to the British. Roman motifs, such as the arch or dome, were 'discovered' in the architecture of medieval Indian Islam. This supposedly culminated in the Mughal palaces, mosques, and tombs of the great emperors, and especially of Akhbar's reign in the sixteenth century.[3] William Hodges's *The Mausoleum of Sher Shah at Sasaram, Bihar* was meant to prove Indian influence on Greek and Roman architecture. Some parallels were far-fetched, but all 'gave' India a shared classical past with Europe. Captain Robert Melville Grindlay in 1830, 'without presuming to ascribe to Hindu sculpture the classical purity and elegant proportions of the Grecian chisel', asserted with reference to the Ellora cave-temples that they displayed 'considerable grandeur of design and intenseness of expression'. In this framework, contemporary India was seen at once as fallen from past glories and inferior to contemporary Europe.[4]

There was apparently limited contact between classical and Near Eastern archaeology on the one hand and Indian archaeology on the other. In British India, awareness of ideas and methodologies current elsewhere was not very wide-spread. When writing about the Bhilsa Topes, Alexander Cunningham seems to have only once referred to Layard's Assyrian discoveries, defining inscriptions and bas-reliefs on the Topes as almost equal in importance to the Mesopotamian discoveries.[5] Henry Creswicke Rawlinson, the diplomat and leading cuneiform scholar in Assyria, classified Assyrian and Indian (as well as Egyptian) sculptures as one category opposed to the classical Greco-Roman canon. In terms of scale, the relation between structural and sculptural features, and attention to ornamental detail, there were indeed similarities between Assyrian and Indian art. But, again, in British India few seemed to invest in such comparisons.[6]

Not only were Indian antiquities held to be of much lesser aesthetic value than classical ones, but neither was India easily assimilated to Christian narratives. Moreover, small religious sculptures were not readily available in detached form as they were mostly in religious use and the British were reluctant to offend religious sensibilities. Agents were not available to mediate acquisitions. British missionar-ies sometimes acquired religious images as trophies of conversion. But only a very few British residents in India in the eighteenth and early nineteenth centuries were interested in collecting Indian religious sculpture, one of the most common forms of Indian antiquity.

Sir William Jones did attempt to assimilate Indian culture to Christian narra-tives. In 1799, the East India Company unveiled a statue of Jones in one of the four corners underneath the dome of St Paul's Cathedral (fig. 40).[7] It depicts the giant of early Orientalism standing in classical dress, leaning on the ancient Indian law book, with a pen in his right hand and a scroll in his left (presumably with his English translations of Indian laws). The bas-relief on another face of the pedestal alludes to Jones's project to match the history of the biblical flood across different cultures and to use independent, Hindu testimony to prove the truth of Christi-anity. The figures of Genius and Study, or History and the new Orientalism, draw back a veil to reveal a scene of Indian mythology. India in a sari, holding a trident, sits underneath a section of the zodiac. An inscription, 'COURMA AVATAR', evokes the tortoise incarnation of Visnu during the cosmic flood. In India's right hand is a three-faced image of God in his three aspects, seen by some interpreters of Hindu-ism at the time as corroboration of the truth of the Christian doctrine of the Trinity. This iconography reflects Jones's successful attempt to make 'Hinduism safe for Anglicans' by giving it a biblical framework. Rejecting the vast cycles of world ages in Hindu doctrine, Jones shortened Indian time to the relatively brief chronology of biblical time; within that frame he granted India great antiquity.[8]

40. John Bacon, relief on the pedestal of the *Statue of Sir William Jones* in St Paul's Cathedral (completed 1799).

Indian and classical archaeology were also differentiated by the ways in which antiquities were investigated and experienced. Westerners considered India to have a past but little history, and to lack datable records and chronicles. India's past was thought to be mostly preserved in manuscripts and oral traditions, and in architectural and archaeological remains: in buildings and in the sites of ancient cities, on coins, and in inscriptions on stone and iron pillars. It was Westerners, including from the eighteenth century increasingly Britons, who started to study those remains with the methods of philology and epigraphy, and by describing sites and sculptures in word and image, rather than through excavations. There was virtually no collecting of large-scale objects, such as was common with classical antiquities. In India, imperial scholars and officials worked very closely with indigenous intellectuals and with assistants possessed of highly valued linguistic and graphological skills. This was very different from what occurred around the Mediterranean and Near East, where locals were almost exclusively employed as labourers or guardians at excavation sites in Britain's spheres of informal influence.

The international contexts in which the Company state and its personnel operated were quite unlike those framing archaeological diplomacy in the Mediterranean and Near East. Indian antiquity was not the focus of cultural nationalism and the rivalry of museum-building nation-states. By the late eighteenth century, Britain exercised virtually exclusive European influence on the Subcontinent. The (Company) state's logistical, material, and diplomatic-military resources were not required in the same ways as for Mediterranean and Near Eastern archaeological campaigns. When Britain briefly occupied the Dutch colony of Java in 1811–16, the conquest created the opportunity for an archaeological mission (chapter 8). Java was relevant in the global conflict as a potential base for Napoleonic France, and in this particular case the Anglo-Dutch relationship was subsumed under the global Anglo-French struggle. Military conquest enabled British scholars to gain control of Dutch and indigenous research assistance and previous scholarship.

Finally, whereas the discovery and collecting of antiquities in the Near East were increasingly presented in accessible language and imagery to comparatively wide and diverse audiences in magazines and museums, oriental learning became more and more a self-contained scholarly discourse within European and Indian learned circles. The Sanskrit scholarship of Jones and Charles Wilkins was continued by Henry Thomas Colebrooke and Horace Hayman Wilson, and the study of the physical remains of ancient Hindu and Muslim cultures took off. But whereas earlier empire-builders in India had communicated their on-the-spot discoveries with excited freshness, the new gentlemanly civil servant or officer's style was characterised more by scholarly rigour than by enthusiastic immediacy.[9] Orientalism was linked to new ideals of governance, which were based on observation, measurement, surveys, and statistics. British officials disseminated dry statistical information, which struck the wider British public as a 'great body of recondite knowledge, daunting and rebarbative'.[10] Indian culture was increasingly only discussed by and for those with current and previous Indian experience. The typical Indian returnee was considered an 'old, yellow-faced, bore', as Thomas Babington Macaulay put it.[11]

In this respect, the story of Indian archaeology is a far cry from the wider appeal of the adventures of a Charles Fellows in Lycia, let alone the thrilling exploits of the Lion of Nineveh, which held the magazine-reading and museum-going British public in their spell.[12] The metropolitan public showed little excitement about the discovery of new languages in southern India, or the decipherment of the Brahmi script or of Buddhist inscriptions. There was also little interest in collecting India's past in the British Museum until A. W. Franks's inspired curatorship in the second half of the nineteenth century.[13] Not until it acquired the spectacular Amaravati Marbles, and the outstanding Stuart collection of Hindu art, at the high point of the raj around 1880, was high-quality sculptural art from India proudly displayed along with that of other ancient worlds.

All these differences notwithstanding, the Company state's investment in British Indian archaeology was remarkable. A variant on the public–private partnerships of classical archaeology developed in British India: private researchers and collectors worked through the sphere of learned sociability in the Orientalist societies of Calcutta, Bombay, and London, and through informal networks of officials. This ensured that the Company state quietly allowed, facilitated, or actively sponsored archaeological research. Official and scholarly circles in British India overlapped because of the peculiar constitutional and political nature of the Company state, and the particular skills and intellectual interests of the service community. The establishment of Orientalist societies in India earlier than in London was one manifestation of this significant overlap on the so-called imperial periphery. The Company state supported archaeological practice especially through the training of officials and officers in drawing and surveying. It provided access to sites, security in the field, and limited, and often implicitly costed, resources.

There was a broad trend from the late eighteenth to the late nineteenth centuries from individual, mostly unsystematic research (observation, sketches, field reports) towards informally collaborative research under the auspices of the Company state. This was closely linked to a shift from private to state-supported archaeological research.[14] Such research was first systematically undertaken in the context of military and administrative surveys, especially from around 1800, in Mysore and Bengal and on Java. Archaeology was a sideline to the primary purposes of these surveys, a sideline that was enabled by the Company state, implicitly or explicitly funded, and more or less directly officially endorsed. Between the 1840s and 1870s, the Company state assumed an increasingly formalised and significant role in imperial archaeology.

Finally, perhaps aided by the absence of international competition, British officialdom began to develop an ethic of imperial care for the antiquities of India. British scholars and officials engaged with the neglect or destruction of ancient remains, with spoliation by Indians and Europeans, and the need to preserve and restore certain sites. By the second third of the century, some argued for the recognition of an imperial duty to care for ancient monuments more generally, although a coherent imperial policy on collecting and preservation only began to emerge a generation later. In brief, empire facilitated access to, and research of, antiquities. In turn, research and the depiction of the antiquities of India helped Britons imagine their Indian empire. To a more limited extent, the antiquities of India were also enrolled in attempts to justify and to help govern that empire.

Learned Officialdom and the Analogy of Science

Within the Indian service community, interest in Indian antiquities was fairly wide-spread from the later eighteenth century onwards. Dr Samuel Johnson enjoined Warren Hastings to sponsor archaeological inquiry: 'it is new for a Governour of Bengal to patronize learning', wrote Johnson, as he exhorted Hastings to 'survey the [remains] of its ancient edifices, and trace the vestiges of its ruined cities' so that '*we shall know the arts and opinions of a race of men*, from whom very little has been hitherto derived'.[15] Hastings had a classical education, was self-taught in Persian (until 1835 the official language in British India), and enjoyed the polite learned sociability of Claude Martin's circle of European connoisseurs at Oudh. Perhaps uniquely among early top British officials, Hastings realised the depth and range of Indian cultures and sponsored Anglo-Indian exchanges not just of commerce but also of ideas. Humanistic scholarship in India by 'men of cultivated talents ... and liberal knowledge' would aid the appreciation of Indian cultures in England. Enlightenment desires to know, order, and classify accompanied a clear imperial imperative for the accumulation of knowledge:

> especially such [knowledge] as is obtained by social communication with people over whom we exercise a dominion founded on the right of conquest, is useful to the state ... it attracts and conciliates distant affections; it lessens the weight of the chain by which the natives are held in subjection; and it imprints on the hearts of our own countrymen the sense and obligation of benevolence.[16]

Overlapping circles of imperial soldiers and administrators on the one hand, and of epigraphers, linguists, numismatists, and archaeologists on the other, studied Indian culture and history from the late eighteenth century.

Governance provided a context for the promotion of Indian learning in the Company state. Alexander Dow and Robert Orme wrote political genealogies and a theory for Anglo-Indian rule to sketch out an 'orientalised British Constitution'. Under Cornwallis and Wellesley, increasingly deep 'formal oriental knowledge [was] promoted ... as an official discourse in office manuals, gazettes and newspapers'. The collating and systematising of Indian knowledge and intelligence in maps, surveys, histories, grammars, translations, and objects was considered vital to British imperial success.[17] A 'high evidentiary value' was ascribed to dona-tive inscriptions in religious sites, which documented the terms of religious gifts, including the rights to collect revenue from taxes. Here, research of sites, texts, objects, and related local traditions could have direct implications for imperial governance.[18]

There was a broad shift in Orientalist studies from philology to archaeology (although one of the linking sciences, epigraphy, the study of inscriptions, remained the 'central pillar'). Closet scholars increasingly became field archaeologists. As in Egypt, where hieroglyphs covered gateways, obelisks, and statues, in India inscriptions on pillars, stones, and coins provided important sources. The French Orientalist Anquetil-Duperron proposed as early as 1759 that the methods of archaeological expeditions practised in Italy, Greece, and Asia Minor be extended to other continents. However, until well into the nineteenth century, the overwhelming interest in Indian archaeology was documenting and deciphering ancient inscriptions and coins, along with translating manuscripts. Excavation was less common, although the collecting of coins and inscriptions was necessitated by the former activities. The occasional empirically and scientifically minded official or officer measured and dated sites, copied inscriptions, and had them translated. Whereas much archaeological research integrated objects, texts, and images, inquirers weighed architectural, epigraphic, aesthetic, and visual evidence differently.[19]

Learned sociability on the model of the Royal Society, Society of Dilettanti, and the Society of Antiquaries was given its first Orientalist institutional framework not in London but in British India. In an example of how empire had centripetal as much as centrifugal tendencies, the Asiatic Society of Bengal was founded in 1784 under the leadership of Sir William Jones and the oversight of Hastings. Its remit was to inquire into 'MAN and NATURE – whatever is performed by the one, or produced by the other', thus encompassing 'the history and antiquities, the natural productions, arts, sciences, and literature of *Asia*'.[20] Members' interests ranged from the mathematical, physical, and earth sciences to botany, zoology, and medicine, and from philosophy, religion, geography, and ethnology to linguistics, history, art, and archaeology.

Jones's own passions were philological and linguistic, but he was aware of the importance of the archaeological sources of Indian history. In his 1786 *Discourse* he reminded the Society of the four media for 'satisfying our curiosity'. Besides languages and letters, philosophy, and religion, there were also the 'written memorials of *Sciences and Arts*' and the 'actual remains of their old *Sculpture and Architecture*'.[21] The Society became a forum for discussion, publication, and, to a very limited extent, for the preservation, too, of the ancient remains of the country. It founded the first journal, the *Asiatick Researches* (from 1788, printed by the superintendent of the Company's press), the first library (1808), and the first museum (1814) in India. The Society became a model for learned societies and scientific institutions in Bombay and Madras and, crucially, London, and conducted correspondence with societies throughout Asia, Europe, and North America.

Like most metropolitan British learned societies, the Asiatic Society was a private body with close ties to officialdom. Civilian and military Company servants were prominently represented. The Governor-General was an *ex officio* member, patron, and sometimes honorary president. The Society received occasional and modest government grants, mostly for publications. And while the Company did not specifically direct the research undertaken or discussed by the Society, occasionally the government requested the Society's advice. More broadly, there was an assumption that in areas such as botany, astronomy, geology, and Indian legal studies the Society and its networks would underpin the Company's transformation from trader to territorial ruler.

It was only in 1823 that Orientalist sociability acquired a formal metropolitan base. Empire came back to the metropolis in the form of the (soon Royal) Asiatic Society. The opening speech was given by the founding director, Henry Thomas Colebrooke (1765–1837), the son of a one-time Company chairman, now one of Europe's foremost scholars of Sanskrit and a former president of the Bengal Asiatic Society, whose research interests and publications covered a breathtaking range across the humanities and sciences.[22] Colebrooke argued that the imperial state had a responsibility towards colonial culture and promoted a model that integrated the spheres of learned sociability and research-active officialdom. He emphasised that the 'civilized' world, and 'England' as 'the most advanced in refinement' in particular, owed much to those Asian countries where civilisation had first developed. The colonial power must promote the exchange of knowledge and return 'in an improved state that which was received in a rudimentary form'. Research in the arts and sciences was instrumental to the project of understanding and improving the colony. Imperial warfare, politics, diplomacy, and commerce enabled 'public functionaries' and other Britons to study in remote spots. On their return home they could preserve their collections and publish their manuscripts. The Society newly founded in Britain, in collaboration with the learned societies in India, was to further research, publication, and preservation, and to increase European knowledge of India and 'knowledge in Asia, by diffusion of European science.' By these means, the Society would both benefit imperial subjects and further British prosperity.[23]

Indeed, many of those engaged in collecting and disseminating information about the empire, both empirically and imaginatively, were gentlemanly officer-scholars and official-scholars.[24] Officers were at the centre of many of the empire's intellectual enterprises. This was due to their training, intellectual curiosity, the sheer boredom of routine army life, the rich opportunities offered for exploration in the field, as well as career incentives for acquiring specialist skills. Their background also influenced the type of information they collected, and the ways in which they observed and represented colonial India. Army officers had a very strong presence in oriental scholarship and in the Orientalist and geographical societies in India and Britain from the late eighteenth century onwards.[25] They published modern battle narratives, travelogues (often with drawings), and hundreds of articles about India in their own trade periodicals and general magazines, and provided numerous surveys and gazettes.

Whereas British officers and officials were patently central to archaeological practices, one can take different views of the role of colonised subjects in the production of colonial knowledge. Most would agree that the power of knowledge or the 'cultural technologies of rule' were integral to European conquest and dominion.[26] Yet, many post-colonial historians and anthropologists assume that the role of the colonised was negligible: at best they were passive informants to Orientalist Europeans who applied their preconceived modes of knowing on Indian raw data. The 'self-perpetuating, reciprocal relationship between colonial knowledge and conquest' entailed an epistemological violence inflicted by the imperial state on the colonised subjects, as indigenous forms of knowledge were displaced by new forms of knowing.[27] Critics of this position assert that indigenous intellectuals contributed actively to the creation of colonial knowledge in complex processes of collaboration and negotiation. Colonial knowledge developed from genuine dialogue, confrontation, and partial accommodation between European and indigenous people, sources, and forms of knowing. Orientalism was thus ambivalent and contested. Colonial encounters were informed as much by British apprehensions over the perennial thinness of the red line, by selective respect for the Orient, by hybridity and dialogue, as by assumptions of European superiority.[28]

Clearly, the role of Indians in this empire of dialogue and collaboration varied. British surveyors, natural historians, and architects relied on Indian language assistants, informants, draughtsmen, and craftsmen. But as the imperial state increasingly replaced the human intelligence of running-spies, news-writers, wandering holy men, physicians, and astrologers with statistical surveys, so scholars too shifted to an extent from relying on the 'embodied knowledge' of informants to the 'institutional knowledge' of European archives, books, and the 'official' memory of Company servants. There were, however, crucial exceptions, most notably in the collecting of literary, ethnographic, and archaeological materials. As we shall see in one of the main case studies below, the surveyor Colin Mackenzie relied overwhelmingly on indigenous agents and draughtsmen who brought particular skills, methodologies, and intellectual traditions to a shared enterprise of producing archaeological knowledge. If the growing knowledge about India, as Peter Marshall puts it, was increasingly 'encased within a framework of European needs and pre-conceptions', in the practices of archaeology at least, British officialdom continued to rely to a significant extent on indigenous input.[29]

The practices of natural history and science in British India provide instructive analogies for the study of archaeological research. Officials with a scientific bent of mind, and often with expertise in drawing, supported by formal institutions such as botanical gardens and by informal networks, worked in fields that had an immediate utilitarian purpose. Although the scientific work of the Company state mostly followed individual enterprise and trade, the importance of science to empire-building was clearly being recognised by the late eighteenth century. Botany was necessary for the cultivation of cash crops and strategic commodities such as teak trees for shipbuilding or for the production of medicines; astronomical observatories aided navigation, and geological surveys prepared the ground for mineral exploitation.[30]

But the Company and its officials also supported science for its own sake, in the fields of theoretical astronomy, publications on natural history, and even in certain exercises in geodesy and trigonometrical surveys which were acknowledged to be not strictly necessary in politico-military terms. In fact, some of this survey work sucked resources from more utilitarian projects as empire sometimes served national science rather than vice versa.[31] If there was a recognition that research was legitimate in its own right, it was rarely conceived as autonomous by its practitioners, who were constantly alive to the imperial possibilities (and constraints) of their research. Natural history and archaeology were also linked in as far as Sanskrit literature was full of plant metaphors which required correct identification to translate Sanskrit drama and poetry. The Madras medical officer Whitelaw Ainslie, who gathered information on indigenous medicine through networks of doctors and surgeons at stations from the Kerala coast to Rajasthan, enlisted help from the Asiatic Society to translate Indian medical texts. Botanical/medical and antiquarian research were thus interlinked; the former was valuable not only for profit and survival (the army was interested in research in Nepalese poison arrows), but to Orientalists too, who in turn learned from their botanical colleagues.

In respect of both science and humanities research, the Company state's contribution started at the very beginning, in the training of officer cadets and budding civil servants. Indeed, the imperial state significantly aided archaeological practice by training a growing proportion of its personnel in drawing. The formalisation of military curricula was led by the artillery and engineers, with cavalry and infantry officer and Company cadet training following suit. Drawing was a polite accomplishment of the British upper and middle classes and a professional requirement for many imperial administrators and soldiers. Naval officers needed drawing skills to sketch coastal outlines for navigational purposes. Surveyors and map-makers, and the army engineers who built the empire's public architecture, had to be able to draw maps, route surveys, topography, fortifications, and assault plans as instruments of war.[32] Engineers in particular were taught military, topographical, and architectural drawing. Among the most versatile of empire-builders, they served extended survey duty in remote, disease-infested jungle, and were called on for varied assignments from building canals or lighthouses, repairing a fort, and designing a palace for a British or Indian ruler, to restoring the odd ancient monument.

Previously, civilian and some military draughtsmen employed in the 'Drawing Room' of the Board of Ordnance had produced military maps; in 1800, those cartographers became the uniformed Corps of Royal Military Surveyors and Draughtsmen. By then, officer cadets and civil servant trainees at Woolwich, Chatham, High Wycombe, Addiscombe, and the Company's civil service academy at Haileybury (1804) also studied drawing and watercolour painting from professional artists such as Paul Sandby R.A., William de la Motte, and William S. Gilpin (Captain John B. Gilpin's son, a talented amateur topographer). By 1796, the East India Company took up 40 per cent of places at Woolwich, which soon had five drawing masters and entrenched drawing and map-making in military culture.[33] In 1802, the Military College at Great Marlow appointed the artist William Alexander, previously the junior draughtsman on Lord Macartney's China mission, as master of landscape drawing.[34] Although it is not entirely clear how systematically drawing and cartographic skills were taught until later in the nineteenth century, this investment in the graphic skills of officials and officers clearly created the potential for cultural endeavours beyond the narrowly defined remit of the Company state.[35] This is evident in the sketches and drawings produced in the context of British diplomatic missions across South-East Asia, as well as by draughtsman employed in the Surveyor-General's office and on surveying tours. Moreover, numerous Company servants and officers have left sketchbooks and drawings; many of these were later worked up into published engravings, aquatints, watercolours, and oil paintings. They depict Indian landscapes, flora and fauna, rulers, village scenes, trades, and ceremonies, as well as European buildings and ancient Hindu and Muslim monuments in virtually any part of India, Afghanistan, and adjacent territories that had ever been ruled by the Company state or traversed by its officials. Artists' materials supplied by Reeves & Son indicated the sheer quantity of official drawing.[36]

Many of the early images document monuments that have since been altered beyond recognition, such as the site of Amaravati discussed below, or have completely disappeared, like the massive circular towers at the Firuz Shah Kotla at Delhi. Maria Graham, who spent the years 1809–11 in India, illustrated her account of Elephanta with an engraving from an on-site sketch, inscribed in handwriting along the top 'frieze': 'Figures in the Great Cave of Elephanta The Trimurti is imperfect in this plate The other figures are as they stood A.D. 1809'. Graham's *Journal* is the pioneering travelogue of an accomplished scholar. For her as much as for the male official-scholar who dominates this section, precise documentation was a form of preservation.[37] Other drawings, by contrast, involve serious representational distortion, either the better to show off certain architectural elements, to open up the perspective, or to include an element that would otherwise not be visible in one and the same view, to exaggerate scale, or to dramatise the remoteness of a location. Some drawings are downright inaccurate, as different draughtsmen rendered the same sculpture very differently in size, physique, or expression.[38]

It is in the immediate physical and ideological contexts of imperial warfare and conquest that officers and artists created some of the earliest visual representations of Indian monuments to find a reasonably wide circulation in metropolitan Britain.

Picturesque Patriotism

In 1782, James Rennell (1742–1830), the first Surveyor-General of India in the 1760s and 1770s and considered the 'father of Indian geography', published the first version of his general map of India, 'Hindoostan'. The title cartouche, which illustrates the artistic, textual, and architectural elements of British Orientalism (artist's palette, mathematical divider, Brahmins handing over legal texts, ziggurat), celebrates British commerce and conquest, both military and intellectual.[39]

As in Rennell's 'Hindoostan', maps made imperial conquest and possession possible in practical ways, but they also visualised and justified them. Rennell was one among several military surveyors who in the second half of the eighteenth century were moved from Scotland to make maps of Ireland, various parts of North America, and Bengal; in all these settings, surveying and mapping were closely related to imperial expansion and consolidation.[40] Rennell's ziggurat indicated that empire facilitated access to, and the documentation of, ancient remains and the dissemination of images of them. Indeed, many of the pictorial and illustrated accounts of the Indian empire that were circulating in the decades around 1800 include depictions of ancient monuments. Most of them were made by officers on campaign, others by professional artists, some of whom also travelled with armies. Empire thus prompted the creation of an early visual archive of picturesque patriotism by both officials and private individuals. It was through views, more than objects as in classical archaeology, that the British Empire in India first circulated among, and could be appropriated by, metropolitan audiences.

Late eighteenth-century educated Britons admired landscapes in books, prints, and paintings. They talked about landscape in highly regulated terms, including those of 'the picturesque'.[41] The picturesque was rough and rugged, it was found in asymmetrical landscapes, and its visual products aimed to elicit emotional responses. India was inherently picturesque, as the surveyor William Lambton asserted: 'to those irregular features of nature, which constitute the picturesque, is added, the ruins of art seldom introduced into landscape painting'. The picturesque was associated with territorial and imperial control. Picturesque representations of conquest helped Britons imagine the Indian empire and understand native geography and peoples, but also to legitimate imperial expansion and dominion. This was in part because such representations could obscure the connections between a place and the needs of its indigenous people: picturesque conquests transformed latently dangerous landscapes of empire into ordered, safe, and legitimate empires of the imagination.[42]

Certain kinds of picturesque views, reinforced by imperialistic narratives in the accompanying text, organised India for patriotic consumption at home. Among the monuments sketched most frequently by officers and artists in Indian theatres of war are hill forts under British siege, attack, or control. Architectural documentation was a by-product of imperial warfare, but architectural subjects were also of interest in their own right. They functioned both as illustrations of campaign narratives and picturesque renditions of ancient monuments which imperial conquest brought under British purview. The representation of ancient and benign imperial landscapes could compensate for, or distract from, the harsher realities of military conquest. The conflation of imperial and artistic interest in topographical art is what Thomas Daniell referred to as 'guiltless spoliations'.[43]

Landscape drawings and engravings of the ancient hill forts of Mysore, Rohilkhand, Bihar, Poona, and Bombay, specifically, allowed Britons back home to participate in imperial conquest and dominion. The forts (called *droogs* in Southern India) commanded narrow passes in the high mountain ranges from the Ghats in the south to the Rajmahal and Himalaya mountains in the north. They were an impressive sight, with their 'stark geology and landscaped admixture of natural mountain and man-made fortification'.[44]

A small number of artists sketched and engraved the forts as views of picturesque patriotism, rendering imminent conquest and imperial dominion over military and cultural sites visible to Britons. Among these men, Francis Swain Ward (c.1734–94) was unusual in that he pursued a dual career as an artist and officer. He was also the first to transform drawings made on the spot in India in 1757–64 into paintings.[45] Ward's *A View of the City of Madurai* 'taken during the siege' of 1763–4 against Muhammad Yusuf Khan is an example of officers on campaign surveying ancient monuments that were (part of) military targets. From the outlook platform of their camp, British soldiers study Madurai with the palace of Tirumala Nayak, most famous of seventeenth-century Madurai rulers, and its temple with *gopuras* (gate with pyramidical tower). The painting has characteristics of a survey study, with its balance of buildings and hills, and the graphic rendering of plain in the middle distance.

The only artist who travelled on a Company salary as well as under army protection to paint official commissions was the painter William Hodges. By the time Hodges arrived in India in 1779, he was already recognised as a painter of exotic scenes who had honed his sense of the sublimity of dramatic landscape with renditions of Alpine scenery and of the extreme climatic conditions and meteorological effects of the South Pacific on Cook's expeditions. The aesthetic idea of the 'sublime' in landscape refers to the 'observation of natural objects – and their artistic representation in landscape painting – which possessed the appropriate characteristics for arousing the kind of strong feelings that would … provoke profound thoughts', and deriving pleasure from fear and danger. By Hodges's generation these were attached to experiences of the unknown, the mysterious, and the obscure; India offered a wide field for discovering and painting the imperial sublime.[46]

Hodges's archaeological views provided some of the first detailed images of Indian architecture, perhaps the closest thing we have to an 'Antiquities of India'. In 1780–85, Hodges covered Madras, Calcutta, and Bihar. He also undertook three tours in north and east India, including participating in Hastings's mission to Benares; with Major Browne's delegation to Delhi, Hodges reached Agra. Hodges produced hundreds of drawings, paintings, prints, a dissertation on cross-cultural comparative architecture, and forty-eight aquatints of *Select Views in India* with descriptions (1785–8). The *Select Views*, many published with detailed notes, aimed at a more popular domestic market. Many prints showed sites referring to recent British military history: they are visual narratives seeking to appeal to the patriotism (and human-interest narratives to evoke the sympathy) of an audience momentarily intrigued by Indian culture and imperial expansion in the East. The *Select Views* also circulated widely in India, where they could be bought new, or at sales of the effects of departed or deceased inhabitants. A travel narrative with fifteen plates from his drawings, *Travels in India* (1793), served to explain and justify the aesthetic and artistic validity of exotic Indian scenes.

Hodges's architectural subjects include Muslim tombs and mosques as well as

Hindu temples, forts, and palaces from Calcutta to Akhbar's tomb. His visual narratives promoted a history that related the Mughal golden age of the middle of the sixteenth century to the early eighteenth to recent military victories and Company rule. His views of ruins contrasted the antiquity of Indian civilisation with progressive European trading nations and their commercial investment, and India as 'decayed, luxuriant and timeless' with England as 'vigorous, rational, and an agent of history'.[47] *A Tomb with Figures* (oil on canvas, *c.*1782) is a sentimental, picturesque scene of natives visiting their ancestors' tombs in evening light. Hodges associated ruins with death, and with imperial and moral decline. *View of the Ruins of a Palace at Gazipoor* (*c.*1785) also suggests antiquity and decay, though a published description admits their early eighteenth-century origins.

Hodges was concerned with the history, morality, and dangers of empires. Although he relied on the military for his security, subject matter, and commissions, in *Travels in India* Hodges considered the dreadful effects of war. The past Mughal empire seemed to him an admonition for contemporary imperial Britain, though Hodges also appreciated the benefits of the Anglo-Indian empire. He saw Hindu culture as unchanged since the earliest stages. Mughal society appeared more evolved, but to Hodges it had not progressed from the feudal stage, because of climate and intermarriage with less developed indigenous populations. Mughal ruins acknowledged that undeveloped potential. In Hodges's ruins of Agra, the viewer experienced a pleasurable melancholy, stemming from realising the loss of a previous political order and social system.

In the tradition of moral landscape painting, Hodges's renderings of Indian monuments invite the viewer to ponder both Indian and British colonial history. In *View of Mosque at Rajmahal*, Hodges attributed the building to 'that liberal patronizer of arts' Sultan Shuha, the third son of the Emperor Shah Jahan, before the supposed decline into Mughal despotism under his brother Aurangzeb. 'To the English' the site, now decaying and gradually overgrown by vegetation, was of 'considerable historical value' as the place where the British army rested after a battle in 1764 which won Britain 'complete possession of the kingdom of Bengal'. Architecture here traces the decline from a supposedly liberal regime that patronised architecture to despotic Mughal rule. It is a barometer of socio-political conditions and a site of British imperial memory.[48]

One of the earliest war artists in India was the painter Robert Home (1752–1834). Home was specifically invited by Cornwallis to accompany the Grand Army in the campaign against Tipu. Being 'embedded' with the forces obviously helped with logistics and security, but even surveyors moving with armies complained that they were frequently restricted from leaving the column without the permission of their

commanding officer and that their schedules were determined by military requirements. Often their vision was obscured by dust clouds 'through which nothing but
the experienced eye can at intervals penetrate'.[49] These constraints must have been
even more true for artists. Home nevertheless managed to publish twenty-nine coloured prints, along with maps and text as *Select Views in Mysore ...* (1794, 2nd edn
1808). The book was dedicated to Cornwallis 'and those gallant officers, by whom
the British dominion in the east has been preserved from the utter destruction
with which it was threatened'. Home advertised his authentic, expensively engraved
views of places both for those yet unfamiliar with them, and also to aid the mem-
ory-work of 'our troops' who recognised places 'where they gallantly fought and
conquered'.[50]

The *Select Views* visualises theatres of war in which ancient architecture forms
the picturesque setting and anchors imperial conquest in time and space. The
accompanying text combines historical and architectural accounts of forts with
campaign narrative. Sequences of engravings visualise the British army (indicated
by a few figures or a tent) approaching fortresses such as Savendroog, through
countryside strewn with ruined monuments. Home concludes on the theme of
commemoration, showing the local burial ground and seven inscriptions of the
'elegant monuments' since erected to British officers who fell in the taking of the
fortress or in its vicinity. The empire had brought ancient Indian monuments under
British purview and established its own more modest memorials.[51]

Home also acted as a guide to two men who would spread the image of India
as a picturesque subject more than any others: the celebrated uncle and nephew
landscapist team, Thomas (1749–1840) and William Daniell (1769–1837).[52] These
artists travelled the most widely and accumulated the broadest visual inventory of
India's cities, landscapes, hill forts, monuments, and cave-temples (fig. 41). Between
1786 and 1793, they worked primarily in Calcutta but undertook three tours: Calcutta to Srinagar, with its Buddhist and Hindu hills overlooking the town, Mysore
to Madras, and to Bombay and its temple sites. They learned from the Sanskrit
scholar Wilkins about Hindu monuments and were impressed with the beauty of
sculptured Hindu pagodas.[53] On the advice of Home, and largely along the route
of Cornwallis's Grand Army, they covered the hill forts and monuments of the
Carnatic and Mysore. As they sketched, drew, and painted a wide range of geographical and cultural sites, they started publishing their first series of views while
still in India, *Views of Calcutta* (1786–8). The 1,400 drawings they brought back to
England served them well for the rest of their careers.

The Daniells sketched twelve *droogs* south of Bangalore from Hosur to Sanka-
ridroog. Their *Oriental Scenery* includes four aquatint views of Trichinopoly, the

41. Thomas Daniell, *Gate of the Tomb of the Emperor Akhbar at Secundra, near Agra* (c. 1795). The tents, high-ranking British officers, and Bengal sepoys in the foreground show that the Daniells toured northern India in a military party. The road from Agra to Sikandra reminded them of the Appian Way, flanked by ruins on both sides.

picturesquely iconic site of imperial military prowess, as well as views of forts under siege by the British.[54] The Daniells followed, and in some cases anticipated, British military expansion with views of monuments which were coming under British control. In 1801, they published several very large aquatints of the Taj Mahal, the primary Mughal monument in Agra. Hodges had displayed paintings of the Taj in 1787 and 1794, but after the fall of Mysore in 1799 Thomas Daniell anticipated further British expansion; indeed, the emperor was duly pensioned off by the British and Delhi and Agra taken in 1803. Already in 1801–3, the Daniells had published a series of engravings of Indian forts, palaces, and mausoleums which were now under British dominion. The views suggest successive conquests and empires in India, and a palimpsest of cultures, religions, and architectural styles: sites of the Mughal and Muslim conquest of India, Muslim architectural appropriation of Hindu religious sites, followed by recent British conquests in Oudh in the north, and views of southern hill forts from the Mysore conquests in 1791–2, now pacified, flying the British standard.[55]

The architecture associated with Britain's key Indian enemies had become of interest in its own right. In the renditions of officers and artists, India's conquered hill forts were among the most striking views of ancient architecture. They were also – in substance and symbolism – significant markers of British imperial conquest, control, and surveillance of the vast and still expanding Indian territory, its ancient remains, and its modern politico-military strongholds.[56] Some depictions, like the Daniells's, pre-empted conquest. But deeper engagement with sites, in the form of descriptions, measurements, transcribing of inscriptions, and collecting of objects, was predicated on the conquest of a territory. Conquest established sustained access and a degree of security. In several cases the conquest of substantial new territories also triggered ambitious surveys of natural and cultural resources. But before the first systematic surveys were being conducted from around 1800, some rudimentary field work had already been carried out.

Closet Archaeologists and Pioneers in the Field

For Alexander Cunningham in the 1860s, archaeological research during the half-century following the foundation of the Asiatic Society in 1784 had remained 'chiefly literary'. That is to say, it mostly involved translations of books and inscriptions, with brief notices of key buildings at Delhi, Agra, and other well-known sites. Exceptions included essays by Jones, Francis Wilford, Colebooke, and Wilson on the religion, geography, and astronomy of the Hindus, but overall the

> early labourers may be called Closet or Scholastic Archaeologists. The travellers of their day gave glowing accounts of the wonders of Ellora, of the massive grandeur of the Kutb Minar, and of the matchless beauty of the Taj Mahal at Agra. But all was vague and indefinite. There were but few measurements and no plans.[57]

William Erskine's study of the cave-temples of Elephanta and Francis Buchanan's surveys of Bengal, judged Cunningham, 'anticipated the period when vague and glowing accounts would give place to accurate descriptions and detailed plans.'[58] Early achievements in British Indian archaeology related indeed less to excavation and surveys, but mostly used manuscripts and inscriptions to establish a basic framework of chronology. Yet Cunningham's assessment did not entirely do justice to the emerging concern, soon to become something of an obsession, with careful description and measurement.[59]

Unsystematic recording of historical sites occurred in the context of military campaigns and by way of 'on-duty-research', as we have already seen with reference to hill forts. Gentlemen-officer-scholars and civil servants sketched, described, and measured monuments. Especially in the case of officers, this often involved the use of (implied and apparently uncosted) resources. Low-key, largely unstructured, unsystematic investment on the part of the imperial state was thus producing cultural outcomes. The Company's amateur archaeologists sent their descriptions, drawings, and the occasional object to the learned societies of India and London, where their findings were discussed and often published.[60]

Without a stated policy or specific instructions, individual officers' judgements usually dictated the extent to which archaeological interests were accommodated on military expeditions. In 1818, the same year that the British Museum and British government considered whether to use British diplomats in a systematic fashion for collection development, Captain Dangerfield from the Bombay establishment wrote of a discovery he had made in the jungle near Baug at a site called Panch Pandoo. He described four caves, giving measurements, their relative state of decay, and the area's geography, topography, geology, and flora. The account was read before the Bombay Literary Society and later published with several competent drawings. An accompanying note by William Erskine (1773–1852), later a famous historian of India, confirmed that the officer was reporting on the first excavation of such a Buddhist site in that region.[61] The editors also printed a letter from Dangerfield to his commanding officer, General Sir John Malcolm, of April 1819. When, on a march, he discovered several pagodas and inscriptions at Wone which had previously not been known to Europeans, Dangerfield had stopped for two days to make rudimentary sketches. He did not dare stay for a fuller survey, which might have been considered incompatible with his military duties. As late as the 1840s, Lieutenant-Colonel William Sleeman of the Bengal army, best known for leading the campaign against *thugee*, stressed that he had had rare 'opportunities of observation' through his 'varied employment', yet he hastily added that few had been 'more exclusively devoted to the service of their masters' and that the 'time of public servants is not their own'.[62] There was at least an implicit expectation that the documentation of India's ancient monuments was of sufficient relevance to justify minor detours or delays, but striking the balance between military duties and archaeological inquiry outside official surveys remained a challenge for officers.

In 1788, the Asiatic Society published the first volume of the *Asiatick Researches*. The issue brought together a variety of archaeological accounts, including Charles Wilkins's translation of the first inscriptions from Bodhgaya, apparently made with the help of Indian assistants.[63] It also included Wilkins's account of a 'decapitated pillar near Buddal' which he had found in a swamp and overgrown with weeds,

42. Anon., *Architectural Model of Tirumala Nayak's Pudu Mandapa, Madurai, India* (1780–89). Adam Blackader, stationed at Madurai, presented this copper alloy model via Sir Joseph Banks to the Society of Antiquaries. It is of a freestanding hall to the east of the great Hindu temple of Minaksi-Sundaresvara. Madurai was a centre for the revival of traditional Hindu architecture, and the model represents an early attempt by an eighteenth-century European antiquarian to comprehend the aesthetics of Hindu temple architecture.

when in charge of a nearby factory; he submitted the translation of an inscription and an 'impression of the column'.[64] Lieutenant Polier's copies of the inscriptions on the monolithic, tapering column of polished sandstone (third century BC), brought to Firuzabad by Firuz Sha from Ambala, sat alongside reports on the Mahabalipuram sanctuaries on the Coromandel coast.[65]

The Asiatic Society discussed and published numerous other reports and drawings of ancient monuments submitted by Company servants, officers, and the occasional civilian from the city of Tagara, the cave inscriptions of Orissa, the Buddhist monument at Bhilsa, and Uttar Pradesh. London's Society of Antiquaries was then also indulging an enlightened antiquarian interest in Hindu art and architecture. In 1789, a Company surgeon, Adam Blackader, stationed at Madurai, presented a model made of copper alloy (complete with scale drawings used in its preparation) of Tirumala Nayak's Pudu Mandapa to Sir Joseph Banks in London (fig. 42). The model is of a freestanding hall to the east of the great Hindu temple of Minaksi-Sundaresvara. Madurai was a centre for the revival of traditional Hindu architecture, and the model represents an early attempt by an eighteenth-century European antiquarian to comprehend the aesthetics of Hindu temple architecture.[66]

The 1790s saw the descriptions, drawings, and reporting on the antiquities of India gain in intensity among scholarly and official circles in British India. From that decade we have architectural drawings by Robert Kyd from Bengal; Sir Alexander Allan's and Colebrooke's drawings of hill forts; Samuel Davis's sketches from

Gaur and of Muslim tombs and mosques at Jaunpur; and Robert Home's views of monuments and sculptured rocks, including the penance of Arjuna, a celebrated, naturalistically carved frieze of figures and animals at Mamallapuram, as well as of Mahabalipuram, then also first measured and its inscriptions reproduced more accurately. In 1794, a Major Moore described the remains of Bijapur; they were to be noticed again in 1808 by Sir James Mackintosh, who called it 'the Palmyra of the Dekkan', and in 1811 by Captain Thomas Sydenham, who measured and described the impressive line-up of fortifications and minarets dominated by the dome of the Gol Gumbaz.[67]

In 1788, Jonathan Duncan, who had joined the Company in 1772 as a minor civil servant aged sixteen, and had helped found the Asiatic Society, was the Resident and Superintendent at Benares. There he curbed Company corruption and ended infanticide, as commemorated in his memorial in Bombay Cathedral. In 1795, the Asiatic Society heard a paper on how Duncan by chance had obtained two urns which had been accidentally discovered in the digging operations of a local *zamindar*, Jagat Singh, who was collecting stones for his new building from the ruins around Sarnath in central India. The site of Varanasi, where Buddha had given his first sermon, 'Turning the Wheel of the Law', rises on the steep western bank of the Ganga river. Pilgrims have worshipped here for two and a half millennia and it is filled with temples, shrines, and sacred images. The stone and marble vessels or urns, found one inside the other, contained some bones and decayed pearls and jewellery. After further digging, again unrelated to archaeological excavations, a stupa emerged.[68]

The Orientalist journals reported these and other discoveries of small objects such as brass images and of inscriptions made by British officials, medical offers, and others when digging tanks or in the course of other duties.[69] In the 1820s came J. Babington's illustrated account of megalithic graves at Malabar and Captain Robert Young's report on megalithic burials near Hyderabad. By the mid-1830s, the engineer and paleontologist Proby Thomas Cautley reported for the first time on the basic stratigraphy of a site, at Behat in Uttar Pradesh.[70] But until the 1840s or 1850s, archaeology was advanced primarily through increasingly thorough and accurate descriptions, often accompanied by site plans and drawings, rather than through excavation or the collecting of objects. It was officers and officials who did most of the field work and forwarded findings for discussion and dissemination in learned circles in India and London, though visiting artists also continued to contribute to building the archaeological archive. They all supported the long-term trend from text-based antiquarian research to material exploration.

The rock-cut cave-temples of western India fascinated British visitors and

43. Henry Salt, *Kenhery, Jagheyseer and Montpezir Caves*. In this folding-out plate in the *Trans-actions of the Literary Society of Bombay* for 1819, an atmospheric view of the entrance to Kan-heri is combined with thumbnail sketches of the figure of Buddha in different attitudes at left. At bottom, the bizarre ensemble over a doorway at Jogeswari shows a five-headed, twelve-handed figure supporting the enthroned figure of a four-handed male, surrounded by attendants and gods. The whole design is framed by 'an arch vomited forth' by a monstrous hybrid of hippo-potamus, elephant, and dragon.

scholars from early on. Buddhist or Jain sanctuaries cut with iron chisels and metals as artificial grottos date back to the third century BC.[71] Henry Salt, familiar to us from Egypt after 1815, had travelled as draughtsman and secretary to Lord Valentia in India in 1802–4, when he explored the cave-temples around Bombay and conducted an extensive survey of ancient monuments on the island of Salsette. A Major Atkins of the Bombay establishment provided a geometrical plan of the hill site and a ground plan and sections of the great cave at 'Kenery' (Kanheri), forty kilometres north of Bombay. Salt drew details of monuments and gave broadly accurate iconographic and descriptive accounts of the caves of Kanheri, Manda-peswar, and Jogeswari (fig. 43).

The history of the British rediscovery of the rock-cut temples of Ellora and Elephanta in the 'long' eighteenth century provides a good case study in the proc-esses of early British-Indian archaeology. The island of Elephanta (Garipuri) lies in the inlet between the mainland and the outer islands of Bombay, and was named after a large black granite elephant with a tiger on its back which stood outside the main portico, just opposite from where the landing place used to be for visitors around 1800. Today it is only an hour's boat journey from Bombay. Elephanta is the smallest, supposedly the oldest, and one of the richest in sculpture of the cave-temples of western India. The famous Hindu site was excavated probably during the Kalachuri period into a high cliff and is reached via a long flight of steps. The main shrine, a sixth-century Shiva temple, is entered through openings on three sides, flanked by courts on two. The key Hindu art on this site is large-scale figurative panels, set deeply recessed into the walls, which depict Shiva's different aspects. There is a triple-headed bust of Shiva and some of the additional courts and porches with side chambers have carved images.

James Forbes was among the earliest of officials, officers, and artists who engaged with Elephanta during the half-century 1770–1820. Forbes worked for the Company as a trader, topographer, diplomat, and revenue administrator, with postings widely spread over western and southern India. He recorded his views of India in 5,000 private letters home and in some 500 on-site sketches over seventeen years. Among the images which reached quite a wide London cultured audience as early as the 1780s was *The Grand Altar Piece, Fronting the Principal Entrance, in the Excavation at the Isle of Elephanta*, 1774, made during a mapping visit to Elephanta and Salsette, which had recently been acquired by the Company. Forbes was overwhelmed by the expanse and depth of the mountain ranges and 'city-sized' spaces carved into the caverns. He admired a high civilisation which preceded European antiquity: 'when India was the muse of art and science' while Europe was all ignorance and barbarism. When once taking an English artist to the site, the visitor said he 'had seen the most striking objects of art in Italy and Greece, but never anything which filled his mind with such extraordinary sensations' regarding the 'general effect', if not 'proportion of form and expression of countenance'.[72]

Apparently prompted into action by the foundation of the Asiatic Society, antiquarian colleagues in the metropolis between 1785 and 1792 printed accounts from the early eighteenth century, alongside fresh ones, of Elephanta and Salsette in *Archaeologia*. The scholarly exercise of retrospective stocktaking included extracts from the Company's manuscript collections compiled by Company official and hydrographer Alexander Dalrymple, with the earliest English drawings of Elephanta by Captain Pyke. Pyke was a Company military cartographer who had visited the island covertly, and hastily measured and drew the architecture and sculpture by candlelight. An account, and Mallet's copies of the inscriptions, from Salsette, and other communications on Salsette and Elephanta, also date from 1785. That same year, the Society of Antiquaries elected Sir John Call, a former East India

Company servant and military engineer, to their membership; they had recently learned that he owned drawings of Indian deities at Elephanta. Hector Macneill, a Scottish-born poet who served as assistant secretary on the flagship of Sir Richard Bickerton in Indian waters in the early 1780s, visited the caves of Cannara, Ambola, and Elephanta in an interval of peace. Macneill shared other visitors' excitement at the romantic location and the aesthetic standards of these monuments 'of genius' in cave-temples which revealed 'new wonder at every step: palaces, statues, giants, monsters, and deities seemed as if starting up from the bowels of the earth to open day ... a scene more like enchantment than reality.'[73]

In addition to Pyke's and Macneill's reports, in 1785 the British antiquarian Richard Gough summarised previous English and French accounts of cave-temples. There was at least one other reference to the temple sculptures in the *Gentleman's Magazine*. Interest in the erotic and sexual symbolism of Elephanta's sculptures also grew. Finally, *Archaeologia* in 1785 published remarks by William Hunter, the Royal Academy's Professor of Anatomy, on the great anatomical accuracy and emotional expressiveness of the Elephanta figures.[74] Western India's cave-temples had clearly achieved considerable currency in London's artistic and intellectual circles.

Views of Elephanta circulated in cultural circles in British India and in Britain in the form of travellers' sketches, engravings, and paintings. James Wales was commissioned to paint a view sketched by the Company servant James Forbes (fig. 44). The central of three rectangular sections is framed by massive receding pillars and beams which enclose chambers receding in long perspective towards the innermost and focal point, a huge sculpted bust of Siva Mahesamurti, the three-faced Hindu symbol of universal creation. Two small human figures point reverentially at the sculptures; a third figure very close to the bust marks its massive scale. Stones have fallen in the middle plain in a picturesque manner. The rectangular space to the right contains three large sculptured manifestations of Siva, to which a single Indian worshipper looks up. The space to the left is devoid of sculptures and humans, but filled with a light from an unknown source leading our view to the painting's margin, a dark recess in the back wall, the innermost sanctum. Vegetation frames this silent scene of Indians and Indian antiquity undisturbed by European visitors.

The Daniells, too, engaged with Elephanta, especially the architectural elements and picturesque effects of the setting and the structures' state of decay. William Westall (1781–1830), official landscape painter to an expedition to Australia in 1801–3, indulged his geological interests by making drawings of rock-cut temples. And Major John Goldingham, a surveyor and the Company's astronomer, argued on the basis of iconographic evidence that Elephanta was a Hindu temple.[75]

44. James Phillips, after James Wales, *Interior View of the Principal Excavated Temple on the Island of Elephanta* (1790).

William Erskine's slightly later study, with plans and copies of sculptures, provided the most exhaustive treatment of Elephanta, but it also denoted a change in the site's appreciation. Erskine, recorder of Bombay from 1804, helped found its Literary Society. He corrected previous accounts on the subject, including those by Pyke, Niebuhr, and Valentia. Erskine's important study was accompanied by a plan and drawings of key figures in the caves. These were by a Mrs Ashburner, whose other drawings of excavated objects in south India, of a ring, brass and earthenware vessels, and vases, were among the many drawings created by the numerous if little-studied female amateur artists in British India. These drawings were distinguished by the fact that they had accompanied a note to Erskine, in which Mrs Ashburner reported on the excavation of these objects near the 'Pandoo Coolies' at Nella Parumba (Malabar). She may have initiated, and certainly was instrumental to, Erskine's scholarly publication.[76] Erskine viewed Elephanta as the product of the dark ages (he dated the site to AD 800), and identified it as Hindu, since Buddhists and Jains did not believe in 'monstrous', multi-headed divine incarnations. He also considered the site less grand architecturally than other monuments and thought the figures lacked polish. Around the same time, James Mill's famous *History of British India* saw in monuments such as Elephanta proof that prior to 'the dawn of taste' magnitude was the only way for barbarian and rude nations to show magnificence in architecture.[77]

Officers, officials, artists, and the occasional individual traveller recorded ancient sites while engaged in varied historical, topographical, geological, aesthetic, and artistic pursuits. Descriptions, images, plans, and, exceptionally, models were made. Picturesque views by officers and artists of hill forts organised India for patriotic consumption at home. Many officers in the field transcribed inscriptions; a few began to conduct extensive, systematic surveys and offered in-depth scholarly discussions. Even those who just cursorily viewed a site were attuned to the regimes of description and sketching.[78] Over subsequent decades, individual officers and officials continued to investigate sites, to copy inscriptions, and to collect coins in various parts of India and Afghanistan. Among other discoveries, these brought to light the inscriptions on Mount Abu in the north-west and disseminated views of Jai Singh's observatory and the Jantar Mantar. They also advanced knowledge of Indo-Greek numismatics. But around 1800, new modes and processes of inquiry had already begun to transform the landscape of archaeology. Ambitious surveys of the natural and cultural resources of newly conquered territories were commissioned. Surveying the empire also prompted some of the most intensive and innovative archaeological research yet.

SURVEYING THE EMPIRE

THE BRITISH EMPIRE made possible archaeological and historical research in India, which was, in turn, expected to help officialdom better understand and run the empire, for instance in terms of historic rights to property or revenue collection. But imperial investment in archaeology produced more than was usable for governance. Indeed, much of the resulting work was of more immediate scholarly than of governmental value.

The gathering of knowledge became a key ambition for the nineteenth-century British imperial state. Imperial surveys were driven, first and foremost, by military, political, and administrative needs. Mapping and surveys aided the execution of military manoeuvres, the construction of fortifications, and the establishment of boundaries. Topographical and statistical surveys facilitated revenue collection and the exploitation of natural resources.[1] Colin Mackenzie's surveys helped organise Mysore for private property in the form of the *ryotwari* system (a class of yeoman farmers), around the same time that the picturesque aesthetics organised British India for consumption in the imperial metropolis.[2]

The first Company surveys of the newly conquered Mysore domains, of parts of Bengal, and of (the briefly British-occupied Dutch island of) Java, allowed the first systematic archaeological research to be carried out under the auspices of the Company state in South-East Asia.[3] Systematic collecting of information about the socio-economic conditions, manufactures, natural resources, and arts of newly conquered territories was in part modelled on Sir John Sinclair's pioneering *Statistical Account of Scotland* (1791–9). This included the location and description of old settlements, buildings, ruins, family histories, and customs. The precise scope and methods of the Company's surveys depended very much on the individual officer in charge. The man who did more than any other to further extensive and innovative archaeological inquiries during the Napoleonic period, first in India and then briefly on Java, was the Scots Colonel Colin Mackenzie.

The Great Mysore Survey of 1799–1809

After the triumph of 1799, Wellesley commissioned three Mysore surveys to fix the boundaries of the new territory and to collect economic, demographic, botanical, geological, as well as cultural data. One survey, led by Lieutenant (later Colonel) Colin Mackenzie, was the first imperial survey to generate significant archaeological knowledge. Born in the Outer Hebrides, Mackenzie came to India as an infantry officer in 1783, but soon transferred to the Army Engineers. He was described as extremely methodical, energetic to the extent of compromising his health, and as somewhat stiff but well respected.[4] His surveying and engineering were instrumental in the defeat of Mysore in 1798–9. A narrowly avoided ambush deepened his friendship with Wellesley, who held him in high esteem. Among Mackenzie's many scholarly achievements are breakthroughs in the study of Jainism, the religion founded by Mahavira in the sixth century BC.[5] He also established the importance of inscriptions to the understanding of land tenures, thus incorporating archaeological inquiry as a means of imperial governance. His hallmarks were careful preparation, thorough and standardised work, and precise record-keeping. In various surveys from the 1780s to 1815, Mackenzie collected vast amounts of information on the climate and natural history, and the history, languages, manners, and antiquities of southern India and the Deccan. A portrait, probably painted on the occasion of Mackenzie's appointment as Surveyor-General in 1816, shows him with three assistants: Kistnaji holding the telescope, his Jain pandit with a palm-leaf manuscript, and a Telugu Brahmin pandit. Towering behind is the huge tenth-century statue of King Bahubali which dominates the holiest Jain site of Shravana Belagola (see plate XVI).

Although Mackenzie described his research as 'foreign to the general habits of military men', he held that 'in the midst of camps and the bustle of war, and of travel and voyages, the human mind may be exercised to advantage'. It was widely accepted that 'science may derive assistance, and knowledge be diffused, in the leisure moments of camps and voyages'. But Mackenzie also wanted to prove that in the vacant moments of an Indian sojourn and campaign in particular (for what is the life of an Indian adventurer but one continued campaign on a more extensive scale) such collected observations may be found useful, at least in directing the observation of those more highly gifted to matters of utility, if not to record facts of importance to philosophy and science.[6]

Even more than other engineers and surveyors, Mackenzie conflated the roles of soldier and scholar. His early discoveries were all made on campaign. Even during his Deccan survey, he was called off four times to advise on the positioning of artillery and on assaults.[7] Mackenzie's military duties, cartographic activities, historiographical curiosity, and visual documentation were all intertwined, as they were in the British imperial project at large. He developed a distinct model of collaborative surveying in which he relied almost exclusively on some twenty indigenous assistants. Mackenzie recognised that investigating Indian history and its material remains could not be separated from the indigenous people, nor from his role as an agent and instrument of imperialism.[8]

Despite the Company's preference for a cheap survey and his complaint about limited resources, Mackenzie defined his terms widely.[9] In the face of harsh conditions of terrain and climate, despite frequent illness, and with limited resources, Mackenzie and his teams amassed historical, ethnographic, and religious texts and traditions, made rubbings and copies of inscriptions, collected coins and some antiquities, and drew hundreds of sketches. Mackenzie's own summary of the achievements of the Mysore survey includes reference to

The design and nature of the monumental stones and trophies ... which illustrate the ancient customs of the early inhabitant, and, perhaps of the early western nations. [Also,] sepulchral tumuli, mounds, and barrows of the early tribes ... illustrated by drawings.[10]

Even before British diplomats were formally instructed to collect antiquities in Greece or Egypt, Mackenzie's officer and Orientalist friends supported his research. On Mackenzie's request in 1808 a memorandum was circulated among senior British officials to solicit materials from natives 'on the ancient history, state, and institutions of the south of India'. This was information which might easily be lost but for the 'interposition of the Gentlemen in the Diplomatic, Judicial, Revenue, and Medical departments'.[11] In more detailed personal memoranda to particular officials, Mackenzie asked for coins, antiquities, drawings of ancient tombs and burial mounds, copies of inscriptions, and other materials relevant to the early history of Buddhism and Jainism. Mackenzie also sent collectors to Poona in 1808, Hyderabad in 1815, and Puri in 1820.

Some in the Company hierarchy in India were aware of the importance of the project for political purposes, especially in terms of understanding the nature of landed property. Others, however, doubted the historical value of anything other than the inscriptional record to date kings, reigns, and wars (most 'historical' texts were considered to be tainted by myth and fable). But since it was thought that, with some notable exceptions, 'regular historical narrations and tracts are seldom found among the Natives, and such notices as exist, are generally preserved in the form of religious legends and popular poems and stories', there was broad support for Mackenzie's project.

Mackenzie pioneered a model of collaborative surveying with teams of native assistants who were crucial to the effectiveness and efficiency of his historical inquiries. Extensive but so far under-used archives survive of field reports, drawings, and other materials which Mackenzie's native assistants sent to him, and of his drawings of ancient buildings and sculpture, and his vast epigraphic collections. These provide important insights into the practice and methods of knowledge production in British India, including the complex personal relations and overlapping (yet not identical) interests of masters and assistants in the archaeological enterprise in British India.[12]

Mackenzie's 'native establishment' consisted of the multilingual, 20-year old Brahmin Borriah Rao (1776–?1803), as head translator, followed by his brother Lakshmiah Rao, with at least seventeen native, mostly Brahmin, assistants. They were trained to collect local histories and traditions, linguistic materials, and information about ancient structures with local lore about them. Mackenzie described them as 'natives trained and instructed by me for this purpose, and with the only charge to government of the postage being franked, and the aid of some of the native writers'.[13] Borriah translated for Mackenzie and directed his native assistants in their collecting. He also recruited and trained several Brahmins, was adept at deciphering 'Hale Kannada' characters, and keenly collected coins. 'I owe to the happy genius of this individual', wrote Mackenzie, 'the encouragement and the means of obtaining what I so long sought'.[14]

Mackenzie's assistants did more than collect and translate materials. They were essential in unlocking knowledge, especially in the face of sceptical locals who felt intimidated by inquisitive British officials, particularly if they approached with sepoys. Mackenzie's assistants reassured and protected 'persons and properties' from 'all violence of any kind', and tried to 'conciliate their minds, which was indeed necessary for easier obtaining my object'.[15] Mackenzie and his teams knew it could be counterproductive to show too much interest in any particular object or to take notes in the presence of locals. Some resistance was encountered in areas of uncertain British authority: local rajas interrupted assistants who were copying temple inscriptions, fearing exposure of the secrets of their kingdoms. Elsewhere, Brahmins tried to suppress certain texts. But there is also evidence of local investment in the collecting project. Petitions were presented to the Company to settle a kingdom as *zamindari* estates, reduce tributes, or have a kingly scion released from a British prison. Narrain Rao initially failed to procure certain materials at the court of the Maharaja of Gadwal, but later obtained them by paying a local acquaintance.[16]

After Borriah's early death his younger brother Lakshmiah directed the team. He later became the first Indian member of the Madras Literary Society and founding president of the Hindu Literary Society there in 1830. In monthly reports, Lakshmiah explained the process of collecting. He was constantly negotiating to enable agents and assistants to persuade locals to share knowledge. Sometimes he turned to local British officials for introductions, or activated wider Company networks in pursuit of materials.[17] He sent lists of items and synopses of traditions, and detailed how he purchased numerous books, prepared translations, and announced the dispatch of copies, texts, or images, as short-term loans to his 'master'. Some locals had materials which they were prepared to sell, or offered in exchange for favours. One day in April 1804, Lakshmiah went to 'the Black Town; to get an explanation of some Persian wards from the head Maleem'. The following day he could speak to the head Mastry of the Maleem, but

> he do not like to get the Copy of that book unless he get some proper ingagement for his service only he gave very few explanation of this [wards] and he told me that he would bring the book to your honor with him two or three days and explain properly the true meaning.[18]

Lakshmiah often went out of his way to accommodate local sensibilities. On one occasion he seemed to agree to secret meetings with a key learned man who understood 'all kind of the Boogalums'. This man had some conditions on who ought to meet with the British-instructed collectors, and whose name must apparently not be connected with them publicly. It is not entirely clear whether he had native or British perceptions in mind, but when trust was established the learned contact promised to send all 'secret books of the Stronomy' and other histories.[19] Similarly, Subarao, one of Mackenzie's Maratha writers, reported on his collecting of histories and inscriptions by Mackenzie's direction in the Mundagada district. With the help of local learned men he gained access to books as well as inscriptions. Repeatedly, Subarao indicates that he patiently had to build delicate relationships of trust with locals who were in possession of interesting materials, as when with one man he 'inquired him slowly that he had any ancient books'.[20]

When Mackenzie's Maratha translator, Baboo Rao, undertook a trip on the Coromandel coast to collect coins and historical information, he also acted as a guide to British officers to the recently discovered temple at Mahabalipuram. He frequently bought or copied books, and when no texts were to be had he asked local chiefs, elders, and learned men about Buddhas and conflicts with the Jains. Baboo Rao followed up stories he heard on the discovery of treasures, old pottery, ruins, or statuary, negotiated over access or objects with temple managers, and sometimes also dug in areas where previously chance discoveries had been made.[21]

Lakshmiah frequently refers to inscriptions, some of which were cut into the rock on hills; others he found in pagodas. Occasionally he left behind a 'writer' to transcribe inscriptions while he himself hurried on. Epigraphy was arguably the central pillar of precolonial Indian history, both owing to the nature of ancient and medieval cultural practices and the documentary function of many such texts, and because of the comparative paucity of other historiographical traditions prior to around 1000. In Calcutta, British scholars and civil servants brought theories and practices derived from the study of the European classical past to bear on new data. Natives served as language teachers, linguistic informants, and understudies to Europeans. Mackenzie conceptualised the value of stone and metal inscriptions as a historical source.[22] By the late eighteenth century, the value of inscriptions was recognised even by those Calcutta Orientalists who had previously focused on the Puranas and other Sanskrit texts in their quest to understand India's ancient history.

One set of some 100 letters and reports by Narrain Rao Brahmin affords us detailed insights into the processes of building the epigraphic archive. The distinctive suffix 'Rao' refers to the Niyogis, a class of secular, multilingual Brahmins in the bureaucracy of the Arcot court.[23] Narrain, who was very likely previously employed in the Arcot administration, was proficient in Telugu, Marathi, Tamil, Sanskrit, Hindustani, Persian, and English. His letters document his travels from Mysore to the Maratha dominions. He was collecting medieval texts in numerous languages and writing original historiographical works, including an antiquarian description of Ellora.[24] Narrain's contributions to Mackenzie's larger project were manifold. His work ethic, professional outlook, and bureaucratic experience are perhaps reflected in the fact that he and other such assistants are referred to not simply as informants but as *munshis* (scholars), *mutasaddis* (accountants), and *gumashtas* (administrative assistants), echoing Persian administrative titles under the Nawab. Donative inscriptions at religious sites shed light on the rights to collect revenue from taxes. Here, research into sites and the related local traditions had direct implications for imperial governance.

The Niyogis were possessed of a heightened awareness of language and writing, an appreciation of the variations of individual speech acts and of lexical and syntactic choices, and high graphological awareness. Such skills often allowed them to date historical documents and judge their authenticity. Some also developed systematic ways to collect, classify, and decipher earlier scripts in inscriptions: by combining comparative formal analysis of samples of graphological norms with the insight that unrecognisable letters in ancient texts were archaic forms of the same letters in a modern script, they worked backwards in palaeographic decipherment. The assistants made faithful copies, so even an undeciphered script was rendered into an important archive for modern epigraphers. In some cases, copper plates or stone stelae were collected, but mostly facsimiles were drawn by hand to reproduce the precise shapes of letters and their arrangement on the inscribed plate, along with sculptural ornaments, borders, or other elements. Finally, their 'awareness of the chronological implications of recurrent stylistic formulae and other distinctive lexical usages' allowed Narrain and others to extend their previous methodology of authenticating administrative documents to dating incomplete inscriptions too.[25]

Narrain Rao trained and 'subcontracted' other Niyogis with similar linguistic skills as assistants or go-betweens; they also made accurate transcriptions when his workload became too great. There are even examples of his assistants employing their own assistants. Mackenzie thus built on his accustomed cartographic and statistical approach to the world and the past, but he shaped a distinct Madras school of epigraphy as a method for historical inquiry. His genuine dialogue with his Niyogi collaborators and their specific skills produced a new class of Niyogis who eventually applied the new modes of imperial knowledge to their own ends.

After Mackenzie's death in 1821, Lakshmiah lobbied the Company to support his continued collecting with a central office and local agents. However, the Asiatic Society advised the Governor-General that the native Indian was unsuited as a 'master head, accustomed to generalisation, and capable of estimating the value and drift of inscription and legendary devices'; they granted he could be a good auxiliary. Instead the Society referred the task of publishing parts of Mackenzie's collection to the Madras missionary William Taylor, who subscribed to spurious eighteenth-century mystical Orientalism rather than post-Jonesian scholarship. Lakshmiah's demotion in Taylor's favour was probably one of the worst decisions taken by British archaeological circles. Taylor's arrogant and bigoted Orientalist rhetoric dramatically highlighted just how prescient Mackenzie's open-minded dialogue with indigenous experts had been.[26]

In 1810, the Company directors had congratulated Mackenzie on his achievements, offered compensation for his expenses, and encouraged him to prepare his materials for publication. They were especially appreciative of the historical collections which, despite some doubts over their veracity, represented the best effort yet to further the understanding of the modern state of the country, and to give indications of historical conditions. The lack of much 'true history' was apparently not yet seen to reflect a lack of historical consciousness, but rather the historical 'commotions and changes' that had played havoc with the preservation of records.[27] In his lifetime, Mackenzie shared his collections with Calcutta Orientalists, some were published in the *Asiatick Researches*, and he corresponded with London scholars.

Mackenzie speaks to us primarily through his very numerous drawings of architectural sites, temples, sculptures, and reliefs.[28] Many drawings are of antiquarian, historical, religious, or ethnographic interest. Officers such as Mackenzie often sketched themselves in the process of measuring or sketching antique sites, as self-conscious, confident, cultured imperial explorers. *A Company Officer about to sketch a ruined temple, perhaps at Vijayanagara*,[29] made by one of Mackenzie's draughtsmen in *c.*1800–1810, appears to show a temple shrine at Vijayanagara, the City of Victory in the Deccan. Two European officers, presumably including Mackenzie, and a European assistant with a drawing portfolio are accompanied by indigenous guides, sepoys, and one very dark-skinned, near-naked porter. The procession approaches a monolithic temple which commands the otherwise plain, flat countryside. They are met by a local delegation of a Brahmin preceded by a white-clad man about to make introductions, and followed by a servant and a very dark-skinned man with a long staff. Closer to the temple stand two more indigenous men whilst another has already climbed on to the temple's stone pedestal to start measuring the surface with a staff. The shrine, with exquisite carvings on all sides, has been colonised by one massive tree, which sits roundly atop the broken temple tower and has embraced the structure with roots driven into the sides and pedestal. We glimpse significantly worse destruction at the rear, where the pedestal and a lower part of the temple are tumbling. The red-coated British officer approaching out of the shadow with his archaeological-artistic-military retinue has come to intervene against inexorable decay, to collect and protect the monument from nature. If he cannot halt erosion or restore the monument, at least he will preserve stone on paper. As in the informal empire in Assyria, the native juxtaposed with ruins is a standard topos in British imperial iconography, of a civilisation in decay being 'rescued' by the enlightened British from neglect, apathy, and destruction by the indigenous people.[30]

In some drawings, Mackenzie visually incorporated his native assistants in the collaborative project of documentation. In *View of the Great Bull at Baswana, cut out of Granite on the Hill of Mysore ... 18 feet high, 1806* and in *Ancient Pagoda at Bisnagar, 1800*, native assistants measure the monuments.[31] In a view of Dindigul (dated 1790), Mackenzie joins a bearded, robed Indian, possibly a Muslim scholar. The authoritatively red-coated Mackenzie is sitting on the ground (though not quite able to sit in the Indian posture), listening respectfully to his guide. This native gestures towards an architectural structure to the left, partially covered by shrubs and palm trees, perhaps the mausoleum of a local Muslim chieftain. Against the background of a towering, heavily fortified grey and white rock, the imperial officer and his native guide are represented as almost equal.[32]

Mackenzie's legacy is very considerable. Over the course of his surveys, he and his teams amassed many thousands of stone and copper plate inscriptions, 1,568 literary manuscripts in thirteen languages and nineteen scripts, 2,070 local tracts, 2,630 drawings and plans, 106 images, forty antiquities, and 6,218 coins. It was the largest collection of sources on the early modern historical anthropology of peninsular India. His collection of inscriptions, estimated at 7,000–8,000, was the first attempt to compile a comprehensive record. Already in 1807, Mackenzie had produced a 'Register of a Collection of Ancient Sassanums or Grants and Inscriptions on Public Monuments', providing tabular analysis of the attributes and contents of some 1,100 inscriptions indexed by reigning kings, with graphic reproductions of selective facsimiles, drawings, and translations. It is a model for many modern epigraphic publications.[33]

Yet Mackenzie wrote relatively little to contextualise his archive and died before he had published much. As Surveyor-General in Calcutta (appointed 1815, Resident 1817–21), Mackenzie had, however, arranged his drawings for publication, some by area, others by subject, viz: the architecture and sculpture of southern India; inscriptions; surveys of Amaravati, Madurai, Mamallapuram. After Mackenzie's death, his collections remained accessible in Madras, where scholars of successive generations were familiar with them. The directors eventually acquired Mackenzie's collections from his widow for £10,000. James Prinsep, a scientist and expert in coins and inscriptions, sought to disseminate Mackenzie's unpublished materials more widely. He illustrated, transcribed, and translated inscriptions from the ten volumes of drawings of sculpture, images, architecture, and inscriptions in the Asiatic Society's Library.[34] If not much of a writer himself, Mackenzie's collections caused others to write. James Fergusson's essay on tree and serpent worship, for instance, was indebted to the Mackenzie collection. Indeed, the Mackenzie archives form the indispensable foundation for much of Victorian and later knowledge of the early history of southern India.[35]

The Java Expedition of 1811–16

The Napoleonic Wars created other opportunities for surveying parts of South-East Asia. In 1811, an amphibious British force captured the Dutch island colony of Java to prevent Napoleon from using it as a naval base. The military expedition allowed an ambitious programme of research to be implemented for the duration of the occupation in 1811–16.[36] On 8 June 1811, Governor-General Lord Minto chaired the Physical and Literary Committee of the Asiatic Society of Bengal at Malacca. Thomas Stamford Raffles, a life-long student of Malayan culture, the philologist Dr J. C. Leyden, Captain John W. Tayler, and the Bengal civilian G. J. Gordon joined the surgeon Dr William Hunter as secretary; local military and naval officers had been invited along, but Colin Mackenzie had sent his apologies as he was already reconnoitring in preparation for the landing.[37] For Minto, the presence of Oriental-ists on the expedition held out the prospect of opening up new fields of research in languages, geography, history, and religion, as well as statistical, juridical, and physical inquiries. Three days later, these men set sail for Singapore and by the end of July they met up with Mackenzie at the Bumbkin Islands. Some eighty transports and their escort vessels made their final approach and descent on Java in the first week of August.[38]

Raffles as Java's British Lieutenant-Governor created an environment very sup-portive of particular disciplines. He introduced far-reaching administrative and economic reforms, convinced that enlightened imperial rule ought to connect the sources of revenue with a colony's prosperity. To ground the reforms in sound knowledge, Raffles commissioned geographical, sociological, ethnographic, his-torical, and cultural surveys. Mackenzie's enormous task was to register the records of the Dutch colonial administration and to direct a land tenure commission as well as fiscal-administrative surveys. As ambitious as ever, he also set out to collect historical and archaeological materials as he had previously done in Mysore.

In 1811–13, Mackenzie toured the island with a team of Dutch engineers, includ-ing Major H. C. Cornelius, and several trained Asian draughtsmen, some of whom had also been on the Mysore survey. Mackenzie mostly focused on detailed note taking while his team measured and sketched monuments.[39] Mackenzie's Indian experience helped him to negotiate religious and other apprehensions on the part of indigenous people. Some locals contributed information and experience freely, pointing out sources and other helpful people. There was a tradition of mutually acquisitive relationships between Javanese 'informants' and European scholars and administrators.[40] Although colleagues had no doubt that Mackenzie's 'experienced eye' allowed him to work much more efficiently than anyone else, he was seriously hindered by the lack of men comparable to India's learned Brahmins. Translations from Dutch, French, as well as Malayan and Javanese were hard to come by. Native translators were not easy to find on account of the genuine linguistic challenges, but also because of their alleged 'indolence'. However, the regents (a kind of official aristocracy) were soon more forthcoming when they realised the surveying was merely about the history, customs, and literatures of the island. Mackenzie reassured his potential collaborators (and his imperial conscience) that he aimed at improving the conditions of the people: 'A more perfect knowledge of their own institutions', he explained, would enable all ranks to support 'what they found attended by no deviation from good faith, and tending to conciliate their feelings and prejudices.'[41]

Other officials too made good use of the brief occupation of Java. The American doctor Thomas Horsfield served the Dutch East India Company from around 1800 to research the *materia medica*, botany, and geology of Java – perhaps another example of a fairly cosmopolitan culture of imperial imagination. He continued under Raffles as a British government naturalist. Archaeology became an important sideline, and Horsfield produced large portfolios of scientific and archaeological drawings, often with the help of native draughtsmen. Major Martin Johnson, an official at Solo, also conducted archaeological research for the British. He discovered the ruins of a temple complex at Suku, east of Surakata, with a truncated pyramid, obelisks, and relief figures. And J. C. Lawrence, in charge of administering Kedu, contributed ancient metal casts which natives had found in large numbers near temple ruins. Mostly made of copper or brass, they represented various deities including a beautiful figure of Brahma with eight arms standing on a male and female figure.[42]

As in India, drawings indicate Western preoccupation with the natural decay of monuments and locals' alleged indifference.[43] In Horsfield's (or a Dutchman's) *The Temple of Singasari*, dense jungle encroaches upon the small, sparsely ornamented, and badly crumbling stone structure. A felled tree at right suggests that locals (or the Dutch?) were defending a small clearing against nature's exuberant approaches, but at least one large-leafed tree has already grown directly out of the stonework; other vegetation is seen peeping out from the top. A single man, perhaps a local assistant, enters the temple, witness of a historic culture whose monument is now quietly eroding back into the landscape. In another of Horsfield's drawings of a very badly ruined temple in east Java, it is not quite clear whether the massive tree, which has driven its roots into the ground underneath and beside the structure, is fatally undermining or precariously holding up the badly tilting temple. Several grotesquely carved heads have tumbled down, the pedestal and sides are fast eroding, while a rooftop garden is developing nicely. A middle-aged, apathetic villager in the foreground gives scale to the huge temple and parallels the depiction of natives indifferent to antiquities in the Near East or India.

Even if there was scope to conceive the scholarly enterprise in South Asia in a cosmopolitan mould, the British now gained control of much of the antiquarian work that the Dutch had done. Cornelius and his assistants provided plans and drawings of temples in central Java to the British. Raffles also obtained drawings of the sculpture collection in the residency's garden of Nicolaus Englehard, the former Dutch governor of the north-east coast. Englehard further gave Mackenzie access to his collections of drawings and translations from Javanese historical works. While the British clearly benefited from Englehard's earlier collecting, Raffles ordered that the monuments of Prambanan and Borobudur (discovered in 1814) be cleaned and repaired, and he apparently attempted to stop the despoiling of sites.[44]

Despite his demanding executive responsibilities, Raffles himself toured Javanese temples and studied and collected images of deities, inscriptions, metal-casting, folk art, coins, and at least one very large, inscribed stone. Raffles further commissioned Captain Geoffrey Phipps Baker of the Bengal Light Infantry to survey the sites of Prambanan and Borobudur. Baker linked military survey work with reports on the state of antiquities. Raffles quoted Baker on his impressions of the key Buddhist site at Borobudur:

> Nothing can exceed the air of melancholy, desolation, and ruin, which this spot presents … The feelings of every visitor must be forcibly in unison with the scene of surrounding devastation, when he reflects upon the origins of this once venerated, hallowed spot.[45]

The short British archaeological mission yielded a rich scholarly harvest. Few of the sites Mackenzie's and Horsfield's teams visited had ever been systematically measured, numerous temples had never been seen by Europeans before. Collections of drawings, inscriptions, specimens of ancient scripts, folk art, and some very large inscribed stones joined extensive archives of reports; some results were presented to the revived Literary and Scientific Society of Batavia. Of the inscriptions discovered by Mackenzie, which used three unknown scripts, only one had previously been known to Europeans. Mackenzie's collections of coins, some Chinese and Japanese, were mostly of a kind previously unknown to European collectors, 'perforated in the centre by a square opening and bearing a variety of figures resembling those of the *voynangs*, or Javanese plays'. None such had previously been found by Europeans, and most had been buried by volcanic eruptions. Similar Chinese coins recently found in India pointed to historic trade connections. Among the ancient sculptures and images discovered, some indicated the presence of Hindu mythology, but most were Buddhist and Jain.[46] The British expedition, which had co-opted Dutch and Javanese help, thus documented key aspects of the archaeology and art of Java. They also demonstrated the existence of Buddhist and Hindu civilisations on the island before the arrival of a Muslim culture, and raised questions about their relations to India.

When the expedition was concluded, Mackenzie argued that the experience on Java showed how political support enabled the best research. Despite the limits of time and local resources, much had been achieved 'under a liberal degree of encouragement and protection' from the British administrators of India and Java, 'which heightens the contrast in other cases, and without any expense to government on that account'. Like his classical archaeological colleagues, Mackenzie was hopeful that he might receive greater official investment. The success suggested to Mackenzie that

> considerable advantage may be derived from following up the same plan of research wherever the influence of the British government affords the same facilities, in the intervals of military operations.[47]

This was a rare, explicit conceptualisation of state involvement in scholarly work. The Society of Sciences (Batavian Society) had been in decline since the French Revolution, and was now revived under the British. It was hoped that, under the patronage of 'the supreme government, should Java remain a British colony', the Society would 'contribute essentially to the general culture of science, and of commercial economy, and of useful knowledge in these parts.'[48]

Very different fates befell the veterans of the Java expedition. Raffles was removed from post in 1815 over controversial policies. Back in England he published a massive, beautifully produced two-volume *History of Java*, the first in English. Eventually exonerated from dishonourable motives by the East India Company, Raffles was elected a Fellow of the Royal Society, knighted by the Prince Regent, and advised King William IV of the Netherlands on governing Java.[49] Colin Mackenzie had taken his collections of Javanese inscriptions to India, where he planned to continue work on the early history of the island, but little of his material reached Raffles. The versatile Horsfield continued his work on Java after the return of the Dutch. He eventually presented archaeological and natural specimens and drawings to the Company's museum in London and became its erudite and efficient keeper in 1820–59. Some, however, never made it back from Java. Among those who died on the expedition were the scholars Drs Leyden and Hunter. But they are not remembered in the official British-Indian site of memory to the Java and Mauritius expeditions, the Greek revivalist Temple of Fame at the tropical park of Barrackpore House. Dedicated 'To the Memory of the Brave', it commemorates only the military conquest, not the intellectual mission.[50]

Research Management

After Mackenzie and Raffles had demonstrated what concerted archaeological efforts could achieve in the context of official surveys, James Prinsep (1799–1840) in the 1830s single-handedly directed an informal yet highly effective network of draughtsmen and collectors of coins and inscriptions. His management of archaeological research combined insights from the systematic survey work of Mackenzie's generation with the practices of learned officialdom and the skills of the closet scholar and the field researcher. Prinsep had been born in Leadenhall Street, not far from East India House, as the tenth child of a former indigo planter turned City merchant and India agent. Prinsep had studied with the first Boden Professor of Sanskrit at Oxford, H. H. Wilson, but became a scientist, assay master, architect of various public buildings in Benares and improver of its sanitation, master of numismatic and epigraphic techniques, and a student of chemistry and mineralogy. Described as enthusiastic, charming, and witty, and with a 'burning, irrepressible enthusiasm' of intellect, in death he was honoured as one of the 'most talented and useful' Englishmen ever to work in India.[51] In the early 1830s, as secretary of the Asiatic Society and editor of its journal, Prinsep oversaw a shift of focus from textual to epigraphic, numismatic, and archaeological studies. Under him, the journal started the key practice of publishing facsimiles of inscriptions.

Prinsep's own main achievements lay in deciphering previously unreadable scripts used in the most ancient Indian inscriptions, such as the Brahmi script on the pillars at Delhi and Allahabad, and on rock inscriptions from west and east India, which revealed that India had enjoyed a long period of Buddhist predominance. He also deciphered the Kharosthi script in coins and inscriptions from the north-west. Prinsep thus furthered historical knowledge of pre-Islamic India. He encouraged systematic survey operations, such as Alexander Cunningham's first excavations of ancient sites, and the work of a Bengal infantryman, Markham Kittoe, in Orissa. Moreover, he helped make Indian archaeology more data-oriented and enhanced the recognition of accurate field work as a means of producing objects for collecting.

As colleagues all over India were obliging Prinsep with coins and copies of inscriptions for decipherment and publication, this led to some breakthroughs.[52] In 1834, Captain T. S. Burt studied the inscriptions on Ashoka's Column at Allahabad. Allahabad, or Prayag, the Place of Sacrifice, is an important Hindu pilgrimage centre where the Ganga and Yamuna rivers meet. Ashoka's Column, a stone pillar originally erected by the emperor at Kausambi, was moved in 1583 by order of Akhbar to the Mughal fort overlooking the confluence. It has edicts of Maurya, Gupta, and Mughal rulers incised on its polished sandstone shaft.[53] On Prinsep's request, Burt sent drawings and facsimiles of the inscriptions. After their colleague Charles Masson had tracked down Greco-Indian connections revealed by coins in Afghanistan and the Punjab, Prinsep collated this data with the Gupta inscriptions and the bilingual coins of Batria. By 1837, when contemplating a stone inscription of King Ashoka, Prinsep was therefore able to date one of Ashoka's edicts and establish the relations between India and Alexander's successors. The pillar and rock inscriptions thus first verified the correlation of Indian and Western history and archaeology. In recognition of his achievements, Prinsep was elected a corresponding member by learned societies throughout Europe.[54]

On occasion, Prinsep used his connections at the highest levels of officialdom to accomplish research. In the late 1830s, he requested Governor-General Lord Auckland (1836–42) to have the Ashokan edict on the rock at Girnar copied. The Girnar mountain, the cone of an extinct volcano, combines Buddhist caves with a Jain temple city on a rocky shelf. Inscribed on a boulder by the path at the foot of the hill is the Ashokan rock edict. On the rock, the edicts of the Maurya emperor are joined by those of later Kshatrapa and Gupta rulers. The imperial authorities in 1838 seconded Captain Thomas Postans (1808–46), a competent linguist and keen amateur archaeologist serving with the Bombay Native Infantry, on special archaeological duty. With his redoubtable wife Marianne, Postans valiantly braved the hot season to provide the requested copies.

Marianne Postans published an account of her time in India. In *Western India*, she described the Girnar mountain as a granite formation, its 'cloud-capt summit [a] bare scarp rock', but 'richly wooded towards the base, blending with a deep ravine, clothed with forest-trees, and intersected by rivers, swollen by the mountain torrents'. The Postans and their party faced the 'majestic peaks of the Girnar, its temples barely distinguishable, and the whole scene closed in by side hills, glowing with the brilliant rays of a departing sun'. Soon after starting the ascent they reached 'the great object of our pilgrimage'. The granite rock was shaped like a flattened cone, some six metres high and over twenty in circumference, and had its surface 'graven with numerous deep but small characters, divided by longitudinal lines'. On the eastern side towards the base it was slightly defaced from blasting during road-works. Postans explained to her readers how King Ashoka sought the conversion of his own people and allies to Buddhism through missionary work and commerce. He also set out Buddhism's main tenets in the vernacular throughout his territories. This was the function of the rocks of Girnar and of Dhauli in Cuttack, and of the *lats* (or pillars) of Delhi and Allahabad. They displayed the Buddhist virtues for all passing pilgrims to read.

The 'celebrated edicts', of which Postans's party now took facsimiles, were the most ancient of the inscriptions on the eastern rock face. Antiquarians had only recently deciphered the inscriptions' now obsolete character of Sanskrit, with important implications for Indian chronology. (The edicts mentioned the king's allies Ptolemy, Antigonus, and Antiochus, and his plan to convert Egypt.) It was through Prinsep's 'indefatigable zeal' that the rock had 'poured forth its hidden springs of wisdom'; the same learning would 'perfect the work, and throw a halo of classic interest around the rude block of the Girnar causeway'.[55]

James Prinseps died on leave in London in 1840. He was commemorated separately by the European and native communities. The Europeans in Calcutta commissioned a bust from Francis Chantrey for the Asiatic Society's rooms. The indigenous community subscribed to an Ionic porch or pavilion on the banks of the Hooghly near Fort William. Designed by one of the Company's engineer-archi-tects, W. Fitzgerald (1843), it is still today known as Prinsep's Ghat.[56] By seeking to publish the Mackenzie archive, with his own systematic collecting and his early interest in preservation, and as a research manager who made ambitious use of semi-official and official networks, Prinsep had shown the next generation of impe-rial officials and archaeologists the way.

Guiltless or Ruthless Spoliation?

There is considerable evidence of natural decay of sites and objects as well as wide-spread neglect and wilful destruction by both Indians and Britons. Manuscripts were lost, inscriptions effaced, and coins melted down to produce ornaments and amulets. Stupas (or funerary mounds) were raided for treasure, buildings were pulled down for bricks, and new structures or whole towns were built over histori-cal sites.[57] Private and public collecting of Indian antiquities was much more limited compared to that of classical antiquities. In response to decay and destruction of antiquities, British officialdom and scholars increasingly recognised an imperial duty of care. It was a challenge, however, to develop and implement coherent policies on the preservation or restoration of antiquities.

As Indian culture became a subject for Western study, early Orientalists collected objects of scientific and antiquarian interest.[58] With a few exceptions – such as the author John Cleland, who in 1736 acquired a set of portraits of Indian rulers in Bombay – the earliest collections of Indian art were made by Company servants from the 1760s.[59] The Indian objects which Europeans in India and in Europe collected were overwhelmingly manuscripts, paintings (especially miniatures), curios, furniture like inlaid ivory chests, jewellery and precious stones, and weapons as decorative items. From the early nineteenth century, collections started to separate out, as manuscripts began to pass into libraries, the India Museum, and other public repositories, while paintings, decorative art, and other objects (weapons, metalwork, jewellery, textiles, carvings) were kept in private hands.[60]

Until well into the nineteenth century there were but few Indian pieces in the British Museum. The first Indian object acquired was an alabaster Shiva linga, with late Mughal-style decorations from the middle of the eighteenth century, presented by Charles Bathurst in 1786. Other objects arrived coincidentally with other collections, such as the eleventh-century relief of an orgiastic scene that came with the Towneley collections in 1805, or the large jade tortoise, which was long kept in the mineralogy department.[61] Edward Hawkins, the Museum's Keeper of Antiquities, considered it 'something of a disgrace to have so few memorials of our Indian empire'.[62] Aside from the British Museum, by 1830, the wide-ranging collections of the Royal Asiatic Society contained some archaeological objects, many donated by officers, such as casts with inscriptions, stone busts, fragments from ancient monuments, sculptures, and coins from India, Burma, China, and Mongolia.[63]

The precise extent of *private* small-object collecting is not easy to ascertain, though it seems clear that it, too, was very limited well into the nineteenth century.[64] The connoisseurs Sir Charles Towneley and Richard Payne Knight possessed Indian sculptures primarily on account of their cross-cultural interests in the relationship between religion and erotica.[65] Towneley purchased several pieces from Elephanta and an entire miniature Hindu temple (probably from Rohilkhand). Knight studied the objects in Towneley's collection and published his comparative study of Greek, Roman, Egyptian, Celtic, and Indian sexual symbols, the *Discourse on the Worship of Priapus* (1786), with detailed illustrations from both the Elephanta sculptures and the temple.[66] Others kept small numbers of Hindu images for scholarly or antiquarian interests, including Jones, Hastings, Charles Wilkins, and the Swiss Lieutenant Polier, who in Lucknow reinvented himself as an Orientalist and lived like a Mughal aristocrat.

Among the few men who had special collections of sculpture early on were the Company servant James Forbes, Governor Lord Clive, and Major-General Charles 'Hindoo' Stuart. Forbes was a scholarly observer of Indian nature, history, and customs. During a stint as Collector at the ancient fortress and temple town of Dabhoi in Gujarat, Forbes restored some dilapidated walls and buildings. When Dabhoi was ceded back to the Marathas in 1783, Forbes was required to depart from the district. At his leaving durbar he refused the presents of local leaders, but asked instead:

> as Dhuboy contained many remains of Hindoo antiquity, in broken columns, mutilated images, and remnants of basso-relievo scattered among dilapidated buildings in the city, I requested they would allow me to select a few of the smallest specimens from the exterior fragments, which I would bring with me to Europe, and erect a temple for their reception in my own garden.

He persuaded the local elders to let him bring to England what was almost certainly the earliest collection of Hindu deities in the country. A supporter of the conversion of Hindus to Christianity, Forbes later built an octagonal Temple of Friendship at Stanmore Hill to display his sculptures in a picturesquely landscaped 'Indian' setting.[67]

Edward, Lord Clive, Governor of Madras (1798–1803), and his wife Henrietta were the first Britons known to have collected Hindu sculpture without being Orientalists. They collected instead in the tradition of aristocratic and genteel Grand Tourists.[68] But by far the most important early collector of Indian sculpture, and definitely the most eccentric, was the Irish Major-General Charles 'Hindoo' Stuart (1757/8–1828), whose collections would eventually form part of the national patrimony in the British Museum.[69] Stuart used his postings over a half-century to amass the most extensive and most significant collection of Indian religious sculpture of any European in this period. His collection contained hundreds of statues, many dating from the eighth to the twelfth centuries; he must have used agents to bring interesting pieces from further away. Stuart was the first European to appreciate the beauty of this sculpture and assembled many high-quality 'examples of each deity as a kind of visual encyclopedia of religion and custom.'[70] His will refers – among fantastically wide-ranging collections – to 'Indian Statues of Stone, Alabaster, Copper, Brass'.[71]

Called 'Hindoo' Stuart for his intense interest in native culture, this daring border-crosser insisted that he was anti-Christian yet had not converted. According to local custom, Stuart also retained two Brahmins in care of his sculptures and later in his life displayed the collection in his house in Calcutta. When Stuart died in 1828, he was given a Christian burial. Against the missionaries' protest, his tomb on Calcutta South Park Street Cemetery was loosely modelled on a north Indian Hindu shrine, embellished with stone sculptures from his collection.[72] Most of Stuart's collection was sent to England in 143 large cases. Fifteen items were donated to the East India Company museum, but the bulk was auctioned off by the heirs at Christie's in 1830. There was only one major bidder for the sculpture, James Bridge, of the goldsmiths Rundell, Bridge and Rundell. The pattern was repeated at the auction of the Bridge heir in 1872. The collection went for the nominal sum of £5 to A. W. Franks, Keeper of British Antiquities at the British Museum, but it was arranged that the Bridge estate donated 115 pieces to the Museum. The majority of Stuart's other pieces were transferred from the India Museum by 1880. Today, the misleadingly named 'Bridge Collection' forms the nucleus of the British Museum's Indian collections in the Hotung Gallery.[73]

Against this background of limited private collecting and the British Museum's slow collection development, India's first colonial museums were conceived in the early modern European spirit of the universal survey museum – a museum as an encyclopedic collection of objects.[74] The beginnings of the first museum were tied to the Asiatic Society, where proposals were discussed from around 1796 as part of a wider move to put the Society on a solid institutional footing.[75] In 1814, a Danish-born amateur botanist, Dr Nathaniel Wallich, called on the Society to collect 'from the abundant matter, which India offers, a Museum that shall be serviceable to history and science'.[76] A museum was established to collect 'all articles that may tend to illustrate Oriental manners and history or to elucidate the peculiarities of Art and Nature in the east'.[77]

The emphasis was on collecting for an initiated, learned circle, not on display for a wider public. The Society specifically solicited donations of ancient monuments, Muslim and Hindu sculpture, coins, and inscriptions on stone and brass, and manuscripts – all 'historical reliques' in short – as well as tools, weapons, musical instruments, animals (alive and dead), minerals, and metals. The geological–zoological collections continued to dominate in status and quantity over the archaeological and ethnological sections until at least the 1860s. By then, a perceived need for more systematic archaeological collections became part of a wider concern to display historical objects scientifically and to bolster the museum's self-image as an imperial institution charged with preserving the heritage of a subject people.[78] The museum collections grew mostly by donation from British officials, although there were early Indian contributors such as Ram Comal, Begam Samroo, Kaikrishna Bahadur, and Mathuranat and Rajendra

Mallick. By the 1820s, regular gifts of coins, copper plates, inscriptions on stone and metal (some originals, most in facsimile), and some wooden, brass, iron, and stone sculptures were received.[79]

The origins of some donations have been controversial since the nineteenth century. A few officials were accused of aggressive collecting methods, none more so than 'Hindoo' Stuart. He was alleged to have offered money for statues to locals, taken them against local resistance, and possibly even separated statues from temples. Stuart's sculptures from Orissa were mostly chlorite schist dating from the eleventh to the thirteenth centuries AD. In 1837–8, Prinsep alleged in the *Journal of the Asiatic Society of Bengal* that two inscribed slabs that Stuart had donated to the Asiatic Society in 1810 turned out to be cut from temples at Bhubaneshwar. In 1835, Lieutenant Markham Kittoe had been copying inscriptions there. He had encountered opposition from the local Brahmins, who were hardened by their past experiences with officials carrying off their images and relics. They pointed out where the commemorative slabs had been cut out from the temple of Ananda Basu Deva 'by a late Colonel Sahib'. Prinsep condemned

> the ruthless spoliation which is often carried on by soi-disant antiquaries, to the direct perversion of the true object of research – the preservation of ancient monuments, and their employment to elucidate the history of the country.

Only accidental discovery revealed the slabs' origins. Prinsep hoped the Society would restore them, in order to build 'confidence in the minds of the people who now watch our explorers with jealousy, and withhold valuable information, lest it should only yield to fresh acts of plunder and demolition.' Through Prinsep's intervention, the two slabs were returned by Lieutenant Kittoe, who explained that the Society would only have sanctioned their removal if they had been 'assured that the objects were going to decay, or held in no estimation where they were.'[80] But the Lieutenant found little 'resulting cordiality or goodwill among the priesthood of the place; on the contrary they brought him a long list of purloined idols and impetuously urged him to procure their return.'[81]

The allegations against Stuart have been repeated ever since. There are some inaccuracies in Prinsep's account.[82] One also wonders whether Stuart was really likely to present slabs taken against the will of local Brahmins to the museum when he had plenty of other objects. His only serious biographer exonerates Stuart as someone who had a 'benevolent and paternalistic relationship' with Hindus and fell foul of missionaries' hateful allegations as an idol-thief.[83] However, the argument that he should be judged against the standards of collecting at a time when there was little interest in Indian sculptures, seems to underestimate incipient contemporary concerns among imperial officials and colonial subjects alike.

Stuart's case demonstrates that potential conflicts between the imperatives of collecting, preservation, and restoration were beginning to sharpen in official circles. Yet 'restoration' clearly was still a very vaguely defined idea and practice. When Lieutenant Kittoe found an inscription in the village of Gusserawa, recently dug from a mound, he bought it for three rupees, made triple facsimiles, and then had it placed in the outer wall of a modern temple. The officer probably considered this a responsible and respectful practice, but we can only speculate how much physical 'reconstruction' of ancient monuments of this kind was going on.[84]

Officialdom began to take a closer interest in the state of Indian antiquities from the 1830s. Men like Prinsep were starting to work out the priorities of preservation and/or restoration in situ versus 'protective collecting' in museums. As in the territories around the Mediterranean and Near East, British officers and researchers complained about locals' indifference to, or active destruction of, ancient remains. Pillars lay on the ground, often without their capitals. Temple structures were frequently discovered completely overgrown with vegetation; inscriptions were partly effaced by the effects of moisture and heat. Local landlords used ancient structures as quarries for their building activities, for instance when Jaga Singh dismantled the Dhamek Tower for its iron cramps.[85] The great brick Mahabodhi temple at Bodhgaya, where Buddha attained enlightenment, was stripped of one or more of its Buddha figures; Mackenzie heard that they had been 'removed by the Bairagis, and some carried off by English gentlemen'.[86] Similarly, William Price, on duty with his corps in Bundelkhand in 1813, found that locals were sharpening their knives and swords on a stone with a Sanskrit inscription near Mow. When Price removed the stone, he found the inscription brought to light the dynasty of Chandelas of Bundelkhand. Alexander Allan versified about the situation:

Despoiled by bigots and through time grown gray,
By wretches pillaged for a bauble's worth.
Still do thine iron-bound walls resist decay.
By fame forgotten – in historic dearth.[87]

Military and sectarian violence were other causes of damage and destruction. At the Elephanta cave-temple, several columns were levelled and figures mutilated 'by the *Portuguese*, who were at the trouble (and no small one) of dragging cannon up the hill, for the better execution of this exploit'.[88] When the Mahrattas retook Salsette, 'to fetch off the plaster with which the Portuguese had covered several of the figures, they fired some cannon in the pagodas'. Realising that this brought down the bas-reliefs, they used hammers instead to clean the plaster from the figures.[89] The Temple at Somnath in western India had been neglected by the Hindus and despoiled by the Muslims before it was used as an ordnance battery to protect the local village against pirates infesting the coast. Although this was already a sad example of the continuous damage suffered by India's ancient remains, Postans – without a trace of irony – quoted the battery as 'proof of the wonderful solidity of this structure'.[90] In Benares, the sectarian destruction of a Hindu monument had the sepoys mobilised. A tall, monolithic-stone, sacred Hindu pillar with exquisite carvings had been suffered to stand in the mosque which replaced the original temple after its destruction by Aurungzebe. Hindu pilgrimages were permitted by the Muslims; but one year some took offence and broke down 'Siva's walking-staff'. Outraged Hindus destroyed a local mosque, the Muslims retaliated by pouring a killed cow's blood into the sacred well, and only sepoys could prevent all-out civil war. Bishop Heber's account conveys scepticism yet proud relief at the (primarily Hindu) sepoys' capacity for 'impartiality' under imperial command.[91]

Despite the neglect or wanton damage of antiquities, the imperial government was slow to formulate any coherent response. Bengal Regulation XIX, sections iii, v (1810), repeated almost verbatim in Madras Regulation VII (1817), gave the government the power to intervene when public buildings were 'exposed to the risk of misuse by private individuals'. But there was no general and effective policy on preservation until the later nineteenth century. Occasionally, a government commission, a one-off subsidy, or the allocation of the proceeds of the sale of government property or of local rents helped conserve or restore a monument or structure.[92]

Some of the earliest attempts at restoration were carried out on Java, first by the Dutch and then the British. A drawing, most likely by a Dutch draughtsman, survives of Major Cornelius's cleaning of the ruins of the central temple of Chandi Sewu, Prambanan, in 1807. A massive temple, with elaborately carved surfaces, fills almost the entire width of the drawing against the background of bare mountains. The scene is teeming with people, as Cornelius and three fellow Dutch officers oversee a complex operation of cleaning and, it appears, restoring parts of the temple. It has suffered structural damage, and profuse vegetation – of softly drawn leafy trees growing on all levels into and out of the structure – is threatening to take over the monument. Two dozen indigenous men work under native overseers and the overall direction of the European officers.[93]

Raffles's beautifully produced *History of Java* made a distinctive visual intervention on the topic of ruination, preservation, and restoration (figs 45a, b). The plates include views of temples in their present state – partially in ruins, overgrown with

45a and b. *One of the Smaller Temples at Prambanan in its Present State* and the same site 'restored to its original state', juxtaposed in Sir Stamford Raffles's *History of Java* (1830). The picturesque drawing shows a temple wildly overgrown, with creepers and roots forcing stones apart, its top about to tumble and join the stone fragments at its base. It is followed by a simple line engraving of the elevation of the temple 'restored to its original state', with a measuring scale at bottom, and full architectural and decorative detail indicated in clear lines. Precise measurement, careful observation of remains, and plausible reconstruction will preserve at least the record, if not the physical structure, of this ancient monument.

vegetation, fragments precariously poised or in danger of falling down – paired with imaginative views.

In India, some of the most iconic monuments were among the earliest to be considered for restoration. Although the documentation is quite patchy, it is clear that the precise meanings and methods of restoration were contentious. In 1808, the Board of Commissioners lamented the 'neglected state' of the famous Taj Mahal and appealed to the 'Government which esteem[ed] the Arts' and was sensitive to the 'national reputation'. The Taj, unique among buildings at Agra, was as yet 'undefiled', and not put to 'vile uses', and 'may yet be preserved to commemorate the glories of a fallen Empire'.[94] It required cleaning, new doors, and repairs to boundary walls and arcades. The Governor-General visited Agra accompanied by Captain Phipps and directed repairs to both the Taj and the imperial tomb at Sikandra.

The work was carried out by Lieutenant-Colonel Joseph Taylor, who combined various postings as an engineer in 1808–35 with intermittent combat assignments and the repair jobs. Detailed discussions ensued between Taylor, local officials, and the Bengal central administration on the appropriate methods and materials. Should marble, coloured stone, or coloured chunam be used? Should the marble slabs of the minarets be pointed with black or coloured stone? And how about painting, and cleaning, and what to do with the inlays? When the initial estimates were exceeded by several tens of thousands of rupees, local administrators advocated the sale of government property or a lottery rather than the alternative: charging admission to the Taj would threaten the dignity of the government and alienate all classes of indigenous people.

Another iconic site 'restored' by Lieutenant-Colonel Taylor was the mausoleum of Emperor Akhbar at Sikandra.[95] A 'judicial letter to Bengal' had asserted in 1817 that 'the credit of our administration is, in some degree, connected with the preservation of these Memorials of the former splendour and majesty of the Indian Empire'.[96] Buildings needed to be 'preserved from all chance of delapidation', if only to encourage the 'polite arts'. But Taylor soon ran foul of officials who took exception to his approach. It was alleged that Taylor 'delapidated an entire building', the tomb of Mulluk Jeha Begum, to remove materials for the repair of the mausoleum. Eventually the regional government granted local agents' request for sepoys to guard the building under threat by Taylor, who reported hastily that he had had the works stopped before the guard had even been applied for. Part of the dispute appears to have been over the respective remits of Taylor, local agents, and the provincial government. But Taylor was also accused of laying claim to a building near the Taj as his private property, and in turn appeared to cast aspersions on local agents over neglecting grass on the dome of the Taj. The Governor-General eventually clarified that the local agents had full control over all buildings and that only material from structurally completely ruined buildings could be used for repairs.

The 'restoration' of the Qutb Minar in the 1820s affords further insights into conflicting contemporary attitudes regarding restoration. The 72-metre-high, tapered tower of red sandstone was constructed from the late twelfth century by order of Qutb-ud-din Aibak, the central Asian conqueror, who asserted: 'He who holds Delhi holds India'. Victory tower to Muslim rule in northern India, Mughal surveillance tower, and minaret, it dominated the area. In 1368, the upper storeys were faced with white marble by Firuz Shah Tughluk, who also added a cupola or small crowning pavilion.

Built as a monument to Islamic hegemony, the Qutb Minar was incorporated by later Mughal rulers into their imperial historiography. The British conquerors of Delhi, too, understood the monument's historic and symbolic meanings: they studied, restored, and reserved it for imperial tourists. In 1794, James Tillyer Blunt of the Bengal Engineers established its height by trigonometrical calculations.

He found the monument in total neglect, 'the battlements in many parts entirely ruined', and 'those that were standing, in such a decayed state as to render it a matter of some danger to venture out from the stair-case'; the inscriptions (on the projecting balconies) were too high to reach.[97] In 1803, just as the British acquired Delhi from the Marathas, the second earthquake in a quarter-century severely damaged the tower, destroying the cupola. In his 1808 aquatint, Daniell showed the monument with only limited damage to some of the battlements and the top: set in a bleak, flat landscape, the imperial monument – measured, drawn, though the name of its builder still waiting to be deciphered (by Walter Ewer in 1820) – asserted the dominion of Britain as the new 'Moghuls' of India.

In the 1820s, Lord Amherst (Governor-General in 1823–8) ordered elaborate works on the Qutb Minar to be carried out by Colonel Robert Smith (1787–1873).[98] Smith was a well-respected engineer who designed buildings and also created images in various media of landscapes and numerous structures encountered throughout his travels in the Punjab, Uttar Pradesh, Lucknow, Nepal, and Penang.[99] The very embodiment of the resourceful, versatile British imperial engineer, Smith was one of the most gifted draughtsmen in the Indian army.[100] Posted to Delhi as garrison engineer and executive officer in 1822, Smith was ordered to repair the Qutb Minar. He restored the entire structure, landscaped the surroundings, and planned to ban Indians from access to the building. It was henceforth to be a site for imperial tourists, with only ten people at a time allowed to view it. This was a radically different approach from that taken by the local officials regarding the Taj Mahal and it is unclear if his proposal was implemented.[101]

Praise for Smith's work in general was mixed with criticism of the cupola, which he had added according to his own design, an octagonal top of sissoo wood and a flagstaff. Contemporaries ridiculed Smith: it looked like a Chinese umbrella, utterly tasteless and unbefitting the ancient monument. Smith defended himself with reference to the common Indian architectural practice of surmounting one dome with another, and to the fact that the original cupola was undocumented. He had steered a middle course between references in the *Asiatick Researches* to a large, harp-shaped stone cupola, and a local tradition of a plain square top on four stone pillars. But Smith's semi-scholarly approach to restoration was overruled in 1847 when his octagonal stone pavilion was removed on the orders of Governor-General Lord Hardinge (1844–8) and placed on a nearby hillock. Some imperial visitors nevertheless admired Smith's restoration of the Qutb, which had been worthily 'preserved and repaired by the liberality of the British government'.[102]

The protracted story of the gradual spoliation and destruction of the great Buddhist stupa at Amaravati on the bank of the river Krishna can serve finally as a means to explore indigenous and British attitudes towards ancient sites and preservation. A stupa is an unadorned hemisphere of earth and rubble raised on a cylindrical base faced with brick(like) stone. At the mount's summit, miniature railings of carved stone mark a square zone with a stone mast in the centre: the mast supports a finial and marks the position of a casket set into the hemisphere which contains ashes, charred bones, gold leaf, and other treasure. Stupas were originally erected to enshrine the cremated remains of Buddha, Mahavira (the founder of Jainism), and their disciples; later, memorial stupas were erected at all Buddhist and Jain holy sites, and also as votive objects in religious or monastic complexes. The Amaravati stupa consisted of a huge solid dome, estimated to have been some forty-three metres in diameter, mounted on an ornate cylindrical platform, surrounded by a railing covered in narrative relief, pillars, and an elaborate coping and other decorative detail, all from various periods. The stupa, originally founded in the third century BC, was celebrated for its fine carvings, especially a narrative series illustrating the life of Buddha. After local pillaging, random digging, and piecemeal removal by indigenous and imperial agents, today hardly anything is left of this famous Buddhist stupa. The Amaravati Marbles, as they are now known, are crucial to the study of the political, religious, and aesthetic developments in the Andradesa. They rank among the most important monuments in the British Museum.

By the 1790s, the stupa had deteriorated to a low hillock and was being incorporated into new dwellings by an enterprising local landlord. Colin Mackenzie in 1797 heard of the site's gradual destruction; there also were reports that statuary was being removed to the raja's new temple. But he could do little to protect the site other than having his assistants document it in drawings. By the time Mackenzie returned in 1816 with a team of trained delineators, the mound at Amaravati had been pillaged further for stonework, and its top dug into by the local landlord to make a water tank. Mackenzie and his team again drew sculptures, plans, and maps. By 1820, eighty finished drawings had been worked up of the sculptures alone.[103]

Yet, while Mackenzie considered local practices unacceptable, he himself had in fact rifled the stupas of eleven sculptural components. He gave two of these to the Asiatic Society, which were later transferred to the museum in Calcutta. The Company purchased the other nine sculptures and housed them at the East India Museum. By the time Sir Walter Elliot (1803–87) visited Amaravati in 1845, the high stupa mound had almost completely disappeared. He nevertheless excavated an area in the north-western part, and found some eighty pieces to remove.[104] He sent them to Madras, but they were left 'uncared for, and exposed to the elements in the green in front of the College'.[105] In 1859, they were eventually shipped at public expense to London, only to again lie exposed to damaging air and climate at Beale's Wharf, Southwark. James Fergusson rediscovered the collection under a rubbish pile in the coach house of the India Museum, after some had been exhibited at the Paris Universal Exhibition. They subsequently lay in the 'India Stores', Belvedere Road, and at the Sculpture Court, South Kensington Museum, before being acquired by the British Museum in 1880, when the India Museum was dissolved. From the 1880s to the 1930s, the Amaravati Marbles were a key display in the imperial metropolis. Many of the best pieces were affixed to the walls of the Great Staircase, 'given pride of place,' as historian Robert Knox has written, with the remains of 'the rest of the ancient world.'[106]

The final destruction of the site occurred when British archaeologists like Robert Sewell dug without making an adequate record of the stratigraphy, coin finds, and so forth. In 1880, the Governor of Madras, the Duke of Buckingham and Chandos, ordered the 'clearing' of the site and had it turned into a large pit with excavated sculpture arranged around it. James Burgess in 1881, as the officer in charge of the Archaeological Survey of Madras, recovered ninety sculptures which joined 300 pieces, excavated by Sewell and the Governor, at the Madras museum. After the activities of Mackenzie, Elliot, Sewell, and the clearance, there was no longer any chance of relating objects to objects and reconstructing the in-situ character of the Great Stupa. Along with the sophisticated methods of modern palaeography, numismatics, and epigraphy, Mackenzie's drawings and descriptions are still key to reconstructing aspects of the stupa. Only Mackenzie was able to estimate the precise shape and height of the dome because he saw it before the mound was more fully excavated for building materials and then gradually destroyed by local and imperial agents. The Amaravati Album at the British Library includes maps, plans, and drawings of sculpture from the stupa (see plate XVII). They provide a reliable record of how the monument's foundations looked before they were disturbed, and where the sculptures used to be positioned.[107] For Mackenzie, both the taking of eleven sculptural pieces *and* documenting Amaravati in sketches, drawings, measurements, and descriptions were means of preserving an archaeological monument that he judged to be in the process of irreversible destruction. Between Mackenzie's death and the arrival of the Amaravati sculptures at the British Museum around 1880, officials and scholars in British India had been defining new priorities with regard to Indian antiquities. Whereas documentation as preservation remained important, the impulse to collect was gradually overruled by the imperative to preserve in situ.

Outlook: The Responsibilities of Empire (*c.*1844–1900)

At iconic sites such as the Taj and the Qutb Minar, the Company state had sporadically started to practise preservation and restoration of antiquities as early as the 1810s and 1820s. But the beginnings of more coherent official interest in the archaeology of ancient India, including issues of preservation and restoration, date from the 1840s. After the Mutiny of 1857, a major programme was inaugurated to systematically record and evaluate ancient sites and monuments, and to construct coherent narratives of Indian pasts from antiquity to the present. This was part of the wider Victorian fascination with ancient worlds, never entirely unrelated to attempts to construct usable pasts. At the time when the fruits of Fellows's and Layard's state-sponsored archaeological campaigns in Lycia and Assyria were becoming abundantly clear at the British Museum, the Company state also began to take an official interest in archaeological matters. With classical and Near Eastern antiquities, anything judged important and movable would be attempted to be shipped to London. But in British India the focus was almost entirely on preservation in situ. Such priorities were in part a function of the perceived lesser aesthetic value of Indian antiquities and of their lesser importance in Western historical narratives. There may also have been practical considerations, as there were far too many sites even to document systematically. Ultimately, a colony posed different issues from ancient lands in spheres of informal imperial influence. British officials were developing a sense of imperial responsibility for the antiquities of British India.

Among the first sites to receive urgent official attention were the cave-temples of western India, where we started out. In 1844, the Royal Asiatic Society urged the Company to consider the caves' poor state and pleaded for their preservation. Around the same time, Fellows had just completed his fourth and final expedition to Xanthus, the quasi-military operation organised jointly by the Admiralty and British Museum, and Layard was about to start his Assyrian campaigns. Travellers such as Maria Graham had decried natural decay and destruction by man in the caves from the middle of the eighteenth century, for instance when 'the Portuguese … made war upon the gods and temples, as well as upon the armies of India'.[108] Captain Thomas Turner Roberts of the Bombay army bemoaned the damage done by those who mutilated figures and 'had not the minds to feel the value of such antiquities, or sense, or decency, to leave what did remain, perfect … for the enjoyment of inquiring minds'.[109]

Company directors asked the Governor-General to protect the caves (and the Ajanta caves in particular) and to have drawings made by 'some of our talented officers'. As a practical measure, they sent a camera obscura to each presidency. The Governor-General instructed local authorities to report on antiquities and make suggestions on preservation; small sums were available for repairs. The Bombay Presidency responded with low-key intervention and had rubbish and undergrowth cleared from the caves at Ajanta and Ellora. Because these were sites of active worship, local authorities were involved. Slightly later sketches suggest this work was indeed done. An artist called 'Mr Fallon' in Bombay was prepared to work at 600 rupees per month (the Company did not want to spare an officer or official), but it was estimated that it would take thirty-two years to draw the main antiquities of western India alone. The Governor-General intimated to the directors that they might not have fully appreciated the scale of the project.[110]

It was in 1847 – Fellows had already been been knighted, Layard was on the diplomatic staff and his first finds were arriving in Bloomsbury – when the Company realised the magnitude of the Indian antiquities problem and the inadequacy of existing resources. They now proposed to collect 'accurate, minute and well classified information as to the nature, extent and state of existing monuments' across India. On the basis of that survey, a commission was to draw up a 'General Plan': in effect, nothing less than a full 'Archaeological Survey of India'.[111] Again, Governor-General Hardinge, writing from Simla, counselled caution and proposed a pilot by officers with 'habits of research, and knowledge of Indian antiquities'. They would prepare preliminary reports on select monuments and rank them for potential publication. They should be given a conceptual framework by an antiquarian commission in England, which was to consult German and French authorities. In the abstract, the notion of the cosmopolitan republic of letters was alive and well, perhaps helped by the fact that there was no imperial competition over the territory or sites concerned.

This was the moment when Alexander Cunningham (1814–93) entered the debate. Cunningham had a distinguished military career in India with the Bengal Engineers from 1833 until 1861, when he was appointed founding director of the Archaeological Survey of India. He had by that time spent some twenty years recording antiquities and collecting coins while serving on boundary commissions. He had worked with Prinsep in deciphering ancient scripts, a stint which laid the foundations for the central role of numismatic and epigraphic evidence in Cunningham's later text-aided archaeology. Cunningham had also 'discovered' the site of Sankissa, and he had perfected the art of opening up stupas from a method pioneered by a French army officer. He donated to the Asiatic Society the coins, Buddha images, and inscriptions he collected while opening up the great Dhamekh stupa at Sarnath, the most imposing of the monuments at that extremely important Buddhist pilgrimage site.[112]

Cunningham's 1840s Sankissa report made the case for a dedicated archaeological survey of India. For Sankissa he explained that he had made his observations on a single march during the rainy season without any halt. A leisurely march, with time to stop at all places of interest, would achieve so much more. He outlined possible itineraries and key sites, from the cave-temples at Ellora and Ajanta, to Buddhist ruins across India, and a route covering Samkassam, Kanjour, Sha-chi, via Benares, and northward – 'opening the Mozurfferpore stupa by the way', for sure – swiftly on to the Gaya caves, Orissa, and so forth. Such work was, he argued, 'an undertaking of vast importance to the Indian government politically, and to the British public religiously'. To the imperial government the explorations would demonstrate that whenever India was divided into numerous chieftains, foreign invaders were successful, but when Indians united under one ruler they repelled invasion. To the British public it would prove that Brahmanism was not an unchangeable religion, but had always adapted and received additions, thus suggesting that Christianity would ultimately succeed.[113]

As the government was gearing up for the pilot research that was to lead to systematic surveys, Cunningham expanded his arguments in favour of an archaeological survey. In addition to points about imperial governance and Christian superiority, he now also made the case for the historical benefit and archaeological duty of the imperial government.[114] The publication of the physical remains of Buddhism would equal in its value for the understanding of the history of India the publication of all Vedas and Puranas:

> It is a duty which the Government owe to the country. The remains of architecture and sculpture are daily deteriorating, and inscriptions are broken or defaced; the sooner therefore that steps are taken for their preservation, the more numerous and consequently the more valuable these remains will be.[115]

The individual presidencies now seconded military officers with archaeological experience. European and Indian draughtsmen supported them. In Bengal, Lieutenant (later General) Frederick Charles Maisey (1825–92, Bengal Native Infantry) and Lieutenant Markham Kittoe (1808–53, Bengal 6th Native Infantry) conducted archaeological surveys. Maisey's excavations at Sanchi in 1851 were a milestone in Buddhist-centred archaeology. During two cold-weather seasons, he excavated, measured, made drawings, and drafted a report on the site, which consists of stupas, shrines, temples, monasteries, and free-standing columns, with some very high-quality sculpture.[116] Kittoe, who returned the slabs allegedly rifled by 'Hindoo' Stuart in the 1830s, served as Archaeological Enquirer to the Government in the North Western Provinces from 1848 until his untimely death in 1853.[117] He carried out extensive excavations in Bihar, Orissa, and in Uttar Pradesh, where he excavated the Buddhist stupa at Sarnath, and added significantly to his earlier collection of sculpture drawings.[118] In Madras, Robert Gill (*c*.1824–75) worked alone from 1842 until his death at 1875 at the Ajanta caves to make a pictorial record. The well-preserved sculptures and paintings of the caves provided the most comprehensive illustration of early Buddhist traditions in India. Many of Gill's large-scale oil paintings of these famous rock-cut cave-temples, which constituted part of the first systematic study of this site, were exhibited in London. And in Bombay, the local branch of the Asiatic Society set up a commission from among its own members to 'collect, receive, and arrange information' for whoever the government would appoint to undertake further inquiries.[119] They oversaw the drawing by Indian draughtsmen of sculptures in the rock temples of Aihole and Badami. Under the superintendence of Lieutenant (later Colonel) Philip Lewis Hart (*c*.1812–97), the civil engineer of Satara, European and Indian draughtsmen such as Harichand Nilaji, Mukhand Ramchanda, and the civil engineer Alexander Cumming also made plans, elevations, and drawings of Muslim monuments in Bijapur.[120] Lieutenant Brett was commissioned to take impressions of cave inscriptions.[121]

Although this pioneering research in the presidencies went mostly according to plan, the commission never sat to consider the reports. The Mutiny of 1857 – during which Maisey had his horse shot out from under him in Delhi – pushed archaeology to the back burner. The projected survey was forgotten until 1861, when Cunningham in a memorandum to Viscount Canning asserted that it would 'not be to our credit as an enlightened ruling power' to allow these sites – many of which were 'studded with ruins more thickly than even the campagna of Rome' – to go unexamined. He urged that the British government in India take charge of the country's ancient monuments:

> During the one hundred years of British dominion in India, the Government had done little or nothing towards the preservation of its ancient monuments, which, in the total absence of any written history, form the only reliable source of information as to the early condition of the country … Some of these monuments … are daily suffering from the effects of time, and … must soon disappear altogether, unless preserved by the accurate drawings and faithful descriptions of the archaeologist … Hitherto the Government has been chiefly occupied with the extension and consolidation of empire … It would redound … to the honour of the British Government to institute a careful and systematic investigation of all the existing monuments of ancient India.[122]

Cunningham advocated support for archaeology with no immediate benefits to imperial governance. However, there was a strong political claim that demonstrating cultural leadership and responsible trusteeship of imperial monuments would do honour to the British government. Canning appointed Cunningham 'Director of Archaeology' with the brief to make accurate descriptions of the most important remains, 'illustrated by plans, measurements, drawings or photographs and by copies of inscriptions', along with their history and traditions as far as they could be traced.[123] His reports were to be published by the Asiatic Society, as no government department was yet established.[124]

The pedigree of the Archaeological Survey of India thus includes the linguistic and textual scholarship in the tradition of Jones, Colebrooke, and Wilson, but also previous surveying activities in Mysore, Bombay, and Madras. Prinsep figures very largely. His systematic collecting of coins and inscriptions for the purpose of extracting historical information marked a shift in Orientalist studies from philology to archaeology, and a parallel move from closet archaeologists to 'travelling antiquarians' or field archaeologists. Both Cunningham and the architectural historian James Fergusson (1808–86) had for some time produced and collected accurate drawings, plans, measurements, and histories. As in earlier, unsystematic documentation by individual officers and officials, all these were modes of 'preserving' the monuments, as Cunningham still put it in the 1860s.

Fergusson's specialisation was comprehensive sets of images of India's architectural heritage in two- and three-dimensional media. From the late 1830s, he had indefatigably been touring architectural sites with a diary, sketching pad, and camera lucida, aiming to record material for a history of architecture. In extracting history from stones, the architectural scholar Fergusson was mostly interested in analysing styles as proof of chronology. Cunningham by contrast gave prime authority to inscriptions and put most emphasis on textual description and narration, attributing only corroborative value to architectural evidence. The relative importance of stylistic versus epigraphic evidence marked the different emerging disciplines, though both sought to 'restore' an authentic past stripped of all later accretions and corruptions. From the 1870s, both projects became part of the Archaeological Survey, as Fergusson, now based in England, collated and compiled a taxonomy of buildings, while Cunningham continued his exhaustive charting of the topography of Indian archaeology.

In 1870, Viceroy Lord Mayo reasserted imperial responsibility, and Cunningham was placed as Director-General over a reinvigorated survey which was now formally constituted as a government department:

The duty of investigating, describing and protecting the ancient monuments of a Country is recognised and acted on by every civilised nation in the world. India has done less in this direction than almost any other nation, and considering the vast materials for the illustration of history which lie unexplored in every part of Hindoostan ... immediate steps should be taken for the creation under the Government of India of a machinery for the discharging a duty, at once so obvious and so interesting.[125]

The survey expanded into new regions, including the Subcontinent's interiors, and took into account the architectural relics of all periods. It would continue being reorganised periodically according to regional, intellectual, and practical consider-ations. Although often underresourced and understaffed, it nevertheless produced impressive results, as an amazing range of materials and sites was covered in great depth. The twenty-three printed volumes of reports published under Cunning-ham's auspices on each season's tour (1861–85) have become a key primary resource on materials from prehistoric archaeology to the architectural remains in the Delhi Sultanate.[126] In 1872, the *Indian Antiquary* was set up to publish inscriptions and their decipherment. In a move that acknowledged Mackenzie's pioneering work and legacy, a government epigraphist was appointed in 1883, albeit only for three years. Cunningham has often been criticised for being too much concerned with art treasures and not enough with ordinary artefacts, for destroying stupas, and accomplishing only very few large-scale scientific excavations of full monuments or whole sites. On the other hand, under Cunningham's direction the accurate description of monuments and sites was standardised, and Cunningham pro-vided site surveys at a vast scale. His method of tracing walls to excavate structural remains was standard well into the twentieth century.[127]

Though preservation was not part of the initial scheme for the survey, in 1863 (Act XX) the government reserved the authority to 'prevent injury to and preserve buildings remarkable for their antiquity or for their historical or architectural value'. Gradually, the government defined its remit for preservation, though with respon-sibility devolved to local governments, little was at first accomplished. In 1880, the central government assumed responsibility for conservation and appointed the highly energetic Captain Henry Cole, RE, as Curator of Ancient Monuments with a three-year research project to survey, register the state of decay, and advise on the conservation and restoration of monuments throughout India. Over time, the priority of preservation in situ over excavation and collecting was established. This echoed what Prinsep had been beginning to work out from the 1830s, but it was by now in part simply the result of the sheer mass of material already known and almost impossible to deal with by the understaffed survey. The impetus for government taking custody of monuments was not only their decay and destruction by time and nature, pillage, and vandalism. There was now also the danger of movable objects such as figures and panels being stolen and sold inside and outside the country. Accusations of robbing the empire of treasure were levelled at natives who foraged for stones and bricks and also at British officers and civilians who decorated private and public places with ancient objects or sold them on the lively international market in Indian antiquities. Contemporaries still considered collecting by the knowledgeable and sensitive private collector one of the many legitimate modes of preservation; the British Museum holds numerous items from the former private collections of Cunningham, Director-General of the Archaeological Survey.[128]

In 1888, a Treasure Trove Act gave the central, provincial, and local governors the 'indefeasible rights' to items of archaeological interest. Cole's images were now also easily reproducible and served as substitutes for objects which remained on site.[129] Since the 1860s, casts and copies had already been produced for museums of objects from all regions, times, and styles. In the 1870s, all casts and drawings produced by art school students of the Orissa temples and the Ajanta caves were also deposited with museums in Calcutta, Bombay, and London. It was thus increasingly difficult to collate survey collections in museums, as conflicting demands – of preservation in situ, continued religious usage, and local and community value – collided with the stated imperative of systematic collecting and safe keeping of loose, endangered, or stray objects.[130]

Under the aegis of Lord Curzon, archaeology became a viceregal priority: 'It is equally our duty to dig and discover, to classify, reproduce and describe, to copy and decipher, and to cherish and conserve.'[131] Curzon declared the 'conservation of the ancient monuments ... an elementary obligation of Government'. Pursuing his preservationist and restorationist mission with his customary zeal and attention to detail, Curzon strengthened the central organisation and funding of the survey, extended preservation legislation and government control over excavations and traffic in antiquities, performed site visits as viceregal progresses, ordered the removal of English clubs and post offices from ancient buildings, brought in a Florentine mosaicist to repair the marble panels of the Red Fort damaged in the Mutiny, and lavished great attention on restoration works at Agra. When in honour of one of his viceregal visits, the famous Jain temples on the Abu plateau were whitewashed and the woodwork a-historically painted in 'gaudy colours', Curzon was furious.[132]

By Curzon's time, the raj had come a very long way in defining its relationship to the antiquities of India. From the late eighteenth century, individual officials and scholars had developed practices and methodologies for the study and documentation of antique remains. They were well connected in the learned societies of the colony and the metropolis, and they were closely tied in from the start with British-Indian officialdom. Reflecting the preponderance of the military on this colonial frontier, military officers – and engineers and surveyors especially – played a disproportionately large role in antiquarian and archaeological studies. Major advances in methodology and the collecting of data were made in the contexts of the innovative surveys led by Mackenzie, Buchanan, and Raffles in Mysore, Bengal, and Java in the decades around 1800. In the next generation, Prinsep experimented with hybrids of both modes of inquiry, using the networks of Orientalism and officialdom to collate accurate data in the field and bring it to bear on epigraphic and linguistic scholarship. Preservation and restoration became a matter of some concern generally for imperial authorities around this time; in Egypt, Muhammad Ali decreed the protection of the built heritage, and the newly independent Greek state established heritage preservation instruments. In India, the imperial master Britain had already been sponsoring the first, highly symbolic restoration projects, such as those at the Taj and the Qutb Minar.

The experience of Mackenzie and others shows the complexity of the cultural and intellectual relationships between imperial officials and indigenous assistants. Orientalists in the field could enable genuine dialogue to take place but could also impose arrogant and domineering command. Even in those cases where indigenous intellectuals or assistants had an important role in shaping research methodologies and practices, they still operated within ultimately unequal imperial–colonial relationships. The precise scope for the construction of knowledge in dialogue and cooperation requires further study in the textual and visual archives of London and India, as does the relationship between scholarly research and its direct or indirect value for imperial governance.[133]

Given the perceived lesser aesthetic, religious, and prestige value of Indian antiquities compared to classical ones, early British-Indian archaeology yielded impressive results. Further research may reveal that collecting, both public and private, and both legal and later illegal, was a somewhat more widespread practice than scholars assume. However, even without major metropolitan collections prior to the high Victorian era, the archaeological practices analysed in these chapters speak to the ingenuity, passion, and persistence of individual officers, and to their ability to use the resources of the Company state.

PART III

CAPITAL OF CULTURE
(1815–*c*.1850)

POMP AND CIRCUMSTANCE
IN LONDON

BEFORE NAPOLEON WAS FINALLY DEFEATED at Waterloo in 1815, he had already abdicated once in the spring of 1814 – after his disastrous Russian campaign and defeat on German territory at the hands of the allies in 1813. With Napoleon exiled on Elba, Britain and its allies celebrated an illusory final victory. The Prince Regent imagined that he was the chief inspiration behind allied triumph, or even that he had personally defeated Napoleon: 'I have fulfilled and done my duty at last', he wrote to his mother, the queen, on receiving news of Napoleon's surrender in 1814. That summer, on the Regent's order, London celebrated.[1]

The Prince Regent (George IV in 1820–30) was an extravagant collector and a lavish and more consistent patron of British painters and sculptors than even his royal father had been; his taste ranged widely from the neoclassical and neo-Gothic to Chinoiserie, but he always retained a particular penchant for eighteenth-century French styles. The prince was also adept at creating stages on which to display himself and his collections, in London, at the Brighton Pavilion, and at Windsor. The sense of style and of occasion of this Francophone, Francophile Regent was inspired more by Versailles and the Tuileries than by St James's. George particularly valued items from the Versailles court and later those associated with Napoleon, though in the 1790s he was quoted as saying he was 'afraid of his furniture being accus'd of Jacobinism'. Largely as the result of his life-long collecting, the British Royal Collections today hold one of the best collections of French art outside France.[2]

George IV's artistic and dramatic sense and his appreciation of ceremony and spectacle manifested themselves in his self-fashioning as the imagined allied leader against Napoleon (see plate XIX).[3] George purchased Napoleonic memorabilia from clocks and furniture to drawings of battles and of the Congress of Vienna. George also indulged a mania for militaria and collected insignia and chivalric orders as well as weapons. He wore uniforms, promoted himself to field marshal in 1811, and surrounded himself with busts and portraits of seventeenth-century French and eighteenth-century British military heroes. George IV's love of France and of militaria combined when he sought to compete with Napoleon. Jacques-Louis David and Thomas Lawrence (1769–1830) fashioned images for public consumption and an enduring fictional iconography for each ruler. Both monarchs also appealed to real and invented heritage.[4] Lawrence was largely responsible for contriving George's royal image from around 1814, when he painted a head and shoulders and one full-length portrait of the Regent. He reduced the overweight royal bulk to a graceful, 'well-fleshed Adonis of thirty-three', in William Hazlitt's politically charged criticism. In fact, the portrait is a good painting which shows off the commanding and dashing figure of the Regent against a tumultuously windy sky, his bare head turned to left, his hands holding a plumed hat and sword.[5] If David was Napoleon's pageant master and Charles Percier and Pierre François Léonard Fontaine were his architects, in Britain Lawrence and John Nash (1752–1835) painted and built on a grand scale for the Regent.

The peace festivities of 1814 soon gave way to plans for more permanent schemes to commemorate the British-led triumph over Napoleonic tyranny. These ranged from the most comprehensive scheme ever to remake the centre of the capital on a grand scale, to free-standing monuments (some built, many more planned), and Sir Thomas Lawrence's painted pantheon of British and allied leaders for what would become the Waterloo Chamber at Windsor Castle. For some two decades after Waterloo, the state was responsible for major metropolitan building projects: as John Summerson wrote, 'so great a proportion of public wealth can rarely have been spent on architecture in the capital in so short a time'.[6] The so-called 'metropolitan improvements' were driven by ministers and the Prince Regent. These developments were complemented by the foundation of the National Gallery, the rebuilding of the British Museum on a grand neo-Greek scale, and the substantial building and rebuilding of several royal residences (see map 4).

In this same period, and inspired by Continental European thinking and practices, the state sought to harness the arts and museums in a quest for both social cohesion and improved manufacturing design. Parliamentary inquiries into national cultural institutions, art, and design acknowledged that certain forms of the arts in Britain had received limited encouragement when compared to some

Continental countries. They called for institutional reform and better access to culture for the many, not just the privileged few.

Post-war cultural politics thus involved examples of the state using art to glorify power in monumental architecture and triumphal arches. It also featured public spaces for the performance and display of power, especially as part of the so-called metropolitan improvements. But in addition to such conventional measures there were also novel uses of art for the purposes of education and social change (galleries, access to art in other public and official spaces). In certain projects like the National Gallery, these purposes overlapped. Such developments rarely came without limitations. There was much criticism of royal frivolity and extravagance. Some building schemes depended on substantial private investment, others remained unbuilt. And the definition of the cultural nation and the ideal scope of access to museums and heritage sites remained matters of contention. But overall, the decades between Waterloo and the Crimean War saw a remarkable outburst of new kinds of state sponsorship of artistic activity in the capital and a sustained rethinking of the relations between politics, society, and culture at the heart of the institutions of British governance. By bringing together different strands of state engagement with art, architecture, and museums, we can better appreciate the unprecedented investment in culture along with new motivations and novel approaches to defining the cultural nation and mechanisms for doing cultural politics.

Victory and Dynasty

Spring 1814 had seen French royal ceremonial in the British capital, as French flags and fleurs-de-lys bedecked Carlton House. On 23 April, Louis XVIII, who had seen out the war in English exile, and had just been invested with the Garter by the Prince Regent, left London for Paris. On 7 June, Tsar Alexander, King Friedrich Wilhelm III of Prussia accompanied by Field Marshal Gebhardt von Blücher, and Prince Metternich representing Austria, along with a range of generals and diplomats, arrived for a state visit. 'The sight was a proud day for old London; three monarchs entering the city at the same time.'[7]

The celebrations gave the British establishment the chance to assert in cultural and symbolic ways British military-diplomatic leadership in Europe and to proudly display characteristics of the British polity. For two months – as 'people from the most distant parts of England' were 'flocking to London to get a peep from a garret window or an area grating at a hero or a Prince as they passed' – 'emperor-hunting' was all the rage. Contemporaries reported how the opera was quite forgotten when an allied leader made an appearance at Covent Garden, tradesmen could not get ordinary business done, and apparently even the cows were too nervous to give milk as usual: 'It is quite ridiculous how wild London is'.[8] On 14 June, the Tsar and the King of Prussia received honorary degrees from Oxford before they were dined at the Radcliffe Camera. The City's financial prowess and civic pride were on display when the Regent, the British cabinet, and the allied dignitaries proc-essed under showy military escort to dine as the Corporation of London's guests of honour at the Guildhall. George Clint painted Europe's victorious monarchs feasting on the first turtle of the season and a baron of beef flying the British royal standard, attended by the Sergeant Carvers. Numerous imperial and royal toasts of mutual congratulations and assurances of friendship were followed by anthems and glees, as the chandeliers and mirrors reflected martial imagery and allegories of universal peace in the crimson-clad Gothic hall.[9]

A review of 12,000 troops in Hyde Park, the scene of military exercises since Elizabethan times, was followed by the re-enactment of a battle at Portsmouth – praised by many as a spectacular entertainment, but condemned by William Cobbett as a typical example of the Regent's wasteful extravagance. On 1 July, 1,700 people attended a ball in the Duke of Wellington's honour at Burlington House. On 7 July, Wellington carried the sword of state as he entered St Paul's – prepared on the model of the 1797 Naval Thanksgiving Service (chapter 3) – alongside the Prince Regent for a Service of General Thanksgiving for the Allied Victory (see plate XIX). Apart from the Duke of Wellington, the Tsar proved a particular favour-ite with the British crowds; he also made the waltz all the rage when he danced it at Almack's Club. But Britons particularly worshipped the old Prussian general Blücher, the energetic opponent of Napoleon, who had been chiefly responsible for the allied drive towards Paris. Wherever he went, people tried to kiss and embrace him, collected locks of his hair, and drew his carriage through the streets like that of a British naval hero. The Prussian enjoyed himself to exhaustion: 'I am still deaf from all the thundering of the cannon and well-nigh beside myself with all the great doings in my honour.' And whereas the French could not kill him, the English, 'the craziest people I know!', and their Regent might well manage through their well-intentioned celebrations; being painted by three portraitists simultaneously, Blücher felt he was 'being fatigued inhumanely'.[10]

The Prince Regent had been disappointed that he himself had not received much popular acclaim so far, and sometimes was even greeted with hisses and groans.[11] On 21 July, he therefore gave a feast for Wellington at his London residence, Carlton

House, which had seen many a splendid celebration since his assumption of regency powers in 1811. For the event, John Nash, the architect of the Brighton Pavilion, built a temporary polygonal hall of brick in the gardens. Various supper tents and a Corinthian temple in the grounds were reached through covered walkways. Their walls were lined with allegorical transparencies (painted cloth through which light could be shone) showing *The Overthrow of Tyranny by the Allied Powers*, *Military Glory*, and *The Arts in England*. The Regent in his gold-embroidered field marshal's uniform and bedecked in the orders of many nations welcomed 2,000 guests, who caroused until 6 a.m. the following morning.[12]

Celebrations of the allied victory were soon combined with the centennial jubilee of the accession of the Hanoverian dynasty in 1714. Extravagant temporary buildings went up in St James's Park, including a picturesque yellow bridge topped with a seven-storey Chinese pagoda over the canal. On 1 August, Windham Sadler's coloured balloon made an ascent from Green Park and sprinkled Jubilee programmes on the crowds. A regatta on Hyde Park's Serpentine was followed by *naumachiae*, staged re-enactments of naval battles using model ships. The siege of Gibraltar and Nelson's victories were particular favourites for these aquatic spectacles, which had become popular at entertainment venues across London beginning in the 1780s. They used scenic devices, music, lighting, and fireworks, as well as rousing renditions of 'Rule, Britannia' with audience participation for the grand finale.[13] In 1814, for the Jubilee, small replicas of men of war, built in the naval dockyards from old ship timber, navigated by sailors and firing blank ammunition from their single row of guns, represented the pivotal stages of the Battle of Trafalgar; French ships sank, engulfed in flames, to the strains of the national anthem. The Battle of the Nile and naval highlights of the War of 1812 with the United States were also showcased. Here the state embraced what had previously been a commercial spectacle as a crowd-pleasing part of the patriotic and royalist celebrations.

Astonished spectators enjoyed two hours of fireworks, with maroons and serpents, Roman candles, Catherine wheels, fire-pots, and girandoles blazing from the thirty-metre-high Gothic Castle of Discord which had been erected in Green Park. People marvelled how the castle, 'with all its horrors of fire and destruction', briefly disappeared behind a cloud of smoke to re-emerge, the fortifications now removed, as the Temple of Concord. This was 'a beautiful structure' which turned on an axis and was adorned with complex transparencies illustrating the origins and effects of war, the deliverance of Europe from tyranny, the restoration of the Bourbons by the aid of the allies, and the triumph of Britain and the Regent's apotheosis.[14]

After the exclusive celebrations at Burlington House and Carlton House, the final events had thus been open to a wider public. Indeed, in some ways the early August events were an extension of the summer theatre of the traditional Bartholomew Fair and other seasonal entertainment at London's commercial venues. Hyde Park featured ornamental booths and stalls, arcades, and kiosks. Trees were hung with coloured lamps, lanterns lined the Mall and Birdcage Walk, and military bands, acrobats, and swings provided entertainment. A ticketing system did filter the crowds at St James's Park to provide those who could afford it with exclusive comfort and safety – at 10s 6d tickets were dearer than the most expensive theatre box – but the conservative press still voiced concerns about potential mob trouble. *The Times* also gloomily predicted that the public would 'first gape at the mummery, then laugh at the authors of it and lastly grumble at the expense'.[15] The 22,874 'illuminating lamps' on the Chinese bridge, pagoda, and pavilions alone cost over £762; the total Jubilee budget exceeded £37,000.[16]

Disaster struck sometime between 10 p.m. and midnight, when the pagoda in St James's Park caught fire and much of the structure tumbled into the lake, killing at least one lamplighter and injuring five, as well as burning some of the royal swans. The applauding crowd assumed this was all part of the spectacle and kept streaming in from the other parks. At least there had not been any riots, and the few troops on standby had not been required, although some newspapers were critical of the proximity of the darlings of Bartholomew Fair, which had been moved from Smithfield to a site near the parks. In defiance of the Home Secretary's order to close the fair on 6 August it remained open for several more days.[17]

The proximity of high and low culture was satirised in prints of John Bull ogling the 'Regency Puppet Show' while his pockets are picked by the fairground manager. Poets criticised the mockery of the sailors' sacrifice and the Prince Regent's populist extravagance:

> I'll have no more sea-fights and sieges,
> No more pagodas, booths, and bridges;
> Nor turn my Park into a camp;
> No, suttlers, players, all shall tramp.[18]

Caricaturists especially lampooned the aquatic spectacles, calling them the Prince Regent playing in his 'washing tub'. A rare engraving, attributed to George Cruickshank and entitled *The Royal Dock Yard, or The Walnut-Shell Squadron* (1814), ridicules the Prince Regent and Lord Liverpool's cabinet, who are making toy ships from walnut shells and paper sails out of petitions presented by a public suffering hardship. The insane George III threatens the frivolously extravagant leaders with deportation to Australia. But the Royal Academician Joseph Farington, for one, thought that the 'pretty appearance' of the ships on St James's Canal by 'no means justified the sour, cavilling remarks profusely made in the opposition newspapers' which criticised the Prince Regent.[19]

Others such as the Dowager Lady Vernon, however, complained that the spectacles would 'spoil our parks for a length of time', a sentiment shared by Charles Lamb, who wrote to Wordsworth about the destruction of natural beauty:

the very colour of green is vanished, the whole surface of Hyde Park is dry crumbling sand ... not a vestige or hint of grass ever having grown there ... the stench of liquors, bad tobacco, dirty people & provisions, conquers the air.

The transformation of Hyde Park made it resemble a repose after battle; 'I almost fancied scars smarting.'[20]

Royal and state spectacle in 1814, then, had adopted the techniques of London's commercial shows and theatrical traditions. They had tolerated, too, the close proximity of, and partial overlap with, traditional popular fairs. This conflation of devices and publics helps explain both their success and the ambiguous responses they attracted. In provincial towns and cities that summer, patriotic peace festivals used elite paternalism and displays of civic hierarchies in the attempt to foster community cohesion during free dinners of beef and plum pudding, amid toasts to the monarchy and Britain's role as the world's naval master and the saviour of Europe.[21] Victory over Napoleonic France was not only celebrated in ephemeral spectacle, however. It also gave rise to enduring schemes for a painted pantheon at Windsor Castle, the radical redesign of London's West End, and fantastical plans for monumental structures which were never realised.

The English Titian

The Prince Regent commissioned Thomas Lawrence, R.A. to paint the portraits of all the major allied sovereigns, statesmen, generals, and diplomats who had helped put an end to Napoleon's dream of European Empire. The project had been prefigured by Henry Bone's miniature copies in enamel of military heroes. The portraits were initially intended for Carlton House, but George IV's plans for Windsor Castle subsequently came to include a display space specially created for Lawrence's portraits (see plates XVIII, XX).

Lawrence had been visiting the Louvre when he was recalled in summer 1814 to paint the Duke of Wellington, the Prussian and Russian generals Blücher and Platov, and the Austrian diplomat Prince Metternich. He exhibited the first three of these with a portrait of the Prince Regent at the 1815 Royal Academy. The full-lengths of the commanding generals Blücher and Platov were probably influenced by Reynolds's *General Granby* at Carlton House. Painted as a loosely conceived pair, they contrast the serene and contemplative Russian after victory with the more energetic if much older Prussian, in whose portrait a sense of action pervades the entire composition, from the general's sash to the sky and the Polish cavalry in the background.[22]

In 1815, Lawrence was knighted in preparation for his European tour to paint the remaining portraits for what would become the Waterloo Chamber. He attended the peace negotiations at Aix-la-Chapelle in 1818, where the British delegation was led by Wellington, Castlereagh, and Lord Stewart. The Austrian emperor, Francis I, took precedence in the protocol at Aix and his portrait by Lawrence is the only full-length of a monarch seated on a throne. It was the Tsar of all the Russias, however, who captivated Lawrence the most. Alexander I chose to be painted in the sombre uniform he had worn at the Battle of Leipzig. With his weight on one leg and his hands characteristically clasped before him, the intensely focused sovereign is silhouetted against the smoke of battle in the background; the portrait acquires a touch of informality by the coat and hat casually thrown over tree branches at right.

In Vienna, now formally travelling as the representative of the Prince Regent, Lawrence moved in the highest circles, helped also no doubt by his own personality and art. But it was in Rome, Europe's traditional capital of art, that the British painter was set to make his greatest artistic and social mark. Colleagues back in England compared him to Van Dyck in terms of the prestige his triumphs shed on English art both nationally and internationally. Lawrence was given splendid apartments in the Papal Quirinal Palace, along with a studio, carriages, a coachman, and the nickname 'Il Tiziano Inglese'. Pope Pius VII, who in 1809 had been imprisoned by Napoleon for opposing his plans for the annexation of the Papal States, symbolised the victory of peace over war after his triumphant return to Rome in 1814. He embodied Europe's hope of spiritual and political renewal. The Pope, portrayed by David and leading Italian painters before, granted Lawrence nine sittings. The masterpiece of the Waterloo Chamber captures the ageing and seemingly frail, but serenely spiritual Pope seated on the magnificent portable papal throne and gazing into the distance. The important pieces of classical sculpture seen in the background were restored under British supervision and escorted by the sculptor Antonio Canova from Paris to Rome; they were about to be displayed in new galleries for the civilised world to admire in peaceful harmony. Moreover, Cardinal Consalvi, the chief papal diplomat whom Lawrence also painted, had tactfully suggested that the papal tiara be omitted from the Pope's portrait: the symbol of the papal claim to authority over all Christian rulers seemed inappropriate in a portrait commissioned for the palace of the head of the Church of England.[23]

The Waterloo Chamber is dominated by Wellington at the head of the room (see plate XX), but otherwise there are few generals who won victories in the field. If the project was intended to celebrate the international alliance that defeated Napoleonic tyranny over Europe, George wanted to see the glory reflect mostly on his own imagined leadership. In the 1830s, a (studio) version of Lawrence's grand portrait hung in the Waterloo Chamber (see plate XIX). Apart from the royal commanders-in-chief and Blücher, there are few serving soldiers; it was only in the 1830s that further British general officers such as Anglesey and Picton were added to the painted pantheon. In brief, with the Waterloo Chamber the Regent had continued British royal patronage of the arts, albeit in a different personal style and with more panache than his father. Lawrence's portraiture won considerable international prestige for British art. The Regent decreed similar symbolic statements about his imagined military leadership to be sculpted on London monuments.

London Triumphant

In the immediate post-war euphoria, the British state made some grand monumental gestures. In 1815–16, Parliament allocated £300,000 for Waterloo and Trafalgar monuments. Dedicated to all the fallen of these two key battles, they were to stand in for all the battles of the French Wars.[24] Among the more fantastical proposals was Andrew Robertson's bombastic design for the Waterloo Monument. On Primrose Hill near the Regent's Park Canal he would rebuild the Parthenon, 'since we have now in this country its most valuable remains'. Robertson envisaged a windowless, square building of solid granite from his native Aberdeen, measuring some fifty-three by twenty-three metres, fourteen metres high, with walls almost one metre thick, and fifty-six colossal Doric columns. Sculptures on the pediment would represent the 'contention of Neptune and Minerva renewed … who shall produce the greatest heroes for Great Britain', Minerva being accompanied by generals like Wellington and Abercromby, and Neptune by Admiral Nelson, Howe et al. On the frieze (in place of the Centaurs) one soldier would represent each cavalry regiment. The London Parthenon would stand on a platform, about half of which was to be arched to accommodate a cemetery for the veterans of the war, cenotaphs for the fallen, and records of every soldier's name. Statues of generals and admirals, statesmen, the king, and the Prince Regent would be erected inside and around the building. A Caledonian Asylum, a Royal Palace, and a chateau for the Duke of Wellington were to be built in the immediate vicinity and the surrounding grounds laid out for 'fêtes to celebrate the battle of Waterloo, and one other victory each year in rotation on its anniversary'.[25]

The London Parthenon, however, lost out to William Wilkins and John P. Gandy's plan for an 'ornamental Tower' to commemorate Waterloo in Regent's Park; Robert Smirke's design for an 'elevated building terminating in an Observatory' was accepted for a Trafalgar memorial in Greenwich Park.[26] In the event, neither monument was built. Political concern with public economy played a part. Too little coherent thought might have been given to the precise object of commemoration: was it the 'collectiv[e] People of England', or the achievement itself, namely the 'Peace of the World', and the 'Majesty of National Virtue', with subordinate roles in the commemorative programme and design for specific battles and leaders?[27] With the St Paul's pantheon, the government had tried to square the circle of promoting culture *by* the nation (represented by the King-in-Parliament) *for* the nation, while at the same time limiting the object of commemoration to officers, and the display to the confined space of the fee-charging Anglican cathedral. By contrast, celebrating ordinary servicemen in outdoor monumental art might have been perceived as a politically risky move in a post-war period of popular unrest. Charles Watkin Williams Wynn, MP had called for the commemoration of the name of every fallen soldier. A member of the public proposed that a new national pantheon ought to have its doors lined with bronze engraved with 'the whole of the official returns of killed and wounded'. But on Castlereagh's insistence a parliamentary decision was deferred to the executive phase of the project – and thus never had to be taken.[28]

In the event, the Monument to the Napoleonic Wars on Edinburgh's Calton Hill by W. H. Playfair, only half finished because its money supply ran out, remained the only general war monument in Britain before Marble Arch was erected in 1828. Originally conceived as a memorial to the fallen soldiers and sailors, then fusing the notions of a memorial church on the Westminster model with the idea of an antique temple, the memorial was to be Scotland's Parthenon. Rather dubious comparisons were drawn between the valour, the military and naval achievements, the patriotism, and the artistic cultures of ancient Athens and modern Scotland. The replica Parthenon was advocated on aesthetic grounds, but also to promote the native arts and, strikingly, on grounds of heritage protection. More than a copy,

the Scottish Parthenon was propagated in terms of transfer, renovation, and restoration: 'while that grand original which they have adopted as the model of their
monument is at this moment perishing amidst the ravages of war, an exact facsimile of that celebrated edifice is now rising in our own metropolis'. A lobbying campaign was facilitated by the Highland Society and by members of both Houses of
the Westminster Parliament. They solicited Scottish expatriates around the world,
from Liverpool, Hamburg, and the Carolinas, to Russia, India, and Australia. Yet,
the modern replica – fittingly, perhaps, for the romantic age – remained even more
of a ruin than its ancient model had by then become.[29]

Even in this era of national pantheon-building, there were some transnational
gestures. James Elmes wanted to build a temple in honour of Wellington on Primrose Hill which was to include a Blücher statue as well as one of the Pope. The
names of other military leaders and those who brought about peace were to be
inscribed and recent history was to be narrated in the four languages of the allies.
And the German architect Leo von Klenze proposed a collective monument of the
united Europe which combined a Christian temple with the burial places of allied
military leaders, including Blücher, Wellington, Kutuzov, and Schwarzenberg.

Most of these fantastically grandiose designs were never built. However, in the
early nineteenth century, London not only acquired numerous monuments, but
became itself a monument.[30] Paris had previously boasted more splendid public
buildings: there was nothing comparable in London to the Louvre, Invalides, École
Militaire, Place de la Concorde, and even the *hôtels particuliers* of unrivalled elegance. London was not even a match for the public buildings of Vienna, the grand
visions of Turin or Lisbon, or the boulevards and piazzas, the wide open squares
or the dramatic vistas of Dresden, Berlin, or St Petersburg. For over half a century,
British architects and urban planners had demanded that London's West End be
developed on a scale fit for an imperial metropolis. As early as 1766, the architect John Gwynn (whom we first encountered when he proposed alterations to
the coronation procession of George III) had published *London and Westminster
Improved*, a far-sighted work with a clear agenda:

The English are now what the Romans were of old, distinguished like them by
power and opulence, and excelling all other nations in commerce and navigation. Our wisdom is respected, our laws are envied, and our dominions are
spread over a large part of the globe. Let us therefore ... employ our riches in
the encouragement of grandeur and elegance.[31]

From the 1810s, with the war still ongoing, British national pride was expressed through an ambitious vision for London's urban design and architecture. At long last, the British metropolis was to be transformed into a triumphant capital city. Indeed, for some two decades after Waterloo, the state was easily the most significant and extravagant sponsor of metropolitan building. It financed thirty-eight new 'Waterloo Churches' (1818–28), seven law courts, new Custom House, Post Office, and Treasury buildings, the substantial aggrandisement of the royal palace, changes to the royal parks, a new British Museum, and a National Gallery. The driving forces were the Prime Ministers Spencer Perceval and the 2nd Earl of Liverpool, and aides such as Sir Charles Long, 1st Baron Farnborough, the Prince of Wales's Francophile artistic adviser who kept parliamentary subsidies flowing for royal and state cultural projects and helped coordinate relations between image-makers and the ruling elite. They were backed enthusiastically by the Prince Regent (George IV in 1820–30).

The only plan ever realised to remake the British capital on a grand scale was put into execution between c.1810–1840: Regent's Park was developed, St James's Park was improved by the Office of Woods, and Regent Street built as London's only boulevard – a royal mile and *via triumphalis* to connect Carlton House with a planned royal pavilion in Regent's Park. Moreover, Trafalgar Square was laid out and the western end of the Strand reconstructed. New buildings were well sited and old ones, like Buckingham House and the British Museum, were brought into relation with the wider plan, all resulting in a greater sense of coherence, order, and circulation.

John Nash, a successful country house architect and property speculator, had twice visited Paris in 1814–15 and admired the straight Rue de Rivoli with its arcades. The influence of the Tuileries, Place de la Concorde, and the Arc du Carrousel are evident in Regent's Park, Regent Street, and Buckingham Palace. While the ambition to rival Napoleon's imperial Paris was the burning motivation of the Prince Regent and a professional challenge for his architect, the immediate impetus for London's metropolitan improvements was the reversion of the lands of the current Regent's Park, then called Marylebone Park, to the crown, and the Office of Woods's decision to develop the land for profitable use. A marked economic shift from the 1810 trade crisis to a revival of credit and a trading boom provided propitious circumstances. The Regent's desire for an adequate approach to his residence, Carlton House, and for a link to a new pleasure palace envisaged in the northerly park shows that urban development was as much part of the creation of the royal image as portraits, palaces, and pageants – a grand stage for a monarch of flamboyant flair unprecedented in the royal House of Hanover.

The guiding idea for Regent's Park was to combine order and countryside. A large open space was to be laid out on picturesque lines with clumps of trees, an irregular lake, and villas, with grand terraces overlooking the park on the periphery, and a royal pavilion facing the present Cumberland Terrace. A variation on the Roman ideal of *rus in urbe*, or countryside in the city, it was nevertheless a stunningly innovative concept in contemporary European urban planning. By 1812, the drives and plantations were largely complete. With the post-war economic revival, the palatial Cornwall, York, Clarence, and Hanover Terraces made good use of the plastic capabilities of stucco. Nash's Sussex Place, surprising with its curving wings, ten pointed and pinnacled domes, and fifty-six Corinthian columns, was followed on the park's eastern borders by the long Chester Terrace and culminated in the grandiose Cumberland Terrace, which combined ideas from Somerset House, Versailles, and Dublin's Four Courts. Even though the royal pavilion was never realised, and only eight of the originally planned fifty-six villas were eventually built, the scheme made a great impact.

Nash's most significant contribution to the redevelopment of London, and the greatest example of town-planning in the capital's history, was Regent Street. The New Street Act of 1813 had decreed a thoroughfare from Pall Mall to Marylebone Park and improved communication through to Charing Cross. In 1817–23, Nash linked Regent's Park with St James's Park, Whitehall, and the Strand. His final plan avoided some of the expensive land purchases initially envisaged, so that the route of the street followed mostly crown land. Nash, a self-described 'thick, squat, dwarf figure, with round head, snub nose and little eyes', was a shrewd businessman but careless in his accounting.[32] He at once was the author of the plan, valued and purchased property on behalf of the commissioners, raised funds for the construction of the sewers and the street, negotiated with developers and builders such as James Burton, and supervised the elevations. To accelerate completion he showed great flexibility in accommodating hotels, shops, office space, and churches, as well as residences.

With its distinctly English blend of formality and the picturesque, of ambitious planning and improvisation, Regent Street by the mid-1820s had achieved its key purposes. It enhanced the income of the crown estate and provided profitable returns for London builders; it marked a social frontier to screen the fashionable West End from the crowded, less affluent Soho; it offered a promenade and shopping area for the idle and wealthy; and it served as a triumphal thoroughfare to impress foreign dignitaries. The street was over twenty-seven metres wide, and it followed a straight line from Carlton House through the strictly formal and residential Waterloo Place on to a circus at the crossing of Piccadilly. Waterloo Place evolved into an impressive piece of town-planning with grandly pillared private houses, the princely residence, the Duke of York's Column, and wide stairs down to St James's Park, flanked by Nash's United Services Club and Decimus Burton's Athenaeum. Lower Regent Street was semi-formal and mostly residential.

The street continued further north with a necessary curve to the north-west, negotiated by Nash's brilliantly sweeping Doric colonnades of the Quadrant, and then again in a straight run, albeit with no uniform façades or rigorous coherence, along the main shopkeeping stretch up to Oxford Street. Here Nash managed another change of direction with All Souls church, Langham Place, whose circular vestibule and tower make it look right from all directions, while masking the street's awkward turn to link up with the Adam brothers' Portland Place, where residential formality once more resumed. Among the individual buildings Nash designed were the Royal Opera House, Haymarket (1816–18) and the Haymarket Theatre (1821), the portico of which closes one of the vistas from Lower Regent Street. Inspired partly by Oxford's sinuous High Street, in its layout and in its architecture Regent Street displayed Nash's mastery of picturesque variety, changes of texture, and the artful management of vistas, such as the domed rotunda at the corner of Vigo Street which arrests the eye at the north end of the Quadrant.

John Soane (1753–1837), meanwhile, had been building seven Courts of Law around Westminster Hall and the classical Scala Regia and Royal Vestibule for the House of Lords. Soane's Board of Trade in Whitehall and the new Law Courts had also been envisaged as components of a triumphant royal route from Windsor to the Houses of Parliament. Nash, with Regent Street completed, in 1826 supplied designs for a second phase of improvements at the southern end of the crown estate. Since taking up residence at Carlton House on coming of age in 1783, George as Prince of Wales and then Regent had remodelled, added to, and redecorated the residence with great frequency. He experimented with every style from Chinoiserie to Gothic, indulged more enduring classical and especially eighteenth-century French inspirations, ordered the creation of a Military Tent Room and an Admirals' Room with emblematic representations of British victories, and had temporary structures built of the kind seen at the 1814 Jubilee.

Yet, after all the costly rebuilding and redecorating, in 1827 Carlton House was demolished. George IV wanted a residence to reflect his grandeur. He claimed that Carlton House lacked in magnificence, comfort, and safety, and settled instead on Buckingham House as his new seat. He persuaded Parliament to authorise a quarter of a million pounds to expand the palace. The main range of the original eighteenth-century house was encased within the new work and by 1828 most of the exterior was complete except for the patriotic sculpture and Marble Arch as the entrance to the forecourt. George IV and Nash continued building with little regard to the moneys available. When the king died, Parliament sacked Nash from the Office of Works. A select committee found in 1831 that the expenditure had been exceeded by £600,000. Edward Blore was appointed to complete the work, though even the next king, William IV (r.1830–37), never got to move in. By 1850, Blore had added a new wing across the forecourt to achieve the courtyard plan resembling English country houses. But the interiors were mostly Nash's idea, with heavily classical forms in the state apartments. The English neoclassical Music Room with its semi-dome sits alongside the Palladian Ballroom or Blue Drawing Room with small domes supported by consoles of coving, and the Rococo White Drawing Room, as well as some Chinese interiors taken from the Brighton Pavilion. Overall the impression is of sumptuous ostentation, coloured in white, with much gold and scagliola for the wall linings, sculptured panels in high reliefs, and crimson, blue, green, and yellow silks. Nash at Buckingham Palace and Wyatville at Windsor used materials from George III's half-finished Gothic Castellated Palace at Kew, which had been demolished in 1827–8 on George IV's orders.[33]

∼

Throughout George III's reign, architects and town planners had proposed monumental gateways to the precinct of the royal residences. In 1816, the Prince Regent acquired models of the three surviving triumphal arches of ancient Rome, of Titus, Septimus Severus, and Constantine. The remodelled Buckingham Palace was then intended to receive triumphal archways as the 'definitive expression of George's fantasy-victory over Napoleon'.[34] Nash planned a processional route for the monarch from Buckingham Palace to Hyde Park, with triumphal arches celebrating British military and cultural prowess achieved under the guidance of the Hanoverian dynasty.

Nash designed Marble Arch in 1825 (built 1827–33) to stand between the projecting wings of Buckingham Palace as a ceremonial gateway to its forecourt (fig. 46). Modelled on Constantine's arch in Rome, and on Percier and Fontaine's Arc du Carrousel (1806–8), erected in the grounds of the Tuileries to celebrate Napoleon's victories, the three archways between monolithic Corinthian columns are clad in white Carrara marble. John Flaxman's sculptural scheme was only partially implemented: there are carved Victories in the spandrels and square panels of standing figures above the side arches by Sir Richard Westmacott and E. H. Baily. One long side of the arch bears high reliefs of the Battle of Waterloo, the other shows scenes from the life of Nelson; on the shorter sides are low reliefs of Fame displaying

46. *Architectural Model of Marble Arch*, after a design by John Nash (*c*.1826).

Britain's naval and military victories. On the east face two reliefs depict the king's approbation of the plans before the Battle of Waterloo and rewarding Wellington afterwards; the naval west side focuses on Nelson. A giant equestrian statue of George IV by Chantrey was to stand on the plinth over the Arch's attic storey, towering over the reliefs of the British heroes and a panel of Napoleon (echoing the arch of Constantine) and classical gods. Once more, the symbolism was of Napoleon's defeat as George's more than the military leaders' achievement. After Nash had been sacked in 1830, Edward Blore substituted a cheap, plain low attic with four weak upright statues for Nash's taller one. Westmacott's *Fame Displaying Britain's Triumphs*, initially intended for the attic of Marble Arch, was incorporated above the bow on the west front of Buckingham Palace. The sculpture in the pediment of its courtyard includes the friezes of Waterloo and Trafalgar, also by Westmacott, somewhat truncated from the arch. Chantrey's George IV was moved to Trafalgar Square. When the palace forecourt was enclosed in 1850–51, the arch was rebuilt at the northern entrance to Hyde Park.

An arch at Hyde Park Corner had previously been suggested by leading architects such as Robert Adam, Jeffrey Wyatt, and John Soane. It was for Decimus

Burton to finally bring Hyde Park into the monumental landscape around the royal residence, with drives, pathways, lodges, and finally a screen and monumental arch.[35] The Park Screen was built in 1826–9 of grey stone on the corner of Hyde Park. Three archways of Ionic columns, coupled in the centre, are separated by screens of five columns each. The sculpted attic frieze is a variation on the Parthenon. The so-called 'Pimlico Arch' is modelled on the Corinthian Arch of Titus, which refers to the conquest of Jerusalem. The single archway with heavy iron gates was initially to be topped by a statue of Britannia Triumphans, a quadriga, and other sculptures, but this was not realised after George IV's death. Neither was the arch's function as an entrance to the grounds of Buckingham Palace from the north. Screen and arch were initially aligned, but the arch was moved in 1883. From 1846 until then, Matthew Cotes Wyatt's much criticised equestrian statue of Wellington had stood on top of the arch. The arch's mostly unexecuted decoration was also to include military figures, possibly with references to Nelson and Wellington, as well as a frieze with horsemen in Grecian-style helmets.[36]

To offset the costs of rebuilding Buckingham Palace, the Carlton House site was laid out for the speculative development of magnificent terraces overlooking the Mall. Carlton House Terrace (1827–33), executed following a general design by Nash, consists of two grand twin stucco blocks each thirty-one bays long and two and a half storeys high (three and a half at the end pavilions), supported by a terrace of projecting servants' quarters facing St James's Park. The park was re-landscaped on picturesque lines, the contours of the lake were softened, and clumps of trees replaced the earlier, more formal layout. Influenced by Ange-Jacques Gabriel's buildings in the Place de la Concorde in Paris, the blocks of Carlton House Terrace flank the broad stone stairs leading to the Duke of York's column (B. D. Wyatt, 1831–4), atop which sit a square balcony, a drum, a dome, and a bronze statue of the Duke in Garter robes by Westmacott, bringing it to a total height of some forty-two metres.

Also from c.1825–6 are Nash's plans for a new connection between Whitehall and the British Museum, linked to the Regent Street scheme by cutting through from Pall Mall, as well as for a new square at the top of Whitehall from which a road was to link directly to Bloomsbury. There, Robert Smirke's sober neo-Greek galleries were gradually taking shape between the 1820s and late 1840s to accommodate the Royal Library and the colossal antiquities arriving from the Mediterranean and Near East. By 1847, the Museum's south front of forty-four gigantic Ionic columns, modelled on the temple of Athena Polias at Priene, was complete.

In the meantime, the new square which Nash had envisaged had been taking shape at Charing Cross (fig. 47). The site faced the Royal Mews at the most important

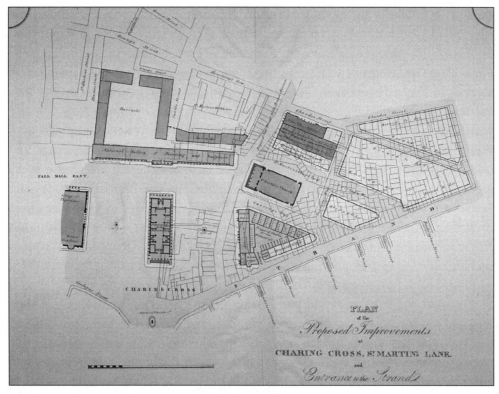

47. *Plan of the Proposed Improvements at Charing Cross, St. Martin's Lane and Entrance to the Strand (c.1824).*

land entrance to Whitehall and the royal precinct. In 1830 it was named Trafalgar Square. Nash's vision for a forum surrounded by public institutions was partially realised: the College of Physicians and the Union Club were already established; on the north side he imagined a National Gallery; on the east an Athenaeum, St Martin's vicarage, the Royal Society of Literature, and the Golden Cross Hotel. In the middle of the square he wanted an imitation of the Parthenon, facing down Whitehall, as the seat of the Royal Academy of Arts, with spaces to either side for statues of George III and George IV.

The National Gallery had been founded in 1824, not by nationalising a royal collection, but through the parliamentary purchase of John Julius Angerstein's outstanding collection of paintings and his Pall Mall home. London finally had a cultural symbol and resource which most European capitals had possessed for decades. Several agendas were served by the gallery's foundation: the preservation of the connoisseurial canon of mostly foreign old master paintings, the desire to reduce pressure for widening access to private collections, and, albeit more

370

indirectly, the improvement of manufacturing design. But a National Gallery was also seen to vindicate the nation's cultural achievement and to offer a monument to military victory, although not of the French kind. As the Chancellor of the Exchequer asserted in the House of Commons, 'every Englishman' viewing the gallery's paintings could proudly reflect 'that they are not the rifled treasures of plundered palaces, or the unhallowed spoils of violated altars', yet another swipe at Napoleon's disreputable collections policy and in particular his ransacking of Italy to make the Louvre Europe's museum.[37] This rhetoric was also apt to disarm those associating national museums with revolutionary tendencies on the earlier French model. At the formerly royal Louvre, from 1793 every *citoyen* was able to view the nationalised former royal, aristocratic, and ecclesiastical collections on (theoretically) equal terms. By 1830, the National Gallery was run by a board of trustees who comprised officers of state, the President of the Royal Academy, as well as collectors and connoisseurs, aristocrats and bankers. It was politically fairly inclusive except for radicals, and broadly mirrored the British Museum's semi-formalised relationship with the state.

In the event, Nash's plans were scaled down considerably, and the National Gallery and Royal Academy occupied one building on the north side of Trafalgar Square – today's National Gallery, built in William IV's short reign by William Wilkins in 1833–7. He was constrained by the obligation to use part of the portico of the former Carlton House. The long, low façade, broken into thirteen sections by a central portico and steps, and several pavilions, domes, and turrets, is competent and pleasant, but fails to entirely command the great square. Some of the friezes intended for Marble Arch were reused on the National Gallery, and several Victories had their spears replaced with paint brushes.[38] After much delay, London finally also acquired an outdoor monument to Admiral Nelson. Nelson's Column, by the little-known architect William Railton, is modelled on a column in Augustus's temple of Mars Ultor in Rome. That temple had celebrated the transformation of Julius Caesar into a god and linked him with the god of war and an ever-lasting empire. With the Prime Minister and Chancellor of the Exchequer sitting on the Nelson memorial committee, the government made the square outside the National Gallery available for the column. The 1,500 subscribers were headed by William IV and included many naval officers as well as numerous sailors, who donated between one and four days' pay. Though a Commons select committee protested that Nelson's Column obstructed the view on to the National Gallery, Parliament subsidised the monument's steps, bas-reliefs, and bronze lions with over £14,000. At the beginning of Queen Victoria's reign, Trafalgar Square therefore resonated strongly with British military *and* cultural prowess. This new space was henceforth appropriated for imperialist display and celebration as well as by anti-colonial protesters, including, in the twentieth century, the India League and Indian Freedom Campaign.

In brief, the Prince Regent, his architect Nash, and successive governments, with parliamentary appropriations more or less enthusiastically forthcoming, had enhanced the splendour of the crown and the display of state authority with the new system of connecting roads and strategically sited royal palaces, triumphal gateways, and cultural institutions to manifest national military and artistic prowess. There were clear limits even to this grandest of state enterprises: it was only partially completed, some elements were soon changed, moved, or demolished, and Regent Street depended as much on the speculative developers of retail and residential quarters as on state sponsorship. Nash and Soane came in for considerable criticism – Soane partly because of his advanced and experimental thinking, Nash mostly for extravagance and lack of strict accounting. Repeatedly his projects had been suspended as Parliament inquired into costs and eventually sacked him. Nevertheless, a patriotic, confident narrative in stone, marble, and stucco of dynastic power and victory over Napoleon had been built. The West End of London had been remade according to a coherent, largely successful plan – which impressed the future Napoleon III, who later commissioned Baron Haussmann to redevelop Paris along not dissimilar principles.

The building for the National Gallery and Royal Academy was placed at the junction between the axes of St Paul's–Strand and Whitehall–Westminster Abbey. This location encapsulates the importance which the arts then held in political thinking. That significance was further reflected in parliamentary inquiries and wide-ranging public discussion about the social and moral uses of the arts and widening access to museums, as well as about organisational reform of art institutions. Such debates assumed prominence at the heart of the institutions of government as well as in the wider public sphere of the cultural nation in the 1820s–40s.

Art for the Nation

In the 1830s and 1840s, British cultural politics converged with Continental European developments in new and crucial respects.[39] In the light of social and political crises, the rationales and purposes of state patronage of the arts as they were advocated in Continental countries focused the attention of the British political elite. There was support for Germanic arguments for the morally and spiritually uplifting qualities of art, and for the social benefits of cultivating public interest in national monuments such as cathedrals, castles, and palaces. In the age of reform, access to art for, and the spread of taste among, all classes was expected to help alleviate social tensions and the consequences of urban poverty. From around 1810, the Prussian Kultusministerium had been putting the arts centre stage in its programmes of national integration and economic development. We can see variants of both strands develop in Britain a generation later.[40]

From the 1800s, the closed culture of the privileged had been coming under increasing scrutiny. Such pressure for change was partly responsible for private owners of paintings granting selective access to their collections, for the foundation of the British Institution (1805) and its loan exhibitions, and, eventually, for the foundation of the National Gallery (1824). Prestigious cultural symbolism had been removed from the exclusive control of primarily aristocratic men to the nation as a whole, although it would take the move to Trafalgar Square in 1837 to give greater numbers physical access, and until the 1850s for fundamental reforms in collections management, cataloguing, cleaning, and preservation to professionalise the operation.[41] Over this same period, the previously restrictive admittance regime of the British Museum underwent radical change, as the ticketing system which had required literacy and leisure was abolished in 1810 and as notions of 'virtual representation of culture' gave way to access for everyone of 'decent appearance' on three days a week; visitor figures, previously at 15,000 per annum, instantly doubled; by 1818 they had reached 50,000.

~

Two further, related developments added pressure for change. First there was increasing demand, both in and out of doors, for reform of institutions that were publicly funded (British Museum, National Gallery) or claimed national status on account of their significance, such as the Royal Academy, but were perceived to be too oligarchic, elitist, and exclusive, and/or inefficient in the ways they operated. Parliamentary select committees conducted extremely thorough inquiries which resulted in thousands of pages of reports (a dozen reports on the British Museum alone in 1835–50) with hundreds of recommendations for improved efficiency, transparency, and accountability, although reform aspirations exceeded actual change until later in the century. But not only had a new mechanism of cultural politics been pioneered by the select committees, but the very fact that cultural institutions which claimed national status by virtue of their statutory mission, self-declared objectives, or funding structures were being held to account by the nation's representatives, and increasingly also in the court of public opinion, was an important new development in cultural politics.

The second impetus for change relates to increasingly inclusive definitions of the cultural nation. Reformers among the political classes established the rhetorical power of notions such as open and free access to cultural institutions. By the 1830s, both the workers' movement and middle-class initiatives for diffusing useful knowledge viewed the arts and museums as means of educational advancement.[42] The post-war disturbances, turmoil over Queen Caroline's trial, and the Reform crisis fuelled a sense of renewed urgency about the neoclassical notion of art and art galleries as instruments of moral improvement. And whereas some thought political crises actually diverted attention from cultural affairs, others supported parliamentary reform in the hope that social and political stability would help revive the arts.[43]

In July 1832, Sir Robert Peel was optimistic that 'the exacerbation of angry and unsocial feelings might be much softened by the effects which the fine arts [have] ever produced upon the minds of men.' The National Gallery allowed people with little leisure the 'most refined species of pleasure' and 'would not only contribute to the cultivation of the arts, but also to the cementing of those bonds of union between the richer and the poorer orders of the State'.[44] Exposing the working classes to art was expected to lessen social tensions and the consequences of urban poverty. From the 1830s, campaigns against the vices of drinking and gambling aimed at their replacement by so-called 'rational recreation', as the working classes were to visit museums and art galleries as well as libraries and public parks.[45] Reformers for the first time used crude visitor statistics to demonstrate the importance of extended opening hours. Even conservatives like Lord Ashley believed that the industrious classes would visit the National Gallery instead of ale houses.[46] Conservatives pursued authoritarian policies to promote the arts as an alternative to drunkenness and crime; reformers and radicals viewed exposure to art and its educative effect as the birthright of Englishmen. Both sides invested in a new kind of cultural politics.[47]

But the function and audiences of galleries also continued to divide both the cultural and political establishments. Among top British Museum officials a bias against the lower orders was deeply engrained, while junior staff were more committed to popular instruction and amusement.[48] Some witnesses before a select committee in 1836 recommended that opening on national holidays would improve the national taste and character, and, if anything, encourage better use of the collections, rather than increase the risk of physical damage.[49] The committees, which brought together evangelicals like the Oxford Tory MP and Museum trustee Sir Robert Inglis with radicals such as Sir Benjamin Hawes, recommended a host of measures to widen access: further extension of opening hours, published synopses and catalogues, and cheap facilities for the public to make casts from coins and antiquities.

Even the reforming camp was split, however. Some like William Cobbett still rejected the very notion of publicly funded galleries as long as they were seen to benefit only an aristocratic elite: 'If the aristocracy [want] the Museum as a lounging place, let them pay for it.'[50] Cobbett's critique was echoed by visual satire portraying tax money wasted on art in the face of widespread poverty and dearness of provisions, a charge levelled both at the acquisition of the Parthenon or Elgin Marbles (1816) and at the exhibition of cartoons for the decoration with frescoes of the Palace of Westminster (1843): 'The poor ask for bread, and the philanthropy of the State accords them – an exhibition.'[51] By contrast, the Christian Socialist penny-paper *Politics for the People* (1848) praised the British Museum. It was 'almost the only place which is free to English Citizens as such … the poor and the rich … a truly equalising place, in the deepest and most spiritual sense.'[52] The rhetoric of the socially levelling museum resonated with the language of rational recreation with which the journal described the sensual and aesthetic experience of the people in the National Gallery, 'the workman's paradise, and garden of pleasure.'[53]

In 1841, a select committee was appointed to inquire into all public buildings containing works of art 'as a means of moral and intellectual improvement for the People'. The chairman was Joseph Hume, the Scottish radical MP for Middlesex, advocate of Catholic Emancipation, repeal of the Test and Corporation Acts, and parliamentary reform, and a consistent champion of the taxpaying public's 'right to insist on every facility of ingress'.[54] The committee pushed for free access to St Paul's Cathedral and its three dozen mostly military monuments in the expectation that this would benefit the population at large by spreading taste, historical understanding, self-improvement, and public morality.[55]

Several developments which had been foreshadowed by Napoleonic-era hero worship peaked in the mid- to late Victorian era. Regency and Victorian war literature – fiction and numerous martial memoirs and campaign accounts – reaffirmed the pantheon's aristo-military code and the centrality of the French Wars to the British self-image and consciousness.[56] It has been suggested that the uncommonly long period of peace in Europe from 1815 to 1854 demanded an adjustment of notions of the heroic and that the vogue for medieval chivalry, in the words of John Tosh, 'displaced valour and danger into a safe haven of agreeable fantasy'.[57] As in the earlier periods discussed in chapters 1 and 4, different notions and codes of masculinity coexisted. In publications such as Stacey Grimaldi's *A Suit of Armour for Youth* (1824), chivalry was presented to English boys as a living code for the present. When the boys had grown up, they would read Kenelm Henry Digby's

Broad Stone of Honour (1822), with subtitles ranging from *Rules for the Gentlemen of England* to *The True Sense and Practice of Chivalry*, and chapters on honour, courtesy, respect for women, hardihood, contempt of luxury, and loyalty to friends and leaders. The Regency sporting journalist Pierce Egan cultivated the manly courage displayed by Nelson's tars and Wellington's soldiers and presented pugilism as a peculiarly English sport. Charles Lever's popular novels of sporting and military adventure frequently drew on examples of heroism (and horsemanship) from the Napoleonic Wars. Thomas Carlyle lectured on heroic qualities such as energy, fearlessness, valour, and tolerance of force and violence. By mid-century, definitions of manliness stressed physical courage, chivalric ideals, and patriotic duty; inspired by a cult of game-playing and a concern with health, they increasingly emphasised a kind of neo-Spartan virility and hardy endurance. By the 1850s, the renewed demands of war (the Crimea) and of consolidating the empire (the Indian Mutiny) heightened national concern with vigorous action and military readiness. In sports, poems, songs, and the classics syllabus, the public schools now taught the moral lessons of self-sacrificial duty to prepare English boys for life on and off the battlefield. Men like General Havelock were also hero-worshipped for their concern for the well-being of their men (linked, of course, with strict discipline); this was, again, a long-term trend dating back at least to the Seven Years War, with a first peak in the Napoleonic period.

What is new in the middle of the nineteenth century is the increasing emphasis on heroes' inner lives and the notion that the more zealously religious, the more morally righteous they were, the better. There was also a trend towards popularising traditional notions of chivalry, courage, and loyalty. British Romantic war prose pioneered by Sir William Napier's hugely popular history of the Peninsular War refined the code of the chivalrous, disinterested, virtuous military hero for a Victorian audience. Napier's bottom-up military history challenged the earlier, almost exclusive concentration on the officer class.[58]

The viewing of the St Paul's statues in the nineteenth century, then, was shaped by official and nostalgic, loyalist modes of commemoration; by Napier's indirect social critique; and by the renewed emphasis on Christian heroics, although there was also growing scepticism of the glorification of military heroes in a Christian temple. The first regimental monuments at St Paul's were erected to commemorate the Crimean War, allowing every serving man a degree of honour. A memorial to the Cavalry Division shows cavalrymen with diverse uniforms in relief; the memorial of the Coldstream Guards killed at Inkerman depicts a battlefield monument with the inscribed names of the fallen barely legible, repeated in larger letters below, thus suggesting distance of the battle from England. Matthew Noble's monument to the 77th Middlesex Regiment shows a long line of soldiers, heads bowed, contemplating the mass grave of their fallen comrades. Statues of statesmen, artists, scientists, and scholars broadened the scope of the pantheon into a more general 'Hall of British Fame' or Valhalla akin to Westminster Abbey.

The values embodied by the military monuments at St Paul's remained prominently on the public mind. Yet different concepts of the Cathedral conflicted – namely its roles as a church, national monument, art gallery, and place of national education and patriotic edification. From the 1820s, political reformers campaigned in Parliament and out of doors to abolish admission fees: why should the taxpayer pay to access a 'National Gallery of … exalted Virtue' funded by Parliament?[59] But the Dean and Chapter protested before select committees: on Sundays between services St Paul's was already no different from a bazaar in Oxford or Regent Street on a weekday afternoon. After access had been somewhat eased in the 1830s, 'hundreds of fashionable loungers' intruded during service hours. St Paul's was notorious for people of the 'lowest description' entering with their hats on, talking, laughing, and eating and thus prone to disturbing those attending divine service. If free access was to be allowed at all times, the Cathedral would turn into a 'Royal Exchange for wickedness' and a Police Act would be required to rid the Cathedral of its salacious clientele and their inappropriate activities, like women knitting, lunch parties, straying dogs, and even men urinating in pews.[60] As for monuments, visitors scribbled their names and other words on to them, and Admiral Rodney's sword was broken by a gentleman probing whether it was made of copper or marble by tapping it with his stick.[61]

Yet, by the time of the report in 1841, it seemed that the conduct of the lower classes in public cultural spaces was in fact improving. Extended and free access appeared to make the populace more caring of the art they experienced; the mob ceased to be the mob, when they acquired taste.[62] *Blackwood's Magazine* considered museums and galleries as schools of 'true politeness'.[63] The 1841 committee was satisfied with the educational and moral potential of cultural experiences for the wider population and demanded extended opening hours at St Paul's. Cathedral authorities resisted the political pressure until admission fees were finally dropped in the context of the Great Exhibition in 1851. While the Cathedral struggled to reconcile its functions as a space of worship and as the national sculpture gallery, the National Gallery of Art, though physically and financially accessible, remained a space of social distinction dependent on the possession of cultural skills. Reformers demanded that the gallery be arranged by schools and periods, as the traditional presentation of Old Masters of individual genius demanded learned connoisseurship on the part of the viewer. A more accessible evolutionary display of art was helped by cheap catalogues, and, from 1856, simple labels.[64] The 1841 committee had also demanded labels and affordable catalogues for the British Museum, whose displays foreign visitors like Ralph W. Emerson from the USA criticised as inadequate, a mere 'warehouse of old marbles'.[65]

Critics complained that poorly dressed, malodorous working-class people visited the national museums in wet weather, often not primarily to experience art. Together with children leaving conspicuous marks on the floors, they damaged the pictures through dust, dirt, and the condensation of vapour on their surfaces. Isolated cases of attacks on works of art in the British Museum and National Gallery in the 1840s were cited as evidence of the trouble that was being invited into the temples of the muses.[66] Increasing visitor numbers – just over and just under three quarters of a million at the British Museum and National Gallery respectively around 1850 – suggested that the ideals of universal access and of good curatorial and preservation practices might conflict with each other.

Another function of the 1841 select committee on fine arts had been to consider the decoration of the new Houses of Parliament. After the Palace of Westminster had burned down in 1834 and was rebuilt, the select committee proposed that it be decorated with fresco paintings.[67] The example was Ludwig I of Bavaria's patronage of art – the grandiose architecture, pioneering museums, splendid collections, and nationalistic and Christian school of painting he sponsored in Munich. Frescopainting in particular had recently attracted much attention among travelling and reading Britons. A royal commission under the chairmanship of Queen Victoria's Consort, Prince Albert, was set up to supervise the scheme. It was hoped, first, that the long-perceived deficiency in drawing in the English school of painting could be corrected. Secondly, fresco was considered a uniquely didactic genre suitable for national education, as it demanded from artists simple compositions and clear effect. After reassurances that only native painters would be employed, extremely popular exhibitions of cartoons from British history and English literature in Westminster Hall fuelled a brief national fresco-mania. In 1846–7, the first frescoes were commissioned and completed: with resonances from George III's Windsor schemes, they were William Dyce's *The Baptism of King Ethelbert* and C. W. Coope's *Edward the Black Prince*, as well as *Chivalry* and *Religion* from Daniel Maclise and J. C. Horsley respectively. Dyce also painted scenes from the legend of King Arthur in the queen's robing room.

However, political and religious hostility to an art form that was both Christian and Germanic, as well as scepticism about Germanically centralised art patronage, soon undermined the patriotic success of the scheme. One of the most significant examples of state promotion of public painting in Britain had briefly attracted widespread support but then fell victim to a moment of politico-cultural panic in the late 1840s. Here, wider concerns about the predominance of the German manner in Britain converged with fears of Romanism during a European revival of the Catholic church. However, the scheme had ensured that national history painting had been in the public eye as rarely before. In the period covered by this book, history painting had not been displayed in official spaces other than royal residences. The scheme also left a permanent legacy in Parliament as an illustrated national history book, even though its potential to develop national culture and models of cultural patronage more widely was ultimately limited.

CONCLUSIONS

CULTURAL POLITICS, STATE, WAR, AND EMPIRE

IN THE BEST BRIEF ANALYSIS of similarities and differences between British and Continental European cultural politics in the late eighteenth century and the first half of the nineteenth, Peter Mandler suggested that Anglo-European cultural politics increasingly diverged in the Napoleonic period and in the aftermath of the great European wars of 1793–1815. After a brief interlude of convergence in the 1830s and 1840s, divergence again prevailed.[1] As outlined in this book, however, there is an alternative way of reading the ballet of Anglo-European cultural politics. This is one which revolves around the Napoleonic period as a crucial transitional period of change. It casts Napoleon as one of the implicit choreographers-general. And it gives greater weight to war and empire in the shaping of the motivations, mechanisms, and outcomes of cultural politics.

The most immediate comparison for Britain's St Paul's pantheon was Napoleon's Les Invalides. His Egyptian expedition spurred Britain's participation in the international race for antiquities around the Mediterranean, and Wellesley's aggressive military and cultural schemes in India. Even private collectors of British art justified their activities with reference to the Napoleonic Wars. As the health of British art was linked with the 'undaunted bravery' of Britain's fleets and armies, Sir John Fleming Leicester – one of the most important early collectors of exclusively modern British paintings (as opposed to foreign Old Masters) – was compared with the Duke of Wellington.[2] Napoleon's European-wide art loot was admired and vilified by British visitors to Paris, among them some who became instrumental in the foundation of a British National Gallery two decades later. And the Prince

Regent sought to out-display and out-build Napoleon in London and at Windsor towards the end of and after the war.

If one looks for direct, formal analogies to Napoleon's Egyptian Commission of Sciences and Arts, or a central government agency distributing international art loot to dozens of provincial museums, then, admittedly, there is little to compare in Britain. But if one takes into account the unique state-sponsored programme of national commemoration in St Paul's Cathedral, the indispensable assistance rendered by the state to Mediterranean and Near Eastern expeditions, investment in the British Museum collections, and the archaeological dimensions of imperial surveys from Mysore to Java, then the contours of the British cultural state can be seen to have been first shaped at the Napoleonic-era peak of fiscal-military expansion.

Such a reading challenges long-standing notions of British cultural exceptionalism. It acknowledges that politicians' cultural commitments blurred the lines between state and society. It is premised on the appreciation of the specific nature of the British state as more porous, more responsive to demands for the provision of infrastructure, and more willing to promote public–private partnerships, to share authority between officialdom and the private and voluntary sectors. It further urges that we consider the cultural politics of the British state not just with respect to the formal institutions of governance, but a wider, loosely connected network of institutions and influence, such as the East India Company, and national cultural organisations. Moreover, overlapping and usually cooperative networks of metropolitan and imperial officialdom and military officers on the one hand, and of scholars, artists, and curators on the other, shaped the practices of archaeology and collection development. In a variant on the public–private partnerships of the otherwise very different field of classical archaeology, military officers, engineers, and surveyors in British India were crucial to the production of cultural knowledge and the development of archaeological practices.

The findings of this book invite further, in-depth comparison with Continental European cultural politics. Such comparison needs to abandon the classic but simplistic dichotomy of a non-state-centred Britain contrasted with a statist France or Prussia. Formal British institutions of state were more significant sites and agents of cultural change than usually acknowledged: the crown, government, Parliament, the Established Church, and the armed services. *Empires of the Imagination* contributes to the ongoing reassessment of the Hanoverian monarchy as a politically and culturally proactive and significant agency. It further highlights Parliament as a distinctly British forum for the discussion of, and source of funding and legitimacy for, cultural projects. And it suggests that associationism as a distinctive feature of British public life, including in art and science, can be profitably investigated in the context of the revised understanding of the state. British cultural politics, as manifested by the St Paul's pantheon, the trajectory of the cult of the heroic, or notions of military masculinity, reflected the country's distinct constitutional arrangements and its political culture. The reluctance to conflate secular heroism too closely with quasi-religious notions and the avoidance of martyrological imagery at St Paul's were some of the ways in which the British state and artists set their national manner and style of commemoration apart from Continental patterns. The politicisation of the London art world during the American Revolution, when American artists were invested in political and artistic agendas, bears further study, including in comparison with other revolutions which were also civil wars.[3]

The practices of commemoration and of collecting reveal a nuanced spectrum of state involvement in cultural endeavour. To take these inquiries further, rather than thinking in terms of the state tampering with the cultural preferences of the market, it is helpful to consider how commerce and state often combined to influence cultural projects. Handelmania in the late eighteenth century was a function both of royal patronage and of musical entrepreneurship. Copyright made relatively cheap editions of literature and music possible, rendering the national cultural patrimony more accessible. Musicians playing in London's theatres and pleasure gardens often also performed for the monarch and the military. And John Nash's 'metropolitan improvements' in the early nineteenth century depended on ministerial and royal drive and public funding as well as on the investment of speculative developers. In other respects, however, official and private cultural practices developed without too much overlap. This was true even in some areas of military commemoration, where the study of private monuments illuminates selective emphases and gaps in the official commemorative effort.

Understanding these practices has required us to overcome modern specialisations between disciplines and indeed between cultural, administrative, and military history. The narratives of war and empire, and the narrative of the cultural politics of the imperial state and its main politico-military protagonists, were closely related. International competition was a key driver of cultural politics. Monument-building and archaeological campaigns were often conducted in comparison and competition with other nations. In certain ways they represented the pursuit of war by other means. The British state sponsored military monuments with a view to promoting national culture and to fostering patriotic morale. Politicians and artists negotiated complex commemorative politics and modes of representing personal and national stories. It is in the interplay of heroic politics and aesthetics that we can best appreciate the practices and discourses of cultural patriotism, masculinity, religion, and national heroic aesthetics.

With respect to the practices of collecting too, war, empire, and the evolution of the cultural state and the cultural nation were inextricably intertwined. The cultural rivalry of nation-states shaped the building of national museums. National antiquities collections were influenced by the rhetorical appropriation of the meanings and physical remains of antiquity *and* by regional military and diplomatic balances of power. Officially sponsored cultural projects depended on the fiscal-military, imperial state, that is, on its logistical, diplomatic, and military capabilities, and on its political capital and rhetoric. Well into the mid-Victorian period, archaeological campaigns relied on individuals with military or diplomatic postings and on Foreign or War Office support.[4] Conversely, cultural endeavour such as appropriating (and claiming to protect) the remains of ancient civilisations could serve informal imperial agendas or legitimate the expanding imperial state. The relationship between state and (semi-)private archaeological endeavour in the Mediterranean and Near East on the one hand, and, on the other, the nature of informal and formal empire, invites further investigation.[5] Moreover, the ambivalent nature of Orientalism requires continued probing: the chapters on India have revealed a complex and mixed story – of recording and professional development, of destruction and preservation, and of both the centripetal and centrifugal tendencies of empire. They have shown a mixed picture, too, of genuine dialogue in knowledge production between officials, Orientalists, and Indians, of imperialist arrogance, and of the use of historical and archaeological knowledge about Indian pasts to inform the practices of imperial governance.

Britain was distinct, it has been said, in lacking a strong concept of cultural patrimony and of its importance to the nation, along with a central-government apparatus to protect it (unlike France, Denmark, Prussia, and some smaller German states). However, British political and cultural figures concerned themselves with notions of heritage, whether in the context of appropriating antiquity or incorporating colonial cultures into British culture. From the beginning of the nineteenth century, British imperial officials and archaeologists were involved in discussions over the respective merits of collecting and preservation or restoration. The British-Indian government was among the first to consider the protection of antiquities in imperial territories. As the ideals and practices of heritage protection were first taking shape, in the Mediterranean and Near Eastern theatres international competition and mutual accusations added urgency to the debates. Both under pressure of international scrutiny, and in the absence of imperial competition in India, British officialdom began to develop an ethic of imperial care for antiquities.[6]

Rarely was there a political or social consensus on the precise place that the arts ought to occupy in public life, and on the role that the state ought to play in cultural affairs. Both philistine and reforming attitudes influenced state funding of antiquities and of royal or national buildings, and debates on the precise scope of public access to cultural sites. Politicians and archaeologists had to engage with critiques of imperial hubris and plunder. Heightened sensitivity to the political potential of art in the public sphere was evinced by attacks on monuments in Revolutionary America and the contemporaneous reception of American art in London. Political strife over heroes could jeopardise official efforts at consensus-building and patriotic celebration, not just at the French Revolutionary Panthéon, but at ostensibly nationally consensual British pantheons, too. Contests over British masculine heroism and its sculptural representation further ensured that the political and aesthetic debate on Westminster Abbey and St Paul's Cathedral remained lively throughout this period. In controversy as much as in consensus, politics and political institutions were significant sites and agents of cultural and artistic change.

If one accepts the period c.1790–1815 as a transitional phase in British cultural politics, then the cultural politics of the immediate post-war period appears less as a temporary deviation from a standard pattern. Instead it suggests greater continuity in state commitment to the arts. New manifestations included grand post-war schemes of reimagining and rebuilding London as a work of art, and investment in the national collections of paintings and antiquities and their spaces of display, as well as in royal residences, parks, and churches. Such new areas of focus in part reflect novel motivations; new mechanisms of cultural politics were developed in the form of parliamentary select committees and royal commissions. In early nineteenth-century Britain, concerns about social divisions were often answered with material solutions such as Poor Law reform, repair of price/wage mechanisms, and state education, rather than with aesthetic or artistic projects. By the 1830s, however, Whig governments acknowledged the need for state intervention on behalf of people's moral and spiritual as well as their material well-being. Widening access to art and museums was recognised as an effective mechanism. Considerable amounts of parliamentary time, political capital, and funds were invested in the quest for social change by cultural means. By the 1850s, national and nationally distinct culture and a reassertion of the voluntarist tradition again trumped the adaptation of foreign models. Following also the revival of European authoritarianism after the 1848 revolutions, British attitudes to Continental modes of governance returned towards traditional resistance to 'bureau and barrack'.[7] A renewed materialism, even if it was now more dressed up in religious language, 'did not exclude aesthetic concerns altogether, but decidedly subordinated them'.[8]

Aesthetically performed politics and politically inflected art and culture interacted in multifarious ways. One of the most versatile languages and practices developed by the overlapping circles of politicians, officers, artists, and patrons charted in this book was that of cultural patriotism. Private initiative could be justified within a framework of patriotic public policy. Diplomats posted from Greece to the outer regions of the Ottoman Empire strove to be recognised as cultural benefactors of the nation. But if patriotism was at stake over acquiring iconic objects and crediting scholarly breakthroughs to the British nation, it also stood in uneasy tension with a more cosmopolitan culture of imperial imagination: when scholars of British and Continental extraction cooperated in South Asia, and authors of various nationalities cross-fertilised each other's work on the historical topography and archaeology of the Mediterranean, they lived the ideals of an enlightened republic of letters in a new age of nationalism.

International cooperation and competition, domestic party politics, religious sensibilities, and aesthetic preferences modulated the language and practices of cultural patriotism. A nuanced understanding of the politico-cultural history of Britain in this period is predicated on appreciating such interplay between aesthetically performed politics and politically inflected art, the nationally introspective and internationally competitive agendas of cultural politics, and the roles of the state, politics, war, and (in)formal empire as powerful agents and sites of cultural change.

A half-century after Abu Taleb's visit, London looked like a truly imperial capital. Along with the scope and nature of the British Empire, the face of its metropolis had undergone fundamental change. War and empire had had a transformative impact on many areas of culture; cultural representations had in turn helped shape political culture and the practices of the cultural state. From George III's coronation at the height of the Seven Years War, to Nelson's funeral among the growing Napoleonic-era pantheon at St Paul's, to the spectacular collections of ancient civilisations in the grandly rebuilt British Museum around 1850, Britons had had opportunities to imagine empire at numerous official and semi-official cultural sites. At the Great Exhibition of 1851 and beyond, the Crystal Palace too staged empires of the imagination.

EPILOGUE

EMPIRES IMAGINED AT
THE GREAT EXHIBITION

All London is astir ... and some part of all the world.

John Ruskin's diary entry for 1 May 1851[1]

The first morning since the creation of the world that all peoples have assembled from all parts of the world and done a common act.

The Times, 2 May 1851

ON 1 MAY 1851, Queen Victoria presided over the opening of the Great Exhibition at the Crystal Palace in Hyde Park. The Great Exhibition had various agendas and has been interpreted and remembered in a number of ways. Yet above all, it was a space where national and imperial identities were imagined.[2] European countries and Dublin had staged manufacturing exhibitions during the previous half-century, but this was the first World Fair, a Gathering of All Nations. The Great Exhibition was yet another example of British public–private partnership in cultural endeavour. It was initiated by the Royal Society of Arts and its chairman, Henry Cole, a civil servant at the Record Office and designer of artistic china and of museum projects. Victoria's Prince Consort, Albert, took a leading role and urged the participation of the government, as a result of which a Royal Commission supervised the project. The Colonial and Foreign Offices and British diplomats facilitated overseas participation, while the East India Company coordinated the Indian displays.[3]

After the mixed results of the parliamentary frescoes scheme (chapter 9), Albert had redirected his cultural work to applied art. He thereby developed a rationale commonly deployed in Continental countries for state promotion of artistic endeavour, namely to harness art and design to industry. There was a perceived urgency to improve British manufacturing design, especially against French and German competition. This ought both to maintain British cultural self-sufficiency and technological supremacy, and, combined with free trade, sustain the empire of well-marketed goods.[4]

Cole argued that, while foreign governments financed similar projects by taxation, it 'would be far nobler for the English people to do the thing well for themselves ... rather than ask the Government for assistance'. When not enough money was raised by public subscription to build the Crystal Palace, leading businessmen underwrote a guarantee against a loss.[5] In the USA, the executive branch handled the country's participation, although detailed coordination was delegated to the National Institute for the Promotion of the Sciences and the Arts in Washington, DC. Congress allocated no funding, and only briefly discussed the cost of navy ships which transported exhibits from New York City to England. The Treasury funded the transport of objects from other Atlantic ports to New York, yet, overall, private individuals shouldered most of the expenses.[6] This arrangement was thus not dissimilar from the British approach, and both contrasted sharply with France, Austria, and the German states, where governments supervised and largely funded the entire programme.[7]

The exhibition building in Hyde Park was an ingenious modular structure of recyclable components of iron, wood, and glass. Some 600 metres in length and 130 metres wide, the total floor area was roughly six times larger than St Paul's Cathedral. Detachments of Royal Engineers tramped over girders to test the strength of gallery floors. Nearly 14,000 exhibitors displayed 100,000 exhibits in four categories: Raw Materials, Machinery, Manufactures, and Sculptures. One half of the palace was reserved for exhibits from Britain and 'British Dependencies', ranging from the Mediterranean, Africa, South-East Asia, and Australia to British North America and the Caribbean. The other half was occupied by countries from across Europe as well as disparate 'exotic' countries such as Egypt, Turkey, and Tunis, China, and Brazil, Chile, and Mexico.[8] Thirty-four juries – each composed evenly of British and foreign members – considered over one million articles and awarded nearly 3,000 Prize Medals, and 170 Council Medals for particularly important innovations in materials, processes, or design; half of these went to UK exhibitors, commensurate with their proportion of participants overall.

By the time it closed in mid-October, the exhibition had received 6 million visitors, including over 27,000 from France, roughly 10,000 from the German states, and some 5,000 from the United States. Some 35,000 British schoolchildren visited in organised groups. Three hundred sets of the five-volume *Illustrated Catalogue* sold for three guineas, plus 7,000 copies of individual volumes. Around 285,000 copies of the *Small Official Catalogue* (one shilling), 84,000 copies of the *Synopsis* (sixpence), and 26,000 copies of the *Popular Guide* (twopence) were also sold. With a large number of guidebooks to London published in 1851, visitor figures increased dramatically, for instance at the British Museum from 720,000 in 1850 to over 2 million, and for the Crown Jewels at the Tower from 32,000 to 209,000.

The Great Exhibition had both internationalist and nationalist meanings – it served to promote international peace and harmony as well as to celebrate British superiority and power. Nearly four peaceful decades after Waterloo, the event was planned as a festival of peace and a symbol of international brotherhood and inter-dependence. Prince Albert was keen to publicise scientific and industrial knowledge with a view to fostering international harmony. Moreover, the exhibition was widely seen to promote 'free trade' in industrial know-how, commercial knowledge, and goods as part of a pacificist and internationalist credo. Finally, it was to project a euphemistic vision of an empire which benefited both Britain, its colonies, and the world economy at large.[9]

Yet, implied in such agendas was the hope that the exhibition would also demonstrate Britain's national progress in arts and manufactures, and help maintain its status as the leading industrialising nation in the face of increasing competition. Britain in 1851 was still the world's leading economic and military power. Yet perceptive analysts could see that the economic basis of Britain's imperial and military supremacy was eroding. It was crucial to remedy deficiencies in manufacturing processes and design, and to educate producers and consumers about the values of industry, mechanisation, and commerce, as well as design and taste.[10] Beyond the competition over goods and markets, at the exhibition British ideals of governance, society, work ethics, and free trade were asserted. What was at stake was whether Britain would decline like some Mediterranean countries, whether it would remain superior in democratic governance and manufacturing to France, and whether it would be overtaken economically by the German states and the United States.[11]

Domestically, the project was promoted as a nationalistic competition and symbol of pride that required the participation of Britons of all classes. It nevertheless reinforced social hierarchies. Accounts in the newspapers and cartoons contrasted social classes in terms of admission fees, attire, and refreshments, as well as the modes in which they viewed and appreciated the exhibits, on the 'day of the great folks, and the day of the little folks … – the day of languid lounging and chatting, and the day of resolute examining and frank amazement – the day of the West-End of London, and the day of all the other ends of the earth'.[12] As an example of the Victorian drive to collect, classify, and spread knowledge, the exhibition focused the ongoing debate on rational recreation between the poles of edification and entertainment (chapter 9). *The Times* criticised aristocratic and wealthy sight-seers for focusing on the wrong objects, such as the crystal fountain or the Indian Koh-i-noor diamond, with mere curiosity rather than a 'businesslike spirit of scru-tiny'. Some reformers demanded that recreation and the very ways of viewing be rationalised; others were concerned about protecting working-class visitors from the provinces from aspects of metropolitan popular culture.[13]

Above all, the Great Exhibition was a space where national and imperial identi-ties were represented and imagined. As a museum or encyclopedia, the exhibition enabled Britons to envision the nation and to experience their empire of goods, places, and peoples. Maps, charts, and floorplans showed Britons their empire. Catalogues and other non-fictional and fictional publications played on the notion of 'walking around the empire' at the Crystal Palace. People's shared physical par-ticipation was enhanced by direct contact with goods whose positioning allowed visitors to appreciate the spread of the empire.

One could also purchase a *Telescopic View of the Great Exhibition 1851*, a device that unfolds through a concertina action. Peeping through a hole in the cover, one sees a three-dimensional view of the interior of the Crystal Palace. On nine planes of hand-coloured cardboard plates, connected at the sides by chintz, appear sumptuous displays, numerous visitors, and decorative elements. Alongside civil-ian Europeans there are some red-coated officers; others wear what appears to be foreign national costume. On the second layer, a prominently positioned black man in a blue overcoat and red headgear is walking with Caucasian gentlemen towards a display of statuary in the centre. The user can choose to see different combinations of levels, and telescope in on particular parts of the display, and thus of the British Empire and the wider world.[14]

There was some discrepancy between the organisers and those commentators who stressed that the festival of peace fostered international harmony, and the jingoistic and xenophobic tone of other publications and cartoons. Some stere-otypically contrasted Britons – a peaceful, industrious, and entrepreneurial people living in a just and free society – with the militaristic if thoughtful and romantic Germans or the handsome, grave, yet irascible Turks. Cartoons lampooned the crudely militaristic Russian Don Cossack and cannibalistic, monkey-faced, dark-skinned savages in Thomas Onwhyn's *Mr and Mrs Brown's Visit to London to See the Great Exhibition of All Nations. How they were … frightened out of their wits, by the*

Foreigners.[15] Imagery circulated of Chinese, Turks, and Indian chiefs overwhelming the capital. Parts of the popular press inflamed fears about foreign threats from Socialists to papal forces, as well as of dirt, epidemics, and plague. They invoked the French invasion scare of 1847 and the European revolutions of 1848, the spectre of Papal Aggression, growing Irish immigration, and the Don Pacifico affair, in which the Royal Navy had blockaded Greek ports in retribution for the ransacking of the Athenian house of the Gibraltar-born Don Pacifico. The Duke of Wellington insisted that seven infantry regiments be stationed in London during the summer, but in fact there was very little trouble; foreign visitor figures in the end barely tripled from 1850 to 1851, from 22,000 to 65,000.

Authors in 1851 offered imaginary views of British culture from the outside. In Henry Sutherland Edwards's long rhyming poem, *An Authentic Account of the Chinese Commission which was sent to report on the Great Exhibition, wherein the opinion of China is shown as not corresponding at all with our own*, the Chinese emperor sends Congou, who has killed four generations of women in his own family, to barbarous Britain. Congou is accompanied by physician-philosopher Sing-Song, who, in the tradition of the Western figure of the *philosophe*, appreciates Western scientific and artistic achievements in a balanced manner. Congou, unable to appreciate cultural differences, condemns Western civilisation as barbarian. The emperor makes him a Mandarin, but has Sing-Song executed for his biased report. Along with caricatures of stereotypical Chinese at the exhibition, Edwards's poem exposed British prejudice against the despotic Chinese while affirming the superiority of British values. W. M. Smith's essay on 'Voltaire in the Crystal Palace' similarly turned the ethnographic gaze on Britain. The resurrected *philosophe*, once a fervent admirer of eighteenth-century England, now casts doubts on the virtues of mechanisation: 'Your iron slave wants many other slaves, unfortunately not of iron, to attend on it.'[16]

Slavery was a touchstone for British responses to America's presence at the Crystal Palace, even though for the United States the Great Exhibition marked its coming of age as an internationally recognised manufacturing and industrialising power.[17] At the start of the exhibition, *Punch* mocked the scattered displays when American contributors used only 40 per cent of their allocated space. The *Athenaeum* offered a symbolic reading of relative emptiness: 'The Belgian and Dutchmen can hardly stir in their well-stored compartments: – the American has wildernesses between his scattered stalls.' Newspapers mapped out the American space as the 'prairie ground of the Exhibition'.[18] The American press moved from apathy and scepticism to appreciating the role of the exhibition as 'the great Test Ground of the World's ingenuity, skill and knowledge', and of the 'morals, systems of religion, modes of government, and intellectual progress of every nation.'[19] The *New York Herald* saw an opportunity to present to the world the quality of American manufacturing as well as the 'superiority of the whole fabric of American free, republican institutions'. Some editorials asserted that Britain, given its national debt, expensive and corrupt government, and unproductive aristocracy could not compete with 'a young, vigorous, athletic, powerful republic' like America.[20]

British commentators commended America for keeping industry free from governmental interference. To some this affirmed Anglo-American ties and pitted Anglo-American *laissez-faire* against *dirigiste* France. Increasingly, it was recognised that the USA was not only a land of vast natural resources but rivalled Europe in terms of machine tools, agricultural implements, and precision-manufactured goods. American exhibitors won five Council Medals, including for the Virginia reaper; the colt revolver received an honourable mention and the *America* beat the British *Titania* in the Royal Yacht Club regatta. British newspapers acknowledged that 'The Yankees are no longer to be ridiculed, much less despised. The new world is bursting into greatness – walking past the old world'. Relative youth of nationhood had advantages, as their 'industrial system [was] unfettered by ancient usage'.[21]

Yet, respect for American progress was tampered by criticism of American hypocrisy. Attention focused on two American sculptural exhibits, Hiram Powers's *The Greek Slave* (c.1843–4) and Peter Stephenson's *The Wounded American Indian* (1848–50).[22] Powers's *Slave* shows a captured Greek woman being sold at a Turkish slave market. The standing nude figure, her gaze directed downward, rests her right hand on a columnar support with symbols of Christian faith; her wrists are bound by a double chain. The statue, which echoed the Venus de Medici, attracted attention as an example of American interpretation of classical beauty as well as for the provocative display of female nudity on a revolving plinth. The obvious contemporary resonances of the subject – nearly two decades after the abolition of the slave trade in the British Empire – also ensured the statue's notoriety. *Punch* famously contrasted the sentiment elicited by the statue with indifference to the plight of real slaves: 'We have the Greek Captive in dead stone. Why not the Virginian slave in living ebony?' Elizabeth Barrett Browning's 1850 sonnet on antislavery was inspired by the *Greek Slave*:

> They say ideal beauty cannot enter
> The house of anguish. On the threshold stands
> An alien Image with enshackled hands,
> Called the Greek Slave!

The statue was exhorted to appeal 'against man's wrong', to 'strike and shame the strong, By thunders of white silence, overthrown.'[23] Discussion of American slavery at the Great Exhibition served as a foil for the British assertion of love of freedom.

Similarly, *The Wounded American Indian* prompted comparative discussion of the treatment of native populations in the British Empire. The statue of a pained, slumped-over Indian, his head bowed over a wound, helped pioneer a national American aesthetics, derived from classical republican ideals. At the same time, it was widely read as a symbol of the permanent decline of the Indian race, on which the settlement of the American Continent was predicated. Exhibition accounts contrasted American mistreatment of indigenous peoples with euphemistic narratives of the humane treatment of the native peoples of British Canada, and of friendly cooperation between natives, settlers, and American loyalist refugees. In the British imagination, America at the Crystal Palace had both presented new strengths and displayed examples of its continuing hypocrisy.[24]

The British Empire occupied one tenth of the British half of the palace. Colonies from the Caribbean to New Zealand showed raw materials and agricultural products alongside ethnographic displays – from Maori artefacts to specimens collected by learned societies in the British West Indies. Africa featured mostly as a reservoir of natural materials, reinforcing the notion of empire as part of a British-centred manufacturing process. Canada displayed a pyramidical trophy of arts, in which a whale jawbone was countered by a gigantic log and surmounted by a birch bark canoe; a chief of the Melicite tribe with his squaw provided the ethnographic element.[25] The only country other than Britain to display colonial goods was France: Algerian exhibitors had sent local textiles and a richly decorated saddle.

At the centre of the British imperial displays were the contributions organised by the East India Company.[26] As the jewel in the imperial crown, India occupied some 30,000 square feet all across the nave, more than twice the floor space of all other colonies combined. India was sumptuously displayed as a fertile land and oriental treasure-trove of natural resources and commodities: jewels, textiles and carpets, musical instruments, raw materials and agricultural produce, arms and elephant trappings.[27] The Company aimed to introduce British manufacturers to new raw materials and to popularise Indian commodities among consumers. Moreover, cultivating cotton in India would free Britain from dependence on American slave labour, linking an imperial civilising mission in the East with a moralistic stance towards the former western colony.[28] India was also imagined as a land with ancient artisanal traditions in cloth- and pottery-making, as well as a living museum of industrial processes and habits that preserved ancient forms into the present. Some considered muslins, calicoes, and chintzes superior to British commodities in design and execution; to others, the displays of arms, jewels, and cloths suggested oriental despotism, barbarity, or wastefulness. In ethnographic displays, besides models of Hindu professions and castes, an Indian government collector was shown on his annual district tour and a European judge was administering the law in a Hindu court of justice.

Trophies of imperial conquest completed the Indian display – from the golden throne of Ranjit Singh, today in the Victoria & Albert Museum, to the Koh-i-noor diamond, the 'Mountain of Light', one of the most famous stones among the British Crown Jewels. Its surrender to Queen Victoria was made a condition in the terms of the capitulation of the Punjab capital Lahore. In Hindu legend for 5,000 years an emblem of dominion and prosperity, the stone is first reliably documented with the Mughal emperors in the early sixteenth century. Its subsequent owners included Persian shahs, Afghan rulers, and various Indian princes, until the Company presented the diamond to Queen Victoria in 1850. Displayed under special police guard, it was appraised as a reminder of 'the forfeit of Oriental faithlessness, and the prize of Saxon valour'.[29]

The diamond trophy notwithstanding, as an international competition at the cultural and symbolic level, the Great Exhibition reflected a shift from art and antiquities to technology and industrial design. Class XXX of exhibits encompassed 'Fine Arts, Sculpture, Models and the Plastic Arts generally, Mosaics and Enamels, illustrative of the taste and skill displayed in such applications of human industry'. Most objects were architectural fittings and decorative art; paintings needed to demonstrate improvements in the preparation of colours; architectural exhibits were mostly linked to materials and building strategies. It would be the French who included the fine arts prominently in the Universal Exhibition at Paris in 1855, thus reasserting the central role of the arts in the French ethos, and the status of Paris as Europe's pre-eminent artistic capital.[30]

Antiquities received pride of place only in the Crystal Palace's second incarnation, when it was revived by a joint stock company and re-erected in 1854 in enlarged form in Sydenham, ten kilometres outside central London.[31] To serve the amusement and instruction of the British people, especially Londoners, accessible displays of art and science echoed the rationale of recent reforms of museums and historical sites. As a three-dimensional, fully coloured encyclopedia of 'the complete history of civilisation', Sydenham featured ten Fine Arts Courts, where architects and archaeologists 'reconstructed' model buildings of brick, plaster, and paint. The Sydenham palace evoked antiquities which British archaeologists and officials had been surveying and collecting for the British Museum over previous generations. Period courts representing the great chain of art from Egypt, Assyria, and

Greece to Rome capitalised on popular interest in recent archaeological discoveries. Yet they also asserted their academic authority through references to scholarly advisers and the authors of official guidebooks – Layard on Assyria, Bonomi and Wilkinson on Egypt, Fellows's illustrator Scharf on Greece and Pompeii.

At Sydenham, techniques of display differed from the connoisseurial British Museum. In the Greek court, archaeology was presented as a new science, which revealed the architectural and engineering innovations of the ancient Greeks. Fellows's historically contextualised display of monuments gave visitors an immersive experience of three-dimensional architectural spaces. The single largest court, the Nineveh or Assyrian court designed by James Fergusson in cooperation with Layard, illustrated Fergusson's thesis that there had been rows of wooden pillars down the interior of palace halls. Indian displays combined models of buildings and artefacts with Gill's large-scale pictures of the sculptures and paintings from the Ajanta caves.

With the transfer to Sydenham, the Crystal Palace, now a commercial venture, has moved away from our main story of state-related cultural endeavour. Yet, the cultural state, empire, and cultural patriotism resonated at Sydenham too. The Crystal Palace Company had acquired sculptures from the excavation site north of Kuyunjik; the British Museum and the Louvre had permitted casts to be made from their collections; the French government had also shared Place's recent Khorsabad discoveries. Among several hundred plaster casts of European sculpture, 500 portrait busts of antique and modern political, military, and cultural figures, and sixteen colossal allegories of cities and nations, one monument held pride of place: near the heart of the palace, a seated statue of Chatham was a reminder of the first global war for empire a century before. In 1857, 81,000 people heard 2,765 singers and 457 orchestral players perform the *Messiah* and *Israel in Egypt*: by reviving the Handel concerts of the 1780s at an even grander scale (and without the controversies prompted by a religious setting), the Handel Festivals consolidated the site's symbolic role in British cultural patriotism. As the Mutiny rang in profound changes in Britain's Indian empire, as British diplomats and archaeologists brought the last Assyrian sculptures and the first marbles from Halicarnassus to London, and as Sir Isaac Brock's Anglo-Canadian monument was being rebuilt at Queenston Heights, Britons were continuously reinventing empires of the imagination.

NOTES

Introduction: Sinews of Power and Empires of the Imagination

1. After returning to Calcutta in 1803, Abu Taleb (1752–1806) wrote a travel narrative in Persian, based on his diaries and letters; it circulated in MS among the Persophone Islamic service elites. Lt-Col. Lennon sent a copy to England, where it was translated selectively by Charles Stewart, Professor of Persian at Haileybury College, and – the romantic and poetic sections omitted – became the first published travel narrative of Europe by a native of South Asia: *The Travels of Mirza Abu Taleb Khan, in Asia, Africa and Europe, during the Years 1799–1803*, trans. Charles Stewart, 2 vols (London: Longman, 1810; 2nd edn 1814); references henceforth are to the 1810 edn as: AT. Translations into French, German, and Dutch followed in 1811–19. The Company commissioned Taleb's son to prepare a Persian edition; abridged Persian editions were in use in Calcutta schools from the 1820s.
2. AT I, 282.
3. *Annual Register*, 52 (1810), 749.
4. For analysis of Taleb's complex positions see Michael H. Fisher, 'Representing "His" Women: Mirza Abu Talib Khan's 1801 "Vindication of the Liberties of Asiatic Women"', *Indian Economic and Social History Review*, 37:2 (2000), 215–37; Fisher, 'Asians in Britain: Negotiations of Identity through Self-Representation', in Kathleen Wilson (ed.), *A New Imperial History: Culture, Identity, and Modernity in Britain and the Empire, 1660–1840* (Cambridge, 2004), 91–112; Fisher, 'From India to England and Back: Early Indian Travel Narratives for Indian Readers', *Huntington Library Quarterly*, 70:1 (2007), 153–72.
5. Thomas Daniell designed the farm buildings, a dairy with a Muslim gateway and minarets, a bridge with Hindu pillars and four small statues of Nandi, as well as a temple of the sun-god Surya. For Dean Mahomet's position in the British Empire and perspectives on India see Michael H. Fisher, *The First Indian Author in English* (Delhi, 1996), and his 'Representations of India, the English East India Company, and Self by an Eighteenth-Century Indian Emigrant to Britain', *Modern Asian Studies*, 32:4 (1998), 891–911.
6. John Brewer, *The Sinews of Power: War, Money and the English State, 1688–1783* (London, 1989); Lawrence Stone (ed.), *An Imperial State at War: Britain from 1689–1815* (London/New York, 1994); Brewer, *The Pleasures of the Imagination: English Culture in the Eighteenth Century* (London, 1997).
7. In the famous *Spectator* no. 412 (1712), Joseph Addison had written about the pleasures of the imagination. These were pleasures provoked by imaginative literature and the fine arts: 'how great a Power … may we suppose lodged in him, who knows all the ways of affecting the Imagination, who can infuse what Ideas he pleases, and fill those Ideas with Terrour and Delight to what Degree he thinks fit? … He can transport the Imagination with such beautiful and glorious Visions, as cannot possibly enter into our present Conceptions.'

8. Miles Ogborn, *Spaces of Modernity: London's Geographies, 1680–1780* (New York/London, 1998); Roy Porter, *London: A Social History* (London, 1994); Celina Fox (ed.), *London – World City 1800–1840* (New Haven, Conn./London, 1992), esp. essay by M. Daunton, 'London and the World', 21–38.

9. For the interrelatedness of trade, naval protection, the mobilisation of men and money, and military capacity see Brewer, *Sinews of Power*, with further references; Linda Colley, *Captives: Britain, Empire and the World, 1600–1850* (London, 2002), introduction. For informal control in the nineteenth-century empire see Andrew Porter, 'Introduction: Britain and the Empire in the Nineteenth Century', in Porter (ed.), *OHBE, vol. III: The Nineteenth Century* (Oxford/New York, 1999), 1–28, at 10–12, 15–16; Peter Sluglett, 'Formal and Informal Empire in the Middle East', in Robert W. Winks (ed.), *OHBE, vol. V: Historiography* (Oxford/New York, 1999), 416–36, at 416–18.

10. See, among others, *OHBE* and recent collections such as Kathleen Wilson (ed.), *A New Imperial History: Culture, Identity, and Modernity in Britain and the Empire, 1660–1840* (Cambridge, 2004); David Armitage and Michael Braddick (eds), *The British Atlantic World, 1500–1800* (Basingstoke, 2002); Martin Daunton and Rick Halpern (eds), *Empire and Others: British Encounters with Indigenous Peoples 1600–1850* (Philadelphia, 1999); and the work of Linda Colley, Matthew Edney, Michael Fisher, Beth Fowkes, Eliga Gould, Maya Jasanoff, Jonathan Lamb, Felicity Nussbaum, Markus Rediker, Joseph Roach, Nicholas Rogers, Sudipta Sen, Kate Teltscher, James Walvin.

11. Eric Hinderaker, 'The "Four Indian Kings" and the Imaginative Construction of the First British Empire', *William & Mary Quarterly*, 3rd ser., 53:3 (1996), 487–526, at 487; Colley, *Captives*; Stone (ed.), *Imperial State at War*, esp. the chap. by Wilson.

12. John E. Crowley, 'A Visual Empire: Seeing the British Atlantic World from a Global British Perspective', in Elizabeth Mancke and Carole Shammas (eds), *The Creation of the British Atlantic World* (Baltimore, 2005), 283–303. For centripetal trends in the empire see below the section on India.

13. Richard H. Drayton, *Nature's Government: Science, Imperial Britain, and the 'Improvement' of the World* (New Haven, Conn./London, 2000); Sidney W. Mintz, *Sweetness and Power: The Place of Sugar in Modern History* (Harmondsworth, 1985); James Walvin, *Fruits of Empire: Exotic Produce and British Taste, 1660–1800* (Basingstoke, 1997); Kathleen Wilson, 'The Good, the Bad, and the Impotent: Imperialism and the Politics of Identity in Georgian England', in Ann Bermingham and John Brewer (eds), *The Consumption of Culture, 1600–1800: Image, Object, Text* (London/New York, 1995), 237–62; Troy O. Bickham, '"A conviction of the reality of things": Material Culture, North American Indians and Empire in Eighteenth-Century Britain', *Eighteenth-Century Studies*, 39:1 (2005), 29–47.

14. Ogborn, *Spaces*, ch. 4, esp. 142–7; Kathleen Wilson, *The Sense of the People: Politics, Culture and Imperialism in England, 1715–1785* (Cambridge, 1995); Jeremy Osborn, 'India and the East India Company in the Public Sphere of Eighteenth-Century Britain', in Huw Bowen, Margarette Lincoln, and Nigel Rigby (eds), *The Worlds of the East India Company* (Woodbridge, 2002), 201–21; Brian Allen, *Francis Hayman* (New Haven, Conn./London, 1987), 66–70.

15. Neil Ramsey, 'Horrid Scenes and Marvellous Sights: The Citizen-Soldier and Sir Robert Ker Porter's Spectacle of War', in *Romanticism on the Net*, 46 (2007), 'Romantic Spectacle', guest-edited by John Halliwell and Ian Haywood: http://id.erudit.org/iderudit/016132ar [accessed 1 Aug. 2008]. The following year, Porter showed the Battle of Alexandria between Napoleon's and Britain's forces. The best brief accounts of Seringapatam art and trophies include Maya Jasanoff, *Edge of Empire: Conquest and Collecting in the East, 1750–1850* (London, 2005), 154–86, and her 'Collectors of Empire: Objects, Conquests and Imperial Self-Fashioning', *Past & Present*, 184 (2004), 109–35, esp. 123–7.

16. AT I, 195.

17. Andrew McClellan, *Inventing the Louvre: Art, Politics, and the Origins of the Modern Museum in Eighteenth-Century Paris* (Cambridge, 1994), 13–25; James Sheehan, *Museums in the German Art World from the End of the Old Regime to the Rise of Modernism* (Oxford, 2000), 21–41.

18. Although free of charge, in practice, until the early nineteenth century, it was accessible primarily to the social elite, the learned, and those possessing a basic education and decent appearance. See Anne Goldgar, 'The British Museum and the Virtual Representation of Culture in the Eighteenth Century', *Albion*, 32 (2000), 195–231.

19. AT I, 126–7, 129; see also 194–5.

20. NMM/KEI/15/4, Elgin to Keith, 15 June and 9 Sep. 1801, 6 Jan. 1802.

21. For the Anglo-French ballet of cultural patriotism and cosmopolitan exchange see Gerald Newman, *The Rise of English Nationalism: A Cultural History 1740–1830* (London, 1987); Derek Jarrett, *The Begetters of Revolution: England's Involvement with France, 1759–1789* (London, 1973); Jeremy Black, 'Britain and the Continent, 1688–1815: Convergence or Divergence?', *British Journal for Eighteenth-Century Studies*, 15:2 (1992), 145–9; J. H. Shennan, 'The Rise of Patriotism in Eighteenth-Century Europe', *History of European Ideas*, 13 (1991), 689–710; Thomas Schlereth, *The Cosmopolitan Ideal in Enlightenment Thought* (London, 1977).

22. Matthew Craske, *The Silent Rhetoric of the Body: A History of Monumental Sculpture and Commemorative Art in England, 1720–1770* (New Haven, Conn./London, 2008). See also Martin Myrone, *Bodybuilding: Reforming Masculinities in British Art 1750–1810* (New Haven, Conn./London, 2006), on how different social and political groups invested in varied notions of heroic conduct.

23. John Gascoigne, *Science in the Service of Empire: Joseph Banks, the British State and the Uses of Science in the Age of Revolution* (Cambridge, 1998); Drayton, *Nature's Government*.

24. See Andrew J. O'Shaughnessy, *An Empire Divided: The American Revolution and the British Caribbean* (Philadelphia, 2000), fig. 3, p. 16, for a sketch of the statue as 'ordered to be Erected': it shows Beckford accompanied by a strangely despondent seated Britannia leaning on him, her helm and spear discarded, while Beckford is trampling a chained slave underneath his right foot. The fullest discussion of the monument is in Philip Jackson-Ward, *Public Sculpture of the City of London* (Liverpool, 2003), 163–5.

25. Madge Dresser, 'Set in Stone? Statues and Slavery in London', *History Workshop Journal*, 64:1 (2007), 162–99; Maaja A. Stewart, 'Inexhaustible Generosity: The Fictions of Eighteenth-Century British Imperialism in Richard Cumberland's *The West Indian*', *The Eighteenth Century: Theory and Interpretation*, 37:1 (1996), 42–55. Sharpe (1752–1806; statue 1816) and Fox (1749–1806; 1822) are commemorated in Westminster Abbey.

26. AT I, 308, 305.

27. Jasanoff, *Edge of Empire*, 108; Richard H. Davis, *Lives of Indian Images* (Princeton, NJ, 1990), 168–74; *Old Humphry's Walks in London* [London, n.d. (?1804)], 149; David Hughson, *Walks through London*, 2 vols (London, 1817), I, 7–8; John Britton and Augustus Charles Pugin, *Illustrations of the Buildings of London*, 2 vols (London, 1825–8), I, 84–9.

28. AT II, 114.

29. T. C. W. Blanning, *The Culture of Power and the Power of Culture* (Oxford, 2002).

30. P. J. Marshall, *The Making and Unmaking of Empires: Britain, India, and America c.1750–1783* (Oxford, 2005); C. A. Bayly, *Imperial Meridian: The British Empire and the World, 1780–1830* (Harlow/New York, 1989).

31. Terry Eagleton, *The Idea of Culture* (Oxford, 2000), 1; Ulrich Gotter, 'Akkulturation als Methodenproblem der historischen Wissenschaften', in Wolfgang Eßbach (ed.), *wir/ihr/sie: Identität und Alterität in Theorie und Methode* (Würzburg, 2000), 373–406, with full references and bibliography. I am also grateful for conversations with Lawrence E. Klein.

32. My thinking has been influenced by imperial historians such as C. A. Bayly, M. Edney, J. Gascoigne (cf. esp. *Science in the Service of Empire*, 136), and D. M. Peers.

33. Benedict Anderson, *Imagined Communities: Reflections on the Origin and Spread of Nationalism* (London, 1983).

34. Eckhart Hellmuth, 'Towards a Comparative Study of Political Culture: The Cases of Late Eighteenth-Century England and Germany', in Hellmuth (ed.), *The Transformation of Political Culture: England and Germany in the Late Eighteenth Century* (Oxford/New York, 1990), 1–38. Paul K. Monod, 'Painters and Party Politics in

England, 1714–1760', *Eighteenth-Century Studies*, 26 (1993), 367–98, on political frag-
mentation in the early eighteenth century as a constraining context which was partly
responsible for the English failure to produce a lasting tradition of history painting;
Peter Brett, 'Political Dinners in Early Nineteenth-Century Britain: Platform, Meeting
Place and Battleground', *History*, 81 (1996), 527–52. For a review of the political culture
approach and more recent work which combines cultural history with emphasis on
political strategy and relational models of sociability see Suzanne Desan, 'Review
Essay: What's After Political Culture? Recent French Revolutionary Historiography',
French Historical Studies, 23:1 (2000), 163–96.

35. James Sheehan, 'Introduction: Culture and Power During the Long Eighteenth
Century', in Hamish Scott and Brendan Simms (eds), *Cultures of Power in Europe
during the Long Eighteenth Century* (Cambridge, 2007), 1–13. Some historians of
France have influentially, if controversially, highlighted the determining power of lan-
guage, ideologies, and representation, see e.g. Keith Baker, Colin Lucas, and François
Furet (eds), *The French Revolution and the Creation of Modern Political Culture*, 4
vols (Oxford, 1987–93). For recent discussions of the analysis of historical change in
social, cultural, and post-social history see the inaugural issue of *Cultural and Social
History*, 1 (2004); V. E. Bonnell and Lynn Hunt (eds), *Beyond the Cultural Turn: New
Directions in the Study of Society and Culture* (Berkeley, Calif., 1999); M. A. Cabrera,
Postsocial History: An Introduction, trans. Marie McMahon (Lanham, Md/Oxford,
2004); Patrick Joyce (ed.), *The Social in Question: New Bearings in History and the
Social Sciences* (London, 2002); see also the issue of *Journal of Social History*, 37:1
(2003), especially essays by Kocka, Charle, Fass, Smith. Joan W. Scott (ed.), *Schools
of Thought: Twenty-Five Years of Interpretative Social Science* (Princeton, NJ/Oxford,
2001), esp. essay by Sewell. Scholars of British history and culture have begun to
show how the visual and performing arts related in complex ways to political discourses, governmental institutions, and imperial expansion: for various approaches
see John Barrell, *The Political Theory of Painting from Reynolds to Hazlitt: 'The Body of
the Public'* (New Haven, Conn./London, 1986); Holger Hoock, *The King's Artists: The
Royal Academy of Arts and the Politics of British Culture, 1760–1840* (Oxford, 2003);
Andrew Hemingway and William Vaughan (eds), *Art in Bourgeois Society 1790–1850*
(Cambridge, 1998); Kate Newey, 'Reform on the London Stage', in Arthur Burns and
Joanna Innes (eds), *Rethinking the Age of Reform* (Cambridge, 2003), 238–53; William
Weber, 'The 1784 Handel Commemoration as Political Ritual', *Journal of British
Studies*, 28 (1989), 43–69; Robert Travers, *Ideology and Empire in Eighteenth-Century
India: The British in Bengal* (Cambridge, 2007). See also references in the chapters on
America and India below.

36. On international cultural relations see Gascoigne, *Science in the Service of Empire*,
117–18, 162–5; Hoock, *King's Artists*, 109–23; Gavin de Beer, *The Sciences Were Never
at War* (London, 1960); for recent art history see e.g. the work of John Bonehill, Sarah

Monks, and Eleanor Hughes. On war as a cultural phenomenon see also from various disciplinary perspectives Linda Colley, *Britons: Forging the Nation 1707–1837* (New Haven, Conn./London, 1992); Scott H. Myerly, *British Military Spectacle: From the Napoleonic Wars through the Crimea* (Cambridge, Mass., 1996); Gillian Russell, *The Theatres of War: Performance, Politics, and Society, 1793–1815* (Oxford, 1995); Wilson, *Sense of the People*.

37. After Peter Mandler, 'Art in a Cool Climate: The Cultural Policy of the British State in European Context, c. 1780–c. 1850', in T. C. W. Blanning and Hagen Schulze (eds), *Unity and Diversity in European Culture c. 1800 (Proceedings of the British Academy*, vol. 134, 2006), 101–20; T. C. W. Blanning, 'The Commercialization and Sacralization of European Culture in the Nineteenth Century', in Blanning (ed.), *The Oxford History of Modern Europe* (Oxford, 2000), 126–52.

38. George M. Frederickson, 'From Exceptionalism to Variability: Recent Developments in Cross-National Comparative History', in *Journal of American History*, 82:2 (1995), 587–604; Wolfgang Reinhard, *Geschichte der Staatsgewalt: Eine vergleichende Verfassungsgeschichte von den Anfängen bis zur Gegenwart* (Munich, 1999); Heinz-Gerhard Haupt and Jürgen Kocka (eds), *Geschichte und Vergleich: Ansätze und Ergebnisse international vergleichender Geschichtsschreibung* (Frankfurt a.M., 1996).

39. Lawrence and Jeanne F. Stone, *An Open Elite? England, 1540–1880* (Oxford, 1984); John Cannon, *Aristocratic Century: The Peerage of Eighteenth-Century England* (Cambridge, 1984); John Brewer and Eckhart Hellmuth (eds), *Rethinking Leviathan: The Eighteenth-Century State in Britain and Germany* (Oxford, 1999); Roy Porter and Mikulás Teich (eds), *The Industrial Revolution in National Context: Europe and the USA* (Cambridge, 1996); Patrick O'Brien (ed.), *The Industrial Revolutions, vols IV–V: The Industrial Revolution in Europe* (Oxford, 1994); Stanley L. Engerman and Patrick O'Brien, 'The Industrial Revolution in Global Perspective', in Roderick Flout and Paul Johnson (eds), *The Cambridge Economic History of Modern Britain* (Cambridge, 2004), 451–64.

40. Brewer, *Pleasures*, 87–122; Bermingham and Brewer (eds), *Consumption of Culture*; Paul Langford, *A Polite and Commercial People: England 1727–83* (Oxford, 1992), 59–121; David Solkin, *Painting for Money: The Visual Arts and the Public Sphere in Eighteenth-Century England* (New Haven, Conn./London, 1993); Neil McKendrick, John Brewer, and J. H. Plumb, *The Birth of a Consumer Society: The Commercialization of Eighteenth-Century England* (London, 1982); John Seed, 'Commerce and the Liberal Arts: The Political Economy of Art in Manchester, 1775–1860', in Janet Wolff and John Seed (eds), *The Culture of Capital: Art, Power and the Nineteenth-Century Middle Class* (Manchester, 1988), 45–81; Geoffrey Clark, 'Commerce, Culture, and the Rise of English Power', *Historical Journal*, 49:4 (2006), 1239–51.

41. Dena Goodman, 'Introduction: The Public and the Nation', *Eighteenth-Century Studies*, 29:1 (1995), 1–4; James Van Horn Melton, *The Rise of the Public in Enlightenment Europe* (Cambridge, 2001), 274.
42. Jonathan White, 'A World of Goods? The "Consumption Turn" and Eighteenth-Century British History', *Cultural and Social History*, 3 (2006), 93–104, for concerns about the consumption turn displacing the focus on power, structure, and agency in social history.
43. Brewer, *Pleasures*; Mandler, 'Art in a Cool Climate'; Janet Minihan, *The Nationalization of Culture: The Development of State Subsidies to the Arts in Great Britain* (New York, 1977), 28, *passim*.
44. T. C. W. Blanning, *The Pursuit of Glory: The Five Revolutions That Made Modern Europe 1648–1815* (New York, 2007), 433–4.
45. Gascoigne, *Science in the Service of Empire*; Drayton, *Nature's Government*; D. MacKay, *In the Wake of Cook: Exploration, Science, and Imperialism* (London, 1985); Robert A. Stafford, *Scientist of Empire: Sir Roderick Murchison, Scientific Exploration and Victorian Imperialism* (Cambridge/New York, 1989); Stafford, 'Scientific Exploration and Empire', in Andrew Porter (ed.), *OHBE, vol. III*, 294–319; Fergus Fleming, *Barrow's Boys* (London, 1998); Charles W. J. Withers, *Geography, Science and National Identity: Scotland since 1520* (Cambridge, 2001); Martin J. S. Rudwick, *Lyell and Darwin, Geologists: Studies in the Earth Sciences in the Age of Reform* (Aldershot, 2005), and the author's wider oeuvre in the history of science. See also the discussion on science in British India, below, 'Empire, Culture, Knowledge'. For examples of the Royal Society advising government see James E. McClellan III, *Science Reorganized: Scientific Societies in the Eighteenth Century* (New York, 1985), 15–16, 26, 29–34; cf. Julian Hoppit, 'Reforming Britain's Weights and Measures, 1660–1824', *English Historical Review*, 108 (1993), 82–104, at 98–100; Richard Sorrenson, 'The State's Demand for Accurate Astronomical and Navigational Instruments in Eighteenth-Century Britain', in Bermingham and Brewer (eds), *Consumption of Culture*, 263–71.
46. Mandler, 'Art in a Cool Climate'. See also below, 'Conclusions: Cultural Politics, State, War, and Empire'.
47. Municipal cultural patronage is a field in need of further investigation. Starting points include Peter Borsay, *The English Urban Renaissance: Culture and Society in the Provincial Town, 1660–1770* (Oxford, 1989); Christopher Chalklin, *The Rise of the English Town, 1650–1850* (Cambridge, 2001); Louise Purbrick, 'The Bourgeois Body: Civic Portraiture, Public Men and the Appearance of Class Power in Manchester, 1838–50', in Alan Kidd and David Nicholls (eds), *Gender, Civic Culture, and Consumerism: Middle-Class Identity in Britain, 1800–1940* (Manchester, 1999), 81–98.
48. Recent assessments include Brewer, *Pleasures*; Blanning, *Culture of Power*, ch. 7; Mandler, 'Art in a Cool Climate'. Hannah Greig's work in progress on 'Institutional

Consumption: A Material History of the Eighteenth-Century British Royal Courts, 1688–1830', considers the court's relationships to suppliers and manufacturers.

49. Although I consider some private monuments in churches, there is no space to explore systematically the church and churches, including regimental churches, as patrons or sites of culture. See Jeremy Gregory, 'Anglicanism and the Arts: Religion, Culture and Politics in the Eighteenth Century', in Jeremy Black and Jeremy Gregory (eds), *Culture, Politics and Society in Britain, 1660–1800* (Manchester, 1991), 82–109; Derek Keene, Arthur Burns, and Andrew Saint (eds), *St Paul's: The Cathedral Church of London 604–2004* (New Haven, Conn./London, 2004), esp. ch. by Aston; Clare Haynes, *Pictures and Popery: Art and Religion in England, 1660–1760* (Aldershot, 2006).

50. The radical MP John Wilkes failed, however, to persuade the Commons to purchase Sir Robert Walpole's art collections in 1777; they went instead to Russia's Catherine the Great: J. G. W. Conlin, 'High Art and Low Politics: A New Perspective on John Wilkes', *Huntington Library Quarterly*, 64 (2001), 357–81; Andrew Moore (ed.), *Houghton Hall: The Prime Minister, the Empress, and the Heritage* (London, 1996).

51. Richard Price, *British Society, 1680–1880: Dynamism, Containment, and Change* (Cambridge, 1999), 195; Peter Clark, *British Clubs and Societies, 1580–1800: The Origins of an Associational World* (Oxford, 2000); R. J. Morris, 'Voluntary Societies and British Urban Elites, 1780–1850', *Historical Journal*, 26:1 (1983), 95–118; Kathleen Wilson, 'Urban Culture and Political Activism in Hanoverian England', in Hellmuth (ed.), *Transformation of Political Culture*, 165–84; cf. the editor's introductory discussion of the English voluntarist tradition of organising public projects on a non-governmental basis, p. 16.

52. Holger Hoock, 'Reforming Culture: National Art Institutions in the Age of Reform', in Burns and Innes (eds), *Rethinking the Age of Reform*, 254–70. For the idea that only the male educated few could acquire taste gradually yielded first to the notion of a virtual representation of culture, which allowed the nation at large to benefit indirectly through the use of national collections by the social and intellectual elites, see Goldgar, 'British Museum'.

53. For collections as extensions of their owners' identities, as semiotics, and as social messages, see, respectively, Werner Muensterberger, *Collecting: An Unruly Passion* (Princeton, NJ, 1994); Jean Baudrillard, 'The System of Collecting', in John Elsner and Roger Cardinal (eds), *The Cultures of Collecting* (Cambridge, Mass., 1994), 7–24; Arjun Appadurai (ed.), *The Social Life of Things: Commodities in Cultural Perspective* (Cambridge, 1986). Pierre Bourdieu, *Distinction: A Social Critique of the Judgement of Taste* (London, 1984), on socio-cultural capital.

54. The binary terms of Edward W. Said's classic *Orientalism* (London, 1978) have been modified to accept a degree of Asian and African agency in self-representation by Said, *Culture and Imperialism* (New York, 1993), xxiv–xxvi; see also Kathleen Wilson,

The Island Race: Englishness, Empire, and Gender in the Eighteenth Century (London, 2002), 4–5. The quotation is from Douglas M. Peers, 'Colonial Knowledge and the Military in India, 1780–1860', *Journal of Imperial and Commonwealth History*, 33 (2005), 157–80, at 161. See also Gyan Prakash, 'Writing Post-Orientalist Histories of the Third World: Perspectives from Indian Historiography', *Comparative Studies in Society and History*, 32:2 (1990), 383–408. John M. MacKenzie, *Orientalism: History, Theory and the Arts* (Manchester/New York, 1995), explores how Western approaches to the Orient were more ambiguous and interactive, with much hybridity and respect for the Orient; see also his 'Edward Said and the Historians', *Nineteenth-Century Contexts*, 18 (1994), 9–25. D. A. Washbrook, 'Orients and Occidents: Colonial Discourse Theory and the Historiography of the British Empire', in Robert W. Winks (ed.), *OHBE, vol. V*, 596–611.

55. Works which address this period in terms of different and related themes include Jasanoff, *Edge of Empire*; Michael W. McCahill, 'Peerage Creations and the Changing Character of the British Nobility, 1750–1850', *English Historical Review*, 96 (1981), 259–84; Deborah Rohr, *The Careers of British Musicians, 1750–1850: A Profession of Artisans* (Cambridge, 2001); Allan Blackstock and Eoin Magennis (eds), *Politics and Political Culture in Britain and Ireland, 1750–1850: Essays in Tribute to Peter Jupp* (Belfast, 2007); Raj S. Amit, *Rule of Sympathy: Sentiment, Race, and Power, 1750–1850* (Basingstoke, 2002); Laurence W. B. Brockliss and David Eastwood (eds), *A Union of Multiple Identities: The British Isles, 1750–1850* (Manchester/New York, 1997); Daniel O'Quinn, *Staging Governance: Theatrical Imperialism in London, 1770–1800* (Baltimore, Md, 2005).

Prelude. London, Autumn 1761

1. Edward Muir, *Ritual in Early Modern Europe* (Cambridge, 1997), 1–7; Max Weber, *Theory of Social and Economic Organization*, ed. with an introduction by Talcott Parsons (New York, 1997).
2. Unless otherwise referenced, my account of the coronation is based on: TNA, WORK 21/1; PC 1/15/20; LC 2/30/1; LC 2/32; *The Form and Order of the Service that is to be performed, and of the ceremonies that are to be observed, in the Coronation of their Majesties King George III. and Queen Charlotte* (London, 1761); *Annual Register ... for 1761* (London, 1762), 201–29; Claude Blair (ed.), *The Crown Jewels: The History of the Coronation Regalia in the Jewel House of the Tower of London*, 2 vols (London, 1998), I; Donald Burrows, *Handel and the English Chapel Royal* (Oxford, 2006), 265–8. Hickey's account is in Alfred Spencer (ed.), *Memoirs of William Hickey*, 4 vols (London, 1913–25), III, 30–33.
3. Jonathan Marsden, 'George III's State Coach in Context', in Marsden (ed.), *The Wisdom of George the Third* (London, 2005), 43–59.

4. BL, Add. MS 32684, fo. 121 [draft, George].

5. Quoted in D. J. Greene (ed.), *The Yale Edition of the Works of Samuel Johnson*, 14 vols (New Haven, Conn./London, 1977), X: *Political Writings*, 290.

6. NMM/MS 52/061, Capt. William Owen, *Narrative [of his] Voyages and Travels: Part 2: 20 July 1761–17 June 1771*, entry for 22 Sep. 1761.

7. Quoted in George S. Rousseau, "'This Grand and Sacred Solemnity ...': Of Coronations, Republics, and Poetry', *British Journal for Eighteenth-Century Studies*, 5 (1982), 1–19, at 10.

8. *London Chronicle*, 12–15, 15–17 Sep. 1761.

9. Paget Toynbee and Leonard Whibley (eds), *Correspondence of Thomas Gray*, 3 vols (Oxford, 1935), II, 755, Thomas Gray to Rev. James Brown, 24 Sep. 1761.

10. Mrs Vernon D. Broughton, *Court and Private Life in the Time of Queen Charlotte, being the Journals of Mrs Papendiek, Assistant Keeper of the Wardrobe and Reader to Her Majesty*, 2 vols (London, 1887), I, 18; Elizabeth Percy, Duchess of Northumberland, *The Diaries of a Duchess: Extracts from the Diaries of the First Duchess of Northumberland, 1716–1776. Edited by James Greig* (London, 1926), 36 (22 Sep. 1761).

11. Judy Rudoe, 'Queen Charlotte's Jewellery: Reconstructing a Lost Collection', in Marsden (ed.), *Wisdom of George the Third*, 179–215, at 184.

12. Horace Walpole to Horace Mann, 10 Sep. 1761, in W. S. Lewis (ed.), *Horace Walpole's Correspondence with Sir Horace Mann*, V (New Haven, Conn., 1960), 528–32, at 529.

13. *The Coronation: A Poem, Humbly Addressed to Nobody who was There, by a Spectator* (London, 1761), 13.

14. *New-York Gazette*, 23 Nov. 1761, 2.

15. Samuel Johnson, 'Thoughts on the Coronation (1761)', in Greene (ed.), *Works of Samuel Johnson*, x, 292–300, at 300.

16. Robert Hay Drummond, *A Sermon Preached at the Coronation of King George III and Queen Charlotte: in the Abbey Church of Westminster, September 22, 1761*, 2nd edn (London, 1761), quotations 8, 9, 10, 16, 20.

17. TNA, WORK 21/1/12v.

18. Count Frederick Kielmansegge, *Diary of a Journey to England in the Years 1761–1762*, trans. Countess Kielmansegge (London, 1902), 30.

19. Lewis (ed.), *Horace Walpole's Correspondence with Sir Horace Mann*, Horace Walpole to Horace Mann, 28 Sep. 1761, vol. V, 534–7, at 535; Toynbee and Whibley (eds), *Correspondence of Thomas Gray*, II, 757, Thomas Gray to Rev. James Brown, 24 Sep. 1761.

20. Secker to Boyce, 14 Aug. 1761, Lambeth Palace Library, MSS 1130/I fo. 80, and Secker, memorandum fo. 173, quoted in Jeremy Black, *George III: America's Last King* (New Haven, Conn./London, 2006), 49 with n. 22.

21. Hannah Smith, *Georgian Monarchy: Politics and Culture, 1714–1760* (Cambridge, 2006), 100.

22. Horace Walpole to the Hon. H. S. Conway, 25 Sep. 1761, in W. S. Lewis (ed.), *Horace Walpole's Correspondence with H. S. Conway,* vol. II (New Haven, Conn., 1974), 119–24, at 121–2.

23. *London Magazine,* 30 (Aug. 1761), 398.

24. *Annual Register* (1762), 233; Toynbee and Whibley, *Correspondence of Thomas Gray,* II, 755, Thomas Gray to Rev. James Brown, 24 Sep. 1761.

25. John Wootton, *King George II at the Battle of Dettingen* (1743), oil on canvas, 145.8 × 163.3 cm, National Army Museum.

26. Horace Walpole to George Montague, 24 Sep. 1761, in W. S. Lewis and Ralph S. Brown (eds), *Horace Walpole's Correspondence with George Montague* (New Haven, Conn., 1941), 386–90, at 387.

27. A letter by James Heming published in *Annual Register* (1762), 229–35, reveals the lack of organisation for the banquet. See also Rousseau, '"This Grand and Sacred Solemnity"', 9.

28. Quoted in Rousseau, '"This Grand and Sacred Solemnity"', 10. See also S. D. Kennedy, 'The Accession and Early Years of George III', *Quarterly Review,* 298 (1960), 435–42.

29. Toynbee and Whibley, *Correspondence of Thomas Gray,* II, 757, Thomas Gray to the Rev. James Brown, 24 Sep. 1761.

30. TNA, LC 5/9/1761.

31. G. A. Tressider, 'Coronation Day Celebrations in English Towns, 1685–1821: Elite Hegemony and Local Relations on a Ceremonial Occasion', *British Journal for Eighteenth-Century Studies,* 15 (1992), 1–16; [Mrs. Elizabeth Thomas], *A Dramatick Pastoral, Occasioned by the Collection at Gloucester on the Coronation Day, for Portioning Young Women of Virtuous Character. By a Lady* (Gloucester, 1762); *London Chronicle,* 10–12 and 26–29 Sep. 1761.

32. *London Chronicle,* 26–29 Sep. 1761.

33. BL, Add. MS 28855, Standing Orders for the Campaigns 1760–61, fos 61–2 (quotation 62), Camp at Wilhelmsdahl, 21 Sep. 1761; *London Chronicle,* 8–10 Oct. 1761.

34. See e.g. *Boston Gazette,* 23 Nov. and 7 Dec. 1761, *New-York Gazette,* 23 and 30 Nov. 1761.

35. Alastair Smart, *Allan Ramsay: Painter, Essayist and Man of the Enlightenment* (New Haven, Conn./London, 1992), 161–6; Alastair Smart, *Allan Ramsay: A Complete Catalogue of His Paintings,* ed. John Ingamells (New Haven, Conn./London, 1999), 111–12; the following pages catalogue several dozen dated copies.

36. *Et spes & ratio Studiorum in Caesare tantum,* Charles Grignion after William Hogarth, frontispiece to *A Catalogue of the Pictures, Sculptures, Models, Drawings, Prints, &c. Exhibited by the Society of Artists of Great Britain,* 1761, etching and engraving. For reproductions see Matthew Hargraves, *'Candidates for Fame': The Society of Artists of Great Britain 1760-1791* (New Haven, Conn./London, 2005), 31–3.

37. Kim Rorschach, 'Frederick, Prince of Wales (1707–51) as a Patron of the Visual Arts: Princely Patriotism and Political Propaganda', unpubl. Ph.D. thesis (Yale, 1985); Francis Vivian, *A Life of Frederick, Prince of Wales, 1707–1751: Connoisseur of the Arts*, ed. Roger White (Lewiston, NY, 2006). For Prince George's education, the king's concern with design, architecture, the hanging of paintings, and collecting, and his involvement with the Royal Academy see Hoock, *King's Artists*, 136–45; David Watkin, 'George III: Enlightened Monarch?', in Marsden (ed.), *Wisdom of George the Third*, 331–46; Watkin, *The Architect King: George III and the Culture of the Enlightenment* (London, 2004).
38. The quotations after Paul Sawyer, 'Processions and Coronations on the London Stage, 1727–61', *Theatre Notebook*, 14:1 (1959), 7–12, at 11–12.
39. Samuel Foote, *The Orators*, new edn (London, 1808, 1st edn 1762), 4.

I. War, Art, and Commemoration
America

1. BL, Eg. 2672, Peter Oliver, 'Journal of a Voyage to England in 1776, and of a Tour through Part of England', 2 vols, 1776–80, entry for Westminster Abbey visit on 21 June 1777, fos 335–6.
2. John Mazzinghy, *The New and Universal Guide through the Cities of London and Westminster, The Borough of Southwark, and Parts Adjacent* (London, 1785), 196.
3. Pierre-Jean Grosley, *A Tour to London, or New Observations on England and its Inhabitants … trsl. from the French by Thomas Nugent*, 2 vols (London, 1772), I, 205.
4. Maurice Halbwachs, *On Collective Memory*, ed., trans., and with an introduction by Lewis A. Coser (Chicago/London, 1992); Daniel Woolf, 'Memory and Historical Culture in Early Modern England', *Journal of the Canadian Historical Association*, 2:1 (1991), 283–308; Barry Schwarz, 'The Social Context of Commemoration: A Study in Collective Memory', *Social Forces*, 61 (1982), 374–402, at 377; Michael Schudson, 'Dynamics of Distortion in Collective Memory', in Daniel L. Schacter (ed.), *Memory Distortion: How Minds, Brains, and Societies Reconstruct the Past* (Cambridge, Mass./London, 1989), 346–64; Alon Confino, 'Collective Memory and Cultural History: Problems of Method', *American Historical Review,* 102:5 (1997), 1386–1403; Marius Kwint, Christopher Breward, Jeremy Aynsley (eds), *Material Memories: Design and Evocation* (Oxford, 1999).
5. Marius Kwint, 'Introduction: The Physical Past', in Kwint, Breward, Aynsley (eds), *Material Memories*, 1–16, esp. 2–3, with references to insights from neurophysiology. The distinctions between communicative and cultural memory are best developed in Jan Assmann, *Das kulturelle Gedächtnis: Schrift, Erinnerung und politische Identität in frühen Hochkulturen*, 6th edn. (Munich, 2007); Aleida Assmann, *Erinnerungsräume: Formen und Wandlungen des kulturellen Gedächtnisses,* 3rd edn (Munich, 2006).

6. Jean A. Rouquet, *The Present State of the Arts in England* (London, 1755), 64. For this section see David Bindman and Malcolm Baker, *Roubiliac and the Eighteenth-Century Monument* (New Haven, Conn./London, 1995); Matthew Craske, 'Making National Heroes? A Survey of the Social and Political Functions and Meanings of Major British Funeral Monuments to Naval and Military Figures, 1730–70', in John Bonehill and Geoff Quilley (eds), *Conflicting Visions: War and Visual Culture in Britain and France* (Aldershot, 2005), 41–60.

7. The fact that Vernon had held a Westminster seat partially explains his commemoration in the Abbey near the monuments of Admirals Wager and Warren, two ministerial Westminster MPs.

8. *London Chronicle*, 4–6 May 1759.

9. *Old England*, 22 Dec. 1750; *Royal Magazine*, 4 (1761), 66.

10. The monument was proposed by a triumvirate formed by the Tory Thomas Carew, George Lyttleton, one of Cobham's Cubs, and James E. Oglethorpe, a former Jacobite who had been honourably acquitted in a court-martial in the wake of the '45, and was classed as a government supporter in 1747. *Parliamentary History*, 14, cols 61–3 (HC, 28 May 1747); *HC Journals*, vol. 25, p. 397 (28 May 1747); H. W. Richmond, *The Navy in the War of 1739–48*, 3 vols (Cambridge, 1920), I, 163–8, II, 1–57; P. A. Luff, 'Mathews v. Lestock: Parliament, Politics and the Navy in Mid-Eighteenth-Century England', *Parliamentary History*, 10 (1991), 45–62. The palm and laurel sprig rising from the stony ground possibly refer to the failure of the rear to support Cornewall's *Marlborough*. Douglas Fordham, 'Raising Standards: Art and Imperial Politics in London, 1745–1776', unpubl. Ph.D. thesis (Yale, 2003), 140. Malcolm Baker, 'Rococo Styles in Eighteenth-Century Sculpture', in Michael Snodin (ed.), *Rococo: Art and Design in Hogarth's England* (London, 1984), cat. no. S.21.

11. BL, OIOC, East India Company, Court Book 72, p. 77; Miscellaneous Letters Received E/1/45, 1763 No. 8. Watson was buried in St John's, Calcutta, in a tomb crowned with a tall painted obelisk: Walter K. Firminger, *Thacker's Guide to Calcutta* (Calcutta, 1906), 137. For the London monument see also Craske, 'Making National Heroes?', 47; *London Chronicle* (1–21 June 1763), 586; Ingrid Roscoe, 'James Athenian Stuart and the Scheemakers Family', *Apollo*, 126 (1987), 178–84.

12. Pierre-Jean Grosley, *A Tour to London, or New Observations on England and its Inhabitants, trsl. from the French by Thomas Nugent*, 2 vols (London, 1772), II, 111.

13. Quoted in Craske, 'Making National Heroes?', 49.

14. Joan Coutu, 'Legitimating the British Empire: The Monument to General Wolfe in Westminster Abbey', in Bonehill and Quilley (eds), *Conflicting Visions*, 61–83; Craske, 'Making National Heroes?', 49–51.

15. Matthew Craske, *The Silent Rhetoric of the Body: A History of Monumental Sculpture and Commemorative Art in England, 1720–1770* (New Haven, Conn./London, 2008), 33–5.

16. Jeremy Black, *George III: America's Last King* (New Haven, Conn./London, 2006), ch. 11; Jack P. Greene, 'Empire and Identity from the Glorious Revolution to the American Revolution', in P. J. Marshall (ed.), *OHBE, vol. II: Eighteenth Century* (Oxford/New York, 1998–9), 208–30; Eliga H. Gould, *The Persistence of Empire: British Political Culture in the Age of the American Revolution* (Chapel Hill, NC, 2000), ch. 4; Stephen Conway, *The British Isles and the American War of Independence* (Oxford, 2000); G. M. Ditchfield, *George III: An Essay in Monarchy* (London, 2002), ch. 5.
17. Stella Tillyard, *A Royal Affair: George III and His Troublesome Siblings* (London, 2006), 314–15. The quotation in a letter from George to Lord Dartmouth, 10 June 1775, in Black, *George III*, 220.
18. Bonamy Dobrée (ed.), *The Letters of King George III* (London, 1935, repr. 1968), 170–71, quotations 171.
19. For celebrations of British victories see Stephen Conway, '"A joy unknown for years past": The American War, Britishness and the Celebration of Rodney's Victory at the Saints', *History*, 86 (2001), 180–99, at 187, 191 n. 71.
20. Troy O. Bickham, 'Sympathizing with Sedition? George Washington, the British Press, and British Attitudes during the American War of Independence', *William & Mary Quarterly*, 59:1 (2002), 101–22; Stephen Conway, 'From Fellow-Nationals to Foreigners: British Perceptions of the Americans, circa 1739–1783', ibid., 65–100; Conway, *British Isles*, ch. 5; Eliga H. Gould, 'A Virtual Nation: Greater Britain and the Imperial Legacy of the American Revolution', *American Historical Review*, 104 (1999), 476–89, at 480.
21. See Mark S. Phillips's forthcoming book with Yale, *"To Make the Distant Near": Distance and Historical Representation* (working title). John Bonehill, 'Exhibiting War: John Singleton Copley's *The Siege of Gibraltar* and the Staging of History', in Bonehill and Quilley (eds), *Conflicting Visions*, 139–68.

Chapter One: The Art of Remembering and Forgetting

1. Anon., *The Propriety of Retaining Gibraltar Impartially Considered* (London, 1783), iv–v.
2. See Dror Wahrman, *The Making of the Modern Self: Identity and Culture in Eighteenth-Century England* (New Haven, Conn./London, 2004), 262–3, citing David Armitage on post-war British 'imperial amnesia'.
3. *Weyman's New York Gazette*, 30 June 1766.
4. William H. W. Sabine (ed.), *Historical Memoirs from 16 March 1763 to 9 July 1776 of William Smith* (New York, 1956), 32–3. For 'royal America', the monarchical, Protestant, imperial political culture of eighteenth-century colonial America up to the 1770s, see Brendan McConville, *The King's Three Faces: The Rise and Fall of Royal America, 1688–1776* (Chapel Hill, NC, 2006).

5. *New York Gazette & Weekly Mercury*, 4 June 1770; Alfred F. Young, *The Shoemaker and the Tea Party* (Boston, 1999), 94–5; Lt-Gov. Cadwallader Colden to the Earl of Hillsborough, 18 Aug. 1770, in E. B. O'Callaghan (ed.), *Documents Relative to the Colonial History of the State of New-York*, 10 vols (Albany, 1857), VIII, 245; Isaac N. Phelps Stokes, *The Iconography of Manhattan Island 1498–1909: Compiled from Original Sources and Illustrated by Photo-Intaglio Reproductions of Important Maps, Plans, Views and Documents*, 6 vols (New York, 1915–28), IV, 813; *New York Journal* or *The General Advertiser*, 23 Aug. 1770.
6. *New York Gazette* or *The Weekly Post Boy*, 10 Sep. 1770.
7. *Morning Chronicle*, 4 Feb. 1775.
8. McConville, *King's Three Faces*, 288–306.
9. Quoted in George F. Scheer and Hugh F. Rankin, *Rebels and Redcoats* (New York, 1957), 166.
10. *New York Gazette*, 22 July 1776; cf. Edward Bangs (ed.), *Journal of Lieutenant Isaac Bangs* (Cambridge, Mass., 1890), entry for 9 July 1776.
11. After the previous break with Parliament, a break with the monarch was required to complete the transfer of political legitimacy in a political culture in which loyalty to the sovereign was such a powerful force. See Jerrilyn Greene Marston, *King and Congress: The Transfer of Political Legitimacy, 1774–1776* (Princeton, NJ, 1987).
12. Wilton would have seen the original in Rome in the 1750s, and been familiar with many derivatives such as Scheemaker's statue of William III at Hull (1734).
13. Capt. John Montressor, quoted in Stokes, *Iconography*, V, 992.
14. Dennis P. Ryan (ed.), *A Salute to Courage: The American Revolution as Seen Through Wartime Writings of Officers of the Continental Army and Navy* (New York, 1979), 33: Orderly book of Major Phineas Porter (1739–1804), entry for 10 July 1776.
15. Quoted in Frank Moore, *Diary of the American Revolution 1775–1781*, abridged, edited, and with an Introduction by John Anthony Scott (New York, 1967), 132.
16. Winthrop D. Jordan, 'Familial Politics: Thomas Paine and the Killing of the King, 1776', *Journal of American History*, 60:2 (1973), 294–308, at 307, quoting *New-England Chronicle*, 18 July 1776, *Maryland Gazette*, 25 July 1776. See also Moore, *Diary*, 132, for *Pennsylvania Journal*, 17 July 1776. The lines from *Paradise Lost* were printed in *Virginia Gazette*, 29 July 1776.
17. Bangs (ed.), *Journal*, entry for 10 July 1776.
18. For examples of removal and destruction see *Constitutional Gazette*, 17 July 1776, quoted in Moore, *Diary*, 130; Charles D. Deshler, 'How the Declaration Was Received in the Old Thirteen', *Harper's New Monthly Magazine*, 85 (July 1892), 165–87, at 166–7, 172; Richard L. Bushman, *King and People in Provincial Massachusetts* (Chapel Hill, NC/London, 1985), 225; *Pennsylvania Journal*, 28 Aug. 1776, quoted in Larry R. Gerlach, *New Jersey in the American Revolution 1763–1783: A Documentary History* (Trenton, NJ, 1975), 225. Occasionally, royal arms were removed quietly for safety,

for instance in the Province House at Hartford, Connecticut, or escaped destruction, especially in some churches, or travelled with their loyalist protectors into exile in New Brunswick and elsewhere: Edmund Slafter, 'Royal Memorials and Emblems in Use in the Colonies before the Revolution', *Massachusetts Historical Society*, 2nd ser., 4 (1887–9), 239–65, at 254–60.

19. Boston: Jordan, 'Familial Politics', 306–8 with further references; *New York Gazette and the Weekly Mercury*, 12 Aug. 1776; *Connecticut Gazette*, 25 Oct. 1776; quotation from William Pynchon Journal in Slafter, 'Royal Memorials', 253 n. 2. Huntington: David Waldstreicher, *In the Midst of Perpetual Fetes: The Making of American Nationalism, 1776–1820* (Chapel Hill, NC/London, 1997), 31. The quotation about Dover in Deshler, 'How the Declaration Was Received', 170. Savannah: *Connecticut Gazette*, 8 Oct. 1776, quoted in Moore, *Diary*, 141–2. See also for Baltimore: Waldstreicher, *Perpetual Fetes*, 31, n. 21, and ibid., p. 25, for mock funerals of stamp distributors. For pre-revolutionary violence see also Gary B. Nash, *The Unknown American Revolution: The Unruly Birth of Democracy and the Struggle to Create America* (London, 2006), esp. chs. 3, 4; Wayne Lee, *Crowds and Soldiers in Revolutionary North Carolina: The Culture of Violence in Riot and War* (Gainesville, Fl., 2001).

20. For the following see Stokes, *Iconography*, V, 992; Susan E. Lyman, 'The Search for a Missing King', *American Heritage Magazine* (1958): http://www.americanheritage.com/articles/magazine/ah/1958/5/1958_5_62.shtml [accessed 13 Mar. 2006].

21. Quoted in A. J. Wall, 'The Statues of King George III and the Honorable William Pitt Erected in New York City 1770', *New York Historical Society Quarterly Bulletin*, 4 (1920), 36–57, at 52.

22. P. O. Hutchinson (ed.), *The Diary and Letters of His Excellency Thomas Hutchinson*, 2 vols (London, 1883–6), II, 167, entry for 22 Nov. 1777.

23. *Pennsylvania Ledger*, 20 July 1776, p. 2. See also *New York Gazette and Weekly Mercury*, 15 July 1776, p. 2. The spicy reference is to a House of Commons speech: a peppercorn in acknowledgement of Britain's right to tax America was more important than millions without it.

24. Ebenezer Hazard to Gen. Gates, 12 July 1776, quoted in Stokes, *Iconography*, V, 992.

25. Julie Spraggon, *Puritan Iconoclasm during the English Civil War* (Woodbridge, 2003), 81, 209–10, 238–9, 262–3; Hannah Smith, *Georgian Monarchy: Politics and Culture, 1714–1760* (Cambridge, 2006), 127. Louis XV's statue, the subject of satiric graffiti from its erection, during the French Revolution was toppled along with that of Louis XIV on Place Vendôme.

26. For the culture of popular opposition before and during the war, including effigy burning, tarring and feathering, large processions, liberty trees and poles, see Young, *Shoemaker*, 92–8; Nash, *Unknown American Revolution*.

27. Waldstreicher, *Perpetual Fetes*, 26–7.

28. Arthur S. Marks, 'The Statue of King George III in New York and the Iconology of Regicide', *American Art Journal*, 13:3 (1981), 61–82, at 70. Modern acts of iconoclasm are also helpfully conceptualised in Dario Gamboni, *The Destruction of Art: Iconoclasm and Vandalism since the French Revolution* (London, 1997).

29. Harriet I. Flower, 'Rethinking "Damnatio Memoriae": The Case of Cn. Calpurnius Piso pater in AD 20', *Classical Antiquity*, 17:2 (1998), 155–86; E. R. Varner (ed.), *From Caligula to Constantine: Tyranny and Transformation in Roman Portraiture* (Atlanta, 2000), esp. the essays by Flower on 'Damnatio Memoriae and Epigraphy', 58–69, and Varner, 'Tyranny and the Transformation of the Roman Visual Landscape', 9–26; Friedrich Vittinghoff, *Der Staatsfeind in der Römischen Kaiserzeit: Untersuchungen zur 'damnatio memoriae'* (Berlin, 1936), 13, 64–74; M. Kajava, 'Some Remarks on the Erasure of Inscriptions in the Roman World (with Special Reference to the Case of Cn. Piso, cos 7 B.C.)', in Heikki Solin et al. (eds), *Acta Colloquini Epigraphici Latini. Helsingiae 3–6. Sept.* (Helsinki, 1995), 201–10.

30. Flower, 'Rethinking "Damnatio Memoriae"', 180.

31. Wolfgang Sofsky, *Traktat über die Gewalt*, 2nd edn (Frankfurt a. M., 1996), 198.

32. John Mack, *The Museum of the Mind* (London, 2003), 116; Flower, 'Damnatio Memoriae and Epigraphy', 59; Kajava, 'Some Remarks on the Erasure', 202–3.

33. [Mackenzie], *Diary of Frederick Mackenzie*, 2 vols (Cambridge, Mass., 1930), II, 535; William H. W. Sabine (ed.), *The New-York Diary of Jabez Fitch of the 17th, Connecticut, Regiment from August 22, 1776 to December 15, 1777* (New York, 1954), 102–3, 229; Marvin L. Brown (trans.), *Journal and Correspondence of a Tour of Duty: Baroness von Riedesel and the American Revolution* (Williamsburg, Va, 1965); Kenneth Silverman, *A Cultural History of the American Revolution: Painting, Music, Literature and the Theater in the Colonies and the United States from the Treaty of Paris to the Inauguration of George Washington, 1763–1789* (New York, 1976), 406, for Charleston in spring 1781.

34. McConville, *King's Three Faces*, 310.

35. Quoted in Wayne Craven, *Sculpture in America* (New York, 1968), 48–9.

36. Stokes, *Iconography*, V, 1058–9; Wall, 'Statues', 54, 56.

37. *New York Daily Advertiser*, 25 July 1825.

38. Craven, *Sculpture*, 48. http://emuseum.nyhistory.org/code/eMuseum.asp?lang=EN, inventory no. 1864.5. Wall, 'Statues', has British officers knocking off the statue's head on 30 Nov. 1776, shortly after British occupation.

39. For the contest over the symbols of liberty see Amelia Rauser, 'Death or Liberty: British Political Prints and the Struggle for Symbols in the American Revolution', *Oxford Art Journal*, 21:2 (1998), 151–71; cf. fig. 10 in this book.

40. Hutchinson (ed.), *Diary and Letters of Thomas Hutchinson*, II, 200.

41. Anon., *An Epitaph on the Late Illustrious Earl of Chatham* (London, 1784), 15–16.

42. [John Almond], *Anecdotes of the Life of … Chatham*, 6th edn, 3 vols (London, 1797), III, Appendix, pp. 330–34; TNA, PRO/30/70/7/470.

43. TNA, WORK 6/19, fo. 179; LC 2/35; Westminster Abbey Muniments, Funeral Fee Book 1760–1783, entries for 1779.

44. George III to Lord North, 12 May 1778, in Sir John Fortescue, *The Correspondence of King George the Third from 1760 to December 1783*, 6 vols (London, 1927–8), IV (1778–9), 139–40, quotation 139.

45. Myrone, *Bodybuilding*, 209; Tobias Smollett, *The History of England from the Revolution to the End of the American* War, new edn, 8 vols (Edinburgh, 1791), VII, 519; Joel Barlow, *The History of England, from the Year 1765, to the Year 1795*, 6 vols (London, 1795), III, 51–2.

46. *Gentleman's Magazine*, 48 (1778), 283–4; *Morning Post*, 10 June 1778; *Annual Register*, 21 (1778), 238–44; [Almond], *Anecdotes*, 434–8; William Hague, *William Pitt the Younger* (London, 2004), xxi–xxiv.

47. For this paragraph see *Parliamentary History*, xix, 1224–9 (House of Commons, 11–21 May 1778). Contract: TNA, T1/554/125–6; T1/559/78–9; *Authentic Memoirs of the Right Honourable the late Earl of Chatham* (London, 1778), 90; *European Magazine*, 5 (1784), 248 (quotation); fine engr. facing: publ. 1 May 1784 by I. Sewell.

48. *Annual Register*, 21 (1778), 240–41; Corporation of London Record Office, Minutes of Committee 1778–83, MSS 55.2: resolution 6 June 1778; [Almond], *Anecdotes*, 338–40; Philip Ward-Jackson, *Public Sculpture of the City of London* (Liverpool, 2003), 166–70.

49. H. Bullock, 'Stringer Lawrence', *Army Quarterly*, 70 (1955), 216–21.

50. Hayman painted Coote as a victorious *and* magnanimous hero, in *Britannia Distributing Laurels to the Victorious Generals* at Vauxhall, and in *The Surrender of Pondicherry to Sir Eyre Coote*, possibly as a modello for an unrealised picture also at Vauxhall. Coote's statue was then also added to the wall of fame at Company HQ, East India House.

51. *Gentleman's Magazine*, 54 (1784), 635, 716–17; HC Journals II (1754–90), 252; *European Magazine*, 18 (1790), 24; ibid., 20 (1791), 163–5 (quotation 164); Allan Cunningham, *The Lives of the Most Eminent British Painters, Sculptors, and Architects*, 6 vols (London, 1829–33), III, 113–15; Charles Francis Bell (ed.), *Annals of Thomas Banks, Sculptor* (Cambridge, 1938), 58–60; Margaret Whinney and John Physick, *Sculpture in Britain, 1530–1830*, 2nd, integrated, edn (London, 1988), 325; E. W. Sheppard, *Coote Bahadur: A Life of Lieutenant General Sir Eyre Coote K.B.* (London, 1956), 179–83. British-built monuments in India, too, often incorporated references to indigenous people: see e.g. monuments to Lord Pigot (1777), Josiah Webbe, Chief Secretary to the Government of Madras (1804), and two casualties of the siege of Mallegaon in 1818, all in the Wren-inspired St Mary's Church at Fort St George, Madras: Joan Coutu, *Persuasion and Propaganda: Monuments and the Eighteenth-Century British Empire* (Montreal, 2008), 291–2, 305–6; BL, IOR/F/4/657 18233.

52. National Library of Ireland, MS 9310, Mary Shackleton, fos 100, 102, quoted in Myrone, *Bodybuilding*, 202.

53. The secret correspondence is transcribed in Carl Clinton Van Doren, *Secret History of the American Revolution* (New York, 1941), 439–81.

54. Harold C. Syrett (ed.), *The Papers of Alexander Hamilton*, 27 vols (New York/London, 1961–87), II, 438–41.

55. André to Washington, Salem, 24 Sep. 1780, quoted in Winthrop Sargent, *The Life and Career of Major John André*, new edition with notes and illustrations, edited by W. Abbatt (New York, 1902), 324–5; Alexander Hamilton to Brigadier Gen. Anthony Wayne, 28 Sep. 1780, in Syrett (ed.), *Papers of Alexander Hamilton*, II, 445.

56. Board's report to Washington, quoted in Sargent, *Life and Career*, 356. For Arnold see his letter to Clinton, 26 Sep. 1780, quoted ibid., 344.

57. André to Washington, Tappan, 1 Oct. 1780, quoted in *Proceedings of a Board of General Officers* (Philadelphia, 1780), 21.

58. Anna Seward, *Monody on the Death of Major Andre* (Litchfield, 1781), 25; William Dunlap, *Andre; A Tragedy in five acts … to which are added, authentic documents respecting Major Andre* (New York, 1798), 23–4, 39, 41.

59. André to Clinton, Tappan, 29 Sep. 1780, quoted in Sargent, *Life and Career*, 360–61.

60. Tallmadge to General Heath, 10 Oct. 1780, quoted ibid., 469–70; Benjamin Tallmadge, *Memoir of Colonel Benjamin Tallmadge* (New York, 1858), 133.

61. Col. Hamilton to Lt-Col. John Laurens, 11 Oct. 1780, in Syrett (ed.), *Papers of Alexander Hamilton*, II, 467–8. Reproduced or extracted in *Pennsylvania Gazette*, 25 Oct. 1780, and in Dunlap's play, *Andre*, 106–9.

62. *Gentleman's Magazine*, 51 (1781), 236, see also 178–9, 235.

63. *Lloyd's Evening Post*, 15 Nov. 1780; *Morning Chronicle*, 16 Nov. 1780, *Gazetteer*, 17 Nov. 1780. The *Morning Herald* of 5 Dec. 1780, called for national revenge.

64. 'Reflections on the Catastrophe of Major André', *Public Advertiser*, as repr. in *Rivington's Royal Gazette*, 14 Mar. 1781, quoted in Judith L. Van Buskirk, *Generous Enemies: Patriots and Loyalists in Revolutionary New York* (Philadelphia, 2002), 103–4.

65. After Buskirk, *Generous Enemies*, 77, 91, 100; see also Sargent, *Life and Career*, 361–2, 384, 386.

66. See references in n. 38 to chapter 4.

67. Readings of André as a demilitarised and feminised British hero seem to me to be pushing a good argument too far: Sarah Knott, 'Sensibility and the American War for Independence', *American Historical Review*, 109 (2004), 19–40; Myrone, *Bodybuilding*, 204.

68. Stanley J. Idzerda (ed.), *Lafayette in the American Revolution: Selected Letters and Papers, 1776–90*, 5 vols (Ithaca/London, 1977–83), III, 180–86, at 182; 195. See for similar comments Joel Barlow to Ruth Baldwin, 10 Feb. 1780, quoted in Silverman, *Cultural*

History, 380; James Thacher, *A Military Journal during the American Revolutionary War from 1775 to 1783* (Boston, 1823), 269–75.

69. Major Benjamin Russell, 62–4, repr. from *New England Magazine*, VI, 363, quoted in Horace W. Smith (ed.), *Andreana. Containing the Trial, Execution and Various Matter Connected with the History of Major John André* (Philadelphia, 1865), 62–3; E. A. Benians (ed.), *A Journal by Thomas Hughes, 1778–1789* (Cambridge, 1947), entry for 10 Oct. 1780; [Anon.], *The History of the War in America, between Great Britain and her Colonies*, 3 vols (Dublin, 1779–85), III, 141; Smollett, *History of England*, VII, 602.

70. *Gazetteer*, 15 Nov. 1780; *Morning Herald*, 18 Nov. 1780.

71. See also Ira D. Gruber (ed.), *John Peeble's American War: The Diary of a Scottish Grenadier 1776–1782* (Stroud, 1997), 411, entry for 6 Oct. 1780; Hon. George Damer to Lord George Germain, 13 Oct. 1780, in R. B. Knowles, W. R. Hewlett, and S. C. Lomas (eds), *Historical Manuscripts Commission: Report on the Manuscripts of Mrs. Stopford-Sackville, of Drayton House, Northamptonshire*, 2 vols (HMC, 49), (London, 1904–10), II, 184; *Gentleman's Magazine*, 50 (1780), 540, 610–16.

72. Seward, *Monody*, 25–6.

73. Myrone, *Bodybuilding*, plate 114, and p. 206 n. 23 for the quoted critic. Westminster Abbey Muniments, Chapter Minutes for Feb. 1782; Funeral Fee Book 1760–1783, 23 Apr. 1782. *Gentleman's Magazine*, 52 (1782), 514.

74. *British Magazine and Review*, 1 (1782), 331–2.

75. *Sophie in London 1786, being the Diary of Sophie v. la Roche*, trans. from the German with an introd. essay by Clare Williams, with a foreword by G. M. Trevelyan (London, 1933), 116–17.

76. *Lady's Magazine*, 13 (1782), 558 (quotation); James Peller Malcolm, *Londinium Redivivum*, 4 vols (London, 1802–7), I, 168; Thomas Maurice, *Westminster-Abbey: An Elegiac Poem* (London, 1784), 8–9. For this paragraph see Myrone, *Bodybuilding*, 204–6.

77. *Sophie in London*, 116.

78. Cf. Myrone, *Bodybuilding*, 208; the Adams quotation, ibid., 207.

79. Edgar P. Richardson, 'Charles Willson Peale and His World', in Edgar P. Richardson, Brooke Hindle, Lillian B. Miller, *Charles Willson Peale and His World* (New York, 1982), 22–105, at 67–8; Waldstreicher, *Perpetual Fetes*, 41; Charles Royster, *A Revolutionary People at War: The Continental Army & American Character, 1775–1783* (Chapel Hill, NC/London, 1979), 291–2, n. 83; Isaac Newton Arnold, *The Life of Benedict Arnold, His Patriotism and His Treason* (Chicago, 1880), 359–66, with reference to Henry Cruger Van Schaack, *Life of Peter Van Schaack, LL.D., Embracing Selections from His Correspondence and Other Writings, during the American Revolution and His Exile in England* (New York, 1942), 147, quoted 365–6.

80. *St James's Chronicle*, 29 Nov. 1781.

81. For this paragraph see Nicholas A. M. Rodger, *The Command of the Ocean: A Naval History of Britain, 1649–1815* (London, 2004), 353–4; *St James's Chronicle*, 29 Nov. 1781;

BMC 5827-8, 6004 (multiple enemies); David Ramsay, *The History of the American Revolution,* 2 vols (London, 1790), II, 296 (quotation); John Andrews, *History of the War with America, France, Spain, and Holland,* 4 vols (London, 1785-6), IV, 288-9.

82. Andrew J. O'Shaughnessy, *An Empire Divided: The American Revolution and the British Caribbean* (Philadelphia, 2000); Kathleen Wilson, *The Sense of the People: Politics, Culture, and Imperialism in England, 1715-1785* (Cambridge, 1995), 159; Vincent Harlow, *The Founding of the Second British Empire, 1763-1793,* 2 vols (London, 1952), I, 256, 281, 312 (my trsl. of French quotation). For the wider imperial context of the war and an exploration of the literary and visual culture of and on the British West Indies, see Geoff Quilley, 'Questions of Loyalty: The Representation of the British West Indian Colonies during the American Revolutionary War', in John Bonehill and Geoff Quilley (eds), *Conflicting Visions: War and Visual Culture in Britain and France c.1700-1830* (Aldershot, 2005), 115-38.

83. Wiltshire RO, 547/1, Diary of Jonathan Adams, 27 May 1782; J. N. Puddicombe, *Albion Triumphant: or, Admiral Rodney's Victory over the French Fleet* (London, 1782), 3-4, 7, 14; Eliza Knipe, 'Ode on Admiral Rodney's Victory, April the 12th, 1782', in *Poems on Various Subjects* (Manchester, 1783), 14-16; Rine Prentice, *A Celebration of the Sea: The Decorative Art Collections of the National Maritime Museum* (London, 1994), 25-7 and colour plates 39-40; *Parliamentary History,* xxiii, 80; York City Archives, Acc. 163, Diary of Dr William White, entry for 21 May 1782. The quotation from Lincolnshire Archives Office, Misc. Don 681/1, Day-book of John Mells, after Conway, *British Isles,* 202.

84. *Gentleman's Magazine,* 52 (1782), 259; *HC Journals,* vol. 25, p. 397; vol. 28, pp. 643-4; vol. 38, pp. 1017, 1020.

85. The following after Kenneth Breen, 'George Brydges, Lord Rodney, 1718?-1792', in Richard Harding and Peter Le Fevre (eds), *Precursors of Nelson: British Admirals of the Eighteenth Century* (London, 2000), 225-48, 401-22; Harding and Le Fevre, 'Sir George Rodney and St. Eustatius in the American War: A Commercial and Naval Distraction, 1775-81', *Mariner's Mirror,* 84 (1998), 193-203; Stephen Conway, '"A joy unknown for years past": The American War, Britishness and the Celebration of Rodney's Victory at the Saints', *History,* 86 (2001), 180-99, at 187-9; Piers Mackesy, *The War for America* (London, 1964), 320; O'Shaughnessy, *An Empire Divided,* 230-32.

86. BMC 5837 (9 Apr. 1781).

87. Rodger, *Command of the Ocean,* 354; Conway, '"A joy unknown for years past"', 185-6.

88. *Parliamentary History of England,* eds Cobbett and Wright, xxiii, 51; [Anon.], *The History of the War in America,* III, 256; Thomas Mante, *The Naval and Military History of the Wars of England,* 8 vols (London, [1795-1807]), VII, 272; William Belsham, *History of Great Britain,* 4 vols (London, 1798), III, 200.

89. TNA, T1/609/226-7; John Kenworthy-Browne, 'A Monument to 3 Captains', *Country Life,* 161 (Jan.-Feb. 1977), 180-82; *Gentleman's Magazine,* 52 (1782), 259, 337; John

Physick, *Designs for English Sculpture 1680-1860* (London, 1969), 146–7; drawing in the V&A Museum: E4379-1920. For the story of Rodney's monuments in Jamaica and Westminster Abbey see Holger Hoock, *The King's Artists: The Royal Academy of Arts and the Politics of British Culture, 1760-1840* (Oxford, 2003), 237–9.

90. For this section, and similar monuments in other parts of the British Isles, see: UKNIWM 10134, 48528, 39789, 5386, 19091, 19743, 23291, 48536, 48559, 16933; NMM M4559, 560, 1700, 3698, 3231, 5205. Katherine Ada Esdaile, *English Church Monuments, 1510 to 1840* (London, 1946), 102–3.

91. Adam Smith, *The Theory of Moral Sentiments* (London/Edinburgh, 1759), ch. 1. For recent contributions in British and British-Indian context see Matthew Craske, *The Silent Rhetoric of the Body: A History of Monumental Sculpture and Commemorative Art in England, 1720-1770* (New Haven, Conn./London, 2008); Robert Travers, 'Death and the Nabob: Imperialism and Commemoration in Eighteenth-Century India', *Past & Present*, 196 (2007), 83–124.

92. Cf. Craske, *Silent Rhetoric*, ch. 11 on grieving female donor figures in funereal sculpture.

93. Anonymous American loyalist in England on the occasion of DeLancey's death, quoted in *Life of Van Schaack*, which is quoted in Lorenzo Sabine, *Biographical Sketches of Loyalists of the American Revolution*, 2 vols (Boston, 1864), I, 365.

94. Esmond Wright, 'The Loyalists in Britain', in Wright (ed.), *A Tug of Loyalties: Anglo-American Relations 1765-85* (London, 1975), 1–25.

95. I have benefited from discussions of this topic with W. H. Foster and Stephen Conway.

96. Some of William Wragg's correspondence appears in *Southern Quarterly Review*, 4 (1843), 97–156; his political polemics from 1769 are in William Henry Drayton et al., *The Letters of Freeman, Etc.: Essays on the Nonimportation Movement in South Carolina*, ed. Robert M. Weir (Columbia, SC, 1977). See also George C. Rogers, Jr, 'The Conscience of a Huguenot', *Huguenot Society of South Carolina Transactions*, 67 (1962), 1–11.

97. TNA, CO 5/396/241v.

98. In 1777, 28 heads of loyalist families from South Carolina are recorded to have arrived in England, with 21 following in 1778, the largest annual figures until the evacuation of Charleston in 1782-3. Robert McCluer Calhoon, *The Loyalists in Revolutionary America* (New York, 1973), 451–2; Robert M. Weir, *Colonial South Carolina: A History* (Millwood, 1983), 252, 266–7, 284, 304, 322; Mary Beth Norton, *The British-Americans: The Loyalist Exiles in England 1774-1789* (London, 1974), 34–8.

99. David Henry, *An Historical Description of Westminster Abbey, its Monuments and Curiosities* (London, 1783), 84; *Southern Quarterly Review*, 4 (July 1843), 97–156, see esp. 118–56, quoting the inscription p. 156, and referring for the origins of the monument to Hon. William Bull to G. Manigault, Bristol, 12 Feb. 1779. Westminster Abbey

Muniments, Chapter Minutes, Chapter Meeting (28 Jan. 1779); Funeral Fee Book 1760–1783, fo. 226.

100. UKNIWM no. 34713.

101. TNA, CO 5/155/18, William Draper, Wimbledon, 26 Jan. 1777.

102. For DeLancey see: TNA, AO 12/19/71–142; L. S. Lanitz-Schürer, 'Whig-loyalists: The De Lanceys of New York', *New York Historical Society Quarterly*, 56 (1972), 179–98; William Gordon, *The History of the Rise, Progress, and Establishment, of the Independence of the United States of America* (London, 1788), 569; Sabine, *Biographical Sketches*, I, 365. His son Oliver was appointed by George III to settle both the military claims of the American loyalists and all army accounts connected with the war.

103. TNA, AO/12/19/200–226.

104. For the Lagrange/Brazier story see TNA, AO/12/13/275–301, quotations at 276–8; La Grange Papers, Alexander Library, Rutgers University, NJ. A 'James B. Lagrange' served as ensign in the various New Jersey Volunteer regiments, either in 1776–8 or later: http://www3.nbnet.nb.ca/halew/Roll_of_Officers.html [accessed: 14.01.2007]. Edward Vaughan Dongan: Lt-Col., 3rd Battalion, New Jersey Vol., died of wounds received Aug. 1777 in a skirmish on Staten Island, aged 29.

105. Burgoyne had been partially rehabilitated by the time of his death, and historians have since warned not to exaggerate the importance of Saratoga, but his funeral at the Abbey was as private as he had directed. Whatever esteem he may have enjoyed at the time of his death, he was not admitted to the pantheon of British heroes in the Abbey's nave. The gravestone was only inscribed in 1960: 'JOHN BURGOYNE | 1723–1792': Westminster Abbey Muniments, Funeral Fee Book 1783–1811, fo. 91 (13 Aug. 1792).

Chapter Two: Transatlantic Journeys

1. William Hayley in *A Catalogue of Pictures, painted by J. Wright, of Derby, and Exhibited at Robins's Room under the Great Piazza, London* (London, 1785), n.p.

2. J. F. Adams, Guernsey Jones, and W. C. Ford (eds), *Letters & Papers of John Singleton Copley and Henry Pelham, 1739–1776* (Boston, 1914), 98, Copley to [Benjamin West], Boston, 24 Nov. 1770.

3. For this paragraph see John Bonehill, 'Reynolds' *Portrait of Lieutenant-Colonel Banastre Tarleton* and the Fashion for War', *British Journal for Eighteenth-Century Studies*, 24 (2001), 123–44; *Morning Chronicle*, 20 May 1783, 3 (quotation); William Cowper, *Poems*, ed. John Baird and Charles Ryskamp, 3 vols (Oxford, 1980), I, 219, ll. 33–6, 39–42. More than half a dozen pictures relating to the siege of Gibraltar were exhibited in 1783 alone, and at least as many more by the time Copley showed his massive *The Siege of Gibraltar* in 1791, commissioned by the Corporation of London. See Bonehill, 'Exhibiting War', and for French and German representations Eve Rosenhaft, 'The Chain of Diamonds and the Trojan Whale: Propaganda, Technology and

National Identity in the Siege of Gibraltar 1782–1783', unpublished paper (2008). For camp spectacle see Stephen Conway, *The British Isles and the American War of Independence* (Oxford, 2000), 120–22; Gillian Russell, *The Theatres of War: Performance, Politics, and Society, 1793–1815* (Oxford, 1995), 33–46; Russell, 'Theatricality and Military Culture: British Army Camps in the 1770s', *Eighteenth-Century Life*, 183:3 (1994), 55–64. For military subjects not covered in this chapter see, on Irish Volunteer imagery: Fintan Cullen, *Visual Politics: The Representation of Ireland 1750–1930* (Cork, 1997), ch. 2; on maritime art: Eleanor Hughes, 'Vessels of Empire: Eighteenth-Century British Marine Painting', unpubl. Ph.D. thesis (University of California, 2002).

4. Quoted in William T. Whitley, *Artists and Their Friends in England 1700–99*, repr., 2 vols (1968; 1st edn 1928), II, 100.

5. David Bindman, 'Americans in London: Contemporary History Painting Revisited', in Christiana Payne and William Vaughan (eds), *English Accents: Interactions with British Art c.1776–1855* (Aldershot, 2004), 9–28, at 11.

6. William L. Pressly, *James Barry: The Artist as Hero* (London, 1983), 60–61 with fig. 12, and reference to *Morning Herald*, 14 Mar. 1782. The painting at Tate Britain, London, measures 76.2 × 63.5 cm.

7. Probably around 1776, West also painted a twin portrait which is supposedly of *Colonel Guy Johnson and Karonghyontye*, the colonial superintendent of Indian affairs who combines the British officer's gentility with the masculinity of native warriors, and the idealised Mohawk subaltern within the British forces in North America.

8. James Thomas Flexner, *America's Old Masters: Benjamin West, John Singleton Copley, Charles Willson Peale and Gilbert Stuart* (New York, 1994), 35, 319; for more detail see Holger Hoock, *The King's Artists: The Royal Academy of Arts and the Politics of British Culture, 1760–1840* (Oxford, 2003), 152–5.

9. Derrick R. Cartwright, *Benjamin West: Allegory and Allegiance* (San Diego, 2005), 20–21. Thanks to Bill and Maddie Foster for bringing this painting to my attention after viewing it at the Timken Art Gallery, San Diego, Calif.

10. *London Courant*, 30 May 1780, [4].

11. Irma B. Jaffe, *Trumbull: The Declaration of Independence* (London, 1976), 56, the longer quotation from *The Morning Post*.

12. John Andrews, *History of the War with America, France, Spain, and Holland*, 4 vols (London, 1785–6), IV, 281.

13. William P. Carey, *The National Obstacle to the National Public Style Considered* (London, 1825), 63.

14. Much research for both these paintings went into the details of arms, heraldry, ships, architecture, and the appearance of participants to convey a sense of historical reality. When working on *La Hogue*, West was reportedly taken to Spithead by an admiral who demonstrated the effect of smoke in a naval battle by ordering several ships to

fire broadsides in manoeuvre. See Cullen, *Visual Politics*, 50; Helmut von Erffa and Allen Staley, *The Paintings of Benjamin West* (New Haven, Conn./London, 1986), 209.

15. Montclair Art Museum, NJ, oil on canvas, 153 × 214 cm.

16. David Hume, *The History of Great Britain*, 2 vols (Edinburgh, 1754; London, 1757), II, 43–4.

17. West was the only painter to exhibit a subject from Cromwell at the Academy before 1801; very numerous Cromwellian subjects appeared throughout the second and last thirds of the nineteenth century: Roy Strong, *And when did you last see your father? The Victorian Painter and British History* (London, 1978), 165–6.

18. Some like John Adams or the Sons of Liberty evoked Cromwell as an 'anti-tyrannical symbol', but most accepted that Cromwell had succumbed to the temptations of power himself.

19. Roger Howell, Jr, 'Cromwell, the English Revolution and Political Symbolism in Eighteenth Century England', in R. C. Richardson (ed.), *Images of Oliver Cromwell: Essays for and by Roger Howell* (Manchester/New York, 1993), 63–73, at 64, 66 (quoting the print), 68, 71; Peter Karsten, *Patriot-Heroes in England and America: Political Symbolism and Changing Values over Three Centuries* (Madison, Wis./London, 1978), 38–56. For satirical depiction of George III as a tyrant in 1778–80 see M. D. George, 'America in English Satirical Prints', *William & Mary Quarterly*, 3rd ser., 10:4 (1953), 511–37, at 528.

20. Robert Alberts, *Benjamin West: A Biography* (Boston, 1978), 150–51; Arthur S. Marks, 'Benjamin West and the American Revolution', *American Art Journal*, 6:2 (1984), 15–35, at 16–18.

21. Erffa and Staley, *West*, cat. 105.

22. Mary-Beth Norton, 'Eardley-Wilmot, Britannia and the Loyalists', *Perspectives in American History*, 6 (1972), 119–31. For both of West's paintings see Erffa and Staley, *West*, cat. 106, 718; Keith Mason, 'The American Loyalist Diaspora and the Reconfiguration of the British Atlantic World', in Eliga H. Gould and Peter S. Onuf (eds), *Empire and Nation: The American Revolution in the Atlantic World* (Baltimore, 2005), 239–59, at 245–6; Maya Jasanoff, 'The Other Side of Revolution: Loyalists in the British Empire', *William & Mary Quarterly*, 65:2 (2008), 207–32, at 217–19.

23. Simon Schama, *Rough Crossings: Britain, the Slaves and the American Revolution* (London, 2005), 177–9, quotation 179.

24. Mary-Beth Norton, *The British-Americans: The Loyalist Exiles in England 1774–1789* (London, 1974), 130; TNA, AO 12/102/56; 13/29/659–69.

25. Jasanoff, 'The Other Side of Revolution', 220–22, quotation 220.

26. Margaretta M. Lovell, *Art in a Season of Revolution: Painters, Artisans, and Patrons in Early America* (Philadelphia, 2005), 58; Jules David Prown, *John Singleton Copley*, 2 vols (Cambridge, Mass., 1966), I, 209.

27. J. F. Adams, Guernsey Jones, W. C. Ford (eds), *Letters & Papers of John Singleton Copley and Henry Pelham, 1739–1776* (Boston, 1914), 98, Copley to [Benjamin West], Boston, 24 Nov. 1770.

28. Anon., *A Candid Review* (London, 1780), 26; Royal Academy of Arts, *Citizens and Kings: Portraits in the Age of Revolution, 1760–1830* (London, 2007), cat. 41, with reference to Hoock, *King's Artists*, 150–64.

29. Descriptions and lists of portraits in 1781: *London Courant*, 2 May; *London Chronicle* 3–5 May; *Morning Chronicle*, 4 May; *Morning Herald*, 8 June

30. William Godwin, *The History of the Life of William Pitt, Earl of Chatham* (London, 1783), 281–3, quotation 283.

31. My discussion of the painting draws on Emily Ballew Neff, with an essay by William L. Pressly, *John Singleton Copley in England* (London, 1996), 36–8; Prown, *Copley*, II, 275–91; Linda Colley, *Britons: Forging the Nation 1707–1837* (New Haven, Conn./London, 1992), 178–80.

32. Edgar Wind, 'The Revolution of History Painting', *Journal of the Warburg and Courtauld Institutes*, 2 (1938–9), 116–27.

33. *Proposal for Publishing, by Subscription, an Engraved Print, from the Original Picture, now Painting by John Singleton Copley, R.A. Elect, Representing the Death of the Late Earl of Chatham, to be Engraved by Mr. John Keyse Sherwin, 29 March 1780*, p. 2, quoted in Neff, *Copley*, 38 n. 46. Lovell, *Art in a Season of Revolution*, argues that late-colonial American painters theorised the act of painting differently from Reynolds and put portraiture on an equal footing with history.

34. *St James's Chronicle*, 9–12 June 1781.

35. *London Courant, and Westminster Chronicle*, 11 June 1781.

36. Emily Ballew Neff, 'The History Theater: Production and Spectatorship in Copley's *The Death of Major Peirson*', in Neff, *Copley*, 60–90, at 83–4 with further references.

37. Norton, *British-Americans*, 81, with reference to Jeffries Diary [Mass. Hist. Soc., Boston], 5 May, 4 July 1781; BL, Eg. 2669, Elisha Hutchinson Diary, Mar. to June 1781, *passim*.

38. The following relies heavily on the excellent discussions by Prown, *Copley*, II, 302–10, and Neff, 'The History Theater', with cat. no. 18; see also Richard Saunders, 'Genius and Glory: John Singleton Copley's "The Death of Major Peirson"', *American Art Journal*, 22:3 (1990), 5–39; Edward Durell, *The Death of Major F. Peirson, 6th January, 1781: Being an Account of the Battle of Jersey. With an Appendix of Historical Documents* (Jersey, 1881).

39. Neff, *Copley*, 62.

40. West's *Wolfe* had similarly combined death scene, runner, and battle/ships in foreground, mid-distance, and background.

41. For an excellent discussion see Mark S. Phillips's forthcoming book with Yale, *"To Make the Distant Near:" Distance and Historical Representation* [working title]. I am

grateful for a preview of chapters and for conversations with the author. See Solkin on West's *Wolfe*, as discussed in the 'Coda' below, with Brock.

42. *Morning Post*, 13 May 1784, 3, and 15 May 1784, 3; *Morning Chronicle*, 13 May 1784, 2, 22 May 1784, 1; *Morning Herald*, 21 May 1784, 1; *Morning Chronicle*, 22 May, 1; *Gazetteer and New Daily Advertiser*, 24 May 1784, 1.

43. *General Evening Post*, 25–27 May 1784, 4; *Whitehall Evening Post*, 25–27 May 1784, 3; *Morning Chronicle*, 27 May 1784, 3.

44. Winslow C. Watson (ed.), *Men and Times of the Revolution, or, Memoirs of Elkanah Watson* (New York, 1856), 176.

45. Elizabeth Mankin Kornhauser, *Ralph Earl: The Face of the Young Republic* (New Haven, Conn./London, 1991); William Benton Museum of Art, *The American Earls: Ralph Earl – James Earl – R. E. W. Earl* (Meriden, Conn., 1972).

46. TNA, AO 13, box 41, no. 245, Memorial of R. Earl and Certificate of J. Money, QMG under Gen. Burgoyne; cf. Kornhauser, *Earl*, 15.

47. See letters J. to C. Smyth, TNA, AO 13/111/469, 437, 7 Apr. and 9 Aug. 1788. James Earl, Ralph's younger brother, is recorded to have been in London in 1787–94; he enrolled at the Royal Academy in 1789, when he married Caroline, the widow of loyalist Joseph Smyth of New Jersey. 34 portraits are recorded for James's English period, primarily of American loyalists and some English sitters. See Robert G. Stewart, 'James Earl: American Painter of Loyalists and His Career in England', *American Art Journal*, 20:4 (1988), 34–59; TNA, AO 13, box 98, bundle 31.

48. For Brown see Dorinda Evans, *Mather Brown: Early American Artist in England* (Middletown, Conn., 1982); Evans, *West and His American Students* (Washington, DC, 1980), 74–83.

49. Evans, *West and His American Students*, pl. 55.

50. *London Chronicle*, 28 Apr. 1789.

51. For Barry see Pressly, *James Barry*, 73–8; Pressly, *The Life and Art of James Barry* (New Haven, Conn./London, 1981), 77–82, 181; Tom Dunne (ed.), *James Barry: 'The Great Historical Painter'* (Cork, 2006), 38, 67, 121, and 142–4 for printmaking techniques. David Bindman, *The Shadow of the Guillotine: Britain and the French Revolution*, with contributions by Aileen Dawson and Mark Jones (London, 1989), cat. no. 6; Marks, 'West', 19; *Morning Herald*, 14 Mar. 1782.

52. There is no space here for the intriguing stories of Joseph and Patience Wright, for which see Hoock, *King's Artists*, 157–64.

53. Robert G. Stewart, *Robert Edge Pine: A British Portrait Painter in America 1784–1788* (Washington, DC, 1979), esp. 16–20, 24–5, 28–31; John Sunderland, 'Pine, Robert Edge (1730–1788)', *Oxford Dictionary of National Biography* (Oxford University Press, 2004), http://www.oxforddnb.com/view/article/22294 [accessed 14 Aug. 2006]; John Sunderland, 'Mortimer, Pine and Some Political Aspects of English History Painting', *Burlington Magazine*, 855 (1974), 317–26. Quotations in this section: William Fairfax

to George Washington, 23 Aug. 1784, quoted in Stewart, *Pine*, 16; ibid., 20, 19, 24; Jaffe, *Declaration of Independence*, 84.

54. See the entry for Aitken in the *ODNB* and Jessica Warner, *John the Painter: Britain's First International Terrorist* (London, 2005).

55. Edgar P. Richardson, Brooke Hindle, and Lillian B. Miller, *Charles Willson Peale and His World* (New York, 1982), esp. Edgar P. Richardson, 'Charles Willson Peale and His World', 22–105, and Lillian B. Miller, 'Charles Willson Peale: A Life of Harmony and Purpose', 170–233; Joseph J. Ellis, 'Charles Willson Peale: Portrait of the American Artist as Virtuous Entrepreneur', in Ellis, *After the Revolution: Profiles of Early American Culture* (New York/London, 1979), 41–71.

56. Charles Coleman Sellers, *The Artist of the Revolution: The Early Life of Charles Willson Peale* (Hebron, Conn., 1939), 86–90, quotation 89, from Peale's broadside describing the engraving after the painting. Sidney Hart, 'A Graphic Case of Transatlantic Republicanism', in Lillian B. Miller and David C. Ward (eds), *New Perspectives on Charles Willson Peale: A 250th Anniversary Celebration* (Pittsburgh, 1991), 73–81, at 75.

57. Broadside, quoted in Lillian B. Miller (ed.), *The Selected Papers of Charles Willson Peale and His Family, vol. I: Charles Willson Peale: Artist in Revolutionary America, 1735–91* (New Haven, Conn./London, 1983), 74, 76.

58. Peale's portrait for Virginia was one of a series of images of Chatham – in oil, stone, and marble – debated or actually commissioned in various American colonies in the run-up to the Revolution, including in Massachusetts, Maryland, and South Carolina: Wayne Craven, *Sculpture in America*, new and rev. edn (Newark, Del./New York/London, 1984), 10–11; A. J. Wall, 'The Statues of King George III and the Honorable William Pitt Erected in New York City, 1770', *New York Historical Society Quarterly Bulletin*, 4 (1920), 36–57, at 57. Joseph Wilton's statue of Pitt in the Guildhall at Cork, Ireland, had been unveiled earlier in 1766: 38.

59. David C. Ward, *Charles Willson Peale: Art and Selfhood in the Early Republic* (Berkeley/Los Angeles/London, 2004), 41–2.

60. Ellis, 'Charles Willson Peale', quotations 60, 51; Ward, *Peale*, 72–4.

61. Gary B. Nash, *First City: Philadelphia and the Forging of Historical Memory* (Philadelphia, 2001), 134–6.

62. Charles Coleman Sellers, *Charles Willson Peale* (New York, 1969), 194–5, description and sketch; Ward, *Peale*, 90–92.

63. For Trumbull see Helen A. Cooper, *John Trumbull: The Hand and Spirit of a Painter* (New Haven, Conn., 1982), esp. the essay by Jules David Prown, 'John Trumbull as History Painter', 22–41, and catalogue pp. 42–92.

64. Theodore Sizer (ed.), *The Autobiography of Colonel John Trumbull, Patriot-Artist, 1756–1843: Containing a Supplement to the Works of Colonel John Trumbull* (New Haven, Conn., 1953), 37–44.

65. Cooper, *Trumbull*, 5–6; Prown, 'John Trumbull as History Painter', 26.

66. Quoted in Cooper, *Trumbull*, 5, after Lewis Einstein, *Divided Loyalties: Americans in England during the War of Independence* (London, 1933), 364.

67. John Trumbull, *Autobiography, Reminiscences and Letters* (New York/London, 1841), 316–17, JT to Gov. Trumbull, Bilboa, 23 Oct. 1781.

68. Trumbull, *Autobiography*, 71–2; cf. Jaffe, *Declaration of Independence*, 25.

69. Sizer (ed.), *Autobiography*, 58–72; Flexner, *America's Old Masters*, 68–70; Trumbull, *Autobiography*, 320–29; Jaffe, *Declaration of Independence*, 27–8; Garry Wills, *Cincinnatus: George Washington and the Enlightenment* (London, 1984).

70. John Trumbull to Andrew Elliot, 4 Mar. 1786, quoted in Prown, 'John Trumbull as History Painter', 31.

71. Trumbull, *Autobiography*, quoting his letter to Jefferson, 11 June 1789, 158–9, quotation 159.

72. Sizer (ed.), *Autobiography*, 88–92, 146–52.

73. Prown, *Copley*, II, 309; Marks, 'West', 33–4; Evans, *West and His American Students*, 89–90; Trumbull, *Autobiography*, 158–9.

74. For this paragraph see Theodore Sizer, *The Works of Colonel John Trumbull, Artist of the American Revolution* (New Haven, Conn., 1950); Prown, 'John Trumbull as History Painter', 32; the quotations from Trumbull, *Autobiography*, 412 and 411–12.

75. Irma B. Jaffe, *John Trumbull: Patriot-Artist of the American Revolution* (Boston, 1975), 84–90.

76. Abigail Adams to Mrs John Shaw, 4 Mar. 1786, in Charles Francis Adams (ed.), *Letters of Mrs Adams, the Wife of John Adams* (Boston, 1840), 324–5, quoted in Prown, 'John Trumbull as History Painter', cat. 6, p. 50, and Jaffe, *Trumbull*, 90.

77. William Dunlap, *A History of the Rise and Progress of the Arts of Design in the United States*, repr. of orig. 1834 edn., 2 vols bound as 3 (New York, 1969), I, 357.

78. Prown, 'John Trumbull as History Painter', 38.

79. Benedict Arnold to General Wooster, 2 Jan. 1776, in Benedict Arnold, 'Colonel Arnold's Letters', 105, cited in Caroline H. Cox, *A Proper Sense of Honor: Service and Sacrifice in George Washington's Army* (Chapel Hill, NC, 2004), 185.

80. Jason Shaffer, 'Making "an Excellent Die": Death, Mourning, and Patriotism in the Propaganda Plays of the American Revolution', *Early American Literature*, 41 (2006), 1–27, at 17.

81. Trumbull, *Autobiography*, 405–39: 'Catalogue of Paintings, by Colonel Trumbull; including Eight Subjects of the American Revolution, with near two hundred and fifty portraits of persons distinguished in that important period. Painted by him from the life. Now exhibiting in the gallery of Yale College, New Haven', at 420.

82. Sizer (ed.), *Autobiography*, 148–50, the first two quotations at 149, the third at 150; Cooper, *Trumbull*, 9.

83. Jaffe, *Trumbull*, 135, 137.

84. Prown, 'John Trumbull as History Painter', cat. 25; Trumbull, *Autobiography*, 95 (quotation); Jaffe, *Trumbull*, 77–8.
85. Sizer (ed.), *Autobiography*, 152. Engravings of *Gibraltar, Bunker's Hill*, and *Quebec* were published in 1797. Later additions to the series: *The Surrender of General Burgoyne at Saratoga, October 16, 1777* (c.1822–32), cat. 30; *The Resignation of General Washington, December 23, 1783* (1824–8), cat. 31; new version of *Bunker's Hill* (1834), cat. 2.
86. The New York State Society of the Cincinnati's attempt to build an equestrian monument to Washington in 1802–3 failed owing to lack of sufficient funds: HUN MSS, HM 9567–85. For the Trumbull portrait see Arthur S. Marks, 'The Statue of King George III in New York and the Iconology of Regicide', *American Art Journal*, 13:3 (1981), 61–82, at 71 and fig. 5; Cooper, *Trumbull*, cat. 41; Sizer (ed.), *Autobiography*, 165–6; Edgar P. Richardson, 'A Penetrating Characterization of Washington by Jonathan Trumbull', *Winterthur Portfolio*, 3 (1967), 1–23.

Interlude. London, Spring and Summer 1784

1. In the medium term, the impact of the loss of the American colonies on the British national psyche was relatively limited. Trade with the new United States soon exceeded pre-war figures; the Empire also asserted itself vigorously in a newly authoritarian vein in the East. See Eliga H. Gould, *The Persistence of Empire: British Political Culture in the Age of the American Revolution* (Chapel Hill, NC, 2000); C. A. Bayly, *Imperial Meridian: The British Empire and the World, 1780–1830* (Harlow/New York, 1989).
2. William Keate, *A Sermon, Preached upon the Occasion of the General Thanksgiving for the Late Peace* (Bath, 1784), 18–19 (quotation 19).
3. William Bennet, *The Divine Conduct Reviewed: A Sermon Preached in the Meeting-House, on the Pavement, Moorfields, July 29, 1784* (London, 1784), 13–15.
4. See e.g. Thomas Scott, *A Thanksgiving Sermon, Preached July 29, 1784, at the Parish Church of Olney, Bucks* (Northampton, 1784), 18.
5. Giuseppe Baretti, *A Guide through the Royal Academy by Joseph Baretti, Secretary for Foreign Correspondence to the Royal Academy* (London, c.1781), 8.
6. Somerset House accommodated the Navy Office, Sick and Hurt, Pay, and Victualling Offices. My account is indebted to Mark Hallett, 'Reading the Walls: Pictorial Dialogue at the Eighteenth-Century Royal Academy', *Eighteenth-Century Studies*, 37:4 (2004), 581–604 (quotation 596), and to Eleanor Hughes, 'Ships of the "Line": Marine Paintings at the Royal Academy Exhibition of 1784', in Tim Barringer, Geoff Quilley, and Douglas Fordham (eds), *Art and the British Empire* (Manchester, 2007), 139–52, 379–82.
7. *Morning Chronicle*, 1 June 1784, 4.

8. Martin Myrone, *Bodybuilding: Reforming Masculinities in British Art 1750–1810* (New Haven, Conn./London, 2005), 213–14; Kathleen Wilson, *The Island Race: Englishness, Empire, and Gender in the Eighteenth Century* (London, 2002), 54–91.

9. For Inglefield see Capt. Inglefield, *Capt. Inglefield's Narrative Concerning the Loss of His Majesty's Ship the Centaur* (London, 1783); *British Magazine and Review*, 2 (1783), 50; Myrone, *Bodybuilding*, 214–17. Stipple engraving by Thomas Gaugain, after Northcote, *Portraits of the Officers and Men who were Preserv'd from the Wreck of the Centaure* (1784); [Anon.], *The History of the War in America, between Great Britain and her Colonies*, 3 vols (Dublin, 1779–85), III, 257–63.

10. Frances Burney, *Evelina, or the History of a Young Lady's Entrance to the World*, ed. M. A. Doody (London, 1994), 116.

11. Ruth Smith, *Handel's Oratorios and Eighteenth-Century Thought* (Cambridge, 1995).

12. William Weber, *The Rise of Musical Classics in Eighteenth-Century England: A Study in Canon, Ritual and Ideology* (Oxford, 1992).

13. The Marsh diaries are in Cambridge UL, Add. MS 7757. I have used Brian Robins (ed.), *The John Marsh Journals: The Life and Times of a Gentleman Composer (1752–1828)* (Stuyvesant, NY, 1998), 313–18 (all subsequent quotations from Marsh are from this section).

14. Charles Burney, *An Account of the Musical Performances in Westminster-Abbey and the Pantheon … in Commemoration of Handel* (London, 1785), viii–xi, 22, 24, 118–22.

15. Simon McVeigh, *Concert Life in London from Mozart to Haydn* (Cambridge, 1993), xiii.

16. Burney, *Account*, 26.

17. Ibid., 10–11.

18. Duncan Sprott, *1784* (London, 1984), 121, without reference.

19. *European Magazine*, suppl. (June 1784), 1.

20. *Morning Post*, 31 May 1784, 2.

21. Basil Cozens-Hardy (ed.), *The Diary of Sylas Neville, 1767–88* (Oxford, 1950), 320.

22. Burney, *Account*, 83–4.

23. Quoted ibid., 115, 123.

24. Richard, 7th Viscount Fitzwilliam, Irish. Sir Watkin Williams Wynn, most fervent Handelian of the Concert of Ancient Music directors, of Welsh Tory gentry stock with former Jacobite sympathies, fell out with George III in 1779. Sandwich (1st Lord Adm. 1771–82), very complicated political career and reputation over prosecution of Wilkes, corruption charges at the Navy Office, scandal over the murder of his mistress 1780, broke with the king in 1783. For previous readings see William Weber, 'The 1784 Handel Commemoration as Political Ritual', *Journal of British Studies*, 28 (1989), 43–69; cf. T. C. W. Blanning, *The Culture of Power and the Power of Culture: Old Regime Europe 1660–1789* (Oxford, 2002), 180–81, 266–9, with reference to

Anna Verena Westermayr, 'The 1784 Handel Commemoration: The Conduct and Interpretation of a Spectacle', unpubl. M.Phil. dissertation (Cambridge, 1996).

25. *Public Advertiser*, 27 May 1784, 2; *Universal Magazine*, 74 (June 1784), 277–8; *Morning Herald*, 27 May 1784, 2; cf. Weber, 'The 1784 Handel Commemoration', 44, 59, 69.

26. *Morning Herald*, 31 May 1784, 2. The paper called the bishops who were subscribers to the Concerts of Antient Music and were prominently seated at the Jubilee the 'Right Reverend Church Militants': 27 May 1784, 2.

27. *Morning Post*, 31 May 1784, 2.

28. *Public Advertiser*, 27 May 1784, 2.

29. James King and Charles Ryskamp (eds), *The Letters and Prose Writings of William Cowper*, 3 vols (Oxford, 1981), II, 254.

30. John Brewer, *The Pleasures of the Imagination: English Culture in the Eighteenth Century* (London, 1997), 405.

31. The quotations in this paragraph from *Morning Post,* 4 June 1784, 2; Cozens-Hardy (ed.), *Diary of Sylas Neville*, 321; *Recollections of the Life of John O'Keefe, Written by Himself* (London, 1826), ii, 95; *European Magazine*, quoted in Christopher Hogwood, *Handel* (London, 1984), 239.

32. Brewer, *Pleasures*, 406.

33. Burney, *Account*, 26, 35, 40.

34. See Howard E. Smither, *A History of the Oratorio,* 4 vols (Chapel Hill, NC, 1977–2000), III, 229–37.

35. For this paragraph see Weber, 'The 1784 Handel Commemoration', esp. 63; George III then also subscribed to the Antient Concerts and raised their social prestige; by 1794 they were called King's Concert, but the political overtones of the king's attendance were also used by commentators and caricaturists for partisan point scoring.

36. Burney, *Account*, 122. See also Anon., *The Commemoration of Handel: A Poem* (London, 1786), 1.

37. Stella Tillyard, *A Royal Affair: George III and His Troublesome Siblings* (London, 2006), 324–5, quotation 324. Cf. Linda Colley, 'The Apotheosis of George III: Loyalty, Royalty and the British Nation 1760–1820', *Past & Present*, 102 (1984), 94–129.

38. David Watkin, *The Architect King: George III and the Culture of the Enlightenment* (London, 2004), 125–32; Roy Strong, *And when did you last see your father? The Victorian Painter and British History* (London, 1978), 78–85; Wendy Greenhouse, 'Benjamin West and Edward III: A Neoclassical Painter and Medieval History', *Art History*, 8:2 (1985), 178–91.

39. Watkin, *Architect King*, 135, with reference to architectural and Masonic traditions of symbolic columns and the anthropomorphic origins of the classical orders.

40. T. C. W. Blanning, *The Pursuit of Glory: The Five Revolutions That Made Modern Europe 1648–1815* (New York, 2007), 318–19.

Chapter Three: 'Pretensions to Permanency'

1. The title refers to Byron's dictum that unlike a picture, a bust 'looks like putting up pretensions to permanency', in *Detached Thoughts,* in Leslie A. Marchand (ed.), *Byron's Letters and Journals,* 13 vols (London, 1973–94), IX, 1821–2 (1979), 11–52, at 21. See Malcolm Baker's discussion in 'Making the Portrait Bust Modern: Tradition and Innovation in Eighteenth-Century British Portrait Sculpture', in Jeanette Kohl and Rebecca Müller (eds), *Kopf/Bild: Die Büste im Mittelalter und Früher Neuzeit* (Munich, 2007), 347–66. For the 1789 service see TNA, WORK 3/3, fos 29–30; 6/21, fos 153, 162; 36/68/68, fos 47–48; T29/60, fos 346; 482; *Gentleman's Magazine,* 59 (1789), 367–70, 459.
2. Beilby Porteus, *A Sermon Preached at the Cathedral Church of St. Paul, London, Before His Majesty and Both Houses of Parliament* (London, 1789), 19, 22.
3. My translations from Michael Maurer (ed.), *Johann Wilhelm von Archenholtz: England und Italien: Nachdruck der dreiteiligen Erstausgabe Leipzig 1785,* 3 vols (Heidelberg, 1993), Teil I [vol. I]: *England,* 144; San Constante, *Londres et les Anglais* (Paris, 1804), 70.
4. James Ralph, *A Critical Review of the Public Buildings, Statues, and Ornaments, in and about London and Westminster* (London, 1783), 54–5; Benjamin Silliman, *A Journal of Travels in England,* 2nd edn, 2 vols (Boston, 1812), I, 195–6 (quotation 196).
5. Jeremy Gregory, 'Anglicanism and the Arts: Religion, Culture and Politics in the Eighteenth Century', in Jeremy Black and Jeremy Gregory (eds), *Culture, Politics and Society in Britain, 1660–1800* (Manchester/New York, 1991), 82–109.
6. *The Public Advertiser,* 25 Apr. 1791, 2, referring to the French Panthéon; ibid., 27 Feb. 1792, 3; 3 Mar. 1792, 3; *The Diary; or, Woodfall's Register,* 28 Mar. 1792, 4.
7. See also Nigel Aston, 'St Paul's and the Public Culture of Eighteenth-Century Britain', in Derek Keene, Arthur Burns, and Andrew Saint (eds), *St Paul's: The Cathedral Church of London 604–2004* (New Haven, Conn./London, 2004), 363–71.
8. *Apar,* 4 Apr. 1791, 543–4. For the Anglo-French dialogue in the creation of pantheons see also Malcolm Baker, 'De Troyes à Westminster: Pierre-Jean Grosley et la commémoration des grands hommes en France et en Angleterre vers 1760', in Thomas W. Gaehtgens and Gregor Wedekind (eds), *Le culte des grands hommes en France et en Allemagne* (Paris, 2009), 00–00.
9. After Avner Ben-Amos, *Funerals, Politics, and Memory in Modern France, 1798–1996* (Oxford, 2000), 25–6.
10. Since his desiccated 'mummy' had been removed from Saint-Denis in 1793, it had been publicly displayed, conserved between the skeletons of a rhinoceros and an elephant at the Natural History Museum, and moved to Lenoir's Museum of French Monuments: Suzanne Glover Lindsay, 'Mummies and Tombs: Turenne, Napoléon, and Death Ritual', *Art Bulletin,* 82:3 (2000), 478–502.

11. In March 1814, as the allies were camped outside Paris, all battle trophies and Frederick II's insignia were burned to prevent them from falling into enemy hands: *Moniteur*, no. 138, 18 May 1807, 541–4; A. Bégis, *Invasion de 1814: Destruction des drapeux étrangers et de l'épée de Frédéric de Prusse à l'Hôtel des Invalides. D'ápres des documents inédits* (Paris, 1897), 14–21.

12. For a tabular overview of all commissions see Holger Hoock, *The King's Artists: The Royal Academy of Arts and the Politics of British Culture, 1760–1840* (Oxford, 2003), table 2.

13. William Attfield, 'Funeral and Sepulchral Honours', in *The Oxford English Prize Essays*, 4 vols (Oxford, 1830), III, 1–27.

14. Ibid., 17–20.

15. Thomas Nipperdey, 'Nationalidee und Nationaldenkmal in Deutschland im 19. Jahrhundert', *Historische Zeitschrift*, 206 (1968), 529–85, esp. 538; Avner Ben-Amos, 'Monuments and Memory in French Nationalism', *History & Memory*, 5:2 (1990), 50–81.

16. Robert A. Nye, 'Review Essay: Western Masculinities in War and Peace', *American Historical Review*, 112:2 (2007), 417–38, at 418.

17. William Wood, *An Essay on National and Sepulchral Monuments* (London, 1808), 21.

18. James A. Leith, *The Idea of Art as Propaganda in France, 1750–1799: A Study in the History of Ideas* (Toronto, 1965).

19. Linda Colley, 'The Apotheosis of George III: Loyalty, Royalty and the British Nation 1760–1820', *Past & Present*, 102 (1984), 94–129, at 109–11.

20. For the service see TNA, WORK 4/18, fos 264–6, 269–70; WORK 21, 36; PC 1/40/130; *Gentleman's Magazine*, 67 (1797), ii, 1057, 1059, 1065; FD III, 931, 945, 948–50. Grenville: Grenville to Lord Spencer, 13 Oct. 1797, in Julian S. Corbett (ed.), *The Private Papers of George, 2nd Earl Spencer*, 4 vols (London, 1913–24), II, 196.

21. FD III, 949–50 (quotation on king 950). See also *Form of Prayer ... used in all Churches upon the nineteenth of December next, being the Day appointed by Proclamation for a general Thanksgiving* (London, 1797).

22. For loyalist press commentary see e.g. *True Briton*, 21 Dec. 1797.

23. Cf. the *Anti-Jacobin*'s vendetta against the 'Jacobin doers of the Morning Chronicle': *Anti-Jacobin*, no. 6, 18 Dec. 1797, 41–2; no. 7, 25 Dec. 1797, 49–51 (quotation 51), with reference to issues of the *Morning Chronicle* of Dec. 1797.

24. James Stanier Clarke, *Naval Sermons Preached on Board His Majesty's Ship Impetueux* (London, 1798), *passim*; HUN MSS, HM 31201, v.1–17, Anna Larpent Diary, 17 vols, 1773–86, 1790–1830, II (1796–8), entry for 19 Dec. 1797.

25. Quoted in J. C. D. Clark, 'England's Ancien Regime as a Confessional State', *Albion*, 21 (1989), 450–74, at 457.

26. Review in *True Briton*, 21 Dec. 1797.

27. TNA, T27/52.169; T1/851.4656, 862.2506, 870.4720, 900.949; T29/81.284; T27/53.21; T27/50.48–50, 186; T27/53.21; T27/58.39, 461; T1/955.6480. BL, Add. MS 39791, fo. 6; 39787, fos 4–6.

28. *HC Journals*, vol. 54, pp. 7, 10; 55, pp. 36, 48; 56, pp. 285, 427, 444.

29. TNA, T27/58.226; T29/78.486–8 (first quotation fo. 487); T27/53.400, 413; FD V, 1781; T1/895.32–4; Prince Hoare, *Epochs of the Arts* (London, 1813), 223–45 (second and third quotations 234); John Bacon, *A Letter to the Right Honourable Sir Robert Peel … on the appointment of a commission for promoting the cultivation and improvement of The Fine Arts* (1843), 6–14; *European Magazine*, 156 (1806), frontispiece and p. 6.

30. TNA, T29/85.265–6, 86.59, 143.213; T27/58.40, 50–51, 278–9; 60.153; 69.315; T1/4029.4572; MPD 1/78.1–29. Royal Academy Archives, Council Minutes, III, 380–83, 387–93; General Assembly Minutes, II, 317–22, 329–30. BL, Add. MS 39780, fos 92–5; 39781, fo. 58; 39791, fo. 215. Ben-Amos, 'Monuments and Memory', 57–8, 64–5. Victoria & Albert Museum, National Art Library, London, R.C. V.11–14, British Institution for Promoting the Fine Arts in the United Kingdom, Minute Books, 4 vols. (1805–22), II, 102; 177–8; III, 39. FD VII, 2660, 2770–71; IX, 3414; X, 3626, 3643; 3669; XI, 3915, 3928.

31. Prince Hoare (ed.), *The Artist; A Collection of Essays, Relative to Painting, Poetry, Sculpture, Architecture*, 2 vols in 1 (London, 1810), 9.

32. *Parliamentary History*, XXXI, 513. TNA, MPD 1/78.56; Guildhall Library, London, Print Room, Box marked 'St. Paul's, Rossi & Burgess'; *Gentleman's Magazine*, 83 (1813), ii, 541; BL, Add. MS 39791, fo. 8; TNA, T29/86.59; T1/4029.4572.

33. *London Scenes, or A Visit to Uncle William in Town* (London, 1824), 26–7.

34. TNA, ADM 101/102/10, Miscellaneous Journal by L. Gillespie, Naval Hospital, Martinique, entry for 24 Nov. 1798; Lt John Aitchison, *An Ensign in the Peninsular War: The Letters of John Aitchison*, ed. W. F. K. Thompson (London, 1981), 118; M. Bailey, *Poems on Westminster Abbey* (London, 1807), 19; *Parliamentary Debates*, new. ser., VIII, 745–9.

35. Nicholas Tracy (ed.), *The Naval Chronicle: The Contemporary Record of the Royal Navy at War*, consolidated edn, 5 vols (London, 1998–9), II, 178–9, 'Biographical Memoir of Sir Thomas Graves, K.B.' (quotation 179); [*Naval Chronicle*, VIII, 370–72, cf. V, 532].

36. Isaac Schomberg, *Naval Chronology: Or an Historical Summary of Naval and Maritime Events, from the Time of the Romans to the Treaty of Peace 1802*, 5 vols (London, 1802), II, 272. NMM/ADM/L/B.187; HOW/11.

37. Formally an honour bestowed by the crown, in this period ministerial influence on the creation of peerages increased: Michael W. McCahill, 'Peerage Creations and the Changing Character of the British Nobility, 1750–1850', *English Historical Review*, 96 (1981), 259–84.

38. Examples of discussions in *Parliamentary Debates*, VI, cols 99, 105–7.

39. 22 large Naval Gold Medals were awarded to admirals, and 117 small Naval Gold Medals to captains in 1794–1815. There were 681 recipients of the army medals: Edward C. Joslin et al. (eds), *British Battles and Medals*, 6th rev. edn (London, 1988), 32–3.

40. Linda Colley, *Britons: Forging the Nation 1707–1837* (New Haven, Conn./London, 1992), 185.

41. *Parliamentary History*, XXXI, 903–4; XXXIII, 977–8; cf. for Trafalgar: *Parliamentary Debates*, vi, cols 97–107.

42. *Gentleman's Magazine*, 75 (1805), 795.

43. Unless otherwise stated, inscriptions are quoted directly from monuments.

44. Martin Papenheim, *Erinnerung und Unsterblichkeit: Semantische Studien zum Totenkult in Frankreich (1715–1794)* (Stuttgart, 1992), 277–8, 297; Joseph Clarke, *Commemorating the Dead in Revolutionary France: Revolution and Remembrance, 1789–1799* (Cambridge, 2007), 243–8.

45. Henry R. Yorke, *Letters from France, in 1802* (London, 1804), 340–47.

46. Simon Schama, *Citizens: A Chronicle of the Revolution* (London, 1989), 546–8, 652; *Monthly Magazine*, 13 (1802), 310; Ben-Amos, *Funerals*, 30–31, 40–44; see 54–7 for the Napoleonic pantheon.

47. Yorke, *Letters from France*, 340–45; Ben-Amos, 'Monuments and Memory', 62.

48. *Parliamentary Debates*, xxvi, col. 1200.

49. On *fama* and *pietà* see Jan Assmann, *Das kulturelle Gedächtnis: Schrift, Erinnerung und politische Identität in frühen Hochkulturen*, 6th edn (Munich, 2007), 32. On the Nelson cult see essays in David Cannadine (ed.), *Admiral Lord Nelson: Context and Legacy* (Basingstoke, 2005), and Holger Hoock (ed.), *History, Commemoration, and National Preoccupation: Trafalgar 1805–2005* (Oxford, 2007).

50. *Parliamentary Debates*, xxvi, cols 1198–1200.

51. For generals commemorated for their role in the suppression of Jacobite rebellions and for Capt. Cornewall see David Henry, *An Historical Description of Westminster Abbey, its Monuments and Curiosities* (London, 1753), 182; Douglas Fordham, 'Raising Standards: Art and Imperial Politics in London, 1745–1776', unpubl. Ph.D. thesis (Yale, 2003), 139–41. See also above, p. 000.

52. Kathleen Wilson, 'Empire, Trade and Popular Politics in Mid-Hanoverian Britain: The Case of Admiral Vernon', *Past & Present*, 121 (1988), 74–109, at 103; James Peller Malcolm, *Londinium Redivivum*, 4 vols (London, 1802–7), I, 100; Gerald Jordan and Nicholas Rogers, 'Admirals as Heroes: Patriotism and Liberty in Hanoverian England', *Journal of British Studies*, 28 (1989), 201–24, at 207–11; John Physick, *Designs for English Sculpture 1680–1860* (London, 1969), 108–9; V&A No. E.433/1946.

53. *Parliamentary History*, XXXI, 903–7; *Parliamentary Debates*, vi, cols 97–107.

54. Sir William F. P. Napier, *History of the War in the Peninsula and in the South of France, from the Year 1807 to the Year 1814*, 6 vols (London, 1828–40), I, 500.

55. Rory Muir, *Britain and the Defeat of Napoleon* (New Haven, Conn./London, 1996), 60–78; Charles W. C. Oman, *A History of the Peninsular War*, 7 vols (Oxford, 1902–30), I, 588–9, 595–602; *Parliamentary Debates*, xii, 131–45, quotation col. 140.

56. *Parliamentary History*, XXXI, 1461; TNA, Pitt Correspondence, 30/8/143, fo. 90.

57. [Robert Southey], *Letters from England, by Don Manuel Alvarez Espriella*, trans. from the Spanish, 2nd edn, 3 vols (London, 1808), I, 312–13.

58. Marquis of Buckingham on Abercromby to Thomas Grenville, Aylesbury, Buckinghamshire CRO, Grenville Papers, D54/13 fo. 6.

59. NMM/COL/14.

60. See also Schomberg, *Naval Chronology*, III, 42, on Burgess.

61. Nelson's dispatch praised the first lieutenant taking command more than the dead captain himself, who was 'killed early in the action'. To be fair, though, Westcott had previously fought on the First of June and served in the West Indies, the Channel, and the Mediterranean, 'THIRTY THREE YEARS OF MERITORIOUS SERVICE' proudly inscribed on to his monument: NMM/JER/4/125; Tracy (ed.), *Naval Chronicle*, I, 255.

62. Quoted in Michael Duffy, *Soldiers, Sugar, and Seapower: The British Expeditions to the West Indies and the War against Revolutionary France* (Oxford, 1987), 74.

63. *Parliamentary History*, XXXI, 1458–64; *Whitehall Evening Post*, 14–16 Apr. 1795, 2; *Morning Post*, 15 Apr. 1795, 2.

64. *HC Journals*, vol. 64, pp. 323–4, 388 (18 May and 7 June 1809); *Parliamentary Debates*, xiv, cols 607–12.

65. For the Foreign Secretary, Castlereagh, this was a theme until the end of the war: *Parliamentary Debates*, xxxi, col. 913.

66. *HC Journals*, vol. 61, p. 16 (28 Jan. 1806); BL, Add. MS 28333, fo. 6, Admiralty to Lady Nelson, 6 Nov. 1805; Anon., *Brief Memoir*, 12; Robert Southey, *The Life of Nelson*, 2 vols (London, 1813), II, 267–8.

67. Nicholas H. Nicolas (ed.), *The Dispatches and Letters of Vice-Admiral Lord Viscount Nelson*, 7 vols (London, 1997–8), III, 86–7; TNA, MPD 1/78, fos 30–31, Charles Rossi to [Treasury], 2 July 1798; and fo. 36: drawing.

68. Hardinge: Gen. T. Maitland, *General Orders*, 13 Mar. 1808, repr. in *Naval Biography*, III, 370. See also for Jervis: Church of England, *Form of Prayer and Thanksgiving for Jervis' Victory* (London, 1797); Brock: *HC Journals*, vol. 68, pp. 663, 672; Ross: *HC Journals*, vol. 70, pp. 12, 28.

69. *A Narrative of my Adventures (1790–1839), by Sir William Henry Dillon, K.C.H., Vice-Admiral of the Red* [ed. Michael A. Lewis], in Dean King with John Hattendorf (eds), *Every Man Will Do His Duty: An Anthology of First-Hand Accounts from the Age of Nelson* (New York, 1997), 12–32, at 31.

70. The quotations are from Tracy (ed.), *Naval Chronicle*, III, 235, 247.

71. Terence M. Freeman, *Dramatic Representations of British Soldiers and Sailors on the London Stage, 1660–1800: Britons Strike Home* (Lewiston, NY, 1995), 65, 114. The

quotation in David Bindman, *The Shadow of the Guillotine: Britain and the French Revolution, with contributions by Aileen Dawson and Mark Jones* (London, 1989), 65; reprod. cat. no. 182. For further analysis see my 'Nelson Entombed: The Military and Naval Pantheon in St Paul's Cathedral', in David Cannadine (ed.), *Admiral Lord Nelson: Context and Legacy* (Basingstoke, 2005), 115–44, at 122–3.

72. *Parliamentary History*, XXXI, 904; XXXIII, 1559; *HC Journals*, vol. 56, p. 428 (18 May 1801); *Parliamentary Debates*, vi, cols 97–107; S. Horsley, *The Watchers and the Holy Ones* (London, 1806), 26.

73. C. H. Kuchler's Nile Medal, 48 mm in diameter, features a figure of Pax supporting a shield depicting Nelson, and on the reverse a victorious fleet sailing into Aboukir Bay. Thomas Wyon's Waterloo Medal (35 mm dia.) shows the laureated head of the Prince Regent, and on the reverse a winged Victory with palm branch. The donor's and the recipient's name respectively would have been impressed around the edge of the former and latter. Cf. Fanny and J. A. de Luc to Mathew Boulton, 24 Oct. 1806, quoted in J. G. Pollard, 'Matthew Boulton and Conrad Heinrich Küchler', *Numismatic Chronicle*, 10 (1970), 259–318, at 309.

74. Christopher Clark, *Iron Kingdom: The Rise and Downfall of Prussia, 1600–1947* (Cambridge, Mass., 2006), 375; cf. Karen Hagemann, 'Mannlicher Muth und Teutsche Ehre': *Nation, Militär und Geschlecht zur Zeit der antinapoleonischen Kriege Preussens* (Paderborn etc., 2002), 449–54.

75. Queen Victoria to Leopold, King of the Belgians, 22 May 1855, in Arthur Benson (ed.), *The Letters of Queen Victoria: A Selection from Her Majesty's Correspondence between the Years 1837–1861*, 3 vols (London, 1906), III, 161.

76. A pendant in Westminster Abbey is John Bacon's East India Company monument to Captain Cooke, who had died in 1800 in a frigate action against the French in the Bay of Bengal. A sailor supports the hero, as if receiving Christ's body from the cross.

77. George L. Smyth, *The Monuments and Genii of St Paul's Cathedral and Westminster Abbey*, 2 vols (London, 1826), II, note on p. 762, 759–60 (Craufurd, Mackinnon), and II, 676 (Moore).

78. Duff: *HC Journals*, vol. 61, pp. 17, 20 (28 and 31 Jan. 1806); Smyth, *Monuments*, II, 684 note. Duncan: Maria Hackett, *A Popular Account of St. Paul's Cathedral, etc.* (London, 1829), 31. See also William Charles Henry Wood (ed.), *Select British Documents of the Canadian War of 1812*, 4 vols (Toronto, 1920–28), I, 14 (on Brock); Sir Denis Le Marchant, *Memoirs of the Late Maj. Gen. Le Marchant* (priv. pr., 1841), 305; J. V. Page (ed.), *Intelligence Officer in the Peninsula: Letters and Diaries of Major the Hon. Edward Charles Cocks, 1786–1812* (Tunbridge Wells/New York, 1986), 166, diary entry 26 Jan. 1811; *The Diary of a Cavalry Officer in the Peninsular and Waterloo Campaigns, 1809–1815*, ed. James Tomkinson (London, 1894), 125; H. B. Robinson, *Memoirs of Lieutenant-General Sir Thomas Picton*, 2nd edn, 2 vols (London, 1836), 401.

79. Roger N. Buckley (ed.), *The Napoleonic War Journal of Captain Thomas Henry Browne* (London, 1987), entry for 16 May 1810, p. 144.

80. Smyth, *Monuments*, II, note on pp. 761–2.

81. Karen Hagemann, 'Der "Bürger" als "Nationalkrieger": Entwürfe von Militär, Nation und Männlichkeit in der Zeit der Freiheitskriege', in Karen Hagemann and Ralf Pröve (eds), *Landsknechte, Soldatenfrauen und Nationalkrieger: Militär, Krieg, und Geschlechterordnung im historischen Wandel* (Frankfurt a.M./ New York, 1998), 74–102, at 87–8; Stefan Dudink, Karen Hagemann, and John Tosh (eds), *Masculinities in Politics and War* (Manchester/New York, 2004), Introduction, 12–15; Arnold Vogt, *Den Lebenden zur Mahnung: Denkmäler und Gedenkstätten* (Hanover, 1993).

82. FD V, 1859.

83. Nicholas Penny, '"Amor publicus posuit": Monuments for the People and of the People', *Burlington Magazine*, 129 (1987), 793–800, at 794.

84. Lars Völcker, *Tempel für die Grossen der Nation: Das kollektive Nationaldenkmal in Deutschland, Frankreich und Grossbritannien im 18. und 19. Jahrhundert* (Frankfurt a. M., 2000), 119–21; Angelika Engbrisch-Styrsch, *Die Madeleine-Kirche in Paris* (Essen, 1989), 77–93; Archives Nationales, Paris, F/13/204; F/21/576.

85. 'Den edlen Hessen, die im Kampf fürs Vaterland Hier siegend Fielen'. See Reinhard Koselleck, 'Einleitung', in Reinhard Koselleck and Michael Jeismann (eds), *Der politische Totenkult: Kriegerdenkmäler in der Moderne* (Munich, 1994), 9–20, at 12. A satirical, anti-monarchical monument demanded the commemoration of all: 'Des trauernden Vaterlandes kummervoller Dank! All denen, deren Namen auf dieser Säule nicht stehen'. [The mourning fatherland's anxious gratitude! To all those whose names are not inscribed on to this column]. 'Monument des Friedens in Rastatt, im Jahre 1798', in *Kameleon, oder das Thier mit allen Farben, Eine Zeitschrift für Fürstentugend und Volksglück*, nos. 1–3 (1798), 54.

86. Geheimes Staatsarchiv Preussischer Kulturbesitz, Berlin, GStA PK/HA I, Rep. 89, 20863, fos 4, 7. Wolfgang Schmidt, 'Denkmäler für die Bayerischen Gefallenen des Russlandfeldzugs von 1812', *Zeitschrift für bayerische Landesgeschichte*, 49 (1986), 303–26; B. Matsche v. Wicht, 'Zum Problem des Kriegerdenkmals in Österreich in der ersten Hälfte des 19. Jahrhunderts', in Koselleck and Jeismann (eds), *Der politische Totenkult*, 51–90; Ulrich Bischoff, *Denkmäler der Befreiungskriege in Deutschland 1813–1815*, 2 vols (Berlin, 1977), I, 40–41; R. L. Alexander, 'The Public Memorial and Godfrey's Battle Monument', *Journal of the Society of Architectural Historians*, 17, 1 (1958), 19–24.

87. *Parliamentary Debates*, xx, cols 531–2 (quotation); TNA, Pitt Correspondence, 30/8/143, fos 84–91; 30/8/144/1, fos 7–12; Timothy Jenks, 'Contesting the Hero: The Funeral of Admiral Lord Nelson', *Journal of British Studies*, 39 (2000), 422–53, at 431–3; Penny, '"Amor publicus posuit"', 797. At St Paul's, only one war-time military monument, to Capt. Willet Miller, was not commissioned by the King-in-Parliament

but by fellow officers. Its pendant in Westminster Abbey is that to a Peninsular War casualty, Lt-Col. George Augustus Lake of the 29th, erected by 'the officers, non-commissioned officers, drummers, and privates of the corps, as a testimony of their high regard and esteem'.

Chapter Four: Modern Heroes

1. *HC Journals*, vol. 28, pp. 643–4 (21 and 22 Nov. 1759). For this section I have relied heavily on the excellent discussion in Douglas Fordham, 'Raising Standards: Art and Imperial Politics in London, 1745–1776', unpubl. Ph.D. thesis (Yale, 2003), 141–57; see also Joan Coutu, 'Legitimating the British Empire: The Monument to General Wolfe in Westminster Abbey', in John Bonehill and Geoff Quilley (eds), *Conflicting Visions: War and Visual Culture in Britain and France, c. 1700–1830* (Aldershot, 2005), 61–83; Matthew Craske, 'Making National Heroes? A Survey of the Social and Political Functions and Meanings of Major British Funeral Monuments to Naval and Military Figures, 1730–70', in ibid., 41–60, at 49–51.
2. The near-nude figure assumes knowledge of Pigalle's citizens on the base of Louis XV's monument at Rheims: Malcolm Baker, 'An Anglo-French Sculptural Friendship: Pigalle and Wilton', in Geneviève Bresc-Bautier, François Baron, and Pierre-Yves Le Pogam (eds), *La Sculpture en Occident: Études offertes à Jean-René Gaborit* (Paris, 2007), 218–25.
3. There is no space here to discuss the well-known Vauxhall paintings, for which see Brian Allen, 'Francis Hayman and the Supper-Box Paintings in Vauxhall Gardens', in Charles Hind (ed.), *The Rococo in England: A Symposium* (London, 1986), 111–33; David Solkin, *Painting for Money: The Visual Arts and the Public Sphere in Eighteenth-Century England* (New Haven, Conn./London, 1993), 191–9. For Robert Adam's monument of Colonel Roger Townshend as a conceptual bridge between the Cornewall and Wolfe monuments see Fordham, 'Raising Standards', 154.
4. On the Wolfe monument see in addition to previous references Malcolm Baker, *Figures in Marble: The Making and Viewing of Eighteenth-Century Sculpture* (London, 2000), 11–12, 45–8; Martin Myrone, *Bodybuilding: Reforming Masculinities in British Art 1750–1810* (New Haven, Conn./London, 2005), 105–20; Matthew Craske and Richard Wrigley, 'Introduction', in Craske and Wrigley (eds), *Pantheons: Transformations of a Monumental Idea* (Aldershot, 2004), 1–10, at 6; Alan McNairn, *Behold the Hero: General Wolfe and the Arts in the Eighteenth Century* (Montreal, 1997), 63–5, plate 5.1, 80–81.
5. *Historical Description* (1788), 57.
6. BL, Add. MS 39790, fos 28–9, John Flaxman to the Rev. William Gunn, [?] Sep. 1814.
7. James Peller Malcolm, *Londinium Redivivum*, 4 vols (London, 1802–7), III, 124.

8. Allan Cunningham, *The Lives of the Most Eminent British Painters, Sculptors, and Architects*, 6 vols (London, 1829–33), III, 114; Cunningham in *Quarterly Review*, 34 (1826), 131, regarding Abercromby; Cockerell quoted in David Watkin, *The Life and Work of C. R. Cockerell* (London, 1974), 20.

9. Cunningham, *Lives*, III, 115.

10. The classicist Thomas Jefferson had recommended modern dress for Jean-Antoine Houdon's statue of Washington for the Virginia Assembly in the 1780s, because a modern hero in antique dress was 'as just an object of ridicule as a Hercules or Marius with a periwig and in a *chapeau bras*'. Quoted in Irma B. Jaffe, *John Trumbull: Patriot-Artist of the American Revolution* (Boston, 1975), 96.

11. For this paragraph see J. E. Cookson, *The British Armed Nation, 1793–1815* (Oxford, 1997), 129; Linda Colley, *Britons: Forging the Nation 1707–1837* (New Haven, Conn./ London, 1992), 127–30, 144; Fintan Cullen, 'The Art of Assimilation: Scotland and Its Heroes', *Art History*, 16:4 (1993), 600–618; Hugh Trevor-Roper, 'The Invention of Tradition: The Highland Tradition of Scotland', in Eric Hobsbawm and Terence Ranger (eds), *The Invention of Tradition* (Cambridge, 1983), 15–41, at 22–8; *Gentleman's Magazine*, 82 (1812), i, 190; *Monthly Magazine*, 4 (1797), 402.

12. George L. Smyth, *The Monuments and Genii of St Paul's Cathedral and Westminster Abbey*, 2 vols (London, 1826), I, 2, 12.

13. On four-nation imperial history see John M. MacKenzie, 'Irish, Scottish, Welsh and English Worlds? A Four-Nation Approach to the History of the British Empire', *History Compass*, 6:5 (2008), 1244–63, with further references to Scots imperial specialisms.

14. Sir William F. P. Napier, *History of the War in the Peninsula and in the South of France, from the Year 1807 to the Year 1814*, 6 vols (London, 1828–40), I, 497; *HC Journal*, vol. 64, pp. 11, 17 (25 and 31 Jan. 1809); BL, Add. MS 30804, fo. 8.

15. George A. Kelly, *Mortal Politics in Eighteenth-Century France* (Waterloo, Ont., 1986), 127–8 (quotation 127). Harvey: Nicholas Tracy (ed.), *The Naval Chronicle: The Contemporary Record of the Royal Navy at War*, consolidated edn, 5 vols (London, 1998–9), I, 107. Nelson: Timothy Jenks, '"Naval Engagements": Patriotism, Cultural Politics, and the Royal Navy, 1793–1815', unpubl. Ph.D. thesis (Univ. of Toronto, 2001), 265–90; William Beatty, *Authentic Narrative of the Death of Lord Nelson* (London, 1807), 68–71, 266; Anon., *Victory in Tears; or, The Shade of Nelson: A Tribute to the Memory of That Immortal Hero* (London, 1805), fn. on p. 20. Cf. for Collingwood: NMM/COL/14/22, Adm. Collingwood to the Rev. Dr Carlyle, 25 Jan. 1801.

16. Bowes: *Gentleman's Magazine*, 82 (1812), ii, 403; Le Marchant: John A. Hall, *A History of the Peninsular War, vol. VIII*, new edn (London, 1998), 341. Cadogan: Wellington, *Dispatches*, x, 447, 454–5. Mackinnon: Wellington, *Dispatches*, viii, 551, 576–7; Major-General Sir John Thomas Jones, *A Journal of the Sieges Carried on by the Army under the Duke of Wellington in Spain: 1811–14*, 3rd edn, 3 vols (London, 1846), I, 128; Arthur H. Haley (ed.), *The Soldier Who Walked Away: Autobiography of Andrew Pearson,*

a Peninsular War Veteran (Liverpool, [1987]), 102; see also for Hoghton: Roger N. Buckley (ed.), *The Napoleonic War Journal of Captain Thomas Henry Browne* (London, 1987), 144; Wellington, *Dispatches*, vii, 590.

17. H. B. Robinson, *Memoirs of Lieut.-Gen. Sir Thomas Picton*, 2 vols (London, 1836), II, 386–7 (quotation 387).
18. I have benefited from discussions with Malcolm Baker and Julia E. Hickey. Richard Westmacott's bronze monument to Nelson in Birmingham (1806–9) is a proud but ungainly representation of corporeal heroism. Westmacott limited his use of allegory to a small Victory and set Nelson against the prow in modern uniform with no effort to conceal the lopped arm. The design may have been influenced by criticism of Committee of Taste-sponsored classicising sculptures, and presents a more rugged hero than those depicted in St Paul's.
19. Not only supporters but also opponents of the war against Revolutionary France argued from religious doctrine: Emma Vincent Macleod, *A War of Ideas: British Attitudes to the Wars against Revolutionary France 1792–1802* (Aldershot, 1998), chs 1, 3, 5, and pp. 137–49.
20. Cf. Craske and Wrigley (eds), 'Introduction', in *Pantheons*, 1–10, at 6.
21. Carolyn D. Williams, *Pope, Homer and Manliness: Some Aspects of Eighteenth-Century Classical Learning* (London/New York, 1993); Anthony Fletcher, *Gender, Sex and Subordination in England, 1500–1800* (New Haven, Conn./London, 1995), ch. 7; Donna T. Andrew, 'The Code of Honour and Its Critics: The Opposition to Duelling in England, 1700–1850', *Social History*, 5 (1980), 409–34; Robert B. Shoemaker, 'The Taming of the Duel: Masculinity, Honour and Ritual Violence in London, 1660–1800', *Historical Journal*, 45:3 (2002), 525–45.
22. James Hervey, 'Meditations among the Tombs', in *Meditations and Contemplations* (London, 1818), 46–50, quotation 49; Edward Young, 'The Complaint Night I. On Life, Death, and Immortality', in *Night Thoughts* (London, 1798), 1–15. Evangelicals had previously pondered that patriotic rhetoric and its visual expression in military monuments ran counter to Christian values: *The Connoisseur*, 19 June 1755.
23. Edmund Butcher, *The Only Security for Peace* (Exeter, 1802), 12–13, quotation 13.
24. Avner Ben-Amos, *Funerals, Politics, and Memory in Modern France, 1798–1996* (Oxford, 2000), 38.
25. Karen Hagemann, *'Mannlicher Muth und Teutsche Ehre': Nation, Militär und Geschlecht zur Zeit der antinapoleonischen Kriege Preussens* (Paderborn etc., 2002), 457–97.
26. Geheimes Staatsarchiv Preussischer Kulturbesitz, Berlin, GStA PK/HA I, GZ, Rep 89, 20854, fo. 6.
27. *Gentleman's Magazine*, 66 (1796), i, 179–81, with plate facing 179; Church of England, *Form of Prayer and Thanksgiving for Jervis' Victory* (London, 1797), 6; Macleod, *War*

of Ideas, 137–49, 74, with reference to *The Sun* (2 Nov. 1793); *Public Advertiser*, 4 Apr. 1791, 3; cf. *Anti-Jacobin*, no. 5 (11 Dec. 1797), 35; *Form of Prayer* (1797), 6.

28. Paul E. Kopperman, 'Religion and Religious Policy in the British Army, c.1700–96', *Journal of Religious History*, 14:4 (1987), 390–405.

29. Jenks, '"Naval Engagements"', 252. For an interesting reading of Clarke see Geoff Quilley, 'Duty and Mutiny: The Aesthetics of Loyalty and the Representation of the British Sailor c.1789–1800', in Philip Shaw (ed.), *Romantic Wars: Studies in Culture and Conflict, 1793–1822* (Aldershot, 2000), 80–109, esp. 100–105.

30. Malcolm, *Londinium Redivivum*, I, 169, quoting from his own review in *Gentleman's Magazine*.

31. For the terminology see Erwin Panofsky, *Tomb Sculpture: Four Lectures on Its Changing Aspects from Ancient Egypt to Bernini*, ed. H. W. Janson (New York, 1964); David Bindman and Malcolm Baker, *Roubiliac and the Eighteenth-Century Monument* (New Haven, Conn./London, 1995), ch. 3.

32. BL, Add. MS 39781, 10–13, Major F[rederick] Maitland to Charles Dundas, 12 June 1794; *HC Journals*, vol. 50, pp. 578, 607; TNA, MPD 1/78, fos 30–31; Prince Hoare (ed.), *Academic Correspondence, 1803* (London, 1804), 28; M. A. McKibbin, 'Citizens of Liberty, Agents of Tyranny: The Dual Perception of Allied Prisoners of War during the French Revolution', *Selected Papers – Consortium on Revolutionary Europe, 1750–1850*, 26 (1996), 112–20.

33. Bryan Edwards, *The History, Civil and Commercial, of the British Colonies in the West Indies*, 3rd edn, 3 vols (London, 1793, 1801), III, 475–7, quotation 475.

34. *The Times*, 7 Jan. 1806.

35. D. A. Bell, 'Jumonville's Death: War Propaganda and National Identity in Eighteenth-Century France', in Colin Jones and Drohr Wahrman (eds), *The Age of Cultural Revolutions: Britain and France, 1750–1820* (Berkeley/London, 2002), 33–61, at 55.

36. The analysis is based on my reading of a random sample of several dozen sermons published across the country throughout the war. Quotations from: [Anon.], *Reflections on Our Late Victory at the Mouth of the Nile* (1798), 8–15; J. Morgan, *A Thanksgiving Sermon [on Ps. III.8] preached in the Parish Church of Towcester on 29th November, 1798* (Towcester, 1798), 18.

37. Among recent discussions of masculinities see Karen Harvey and Alexandra Shepard, 'What Have Historians Done with Masculinity? Reflections on Five Centuries of British History, circa 1500–1950', *Journal of British Studies*, 44 (2005), 274–80; Karen Harvey, 'The History of Masculinity, circa 1650–1800', *Journal of British Studies*, 44 (2005), 296–311; Robert A. Nye, 'Review Essay: Western Masculinities in War and Peace', *American Historical Review*, 112:2 (2007), 417–38; Michael Roper and John Tosh (eds), *Manful Assertions: Masculinities in Britain since 1800* (New York, 1991).

38. Matthew Craske, *Art in Europe 1700–1830: A History of the Visual Arts in an Era of Unprecedented Urban Economic Growth* (Oxford/New York, 1997), 263–4; David

Solkin, *Painting for Money: The Visual Arts and the Public Sphere in Eighteenth-Century England* (New Haven, Conn./London, 1993), ch. 5; Bindman and Baker, *Roubiliac*, 147–72, 189.

39. Mark Girouard, *The Return to Camelot: Chivalry and the English Gentleman* (New Haven, Conn./London, 1981), chs 2–4; Fletcher, *Gender, Sex and Subordination*, 297–321.

40. Wordsworth's 'Happy Warrior' was strong and brave, yet selfless, compassionate, and gentle, transmuting the horrors of war to 'glorious gain'. William Wordsworth, 'Character of the Happy Warrior', in *Wordsworth: Poetical Works*, with Introduction and Notes edited by Thomas Hutchinson. A New Edition, Revised by E. de Selincourt (Oxford, 1974), 386–7.

41. J. G. W. Conlin, 'Benjamin West's *General Johnson* and Representations of British Imperial Identity, 1759–1770: An Empire of Mercy?', *British Journal for Eighteenth-Century Studies*, 27 (2004), 37–59; Solkin, *Painting for Money*, 190–213.

42. Gibraltar (on the occasion of the unveiling of Copley's painting at the Guildhall): [John Boydell], *A Description of Several Pictures presented to the Corporation of the City of London* (London, 1794), viii, quoted in Margarette Lincoln, *Representing the Royal Navy: British Sea Power, 1750–1815* (Aldershot, 2002), 102. 1794: William Henry Dillon, in Dean King with John Hattendorf (eds), *Every Man Will Do His Duty: An Anthology of First-Hand Accounts from the Age of Nelson* (New York, 1997), 31. See for the Battle of the Nile: NMM/HIS/35/10. The quotation from *Parliamentary Debates*, vi, cols 97–107.

43. Countess of Minto (ed.), *Life and Letters of Sir Gilbert Eliot, First Earl of Minto from 1751 to 1806*, 2 vols (London, 1874), II, 290–91.

44. Philip Carter, *Men and the Emergence of Polite Society, 1660–1800* (New York, 2000), 76.

45. Westcott: TNA, ADM 101/102/10, Miscellaneous Journal by L. Gillespie, Naval Hospital, Martinique, entry for 24 Nov. 1798. Moore: Charles Steevens, *Reminiscences of My Military Life from 1795 to 1818, by the Late Lieut.-Col. Chas. Steevens*, ed. Nathaniel Steevens (Winchester, 1878), 78. Smith: HUN MSS, POR 2168, Jane Porter [1803].

46. NMM/RUSI/NM/235/r/6, Philip Riou, Col. RA, scrapbook has MS extract or copy from *Quarterly Review*, no. 5, Suppl. 253, Life of Nelson.

47. Michèle Cohen, '"Manners Make the Man: Politeness, Chivalry, and the Construction of Masculinity, 1750–1830', *Journal of British Studies*, 44 (2005), 312–29.

48. *Military Mentor* (London, 1804), I, Letter XXIV, 'On Anger', 270–72.

49. See Carter, *Men*, 108.

50. Joseph A. Whitehorne, *The Battle for Baltimore, 1814* (Baltimore, 1997); Anthony S. Pitch, *The Burning of Washington: The British Invasion of 1814* (Annapolis, Md, 1998); Donald R. Hickey, *The War of 1812: A Forgotten Conflict* (Urbana, Ill., 1989); W. A.

7. They also commissioned a full-length portrait in oil. For this section see Royal Academy Archives, Burlington House, London, Council Minutes II, 183, 218–22, 230–31, 233, 327–8, 365–6; General Assembly Minutes I, 352; FD II, 317, 319, 321, 374–5, 398, 636; Mary Ann Steggles, 'The Empire Aggrandized: A Study of Commemorative Portrait Statuary Exported from Britain to Her Colonies in South Asia, 1800–1939, unpubl. Ph.D. thesis (Leicester, 1992), 12–15; *Madras Courier*, 21 May 1800, 1; *Calcutta Gazette*, 5 June 1800, 3; Joan Coutu, *Persuasion and Propaganda: Monuments and the Eighteenth-Century British Empire* (Montreal, 2008), 300–304, 309–12; Barbara Groseclose, *British Sculpture and the Company Raj* (Newark/London, 1995), 64–6.

8. BL, OIOC, P&D, P248/(33). A print by Dawe was reviewed by the *Monthly Magazine*, 15 (1803), 565. Royal Academy of Arts Catalogues for 1800: 1087–8, 1096; 1801: 915; 1802: 1042.

9. *Monthly Magazine*, 15 (1803), 58; BL, IOR/F/4/186/3905, fos 1–27, quotations fos 9, 17; Roger Hudson (ed.), *Memoirs of a Georgian Rake* (London, 1995), 400. The British merchants in Bombay later commemorated Wellesley as imperial protector of indigenous cultural traditions with a statue by Bacon and Mannings for £5,000. In 1820, a statue of Hastings by Flaxman was commissioned for East India House; it too shows Hastings the statesman and scholar, with a map and the laws of India.

10. BL, IOR/F/4/193/4377, fos 5–7; *Calcutta Gazette Extraordinary*, 12 Oct. 1805; *Government Gazette Extraordinary* (Madras), 1 Nov. 1805. For the full mourning regime see BL, IOR/F/4/193/4333, 4359, 4377; F/4/188/4119.

11. *European Magazine*, 56 (1806), 156, quoting the *Calcutta Gazette*.

12. *Calcutta Gazette Extraordinary*, 12 Oct. and 4 Nov. 1805; *Madras Gazette Extraordinary*, 5 Nov. 1805 (first quotation); *Government Gazette* (Madras), 14 Nov. 1805; supplement 27 Nov. 1805 (second quotation); 12 Dec. 1805; *Government Gazette Extraordinary*, 1 Nov. 1805.

13. BL, IOR, P&D, Add. Or. 4174–6, P3110. For government contributions to the Madras cenotaph project see BL, IOR/F/4/222/4861; IOR/F/4/232/5281 [Aug.–Oct. 1806].

14. Franklin and Mary Wickwire, *Cornwallis: The Imperial Years* (Chapel Hill, NC, 1980), 267.

15. Mary Ann Steggles, *Statues of the Raj* (London, 2000), 64–6. As late as 1843 it was also said of the statue which the British military officer of the Bombay Presidency had built on the Bombay Green that the 'old practice of worshipping the statue of Cornwallis is still in high value among the natives of Bombay'. Quoted in Steggles, *Statues*, 18, without reference. John Bacon the Younger's seated statue of Cornwallis in military uniform under the robes and orders of the Governor-General is accompanied by female allegories, possibly Truth and Duty (or Fame).

16. W. C. H. Wood (ed.), *Select British Documents of the Canadian War of 1812*, 3 vols in 4 (New York, 1968), I, 13–14; see also Robert Malcolmson, '"It remains only to fight": The Battle of Queenston Heights', in Donald E. Graves (ed.), *Fighting for Canada:*

Seven Battles, 1758–1945 (Toronto, 2000), 89–130; R. Arthur Bowler, 'Propaganda in Upper Canada in the War of 1812', *American Journal of Canadian Studies*, 18 (1988), 11–32; *The Journal of Major John Norton, 1816*, ed. with introductions and notes by Carl F. Klinck and James J. Talman (Toronto, 1970), 286.

17. For this paragraph see Gerald M. Craig, *Upper Canada: The Formative Years, 1784–1841* (Oxford, 1963), 70; Robert S. Allen, *His Majesty's Indian Allies: British Indian Policy in the Defence of Canada, 1784–1815* (Toronto/Oxford, 1992), 120–27, 140; David Mills, *The Idea of Loyalty in Upper Canada 1784–1850* (Kingston, Ont., 1988), 26; Carl Benn, *The Iroquois in the War of 1812* (Toronto/London, 1998), 88; Sandy Antal, *A Wampum Denied: Procter's War of 1812* (Ottawa, 1997), 105; Colin G. Calloway, *Crown and Calumet: British–Indian Relations, 1783–1815* (Norman, Okla/London, 1987), 208–9.

18. Wood, *Select British Documents*, I, 623: Lt-Col. Thomas Evans, Fort George, 15 Oct. 1812; Allen, *His Majesty's Indian Allies*, 139; Ernest A. Cruikshank (ed.), *The Documentary History of the Campaigns upon the Niagara Frontier in 1812–14*, 9 vols (Welland, Ont., 1896–1908), II, 83 (quotation); John K. Mahon, *The War of 1812* (Gainesville, 1972), 76–81.

19. District General Orders, Fort George, 16 Oct. 1812, and Major-General Van Rensselear to Major-General Sheaffe, 16 Oct. 1812, in Cruikshank (ed.), *Documentary History*, II, 129–31.

20. Joseph R. Roach, *Cities of the Dead: Circum-Atlantic Performance* (New York/Chichester, 1996), 137.

21. Wood, *Select British Documents*, I, 636–7.

22. *Parliamentary Debates*, xxvi, cols 1199–1200; *HC Journals*, vol. 68, p. 663 (13 July 1813); TNA, MPD 1/78, fos 8–10; T1/1411.11560.

23. David Solkin, *Painting for Money: The Visual Arts and the Public Sphere in Eighteenth-Century England* (New Haven, Conn./London, 1993), 210–13, quotations 212–13.

24. George Sheppard, *Plunder, Profit, and Paroles: A Social History of the War of 1812 in Upper Canada* (Montreal/London, 1994), 181–2, 208; *New-York Spectator*, 4 May 1840, col. F; *Cleveland Daily Herald*, 12 Oct. 1841, col. C; *North American and Daily Advertiser*, 12 Oct. 1842, col. D (first quotation); *North American and United States Gazette*, 19 Oct. 1853, col. F; *Vermont Patriot & State Gazette*, 12 Oct. 1855, col. H; *Daily Cleveland Herald*, 12 Oct. 1855, col. C, and 18 Oct. 1859, col. B; *New York Herald*, 19 Dec. 1858, p. 5; *New York Times*, 18 Oct. 1859 (second quotation). http://www.ontarioplaques.com/Plaques_MNO/Plaque_Outside05.html [accessed 9 Dec. 2008].

25. Quoted in John E. Walsh, *Execution* (London, 2001), 148. See also Winthrop Sargent, *The Life and Career of Major John André*, new edition with notes and illustrations, edited by W. Abbatt (New York, 1902), 408–10.

26. *Maryland Gazette and Political Intelligencer*, 2 Aug. 1821, col. B; 23 Aug. 1821, col. E.

27. Robert E. Cray, Jr, 'Major John André and the Three Captors: Class Dynamics and Revolutionary Memory Wars in the Early Republic, 1780–1831', *Journal of the Early Republic*, 17:3 (1997), 371–97; Susan Gray Davis, *Parades and Power: Street Theatre in Nineteenth-Century Philadelphia* (Philadelphia, 1986), 59–60, 64; John P. Resch, 'Politics and Public Culture: The Revolutionary War Pension Act of 1818', *Journal of the Early Republic*, 8:2 (1988), 139–58; Lydia Maria Child, *Letters from New York* (New York, 1843), 177–80 (quotation 179); Michael Meranze, 'Major Andre's Exhumation', in Nancy Isenberg and Andrew Burstein (eds), *Mortal Remains: Death in Early America* (Philadelphia, 2003), 123–35, 229–31.

28. Child, *Letters*, 172–3; *Maryland Gazette and Political Intelligencer*, 13 June 1822, col. A.

29. Horatio Spafford, *A Gazetteer of the State of New York* (New York, 1824), 331–2, quoted in Cray, 'Major John André', 391.

30. Child, *Letters*, 170–71.

31. Allan Cunningham, *The Lives of the Most Eminent British Painters, Sculptors, and Architects*, 6 vols (London, 1829–33), III, 73.

32. Edward Wedlake Brayley and John Preston Neale, *The History and Antiquities of the Abbey Church of St Peter, Westminster*, 2 vols (London, 1818, 1823), II, 241 ('wantonly damaged'); James Peller Malcolm, *Londinium Redivivum*, 4 vols (London, 1802–7), I, 167–8 ('proof of the necessity'); B. Lambert, *The History and Survey of London and its Environs: From the Earliest Period to the Present Time*, 4 vols (London, 1806), III, 413; Arthur Penrhyn Stanley, *Historical Memorials of Westminster Abbey* (London, 1868), 256–7 ('Often has the head …' and 'many a citizen').

33. The Dean of Westminster Abbey, quoted in Richard Jenkyns, *Westminster Abbey* (London, 2004), 158.

34. *The Times*, 9 June 1884, 9, quoted in Martin Myrone, *Bodybuilding: Reforming Masculinities in British Art 1750–1810* (New Haven, Conn./London, 2005), 351 n. 25.

35. At the same time the Castledownshend Nelson monument, pulled down in 1920, re-erected in 1926, was blown up by the IRA.

36. In a pre-development environmental impact assessment before the Spire was built, archaeologists with the Dublin Corporation recovered the dedication plaque which records the laying of the foundation stone and the names of the subscriber committee.

37. *Barbados Mercury*, 21 and 24 Dec. 1805, 7 and 14 Jan. 1806. David Lambert, '"Part of the Blood and Dream": Surrogation, Memory and the National Hero in the Postcolonial Caribbean', *Patterns of Prejudice*, 43:3 (2007), 345–71, esp. 346–50. http://www.barbados.gov.bb/bdosnathero.htm; http://www.yalealumnimagazine.com/issues/02_04/letters.html; http://www.rose-hulman.edu/~delacova/caribbean/statue.htm; http://wwwsoc.uwimona.edu.jm:1104/government/Henke.pdf; http://susan.chin.gc.ca/~intercom/cumins.pdf; http://barbadosfreepress.wordpress.com/2008/07/24/barbados-national-trust-votes-to-leave-nelsons-statue-where-it-is/ [all accessed Nov. 2008].

II. Empire, Archaeology, and Collecting
The Mediterranean and the Near East

1. HUN MSS, FB 52.
2. Michael Ledger-Lomas, 'Shipwrecked: James Smith and the Defence of Biblical Narrative in Victorian Britain,' in Rüdiger Görner (ed.), *Angermion: Jahrbuch für britisch-deutsche Kulturbeziehungen* (Berlin, 2008), 83–110.
3. Jonathan Scott, *The Pleasures of Antiquity: British Collectors of Greece and Rome* (New Haven, Conn./London, 2003), 172–9. For Sloane as an Enlightenment virtuoso in the context of imperial expansion see Arthur Macgregor (ed.), *Sir Hans Sloane: Collector, Scientist, Antiquary, Founding Father of the British Museum* (London, 1994).
4. Simplistic dichotomies of a 'French model' versus a 'British model' persist in the historiography, e.g. Margarita Diaz-Andreu, 'Britain and the Other: The Archaeology of Imperialism', in Helen Brocklehurst and Robert Phillips (eds), *History, Nationhood and the Question of Britain* (Basingstoke, 2004), 227–41, at 228.
5. Mogens T. Larsen, *The Conquest of Assyria: Excavations in an Antique Land, 1840–1860* (London/New York, 1994), 21; cf. Ian Jenkins, *Archaeologists and Aesthetes: The Sculpture Galleries of the British Museum 1800–1939* (London, 1992); Maya Jasanoff, *Edge of Empire: Conquest and Collecting in the East, 1750–1850* (London, 2005), 216–26; Holger Hoock, 'The Battle of the Nile and Its Cultural Aftermath', in Margarette Lincoln (ed.), *Nelson & Napoléon* (London, 2005), 65–71, 273.
6. Legrand, *Revue archéologique* (1897), 57.
7. Philip Mansel, 'The Grand Tour in the Ottoman Empire, 1699–1826', in Paul and Janet Starkey (eds), *Unfolding the Orient: Travellers in Egypt and the Near East* (Reading, 2001), 41–64, at 51–2.
8. Adolf Michaelis, *Ancient Marbles in Great Britain* (Cambridge, 1882), 182–3.
9. Scott, *Pleasures*; Viccy Coltman, *Fabricating the Antique: Neoclassicism in Britain, 1760–1800* (Chicago/London, 2005), is an excellent exploration of neoclassicism as a late eighteenth-century style of thought translated into material possessions. On nineteenth-century Hellenism see Richard Jenkyns, *The Victorians and Ancient Greece* (Oxford, 1980).
10. Donald M. Reid, *Whose Pharaohs? Archeology, Museums, and Egyptian National Identity from Napoleon to World War I* (Berkeley, Calif./London, 2002), 27, 43, 81. Cf. Holger Hoock, *The King's Artists: The Royal Academy of Arts and the Politics of British Culture, 1760–1840* (Oxford, 2003), ch. 4, for the tense marriage between patriotism and cosmopolitanism in the British and European art worlds.
11. Ian Jenkins and Kim Sloan, *Vases and Volcanoes: Sir William Hamilton and His Collection* (London, 1996). In 1799, the Society of Dilettanti commissioned Knight and Towneley to publish the best marbles and bronzes imported by private collectors over the previous half-century. The first volume appeared in 1809 as *Specimens of Antient*

Sculpture, covering the collections of Towneley, the Marquis of Lansdowne, Knight, Thomas Hope, and Lord Yarborough.

12. Lionel H. Cust, *History of the Society of Dilettanti*, ed. Sir Sidney Colvin (London, 1914), 77–96.

13. William Roy, *Military Antiquities of the Romans in Britain* (London, 1793); R. A. Gardiner, 'William Roy: Surveyor and Antiquary', *Geographical Journal*, 143 (1977), 439–50; Helen C. Adamson, *William Roy, 1726–1790: Pioneer of Roman Archaeology in Scotland* (Glasgow, 1984); George MacDonald, 'General William Roy and His Military Antiquities of the Romans in North Britain', *Archaeologia*, 68 (1917), 161–228; Richard Hingley, 'Projecting Empire: The Mapping of Roman Britain', *Journal of Social Archaeology*, 6:3 (2006), 328–53, at 339–40. Thanks to Rachel Hewitt for most of these references.

14. On Leake and Gell see J. M. Wagstaff, 'Colonel Leake: Traveller and Scholar', in Sarah Searight and J. M. Wagstaff (eds), *Travellers in the Levant: Voyagers and Visionaries* (Durham, 2001), 3–15; Charles Plouviez, 'Straddling the Aegean: William Gell 1811–1813', in ibid., 43–55. There is no space here to explore the full disciplinary and institutional contributions of geography and geology to the project of classical and Near Eastern British archaeology. For the relationship between the Geological Survey under the Director-Generalship of Sir Roderick Murchison and the Colonial, Foreign, India, and War Offices, and the Admiralty, see Robert A. Stafford, *Scientist of Empire: Sir Roderick Murchison, Scientific Exploration and Victorian Imperialism* (Cambridge/New York, 1989); Donald Gordon Payne, *The History of the Royal Geographical Society, 1830–1930: To the Farthest Ends of the Earth* (London, 1980).

15. BM, G.M. 1167 (9 May 1818).

16. Giovanni d'Athanasi, *Researches and Discoveries in Upper Egypt Made under the Direction of Henry Salt* (London, 1836), 23–4.

17. BM, O.P. XLII, Sir Charles Murray to Lord Lansdowne, Cairo, 1 Aug. 1849.

18. BL, Add. MS 38981, fos 106–8, Newton to Layard, 16 Aug. 1852.

19. Coltman, *Fabricating*; Scott, *Pleasures*; Philip Ayres, *Classical Culture and the Idea of Rome in Eighteenth-Century England* (Cambridge, 1997); Richard Jenkyns, *The Victorians and Ancient Greece* (Oxford, 1980), 60–61, 65.

20. *The Travels of Mirza Abu Taleb Khan, in Asia, Africa and Europe, during the Years 1799–1803*, trans. Charles Stewart, 2 vols (London, 1810), I, 120.

21. Magazines such as *Chambers's Edinburgh Journal*, 8 (1838–9), 90–92, also gave detailed accounts of domestic and personal Egyptian objects and crafts as documents of Egyptian civilisation.

22. Quoted in John Ray, *The Rosetta Stone and the Rebirth of Ancient Egypt* (London, 2007), 55.

23. [National Illustrated Library], *The Buried City of the East: Nineveh* (London, 1851), 293.

24. *Synopsis of the Contents of the British Museum* (London, 1808), xxx–xxxii.

Chapter Five: The Spoils of War

1. For the overlapping military, scientific, and Egyptological contexts see Maya Jasa-noff, *Edge of Empire: Conquest and Collecting in the East, 1750–1850* (London, 2005); Brian Lavery, *Nelson and the Nile: The Naval War against Bonaparte, 1798* (London, 1998); Piers Mackesy, *British Victory in Egypt* (London/New York, 1995); Patrice Bret, *L'expédition d'Égypte, une entreprise des Lumières 1798–1801* (Paris, 1999); Marie-Noëlle Bourguet, 'Science and Memory: The Stakes of the Expedition to Egypt (1798–1801)', in Howard G. Brown and Judith A. Miller (eds), *Taking Liberties: Problems of a New Order from the French Revolution to Napoleon* (Manchester/New York, 2002), 92–109; James S. Curl, *Egyptomania: The Egyptian Revival, a Recurring Theme in the History of Taste* (Manchester, 1994); Patrick Conner (ed.), *The Inspiration of Egypt: Its Influence on British Artists, Travellers and Designers, 1700–1900* (Brighton, 1983).
2. Quoted in Peter A. Clayton, *The Rediscovery of Ancient Egypt: Artists and Travellers in the 19th Century* (London, 1982), 19.
3. Brian M. Fagan, *The Rape of the Nile: Tomb Robbers, Tourists, and Archaeologists in Egypt* (New York, [1975]), 74, quoting a lieutenant without reference.
4. Bourguet, 'Science and Memory', 105.
5. National Archives of Scotland, Edinburgh, GF45/4/45, Meredith to Cavan, 6 Dec. 1801; Arthur H. Haley (ed.), *The Soldier Who Walked Away: Autobiography of Andrew Pearson, a Peninsular War Veteran* (Liverpool, [1987]), 30–39 (quotations 31, 39); see also Charles Steevens, *Reminiscences of My Military Life from 1795 to 1818, by the late Lieut.-Col. Chas. Steevens, Formerly of the XX Regiment*, ed. N. Steevens (Winchester, 1878), 27–30; National Archives of Scotland, Acc 12054, Sergeant William Newman's Journal, 'The Hardships of War', 2 vols, I, 63, references 'Pompy's Pillor'.
6. Archives Nationales, Paris, F17 1101, dossier 3T.
7. Robert T. Wilson, *History of the British Expedition to Egypt*, 2nd edn (London, 1803), 228 and note; BL, Add. MS 30095, 284, Wilson Journal, 7 Sep. 1801.
8. Quoted in John Ray, *The Rosetta Stone and the Rebirth of Ancient Egypt* (London, 2007), 36.
9. TNA, WO 1/345, p. 450, 'Articles de la Capitulation proposée par Abdoulahy Jacques François Menou Général en Chef de l'armée française actuellement à Alexandrie'; BL, Add. MS 46839, fos 12–13, 'Inventory of Egyptian antiquities in the possession of the French authorities at Alexandria'; Society of Antiquaries, *Archaeologia*, 27 (London, 1812), 213–14; [Prospectus], 'Under the patronage of His Majesty. Engravings with a descriptive account, in English and French, of Egyptian Monuments, in the *British Museum*'; British Museum, *Acts and Votes* (London, 1805), 83.
10. *Notice de la Galerie des Antiques du Musée Napoléon* (Paris, an 11), 4.

11. Dorothy Mackay Quynn, 'The Art Confiscations of the Napoleonic Wars', *American Historical Review*, 50 (1945), 437–60, at 437–9; Andrew McClellan, *Inventing the Louvre: Art, Politics and the Origins of the Modern Museum in Eighteenth-Century Paris* (Cambridge, 1994), 121–3; Ian Jenkins, *Archaeologists and Aesthetes: The Sculpture Galleries of the British Museum 1800–1939* (London, 1992), 105. An exemplary study of an aspect of Napoleon's art loot is Benedicte Savoy, *Patrimoine annexé: Les biens culturels saisis par la France en Allemagne autour de 1800*, 2 vols (Paris, 2003).

12. For this, and Herder's challenge to Winckelmann's insistence that Egyptian art should be judged according to Greek standards, see Nigel Leask, *Curiosity and the Aesthetics of Travel Writing, 1770–1840* (Oxford, 2002), 107–8, and Jenkins, *Archaeologists and Aesthetes*, 10.

13. George R. Gliddon, *An Appeal to the Antiquaries of Europe: On the Destruction of the Monuments of Egypt* (London, 1841), 111.

14. Quoted in Stanley Mayes, *The Great Belzoni* (London, 1959), 225.

15. For Anglo-French rivalry in Egypt, and key characters, see Jasanoff, *Edge of Empire*; Mayes, *Great Belzoni*; Deborah Manley and Peta Rée, *Henry Salt: Artist, Traveller, Diplomat, Egyptologist* (London, 2001); Ronald T. Ridley, *Napoleon's Proconsul in Egypt: The Life and Times of Bernardino Drovetti* (London, [1998?]).

16. BL, Add. MS 25658, fos 47, 54–6, 64; 30129, fos 4–14; TNA, FO 566/449, Register FO Correspondence from Turkey, 1818–33, entries Barker, 30 June 1830; FO 78/89/64, 72, 82; 91/113–14; BM, C2691–2 (14 Mar. 1818); [G. Long], *British Museum*, II, 375–6; *Annals of the Fine Arts*, 3 (1819), 494–8; Jasanoff, *Edge of Empire*, 249–55.

17. TNA, FO 24/6/66, Society of Antiquaries, Memorandum on the Rosetta Stone [n.d.].

18. BL, Add. MS 21026, fos 32–3, Salt to W. Hamilton, 1 May 1819, 'extract', 33v; 25658, fos 21–3, Burton to Barker, 15 Feb. 1828.

19. Correspondence between Burton, Salt, Barker, and British government officials (1827–8): TNA, HO 44/17/78, FO 78/160/55–7; FO 78/170/72; FO 352/19A, 2/384; BL, Add. MS 25658, fos 17–20, 24, 32; 25659, fos 21–3; fos 2–4, 'Mem.: regarding a Trilingual Stone at Grand Cairo' [n.d., early 1829?] (first quotation); Robert Solé and Dominique Valbelle, *The Rosetta Stone: The Story of the Decoding of Hieroglyphics* (London, 2002), 96–8 (second quotation, 98). For the Rosetta Stone see also Richard Parkinson, *Cracking Codes: The Rosetta Stone and Decipherment* (London, 1999).

20. British and international correspondence in 1829: BL, Add. MS 25658, fos 39, 42–53 (first quotation, 45r); 25659, fos 44v–47 (second and third quotations, 44v, 47r); TNA, FO 78/184/89; Royal Society of Literature [RSL], Council Minutes II, 79–82; Emmanuel de Rougé, *Notice des monuments exposés dans la galerie d'antiquités égyptiennes … au Musée du Louvre* (Paris, 1849), cat. C122.

21. *Report, Select Committee on the British Museum*, 1836, [10]:1, sec. 10: 56–7.

22. Along with measures following Greek independence in 1830, his ordinance was one of the earliest laws to preserve any country's cultural patrimony. Between 1800 and 1815,

Papal decrees and Napoleonic legislation banned the export of Roman antiquities, regulated excavations, and planned for the protection and restoration of sites. Stephanie Moser, *Wondrous Curiosities: Ancient Egypt at the British Museum* (Chicago/London, 2006), 139, 141; Margarita Díaz-Andreu, *A World History of Nineteenth-Century Archaeology: Nationalism, Colonialism, and the Past* (Oxford, 2007), 72.

23. *Quarterly Review*, 11 (1814), 458, quoted in Terence Spencer, *Fair Greece, Sad Relic: Literary Philhellenism from Shakespeare to Byron* (Bath, 1974), 229. Philip Mansel, 'The Grand Tour in the Ottoman Empire, 1699–1826', in Paul and Janet Starkey (eds), *Unfolding the Orient: Travellers in Egypt and the Near East* (Reading, 2001), 41–64.

24. For the Aegina and Bassae Marbles see William St Clair, *Lord Elgin and the Marbles: The Controversial History of the Parthenon Sculptures*, 3rd rev. edn (Oxford, 1998), 201–4; Raimund Wünsche, 'Ludwigs Skulpturenerwerbungen für die Glyptothek', in Klaus Vierneisel and Gottlieb Leinz (eds), *Glyptothek München 1830–1980* (Munich, 1980), 23–83, at 49–70; Hansgeorg Bankel (ed.), *Carl Haller von Hallerstein in Griechenland 1810–1817* (Berlin, 1986), 83–91, 122–31; Samuel Pepys Cockerell (ed.), *Travels in Southern Europe and the Levant, 1810–1817: The Journal of C. R. Cockerell, R.A.* (London, 1903), repr. as Charles Robert Cockerell, *Travels in Southern Europe and the Levant, 1810–1817*. (*Museums and Their Development: The European Tradition 1700–1900*, ed. and introduced by Susan M. Pearce, vol. IV) (London, 1999), 56–7, 214–15.

25. Cockerell, *Travels*, 56–7.

26. NMM/KEI/15/4, Elgin to Keith, 15 June and 9 Sep. 1801, 6 Jan. 1802; St Clair, *Lord Elgin*, 93–4, 129; BL, Add. MS 38246, fo. 119.

27. St Clair, *Lord Elgin*, 113.

28. Ibid., 116, 123–4, 132–4, 153–7; A. H. Smith, 'Lord Elgin and His Collection', *Journal of Hellenic Studies*, 36 (1916), 163–372, at 358–9; BL, Add. MS 56486, fo. 3.

29. Robert Wood, *The Ruins of Balbec, otherwise Heliopolis, in Coelosyria* (London, 1757), 1.

30. Society of Dilettanti, *Report of the Committee of the Society of Dilettanti, appointed by the Society to superintend the expedition lately sent by them to Greece and Ionia* (London, 1814), 16.

31. RSL, Council Minutes II, 51–3, 59–61; Alain Schnapp, *The Discovery of the Past: The Origins of Archaeology* (London, 1996), 305–7.

32. Kenneth R. H. Mackenzie (ed.), *Discoveries in Egypt, Ethiopia and the Peninsula of Sinai in the Years 1842–1845* (London, 1852), 31.

33. Clarke in a private letter to a friend, quoted in Brian Dolan, *Exploring European Frontiers: British Travellers in the Age of Enlightenment* (Basingstoke, 2000), 135–6: 'We have the better Orientalists than the French.'

34. *Descriptive Account of a Series of Pictures … now Exhibiting at the Egyptian Hall* (London, 1828), 38 (quotation); BL, Add. MS 25659, fo. 3; 30977, fos 14–17.

35. *Quarterly Review*, 28 (Oct. 1822), 76, footnote; Sébastien L. Saulnier Fils, *Notice sur le voyage de M. Lelorrain en Égypte et observations sur le zodiaque circulaire de Denderah* (Paris, 1822).
36. Quoted in Dietrich Wildung, *Preussen am Nil* (Berlin, 2002), 15.
37. Leask, *Curiosity*, 126, 151.
38. BL, Add. MS 25658, 50–56 (quotations 50r, 50v); BL, Add. MS 29859, fo. 32v.
39. *Edinburgh Review*, 6 (1807), 481.
40. Wilson, *History*, 269; BL, Add. MS 30129, fos 4–14 (quotations at 4–5); cf. Haley (ed.), *Soldier*, 31–2.
41. *European Magazine*, 80 (1821), i, 90–91. Repeated attempts by travellers, military officers, and others in the 1820s–40s to get the British government to transport the obelisk to Britain failed, despite the fact that the French were successfully removing prize obelisks to Paris. The obelisk was finally transported to London in 1877/8 and erected on the north bank of the river Thames, where it still stands today; the operation was financed privately by the foremost mid-Victorian dermatologist and leading philanthropist Erasmus Wilson. See William Rae Wilson, *Travels in Egypt and the Holy Land*, 2nd edn (London, 1824), 26; BL, Add. MS 25658, fo. 47, Burton to Earl of Aberdeen, 3 Aug. 1829; fos 54–6, Barker to Burton, 15 Aug. 1829, with addendum 28 Aug.; fo. 64, Barker to Burton, 14 June 1830; TNA, FO 566/449, Register FO Correspondence from Turkey, 1818–33, entries Barker, 30 June 1830; Todd Porterfield, *The Allure of Empire: Art in the Service of French Imperialism 1798–1836* (Princeton, NJ, 1998), ch. 1.
42. *European Magazine*, 80 (1821), i, 91–2; cf. ii, 422–3 with note. For Quatremère see the wide-ranging discussion in Daniel J. Sherman, 'Quartremère/Benjamin/Marx: Art Museums, Aura, and Commodity Fetishism', in Daniel J. Sherman and Irit Rogoff (eds), *Museum Culture: Histories, Discourses, Spectacles* (Minneapolis, 1994), 123–43.
43. William St Clair, 'Imperial Appropriations of the Parthenon', in John H. Merryman (ed.), *Imperialism, Art and Restitution* (Cambridge, 2006), 65–98, at 79.
44. *Parliamentary Debates*, 1st ser., xxxii, cols 577–8 (15 and 23 Feb. 1816), at pp. 823–8, quotation 824. For an analysis of the select committee proceedings and further reading see my *King's Artists*, 288–92.
45. Jenkins, *Archaeologists and Aesthetes*, 17.
46. P.P. 1816, iii (161), 49, 'Report from the Select Committee on the Purchase of the Earl of Elgin's Collection of Sculptured Marbles', 15.
47. St Clair, 'Imperial Appropriations of the Parthenon', 81.
48. Dolan, *Exploring*, 138, with reference to Hamilton's pamphlet *Memorandum on the Subject of the Earl of Elgin's Pursuits in Greece* (1811), and Clarke's published travel accounts.
49. Gillen D'Arcy Wood, *The Shock of the Real: Romanticism and Visual Culture, 1760–1860* (Basingstoke, 2001), 157, quoting *The Curse*, ll. 143–8.

50. For this complex, and the notion of temporalising antique lands, topographies, and their modern inhabitants by comparing them with biblical or classical worlds, see Leask, *Curiosity*.

51. Richard Chandler, *Travels in Greece; or, An Account of a Tour Made at the Expense of the Society of Dilettanti* (Oxford, 1775), 50, 'ignorant contempt and brutal violence'. W. Eton, *A Survey of the Turkish Empire* (London, 1799), e.g. 348–50; Pierre-Augustin Guys, *Voyage littéraire de la Grèce, ou Lettres sur les Grecs, anciens et modernes, avec un parallèle de leurs moeurs*, 2 vols (Paris, 1771). 'Modern Greece …': one such report quoted in William St Clair, *That Greece Might Still be Free: The Philhellenes in the War of Independence* (London/New York/Toronto, 1972), 116. Hughes: Thomas Smart Hughes, *Travels in Sicily, Greece, and Albania*, 2 vols (London, 1820), quoted in Christopher M. Woodhouse, *The Philhellenes* (London, 1969), 27; cf. H. N. Angelomatis-Tsougarakis, *The Eve of the Greek Revival: British Travellers' Perceptions of Early Nineteenth-Century Greece* (Oxford, 1986), ch. 3; Leask, *Curiosity*, 114, 146–7; Catherine P. Bracken, *Antiquities Acquired: The Spoliation of Greece* (Newton Abbot, 1975), 40–41.

52. On indigenous archaeologies see Yannis Hamilakis, *The Nation and Its Ruins: Antiquity, Archaeology, and National Imagination in Greece* (Oxford, 2007), ch. 3, with further references; Richard Clogg, 'Sense of the Past in Pre-Independence Greece', in Roland Sussex and J. C. Eade (eds), *Culture and Nationalism in Nineteenth-Century Eastern Europe* (Columbus, Ohio, 1983), 7–30, at 9–10; Yannis Hamilakis, 'Decolonizing Greek Archaeology: Indigenous Archaeologies, Modernist Archaeology and the Post-Colonial Critique', in Dimitris Plantzos and Dimitris Damaskos (eds), *A Singular Antiquity: Archaeology and Hellenic Identity in Twentieth-Century Greece* (Athens, 2008), 273–84, with a good reading of the clash of indigenous and Western archaeologies over Clarke's 1801 removal of the so-called Ceres or Demeter from Eleusis to Cambridge.

53. St Clair, *That Greece Might Still be Free*, note on p. 317.

54. Díaz-Andreu, *A World History of Nineteenth-Century Archaeology*, 82–6, on the relation between western Philhellenism, Greek intellectuals, and Greek antiquity.

55. On the importance of the new archaeology and of classical antiquities to the new state see Hamilakis, *Nation and Its Ruins*, 53, 79–99; Yannis Hamilakis and Eleana Yalouri, 'Sacralizing the Past: The Cults of Archaeology in Modern Greece', *Archaeological Dialogues*, 6:2 (1999), 115–35.

56. Captain E. de Verninac Saint-Maur, *Voyage de Luxor* (1835), quoted in Donald M. Reid, *Whose Pharaohs? Archeology, Museums, and Egyptian National Identity from Napoleon to World War I* (Berkeley, Calif./London, 2002), 1.

57. Quoted in Jonathan Scott, *The Pleasures of Antiquity: British Collectors of Greece and Rome* (New Haven, Conn./London, 2003), 225.

58. For Denon see his *Travels*, 1801, trans. A. Aikin, 3 vols, III, 187, quoted in Leask, *Curiosity*, 118. For the second quotation see Frédéric Caillaud (1822) in Peter France, *The Rape of Egypt: How the Europeans Stripped Egypt of Its Heritage* (London, 1938), 107. See also Mackenzie (ed.), *Discoveries*, note on p. 10, for Lepsius.

59. BL, Add. MS 43233, fos 44–5, Aberdeen to Lt-Col. Leake, 4 Apr. 1829, quotations 45.

Chapter Six: Antique Diplomacy

1. For Chandler see Brian Dolan, *Exploring European Frontiers: British Travellers in the Age of Enlightenment* (Basingstoke, 2000), 124–7.

2. Francis Beaufort, *Karamania, or a Brief Description of the South Coast of Asia-Minor and of the Remains of Antiquity* (London, 1817), viii–ix. See HUN MSS, FV 51, for his topographical watercolour sketches of Mediterranean sites with commentary, 1810–12.

3. Beaufort, *Karamania*, x.

4. HUN MSS, FB 458, Malta, Frederiksteen, [?20] Oct. 1811.

5. Beaufort, *Karamania*, 2–7, quotation 6–7, referring to Herodotus, Plutarch, and Appian. See HUN MSS, FB 15–17, Journals Frederiksteen, July 1811–June 1812, for Beaufort's detailed notes on topography and archaeological discoveries, including Patara, with some ink and ink and wash sketches of topography, ancient sites, specific monuments, transcriptions of inscriptions.

6. HUN MSS, FB 17/100–103, quotation 101–3.

7. Samuel Pepys Cockerell (ed.), *Travels in Southern Europe and the Levant, 1810–1817: The Journal of C. R. Cockerell, R.A.* (London, 1903), repr. as Charles Robert Cockerell, *Travels in Southern Europe and the Levant, 1810–1817.* (*Museums and Their Development: The European Tradition 1700–1900*, ed. and introduced by Susan M. Pearce, vol. IV) (London, 1999), 190–99.

8. Edward Forbes and Thomas Spratt, *Travels in Lycia, Milyas, and the Cibyratis*, 2 vols (London, 1847); Thomas Spratt, *Travels and Researches in Crete*, 2 vols (London, 1865). Cf. Michael Ledger-Lomas, 'Shipwrecked: James Smith and the Defence of Biblical Narrative in Victorian Britain', in *Angermion: Jahrbuch für britisch-deutsche Kulturbeziehungen*, ed. Ruediger Goerner (Berlin, 2008), 83–110.

9. TNA, ADM 1/4282, J. Forshall, Secretary BM, to Lords Commissioners ADM, 10 Apr. 1839, enclosing correspondence between all parties; quotations from J. Forshall to Lord Commissioners of the Admiralty, 9 March 1839 and Edward Hawkins to Charles Wood, MP, 1 Aug. 1839; Charles Fellows, *The Xanthian Marbles; their Acquisition and Transmission to England* (London, 1843), 3; see also Fellows, *An Account of Discoveries in Lycia, Being a Journal Kept During a Second Excursion in Asia Minor by Charles Fellows 1840* (London, 1841), 241–2.

10. P. J. Vatikiotis, *The History of Modern Egypt: From Muhammad Ali to Mubarak*, 4th edn (London, 1991), 68.

11. Jonathan P. Parry, *The Politics of Patriotism: English Liberalism, National Identity and Europe, 1830–1886* (Cambridge, 2006), 152–3.

12. BL, Add. MS 40565, fo. 242v; BM, O.P. XXIV, Fellows to Trustees, 31 May 1841. Fellows's plea was reinforced by William R. Hamilton: Ian Jenkins, *Archaeologists and Aesthetes: The Sculpture Galleries of the British Museum 1800–1939* (London, 1992), 142 with reference to BM, O.P. XXIV, 8 and 10 June 1841; Fellows, *Xanthian Marbles*, 5–6, 41; Enid Slatter, *Xanthus: Travels of Discovery in Turkey: Original Illustrations by Charles Fellows and George Scharf Junior* (London, 1994), 226, 231; BL, Add. MS 70849, fo. 12, Forshall to Fellows, c/o British Consulate, Smyrna, 20 Dec. 1841; fo. 14, Forshall to Fellows, c/o British Consulate, Rhodes, au soins Smyrna, 15 Jan. 1842.

13. Fellows, *Xanthian Marbles*, 7–11; BM, O.P. XXV, Charles Bankhead to [My Lord], 24 Nov. 1841. Cf. Hamilton's brief in BM, O.P. XXIV, 10 June 1841; Slatter, *Xanthus*, 215–17.

14. Fellows, *Xanthian Marbles*, 22–4, 31–2, 40–41 (quotation 23–4).

15. Slatter, *Xanthus*, 231–4; Jenkins, *Archaeologists and Aesthetes*, 142–3.

16. These included Xanthian mammals, birds, reptiles, fishes, and annulosa, Sicilian shells and sponges, as well as British insects. In Rome in summer 1843 the inveterate collector also procured moulds of bas-reliefs in the Villa Albani as comparative material for the Lycian marbles, complete with suggestions for the colouring of the restored parts. BL, Add. MS 53724, fos 3, 5, 21, 23, 25–7.

17. P.P. 1850, xxiv, 'Report of the Commissioners Appointed to Inquire into the Constitution and Government of the British Museum with Minutes of Evidence', 40.

18. BM, O.P. XXVIII, 26 May 1843.

19. BL, Add. MS 53724, fos 25v–26, Forshall to Fellows, 16 May 1843; Add. MS 40565, fos 242–5. TNA, ADM 1/5530/no. 291.

20. TNA, ADM 1/5530/no. 291 (quotation); ADM 53/422; Slatter, *Xanthus*, 298.

21. Armstrong's reports are filed in TNA, ADM 1/5540 (Med. 1844) In-letters and papers.

22. TNA, ADM 1/5540.

23. Fellows, *Xanthian Marbles*, 31.

24. Thanks to Michael Ledger-Lomas for pointing this out.

25. TNA, ADM 1/5540; ADM 51/3637, Journal of HMS *Medea*, 14 Aug. 1840–8 July 1850.

26. Popular song written and sung by Edwin Ransford to music by N. J. Sporle. BL, Add. MS 36488 C, George Scharf, Journal of Journey to Asia Minor, 5 Aug. 1843–20 May 1844, this account from fos 40–59, 27 Oct. 1843–end of Jan. 1844; quotations: 43v, 48r, 58v–59r.

27. TNA, ADM 51/33704, log HMS *Warspite*; BM, O.P. XXX, Fellows to Forshall, 29 June 1844; C.6475, 29 June 1844; C6519, 9 Nov. 1844; BL, Add. MS 53724, fos 7, 9, 15. The quotation from BL, Add. MS 40565, fo. 247, Peel to Fellows.

28. For the early rediscovery of the ancient Near East see St John Simpson, 'From Perse-
    polis to Babylon and Nineveh: The Rediscovery of the Ancient Near East', in Kim
    Sloan with Andrew Burnett (eds), *Enlightenment: Discovering the World in the Eigh-
    teenth Century* (London, 2003), 192–201. I have used Layard's very extensive papers at
    the BL only selectively. Jonathan P. Parry, Cambridge, is preparing a full account. See
    also Henry Layard, *Discoveries in the Ruins of Nineveh and Babylon* (London, 1853);
    Cyril John Gadd, *The Stones of Assyria: The Surviving Remains of Assyrian Sculpture,
    Their Recovery and Their Original Positions* (London, 1936); Mogens T. Larsen, *The
    Conquest of Assyria: Excavations in an Antique Land, 1840–1860* (London/New York,
    1994); William K. Loftus, 'Warkah: its Ruins and Remains (With a Plan)', *Transactions
    of the Royal Society of Literature*, 2nd ser., 6 (1859), 1–64.
29. A. Henry Layard, *Nineveh and its Remains*, 2 vols (London, 1849), I, 71.
30. *Athenaeum*, 24 June 1843, 543; *The Times*, 14 Dec. 1844, 5.
31. BL, Add. MS 38976, fo. 234, Rawlinson to Layard, 15 Oct. 1845 (quotation); Layard,
    Nineveh, 40, 70–71; Larsen, *Conquest*, 24–5; Paul Emile Botta, *Monuments de Ninivé*,
    5 vols (Paris, 1847–50); Gordon Waterfield, *Layard of Nineveh* (London, 1963), 114.
32. BL, Add. MS 38941, fo. 36.
33. BL, Add. MS 47490, fo. 107, John Barker to Dr John Lee, 27 Sep. 1827.
34. *Quarterly Review*, 19 (Dec. 1818), 391. Canning's Consular Act of 1825 had completed
    the transformation of the previous hybrid 'Cinderella Service' of consuls partly
    appointed by the trading companies, partly by the state, into a professional govern-
    ment service. D. C. M. Platt, *The Cinderella Service: British Consuls since 1825* (London,
    1971).
35. Robert A. Stafford, *Scientist of Empire: Sir Roderick Murchison, Scientific Exploration
    and Victorian Imperialism* (Cambridge/New York, 1989), 94–7. For the wider context
    see Peter Sluglett, 'Formal and Informal Empire in the Middle East', in Robert W.
    Winks (ed.), *OHBE, vol. V: Historiography* (Oxford/New York, 1999), 416–36, esp.
    416–18.
36. BL, Add. MS 38941, fo. 36, Layard to Henry Ross [begun on 3 Dec. 1848]; 40574, fos 21–6,
    correspondence between Stratford Canning and Peel, Sep. 1845–Jan. 1846.
37. BL, Add. MS 40637, fos 20–21, 28–9, Layard to Canning, 1 and 15 Dec. 1845; cf. Stanley
    Lane-Poole, *The Life of the Right Honourable Stratford Canning*, 2 vols (London, 1888),
    II, 149; Layard, *Nineveh*, 87–8; Waterfield, *Layard*, 124, 134.
38. *Athenaeum*, 10 Oct. 1846, 1046–7, quoted in Larsen, *Conquest*, 113.
39. BL, Add. MS 30977, fos 18–19 (quotation fo. 9).
40. BL, Add. MS 38976, fos 369–70; A. Henry Layard, *Popular Account of the Discoveries
    at Nineveh* (London, 1851), 91.
41. BL, Add. MS 38976, fo. 355, Stratford Canning to Layard, 6 May 1846.
42. BM, O.P. XXXIV, 12 Mar. 1846; XXXV, 21 Aug. 1846.

43. Lane-Poole, *Stratford Canning*, II, 149–50; BL, Add. MS 38977, fo. 47, Canning to Layard, 7 Sep. 1846.

44. BL, Add. MSS 30977, fos 14–17, Memorandum for the consideration and use of M.:r Layard, 21 Sep. 1846.

45. BL, Add. MS 30977, fos 97–9, 158; 38942, fos 9, 12.

46. BL, Add. MS 30977, fo. 9, Layard to Capt. Jones, 25 Oct. 1849; fo. 12, Layard to Capt. Kambell, 10 Jan. 1850; fo. 39v, Layard to Sir Henry Ellis, 2 June 1850 (quotation). TNA, ADM 53/2710–11, HMS *Jumna*'s logs, entries 18 Mar., 13 Oct. 1848; BM, O.P. XLII, 10 and 14 Aug. 1849; C7844, 18 Aug. 1849; O.R. 41, 8 Nov. 1848; C.7628, 11 Nov. 1848. O.P. LXII, 10 Aug. 1849; C7844, 18 Aug. 1849.

47. BL, Add. MS 39096, fo. 189, Hawkins to Layard, 24 Oct. 1848. I owe the reference to this dispute to Jonathan P. Parry.

48. BL, Add. MS 58174, *Bombay Times*, 24 Mar. and 28 Apr. 1849.

49. Transcripts of Botta's remuneration had been put in ministers' hands during their special Museum tour; but the Cotton Spinners protests had distracted government attention away from antiquities. BL, Add. MS 39096, fo. 349, Birch to Layard, 17 Jan. 1849 (quotations). For readings of the *Illustrated London News* see Shawn Malley, 'Shipping the Bull: Staging Assyria in the British Museum', *Nineteenth-Century Contexts*, 26:1 (2004), 1–27; Frederick N. Bohrer, *Orientalism and Visual Culture: Imagining Mesopotamia in Nineteenth-Century Europe* (Cambridge, 2003), ch. 5.

50. Larsen, *Conquest*, 192; BL, Add. MS 30977, fo. 158, 'Expences on the last Lion & Bull sent to England'; BL, Add. MS 38942, fos 9, 12; Layard, *Discoveries in the Ruins of Nineveh and Babylon*, 2; *Illustrated London News*, 26 June 1847, 409–10 (quotations).

51. Layard, *Popular Account*, 380–81; also in [National Illustrated Library], *The Buried City of the East: Nineveh* (London, 1851), 293–4.

52. BM, O.P. XLII, 20 Mar. 1849.

53. Lord Ellesmere in Feb. 1849, quoted in Waterfield, *Layard*, 194 (from BL, Add. MS 38977).

54. Stafford, *Scientist of Empire*, 95–7.

55. BM, O.P. XLII, 20 Mar. 1849; BL, Add. MS 38980, fos 29–32. The quotations in Waterfield, *Layard*, 222, 227.

56. Geheimes Staatsarchiv Preussischer Kulturbesitz, Berlin, GstA PK, GZ I, 44a.

57. BL, Add. MS 38979, fos 411–12, Stratford Canning to Palmerston, 18 Dec. 1850; cf. fos 409–10 for translations of vizierial letters.

58. BM, O.P. XXXII, 11 Mar. 1845.

59. *British Quarterly Review*, 9 (1849), 399–442, esp. 414, 417–18; *North British Review*, 11 (1849), 111–35; cf. Shawn Malley, 'Austen Henry Layard and the Periodical Press: Middle Eastern Archaeology and the Excavation of Cultural Identity in Mid-Nineteenth Century Britain', *Victorian Review*, 22:2 (1996), 152–70, at 161; William Ainsworth, *Researches in Assyria, Babylonia, and Chaldaea* (London, 1838), 4.

60. BM, O.P. XXXV, 21 Apr. 1846; XXXIV, 14 Sep. 1845.
61. BM, O.P. XXXVI, 19 Aug. 1846.
62. Quoted in Jonathan Parry, 'Layard, Sir Austen Henry (1817–1894)', *Oxford Dictionary of National Biography* (Oxford, 2004), http://www.oxforddnb.com/view/article/16218 [accessed 26 Sep. 2005].
63. Quoted in Larsen, *Conquest*, 105.
64. A. H. Layard, *Original Drawings*, Vol. III, number NW43 (1845–7), based on relief of Ashurnasirpal on his throne, BM 12565.
65. Frederick N. Bohrer, 'Inventing Assyria: Exoticism and Reception in Nineteenth-Century England and France', in Donald Preziosi and Claire Farago (eds), *Grasping the World: The Idea of the Museum* (Aldershot, 2004), 191–226; Bohrer, *Orientalism*, ch. 4, and p. 209 for Sidney Smirke's assessment of the greater indebtedness of Greek decorative motifs and sculpture to Assyrian than to Egyptian art.
66. Quoted in Julian Reade, *Assyrian Sculpture* (London, 1998), 15.
67. The collection which eventually did reach Berlin had initially been acquired by the Crystal Palace Company. Gadd, *Stones of Assyria*, 74–7, 87–8, 93–6, 105–10, 118–19, Appendix.
68. My account in this section largely follows Jenkins, *Archaeologists and Aesthetes*, ch. 8, with very full documentation from the British Museum Archives. I have also consulted Charles Thomas Newton, *A History of Discoveries at Halicarnassus, Cnidus, and Branchidae*, 2 vols (London, 1862–3); Brian F. Cook, 'Sir Charles Newton, KCB (1816–1894)', in Ian Jenkins and G. B. Waywell (eds), *Sculptors and Sculpture of Caria and the Dodecanese*, with assistance from M. Gisler-Huwiler and Peter Higgs (London, 1997), 10–21; William Kirk Dickson, *The Life of Major-General Sir Robert Murdoch Smith* (London, 1901); Lane-Poole, *Stratford Canning*.
69. BL, Add. MS 34582, fo. 329, Newton to Dr Bliss, 9 Jan. 1852.
70. W. B. Stanford and E. J. Finopolou, *The Travels of Lord Charlemont in Greece and Turkey in 1749* (London, 1984); Mayer's drawings were published as prints in London in 1801–10.
71. Quoted in Lane-Poole, *Stratford Canning*, II, 148.
72. BL, Add. MS 34582, fo. 329, 9 Jan. 1852.
73. Quoted in Jenkins, *Archaeologists and Aesthetes*, 183.
74. In 1847, an Admiralty-sponsored hydrographic expedition led by Graves and Spratt used ancient topographical references and recent British charts to seek to determine the location of the Mausoleum at Halicarnassus: Thomas Spratt, 'On Halicarnassus', *Transactions of the Royal Society of Literature*, 2nd ser., 5 (1856), 1–23.
75. In 1865, Newton had acquired a stray piece of the Mausoleum frieze in the Viletta of the Marchese di Negro at Genoa through Consul Brown for £720, having first tried for it for £200 in the late 1840s. The same year, Salzmann and Biliotti excavated on

behalf of the Museum further sculptural and architectural fragments at Bodrum and sent them on HMS *Orontes* and *Chanticleer*.

76. David Gange, 'Religion and Science in Late Nineteenth-Century British Egyptology', *Historical Journal*, 49:4 (2006), 1083–1103, demonstrates that late nineteenth-century British Egyptology was more influenced by religious considerations than has hitherto been supposed.

77. Bernard Porter, '"Bureau and Barrack": Early Victorian Attitudes towards the Continent', *Victorian Studies*, 27 (1983–4), 407–33.

78. See the discussions in Leask, *Curiosity*; Dolan, *Exploring*.

India

1. Quoted in Matthew H. Edney, *Mapping an Empire: The Geographical Construction of British India, 1765-1843* (Chicago/London, 1997), 291.
2. BL, IOR/Eur MSS D809.
3. Thomas and William Daniell, *A Picturesque Voyage to India* (London, 1810), i–ii.
4. Quoted in Douglas M. Peers, 'Colonial Knowledge and the Military in India, 1780–1860', *Journal of Imperial and Commonwealth History*, 33 (2005), 157–80, at 161.
5. Nicholas B. Dirks, e.g. in *The Scandal of Empire: India and the Creation of Imperial Britain* (Cambridge, Mass., 2006), stresses the former; P. J. Marshall, C. A. Bayly, and their pupils emphasise the latter dimension of colonial state formation.
6. Richard Drayton, 'Knowledge and Empire', in P. J. Marshall (ed.), *OHBE, vol. II: Eighteenth Century* (Oxford/New York, 1998–9), 231–52; Thomas R. Trautmann, *Aryans and British India* (Berkeley, Calif./London, 1997); Peers, 'Colonial Knowledge'.
7. The Company was run from London by a board of 24 directors, mostly substantial City businessmen and men who had returned from India. By the end of the eighteenth century there were some 3,000 shareholders. See Lucy Sutherland, *The East India Company in Eighteenth-Century Politics* (Oxford, 1952); Huw Bowen, *The Business of Empire: The East India Company and Imperial Britain, 1756-1833* (Cambridge, 2006); K. N. Chaudhuri, *The Trading World of Asia and the English East India Company* (Cambridge, 1978); P. J. Marshall, *East Indian Fortunes: The British in Bengal in the Eighteenth Century* (Oxford, 1976); Huw Bowen, Margarette Lincoln, and Nigel Rigby (eds), *The Worlds of the East India Company* (Woodbridge, 2002); Philip Lawson, *The East India Company: A History* (London, 1993).
8. Douglas M. Peers, 'Soldiers, Scholars, and the Scottish Enlightenment: Militarism in Early Nineteenth-Century India', *International History Review*, 16:3 (1994), 441–65; Peers, 'Between Mars and Mammon: The East India Company and Efforts to Reform Its Army, 1796-1832', *Historical Journal*, 33:2 (1990), 385–401; Peers, 'The Indian Army and the British Garrison State in India, c.1800-1858', in Alan Guy and Peter B. Boyden (eds), *Soldiers of the Raj: The Indian Army, 1600-1947* (London, 1997), 57–67.

9. Robert Travers, *Ideology and Empire in Eighteenth-Century India: The British in Bengal* (Cambridge, 2007), shows how the English political language of 'ancient constitution-alism' was transplanted to Bengal, where the British sought to justify imperial rule by reference to an ancient Mughal constitution.

10. Kaushik Roy, 'Introduction: Armies, Warfare, and Society in Colonial India', in Roy (ed.), *War and Society in Colonial India* (New Delhi, 2006), 1–52, at 1. For the largely Indian nature of the Company army see Seema Alavi, *The Sepoys and the Company: Tradition and Transition in Northern India 1770–1830* (Oxford, 1995). For the 'garrison state' see Peers, 'The Indian Army and the British Garrison State'.

11. On Company reform see P. J. Marshall, 'The British in India', in Marshall (ed.), *OHBE, vol. II*, 485–507; see in the same vol. the essays by Rakat K. Ray, 'Indian Society and the Establishment of British Supremacy, 1765–1818', 508–29, and Huw Bowen, 'British India, 1765–1813: The Metropolitan Context', 530–51. Cf. Linda Colley, *Captives: Britain, Empire and the World, 1600–1850* (London, 2002), 242–4, 249, 257. Historians detect parallels between the British state's reactions to change at home and imperial activity. A 'more conservative and militaristic nationalism, a new emphasis on cer-emonial display and religious seriousness', together with a proliferation of 'barracks and prisons' was fostered by the governing classes at the same time as 'a more rigorous policy of control and greater ideological assertiveness was practised by British impe-rial activists' (ibid., 314).

12. BL, IOR, PD P2203; *Monthly Magazine*, 5 (1798), pt 1, frontispiece; *European Maga-zine*, 43 (Mar. 1803), 167.

13. Geoff Quilley, 'Signs of Commerce: The East India Company and the Patronage of Eighteenth-Century British Art', in Bowen, Lincoln, and Rigby (eds), *Worlds of the East India Company*, 183–99.

14. Campbell's *Vitruvius Britannicus*, Gibbs's *A Book of Architecture*, works by Chambers, Stuart and Revett, the Adam brothers, Paine, Soane, and Wood, as well as French and Italian studies, and magazines such as *The Builder*. Gibbs was used by Lt James Agg for the construction of St John's-in-the-Swamps in Calcutta (1786) after designs of St Martin-in-the-Fields, London (a common model for Anglican churches through-out the empire), and for Thomas Fiott de Havilland's design of a portico with Ionic columns for St Andrew's Kirk, Madras.

15. This was headed by C. W. Pasley, whose handbook for civil engineers and architect officers, *Course of Practical Architecture for the Use of Junior Officers*, saw numerous editions in the nineteenth century.

16. C. A. Bayly, *The New Cambridge History of India II. 1: Indian Society and the Making of the British Empire* (Cambridge, 1988), 81.

17. Quoted in Thomas R. Metcalf, 'Architecture in the British Empire', in Robert W. Winter (ed.), *OHBE, vol. V: Historiography* (Oxford/New York, 1999), 584–95, at 590.

18. J. P. Losty, *Calcutta City of Palaces: A Survey of the City in the Days of the East India Company 1690–1858* (London, 1990).

19. C. A. Bayly, 'The British Fiscal-Military State and Indigenous Resistance', in Lawrence Stone (ed.), *An Imperial State at War: Britain from 1689 to 1815* (London, 1994), 322–54, at 341–2.

20. Kedleston was designed by Robert Adam in 1759–70 on the basis of earlier designs by James Paine. Its original plan of a central block and four detached wings linked to the centre by curving corridors allowed for good circulation of air. Whereas Kedleston only had two of the planned four pavilions built, Government House had all four.

21. Lord Valentia, *Voyages and Travels*, 2 vols (London, 1811), I, 192. Cf. George Nathaniel Curzon, *British Government in India: The Story of the Viceroys and Government Houses*, 2 vols (London, 1925), I, 208.

22. Sten Nilsson, *European Architecture in India 1750–1850* (London, 1968), 158.

23. Quoted in Philip Davies, *The Penguin Guide to the Monuments of India, vol. II: Islamic, Rajput, European* (Harmondsworth, 1989), 80.

24. For this paragraph see Robert Travers, 'Death and the Nabob: Imperialism and Commemoration in Eighteenth-Century India', *Past & Present*, 196 (2007), 83–124; Ashish Chadha, 'Ambivalent Heritage: Between Affect and Ideology in a Colonial Cemetery', *Journal of Material Culture*, 11:3 (2006), 339–63.

25. For these and similar monuments see Asiaticus [i.e. John Hawkesworth], *Asiaticus ... Part the first. Ecclesiastical ... and historical sketches respecting Bengal. Part the second. The Epitaphs in the different burial grounds in and about Calcutta* (Calcutta, 1803), part II, 13, 38, 26, 68, 28, 40.

26. *Bengal Obituary* (1848), 268.

27. Lady Maria Nugent, *A Journal from the Year 1811 till the Year 1815, including a Voyage to, and Residence in India*, 2 vols (London, 1839), II, 67–8.

28. Jan Morris, *Stones of Empire: The Buildings of the Raj* (Oxford, 1983), 25. For hybridity as a productive reconciliation between imperial and colonised cultures see the work of Homi Bhabha.

29. Thomas R. Metcalf, *An Imperial Vision: Indian Architecture and Britain's Raj* (Berkeley, Calif., 1989), 110.

30. Indira Viswanathan Peterson, 'The Cabinet of King Serfoji of Tanjore: A European Collection in Early Nineteenth-Century India', *Journal of the History of Collections*, 11:1 (1999), 71–93.

31. Maya Jasanoff, *Edge of Empire: Conquest and Collecting in the East, 1750–1850* (London, 2005), 317.

32. The gat of the Sikandarbagh, by contrast, is primarily a classical composition with an Indian roofline. Banmali Tandan, *The Architecture of Lucknow and Its Dependencies, 1722–1856* (Delhi, 2001), 192–218; G. H. R. Tillotson, *The Tradition of Indian Archi-*

tecture: Continuity, Controversy and Change since 1850 (New Haven, Conn./London, 1989), 6–11.

33. William Dalrymple, *White Mughals: Love and Betrayal in Eighteenth-Century India* (London, 2002), 33.

34. See Marshall's moderate version of the overstated case in Raymond Schwab, *The Oriental Renaissance: Europe's Rediscovery of India and the East, 1680–1880*, trans. Gene Patterson-Black and Viktor Reinking; foreword by Edward W. Said (New York/Guildford, 1984), to add the issue of indifference and ignorance to Trautmann's argument for a shift from Indomania to Indophobia: P. J. Marshall, 'British-Indian Connections c.1780 to c.1830: The Empire of the Officials', in Michael J. Franklin (ed.), *Romantic Representations of British India* (London, 2006), 45–60; Trautmann, *Aryans*, 10. See also Elinor S. Shaffer, *'Kubla Khan' and 'The Fall of Jerusalem': The Mythological School in Biblical Criticism and Secular Literature 1770–1880* (Cambridge, 1975).

35. Catherine Hall, *Civilising Subjects: Metropole and Colony in the English Imagination, 1830–1867* (Oxford, 2002), 142, contrasts the notion of India as an ancient civilisation with Africa as a place 'without culture' as 'deeply embedded in missionary discourse' in the 1830s.

36. Susan Bayly, 'The Evolution of Colonial Cultures: Nineteenth-Century Asia', in Andrew Porter (ed.), *OHBE, vol. III: The Nineteenth Century* (Oxford/New York, 1999), 447–69, at 467–8. For the complex history of the concept of race and its relation to Orientalism see Shruti Kapila, 'Race Matters: Orientalism and Religion, India and Beyond c.1770–1880', *Modern Asian Studies*, 41:3 (2007), 471–513. The quotation from Jasanoff, *Edge of Empire*, 308.

37. On Said and revisionism see introduction, note 54. The quotation is from Peers, 'Colonial Knowledge', 161. See also Gyan Prakash, 'Writing Post-Orientalist Histories of the Third World: Perspectives from Indian Historiography', *Comparative Studies in Society and History*, 32:2 (1990), 383–408.

38. Bernard S. Cohn, *Colonialism and Its Forms of Knowledge: The British in India* (Princeton, NJ, 1996).

39. C. A. Bayly, *Empire & Information: Intelligence Gathering and Social Communication in India, 1780–1870* (Cambridge, 1996); Michael Dodson's *Orientalism, Empire and National Culture: India, 1770–1880* (Basingstoke/New York, 2007) argues that Orientalism was potentially subversive, as Indian Sanskrit scholars adapted the social and institutional underpinnings of colonial rule to forge sometimes anti-colonial Hindu identities. See also Eugene Irschick, *Dialogue and History: Constructing South India, 1795–1895* (Berkeley, Calif., 1994). On the weaknesses of the term 'indigenous knowledge' see, with respect to science, Colin Scott, 'Science for the West, Myth for the Rest? The Case of James Bay Creet Knowledge Construction', in Laura Nader (ed.), *Naked Science: Anthropological Inquiry into Boundaries, Power and Knowledge* (London, 1996), 69–86. For a perceptive reading of science practised in a non-London-centred

461

manner and fostering dialogue between European and indigenous traditions see Sujit Sivasundaram, '"A Christian Benares": Orientalism, Science and the Serampore Mission of Bengal', *Indian Economic and Social History Review*, 44:2 (2007), 111–45.

40. Peers, 'Colonial Knowledge', 162. Cf. Susan Bayly, 'Caste and "Race" in the Colonial Ethnography of India', in Peter Robb (ed.), *The Concept of Race in South Asia* (Delhi/ Oxford, 1996), 165–218.

41. Bayly, *Empire & Information*, 56; Peers, 'Colonial Knowledge'.

42. BL, IOR/Eur D/809.

43. Katherine Prior, 'Clevland, Augustus (1754–1784)', *Oxford Dictionary of National Biography* (Oxford), 2004, http://www.oxforddnb.com/view/article/5634 [accessed 26 Nov. 2008]; *Bengal Obituary* (1848), 72; Kate Teltscher, *India Inscribed: European and British Writing on India, 1600–1800* (Delhi/Oxford, 1996), 121–4; Chadha, 'Ambivalent Heritage', 351; Nugent, *Journal*, I, 204–6, quotations 205. William Hodges's painting *A Camp of a Thousand Men* (1782) also celebrates Clevland's 'supposedly benign authority as a civilizing influence': Geoff Quilley and John Bonehill (eds), *William Hodges, 1744–1797: The Art of Exploration* (London, 2004), cat. 62, pp. 172–3. Amal Chatterjee, *Representations of India, 1740–1840: The Creation of India in the Colonial Imagination* (Basingstoke, 1998), 18. Joan Coutu, *Persuasion and Propaganda: Monuments and the Eighteenth-Century British Empire* (Montreal, 2008), 312–15, ill. 9.27, 9.28; see also pp. 307–9 for the magnanimity narrative in the commemoration of tax collector Charles Robert Ross at Madras (d.1816).

44. Travers, *Ideology and Empire*, 244–6 (quotation 246).

45. The scholarly and administrative careers of Leyden and Craufurd depended heavily on the patronage of fellow Scot Lord Minto. Hardly anything is known about Colin Mackenzie's education. Francis Hamilton studied at Glasgow and Edinburgh. Jane Rendall, 'Scottish Orientalism: From Robertson to James Mill', *Historical Journal*, 25:1 (1982), 43–69. More generally see John M. MacKenzie, 'Essay and Reflection: On Scotland and the Empire', *International History Review*, 15:4 (1993), 714–39, and MacKenzie, 'Irish, Scottish, Welsh and English Worlds? A Four-Nation Approach to the History of the British Empire', *History Compass*, 6:5 (2008), 1244–63; on Scottish thought and governance: Martha McLaren, *British India & British Scotland, 1780–1830: Career Building, Empire Building, and a Scottish School of Thought on Indian Governance* (Akron, Ohio, 2001).

Chapter Seven: Antiquities of India

1. Nigel Leask, *Curiosity and the Aesthetics of Travel Writing, 1770–1840* (Oxford, 2002); Margarita Díaz-Andreu, *A World History of Nineteenth-Century Archaeology: Nationalism, Colonialism, and the Past* (Oxford, 2007).

2. Leask, *Curiosity*, 31.

3. Ebba Koch, *Mughal Architecture: An Outline of Its History and Development (1526–1858)* (Munich, 1999); cf. Koch, *Mughal Art and Imperial Ideology: Collected Essays* (Oxford, 2001); Thomas R. Metcalf, *An Imperial Vision: Indian Architecture and Britain's Raj* (Berkeley, Calif., 1989), 24–105.

4. Hodges's painting is in the Earl of Plymouth's collections at Oakly Park; oil on canvas, 292 × 457 cm. Richard Gough, *A Comparative View of the Ancient Monuments of India, Particularly those in the Islands of Salset near Bombay, as Described by Different Writers, Illustrated with Prints* (London, 1785); Mildred Archer and Ronald Lightbown, *India Observed: India as Viewed by British Artists, 1760–1860* (London, 1982), cat. 110–12; Dilip K. Chakrabarti, *A History of Indian Archaeology: From the Beginning to 1947* (New Delhi, 1988), 31 (quotation); Lady Maria Nugent, *A Journal from the Year 1811 till the Year 1815, including a Voyage to, and Residence in, India*, 2 vols (London, 1839), I, 247–80, esp. 267; Hermione de Almeida and George H. Gilpin, *Indian Renaissance: British Romantic Art and the Prospect of India* (Aldershot/Burlington, Vt, 2006), 119; Giles Tillotson, 'Hodges and Indian Architecture', in Geoff Quilley and John Bonehill (eds), *William Hodges, 1744–1797: The Art of Exploration* (London, 2004), 49–60; Thomas R. Metcalf, *Ideologies of the Raj* (Cambridge, 1994), 1–13.

5. Upinder Singh, *The Discovery of Ancient India: Early Archaeologists and the Beginnings of Archaeology* (Delhi, 2004), 339–40, speculates this may in part be the result of different sets of personnel as officers in India had little in common with European archaeologists.

6. BL, Add. MS 38977, fo. Rawlinson to Layard, 5 Aug. 1846.

7. It is one of the four initial monuments admitted to the cathedral in the 1790s, all by John Bacon the Elder, of intellectual and artistic figures; the others are Sir Joshua Reynolds, Dr Samuel Johnson, and John Howard, prison reformer. Jones's tomb on South Park described the stoic manner of his death: *Bengal Obituary* (1848), 81. It is illustrated in Robert Travers, 'Death and the Nabob: Imperialism and Commemoration in Eighteenth-Century India', *Past & Present*, 196 (2007), 83–124, at 117. For the inscription see Beinecke Library, Yale University, New Haven, Beinecke MSS Vault Hilles 2, John Bacon to Charles Grant, 25 July 1804.

8. Thomas R. Trautmann, 'The Lives of Sir William Jones', in Alexander Murray (ed.), *Sir William Jones, 1746–94: A Commemoration* (Oxford, 1998), 91–122, at 109–111, quotation 111; Trautmann, *Aryans and British India* (Berkeley, Calif./London, 1997), 76–80. In 'On the Gods of Greece, Italy and India' (*Asiatick Researches*, 2 (1790), 111–47), Jones had argued that Hinduism was the contemporary representative of the ancient paganism of Greece and Rome; he made a claim for secular literary criticism as a *sine qua non* for scriptural authority. See Alun David, 'Sir William Jones, Biblical Orientalism and Indian Scholarship', *Modern Asian Studies*, 30:1 (1996), 173–84.

9. P. J. Marshall, 'British-Indian Connections c.1780 to c.1830: The Empire of the Officials', in Michael J. Franklin (ed.), *Romantic Representations of British India* (London, 2006), 45–60, at 54, with reference to Douglas M. Peers, 'Colonial Knowledge and the Military in India, 1780–1860', *Journal of Imperial and Commonwealth History*, 33 (2005), 157–80, at 158; T. E. Colebrooke, *The Life of H. T. Colebrooke* (London, 1873), 235.

10. Marshall, 'British-Indian Connections', 60. For an excellent study of how Orientalism and its public appeal in the metropolis continued to thrive in the more popular sphere of exhibitions, theatre, periodical press, and menageries see Sujit Sivasundaram, 'Trading Knowledge: The East India Company's Elephants in India and Britain', *Historical Journal*, 48 (2005), 27–63.

11. Thomas Pinney (ed.), *The Letters of Thomas Babington Macaulay*, 6 vols (Cambridge, 1976), III (January 1834–August 1841), 203–5, at 204, letter to Charles Macaulay, Calcutta, 5 Dec. 1836.

12. See above, pp. 00–00, 58.

13. Michael D. Willis, 'Sculpture from India', in Marjorie L. Caygill and John Cherry (eds), *A. W. Franks: Nineteenth-Century Collecting and the British Museum* (London, 1997), 250–61.

14. Throughout the nineteenth century, individual officials continued to make drawings of monuments throughout British India in the course of their duties: Sir Henry Yule (Bengal Engineers 1840–62), irrigation engineer, and historical geographer, made drawings of forts and tombs in the Punjab. The Rev. Charles S. P. Parish, a chaplain in Burma in 1852–78, sketched monasteries, pagodas, and Buddha statues. Capt. (later Col.) Henry Francis Ainslie on army duty in Poona and Karachi, various members of the Bombay Civil Service in western India in the early 1850s, and Claudius R. W. F. Harris, a military interpreter in Central India, all drew monuments. Lt Alex Nash (Bombay Engineers, in India 1834–46), made drawings on the Deccan revenue survey of monuments of Bijapur and the great hill forts of Dejouri and Purandhar. Herbert Benjamin Edwardes, an officer in the Bengal European Fusilier Regiment and political agent in trans-Indus British India, illustrated his diary on the 1847 campaign to pacify Bannu with views of forts at Nanipore, Khooshab, and Lukkee. Henry Ambrose Oldfield, from the Indian Medical Service (1846–68), during his leisure hours sketched architecture in Bengal, the Punjab, and Nepal until his eyesight deteriorated around 1860, when he trained a native assistant to sketch and copy for him. See AI, 352–64, 275, 91, 198, 223, 259–60, 262–72.

15. *Boswell's Life of Johnson* (London/New York/Toronto, 1953), 1120, 1117–18. For a complaint about how little was known of Indian antiquity as the Company did not even engrave monuments, see Gough, *Comparative View*, v.

16. Hastings to Nathaniel Smith, Chair EIC, 1784, quoted in O. P. Kejariwal, *The Asiatic Society of Bengal and the Discovery of India's Past* (New Delhi, 1988), 24.

17. C. A. Bayly, *Empire & Information: Intelligence Gathering and Social Communication in India, 1780-1870* (Cambridge, 1996), 53-4.
18. Most of the men studying India's pasts discussed in this chapter collected texts and traditions as well as describing and collecting other physical remains.
19. The antiquarian coordination of text with artefact remained crucial to archaeology well beyond this period: David Percy Dymond, *Archaeology and History: A Plea for Reconciliation* (London, 1974), 56, 109; Philippa Levine, *The Amateur and the Professional: Antiquarians, Historians and Archaeologists in Victorian England, 1838-1886* (Cambridge, 1986), 98-9. For Anquetil see G. Sarton, 'Anquetil-Duperron (1731-1805)', *Osiris*, 3 (1938), 193-223. His reports from India take up much space in Gough's 1785 compilation.
20. William Jones, *A discourse on the institution of a Society for enquiring into the history ... antiquities, arts, sciences, and literature of Asia, delivered at Calcutta, January 15th, 1784* (London, 1784), 8, 5. *Proceedings*, I, 2-3 (pagination starting with transcription of actual proceedings). For the centripetal effects of empire see the work of John M. MacKenzie.
21. William Jones, *Discourses Delivered at the Asiatick Society, 1785-92*, with a new introduction by Roy Harris (London, 1933), 'The Third Anniversary Discourse', 24-46, at 32.
22. Colebrooke had worked in the administrative, diplomatic, and judicial branches of the Indian service, reaching the positions of chief justice of the superior court of appeal in Calcutta and member of the supreme council before returning to England in 1814. He donated 2,749 Indian manuscripts to the East India Company library in 1819.
23. *Transactions of the Asiatic Society of Great Britain and Ireland* [henceforth: *TRAS GB&IR*], I, pt 1 (1824), quotations xviii, 22, 23. The Madras society merged with the London society in 1828.
24. This paragraph is indebted to Peers, 'Colonial Knowledge'.
25. Peacetime advancement could come through secondment requiring specialist skills. See also Rosane Rocher, 'Sanskrit for Civil Servants, 1806-1818', *Journal of the American Oriental Society*, 122 (2002), 381-90. Of the Asiatic Society's 92 members in 1789, at least 26 were officers, 3 surgeons. In the *Asiatic Researches*, vol. 7, seven out of ten articles were by officers, one by a surgeon (vol. 9: 5/11 articles); similar patterns apply to other journals and to donations to the Asiatic Society museum.
26. The phrase is Nicholas B. Dirks's in *Castes of Mind: Colonialism and the Making of Modern India* (Princeton, NJ, 2001), 9.
27. Nicholas B. Dirks in Bernard S. Cohn, *Colonialism and Its Forms of Knowledge: The British in India* (Princeton, NJ, 1996), xii, discussed in Phillip B. Wagoner, 'Precolonial Intellectuals and the Production of Colonial Knowledge', *Comparative Studies in Society and History*, 45:4 (2003), 783-814, at 783-4; Ronald Inden, 'Orientalist

Constructions of India', *Modern Asian Studies*, 20:3 (1986), 401–46; Inden, *Imagining India* (Oxford, 1990); Bernard S. Cohn, 'The Census, Social Structure and Objectification in South Asia', in his *An Anthropologist among the Historians and Other Essays* (Delhi/Oxford, 1987), 224–54; Nicholas B. Dirks, 'The Invention of Caste: Civil Society in Colonial India', *Social Analysis*, 25 (1989), 42–52; Dirks, 'Colonial Histories and Native Informants: Biography of an Archive', in Carol A. Breckenridge and Peter van der Veer (eds), *Orientalism and the Postcolonial Predicament: Perspectives of South Asia* (Philadelphia, 1993), 279–313; Dirks, *Castes of Mind*; Gauri Viswanathan, *Masks of Conquest: Literary Studies and British Rule in India* (London, 1990); Metcalf, *Ideologies*.

28. Peers, 'Colonial Knowledge', 161. For wide-ranging examples of indigenous intellectual agency and genuine colonial-imperial dialogue see Wagoner, 'Precolonial Intellectuals', 784–5; Norbert Peabody, 'Cents, Sense, Census: Human Inventories in Late Precolonial and Early Colonial India', *Comparative Studies in Society and History*, 43:4 (2001), 819–50; Thomas R. Trautmann, 'Hullabaloo about Telugu', *South Asia Research*, 19:1 (1999), 53–70; Kumkum Chatterjee, 'History as Self-Representation: The Recasting of a Political Tradition in Late Eighteenth-Century Eastern India', *Modern Asian Studies*, 32:4 (1998), 913–48, at 915; Michael S. Dodson, *Orientalism, Empire, and National Culture: India, 1770–1880* (Basingstoke, 2007); E. F. Irschick, *Dialogue and History: Constructing South India, 1795–1895* (Berkeley, Calif., 1994); Bayly, *Empire & Information*; W. R. Pinch, 'Same Difference in India and Europe', *History and Theory*, 38:3 (1999), 389–407; Richard M. Eaton, '(Re)imag(in)ing Other²ness: A Postmortem for the Postmodern in India', *Journal of World History*, 11:1 (2000), 57–78; Mohamad Tavakoli-Targhi, *Refashioning Iran: Orientalism, Occidentalism and Historiography* (Basingstoke, 2001), esp. 18–34.

29. Marshall, 'British-Indian Connections', 54; Bayly, *Empire & Information*, 212–14, *passim*. For the alternative model, in the Great Trigonometrical Survey of 1818, and its scientific mapping, which exceeded the company's military or revenue requirements in an imperialist assertion of British scientific and rational superiority, see Matthew H. Edney, *Mapping an Empire: The Geographical Construction of British India, 1765–1843* (Chicago/London, 1997), 16–25, 319, 335–6, *passim*.

30. Sibpur (1786/7), Calcutta; at Madras, Company surgeon James Anderson sought to break the Spanish monopoly of cochineal dye production; at Bombay Dr Helenus Scott conducted experiments with sugar, coffee, tobacco, and indigo; at Saharanpur, the Company took over the Mughal gardens for medicinal plant cultivation in 1818.

31. Deepak Kumar, 'The Evolution of Colonial Science in India: Natural History and the East India Company', in John MacKenzie (ed.), *Imperialism and the Natural World* (Manchester/New York, 1990), 51–66; Mildred Archer, *Natural History Drawings in the India Office Library* (London, 1962); Edney, *Mapping*, 294–9; Bayly, *Empire & Information*, 307.

32. John Bonehill, 'Shows of Strength: War and the Military in British Visual Culture, circa 1775–1803', 2 vols, unpublished Ph.D. thesis (University of Leicester, 2001), 212–31.
33. The Royal Military Academy, Woolwich (1741), trained cadet officers of the artillery and engineering corps, future surveyors and draughtsmen in military and architectural drawing, surveying, and levelling. Paul Sandby, chief drawing master, had been draughtsman to the Scottish Highlands Survey, the mapping by the Board of Ordnance which had been commissioned after the 'Forty-Five'. His classes included topographical drawing and sketching in the field, as well as figures, perspective, and 'military embellishments'.
34. AII, 371–91.
35. Ann Bermingham, *Learning to Draw: Studies in the Cultural History of a Polite and Useful Art* (New Haven, Conn./London, 2000), 79–85; Kim Sloan, *A Noble Art: Amateur Artists and Drawing Masters, 1600–1800* (London, 2000), 106–9; Matthew H. Edney, 'British Military Education: Mapmaking, and Military "Map-Mindedness" in the Later Enlightenment', *The Cartographic Journal*, 31:1 (1994), 14–20.
36. Embassies: AI, 25–6, II, 419–23; Michael Aris (ed.), *Views of Medieval Bhutan: The Diary and Drawings of Samuel Davis, 1783* (London/Washington, 1982). Artists' materials: BL, IOR/L/AG/1/1/1–87.
37. Maria Graham, *Journal of a Short Residence in India* (Edinburgh, 1812), plate inserted between pp. 54 and 55; quotation p. 57. For a discussion of gender, aesthetics, and ethics in Graham see Leask, *Curiosity*, 205–17.
38. George Michell and Antonio Martinelli, *Oriental Scenery: Two Hundred Years of India's Artistic and Architectural Heritage* (New Delhi, 1998), 'Introduction'.
39. Edney, *Mapping*, 13–15, with plate 1.5. The cartouche is a copper-engraving drawn by E. Edwards and engraved by J. Hall at 26.7 × 18.4 cm.
40. Edney, *Mapping*; Ian J. Barrow, *Making History, Drawing Territory: British Mapping in India, c.1756–1905* (New Delhi/Oxford, 2003), 67.
41. For introductions to the picturesque see Malcolm Andrews, *The Search for the Picturesque: Landscape Aesthetics and Tourism in Britain, 1760–1800* (Aldershot, 1989); Stephen Daniels, 'Re-Visioning Britain: Mapping and Landscape Painting, 1750–1820', in *Glorious Nature: British Landscape Painting, 1750–1850*, catalogue by Katharine Baetjer, essays by Michael Rosenthal et al. (New York, 1993), 61–72; Stephen Copley and Peter Garside (eds), *The Politics of the Picturesque: Literature, Landscape, and Aesthetics since 1700* (Cambridge, 1994).
42. On the picturesque and scientific gaze see Edney, *Mapping*, 57–61 (quotation from Lambton at 61); Barbara M. Stafford, *Voyage into Substance: Art, Science, Nature and the Illustrated Travel Account, 1760–1840* (Cambridge, 1984), 31–56, 348–9; Tapati Guha-Thakurta, *Monuments, Objects, Histories: Institutions of Art in Colo-

nial and Postcolonial India (New York/New Delhi, 2004), 9–12; Monica Juneja (ed.), *Architecture in Medieval India: Forms, Contexts, Histories* (New Delhi, 2001), 13–23.

43. John E. Crowley, 'A Visual Empire: Seeing the British Atlantic World from a Global British Perspective', in Elizabeth Mancke and Carole Shammas (eds), *The Creation of the British Atlantic World* (Baltimore, 2005), 283–303, at 295.

44. Almeida and Gilpin, *Indian Renaissance*, 176–80, quotation 176.

45. Pauline Rohatgi, 'Preface to a Lost Collection: The Pioneering Art of Francis Swain Ward', in Pauline Rohatgi and Pheroza Godrej, *Under the Indian Sun: British Landscape Artists* (Bombay, 1995), 32–51.

46. Almeida and Gilpin, *Indian Renaissance*, 115–16.

47. Beth Fowkes Tobin, 'The Artist's "I" in Hodges's *Travels in India*', in Quilley and Bonehill (eds), *Hodges*, 43–8, quotations at 48.

48. Quilley and Bonehill (eds), *Hodges*, cat. 49, quoting Hodges's letterpress to the aquatint in *Select Views* (14), 1786. For Hodges's views of forts as sites of strategic significance, military use, and successive imperial conquests see ibid., cat. 59. For officers publishing influential illustrated narratives see Robert Hyde Colebrooke (1762–1808, Bengal Infantry, Surveyor-General, 1800–1808), *Twelve Views of Places in the Kingdom of Mysore, The Country of Tippoo Sultan, from Drawings Taken on the Spot. To which are annexed, concise descriptions of the places drawn, with a brief detail of the operations of the army under Marquis Cornwallis, during the war* (London, 1794); Sir Alexander Allan (1764–1820), Madras Native Infantry 1780–1804, fought in the third and fourth Mysore Wars: *Views in the Mysore Country* (London, 1794).

49. John A. Hodgson, 'Remarks on the Surveys in India', 21 Nov. 1821, BL, IOR F/4/682 18864, 500–525.

50. Robert Home, *Select Views in Mysore, the Country of Tippoo Sultan; From Drawings Taken on the Spot by Mr. Home; with Historical Descriptions* (London, 1794), vi, 8, vii. The original drawings, engraved by various hands, are probably those in BL, WD 3775.

51. Home included other sites, such as the Maugree Hindu Pagodas, ostensibly because Cornwallis had pitched his camp nearby several times during the campaign. Home seems to choose an architectural site rather than the camp as a site of visual interest. See also F. W. Blagdon, *A Brief History of Ancient and Modern India* (London, 1805), a massive volume with plates of architecture associated with Tipu, several artillery encampments, and the residences of imperial administrators. They show architecture in landscape with generic, very dark-skinned locals and sepoys.

52. Mildred Archer, *Early Views of India: The Picturesque Journeys of Thomas and William Daniell 1786–1794* (London, 1980).

53. See the 1789 drawing, engraved 1795, *Hindoo Temples at Bindrabund on the River Jumna*, aquatint in sombre, dark colours.

54. *The Great Pagoda, Trichinopoly* (aquatint, 1797), Pierpont Morgan Library.

55. de Almeida and Gilpin, *Indian Renaissance*, 204–5.
56. Ibid., 178.
57. Alexander Cunningham, *Archaeological Survey of India. Four Reports Made during the Years 1862–63–64–65*, vol. I (Delhi, 1972), xviii–xix (henceforth: Cunningham, *Report*).
58. By 1860, Erskine's Elephanta essay had been corrected in some details but remained the best overall account. Erskine's article is in *Transactions of the Literary Society of Bombay*, I (London, 1819), 198–250 [henceforth: *Tr. Lit. Soc. of Bombay*]. Cunningham, *Report,* vi, footnotes a forthcoming essay by Burgess.
59. Sujit Sivasundaram, 'Buddhist Kingship, British Archaeology and Historical Narratives in Sri Lanka, c.1750–1850', *Past & Present*, 197 (2007), 111–42. Cf. Gough, *Comparative View*, preface.
60. *Proceedings*, I, 125 (27 Mar. 1788); *AR*, I (1788), 331–2; cf. *Archaeologia*, 9 (1789), 81–3.
61. *Tr. Lit. Soc. of Bombay*, II (London, 1820), 194–204.
62. W. H. Sleeman, *Rambles and Recollections of an Indian Official*, 2 vols (London, 1844), I, v.
63. In 1785, John H. Har[r]ington, the Society's Secretary, presented 'Description of a Cave near Gaya' (probably the Nagarjuni caves). The caves had been noticed by the Collector of Gaya, who sent drawings of temples and images, and an inscription from a stone: *Proceedings*, I, 69 (29 Dec. 1785). *AR*, I, 276–83. The site, some 10 km from Bodhgaya, and hence associated with Buddhism, from the tenth century was also an important Hindu centre; no monument survives that predates the eighteenth century, but there are ninth- and tenth-century Pala sculptures and votive inscriptions inserted in pavements and walls. Charles Wilkins, a founder of the Bengal Society and later first curator of the East India House Museum, laid the foundations of epigraphy by establishing the existence of the Pala and Maukhari dynasties.
64. *AR*, I (1788), 131–41.
65. The Firuzabad transcriptions were corrected in 1798 through copies by Capt. James Hoare, though he died before he could present his Book of Drawings and Inscriptions to the Asiatic Society. The Society in 1798 considered a translation of the pillar inscriptions by Henry Colebrooke with an introduction by Harington and the inscriptions were deciphered as Brahmi by James Princep in the 1830s. For Mahabalipuram see *AR*, I (1788), 145–70.
66. The letter is printed in *Archaeologia*, 10 (1792), 449–59; for the model see reproduction in Malcolm Baker and Brenda Richardson (eds), *A Grand Design: The Art of the Victoria & Albert Museum* (London, 1997), cat. no. 87 and fig. 108 for a scale drawing of a pillar from the model depicting the patron and his wives. Cf. John Guy, 'Tirumala Nayak's Choultry and an Eighteenth-Century Model', in Claudine Bautze-Picron (ed.), *Makaranda: Essays in Honour of Dr James C. Harle* (Delhi, 1990), 207–13. For the function of models see Malcolm Baker, 'Representing Invention, Viewing Models', in Soraya de Chadarevian

and Nick Hopwood (eds), *Models: The Third Dimension of Science* (Stanford, Calif., 2004), 19–42.

67. AII, 468; AI, 161, drawings 2414, 1261; AI, 333. Cf. *Proceedings*, I, 255.

68. *AR*, V (1797), 131–2; cf. *Proceedings*, I, 252.

69. *TRAS GB&IR*, I (1827), 527.

70. Joyce Brown, 'A Memoir of Colonel Sir Proby Cautley, FRS, 1802–1871, Engineer and Palaeontologist', *Notes and Records of the Royal Society*, 34 (1979–80), 185–225.

71. For the rediscovery of Ellora by British military officers who made sketches, took descriptive notes, and sent tracings of inscriptions to the Asiatic Society for translation and publication see *Proceedings*, I, 51 (28 Apr. 1785); *AR*, V (1797), 135–40; *Tr. Lit. Soc. of Bombay*, III (1823), 265–323; *TRAS GB&IR*, II (1830), 326–39, with descriptive account by Lt-Col. James Tod, 328–39, and four fine lithographic plates of sculptural figures in the temple. As early as 1785, an account by Company Servant Malet of the Salsette Caves and their inscriptions in an unknown character had been read at the Asiatic Society. For the proceedings see also *Proceedings*, I, 57 (30 June 1785); 247 (7 Aug. 1794); *AR*, VI (1799), 389–423.

72. James Forbes, *Oriental Memoirs*, 4 vols (London, 1813–15), I, 433–4.

73. MacNeill, quoted in Almeida and Gilpin, *Indian Renaissance*, 50; MacNeill's account was published in *Archaeologia*, viii (1787), 251–89.

74. *Archaeologia*, 7 (1785), 323–33. The issue also contains drawings and bas-reliefs from the caves in Sir Ashton Lever collection, 333–6; Lethieullier's extract from the MSS of the late Gov. Boon of Bombay on the Pagoda at Salset, 286–392.

75. He was elected a member, and the paper was published in the *Asiatic Researches*. *Proceedings*, I, 250–51 (20 Aug., 10 Sep. 1795). *AR*, IV (1795), 409–15.

76. BL, MSS. Eur. C. 9 [= AI, 95]. For competent drawings by other women who accompanied their husbands, fathers, or brothers on tours of duty see e.g. AI, 94–5, 129–31.

77. James Mill, *The History of British India*, 3 vols (London, 1817), I, 335–9, quotation 335.

78. Among administrators who paid brief visits to Elephanta was Edward Strachey. His papers contain notes, measurements, sketches, and inscriptions from Elephanta and Karli, all messily scribbled onto scraps of paper of various sizes and shapes, apparently made during a journey with Governor Elphinstone: BL, OIOC, MSS Eur F128/202.

Chapter Eight: Surveying the Empire

1. Zaheer Baber, *The Science of Empire: Scientific Knowledge, Civilization, and Colonial Rule in India* (Albany, NY, 1996), 139, 153; Matthew H. Edney, *Mapping an Empire: The Geographical Construction of British India, 1765–1843* (Chicago/London, 1997), 105, 147.

2. Nigel Leask, *Curiosity and the Aesthetics of Travel Writing, 1770–1840* (Oxford, 2002), 169.

3. Around the time of Mackenzie's death in 1821, George Boyd (1800–1850), Bombay Infantry, started over three decades of surveying activity, in the course of which he drew monuments mostly in western India and Afghanistan in 1821–44: AI, 137–9.

4. Reginald H. Phillimore, *Historical Records of the Survey of India*, 4 vols (Dehra Dun, 1945–58), II, 419–28; Phillimore, 'Introduction', in the largely derivative W. C. Mackenzie, *Colonel Colin Mackenzie, First Surveyor-General of India* (Edinburgh/London, 1952), ix.

5. From the mid-1790s, he contributed occasional papers on antiquities in India and Ceylon to the Asiatic Society and the *Asiatick Researches. Proceedings*, I, 249–51, 268 (Jan.–Sep. 1795, Oct. 1796); *AR*, V (1797), 303–14. Ceylon: *Proceedings*, I, 287 (8 Mar. 1798), printed *AR*, VI (1799), 424–54 with illustrations.

6. Colin Mackenzie, 'Biographical Sketch of the Literary Career of the Late Colonel Colin Mackenzie', *JRAS*, 1 (1834), 333–64, at 334.

7. Nicholas B. Dirks, 'Guiltless Spoliations: Picturesque Beauty, Colonial Knowledge, and Colin Mackenzie's Survey of India', in C. B. Asher and T. R. Metcalf (eds), *Perceptions of South Asia's Visual Past* (New Delhi, 1994), 211–32, at 212–13.

8. See also Nicholas B. Dirks, *Castes of Mind: Colonialism and the Making of Modern India* (Princeton, NJ, 2001), 82, 84, 104.

9. Mackenzie, 'Biographical Sketch', 337.

10. Ibid., 339–40.

11. Dirks, *Castes of Mind*, 88.

12. The originals in Madras (Chennai) are in Telugu, Marathi, Tamil; the translations, apparently done by the assistants themselves, are in BL, OIOC, Mack Translations XII (henceforth: Mack Translations). B. S. Cohn used a brief example from Lutchmiah's 1804 reports and from H. H. Wilson's 1828 account, appended to his catalogue of the Mackenzie collection, of Baboo Rao's inquiries on the Coromandel coast. N. Dirks considered at least eight collaborators, but there are some inaccuracies in his representation of some reports, for which see the best discussion of this archive thus far in Phillip B. Wagoner, 'Precolonial Intellectuals and the Production of Colonial Knowledge', *Comparative Studies in Society and History*, 45 (2003), 783–814, at 793 nn. 17, 18.

13. All purchases had also been made at his 'private expense': Mackenzie, 'Biographical Sketch', 342.

14. Quoted in Dirks, *Castes of Mind*, 99. Borriah also wrote scholarly articles in English on ancient Indian history, and Telugu literary works. The occasional drawing in Mackenzie's collections is ascribed to Borriah: Mackenzie, 'Biographical Sketch', 335–6; AII, 531: WD 1062/21.

15. Mackenzie quoted in Dirks, *Castes of Mind*, 90.

16. Mack Translations XII, 14 [3, 5].

17. Ibid., XII, 2–11 for 1804–6.

18. Ibid., XII, 9, fos 48v–49r, 26 Apr. 1804
19. Ibid., XII, 9, fos 61v–63r.
20. Ibid., XII, 11, fo. 108r. The reports of Notalac Naima Brahmin for parts of 1804 through 1806 also detail complex negotiations between the assistant, other Brahmins, and locals to obtain access, information, or opportunities to copy or buy books: ibid., XII, 3, fos 11–33.
21. H. H. Wilson, *The Mackenzie Collection: A Descriptive Catalogue of the Oriental Manuscripts and Other Articles* (Calcutta, 1828), 600, 602.
22. Mack Translations XII, 9, fos 72, 79v; 10, fo. 113; Wagoner, 'Precolonial Intellectuals', 787–8, with further references; BL, OIOC, MSS Eur F218/213, 'Hints or Heads of Enquiry into facilitating our knowledge of the more southerly parts of the Deckan', pp. 3–6.
23. Persian and English for written communication, Persian and Marathi for accounting, Telugu and Tamil among bureaucrats and with local correspondents. This group also included the Cavelly brothers Borriah and Lakhsmiah although they were not themselves from Arcot. The following largely after Wagoner, 'Precolonial Intellectuals', 799–803.
24. Co-authored with Ananda Row, 'Memoir Descriptive of the Ancient Place of [Ellora] near Dolwatabad ...' = Mack Gen, XIV, no. 8.
25. See Wagoner, 'Precolonial Intellectuals', 790.
26. 'Report of the Committee of Papers on Cavelly Venkata Lachmia's Proposed Renewal of Colonel Mackenzie's Investigations', Proceedings of the Asiatic Society of Bengal, printed in *Madras Journal of Science and Literature* (1836), 437–42.
27. After Dirks, *Castes of Mind*, 96.
28. The Mackenzie collections include his own field sketches as well as drawings sent to him whenever a colleague on military duty elsewhere discovered a new monument, e.g. Thomas F. De Havilland (1775–1866), who concluded Mackenzie's survey of the Deccan. At various stages, engineers and surveyors assisted Mackenzie: Lts George Rowley (as ensign Madras Eng., 1797–1803, assists Mackenzie), William Ward (India since 1801, assistant on Mysore survey), R. H. Fotheringham (Madras engineer 1792–1815, assistant Mysore survey), William George Stephen, Thomas and Benjamin Sydenham, and John L. Caldwell (engineers from 1788), as well as surveyors Henry Hamilton and J. Newman. He employed young civilian assistants, some of whom had trained at the Madras surveying school. His own draughtsmen John Newman, John Gould, C. Ignatio, J. H. Schenks, John Mustie, Sheik Abdullah, and Pyari Lal drew on the spot or worked up drawings at headquarters. Even in his assistants' work, Mackenzie determined the subjects and general style. AII, 473–552 lists hundreds of drawings of antiquities, chiefly in southern India and Deccan, as well as Java, but also northern India and some other territories. These include very numerous drawings by Mackenzie himself. Among the drawings of the temple and choultry of Tirumala Nayak at

Madura, c. 1801–05, are some by a South Indian (probably Madura) artist, see AII, 531; others are copies from native people, e.g. from a Ceylonese priest: AII, 521, WD 2621.

29. Sometimes this is titled *Engineer officers of the British army with a draughtsman and a guide surveying a Hoyasala temple in South India.*

30. AII, 477, WD 586; cf. AII, 478, WD 597, 'Ruined palace and temple at Vijayanagar' (Madras), 1800. Tapati Guha-Thakurta, 'The Compulsion of Visual Representation in Colonial India', in Maria Antonella Pelizzari (ed.), *Traces of India: Photography, Architecture, and the Politics of Representation, 1850–1900* (New Haven, Conn./London, 2003), 110–39, at 117; cf. Dirks, '"Guiltless Spoliations"', 223.

31. BL, WD 577, 596.

32. AI, 484, WD 640, 'View of Dindigul (Madras)'. Cf. Dirks, '"Guiltless Spoliations"', 223. For the site see George Michell, *The Penguin Guide to the Monuments of India, vol. I: Buddhist, Jain, Hindu* (London, 1990), 397–404. For representations of imperial officials with Hindu and Muslim scholars in monuments see Barbara Groseclose, 'Imag(in)ing Indians', *Art History*, 13:4 (1990), 488–515.

33. For the collections see Wilson's catalogue; for the inscriptions see Wagoner, 'Precolonial Intellectuals', 805–7. For the two MSS copies of the 1807 register see BL, OIOC, MSS Eur, Mack Gen, vol. XVIII (recensions A and B).

34. *Journal of the Asiatic Society of Bengal*, 7 (1837), i, 88–97, 218–23, 278–80. Prinsep would have liked to have them all edited, especially since the cheap lithographic technique was now available.

35. Cunningham, *Report*, vii.

36. For the expedition and British archaeological research see BL, OIOC, MSS Eur F148, including folder 46 for Mackenzie's archaeological records; Mack Misc 90 'Affairs of Java', fos 157–229. BL, OIOC, Mack Private 2, 16 (henceforth: Mack Private). BL, OIOC, Mack Misc 89/5, 6; Misc 91/4, fos 55–9; E. Wurtzburg, *Raffles of the Eastern Isles*, ed. for publication by C. Witting (London, 1954), 157–400.

37. See Jane Rendall, 'Scottish Orientalism: From Robertson to James Mill', *Historical Journal*, 25:1 (1982), 43–69, at 50–51 for Minto's support of Orientalists, and at 54–5 for Leyden's comparative philology in an evolutionary historical framework.

38. P. Thankappan Nair (ed.), *Proceedings of the Asiatic Society*, II (Calcutta, 1995), 243–9.

39. Mackenzie's close control over processes is evident in his correspondence with assistants who received detailed instructions on the methodology of making tracings and drawings of inscriptions. Mack Misc 90, 'Affairs of Java', fos 157–229 (8), Misc. notes and correspondence relating to Javanese antiquities, histories, and geography, e.g. at 167; Mack Private 74, fos 329–30, 332.

40. *The British in Java, 1811–1816: A Javanese Account* by Peter Carey. BL, Add. MS 12330, family chronicle of senior prince, Panular, during British occupation 1812–16.

41. Mackenzie, 'Biographical Sketch', 356, footnote: one native followed Mackenzie to India to continue translating.

42. Thomas Stamford Raffles, *The History of Java*, 2 vols (London, 1817), II, 45–6, 56. John Crawford, Resident at Djocjocarta, also studied the cultures of Java, Bali, and other regions and developed the concept of greater India. His account of the ruined Hindu temple at Borobudur was published with beautiful drawings in *Tr. Lit. Soc. of Bombay*, I (London, 1819), 154–66.

43. For Horsfield sending drawings to Raffles see Raffles, *History*, II, 33–51. Horsfield's main report is in BL, OIOC, MSS Eur F148/46, 'Dr Horsfield. Narrative of a Journey through Java, with a view to Mineralogical and other researches …'. For the drawings discussed here see AII, 453–6, WD 957/9, 956/19, 957/16.

44. Raffles, *History*, II, 55; BL, OIOC, MSS Eur F148/47, 12. Mildred Archer, 'Archaeology and the British Interlude in Java', *Geographical Magazine* (1958), 460–72.

45. Raffles, *Memoir*, 158. See also Raffles, *History*, II, 7–33.

46. BL, OIOC, MSS Eur F148/47, 11–12.

47. Mackenzie, 'Biographical Sketch', 342.

48. Ibid., 355–60.

49. Lady Sophia Raffles, *Memoir of the Life and Public Services of Sir Thomas Stamford Raffles*, with an Introduction by John Bastin (Oxford, 1991), 261–5. A second, posthumous edition of the *History* added to the drawings of sculptures and stone objects; also an architectural supplement, based in part on drawings by Capt. Baker, which had first been promised for the first edition.

50. By order of Governor-General Ellenborough, the temple was later also dedicated to nine casualties of the battles of Maharajpur and Panniar in 1843. See Andreas Volwahsen, *Splendours of Imperial India: British Architecture in the 18th and 19th Centuries* (Munich/London, 2004), 31–2, 125, with plans, drawings, and photographs.

51. Malconer, *Colonial Magazine* (Dec. 1840), quoted in J. P. Losty, 'Prinsep, James (1799–1840)', *Oxford Dictionary of National Biography* (Oxford, 2004), http://www.oxforddnb.com/view/article/22812 [accessed 26 June 2008]. Both in *Gleanings in Science* and in its successor, the *Journal of the Asiatic Society of Bengal* (1832–), which now took precedence over the *Asiatic Researches* for publications on Indian history and culture, Prinsep did much of the drawing and lithography of the accompanying plates himself.

52. Col. Stacy in Chittor and Udaipur, Lt Conolly in Jaipur (Sawai Jai Singh's 1727 foundation), Capt. Cautley in Saharanpur, Col. Smith in Patna, Tregear in Jaunpur, Lt Alexander Cunningham at Sarnath and Banaras, Gen. Ventura, A. Court, Dr Gerard, Charles Masson, and others in the Punjab and Afghanistan, and others collecting in various districts. Ventura, the French general of Ranjit Singh, used his influence to get permission to dig into topes, towers in the Punjab plains and frontier hills.

53. Michell, *Penguin Guide*, 152–3.

54. Jones had established points of synchronisation between Greek and Indian history, identifying, for instance, Chandragupta Maurya with the Sandrokottos of ancient

Greek historians. Many Company officers and officials and scholars contributed genealogies of dynasties.

55. This section is based on Mrs Postans, *Western India in 1838*, 2 vols (London, 1839), II,
    33–81, quotations on 34–5, 35–6, 36, 46.

56. George W. Johnson, *Three Years in Calcutta, or a Stranger in India* (London, 1843),
    quoted in Laura Sykes (ed.), *Calcutta through British Eyes 1690–1990* (Madras/Oxford,
    1992), 18. For an illustration see Prinsep's brother William's painting in C. A. Bayly
    (ed.), *The Raj: India and the British, 1600–1947*, with contributions by Brian Allen …
    [et al.] (London, 1990), cat. 270. For their intellectual prowess, the British community
    by public subscription, and occasionally the Company officially, erected monuments
    to other scholars, judges, and scientists. South Park Street: James Kerr, Company
    surgeon, 'distinguished as well by his Medical | knowledge as by his improving the
    Arts and enriching | Science by his discoveries in India' (d.1782, aet. 42). Calcutta
    Botanical Gardens: urn by Thomas Banks to superintendent Lt-Col. Robert Kyd
    (1746–93), military secretary in Bengal. There is also a stone pillar, inscribed in Latin,
    in the memory of his botanical colleague William Roxburgh.

57. Bernard S. Cohn, 'The Transformation of Objects into Artifacts, Antiquities, and Art
    in Nineteenth-Century India', in Cohn, *Colonialism and Its Forms of Knowledge: The
    British in India* (Princeton, NJ, 1996), 76–105, esp. 78–80.

58. Richard H. Davis, *Lives of Indian Images* (Princeton, NJ, 1990), 158–9. For European
    collecting in India, and parallels between European princely cabinets of curiosities
    and Mughal libraries and treasure-houses see Maya Jasanoff, 'Collectors of Empire:
    Objects, Conquests and Imperial Self-Fashioning', *Past & Present*, 184 (2004), 109–35;
    Jasanoff, *Edge of Empire: Conquest and Collecting in the East, 1750–1850* (London,
    2005), 316–18.

59. For Company officials collecting MSS, miniatures, metalwork, drawings, and paint-
    ings see Mildred Archer, 'British as Collectors and Patrons in India, 1760–1830', in
    Archer, *Treasures from India: The Clive Collection at Powis Castle* (London, 1987),
    9–16.

60. Jasanoff, *Edge of Empire*, 109.

61. Capt. Frederick Maryat (1792–1848) gave a large lacquer Buddha and a colossal stone
    carving of Buddha's footprint in 1826. Sometimes, an officer's offer of objects was
    declined for purchase: BM, O.P. 2 Feb. 1833, Standing Committee Minutes C.3560, 9
    Feb. 1833.

62. BM, O.P. 18 July 1836. He didn't recommend purchase of the sculpture in question as
    it was too expensive.

63. *Transactions of the Asiatic Society of Great Britain and Ireland* [henceforth: *TRAS
    GB&IR*], I (1827), 600–630; II (1830), cxviii.

64. The best assessment is in Jasanoff, *Edge of Empire*, 328, on the basis of Christie's sales
    1766–1835: the market for small Indian objects was marginal to European art and

artefacts. Among late eighteenth-century Bengali wills and inventories, only 5 per cent had small collections of Indian art and artefacts.

65. Partha Mitter, *Much Maligned Monsters: History of European Reactions to Indian Art* (Oxford, 1977), 73–104, esp. 85–93, with good illustrations. Capt. Alexander Allan, military artist, cartographer, and commander of the man-of-war *Cumberland* in the second Mysore War, had brought some sculptures to England.

66. Hermione de Almeida and George H. Gilpin, *Indian Renaissance: British Romantic Art and the Prospect of India* (Aldershot/Burlington, Vt, 2006), with excellent reproductions in pl. 4, figs pp. 41, 43, 51.

67. James Forbes, *Oriental Memoirs*, 4 vols (London, 1813–15), III, 361. The best brief introduction is Davis, *Lives*, 160–63.

68. For the best account of private collectors see Jasanoff, *Edge of Empire*, here esp. 186–95.

69. Jörg Fisch, 'A Solitary Vindicator of the Hindus: The Life and Writings of General Charles Stuart (1757/8–1828)', *JRAS* (1985), no. 1, 35–57; Davis, *Lives*, 163–7; Jasanoff, *Edge of Empire*, 195, 309–10; [Anon.], 'Major Gen. Chas. Stuart', *Asiatic Journal*, 16 (1828), 606–7; *Gentleman's Magazine*, 100 (1830), i, 470. For border-crossers see also William Dalrymple, *White Mughals: Love and Betrayal in Eighteenth-Century India* (London, 2002), 23–43, 391–2.

70. Michael D. Willis, 'Sculpture from India', in Marjorie L. Caygill and John Cherry (eds), *A. W. Franks: Nineteenth-Century Collecting and the British Museum* (London, 1997), 252.

71. Jasanoff, *Edge of Empire*, 164.

72. Davis, *Lives*, fig. 25, p. 166. The tomb is also pictured in Jasanoff, *Edge of Empire*, 310.

73. BL, IOR L/AG/34/27/93, 790; H. E. A. Cotton, '"Hindoo" Stuart: A Discovery at the British Museum', *Bengal, Past & Present*, 48 (1934), 78–80.

74. Tapati Guha-Thakurta, 'The Museumised Relic: Archaeology and the First Museum of Colonial India', *Indian Economic and Social History Review*, 34:1 (1997), 21–52, at 23.

75. Postponed in 1798 to consolidate the finances; priority was given to publishing the *Transactions*: *Proceedings*, I, 291.

76. Quoted in O. P. Kejariwal, *The Asiatic Society of Bengal and the Discovery of India's Past* (New Delhi, 1988), 116.

77. *Proceedings*, II, 127; Guha-Thakurta, 'The Museumised Relic', 24–5.

78. Guha-Thakurta, 'The Museumised Relic'; Kejariwal, *Asiatic Society*.

79. *Proceedings*, III/1: 124, 197–9, 206–7, 363, 670.

80. *Journal of the Asiatic Society of Bombay* [henceforth: *JASB*], 6 (1837), 280 and footnote.

81. Ibid., 7 (1838), i, 558. On Bhubaneshwar see Michell, *Penguin Guide*, 219–26; on Stuart's collecting see Davis, *Lives*, 164–5; Ramaprasad Chanda, *Medieval Indian Sculpture in the British Museum*, with an introduction by R. L. Hobson (London, 1936), 69–70.

82. The appendix to vol. XI (1810) of *AR* supposedly mentioning Stuart's donation does not exist; a list of donors and donations to the Society dated 1822, published *AR*, XV (1825), however, mentions among several of Stuart's donations 'Two Stones from Bhu-vaneswara in Orissa with Sanscrit Inscriptions' (xxxv). For later nineteenth-century references to the story see Fisch, 'Solitary Vindicator', nn. 42-3.

83. Fisch, 'Solitary Vindicator', 52.

84. *JASB*, 17 (1848), i, 537. In the 1840s, however, Taylor's repair jobs were praised as a great achievement in the face of limited resources; nothing had been done since to main-tain the tomb's state of repair: S. Roy, 'Indian Archaeology from Jones to Marshall (1784-1902)', *Ancient India*, special number, 9 (1953), 4-28; *Bengal Obituary* (1848), 378.

85. Quoted in Kejariwal, *Asiatic Society*, 201.

86. Colin Mackenzie, 'Extracts from the Journal of Col. Colin Mackenzie's Jain Pandit of his Route from Calcutta to Gaya in 1820', quoted in Alan Trevithick, 'British Archae-ologists, Hindu Abbots, and Burmese Buddhists: The Mahabodhi Temple at Bodh Gaya, 1811-1877', *Modern Asian Studies*, 33:3 (1999), 635-56, at 643. Site: Michell, *Penguin Guide*, 228-9, ill. 209.

87. Alexander Allan, 'To Sarnath', *The Bengal Annual* (1836), 195, quoted in Kejariwal, *Asiatic Society*, 8.

88. J. Goldingham, 'Some Account of the Cave in the Island of Elephanta', *AR*, IV (1795), 407-15, at 407.

89. Richard Gough, *A Comparative View of the Ancient Monuments of India, Particularly Those in the Islands of Salset near Bombay, as Described by Different Writers, Illustrated with Prints* (London, 1785); footnote 'g' at p. 14.

90. Captain Postans, 'A Few Observations on the Temple of Somnath', *TRAS GB&IR*, VIII (1846), 172-5. Postan's request to the Court of Directors for publication subsidies for sketches and for permission to dedicate his book on Sind to them was rejected, although in 1844 the Company paid him £50 for drawings of buildings, scenery, and costumes in Sind, Cutch, and Bombay.

91. Reginald Heber, *Narrative of a Journey Through the Upper Provinces of India, from Calcutta to Bombay, 1824-1825 (with notes upon Ceylon)*, 2 vols (London, 1828); Heber, *An Account of a Journey to Madras and the Southern Provinces, 1826; and Letters Written in India*, 2 vols (London, 1828), I, 323-4.

92. BL, OIOC, F/4/701, 19025; F/4/1118, 30049. *First Report of the Curator of Ancient Mon-uments in India for the Year 1881-82* (Simla, ?1882).

93. AII, 455, WD 957/f.1 (82). Also AII, plate 91. The same image without figures seems to be the basis for a plate in Raffles, *History*, II, second plate after 18. Another copy was owned by Mackenzie.

94. BL, OIOC, F/4/620 (quotation); F/4/2645; F/4/776, 20985; Ben Pub 11.5.1825, draft 256/1824-25, E/4/714 p. 721.

95. BL, OIOC, F/4/699, 18956; Ben Pub 10.12.1823, draft 73/1823–24, E/4/710, pp. 57–8. F/4/714, 19482; Ben Pub 17.3.1824, draft 245/1823–24, E/4/711 pp. 215–16.

96. BL, OIOC, F/4/620 (23 Feb. 1817).

97. *Proceedings*, I, 247–8 (7 Aug., 18 Sep. 1794); AR, IV (1795), 313–16 (in 1807 edn, 305–7, quotation 306).

98. Mildred Archer, 'An Artist Engineer – Colonel Robert Smith in India (1805–1830), *The Connoisseur* ([Feb.] 1972), 78–88.

99. Bayly (ed.), *Raj*, 208–9, cat. 257; AI, 317–23. For a pictorial journal of his travels in Hindustan see V&A Museum, I.M. 15–1915.

100. Smith's oil painting *Inside the Main Entrance of the Purana Quila, Delhi* (1823, Yale Center for British Art, 81.9 × 107.3 cm) shows the inner face of the northern gate of the fort built mostly by the captor of Delhi, Sher Shah Sur, after 1540.

101. The cost of the repair programme, including standstone, sand, iron and copper cramps, and equipment, totalled 22,262 rps: BL, IOR, Board's collection, Bengal Political Dept, vol. 1324, no. 52472.

102. On the Qutb see W. H. Sleeman, *Rambles and Recollections of an Indian Official*, 2 vols (London, 1844), II, 251–6, quotation 252; see also on other repair work E. C Archer, *Tours in Upper India, and in Parts of the Himalaya Mountains*, 2 vols (London, 1833), I, 107–8.

103. The Mackenzie collections include Amaravati plans and drawings by assistants and draughtsmen T. Anderson, C. Barnett, M. Bourke, Gould, Hamilton, Mustie, Newman, W. Sydenham, Najbulah, Pyari Lal, Sheik Abdullah.

104. Elliot had been collecting coins and inscriptions since assignments in south Maratha in the 1820s.

105. James Burgess, *The Buddhist Stupas of Amaravati and Jaggayyapet ... Surveyed in 1882 ... With Translations of the Ashoka Inscriptions at Jaugada and Dhauli, by Georg Bühler* (London, 1887), 18.

106. Robert Knox, *Amaravati: Buddhist Sculpture from the Great Stupa* (London, 1992).

107. Ibid., 23–41, for architecture and sculpture. Cohn, 'The Transformation of Objects into Artifacts, Antiquities, and Art in Nineteenth-Century India', 76–105.

108. Maria Graham, *Journal of a Short Residence in India* (Edinburgh, 1812), 57–8.

109. BL, OIOC, MSS Eur D123, pp. 9–49, quotations 11, 16–17 on Elephanta.

110. BL, OIOC, L/P&J/3/998, Public desp. to Bengal, no. 15 of 1844, 29.5.1844. L/P&J/3/37, Public Letters from Bengal, nos. 13, 14, 34 of 1845, 26 Mar., 24 May, 27 Dec. 1845. For comparison, the cost of building a comfortable bungalow in 1830s Bombay was about 600–800 rupees according to Postans, *Western India*, I, 14.

111. BL, OIOC, L/P&J/3/1001 [27 Jan. 1847].

112. *JRAS* (1843), 241–7, 'Account of the Discovery of the Ruins of the Buddhist Site of Sankassa, by Lt Alex. Cunningham, of the Bengal Engineers, in a Letter to Colonel Sykes, F.R.S.' [read 3.12.1842]; Tapati Guha-Thakurta, *Monuments, Objects, Histories:*

Institutions of Art in Colonial and Postcolonial India (New York/New Delhi, 2004), 27–8, 32–3; Abu Imam, 'Sir Alexander Cunningham (1814–1893): The First Phase of Indian Archaeology', *JRAS* (1963), 194–207. For an 1814 drawing of Sarnath in the Mackenzie collection see AII, 491, WD 694.

113. *JRAS* (1843), 246–7, 'Account of the Discovery'.

114. *JASB*, 17 (1848), i, 535–6, 'Proposed Archaeological Investigation'.

115. Ibid., 535.

116. Ibid., 171–201, for a very detailed report by Maisey on antiquities at Kalinjar. Maisey's report on Sanchi (BL, OIOC, MSS Eur D 618) was accompanied by two series of drawings: AII, 553–6; cf. AII, plate 113: Sculpture from the Eastern Gateway of the Great Stupa, Sanchi, C.I. (c.1849–52.). Further drawings listed in *British Drawings* III, 218–24, incl. some related to the Sanchi report. In the 1870s, a cast of the Eastern Gateway of the Sanchi Stupa was installed in the east Cast Court of the South Kensington Museum. Maisey's assistant from early 1851 was Alexander Cunningham, who excavated with him at Sanchi and other sites, collected caskets, coins, pieces of bone, beads, and pottery, and helped with plans and sections of the stupas and drawings of sculpture and relic baskets. These were intended to become the subject of a second report, but after the Asiatic Society failed to send translations of the inscriptions, and Maisey went on campaign in Burma 1852–4, it was never written.

117. He had previously studied Muslim architecture and now worked in Bihar and Shahabad. In 1836 he copied the Khandagiri rock inscriptions for Prinsep, then made drawings of the stupa rail at Bodhgaya, and offered to collect for the Calcutta museum.

118. The British Library collection is listed in AII, 466–8, a total of 212 drawings from Bengal, Bihar, U.P., 1846–53. These include WD 2876/fos 1–34 Sculpture at Sarnath, U.P. See also Cunningham, *Report*, xxvii.

119. AI, 35, quotes 1848 correspondence in BL, OIOC, Bombay General Proceedings, III, no. 1004; VI, nos 2570–72; IX, nos 4447–9, 4451.

120. AII 442–6, including of the tomb, mosque, and large tank of Ibrahim Adil Shah II, and the Jami Masjid (1851/2).

121. Bombay Govt Resolution, 31 July 1848. In the 1850s, the Company first employed official photographers on archaeological surveys in the various presidencies.

122. 'Memorandum from Col. A. Cunningham of the Bengal Engineers to the Governor-General, Lord Canning, Regarding a Proposed Investigation of the Archaeological Remains of Upper India', in *Archaeological Survey of India, Four Reports*, 3 vols (Simla, 1871), preface, I: ii. For this section see Guha-Thakurta, *Monuments*, 1–70.

123. Quoted by Stephen Bann, 'Antiquarianism, Visuality, and the Exotic Monument: William Hodges's A Dissertation', in Maria Antonella Pelizzari (ed.), *Traces of India: Photography, Architecture, and the Politics of Representation, 1850–1900* (New Haven, Conn./London, 2003), 62–85, at 66.

124. The Archaeological Survey was but one of numerous surveys commissioned by government in the second half of the nineteenth century, including also geological, meterological, tidal, geodetic, and marine surveys as well as the first general census (1871-2).

125. Quoted in Margarita Díaz-Andreu, *A World History of Nineteenth-Century Archaeology: Nationalism, Colonialism, and the Past* (Oxford, 2007), 228.

126. Their focus is primarily on coins, seals, and inscriptions, at the expense of sculpture.

127. A summary of contemporary and later assessments in Upinder Singh, *The Discovery of Ancient India: Early Archaeologists and the Beginnings of Archaeology* (Delhi, 2004), 341-8.

128. Guha-Thakurta, *Monuments*, 55-6; Singh, *Discovery of Ancient India*, 353.

129. A new type of photographic album was produced by the London firm Griggs from 1880.

130. There is no space here to explore the lively debate and reform of 'treasure trove' in mid- and late nineteenth-century Britain, for which see George Francis Hill, *Treasure Trove in Law and Practice from the Earliest Time to the Present Day* (Oxford, 1936); John Carman, *Valuing Ancient Things: Archaeology and Law* (London, 1996).

131. Lord Curzon quoted in Douglas M. Peers, 'Colonial Knowledge and the Military in India, 1780-1860', *Journal of Imperial and Commonwealth History*, 33 (2005), 157-80, at 161 n. 14. See C. R. Wilson (ed.), *Old Fort William in Bengal, a Selection of Official Documents Dealing with Its History*, 2 vols (Calcutta, 1906), I, xxix-xxii, for Curzon's speech, 19 Dec. 1902.

132. Derek Linstrum, 'The Sacred Past: Lord Curzon and the Indian Monuments', *South Asian Studies*, 11 (1995), 1-17, quotation 6; David Gilmour, *Curzon* (London, 1994), 178-81.

133. Phiroze Vasunia is working on a book on Greece, Rome, and the British Empire for Oxford University Press.

III. Capital of Culture

Chapter Nine: Pomp and Circumstance in London

1. Quoted in Steven Parissien, *George IV: The Grand Entertainment* (London, 2001), 264.

2. The Queen's Gallery, *George IV and the Arts of France* (London, 1966). The quotation from Lady Bessborough on p. 5.

3. For the caption to plate XX I am indebted to archival research that has reattributed the Dublin portrait, long thought to have been the prime original, but now considered an 1821 copy: correspondence with Dr Mary Clark, Dublin City Archives, March 2009.

4. Parissien, *Grand Entertainment*, 265.

5. Ibid., 250, quoting Hazlitt from *The Champion* (1815).

6. John Summerson, *Georgian London*, ed. Howard Colvin (New Haven, Conn./London, 2003), 227.

7. R. W. Jeffery (ed.), *Dyott's Diary 1781–1845*, 2 vols (London, 1907), I, 311.

8. Harriot G. Mundy (ed.), *The Journal of Mary Frampton, from the Year 1779, until the Year 1846* (London, 1885), 218.

9. *An Account of the Visit of His Royal Highness the Prince Regent, with Their Imperial Majesties the Emperor of all the Russias and the King of Prussia, to the Corporation of London* (London, 1814).

10. The quotations from Blücher's correspondence are taken from Ernest F. Henderson, *Bluecher and the Uprising of Prussia against Napoleon* (New York/London, 1911), 259–60.

11. *The Jerningham Letters (1780–1843) being Excerpts from the Correspondence and Diaries of the Honourable Lady Jerningham and of Her Daughter Lady Bedingfeld*, ed., with notes, by Egerton Castle, 2 vols (London, 1896), II, 54.

12. John Summerson, *The Life and Work of John Nash Architect* (London, 1980), 98; Christopher Hibbert, *George IV* (London, 1998); Gillian Russell, *The Theatres of War: Performance, Politics, and Society, 1793–1815* (Oxford, 1995), 89.

13. Eleanor Hughes, 'Vessels of Empire: Marine Painting in Eighteenth-Century Britain', unpubl. Ph.D. thesis (Berkeley, Calif., 2001), 210–15; G. D. Glenn, 'Nautical "Docudrama" in the Age of the Kembles', in J. L. Fisher and S. Watt (eds), *When They Weren't Doing Shakespeare: Essays on Nineteenth-Century British and American Theatre* (Athens, Ga/London), 137–51; Terence M. Freeman, *Dramatic Representations of British Soldiers and Sailors on the London Stage, 1660–1800: Britons Strike Home* (Lewiston, NY, 1995).

14. FD XIII, 4570; *Gentleman's Magazine*, 84 (1814), ii, 181–2.

15. Quoted in Hibbert, *George IV*, 460; cf. Mundy (ed.), *Journal of Mary Frampton*, 235–6.

16. TNA, WORK 21/8/1.

17. *Gentleman's Magazine*, 84 (1814), ii, 183.

18. Peter Pindar, *The R---t's Fair, or Grand Galante-Show!!* (London, 1814), 11, 27 (quotation). *Radical Statesman* (26 July 1814), 'The Soliloquy of a Sailor'. For this section see Russell, *Theatres of War*, 89–93.

19. FD XIII, 4569.

20. Mundy (ed.), *Journal of Mary Frampton*, 230, Dowager Lady Vernon to Mary Frampton, 29 June 1814; Charles Lamb to Wordsworth, in Charles Lamb, *The Letters of Charles and Maria Lamb*, ed. Edwin W. Marrs, 3 vols (Ithaca, NY, 1975–8), III, 96.

21. J. E. Cookson, *The British Armed Nation, 1793–1815* (Oxford, 1997), 241–3.

22. Michael Levey, *Sir Thomas Lawrence* (New Haven, Conn./London, 2005), 188, 190–91.

23. *Pope Pius VII* (1819), 262.2 × 177.9 cm., HM The Queen, RC 404946. Levey, *Sir Thomas Lawrence*, 224–32. In 1813–16 Nash had enlarged an old lodge in Windsor Great Park

as a picturesque, thatched-roof *cottage orné* at a total cost of over £40,000, but then in 1828 the king moved back into the castle. The castle was elaborately restored and embellished by Wyatville for some £800,000, largely following a scheme devised by Charles Long, who suggested the famous Grand Corridor, over 160 metres long, to revolutionise communication in the castle. Long was also involved in purchases of art works and possibly of *boiseries* in Paris for the panelling in the Grand Reception Room. The private royal apartments continued to reflect George's French preferences and personal involvement in design decisions. St George's Hall was remodelled to accommodate the former chapel and provided a Gothic setting for the Order of the Garter, presided over by the king's portrait in yet another example of the king-hero.

24. *Parliamentary Debates*, 1st ser., xxxi, cols 1049–53 (29 June 1815); *HC Journals*, vol. 70, pp. 446, 448; vol. 71, pp. 11, 12. TNA, T27/74.174.

25. Andrew Robertson (ed.), *Letters and Papers of Andrew Robertson, Miniature Painter* (London, 1895), 280–83, letters to John Ewen at Aberdeen, 22 May–24 July 1816.

26. TNA, T1/4029.6968.

27. Cambridge University Library, Add. 9389/6/H/16, Prince Hoare to Ignatius Bonomi, 10 Apr. 1816. See also 'Publius', 'On the Waterloo Monument', *Annals of the Fine Arts*, 2 (1818), 146–60.

28. *Gentleman's Magazine*, 87 (1817), i, 501–2 (quotation 502); *Parliamentary Debates*, 1st ser., xxxi, cols 1052–3 (1815).

29. Directors' Meeting 30 Apr. 1828, Committee on the National Monument of Scotland, Minute Book, I, 256.

30. Dana Arnold, 'George IV and the Metropolitan Improvements: The Creation of a Royal Image', in Arnold (ed.), *'Squanderous and Lavish Profusion': George IV, His Image and Patronage of the Arts* (London, 1995), 51–6; Summerson, *Nash*, 58–100, 114–45.

31. John Gwynn, *London and Westminster Improved* (London, 1766), xv.

32. Quoted in Roy Porter, *London: A Social History* (London, 1994), 127.

33. David Watkin, *The Architect King: George III and the Culture of the Enlightenment* (London, 2004).

34. Parissien, *Grand Entertainment*, 274.

35. Summerson, *Georgian London*, 230–31.

36. Ibid., 231–2.

37. For the National Gallery see J. G. W. Conlin, *The Nation's Mantelpiece: A History of the National Gallery* (London, 2006), on Angerstein see 50–52; Holger Hoock, 'Old Masters and the English School: The Royal Academy of Arts and the Notion of a National Gallery at the Turn of the Nineteenth Century', *Journal of the History of Collections*, 16:1 (2004), 1–18; Gregory Martin, 'The Founding of the National Gallery, London', *The Connoisseur*, 185–7 (Apr.–Dec. 1974).

38. Conlin, *Nation's Mantelpiece*, 60–61.

39. Shannon Hunter Hurtado, 'The Promotion of the Visual Arts in Britain, 1835–60', *Canadian Journal of History*, 27 (1993), 59–80, for a Marxian analysis.

40. For the limits see e.g. the reception of Gladstone's proposal for the National Gallery as a model of state responsibility for the citizenry's spiritual well-being, derided as a crypto-Catholic Tory idea: J. G. W. Conlin, 'Gladstone and Christian Art, 1832–1854', *Historical Journal*, 46:2 (2003), 341–74. The association of the National Gallery with national education also drew opposition from those favouring voluntarist, denominational education over central government direction: Conlin, *Nation's Mantelpiece*, 68–9.

41. I discuss these developments in detail in 'Old Masters and the English School' and in 'Reforming Culture: National Art Institutions in the Age of Reform', in Arthur Burns and Joanna Innes (eds), *Rethinking the Age of Reform: Britain 1780–1850* (Cambridge, 2003), 254–70.

42. *The Penny Magazine of the Society for the Diffusion of Useful Knowledge*, new ser. (1841), 11, 21, 52, 68, 89, 217, 241, 265, 289, 377, 425; *Edinburgh Review*, 65 (1837), viii; Anthony Burton, *Vision & Accident: The Story of the V&A* (London, 1999), 14.

43. James V. Millingen, *Some Remarks on the State of Learning and the Fine Arts in Great Britain; on the Deficiency of Public Institutions and the Necessity of a Better System for the Improvement of Knowledge and Taste* (London, 1831), 3, 5, 72.

44. *Parliamentary Debates*, 3rd ser., xiv, col. 645 (23 July 1832).

45. Peter Bailey, *Leisure and Class in Victorian England: Rational Recreation and the Contest for Control, 1830–1885* (London, 1978); Hugh Cunningham, *Leisure in the Industrial Revolution, c.1780–c.1880* (London, 1980), ch. 3. Tony Bennett, *The Birth of the Museum: History, Theory, Politics* (London/New York, 1995), 19–20.

46. *Parliamentary Debates*, 3rd ser., xii, cols 468–9 (13 Apr. 1832).

47. For a disciplinarian reading of the National Gallery see Colin Trodd, 'Culture, Class, City: The National Gallery, London and the Spaces of Education, 1822–57', in Marcia Pointon (ed.), *Art Apart: Art Institutions and Ideology across England and North America* (Manchester, 1994), 33–49.

48. P.P. 1835, vii (479), 1–623, 'Report on the British Museum', paras 612, 1287–9, 1313–14, 1320–22, 1328, 2908, 3916–19.

49. P.P. 1836, x (440), 1–931, 'Report on the British Museum', iii–v; cf. evidence paras 2302–12 (Richardson); cf. Cunningham, *Leisure*, 91, 106–7.

50. *Parliamentary Debates*, 3rd ser., xvi, cols 1003–4 (25 Mar. 1833); cf. xvi, col. 1341 (1 Apr. 1833), for Cobbett on the foundation of Sir John Soane's Museum.

51. 'The Elgin Marbles! Or John Bull buying Stones at the time his numerous Family want Bread!!': BMC 12787 [?June 1816]. The quotation from 'Substance and Shadow, Cartoon No. 1', *Punch*, 5 (1843), 22.

52. *Politics for the People*, no. 11 (1 July 1848), 183.

53. Ibid., no. 1 (6 May 1848), 5–6, quotation 5; no. 2 (13 May 1848), 38–41.

54. *Parliamentary Debates*, new ser., xxii, cols 1352–3 (8 Mar. 1830), quotation 1353; cf. 3rd ser., xxvii, col. 1186 (18 May 1835). Among active members were the radical Liverpool MP William Ewart, Henry Gally Knight, a moderate Whig, and the Tories Henry Goulburn and Henry Thomas Hope.

55. P.P. 1841, vi (416), 437–635, 'Report on National Monuments', paras 119–20, 246–50, 439–44, 1931, 2183, 2185 (henceforth: 'Report on National Monuments').

56. For this paragraph see William Matthews, *British Autobiographies: An Annotated Bibliography of British Autobiographies Published or Written before 1851* (Berkeley, Calif./London, 1955); James A. Mangan and James Walvin (eds), *Manliness and Morality: Middle-Class Masculinity in Britain and America, 1800–1940* (Manchester, 1987), esp. introduction and essay by R. J. Park, 'Biological Thought, Athletics and the Formation of a "Man of Character"', 7–34; Norman Vance, *The Sinews of the Spirit: The Ideal of Christian Manliness in Victorian Literature and Religious Thought* (Cambridge, 1985); Graham Dawson, *Soldier Heroes: British Adventure, Empire and the Imagining of Masculinities* (London, 1994); Dawson, 'Stars of Empire: Victorian Soldier Heroes and Boyhood Masculinity', *Journal for the Study of British Cultures*, 3:2 (1996), 117–31; C. I. Hamilton, 'Naval Hagiography and the Victorian Hero', *Historical Journal*, 23:2 (1980), 381–98.

57. John Tosh, 'The Old Adam and the New Man: Emerging Themes in the History of English Masculinities, 1750–1850', in Tim Hitchcock and Michèle Cohen (eds), *English Masculinities 1660–1800* (London/New York, 1999), 217–38, at 222.

58. Sir William F. P. Napier, *History of the War in the Peninsula and in the South of France, from the Year 1807 to the Year 1814*, 6 vols (London, 1828–40).

59. Discussion of admission fees was linked to the complex internal economic functioning of the Cathedral. On compensation for loss of revenue see e.g. Edward Edwards, *A Letter to Sir Martin Arthur Shee … on the Reform of the Royal Academy, with Observations on the Evidence Respecting the Academy given before the Select Committee of the Commons* (London, 1839), 7.

60. P.P. 1837–8, xxxvi (119), 447–60, 'Correspondence between the Secretary of State and the Dean and Chapter of St. Paul's', quotations 451–2. An average of some 60,000 visitors annually were registered in the 1820s and 1830s: figure calculated from P.P. 1837, xli (242), 'Amount of Fees received at the Door of St. Paul's, and for seeing the Monuments', 479; for criticism see John Smith, *Nollekens and his Times*, 2 vols (London, 1829), I, 376–7.

61. 'Report on National Monuments', paras. 11, 23–34, 43–9, 75, 78, 97, 117–18, 150–51, 331, 339, 344, 544–51. Cf. William Wilkins, 'A Letter to Lord Viscount Goderich, on the Patronage of the Arts by the English Government', *Library of the Fine Arts*, 3 (May 1832), 291–307, 367–78, 472–83, here at 372.

62. 'Report on National Monuments', paras 355, 417–18, 719–22, 1361–2, 1845, 1847, 1849, 1856, 2003, 2538, 2585–7, 2640, 2650–53, 2672–3, 2869–71.

63. Quoted in Richard D. Altick, *The Shows of London* (Cambridge, Mass., 1978), 244.
64. Trodd, 'Culture, Class, City', 39–40. Carmen Stonge, 'Making Private Collections Public: Gustav Friedrich Waagen and the Royal Museum in Berlin', *Journal of the History of Collections*, 10:1 (1998), 61–74, here 65.
65. Ronald A. Bosco and Joel Myerson (eds), *The Later Lectures of Ralph Waldo Emerson*, 2 vols, vol. I, 1843–54 (Athens, Ga, 2001), 222. The social profile of the National Gallery's early audiences, exceeding half a million by 1840, is difficult to ascertain, though the *Art Union*, 2 June 1840, 90, approved of working-class visitors on Mondays. For Godwin see Duncan Forbes, '"The Advantages of Combination": The Art Union of London and State Regulation in the 1840s', in Paul Barlow and Colin Trodd (eds), *Governing Cultures: Art Institutions in Victorian London* (Aldershot, 2000), 128–42, here 132. Emerson is quoted in Altick, *Shows of London*, 252.
66. Altick, *Shows of London*, 250–51.
67. P.P. 1841, vi, 'Report from the select committee on the fine arts'. This paragraph follows Emma L. Winter, 'German Fresco Painting and the New Houses of Parliament at Westminster, 1834–1851', *Historical Journal*, 47:2 (2004), 291–329, an excellent example of cultural transfer analysis, although like many she tends to exaggerate the lack of 'any tradition of public patronage of the arts' in Britain (293).

Conclusions: Cultural Politics, State, War, and Empire

1. Peter Mandler, 'Art in a Cool Climate: The Cultural Policy of the British State in European Context, c. 1780–c. 1850', in T. C. W. Blanning and Hagen Schulze (eds), *Unity and Diversity in European Culture c. 1800 (Proceedings of the British Academy*, vol. 134, 2006), 101–20.
2. William Paulet Carey, *A Descriptive Catalogue of a Collection of Paintings by British Artists in the Possession of Sir John Fleming Leicester* (London, 1819), xii.
3. See Holger Hoock, *The King's Artists: The Royal Academy of Arts and the Politics of British Culture, 1760–1840* (Oxford, 2003), ch. 6, for the politics of the London art world during the French Revolution.
4. As late as the 1860s, the Palestine Exploration Fund, mostly military men and clerics, carried out topographical tasks in the Holy Land for the War Office.
5. For intellectual pursuits facilitated by the Victorian informal empire in the Far East see Fa-Ti Fan, 'Victorian Naturalists in China: Science and Informal Empire', *British Journal for the History of Science*, 36:1 (2003), 1–26.
6. For the former claim see Peter Mandler, 'Art in a Cool Climate'. The Cambridge Victorian Studies Group is conducting and promoting innovative work on heritage in Britain and the Empire: http://www.victorians.group.cam.ac.uk/index.html.
7. Bernard Porter, '"Bureau and Barrack": Early Victorian Attitudes Towards the Continent', *Victorian Studies*, 27 (1983–4), 407–33.

8. Mandler, 'Art in a Cool Climate', 119.

Epilogue: Empires Imagined at the Great Exhibition

1. Joan Evans and John Howard Whitehouse (eds), *The Diaries of John Ruskin, 1848–1873* (Oxford, 1958), 468.

2. I have drawn heavily on Jeffrey A. Auerbach, *The Great Exhibition of 1851: A Nation On Display* (New Haven, Conn./London, 1999), esp. ch. 6. Numerous pressure groups used the Great Exhibition to showcase their causes, from pacifists, the temperance movement (who liked the ban on alcohol from displays and the refreshment rooms), proponents of metrication and a single trade currency to various religious proselytisers: Nicholas Fisher, '"Nothing Can be More Successful": Were the Political and Cultural Aims of the Great Exhibition Fulfilled?', in Franz Bosbach (ed.), *Die Weltausstellung von 1851 und ihre Folgen. The Great Exhibition and Its Legacy* (Munich, 2002), 243–53, esp. 250.

3. The commission combined aristocrats, with the Whig grandee Earl Granville as deputy to Prince Albert as chairman, politicians of all complexions, including Lord John Russell and Gladstone for the government, and men distinguished in the arts, science, and agriculture.

4. There is no space here to discuss the parliamentary select committees, which led to the Government School of Design and local schools and museums of art and design being founded in the 1830s. See with full references Thomas Gretton, '"Art is Cheaper and Goes Lower in France": The Language of the Parliamentary Select Committee on Arts and Principles of Design of 1835–1836', in Andrew Hemingway and William Vaughan (eds), *Art in Bourgeois Society 1790–1850* (Cambridge, 1998), 84–100; Quentin Bell, *Schools of Design* (London, 1963). For Albert and the Great Exhibition see David G. C. Allan, '"A Duty and a Pleasure": Prince Albert and the Society of Arts', and Susan Bennett, 'Prince Albert, the Society of Arts and the Great Exhibition of 1851', both in Bosbach (ed.), *Weltausstellung*, 91–8, 99–106.

5. The general background after Hermione Hobhouse, *The Crystal Palace and the Great Exhibition: Art, Science and Productive Industry. A History of the Royal Commision for the Exhibition of 1851* (London/New York, 2002), quotation on p. 14.

6. John E. Findling, 'America at the Great Exhibition', in Bosbach (ed.), *Weltausstellung*, 197–204, at 197–8.

7. In the German states, discussion of which government or institutions ought to represent 'Germany' seemed to suggest that if national unity could not be achieved in the virtual world, Germany was far from achieving it in reality: Abigail Green, 'The Representation of the German States at the Great Exhibition', in Bosbach (ed.), *Weltausstellung*, 267–77.

8. Egypt sent 50 exhibits, Turkey 216, America 1,023, the Zollverein (Prussia, Bavaria, Saxony, Württemberg, and 22 other German states) 1,874, France 3,459.

9. Wolfram Kaiser, 'Inszenierung des Freihandels als Weltgesellschaftliche Entwicklungsstrategie: Die "Great Exhibition" 1851 und der politische Kulturtransfer nach Kontinentaleuropa', in Bosbach (ed.), *Weltausstellung*, 163–80; John R. Davis, 'The International Legacy of the Great Exhibition', ibid., 337–47.

10. On technology transfer see David J. Jeremy, 'The Great Exhibition, Exhibitions, and Technology Transfer', in Bosbach (ed.), *Weltausstellung*, 127–39.

11. Some European governments, especially in the German states and Austria, were concerned that London in the summer of 1851 could became the venue for international socialists and revolutionaries. The Prussian king worried for the safety of his heir, sending a hysterical warning to Queen Victoria and Prince Albert that 'countless hordes of desperate proletarians, well-organised and under the leadership of blood-red criminals, are on their way to London now': quoted in Hobhouse, *Crystal Palace*, 59; cf. Davis, 'International Legacy'.

12. *The Five Shilling Day at the Exhibition*, in *The Illustrated London News* (19 July 1851), 100–101.

13. Andrea Hibbard, 'Distracting Impressions and Rational Recreation at the Great Exhibition', in James Buzard, Joseph W. Childers, and Eileen Gillooly (eds), *Victorian Prism: Refractions of the Crystal Palace* (Charlottesville, Va, 2007), 151–67, at 161–2, the *Times* quotation on p. 161. Cf. 'The Great Exhibition of 1851', *New Monthly Magazine*, 92 (1851), 103–26, at 126.

14. Thomas Rawlins, *Lane's Telescopic View of the Interior of the Great Industrial Exhibition* (London, 1851). For a view see http://billdouglas.ex.ac.uk/eve/di/69417.htm [accessed 4 Jan. 2009].

15. Auerbach, *Great Exhibition*, 166–7. Some foreigners remarked upon Britain's relative social and political stability against the background of recent Continental revolutions, see e.g. Edmond Texier, *Lettres sur l'Angleterre* (Paris, 1851).

16. *Blackwood's Edinburgh Magazine*, 70:430 (1851), 142–53, at 143.

17. For this section see John E. Findling, 'America at the Great Exhibition', in Bosbach (ed.), *Weltausstellung*, 197–204; Robert F. Dalzell, *American Participation in the Great Exhibition of 1851* (Amherst, 1960).

18. *Athenaeum*, 3 May 1851, 478; *The Times*, 15 May 1851, 5; cf. *Morning Chronicle*, 31 May 1851, 2.

19. *New York Tribune*, 25 Jan. 1851; *Springfield Republican*, 27 Nov. 1850, quoted in Dalzell, *American Participation*, 31, 29.

20. Quoted in Dalzell, *American Participation*, 29.

21. The second world fair was held in 1853 in the USA; as the *Cleveland Plain Dealer* asserted: 'No country is better fitted than the United States to give the next impetus to this great idea of modern civilization.' The quotations are from the *Liverpool Times*,

London Observer, and *Cleveland Plain Dealer*, after Dalzell, *American Participation*, 51–2, 64.

22. Kate Flint, 'The Native American and the Crystal Palace', in Buzard, Childers, and Gillooly (eds), *Victorian Prism*, 171–85; Richard P. Wunder, *Hiram Powers: Vermont Sculptor, 1805–1873*, 2 vols (Newark/London/Toronto, 1991), II, 157–68.

23. Elizabeth Barrett Browning, *Poetical Works*, 14th edn, 5 vols (London, 1886), III, 302.

24. *Illustrated London News*, 24 May 1851, 459–60.

25. For a narrative of the progress of civilisation reversed in an account of the British North American section, moving from agricultural produce of British settlers to the 'evidence of wilderness' in the form of 'birch canoes, snow shoes, the wampum belt, the tomahawk, and the moccasin of the Indian', see *Morning Chronicle*, 16 May 1851, 6.

26. A. M. Dowleans, *Catalogue of the East Indian Productions Collected in the Presidency of Bengal, and Forwarded to the Exhibition of Works of Art and Industry to be Held in London in 1851* (London, 1851); Lara Kriegel, 'Narrating the Subcontinent in 1851: India at the Crystal Palace', in Louise Purbrick (ed.), *The Great Exhibition of 1851: New Interdisciplinary Essays* (Manchester/New York, 2001), 146–78.

27. [John Tallis], *Tallis's History and Description of the Crystal Palace and the Exhibition of the World's Industry in 1851*, 3 vols (London, 1852), I, 33.

28. Lara Kriegel, 'The Pudding and the Palace: Labor, Print Culture, and Imperial Britain in 1851', in Antoinette M. Burton (ed.), *After the Imperial Turn: Thinking with and through the Nation* (Durham, NC, 2003), 230–45, at 234.

29. *Tallis's History and Description of the Crystal Palace*, I, 36, 150.

30. A gallery mainly of French paintings apparently planned by a British firm failed when the French government refused to pay for the shipment of works: Patricia Mainardi, 'The Unbuilt Picture Gallery at the 1851 Great Exhibition', *Journal of the Society of Architectural Historians*, 45:3 (1986), 294–9. There was no space at the Crystal Palace for sculptures from colonial territories such as India. Instead, as *The Illustrated London News*'s visual guide showed, works of Western sculpture stood next to displays from India, Turkey, or China. Depicting most sculptures only rather crudely, it contrasted classical sculpture with Indian textiles, arms, and armour: *Illustrated London News*, 6 Mar. 1852, 1.

31. For the Sydenham palace see J. R. Piggot, *Palace of the People: The Crystal Palace at Sydenham, 1854–1936* (London, 2004); Samuel Phillips, *Guide to the Crystal Palace and Park* (London, 1854); Andrew Hassam, 'Portable Iron Structures and Uncertain Colonial Spaces at the Sydenham Crystal Palace', in Felix Driver and David Gilbert (eds), *Imperial Cities: Landscape, Display and Identity* (Manchester/New York, 1999), 174–93; Debbie Challis, 'Modern to Ancient: Greece at the Great Exhibition and the Crystal Palace', in Jeffrey A. Auerbach and Peter H. Hoffenberg (eds), *Britain, the Empire, and the World at the Great Exhibition of 1851* (Aldershot, 2008), 173–90.

INDEX

mausoleum 192, 197, 265–7, 289, 305
  monuments, commemoration, and notion of
    136–7, 186
Mayer, Luigi 266
Mayo, Lord 346
medals 18, 25–6, 232, 387, 391
  commemorating acquisition of antiquities 237
  as reward for military service 135, 145, 151, 155,
    161
  see also chivalric orders; Prussia
mediation, of experience of monuments 137–8
Mediterranean, see entries for specific territories;
  Map 2
  British geostrategic interests 206
  Corfu 206
  Cyprus 210
  Gibraltar 4, 46, 48, 68, 70, 83–4, 96, 113–14, 119,
    180, 357
  Malta 206, 228, 245, 247, 252, 266
  Minorca 4, 46, 68, 206
  see also Greece; Italy
memorialisation, see commemoration
memory 9
  contestation 43, 58–9, 81–2, 68–71, 147–50
  distortion, erasure, forgetting II, III, IV, 40, 54–7,
    81
  historiography and theory 40–41, 136, 408 n. 5
  popular memorabilia 6, 68–9, 84
  see also commemoration; death; heroism;
    monuments; St Paul's Cathedral; wampum;
    Westminster Abbey
Menou, General 221
Meredith, Lt George 220–21
Metternich, Prince 355, 360
Michaelis, Adolf 209
Middle East:
  Acre 143, 206, 246, 266
  Aleppo 206
  Balbec 210
  crisis 1830–40s 245
  Holy Land 485 n. 4
  Jerusalem 253
  Palestine Exploration Fund 485 n. 4
  Syria 246, 266
Mill, James 313
military:
  American Continental army 50, 107
  American militias 53, 103, 107
  British forces in American Revolutionary War 46
  British in India (garrison state) 9, 275
  and British Museum 29
  Coldstream Guards 376

Dutch navy 86, 144, 146, 165
English militias 139, 148
escort for cultural and scientific expeditions 41,
  302–5
French army, navy 18, 149, 176, 178, 221, 265,
  343; see also wars
  at George III's coronation 27
  gunners install objects at British Museum 29
Hessians 50, 107, 113, 116, 160
Highlanders X, 18, 156, 164, 168
Highland regiments 95, 156, 168–9
Indian arms as spoils of war 279
loyalist regiments 75, 78–9
mobilisation during French Revolutionary Wars
  159
and music 14
officers with antiquarian and archaeological
  interests 213–14, 288, 294–7, 306–7, 349
Ordnance stores 125
Prussian 155, 160, 181–2
Royal Engineers 387
Royal Engineers Institution, Chatham 278
Royal Military Academy, Woolwich 467 n. 33
sepoys 41, 275, 318, 322, 336, 338
service of MPs 145–6
veterans 71, 75, 112, 117, 135, 155, 159–60, 200,
  216, 235, 282, 327, 362
see also army; battles; chivalric orders; honour;
  India, Company state; Parliament; Royal Navy;
  science; Scotland; soldiers; war; wars
Milman, Henry 185
Milton, John 10, 121
Minto, Lord 324
Mirabeau, Comte de 147, 148
model, architectural 42, 46
Mohl, Julius 253
Moira, Lord 150
monarch, monarchy V, 1, 4, 11–12, 20, 41, 45, 50, 52,
  54–5, 58, 84, 86, 88, 97, 100–101, 103, 105, 120, 122,
  124–5, 128–9, 134, 138–9, 146, 160–61, 351, 354–6,
  359–60, 364, 367, 381–2
  centennial of Hanoverian accession (1814) 357–9
  cultural patronage 14, 17–18, 84, 122, 128, 367,
    381
  destruction of royal symbols 51–3
  head of armed services 32, 84
  and national identity and integration 5, 134, 138
  and recognition of military service 144–5
  see also coronation; Charles I; Charles II; George
    II; George III; George IV; monuments,
    equestrian; William IV; Victoria
Montesquieu, Charles de Secondat, Baron de 11, 105